ENGLISH

COMMUNICATION SKILLS IN THE NEW MILLENNIUM

LEVEL II

J.A. Senn
Carol Ann Skinner

BARRETT KENDALL PUBLISHING
AUSTIN, TEXAS

Educating tomorrow today

PROJECT MANAGER
Sandra Stucker Blevins

EDITORIAL DIRECTOR
Sandra Mangurian

EDITORIAL STAFF
Marianne Murphy
Marlene Greil
Donna Laughlin
Susan Sandoval
Vicki Tyler
Catherine Foy
Michelle Quijano
Elizabeth Wenning
Cheryl Duksta
Margaret Rickard

PRODUCTION DIRECTORS
Gene Allen, Pun Nio

PHOTO RESEARCH AND
PERMISSIONS
Laurie O'Meara

ART AND DESIGN
Pun Nio
Leslie Kell
Rhonda Warwick

PRODUCTION
Bethany Powell
Isabel Garza
Rhonda Warwick

COVER
Leslie Kell Designs
Pun Nio
Images © Photodiscs, Inc.

EDITORIAL AND PRODUCTION
SERVICES
Book Builders, Inc.
Gryphon Graphics
Inkwell Publishing
   Solutions, Inc.
NETS

ISBN 1-58079-111-5   2 3 4 5 6 7 RRD 06 05 04 03 02 01

SENIOR CONSULTANTS

Tommy Boley, Ph.D.
Director of English Education
The University of Texas at El Paso
El Paso, TX

Deborah Cooper, M.Ed.
Coordinating Director of PK-12
    Curriculum
Charlotte-Mecklenburg Public Schools
Charlotte, NC

Susan Marie Harrington, Ph.D.
Associate Professor of English,
    Director of Writing, Director of
    Placement and Assessment, and
    Adjunct Assistant Professor
    of Women's Studies
Indiana University-Purdue University,
    Indianapolis
Indianapolis, IN

Carol Pope, Ed.D.
Associate Professor of Curriculum
    and Instruction
North Carolina State University
Raleigh, NC

Rebecca Rickly, Ph.D.
Department of English
Texas Tech University
Lubbock, TX

John Simmons, Ph.D.
Professor of English Education and
    Reading
Florida State University
Tallahassee, FL

John Trimble, Ph.D.
University Distinguished Teaching
    Professor of English
The University of Texas
Austin, TX

CONTRIBUTING WRITERS

Jeannie Ball

Grace Bultman

Richard Cohen

Elizabeth Egan-Rivera

Laurie Hopkins Etzel

Bobbi Fagone

Lesli Favor

Nancy-Jo Hereford

Susan Maxey

Linda Mazumdar

Elizabeth McGuire

Shannon Murphy

Carole Osterink

Michael Raymond

Duncan Searl

Jocelyn Sigue

Lorraine Sintetos

James Strickler

Diane Zahler

Kathy Zahler

CRITICAL READERS

Alan Altimont
St. Edwards University,
Austin, TX

Larry Arnhold
Deer Park High School,
Houston, TX

Kerry Benson
Santa Fe Public School,
Santa Fe, NM

Elaine Blanco
Gaither High School,
Lutz, FL

Peter Bond
Randolph School,
Huntsville, AL

Christina M. Brandenburg
Rancho Cotate High
School, Rohnert Park, CA

Paulette Cwidak
John Adams High
School, South Bend, IN

Jean Ann Davis
Miami Trace High
School, Washington
Courthouse, OH

Terri Dobbins
Churchill High School,
San Antonio, TX

Susan Drury
Springwood High
School, Houston, TX

David Dunbar
Masters School,
Dobbs Ferry, NY

Chuck Fanara
Brebeuf Preparatory,
Indianapolis, IN

Jason Farr
Anderson High School,
Austin, TX

Marilyn Gail
Judson High School,
San Antonio, TX

Gary Gorsuch
Berea High School,
Berea, OH

Monica Gorsuch
MidPark Sr. High School,
Cleveland, OH

Donna Harrington
Churchill High School,
San Antonio, TX

Janis Hoffman
John Adams High
School, South Bend, IN

Norma Hoffman
John Adams High
School, South Bend, IN

David Kidd
Norfolk Academy,
Norfolk, VA

Kate Knopp
Masters School,
Dobbs Ferry, NY

Suzanne Kuehl
Lewis-Palmer High
School, Monument, CO

Michelle Lindner
Milken Community High
School, Los Angeles, CA

Stephanie Lipkowitzs
Albuquerque Academy,
Albuquerque, NM

Sarah Mannon
Hubbard High School,
Chicago, IL

Linda Martin
Valley Torah, North
Hollywood, CA

Lisa Meyer
Lincoln High School,
Tallahassee, FL

Karla Miller
Durango High School,
Durango, CO

Stacy Miller
Santa Fe High School,
Santa Fe, NM

Eddie Norton
Oviedo High School,
Oviedo, FL

Diana Perrin
Johnson High School,
Huntsville, AL

William Petroff
R. Nelson Snider High
School, Ft. Wayne, IN

Linda Polk
Deer Park High School,
Houston, TX

Lila Rissman
Suwanne Middle School,
Live Oak, FL

Carmen Stallard
Twin Springs High
School, Nickelsville, VA

Jeanette Taylor
Rye Cove High School,
Duffield, VA

Eric Temple
Crystal Springs Uplands
School, Hillsborough, CA

Sherry Weatherly
Denton High School,
Denton, TX

Exploring Writer's Craft

CHAPTER 3 Writing Informative Paragraphs

CHAPTER 4 Writing Other Kinds of Paragraphs

CHAPTER 5 Writing Effective Compositions

ix

Achieving Writer's Purpose

CHAPTER 6 Personal Writing:
                Self-Expression and Reflection

CHAPTER 7 Using Description: Observation

CHAPTER 8 **Creative Writing: Stories, Plays, Poems**

CHAPTER 9 Writing to Inform and Explain

CHAPTER 10 Writing to Persuade

CHAPTER 11 Writing About Literature

Applying Communication Skills

CHAPTER 12 Research Reports

Communication Resource

CHAPTER 15   Vocabulary

CHAPTER 16   Reference Skills

Grammar

CHAPTER 1 The Parts of Speech

CHAPTER 2 The Sentence Base

CHAPTER 3 Phrases

CHAPTER 4 Clauses

Usage

CHAPTER 5 Using Verbs

CHAPTER 6   Using Pronouns

CHAPTER 7 Subject and Verb Agreement

CHAPTER 8 Using Adjectives and Adverbs

Mechanics

CHAPTER 9 Capitalization

CHAPTER 10   End Marks and Commas

Spelling

CHAPTER 13 **Spelling Correctly**

Study and Test-Taking Skills Resource

COMPOSITION

first
nd almo
oped for so
hless. The ho
miraculo
o fe

CHAPTER 1

Using Your Writing Process

Creativity is always something of a mystery, but it is safe to say that writers of all genres go through a process as they search for inspiration. That is, they start by exploring their ideas and then work on expressing those ideas in new and interesting ways—until they get their writing just right.

This chapter will help you explore *your* ideas by showing a process for writing—a way to plan, draft, revise, edit, and publish your work. You will not always follow the stages of this process in the same order for each composition you write. For instance, you may get an inspiration for your introduction and draft it even before you have finished planning the rest of the composition. You may even decide to return to the planning stage while revising. Writers rarely march step-by-step through the writing process. Instead, recognizing the flexibility of the process, they move in and out of the various stages as needed.

This chapter offers you some writing strategies that have been successful for many writers. You will have an opportunity to practice these strategies and choose those that work best for you.

Reading with a Writer's Eye

Read through the following profile in which the author, Lois Rosenthal, explores the writing process of poet Nikki Giovanni. As you read, you will see that creating a poem is a way of thinking as well as a process of putting words on paper. What does it mean to think like a poet?

FROM
Nikki Giovanni

Lois Rosenthal

Nikki Giovanni is one of America's most widely read living poets, and one of the most outspoken. From the sixties, when she gained notoriety as one of the prime forces in the civil rights movement to the present, when she travels all over the world to teach and to give scores of poetry readings and lectures each year, she speaks out on whatever issues she believes are crucial. Her awards, both literary and for being an outstanding woman of achievement, are legion.

Says Giovanni: "I use poetry as an outlet for my mind. It's my justification for living. But speaking my mind is an important part of my life as well, even when it's not a popular view. Everyone has a right to the dictates of her own heart. The one thing you cannot take away from people is their own sense of integrity. I don't want my integrity impinged upon nor will I impinge on the integrity of someone else.

"Though you cannot live your life to be intimidated by lesser people under any circumstances, I don't think you should shout people down if you disagree with them." Giovanni's caring but no-holds-barred approach to life extends to her poetry, and to her way of teaching poetry to her students. When poems are read, critical comments can be honest but

they must also be kind. She forbids vicious attacks on anyone's work—the work must not be "shouted down."

"Students need to realize their feelings are valid," says Giovanni. "From there, I begin asking them what they are trying to say in each particular poem. What started it? They are required to take their thought to the furthermost point, to push themselves a little bit beyond what makes sense to them. By the time their explanation is finished, they often wind up with a very different poem.

"If one writes that he is in love with a red-headed girl, I want to know if her mother and her sister are redheads. I want information about the girl's background. How did he meet her? How did this affair end? What is he envisioning?

"I'm trying to teach students to see the whole scene and bring all the information to bear on this love poem. Then we might have something, because it's insufficient to just write that you are in love. Nobody cares. We care about what's around it, what triggered the poem.

"If you are working on your own—not as part of a workshop—and if, for instance, you are writing about raindrops, have this conversation with yourself:

QUESTION: Where does the rain go?

ANSWER: It falls to the ground.

QUESTION: Then what?

ANSWER: The rain comes back as a bud.

QUESTION: What does the bud do?

ANSWER: The bud gives off oxygen and oxygen goes back up into space.

"Follow your image as far as you can no matter how useless you think it is. Push yourself. Always ask, 'What else can I do with this image?,' because you have images before you have poems. Words are illustrations of thoughts. You must think this way."

Giovanni suggests you make a checklist of questions for yourself. For instance, when you finish a poem, ask:

1. Did you say all you needed to?
2. Did you say more than you should have? (More is better than less because it's easier to subtract than add.)
3. Is this a poem you actually like reading?
4. If you didn't write it, would it still make sense to you?
5. Is it boring? "Most writers know when they're being boring because that's the first question they ask. My answer—'Yes, dear, it is.'"

"Learn to listen when you're talking to people. So many people listen poorly. Listen to how people say things, to what they really mean, because people frequently say one thing and mean another. Learn to separate the wheat from the chaff and look at your own poetry in the same way."

Thinking as a Writer

Analyzing a Writer's Process

- Why do you think that Lois Rosenthal chose to write this article?
- Think about how Nikki Giovanni makes the process of writing appealing to her students. Does she inspire *you* to write? What does she say about writing that prompts your response?

Saying What You Mean

Oral Expression Giovanni advises her students to "listen when you're talking to people. . . . Listen to how people say things, to what they really mean, because people frequently say one thing and mean another."

- Think about a project or assignment you have worked on with a classmate. Talk with that classmate about the process of working together. Did you communicate your ideas clearly in an appropriate way? Did you misinterpret anything your partner said? How can you put Giovanni's advice to use?

Envisioning Thoughts

Viewing Nikki Giovanni uses the example of raindrops to help her students understand that "words are the illustrations of thought."

- Observe the raindrops on the leaf in this photograph. What  thoughts, feelings, or memories do you associate with the image? What words immediately come to mind?

Refining Your Writing Process

In Rosenthal's essay, Nikki Giovanni characterizes writing as a powerful means of self-expression and a "justification for living." By the end of the essay, we realize that writing does not have to be difficult or mysterious. It's something that everyone can and should enjoy doing.

To help you get your words down on paper, Chapter 1 introduces the writing process. Like Rosenthal's essay, the writing process is a "how-to" for writers. This process is not just for poems though. It is a series of stages or steps that will help you write stories, essays, and reports too.

Your **writing process** is the recursive series of stages that you, as a writer, proceed through when developing your ideas and discovering the best way to express them.

The word *recursive* indicates that, as a writer, you may often move back and forth from one stage of the process to another, depending upon the needs of the specific work, rather than simply proceeding from the first stage straight through to the last. Writing is a creative process. As a writer you can shift from one stage to another or change the order of stages that you follow. For example, you may choose to revise as you draft, or edit as you revise.

Each stage has its own distinct characteristics. The diagram on the following page illustrates and describes these stages and shows the relationship between them. As you review the diagram, think about the steps you go through when you create a piece of writing.

Throughout this book, as you work through the stages of writing various essays, you will notice this icon. It will remind you to save your work in a convenient place so you can return to it and continue to work on it, or simply use it later for inspiration. You may wish to use a manila folder or a pocket in your binder to store your work. If you actually work on a computer, you will probably want to create a folder on your hard drive, along with some kind of backup copy on a removable storage disk. Use whatever kind of storage system will be most convenient for you.

● Process of Writing

The following diagram illustrates the elements, or processes, writers use as they create. Notice that the diagram loops back and forth. This looping shows how you often move back and forth among various stages of writing instead of going step-by-step from beginning to end. You can go back to any stage at any point until you are satisfied with the quality of your writing.

Prewriting includes the invention you do before writing your first draft. During prewriting you find and develop a subject, purpose, and audience; collect ideas and details; and make a basic plan for presenting them.

Prewriting

Drafting

Revising

Publishing

Editing

Drafting is expressing your ideas in sentences and paragraphs following your plan, as well as incorporating new ideas you discover while writing. Drafting includes forming a beginning, a middle, and an end—an introduction, a body, and a conclusion.

Revising means rethinking what you have written and reworking it to increase its clarity, smoothness, and power.

Editing involves checking and reworking sentences and sentence structure. It also includes looking for, and correcting, errors in grammar, usage, mechanics, and spelling, and then proofreading your final version before making it public.

Publishing is sharing your work in an appropriate way.

Your Writer's Portfolio

As you begin your writing this term, think of yourself as an apprentice learning a craft. Ideally, with each new essay you write, you come a step closer to developing your own composing processes. A good way to track your progress is to keep a **portfolio**— a collection of your work that represents various types of writing and your progress in them.

PORTFOLIO This icon represents a reminder throughout the book to place your work in your writing portfolio. When you add a piece to your portfolio, be sure to date it so you will later have an accurate chronological record of your work. You will also be reminded in the chapter-closing checklists to consider including the essay in your portfolio you have been working on, but the choice is always yours, possibly with guidelines from your teacher.

As you work through the writing assignments in your class, you will be asked to do many kinds of writing—sharing a story from your own life, writing a poem, urging a solution to some social problem, describing a scene from nature, researching a complex topic, writing a letter, and much more. No single assignment could show all your skill as a writer, but collecting various compositions along the way can demonstrate the range of your growing skills.

You may be asked to write evaluations of your progress as a writer throughout the year. You should include these evaluations in your portfolio along with your various writings. This activity will help you examine both your successes as a writer and the areas of your work that could be stronger still. At the term's end, you may be asked to write a "cover letter" for your portfolio in which you summarize its contents, explain why you included each piece, and evaluate your overall progress, strengths, and weaknesses.

Throughout the writing activities, you will be asked to take "Time Out to Reflect." Reflecting on your experience as a writer will give you an opportunity to develop your process even further. Use these reflections to think about what you have learned, what you want to learn, and how you can continue to grow as a writer. Your written reflections are suitable additions to your portfolio.

On the following page are a few guidelines for including work in your portfolio.

- Date each piece of writing so you can see where it fits into your progress.
- Write a brief note to yourself about why you have chosen to include each piece—what you believe it shows about you as a writer.
- Include unfinished works if they demonstrate something meaningful about you as a writer.

Prewriting Writing Process

The novelist Ernest Hemingway wrote, "My working habits are simple: long periods of thinking, short periods of writing." As Hemingway knew, much of the work in producing a good piece of writing takes place before the writer ever sits down and actually drafts the story, article, or essay.

Prewriting includes all of the thinking, imagining, and planning you do before attempting a first draft. Much of your prewriting may occur only in your mind. But prewriting can also mean creating lists, notes, outlines, and graphic organizers as you (1) clarify your subject; (2) consider your occasion, purpose, and audience; and (3) organize your material.

Keep a writing folder as you work through the following prewriting strategies. At some later time you may be able to draw on many of the ideas in your folder.

Strategies for Finding a Subject

Subjects for writing are all around you—in current events, in conversations with friends, in the day-to-day life of your family, in sporting events, on the television and radio, and on the Internet. Finding subjects to write about is simply a matter of keeping your mind and eyes open. The following strategies will help you do both.

Taking an Inventory of Your Interests   Good writing is usually fresh and original. If you draw on material from your personal experiences, you are bound to discover good subjects for writing.

Practice Your Skills

● *Exploring Personal Experiences*

Answer each question as completely as you can. Be sure to save your notes in your writing folder for later use.

1. What three people have played the most important roles in my life? What has each done to direct me along my current path?

2. What three national problems (poverty, pollution, racism, for example) seem to have the greatest impact on my life? What is that impact? What can I do about it?

3. What three subjects do I always like to read about? Why?

4. What three talents or skills do I have?

5. What two interests have I had for most of my life? What new interest have I developed in recent years?

Freewriting   Freewriting is another strategy for discovering possible subjects for writing. **Freewriting** means writing freely about ideas as they come into your mind. You can start writing with no premeditation whatsoever, or you can do **focused freewriting**— that is, beginning with a specific idea, word, or phrase.

Select a time limit, such as five or ten minutes, and write without stopping for that entire period. Write whatever comes to mind. Do not censor your thoughts and do not worry about complete sentences or proper punctuation. It is all right if your thoughts seem disorganized or if you feel that you are repeating yourself—the important thing at this point is to get your thoughts out and down on paper. Even if ideas seem to dry up, jot down that your brain is suddenly feeling empty. Keep writing that very thought until a new idea occurs to you. Freewriting works best with practice, and it can help you discover subjects you never expected to write about.

Recalling

Your writing can be original and convincing if you enrich it with as many details from your past as possible. If you concentrate, you can recall a surprising number of details from half-forgotten scenes from your own life. Just think of your memory as a photographic film. All of your experiences have made an impression on the mind's film, and everything you have ever seen, touched, tasted, smelled, or heard has left an impression, however slight, in your memory.

The challenge is to learn to develop some of the images stored in your mind and to use them to enliven your writing. For instance, concentrate on the last year and recall an experience you have had. Perhaps you visited an underground cave such as Mammoth Cave in Kentucky. Make a chart like the following one to help you recall a past experience. Next to each heading, list all the details you can recall.

EXPERIENCE: VISIT TO MAMMOTH CAVE	
Sights	huge room, pale light, dark shadows, stalactites, stalagmites, tourists' faces
Sounds	echoes/voices, dripping, guide's voice
Touch	cool, clammy, sticky hands, limp clothes
Smells	musty, odor of sulfur gas (like rotten eggs)
Reactions	awe, curiosity, uneasiness; fear of large, dark places

THINKING PRACTICE

Choose one of the following topics or another from your past and list as many details as you can recall. Make a chart like the one above to help unlock your memories.

1. the first time I ever went swimming
2. my first dance
3. a childhood birthday party

By writing whatever was on her mind, this student writer soon found her thoughts focusing on a classical piano concert. She had the first glimmer of a very promising subject to write about.

MODEL: Freewriting from Scratch

I don't feel that I have much to say, but I'll keep writing so one idea will lead to another. How could anyone not like music? My favorite instrument is the piano, especially jazz and blues piano. I love Heavy Metal music too. I never much liked classical music. Then I went to a classical concert. I expected to have a boring time. Strange how wrong you can be about something. I had a great time. The soloist was amazing. It was a special date with a special person in a special place. Same applies to people. Someone you think you have nothing in common with turns out to become your best friend.

Freewriting can also be done on a specified subject. This type of writing, called **focused freewriting**, is another good way to let one idea lead to another—sometimes with surprising results.

The following is an example of focused freewriting. By starting out writing about the subject of classical music, the student found herself writing about a concert.

MODEL: Focused Freewriting

Classical music—what can I write about classical music? I love the piano. I went to hear a piano concerto by Beethoven, expecting to be totally bored. Beethoven wrote over a century ago. I was pleasantly surprised. The concert hall was spectacular. The pianist was a virtuoso. He played Beethoven's Emperor Concerto. Beethoven's music is intense and modern sounding. There was even a section of improvisation. I still love Heavy Metal, but I have started a collection of classical CDs. First impressions can be deceiving.

PRACTICE YOUR SKILLS

● *Freewriting from Scratch*

Freewrite for five minutes by writing down everything that passes through your mind. Relax and let your mind run free. If you come to a dead end, write anything that comes to mind— even if it is "I don't know what to write about." At the end of five minutes, stop writing and place a star next to any item that you feel you might want to further explore. Place your work in your writing folder for later use.

● *Freewriting with a Focus*

This time freewrite for five minutes on one of the subjects you started in the previous activity. Start by focusing on that subject alone but then let your mind take you where it will.

Keeping a Journal   Another good way to discover worthwhile writing is to keep a **journal**. The types of entries can vary widely, from simple recall of the day's events to more complex analyses of your thoughts, feelings, relationships, hopes, and dreams.

Journals can record observations:

October 30, 1918

Just in from a walk in the Park on this incredibly lovely autumn day. Various houses have orange berries growing upon them, the beech trees are so bright that everything looks pale after you have looked at them.

—*Virginia Woolf, author*

They can record frustration:

January 29, 1915

Again tried to write, virtually useless. The past two days went early to bed, about ten o'clock. Something I haven't done for a long time now.

—*Franz Kafka, author*

They can record reflections:

> May 1, 1858
>
> The rain is pattering on the roof, the clouds are dark and lowering, making all objects look gloomy, and causing my spirits to be depressed, so much are we affected by the things with which we are surrounded.
>
> *—Sallie McNeill, diarist*

Or the news of the hour:

> April 26, 1865
>
> For the present, everything is forgotten in the assassination of President Lincoln, the [news] of which came today.
>
> *—Henry Crabb Robinson, diarist*

Choose a notebook you will enjoy writing in. Date each entry. Write about whatever is on your mind, or use the ideas offered in this text. Your **journal** will become a rich resource to mine for writing ideas.

PRACTICE YOUR SKILLS

⬤ *Writing in Your Journal*

Look through old magazines for images that evoke a strong reaction in you. In your journal, freewrite everything that comes to mind as you look at those images.

You will also use your **journal** in other ways with this book. The chart on page C16 outlines some additional purposes for the **journal**.

Keeping a Response Log   Your **journal** is a good place to write your responses and reactions to what you read. You may want to set aside a certain part of your **journal** as your Response Log. Here are a few ways you can record your responses.

Exploring Literature in a Response Log

Fiction, Drama, and Poetry

- Write about a piece of literature, or a script for television or film, exploring the character, the action, the setting, or some other aspect of the medium.

- Write about the theme, or central message, of a story, poem, or play. If a story concerns family relations, for example, you may choose to address this issue in your own writing.

- Write about a conflict one of the characters faced and the outcome. Would you have acted or responded in the same way?

- Write about an aspect of the work that you really enjoyed.

Nonfiction

- Decide whether you agree with an editorial in a newspaper or with an expression of opinion in some other medium, such as a magazine, the radio, or television.

- Comb newspapers and magazines and surf the Internet to find issues or subjects that you could explore and write about.

- Think about biographies and autobiographies you have read. Write about the subject of any of them: What does that person mean to you?

PRACTICE YOUR SKILLS

Responding to Reading

Create a section in your journal called Response Log. Tape a tab on the side of a page about halfway through your journal. Then read some articles or editorials in today's newspaper. Use the Response Log to list five subjects you could write about.

Keeping a Learning Log   A Learning Log is a section of your **journal** where you can write ideas that interest you. One important function of a Learning Log is to help you distinguish between what you already know about a subject and what you still need to learn. For example, suppose you were interested in learning more about the style of music popular in the late 1700s and early 1800s. Your entry might look like the model below by the student writing about classical music. Note the questions the student asks as well as the resources she notes for answering them.

MODEL: Learning Log Entry

> I really like classical piano music. I think of Beethoven and Mozart when I think of that style of music. But I don't know exactly how to define it. How is it different from rock and roll? Why is it called classical music? I guess I could look it up in some kind of music dictionary or encyclopedia, or on the Internet. Maybe I could do a keyword search at the library database, too, and find some books on it. My best friend's mother is a professional pianist—maybe I could ask her if she can recommend some good leads.

PRACTICE YOUR SKILLS

● *Learning More About a Subject*

Create a Learning Log section in your journal. Attach a tab labeled Learning Log on a page about three-quarters of the way through your journal. Think of a subject about which you know a little but would like to know more, what you'd still like to find out, and where and how you could find out what you need to know.

Creating a Personalized Editing Checklist A Personalized Editing Checklist is a section of your **journal** where you can keep a list of errors that recur in your writing. You might include words you frequently misspell, usage mistakes, mechanical and grammatical errors, and so forth. When you edit an essay, you should refer to this checklist.

You can learn more about the Personalized Editing Checklist on page C46.

● *Keeping Track of Errors*

Create another section in your journal called Personalized Editing Checklist. Add to your Personalized Editing Checklist as you work on the writing assignments in this book.

Choosing and Limiting a Subject

Writing gives you the opportunity to know yourself better and to present your ideas and interests to others. You should make the most of this opportunity by writing about subjects you find personally stimulating and challenging.

> ### Guidelines for Choosing a Subject
>
> - Choose a subject that genuinely interests you.
> - Choose a subject that will most likely capture the interest of your readers.
> - Choose a subject you can cover thoroughly through your own knowledge or with a reasonable amount of research.

Limiting a Subject   Once you have selected your subject, you may have to limit it so that it is more manageable. For example, a very broad subject like "the federal government" or "the Olympic Games" cannot be covered in a paragraph or a short essay. To limit such a broad subject, use the strategies suggested in the following box.

> ### Strategies for Limiting a Subject
>
> - Limit your subject to one person or one example that represents the subject.
> - Limit your subject to a specific time or place.
> - Limit your subject to a specific event.
> - Limit your subject to a specific condition, purpose, or procedure.

Notice how the student writer automatically limited the subject she came up with in her freewriting.

MODEL: Limiting a Subject

GENERAL SUBJECT:
music

MORE LIMITED:
classical music

LIMITED SUBJECT:
attending
a concert

PRACTICE YOUR SKILLS

● *Limiting a Subject*

The following subjects are each too broad for a paragraph or an essay. On your paper write three limited subjects for each broad subject, using the strategies from the box above.

Example:

GENERAL SUBJECT   aerobic exercise
LIMITED SUBJECTS   aerobic classes at town hall (place)
                         aerobic dancing (example)

1. dieting
2. holidays
3. hobbies

4. sports
5. movies
6. crafts

Children's Storybooks

Review your writing ideas from earlier in this chapter (*pages C11–C17*). Select a subject for a story that you think would interest a five- or six-year-old child, and plan a story that is about one paragraph long. Recall a child you know—maybe a sibling, a cousin, or even a neighbor—and ask yourself, Would this child understand the ideas in this story? Would he or she enjoy it?

Next plan your illustrations. Which ideas might be clearer with an illustration? Which ideas might be expressed better in a picture than in words? What style of illustration might be appropriate for children of this age? Create rough sketches of your illustrations.

Then write your one-paragraph story. As you write, choose your words carefully and use short, interesting sentences, keeping in mind that you are writing for a young child.

Now plan the layout of your book. Thumbnails—small representations of each page—will help you decide on the appropriate amount of text for each page. For this age group, one or two sentences per page is enough copy. Your thumbnails will also help you determine the best position for your illustrations. Strive to keep the page layout clean and easy for a young child to follow.

At last you are ready to create your book. Choose a type style that will appeal to children. Be sure the type size is appropriate for a young child. Then type and illustrate your story, following the suggestions in <u>A Writer's Guide to Electronic Publishing</u> (pages C698–C721). You may wish to staple the left-hand side or bind your book in a folder. After your teacher and classmates have reviewed your book, give it to the child you had in mind.

Considering Your Occasion, Audience, and Purpose

Often your writing has a specific purpose, such as completing a school assignment or writing a letter to the editor of a newspaper. At the same time, every piece of writing has a general purpose. **Purpose** is your reason for writing or speaking. For example, the purpose of your school assignment may be to explain something; the purpose of your letter to the editor may be to persuade readers. Whatever your purpose may be for a particular piece of writing, it is important to define it clearly before you begin writing. In successful communication, the purpose of your message is appropriate to both the occasion that prompts it and the audience who will receive it. The following chart lists the most common purposes and forms, although writing purpose can take almost any form in the hands of a creative writer.

WRITING PURPOSES	POSSIBLE FORMS
Informative to **explain** or **inform**; to focus on your subject matter and audience	**Factual writing** scientific essay, research paper, business letter, summary, descriptive essay, historical narrative, news story
Creative (literary) to **create**; to focus on making imaginative use of language and ideas	**Entertaining writing** short story, novel, play, poem, dialogue
Persuasive to **persuade**; to focus on changing your readers' minds or getting them to act in a certain way	**Convincing writing** letter to the editor, persuasive essay, movie or book review, critical essay (literary analysis), advertisement
Self-expressive to **express** and **reflect** on your thoughts and feelings	**Personal writing** journal entry, personal narrative, reflective essay, personal letter

Sometimes writing purposes overlap. For example, you can give people information *and* express your thoughts at the same time. You can write informatively about a place you have visited *and* persuade your audience to visit that place. Being clear about your purpose is important because it will affect many of the writing decisions you make.

Occasion is your motivation for composing—the factor that prompts or forces you, as a writer, to decide on your process for communicating. In other words, do you put a message in writing, or do you prepare a speech? Suppose you are writing in your **journal** about a memorable experience, which involves writing an essay. In this case, creating the journal entry is the occasion for writing.

Occasion usually can be stated well using one of the following sentences.

- I feel a need to write for my own satisfaction.

- I have been asked to write this by [name a person].

- I want to write an entry for [name a publication].

- I want to enter a writing contest.

As you plan your writing, you also need to remember the **audience** you will be addressing, or who will be reading your work. What are their interests and concerns? How can you best communicate to this particular audience? For example, if you were writing a description of some place you had visited, you would present details in a different way for an eight-year-old than for someone your own age.

> **Audience Profile Questions**
> - Who will be reading my work?
> - How old are they? Are they adults? teenagers? children?
> - What do I want the audience to know about my subject?
> - What background do they have in the subject?
> - What interests and opinions are they likely to have?
>   Are there any words or terms I should define for them?

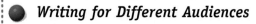

PRACTICE YOUR SKILLS

● *Writing for Different Audiences*

> **Write two paragraphs that describe an important event of the last 50 years, such as the fall of the Berlin Wall. Address your first paragraph to a third-grade student. Address the second paragraph to an adult living in the 1800s.**

Writing Tip

Make sure the **purpose** of your message is appropriate to the **occasion** that prompts it and the **audience** who will receive it.

Developing Your Voice

Writing is a way to give voice to your thoughts. Growing as a writer requires the ability to use the appropriate voice for each writing situation. Part of a writer's growth involves the discovery of his or her own distinctive voice and the ability to adapt that individual voice appropriately to different situations. **Voice** in writing is the particular sound and rhythm of the language the writer uses. Voice is an important part of your writing style that has to do with word choice. There are times, however—for example, when writing dialogue or writing from the point of view of a particular narrator— that you might want to imitate someone else's voice.

Voice can and should be affected by the writer's subject, occasion, audience, and purpose. In speaking, you probably use a different voice when asking your teacher to clarify an assignment than when comforting a friend about a disappointment. Similar differences in voice would be appropriate if you were approaching those same tasks on paper. In your **journal** you might use one voice when you are in a good mood and another when you are feeling irritable, one voice when recording a private hope and another when responding to a short story. For example, when writing to a company to complain about a defective product, you would use a voice of authority and power. When writing to your younger brother at camp, however, you would use a softer, caring voice. In your **journal** the mood of the day and your own natural style will determine your voice.

PRACTICE YOUR SKILLS

● *Recognizing Writers' Voices*

Reread the journal selections on pages C14–C15. Then write the name of the journal writer whose voice is best described by each of the following words. Be prepared to give reasons for your answers.

1. somber   **3.** joyful

2. shocked   **4.** irritable

● *Finding Your Natural Voice*

Pair up with a partner. For about five minutes, compare your feelings about television. At the end of your conversation, write freely for five minutes. Repeat your feelings about television, this time putting them into writing instead of speech. Try to use the same words and sentence structures you used in your conversation, but eliminate the pauses and fillers that probably came up in your speech.

● *Developing Different Voices*

Freewrite for three minutes on each of the following situations.

1. A bully is giving your younger brother a hard time. What do you say to the bully so that he will leave your brother alone?

2. A girl has moved in next door to you. She goes to your school and is the same age. You want to be friendly but sense she is very shy. You decide to leave a note for her in her mailbox. What do you say?

3. A teacher has asked you to be president of the computer club. Although honored, you have so much to do already you must turn the job down. What will you say?

4. In one subject you received a low grade on your report card. How do you explain your grade at home?

5. You have just won an important race in a track-and-field competition. Your cousin, who is also a runner, lives in another state and could not attend the event. How will you describe your triumph in your weekly letter to him?

Reading your work aloud will help you hear whether your writing voice sounds the way you want it to sound. The work becomes a slightly different piece, and you will detect features that you missed in a silent reading.

Writing Tip

To evaluate your written **voice,** read your work aloud.

Strategies for Developing a Subject

After choosing and limiting a subject and establishing your purpose and audience, you can begin to collect information such as facts, examples, incidents, and reasons about your subject. The strategies that follow will help you collect interesting and lively details.

Observing   A helpful strategy for collecting details about your subject is to use your own powers of observation. Observing is especially useful if your purpose is to describe a person, place, or object. Observing, though, involves more than merely looking. When you observe, you open your senses. The sensory impressions—including sights, sounds, smells, tastes, and feelings—associated with a subject are vital to bringing that subject to life. On the following page are some techniques that will help you gather details through observation.

Techniques for Observing

- Be aware of the reason why you are observing. Keep your purpose in mind as you decide what and how to observe.
- Use all your senses. Look, listen, smell, touch, taste.
- Use your mind. Think about what your observations mean.
- Observe from different viewpoints. Look at your subject from all angles: near and far, above and below, inside and out.
- Sketch your subject. Make a drawing of what you observe.
- Take notes, keeping a record of your observations.

It is important to know how to collect and organize the information you get from observing. Taking notes using note cards or computer files is a convenient way to keep information so that it is easy to arrange and rearrange when drafting. The following note card shows how a student took notes on the piece about Nikki Giovanni.

	Nikki Giovanni
	Poet
SUMMARIES OF MAIN IDEA:	Students must listen to themselves.
	One's feelings are one's own.
YOUR NOTES RECORD THE WRITER'S MAIN MESSAGE AND FACTS	Listen to feelings.
	Confront life.
	Look beyond the obvious.

PRACTICE YOUR SKILLS

● *Observing*

Use the preceding guidelines to observe the scene in the picture on the following page. Place yourself in the scene so that you can use all your senses. Then record ten or more details that you could use to describe the scene. Take time to include details that may not be obvious at first. Save your notes in your folder for possible later use.

Brainstorming for Details   Brainstorming is another effective way to discover details for an essay once you have chosen and limited your subject. In **brainstorming** your goal is to work with a partner or a group of classmates and freely list all ideas related to your subject as they occur to you. Just let them flow from one to another until you have unlocked a large store of ideas. The following guidelines will help you brainstorm.

Guidelines for Brainstorming

- Set a time limit, such as 15 minutes.
- Write the subject on a piece of paper and ask someone to be the recorder. If your group meets frequently, take turns recording ideas.
- Start brainstorming for details—facts, examples, incidents, reasons, connections, and associations. Since you can eliminate irrelevant ideas later, contribute and record any and all ideas.
- Build on the ideas of other group members. Add to those ideas or modify them to make them better.
- Avoid criticizing the ideas of other group members.

When you have finished brainstorming, you should get a copy of all the supporting details from the group recorder. Then, from the group list, select the details that are best for your own essay.

Following is part of a brainstorming list made by a small group on the subject of a classical music concert.

MODEL: Brainstorming List

> Classical Piano Concert
> —formal, everyone dressed up
> —concert hall like a palace, beautiful architecture
> —subdued crowd—does not jump up and down or run up to stage
> —quietly respectful audience
> —conductor leading orchestra
> —instruments synchronized, like a dance
> —instruments beautifully crafted
> —pianist's fingers flying across keyboard
> —improvisation by pianist
> —the music with variations on a theme, like jazz

PRACTICE YOUR SKILLS

● *Brainstorming for Ideas*

Form a small group and brainstorm to find a clever title for a new television comedy about a songwriting team—a sophomore from an American high school and a fifteen-year-old from outer space. Think of at least five possible titles. Then brainstorm again to decide how the two characters should meet in the first episode.

Clustering   Another strategy for developing supporting details is clustering. **Clustering**—the visual form of brainstorming—is a good strategy for developing details. When you cluster ideas, however, you connect them rather than list them. You begin with a single word or phrase enclosed in a box or circle and then arrange associated ideas around that nucleus, linking the ideas to the original word or phrase. You then go on to link each of these words or phrases, in turn, to other words as they occur. In the end you have a diagram that provides you not only with details but with groups or clusters of related details. Following is a cluster diagram on the subject of observing a classical music concert.

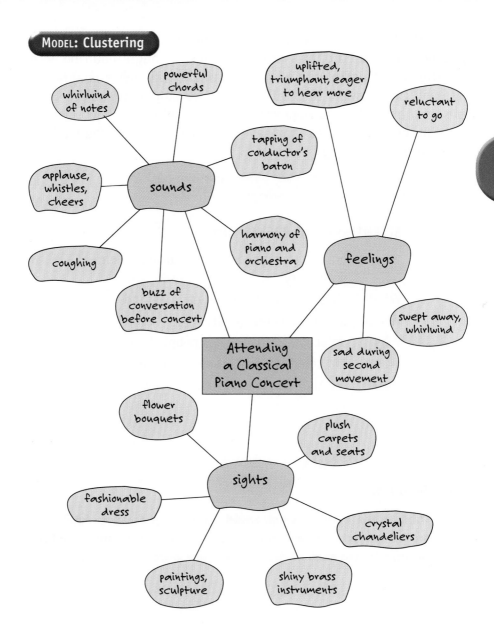

whirlwind of notes

powerful chords

uplifted, triumphant, eager to hear more

reluctant to go

applause, whistles, cheers

tapping of conductor's baton

sounds

coughing

harmony of piano and orchestra

feelings

buzz of conversation before concert

swept away, whirlwind

Attending a Classical Piano Concert

sad during second movement

flower bouquets

plush carpets and seats

sights

fashionable dress

crystal chandeliers

paintings, sculpture

shiny brass instruments

PRACTICE YOUR SKILLS

🔴 *Using a Cluster Diagram*

Create a cluster on the subject of your achievements at home, at school, or in your community. Write the words *My Achievements* in a box in the middle of a paper. Then write whatever comes to mind and circle your ideas. Connect related ideas with lines.

Inquiring   You can also develop supporting details by using the strategy of **inquiring,** or asking questions. Through inquiring with questions that begin with *who, what, where, why, when,* and *how,* you will find answers that will help you develop your subject. Suppose, for example, you were writing on the subject of how scientists study past cultures that have no written records. You might think of the following questions.

MODEL: Inquiring to Develop Supporting Details

SCIENTISTS AND PREHISTORY

Who   are some of the scholars learning about prehistory?

What   clues did early people leave behind?

Where are these clues found?

Why   do scholars study early people?

When   did scientists first study prehistory?

How   are the ages of clues determined?

PRACTICE YOUR SKILLS

 Inquiring

Think of ten questions you could ask to help develop details on the subject of how teenagers are portrayed in movies today. Be sure to use each of the six question words listed above at least once.

Strategies for Organizing Details

In order to collect ideas and details about your subject, you have to let your mind run free through such activities as brainstorming, clustering, and observing. Now it is time to provide a focus, or main idea, and to organize your ideas so that they will make sense to a reader. The following strategies will help you do just that.

Focusing Your Subject   Before you can decide how best to organize your details, you need to zero in on an exact focus for your essay. To do so, ask yourself what you want to say about your subject. For example, you might think of a meaningful generalization that can be drawn from the specifics you have developed in your prewriting work. This main idea will help you organize your entire essay. The guidelines below will help you focus your subject.

> ### Guidelines for Deciding on a Focus
>
> - Look over your details. Can you draw meaningful generalizations from some or all of the details? If so, the generalization could be the focus of your writing.
> - Choose a main idea that intrigues you.
> - Choose a main idea that suits your purpose and audience.

The student who brainstormed and clustered her observations about classical music chose as her main idea the experience of attending a classical concert. She established that her writing purpose was to inform and entertain and that her audience was her classmates. Her main idea, then, suited both her purpose and audience.

PRACTICE YOUR SKILLS

● *Focusing a Subject*

Review the questions that you wrote on page C30 on the subject of how teenagers are portrayed in movies today. Circle the three questions you think have the most potential for expansion into essays. Then choose the one you prefer, and rephrase it as a main idea.

Classifying Your Details   To organize your material, you should begin by classifying your details—that is, grouping related details that support the main idea. For example, if you were writing about your interests, you might see that your supporting details break down into such large categories as swimming, music, computers, and movies. Some of this grouping automatically occurs in clustering. For example, the sample cluster on page C29 shows three categories of details—sounds, sights, and feelings—for observing a classical music concert. Grouping your supporting details in logical categories will help your reader easily follow your thoughts. You may also see that, because certain details do not fall into a category, they should be eliminated.

Ordering Your Details   Finally, after grouping your supporting details in categories, decide on the best order to use. The following chart shows some common ways to order material.

WAYS TO ORGANIZE DETAILS		
Types of Order	**Definition**	**Examples**
Chronological	the order in which events occur	story, explanation, history, biography, drama
Spatial	location or physical arrangement	description (top to bottom, near to far, left to right, etc.)
Order of Importance	degree of importance, size, or interest	persuasive writing, description, evaluation, explanation
Logical	logical progression, one detail growing out of another	classification, definition, comparison and contrast

After deciding on the best order in which to present your supporting details in your composition, make a simple list or chart showing the details in that order. The following list shows the order in which the student writing about the classical music concert chose to present her details. Because she wanted to give the feeling of the concert from start to finish, she chose chronological order.

When I first arrived

—not looking forward to the experience

—beautiful building, paintings and sculptures inside

—chairs onstage, music on stands

—crystal chandeliers hanging from ceiling

—beautiful hand-crafted instruments

—musicians tuning: playing scales

—audience in jewels and formal wear

—applause for arrival onstage of conductor and soloist

—stillness before the concert starts

Once concert was under way

—lights dimmed

—strings and woodwinds seeming to echo each other

—instruments seeming to move in response to the conductor's baton

—the piano and the orchestra joining in a musical dance

—the pianist immersed in the performance

—fingers moving like lightning

—an incredible improvised piano solo

—audience applauding, whistling, and cheering

—fans throwing flowers onstage

—woman crinkling a candy wrapper

After the concert

—reflections on how misleading first impressions can be

PRACTICE YOUR SKILLS

● *Organizing Details*

For each of the subjects listed on the following page, decide which method of organization would be most appropriate. Indicate your answer by writing *chronological, spatial, logical,* or *order of importance or degree* after the proper number.

1. reasons people should avoid smoking
2. description of sky theater at the planetarium
3. story about the first time you tried to ski
4. news account of an earthquake
5. tallest buildings in the United States
6. description of how binoculars work

Drafting   Writing Process

During the drafting stage of the writing process, you review all the prewriting work you have done and put your ideas and supporting details into complete sentences. As you write your first draft, you will soon be able to tell whether you have a workable subject or whether you need to go back and rethink your ideas. Follow these strategies to produce your first draft.

Strategies for Drafting

- Write an introduction that will capture the reader's interest and express your main idea.
- Use your organized prewriting notes as a guide, but depart from them when a good idea occurs to you.
- Write fairly quickly. Do not worry about spelling or phrasing. You will have a chance to fix such problems when you revise.
- Stop frequently and read what you have written. This practice will help you move logically from one thought to the next as you draft.
- Try to write a conclusion that drives home to the reader the main point of the essay.

The following model shows the first draft by the student attending a concert. Notice that a number of mechanical errors will need to be corrected in a later stage.

I went to a classical concert. I didn't want to go at first. I was a diehard Heavy Metal fan and this would not be good for my image. The concert hall was elegant, like a palace. Inside, there were paintings, sculptures and plush carpeted floors.. He people there are all dressed up. Some people are in formal evening clothes. I felt like was at a fashion show.

The orchestra come onstage and began to tune their instruments fragments of different songs,miscellaneous scales and chords filled the air. The string section had beautiful handcrafted wooden instruments. Ushers handed out porgrams that told all about the piece we were about to hear- beethoven's "Emperor" piano concerto. The conductor and the soloist entered. There was applause, but not too much. This was followed by a moment of silence.

The conductor taps his stick and the concert begins. The pianist struck a loud chord. He flew off into a wild introduction. The orchestra answered, picking up the theme. Soon the piano and orchestra are trading licks back and forth. The pianist played with power and authority. The instrument can be heard even when playing with the full orchestra. The first part of the concert is a quick movement. The piano player's fingers move quickly across the keyboard. At times the music seemed abstract and difficult to follow, but whenever I was beginning to feel lost, a familiar theme wood survived reappear. When the first movement ended I felt exhilarated as though I had been swept off into the clouds by a hurricane.

The second section was slow and songlike. It made me feel sad. That mood changed abruptly with the third section which was really driving and built up to a big conclusion. The music toyed with the audience with a series of false endings. By the time it was over the audience were leaping to their feet cheering, aplauding and whistling. . Some fans even threw flowers onto the stage as the pianist took his bow.

By the time the concert was over, I felt I had been transported to somewhere I had never been. First impressions can be misleading. I thought I would have a lousy time but wound up really enjoying myself. It was like when you start out disliking someone and end up as best of friends. The concert pianist improvised at times like a jazz or rock musician. This guy is in the same league as my favorite jazz artists. I didn't know that classical musicians were so creative. I went right out and bought three different recordings of Beethoven's Emperor Concerto. I can't wait to go to my next concert. I learned something new about music and about myself.

Drafting a Title   After you have completed your first draft, think of several possible titles for your essay. A good title should interest and inform your audience and also arouse your reader's curiosity. At the same time, a title must give some idea of the subject matter of your paragraph or essay. The student who wrote the sample draft decided on the title "A Classical Concert."

PRACTICE YOUR SKILLS

● *Drafting a Title*

Review the draft of the essay about attending a classical music concert, and write three possible titles for that essay. You may also want to brainstorm for ideas with your classmates.

If you drafted your essay on a computer, save a copy of the first draft in a separate file before you begin to revise. You never know when you may need to refer to your first draft as you work. Also,

File	Edit	View	Insert	Format
New...				⌘N
Open...				⌘O
Open Web Page...				
Close				⌘W
Save				⌘S
Save As...				
Save as HTML...				
Versions...				

contrasting the first draft with the final revisions will help you evaluate your skills as a writer. Of course, the revised draft will replace the original one.

To save a copy of the first draft, use the Save As command. Click File and Save As to display the Save As dialog box. In the file name text box, type the desired name of the file. For example, if the file with your first draft is named Essay, you can save the file you plan to revise as Essay Rev.

Revising Writing Process

The writer Dorothy Canfield Fisher once remarked, "Very young writers often do not revise at all. . . . They are hypnotized by what they have written. 'How can it be altered?' they think. 'That's the way it was written.' Well, it has to be altered. You have to learn how. That is chiefly what English classes can teach you."

Revising means "seeing again." When writers revise, they stand back from their work and "see it again" with fresh, new eyes. To do this, you should put your first draft away for a few days. Then you will be able to read it over and evaluate it objectively. Reading the composition aloud will also help you evaluate it, because you can often hear awkward sentence structure and other problems.

Revising on Your Own

Some of the strategies for revising that writers use are described below. You may need to use some of these techniques more than others or vary them according to your writing needs.

Adding Ideas   As you look over your draft, ask yourself whether you need to **elaborate**. Have you covered every aspect of the subject? Are your ideas fresh and original enough to interest your audience? Have you explored the subject in depth, not just superficially? If not, you may need to think of new ideas. Freewrite about the subject or discuss it with someone more knowledgeable about the subject than you.

Adding Supporting Details   Look over your draft again. Have you fully developed your subject? Have you included enough supporting details? Are the supporting details specific enough to make your ideas clear and interesting? If not, you may need to **elaborate** by adding fresh details and information to your draft.

Rearranging   Check the organization of your ideas and details. Are all your details in the proper order? Does one idea lead to another so that the reader can easily follow your train of thought? If not, rearrange your material so that one idea flows logically into another.

Deleting Unnecessary Words or Ideas   Is all the information you have provided necessary? Have you avoided repeating yourself? Are all the details related to the main point? If not, delete any unnecessary words or details.

Substituting Stronger Words and More Varied Sentences
Once again read over your draft. If any part seems confusing, think of a clearer way to express the same idea. Replace any dull, boring words and phrases with more original ones. Use vivid adjectives, strong action verbs, and the active voice instead of the passive voice. Vary your sentence structure and length to keep from sounding monotonous.

Using an evaluation checklist like the one below is a handy way to see whether your latest draft exhibits all the qualities of a good essay. Throughout this book, you will find several evaluation checklists to guide you through the revising stage. Personalize these checklists by adding or modifying items to suit your writing needs.

> ### Evaluation Checklist for Revising
> ✓ Did you clearly state your main idea?
> ✓ Does your essay have a strong introduction, body, and conclusion?
> ✓ Did you include enough interesting details to elaborate, or explore your subject in depth and support your main idea? *(pages C25–C30)*
> ✓ Did you present your ideas in a logical order? *(pages C30–C33)*
> ✓ Do any of your sentences stray from the main idea?
> ✓ Are your ideas clearly explained?
> ✓ Are your words specific?
> ✓ Are any words or ideas repeated unnecessarily? *(page C38)*
> ✓ Are your sentences varied and smoothly connected? *(page C38)*
> ✓ Is the purpose of your essay clear? *(pages C21–C22)*
> ✓ Is your writing suited to your audience? *(page C22)*
> ✓ Is your title effective? *(page C36)*

PRACTICE YOUR SKILLS

 Studying a Revision

Carefully read the following portion of a revised draft on the classical music concert. (Any remaining errors in spelling, capitalization, and usage will be corrected later.) Then answer the questions that follow.

A classical concert

~~I went to a~~ classical concert. ⌐I was reluctant to attend my first⌐ ~~I didn't want to go at first.~~ I was a diehard Heavy Metal fan ~~and this would~~ _and jazz keyboard_

~~not be good for~~ my image. _I had my = to consider_ The concert hall was ~~elegant, like a~~ palace. _tial_ Inside, ~~there were~~ _It was adorned with_ paintings,

sculptures and plush ~~carpeted floors.~~ _velvet seats and cryst[l] chandeliers_ ~~No people~~

~~there are~~ all dressedup. _The audience was_ ~~Some people are~~ in formal

evening clothes. I felt like _I_ was at a fashion show. _glamorous_

The orchestra ~~come~~ _members filed_ onstage and began to tune

their instruments fragments of different songs,

miscellaneous scales and chords filled the air. _and the buzz of conversation_ ~~The~~

~~string section had beautiful handcrafted wooden~~

~~instruments.~~ Ushers handed out porgrams that _in tuxedos_

~~told all about~~ _described_ the piece we were about to hear—

beethoven's "Emperor" piano concerto. The conductor

and the soloist entered. There was applause, ~~but not~~ _a ripple of_

~~too much.~~ This was followed by a ~~moment of~~ silence. _n expectant_

1. Where did the writer combine two sentences into one?
2. What specific words did the writer use to replace vague words?
3. Which idea was out of place?
4. Where did the writer add details? Why? What were those details?
5. What words were deleted? Why?

Revising Through Conferencing

Conferencing is another excellent strategy you can use for revising. **Conferencing** is a meeting for a variety of purposes, such as sharing information and evaluating one another's work.

One way to conference is to use a test reader. Ask a friend, family member, or classmate to read your draft and tell you specifically what was good and what could be improved. When your reader responds, do not try to defend your work. Just listen to the comments. Afterward you should decide which suggestions are worth taking.

Peer Conferencing   Another way to conference is to form a group with three or four other students and read one another's drafts. Then take turns discussing each person's draft, offering praise for what each person has done well and providing suggestions to make the drafts better.

Whether you choose to conference with one other person or in a small group, the following guidelines will help you get the most out of this revising technique.

Guidelines for Conferencing

Guidelines for the Writer

- List some questions for your classmate. What aspects of your essay most concern you?

- Try to be grateful for your critic's candor rather than being upset or defensive. Keep in mind that the criticism you are getting is well intended.

Guidelines for the Critic

- Read your partner's work carefully. What does the writer promise to do in this essay?

- Point out strengths as well as weaknesses. Start your comments by saying something positive like "Your opening really captured my interest."

- Be specific. Refer to a specific word, sentence, or section of the essay when you comment.

- Be sensitive to your partner's feelings. Phrase your criticisms as questions. You might say, "Do you think your details might be stronger if . . . ?"

PRACTICE YOUR SKILLS

● *Revising and Conferencing*

Pair up with a partner and use the preceding strategies and the Evaluation Checklist for Revising on page C39 to review the continuation of the writer's draft about attending a classical music concert. Errors in spelling, punctuation, capitalization, and usage will be corrected later. Using the preceding guidelines, look at each other's revisions. Check to see if there are any areas in which you could make improvements that either of you may have left uncorrected.

The conductor taps his stick and the concert begins. The pianist struck a loud chord. He flew off into a wild introduction. The orchestra answered, picking up the theme. Soon the piano and orchestra are trading licks back and forth. The pianist played with power and authority. The instrument can be heard even when playing with the full orchestra. The first part of the concert is a quick movement. The piano player's fingers move quickly across the keyboard. At times the music seemed abstract and difficult to follow, but whenever I was beginning to feel lost, a familiar theme wood survived reappear. When the first movement ended I felt exhilarated as though I had been swept off into the clouds by a hurricane.

The second section was slow and songlike. It made me feel sad. That mood changed abruptly with the third section which was really driving and built up to a big conclusion. The music toyed with the audience with a series of false endings. By the time it was over the audience were leaping to their feet cheering, aplauding and whistling. . Some fans even threw flowers onto the stage as the pianist took his bow.

Prewriting Workshop
Drafting Workshop
Revising Workshop
Editing Workshop ▶
Publishing Workshop

Sentences

"If you write anything, read it through a second time, for no one can avoid slips, . . . and mistakes in writing will bring you into disrepute." A scholar named Ibn Tibbon made those remarks almost 800 years ago, but his advice is still important today. Correcting errors in your writing—or editing—is an important part of the writing process.

When you edit, you pull together, or integrate, what you know about a variety of usage and mechanics skills. As you review different skills in each composition chapter, add them to your Personalized Editing Checklist. Then, at the end of the course, you will have covered virtually every major skill.

Sentence Fragments

Some writers begin their editing with subjects and verbs, because they are the foundation of every sentence. If a subject or a verb is missing from a group of words, you no longer have a sentence at all. Instead, you have a **sentence fragment**, or only part of a sentence. Because sentence fragments can create misunderstanding, always check your work for any missing subjects and verbs.

SENTENCE FRAGMENT	Musicians in worn-out jeans and scruffy sneakers.
	(The verb is missing. You do not know what the musicians are doing.)
SENTENCE	Musicians in worn-out jeans and scruffy sneakers **are practicing their instruments.**

Subject and Verb Agreement

The next logical step in editing is to check if the subject and verb in each sentence agree in number. **Number** refers to whether the subject and the verb are singular (one) or plural (more than one). To agree, therefore, both the subject and the verb must be either singular or plural.

In the following examples, the subject is underlined once, and the verb is underlined twice.

SINGULAR SUBJECT AND VERB   The drummer sits in a chair.

PLURAL SUBJECT AND VERB   The guitar players stand in the front.

Words Interrupting a Subject and Verb

Checking for subject and verb agreement, of course, is not always as easy as in the examples above. Sometimes, for instance, words separate the subject from the verb. As a result, you can easily make a mistake by having the verb agree with a nearby word—rather than with the subject.

AGREEMENT ERROR   That horn by the speakers belong to Jim. (The verb must agree with the subject *horn*, not with the word *speakers*—even though that word is closer to the verb than the subject is.)

CORRECT   That horn by the speakers belongs to Jim. (The singular verb *belongs* now agrees with the singular subject *horn*.)

If you want your writing not only to be true but also to be clear and easy to understand, never skip the editing stage of the writing process.

Editing Checklist

✔ Are there any sentence fragments?

✔ Do the subject and verb in each sentence agree—even if words interrupt them?

Throughout prewriting, drafting, and revising stages, you have been concentrating on the form and substance of your work. While you may have noticed—and sometimes corrected—slips in spelling, punctuation, capitalization, and usage, your focus has been on the more substantive concerns of presenting your ideas clearly and refining your words. **Editing** is the stage in which you locate and correct your mechanical errors.

Strategies for Editing

By the time you reach the editing stage, you will have a draft that reflects your best effort. Along the way you probably tried to follow all the rules you know for correct mechanics, but for the most part you concentrated on the content of your essay rather than on its form. Now that you are satisfied with your content, you need to correct errors in grammar, usage, mechanics, and spelling. Such errors can ruin the good impression you have tried to make in your writing.

COMPUTER TIP

Use the Grammar Checker feature of your word-processing software to check your writing for technical errors. But use caution: you know best what you mean to say. A Grammar Checker may not always give the right solution.

Using an Editing Checklist   When you edit, you should slowly proofread your work at least three times, concentrating on one kind of error at a time. For example, read each sentence first for errors in usage, such as agreement of subject and verb, consistency of verb tense, agreement of pronoun and antecedent, and comparison of adjectives and adverbs. Then read each sentence a second time, looking for spelling problems. Finally, read over your paper and check for errors in punctuation and capitalization. The checklist on the next page will help you concentrate on particular types of errors.

> ### Editing Checklist
>
> ✓ Are your sentences completely free of errors in grammar and usage?
>
> ✓ Did you spell each word correctly?
>
> ✓ Did you use capital letters where needed?
>
> ✓ Did you punctuate each sentence correctly?
>
> ✓ Did you indent your paragraphs as needed and leave proper margins on each side of the paper?

Using a Manual of Style   Writers often consult style guides or handbooks to review rules for grammar, spelling, mechanics, and usage. As you edit, you may wish to consult one of the following:

- *APA Publication Manual of the American Psychological Association.* 4th ed. Washington, DC: American Psychological Association, 1994.
- *The Chicago Manual of Style: The Essential Guide for Writers, Editors, and Publishers.* 14th ed. Chicago: University of Chicago Press, 1993.
- *MLA Handbook for Writers of Research Papers.* 5th ed. New York: Modern Language Association of America, 1999.

Creating a Personalized Editing Checklist   You may also want to reserve an eight-page section at the end of your **journal** to use as a Personalized Editing Checklist. Write the following headings on every other page: *Grammar Problems, Usage Problems, Spelling Problems, Mechanics Problems* (capitalization and punctuation)—two pages for each type of problem. Throughout the year, record on these pages any mistakes that recur in your writing. Look up those problems in the index, and next to each error write the page in this textbook that helps you correct it. It is a good idea to include a few examples of the corrected problem. Refer to this checklist each time you edit a composition.

Proofreading   While editing their work, writers use a shorthand method to correct their errors. Some of the most common symbols of this shorthand, called proofreading symbols, are shown in the chart on the next page.

Proofreading Symbols

∧	insert	Meet me _{at} three o'clock.
⋏	insert comma	Hello‸my name is Claire.
⊙	insert period	Dr‸Chan told me to call.
ℐ	delete	Where is ~~is~~ that dog?
¶	new paragraph	¶Before dawn the fog had lifted.
⋯	let it stand	What ~~surprising~~ news!
#	add space	Jack hit a home#run.
⌒	close up	I'll do it my◡self.
∿	transpose	I did͡nt hear the phone ring.
≡	capital letter	The party is on ≡saturday.
/	lowercase	Where is the highest /Mountain?
(SP)	spell out	I ate (SP)2 oranges.
⌄⌄	insert quotes	⌄I hope you can join us⌄said my brother.
⌃	insert hyphen	I attended a school⌃related event.
⌄	insert apostrophe	The ravenous dog ate the cats⌄ food.
⌒	move copy	I usually(on Fridays)go to the movies.

The following model shows how a student edited with proofreading symbols.

MODEL: Edited Draft

A ≡classical ≡concert

A diehard Ⱨeavy Ⱨetal and jazz keyboard fan
I was reluctant to attend my first classical
concert. I had my my image to consider. The
concert hall was palatial. It was adorned with
paintings, sculptures, and plush velvet seats and
cryst̸l chandeliers.¶ The audience ~~were~~ was all
dressed∧#up¶ in formal evening clothes. I felt like I
was at a glamorous fashion show.

The orchestra members filed onstage and began to tune their instruments⌢fragments of different songs, miscellaneous scales⌃and chords and the buzz of conversation filled the air. Ushers in tuxedos handed out porgrams ~~that~~ describ*ing*ed the piece we were about to hear—beethoven's ⸙"Emperor" ~~piano~~ concerto. The conductor and the soloist entered. There was a ripple of applause⸳ ~~This was~~ followed by an expectant silence.

PRACTICE YOUR SKILLS

● *Using Proofreading Symbols*

Copy the following paragraph and edit it, using proofreading symbols.

I still am not sure what I should do after I graduate from High school. While I plan to go to college I am not ready to start immediately since I love to paint, I want to attend artschool for at least one year. Through out school all my art teachers thought I had talent and they told me to spend more time at my easel. I also want to read and study my favorite artist's techniques. My mom and dad, however, say that I should wait to study art until after I finish college. Its a dilemma!

☐	**Publishing**	**Writing Process**	☐

Publishing is the final stage in the writing process. When you publish your work, you present it in neat final form to an audience. Some writing is not meant for an audience. Diaries, for example, are written for the sake of the writer. Most writing, however, is an act of communication—of sending a message to someone. As such it would be incomplete without an audience at the receiving end. Publishing your work, therefore, is the best way to deliver your message. The following chart has many good suggestions for publishing.

Ways to Publish Your Writing

In School

- Read your work aloud to a small group in your class.
- Display your final draft on a bulletin board in your classroom or school library.
- Read your work aloud to your class or present it in the form of a radio program or videotape.
- Create a class library and media center to which you submit your work. The library and media center should have a collection of folders or files devoted to different types of student writing and media presentations.
- Create a class anthology to which every student contributes one piece. Use electronic technology to design a small publication. Share your anthology with other classes.
- Submit your work to your school literary magazine, newspaper, or yearbook.

Outside of School

- Submit your written work to a newspaper or magazine.
- Share your work with a professional interested in the subject.
- Present your work to an appropriate community group.
- Send a video based on your written work to a local cable television station.
- Enter your work in a local, state, or national writing contest.

Using Standard Manuscript Form

The appearance of your essay may be almost as important as its content. A marked-up paper with inconsistent margins is difficult to read. A neat, legible paper, however, makes a positive impression on your reader. When you are using a word-processing program to prepare your final draft, it is important to know how to lay out the page and how to choose a typeface and type size.

Use the following guidelines for standard manuscript form to help you prepare your final draft. The model on the following pages shows how the writer used these guidelines to prepare her final draft on attending a classical music concert.

Standard Manuscript Form

- Use standard-sized 8½-by-11-inch white paper. Use one side of the paper only.

- If handwriting, use black or blue ink. If using a word-processing program or typing, use a black ink cartridge or black typewriter ribbon and double-space the lines.

- Leave a 1¼-inch margin at the left and right. The left margin must be even. The right margin should be as even as possible.

- Put your name, the course title, the name of your teacher, and the date in the upper right-hand corner of the first page. Where applicable, follow your teacher's specific guidelines for headings and margins.

- Center the title of your essay two lines below the date. Do not underline or put quotation marks around your title.

- If using a word-processing program or typing, skip four lines between the title and the first paragraph. If handwriting, skip two lines.

- If using a word-processing program or typing, indent the first line of each paragraph five spaces. If handwriting, indent the first line of each paragraph 1 inch.

- Leave a 1-inch margin at the bottom of all pages.

- Starting on page 2, number each page in the upper right-hand corner. Begin the first line 1 inch from the top. Word-processing programs give you the option of inserting page numbers.

1 INCH

Claudia Gonzalez
English: Ms. Robbins
September 20, 2000

2 LINES

A Classical Concert

4 LINES

    A die-hard heavy metal and jazz keyboard fan, I was reluctant to attend my first classical piano concert. This would not be good for my image. Soon, however, my attitude changed. The concert hall was palatial. It was adorned with paintings, sculptures, plush velvet seats, and crystal chandeliers. The audience was all dressed up in formal evening clothes. I felt like I was at a glamorous fashion show.

1.25 INCHES

    The orchestra members filed onstage and began to tune their instruments. Fragments of songs, scales, and chords and the buzz of conversation filled the air. Ushers in tuxedos handed out programs describing the piece we were about to hear—Beethoven's *Emperor Concerto*. The conductor and the soloist entered. There was a ripple of applause, followed by an expectant silence.

    The conductor tapped his baton and the concert began. The pianist struck a resounding chord and then sped off in a whirlwind of notes. The soloist's fingers raced like lightning up and down the keyboard. The orchestra followed his lead, and before long, the piano and the orchestra were responding to each other like a pair of graceful but

1 INCH

frenzied dancers. At times the music seemed abstract and difficult to follow, but whenever I was beginning to feel lost, a familiar theme would resurface. When the first movement ended, I felt as though I had been swept away by a storm to another world.

The musical tempest subsided. The second movement was slow and songlike. It made me feel sad. That mood changed abruptly, though, as the third section drove relentlessly to a climactic grand finale. A series of false endings kept us at the edge of our seats. When the last note sounded, the audience were leaping to their feet cheering, applauding, and whistling. Some fans even threw flowers onto the stage as the pianist took his bow.

1.25 INCHES ↔

1.25 INCHES ←→   First impressions can be misleading. I thought I would spend a dull evening but ended up really enjoying myself. It was like becoming best friends with someone you could not stand at first. The next day, I went right out and bought three different recordings of Beethoven's *Emperor Concerto*. I can't wait to go to my next concert. I discovered something new about music and about myself.

↕ 1 INCH

Time Out to Reflect

You have now traveled through the five stages of the writing process. At the beginning of this chapter *(page C8)*, you saw a diagram. Take a moment to write down your understanding of the writing process. How closely does this process match your previous experiences as a writer? What might account for any differences between the writing process as described in this chapter and the writing process as you have previously experienced it?

◢ Writing Process Checklist

Remember that the writing process is recursive—you can move back and forth among the stages of the process to achieve your purpose. The numbers in parentheses refer to pages where you can get help with your writing.

PREWRITING

- Find a subject to write about by taking an inventory of your interests, freewriting, exploring the Internet, keeping a **journal**, and reading and thinking about literature. *(pages C10–C17)*
- Choose and limit a subject. *(pages C18–C19)*
- Consider your purpose, audience, and occasion. *(pages C21–C22)*
- Be aware of the voice you choose. *(pages C23–C25)*
- Develop your subject by observing, brainstorming for details, clustering, and inquiring. *(pages C25–C30)*
- Organize your material by focusing your subject, classifying your details, and ordering your details. *(pages C30–C33)*

DRAFTING

- Write a first draft and choose a title. *(pages C34–C36)*

REVISING

- Elaborate by using facts, details, quotations, or examples to develop an idea or support a statement.
- Rearrange sentences and paragraphs for logical order.
- Delete needless words and ideas, and substitute precise, vivid words for dull, general language.
- Use the <u>Evaluation Checklist for Revising</u> as a reminder and guide. *(page C39)*
- Use conferencing to help you revise your draft. *(pages C41–C42)*
- Revise your draft as often as needed. Repeat some of the prewriting and drafting strategies if necessary.

EDITING

- Use the <u>Editing Checklists</u> to look for errors in grammar, usage, spelling, capitalization, and punctuation. *(pages C44 and C46)*
- Use proofreading symbols to correct errors. *(page C47)*

PUBLISHING

- Follow standard manuscript form and make a neat final copy of your work. Then find an appropriate way to share your work with others. *(pages C48–C50)*

CHAPTER 2

Developing Your Writing Style

"All writing is communication," said the American writer E. B. White; ". . . it is the Self escaping into the open." In other words, how you write is just as important as what you write, because your reader can see only what is on the page. Whether your reader is an old friend or someone whom you have never met, your word choices and sentence structures reveal a great deal about the way you think and organize your ideas. In this sense, your reader gets to know you by your writing style.

Developing a clear and original writing style will help you communicate to your reader in a way that is easily understood and appreciated. This chapter will give you the tools you need to develop a writing style so you can communicate your thoughts in a way that will capture your reader's interest.

Reading with a Writer's Eye

In her memoir, Jade Snow Wong reflects on her experiences growing up in a Chinese American family. As you read the following portion of Wong's memoir, think about how the merging of Asian and Western cultures plays a major role in Wong's reflections on her upbringing. On a second reading, notice how Wong's straightforward, direct writing style helps you understand what it was like for her to be the "fifth Chinese daughter."

Fifth Chinese Daughter

Jade Snow Wong

From infancy to my sixteenth year, I was reared according to nineteenth century ideals of Chinese womanhood. I was never left alone, though it was not unusual for me to feel lonely, while surrounded by a family of seven others, and often by ten (including bachelor cousins) at meals.

My father (who enjoyed our calling him Daddy in English) was the unquestioned head of our household. He was not talkative, being preoccupied with his business affairs and with reading constantly otherwise. My mother was mistress of domestic affairs. Seldom did these two converse before their children, but we knew them to be a united front, and suspected that privately she both informed and influenced him about each child.

In order to support the family in America, Daddy tried various occupations—candy making, the ministry to which he was later ordained—but finally settled on manufacturing men's and children's denim garments. He leased sewing equipment, installed machines in a basement where rent was cheapest, and there he and his family lived and worked. There was no thought that dim, airless quarters were terrible conditions for living and working, or that child labor was unhealthful. The only goal was for all in the family to work, to save, and to become educated. It was possible, so it would be done.

My father, a meticulous bookkeeper, used only an abacus, a brush, ink, and Chinese ledgers. Because of his newly learned ideals, he pioneered for the right of women to work. Concerned that they have economic independence, but not with the long hours of industrial home work, he went to shy housewives' apartments and taught them sewing.

My earliest memories of companionship with my father were as his passenger in his red wheelbarrow, sharing space with the piles of blue-jean materials he was delivering to a worker's home. He must have been forty. He was lean, tall, inevitably wearing blue overalls, rolled shirt sleeves, and high black kid shoes. In his pockets were numerous keys, tools, and pens. On such deliveries, I noticed that he always managed time to show a mother how to sew a difficult seam, or to help her repair a machine, or just to chat.

I observed from birth that living and working were inseparable. My mother was short, sturdy, young looking, and took pride in her appearance. She was at her machine the minute housework was done, and she was the hardest-working seamstress, seldom pausing, working after I went to bed. The hum of sewing machines continued day and night, seven days a week. She knew that to have more than the four necessities, she must work and save. We knew that to overcome poverty, there were only two methods: working and education.

Having provided the setup for family industry, my father turned his attention to our education. Ninety-five percent of the population in China had been illiterate. He knew that American public schools would take care of our English, but he had to be the watchdog to nurture our Chinese knowledge. Only the Cantonese tongue was ever spoken by him or my mother. When the two oldest girls arrived from China, the schools of Chinatown received only boys. My father tutored his daughters each morning before breakfast. In the midst of a foreign environment, he clung to a combination of the familiar old standards and what was permissible in the newly learned Christian ideals.

My eldest brother was born in America, the only boy for fourteen years, and after him three daughters—another older sister, myself, and my younger sister. Then my younger brother, Paul, was born. That older brother, Lincoln, was cherished in the best Chinese tradition. He had his own room; he kept a German shepherd as his pet; he was tutored by a Chinese scholar; he was sent to private school for American classes. As a male Wong, he would be responsible some day for the preservation of and pilgrimages to ancestral graves—his privileges were his birthright. We girls were content with the unusual opportunities of working and attending two schools.

For by the time I was six, times in Chinatown were changing. The Hip Wo Chinese Christian Academy (in the same building as the Methodist Mission) had been founded on a coeducational basis, with nominal tuition. Financial support came from three Protestant church boards: the Congregational, Presbyterian, and Methodist churches contributed equal shares. My father was on the Hip Wo School Board for many years. By day, I attended American public school near our home. From 5:00 P.M. to 8:00 P.M., on five weekdays and from 9:00 A.M. to 12 noon on Saturdays, I attended the Chinese school. Classes numbered twenty to thirty students, and were taught by educated Chinese from China. We studied poetry, calligraphy, philosophy, literature, history, correspondence, religion, all by exacting memorization. The Saturday morning chapel services carried out the purposes of the supporting churches.

Daddy emphasized memory development: he could still recite fluently many lengthy lessons of his youth. Every evening after both schools, I'd sit by my father, often as he worked at his sewing machine, sing-songing my lessons above its hum. Sometimes I would stop to hold a light for him as he threaded the difficult holes of a specialty machine, such as one for bias bindings. After my Chinese lessons passed his approval, I was allowed to attend to American homework. I was made to feel luckier than other Chinese girls who didn't study Chinese, and also luckier than Western girls without a dual heritage. . . . There was little time for play, and toys were unknown to me. In any spare time, I was supplied with embroidery and sewing for my mother. The Chinese New Year, which by the old lunar calendar would fall sometime in late January or early February of the Western Christian calendar, was the most special time of the year, for then the machines stopped for three days. Mother would clean our living quarters very thoroughly, decorate the sitting room with flowering branches and fresh oranges, and arrange candied fruits or salty melon seeds for callers. All of us would be dressed in bright new clothes, and relatives or close friends, who came to call, would give each of us a red paper packet containing a good luck coin—usually a quarter. I remember how my classmates would gleefully talk of *their* receipts. But my mother made us give our money to her, for she said that she needed it to reciprocate to others.

Yet there was little reason for unhappiness. I was never hungry. Though we had no milk, there was all the rice we wanted. We had hot and cold running water—a rarity in Chinatown—as well as our own bathtub. Our sheets were pieced from dishtowels, but we had sheets. I was never neglected, for my mother and father were always at home. During school vacation periods, I was taught to operate many types of machines—tacking (for pockets), overlocking (for the raw edges of seams), buttonhole, double seaming; and I learned all the stages in producing a pair of jeans to its final inspection, folding and tying in bundles of a dozen pairs by size, ready for pickup. Denim jeans are heavy—my shoulders ached often. My father set up a modest nickel-and-dime piecework reward for me, which he recorded in my own notebook, and paid me regularly.

Only Daddy and Oldest Brother were allowed individual idiosyncrasies. Daughters were all expected to be of one standard. To allow each one of many daughters to be different would have posed enormous problems of cost, energy, and attention. No one was shown physical affection. Such familiarity would have weakened my parents and endangered the one-answer authoritative system. One standard from past to present, whether in China or in San Francisco, was simpler to enforce.

Thirty-five years later, I have four children, two sons and two daughters. In principle we remain true to my father's and mother's tradition, I believe. Our children respect my husband and me, but it is not a blind obedience enforced by punishment. It is a respect won from observing us and rounded by friendship. My parents never said "please" and "thank you" for any service or gift. In Chinese, both "please" and "thank you" can be literally translated as "I am not worthy" and naturally, no parent is going to say that about a service which should be their just due. Now I say "thank you," "please," and "sorry" to my children, in English, and I do not think it lessens my dignity. The ultimate praise I ever remember from my parents was a single word, "good." We do not abhor a show of affection. Each child looks forward to his goodnight kiss and tuck-in. Sometimes one or more of them will throw his arms around one of us and cry out, "I love you so."

Traditional Chinese parents pit their children against a standard of perfection without regard to personality, individual ambitions, tolerance for human error, or exposure to the changing social scene. It never occurred to that kind of parent to be friends with their children on common ground. Unlike our parents, we think we tolerate human error and human change. Our children are being encouraged to develop their individual abilities. They all draw and can use their hands in crafts, are all familiar with our office and love to experiment with the potter's wheel or enameling supplies at our studio. Sometimes I have been asked, "What would you like your children to be?" Let each choose his or her career. The education of our girls will be provided by us as well as that of our boys.

Thinking as a Writer

Analyzing Writing Style

Think about how Jade Snow Wong's words and sentence construction contribute to your interpretation of her feelings about the influence of Chinese culture on her upbringing.

- How might the author's writing style be different if she were writing about growing up in China as opposed to growing up as a Chinese American in the United States? What, if anything, would remain the same?

Convey Author's Style

Oral Expression • Choose a paragraph from the excerpt from Jade Snow Wong's memoir that you find particularly interesting or striking and read it aloud. How does Wong's style affect your delivery of the paragraph? How does her style influence the reaction you have to that particular paragraph? Explain your answers.

Comparing Visual and Writing Styles

Viewing Elements of art—line, shape, color, texture—are to a visual artist what words are to a writer. Both the artist and the writer use these means to express their thoughts and feelings. Principles of design— pattern, variety, rhythm—are to an artist what sentences and paragraphs are to a writer. They mandate the way the elements are used to convey ideas and feelings.

Artist unknown, Chinese. *Winged Tiger,* 19th century. One of a pair of banners, silk embroidery on silk, 46$\frac{1}{2}$ by 46 inches. The Metropolitan Museum of Art.

- Observe this banner depicting a winged tiger. What does the banner convey to you? How does the artist's style, or unique way of using the elements, contribute to your interpretation of the banner?

Developing Your Stylistic Skills

The selection you have recently read and the accompanying activities should suggest to you the importance of communication in daily life. It is fair to say that carefully chosen words and sentences are the tools of skillful communication.

> "When *I* use a word," Humpty Dumpty said, in rather a scornful tone, "it means just what I choose it to mean—neither more nor less."
>
> "The question is," said Alice, "whether you *can* make words mean so many different things."
>
> "The question is," said Humpty Dumpty, "which is to be master—that's all."
>
> —Lewis Carroll, *Through the Looking Glass and What Alice Found There*

Are you a master of the words and sentences that you use in your writing? Speakers use facial expressions and subtle changes in tone of voice to communicate their meaning. When you write, though, you must choose your words and shape your sentences in such a way that your message is clear. This chapter will help you become a master of the words and sentences you write.

Your writing **style** is the distinctive way you express yourself through the words you choose and the way you shape your sentences.

 Your Writer's Journal

In your journal, freewrite a list of memories from your childhood. Make a list of topics related to the theme of childhood and growing up. Your topics may include anything that you remember clearly and vividly. You can write about a family vacation, a sporting event, or a surprise party. Choose one experience from your list and write down everything you remember about it. What was your reaction to the event? Describe any sights, sounds, or other sensations in as much detail as you can.

● Choosing Vivid Words

Precise, vivid language helps to etch a writer's message in the reader's mind. Using general words is like sketching the outline of a person without adding the distinguishing features. Vivid words, on the other hand, supply details that convey an image precisely. The vivid words in the following passage create a mood and make the scene from the novel *Ethan Frome* easy to picture.

MODEL: Vivid Words

> They walked on in silence through the blackness of the **hemlock-shaded** lane, where Ethan's sawmill **gloomed** through the night, and out again into the comparative clearness of the fields. On the farther side of the hemlock belt the open country **rolled** away before them grey and lonely under the stars. Sometimes their way led them under the shade of an overhanging bank or through the thin obscurity of a **clump** of leafless trees. Here and there a farmhouse stood far back among the fields, **mute** and **cold** as a grave-stone. The night was so still that they heard the frozen snow **crackle** under their feet.
>
> —*Edith Wharton,* Ethan Frome

Specific Words

In the following examples, notice how specific words leave a deeper impression than dull, general words do.

GENERAL NOUN   noise
SPECIFIC NOUNS   crash, whisper, clang

GENERAL VERB   walked
SPECIFIC VERBS   ambled, strolled, lumbered

Writing Tip

Choose **specific words** over general words.

PRACTICE YOUR SKILLS

● *Choosing Specific Words*

Write two specific words for each of the following general words.

1. tree	**6.** nice	**11.** went	**16.** excellent
2. car	**7.** cute	**12.** saw	**17.** wanted
3. clothes	**8.** pretty	**13.** said	**18.** looked
4. books	**9.** great	**14.** thought	**19.** moved
5. airplane	**10.** ran	**15.** walked	**20.** disagreed

● *Using a Sentence Pyramid to Write with Specific Words*

Copy the pyramid below. In the first box, copy an underlined word from the sample sentence. Brainstorm and use a thesaurus to come up with specific words for the second box. In the third box, use the new words in phrases. Write a new sentence in the fourth box.

SAMPLE SENTENCE   The <u>police officer</u> <u>lit</u> <u>flares,</u> which <u>gave</u> the <u>scene</u> a <u>theatrical, tragic</u> air.

Copy General Word:

> Scene

Choose Specific Words:

> environment   theater
> milieu   locale
> site   <u>climate</u>
> arena   setting
> <u>circumstances</u>   outburst

Write Phrases:

> <u>in a warm climate</u>
> under strange circumstances

Write New Sentence:

> Michael's grandparents prefer living <u>in a warm climate</u> over a cold one.

Figurative Language

Good writers create **figurative language**—words and phrases employed for a highly imaginative rather than a literal meaning. Figurative language uses words in inventive ways to create strong images.

Similes and Metaphors Both of these figures of speech express a similarity between two essentially different things. **Similes** use *like* or *as* to state the comparison. **Metaphors**, on the other hand, *imply* a comparison without using *like* or *as*. Notice how the use of a simile or a metaphor enlivens the following sentence.

DULL	After her chores Karen quickly ran out of the house.
SIMILE	After her chores Karen exploded out of the house **like a Fourth of July firecracker.**
METAPHOR	**Karen became a Fourth of July firecracker,** exploding out of the house after her chores.

Clichés Overused, worn-out comparisons or figures of speech drain life from your writing. Such worn-out expressions are called **clichés**. You should always replace clichés with fresh similes or metaphors or with specific words.

CLICHÉ	One club member spoke for half an hour, **making a mountain out of a molehill.**
FRESH METAPHOR	One club member spoke for a half an hour, **making a blaze out of an ember.**
SPECIFIC WORDS	One club member spoke for half an hour, **making a dilemma out of a small problem.**

Writing Tip

Use **similes** and **metaphors** to enliven writing. Avoid **clichés**.

PRACTICE YOUR SKILLS

● *Identifying Similes and Metaphors*

Write *simile* or *metaphor* to indicate which figure of speech is used in each of the following sentences.

1. The afternoon light entered the room like a shy visitor.

2. Dim rivers of light were flowing from horizon to horizon.
   —*Arthur C. Clarke,* 2001: A Space Odyssey

3. Japan is a necklace of islands.

4. The sunset was a treasure chest of gold laid in the meadow.

5. Somewhere at the end of the column a driver sang—the wailing toneless voice rose and fell like a wind through a keyhole.
   —*Graham Greene,* The Heart of the Matter

6. We settle down, like walruses stranded on rocks.
   —*Virginia Woolf,* The Waves

7. The child stood like a lost pup in the street.

8. The drumbeat of her blood was urging her on to the finish line.

9. Catching the sunlight, the raindrops seemed like cat's-eye marbles.

10. She was very old and small and she walked slowly . . . with the balanced heaviness and lightness of a pendulum in a grandfather clock.
    —*Eudora Welty,* "A Worn Path"

● *Revising to Eliminate Clichés*

Replace the underlined clichés in the following sentences with fresh similes or metaphors or with specific words.

11. Mom's smile is as <u>sweet as pie</u>.

12. This book is <u>right up your alley</u>.

13. Losing the straw poll by 30 percentage points <u>took the wind out of the candidate's sails</u>.

14. Sally still saw <u>a ray of hope</u>.

15. The television show was as <u>dull as dishwater</u>.

Comparing

When you **compare,** you find similarities between people, places, things, or events. When you write a simile or metaphor, however, you compare in a particular way—you show how two unlike subjects are alike. You find qualities that the subjects share. For example, a baseball glove and a butterfly net both require the use of hand and arm and the skill to catch flying objects, and both are used by someone pursuing an object. Effective similes and metaphors, then, use original, thought-provoking comparisons that cause people to look at things in new and different ways.

> Daniel leaped with the silent, sleek agility of a panther.

Making a chart like the one that follows will help you construct similar comparisons.

COMPARISON CHART

Person, Place, Thing, Animal, Event	Comparison	Similar Qualities
Subject 1 DANIEL	leaps with silent, sleek agility	DANIEL = PANTHER
Subject 2 PANTHER	leaps with silent, sleek agility	

THINKING PRACTICE

Create your own comparison chart for one of the following phrases. Then write your simile or metaphor.

1. My best friend walks . . .
2. The thunderclouds hovered . . .
3. The bus lurched . . .
4. The wooded path stretched . . .

▶ Writing Concise Sentences

Referring to a truly effective piece of writing, the English writer Katherine Mansfield once remarked, "There mustn't be one single word out of place or one word that can be taken out." Writing that follows this advice is concise; it contains no unnecessary words or phrases.

Writing Tip

Express your meaning in as few words as possible.

Redundancy

One way to revise wordiness is to eliminate unnecessary repetition, or **redundancy.** In a redundant sentence, the same idea is repeated without any new shades of meaning.

REDUNDANT	The **slowly moving** train crawled into the station.
CONCISE	The train **crawled** into the station.
REDUNDANT	She grew four **inches in height** in one year.
CONCISE	She grew four **inches** in one year.

PRACTICE YOUR SKILLS

● *Eliminating Redundancy*

Revise each of the following sentences by eliminating the redundant words or phrases.

1. Jonathan scowled angrily when Stephanie insulted him.

2. The strange feeling was very peculiar.

3. Dogs can hear sounds that are inaudible to the human ear and cannot be heard by people.

4. Sharks blink their eyes at strong light by closing a membrane over their eyeballs.

5. We packed the necessary things we needed for the trip.

6. Terry was alone in the damp cave because there was no one else in it.

7. The student was given a medal for his brave heroism.

8. The wave was huge in size and awesome in nature.

9. She set her alarm for 3 A.M. in the morning so she could watch the meteor shower.

10. The fog over the city was thick because low clouds hung over the buildings.

Wordiness

When you revise your writing, streamline the sentences by eliminating expressions that add no meaning and by reducing wordy phrases.

Empty Expressions   Fillers often take up space in a sentence without adding any meaning. When you revise, eliminate such empty expressions.

WORDY	Despite **the fact that there has been** a drought in the food bowl of the Great Plains, most crops are surviving.
CONCISE	Despite the drought in the food bowl of the Great Plains, most crops are surviving.
WORDY	**In my opinion** the high-fashion clothes advertised in most magazines are like costumes.
CONCISE	The high-fashion clothes advertised in most magazines are like costumes.
WORDY	**What I'm trying to say is that** little lies lead to big lies.
CONCISE	Little lies lead to big lies.

EMPTY EXPRESSIONS	
on account of	due to the fact that
what I want is	the reason that
in my opinion	the thing/fact is that
it seems as if	there is/are/was/were
it is/was	what I'm trying to say is that
because of the fact that	I believe/feel/think/that

PRACTICE YOUR SKILLS

● Revising to Eliminate Empty Expressions

Revise the following paragraph by eliminating the empty expressions or by replacing them with more precise language.

EXAMPLE   In my opinion Ernest Hemingway's house in Key West, Florida, is part of history.

POSSIBLE   Ernest Hemingway's house in Key West, Florida,
REVISION   is part of history.

A Writer's Home

Key West is an interesting place to visit for the reason that it is the southernmost city in the continental United States. On account of the fact that it has the Atlantic Ocean on one side and the Gulf of Mexico on the other, Key West is a popular boating, fishing, and snorkeling spot. It was Key West's great fishing that was what drew writer Ernest Hemingway to the area in the 1920s. The fact is that Hemingway was the first writer of renown to set up a home in Key West, although the famous naturalist John James Audubon had lived there earlier. The fact of the matter is that Hemingway owned his home in Key West from 1931 to

1961. Because of the fact that Hemingway was very much interested in Spain, his home has many beautiful Spanish objects. It seems as if his wife wanted a swimming pool, so the home also has the first pool built in Key West. On account of the fact that he needed privacy, Hemingway had a studio in the loft above his pool house. It was there that he would work on his writing in the company of some of his 50 cats. Due to the fact that they were so much a part of the home, the cats were allowed to stay, and their offspring now wander contentedly around their famous home.

Wordy Phrases and Clauses   Some sentences can be reduced by eliminating wordy sentences or clauses so that the same meaning is expressed in fewer words. Notice how the following sentences with wordy phrases and clauses can be written more concisely.

WORDY   Kristin danced **with a graceful style.** (prepositional phrase)

CONCISE   Kristin danced **gracefully.** (adverb)

WORDY   Ricky wore a jacket **made of suede.** (participial phrase)

CONCISE   Ricky wore a **suede** jacket. (adjective)

WORDY   The tree **that is in my backyard** is older than my grandmother. (adjective clause)

CONCISE   The tree **in my backyard** . . . (prepositional phrase)

WORDY   *Nicholas Nickleby,* **which is a novel by Charles Dickens,** was made into a nine-hour play. (adjective clause)

CONCISE   *Nicholas Nickleby,* **a novel by Charles Dickens** . . . (appositive phrase)

PRACTICE YOUR SKILLS

● **Deleting Unnecessary Words**

Revise the following paragraph by eliminating redundancy, empty expressions, and wordy phrases and clauses.

Robots at Work

Automated robots are not just a fantasy of the future. Today there are already 40,000 robots in the United States that perform repetitive jobs in factories. Robots are also used in other industrialized countries where industry has developed. The fact of the matter is that these robots are controlled by computers. Some robots can even distinguish shapes and colors due to the fact that they use television cameras as eyes. Robot experts who know a lot about these things predict that the use of robots will increase dramatically in the next ten years.

COMPUTER TIP

The Grammar Checker in your word-processing software analyzes your text for many of the sentence problems that you have been reading about in this chapter. These include wordiness, unclear phrasing, sentence structure, and misused words. To check your sentences for these and other specific problems, you can customize your Grammar Checker. Find the Settings feature in the Grammar Checker and click the box next to any option. Check your Personalized Editing Checklist for recurring errors to determine how to adjust the settings.

Flyers

You see them all over—stuck inside newspapers, placed on desks or seats, handed out at exits. What is it about flyers that makes them a popular way to spread information? They are called *flyers* because of their tendency to fly or fall onto the floor. Then someone must bend down and pick them up, and in the process the flyers and their message get noticed.

They also get noticed because of their economy of words. All the extra, unnecessary words and phrases are sifted out on a flyer, leaving the words and phrases with the most impact to communicate clearly. Less is more.

Consider the following flyer.

easy-to-read type; brief phrases

attention-getting headline

essential information

symbols that convey ideas

Media Activity

For practice in making each word count, make a flyer of your own. Instead of advertising a garage sale, advertise the best qualities of a special friend or relative. Make a rough draft that includes all the elements above (headline, bulleted list, boxed information, symbols). Choose words with impact and be as concise as possible.

Use a word-processing program to create the final version of your flyer. (Many have flyer templates included. Feel free to experiment with the design of your flyer.) Choose the headline and text size for maximum effect. Add clip art symbols to convey meaning through graphics. Carefully proofread your flyer and then print it out. After your teacher and peers have reviewed it, give it to the person whose qualities you praised.

⬤ Creating Sentence Variety

Sentences are the building blocks of paragraphs. If all sentences in a composition were the same length and structure, the composition would undoubtedly be drab and uninteresting. If the sentences are varied, however, the composition will more than likely hold the reader's attention.

Sentence-Combining Strategies

Good writing uses a mixture of short and long sentences to imitate the natural rhythms of speech. Therefore, whenever possible, use the following strategies to combine short and choppy sentences into longer ones.

Combining Sentences with Phrases   One way to combine short sentences is to express some of the information in a prepositional phrase, an appositive phrase, or a participial phrase.

A. The Blue Angels perform spectacular stunts. They are part of the United States Navy. They perform aviation stunts at air shows. The shows are held around the world.

The Blue Angels **of the United States Navy** perform spectacular aviation stunts **at air shows around the world.** (prepositional phrases)

B. Blue Angel pilots must have at least 1,500 hours of flying time. They are some of the best-trained pilots.

Blue Angel pilots, **some of the best-trained pilots,** must have at least 1,500 hours of flying time. (appositive phrase)

C. The Blue Angels usually please the audience most. They bring the show to a thrilling finish.

Bringing the show to a thrilling finish, the Blue Angels usually please the audience most. (participial phrase)

PRACTICE YOUR SKILLS

● *Combining Sentences with Phrases*

Combine each of the following sets of short sentences, using the models on page C73. (The letter in parentheses indicates which model to use.) Remember to use commas where needed.

1. The Blue Angels' Skyhawks gain speed quickly. They speed from 0 to 140 miles per hour in two seconds. (C)

2. Six Blue Angels perform together. They perform in tight formation. There are only three feet between planes. (A)

3. The seventh Blue Angel does not fly. He is the announcer. (C)

4. These superb flyers carefully watch the weather. They choose either their high show or their low show. (C)

5. High-speed climbs and starbursts require clear skies. High-speed climbs and starbursts are part of the high show. (B)

6. One pilot gives all the orders. He is the leader. (B)

7. The Blue Angels communicate in flight. They use microphones and earphones. (A)

8. The soloists follow orders from the leader. They sometimes take off from the formation. (C)

9. Two soloists sometimes travel at speeds of nearly 1,000 miles per hour. They approach from opposite directions. (C)

10. In upside-down stunts, the Blue Angels are held in the pilot seat. They are held in place by harnesses. (A)

Combining Sentences by Coordinating   Another way to combine your sentences is to link items of equal importance with one of the following coordinating conjunctions: *and, but, or, for, yet,* or *so.* The resulting combinations will contain compound elements.

A. John Adams died on July 4, 1826. Thomas Jefferson died on July 4, 1826.

John Adams and Thomas Jefferson died on July 4, 1826. (compound subject)

B. Coincidences often intrigue people. Coincidences often frighten people.

Coincidences often **intrigue and frighten** people. (compound verb)

C. The number 88 was thought to be unlucky for James II of Scotland. The number 88 was thought to be unlucky for Mary Stuart, Queen of Scots.

The number 88 was thought to be unlucky for **James II of Scotland and Mary Stuart, Queen of Scots.** (compound object of the preposition)

D. James II died in battle in 1488. Mary Stuart was beheaded in 1587.

James II died in battle in 1488, **but** Mary Stuart was beheaded in 1587. (compound sentence)

E. Superstitions are foolish. Superstitions can be interesting, though.

Superstitions are **foolish but interesting.** (compound predicate adjective)

F. In superstitious societies the people most feared are magicians. In some superstitious societies, however, the people most feared are witch doctors.

In superstitious societies the people most feared are **either magicians or witch doctors.** (compound predicate nominative)

PRACTICE YOUR SKILLS

● *Combining Sentences by Coordinating*

Combine each of the following pairs of sentences, using the preceding models. Within the parentheses are the letter indicating which model to use and the correct conjunction. Use commas where needed.

EXAMPLE   The earliest electronic computers were not compact. They were not reliable. (E—*neither/nor*)

ANSWER   The earliest electronic computers were neither compact nor reliable.

1. The first electronic digital computer contained 18,000 vacuum tubes. It filled a room the size of a gymnasium. (B—*and*)

2. This huge machine was invented at the University of Pennsylvania by J. Presper Eskert. It was also invented by John W. Mauchly. (C—*and*)

3. Overheated wires were a constant problem. Burned-out bulbs were a constant problem. (A—*and*)

4. The solution was a large team of technicians. An air-conditioning system powerful enough to cool the Empire State Building also helped. (F—*and*)

5. Today's much smaller computers are more powerful and more reliable than the old giant machines. They use less energy. (B—*yet*)

Combining Sentences by Subordinating   When ideas in two short sentences are of unequal importance, you can combine them by subordinating. To **subordinate**, express the less important idea in a dependent adjective clause or adverb clause. The words below are often used to introduce dependent clauses.

FOR ADJECTIVE CLAUSES	FOR ADVERB CLAUSES
Relative Pronouns	**Subordinating Conjunctions**

who	which	after	unless
whom	that	although	until
whose		because	whenever

A. Ludwig van Beethoven began to lose his hearing at the age of 26. Many regard him as the world's greatest composer.

Ludwig van Beethoven, **whom many regard as the world's greatest composer,** began to lose his hearing at the age of 26. (adjective clause)

B. He suffered this misfortune throughout his life. His last words sang of hope: "I shall hear in Heaven."

Although he suffered this misfortune throughout his life, his last words sang of hope: "I shall hear in Heaven." (adverb clause)

● *Combining by Subordinating*

Revise the following paragraph. Combine each pair of sentences, using the preceding models. The parentheses tell which model to use and the correct joining word. Use commas where needed.

Saving Lady Liberty

The Statue of Liberty needed extensive repair work. It was built more than 100 years ago. (A—*which*) The monument was badly corroded. Its uplifted arm has welcomed millions to the United States. (A—*whose*) The statue needed work from head to toe. Pollution had caused it to rust. (B—*because*) Liberty cost only $500,000 to build. It cost millions of dollars to repair. (B—*although*) The improvements should last. The statue celebrates its 200th birthday in the year 2086. (B—*until*)

Varying Sentence Structure

To avoid monotony and keep your reader's interest, strive to use a mixture of sentence structures in your essays. Notice the variety in the following passage. To enhance your appreciation of the sentence variety, read the paragraph aloud and notice the various rhythms you hear.

Encounter with Gorillas

SIMPLE

COMPLEX

COMPOUND-
COMPLEX

Suddenly the air was shattered by the screams of five male gorillas bulldozing down the foliage toward me. Their screams were so deafening that I could not locate the source of the noise. I knew only that the group was charging from above; then the tall vegetation gave way as though an out-

SIMPLE

SIMPLE
COMPOUND

COMPOUND

COMPLEX

SIMPLE

of-control tractor were headed directly for me. Only on recognizing me did the group's dominant silverback swiftly brake to a stop three feet away, causing a five-gorilla pileup. I then sank to the ground submissively. The hair on each male's headcrest stood erect; canines were fully exposed. The irises of their eyes, ordinarily soft brown, glinted yellow, and an overpowering fear odor filled the air. For a good half hour, all five males screamed if I made even the slightest move. After a 30-minute period, the group allowed me to pretend to feed meekly on vegetation and then finally moved rigidly out of sight.

—*Dian Fossey,* Gorillas in the Mist

PRACTICE YOUR SKILLS

● *Revising to Vary Sentence Structure*

The following paragraphs contain only simple sentences. Using the sentence-combining techniques on pages C73–C76, revise the paragraphs so that they contain a mixture of simple, compound, complex, and compound-complex sentences. Remember to use commas where needed. When you have finished, read your revisions aloud to check for sentence variety. Then exchange papers with a classmate and compare your revisions.

1. Handwriting Analysis

Experts at handwriting analysis use only their eyes and a microscope as tools. Handwriting analysis is an inexact science. Experts are called on to discover forgery. They compare two documents side by side. They look for telling details about the handwriting. They look for the dots above *i*'s and the crosses through *t*'s. They look for the angle of the pen. Sometimes experts disagree. Many people doubt the reliability of handwriting analysis. These doubts will not disappear. Courts allow experts to testify. Juries are often persuaded by the testimony of handwriting experts.

2. Today's Armor

Armor of the past was heavy and prone to rusting. Today's armor is, in contrast, lightweight and rustproof. Most bullet-proof vests for police officers, for example, are made from a fabric called Kevlar. Kevlar is five times stronger than steel. The fabric has a coating of resins on the surface nearest the body. This coating adds extra strength. Rust on armor of the past had to be cleaned and treated with sand and vinegar. Today's armor is machine washable. Police officers are not the only people who wear armor today. Goalies on hockey teams suit up in padded armor that protects them from the fast-moving puck. Welders protect their faces from dangerous sparks with a medieval-looking face shield. Firefighters and construction workers wear helmets. These helmets are tough. They are also lightweight. Probably the most advanced armor of today is the space suit. The space suit protects astronauts from the uninhabitable environment of outer space.

Varying Sentence Beginnings

Sentences that always begin with subjects become tiresome to read or hear. When you revise, begin your sentences in a variety of ways, such as those shown in the following examples.

SUBJECT	The Greek **city-states** of Elis and Pisa were at war in the spring of 776 B.C.
ADVERB	**Finally** they made peace in the summer.

INFINITIVE PHRASE	**To celebrate the peace,** each city decided to hold athletic games.
PARTICIPIAL PHRASE	**Wishing to honor the gods,** they held their games jointly in Olympia.
PREPOSITIONAL PHRASE	**In this first Olympic match,** the only sport was foot racing.
ADVERB CLAUSE	**Because the Greeks cared only about winning,** no speed records were kept.
INVERTED ORDER	**Out of this match** grew the Olympic Games.

PRACTICE YOUR SKILLS

● *Varying Sentence Beginnings*

Revise the following paragraph. Vary the beginnings of the sentences by using the openers suggested in the parentheses.

Basic Signals

There are two basic types of signals in the field of electronics, analog and digital. *(prepositional phrase)* You can observe familiar appliances to understand their difference. *(infinitive phrase)* A car speedometer is an analog device, registering a continuous range of speed. *(participial phrase)* The channel selector on your television set is digital because it can work only in certain set positions. *(adverb clause)* Digital clocks give more accurate readouts than analog clocks because they tell you in numbers the hour, minutes, and second. *(adverb clause)* You must estimate these details to read the time from an analog clock's hands. *(infinitive phrase)*

Vary the length, structure, and beginnings of your sentences.

 ## Eliminating Sentence Faults

Good writers, like trail guides, blaze clear paths for readers to follow. To help readers through the paths of your ideas, revise your sentences to eliminate clutter and confusion.

Faulty Coordination and Subordination

When joining ideas of equal importance, use the correct coordinating conjunction because faulty coordination leaves readers confused. In the following example, the conjunction *and* does not clearly express the relationship between the two ideas.

FAULTY COORDINATION	The Boston Marathon was draining, **and** I am looking forward to next year's run.
PRECISE COORDINATION	The marathon was draining, **but** I am looking forward to next year's run.

You can also use a semicolon and a transitional word to join ideas of equal importance.

PRECISE COORDINATION	The Boston Marathon was draining; **nevertheless,** I am looking forward to next year's run.

The chart on the following page shows words that express coordination precisely.

TO SHOW SIMILARITY	TO SHOW CONTRAST	TO SHOW RESULT
and	but	so
both/and	yet	thus
not only/but also	or, nor	hence
besides	however	therefore
indeed	instead	consequently
furthermore	still	accordingly
moreover	nevertheless	as a result

Faulty coordination also results if unrelated ideas are joined.
When you revise, express the unrelated idea in a separate sentence.

FAULTY COORDINATION   My basset hound had five puppies,
and we have had her for two years.

IMPROVED   My basset hound had five puppies.
We have had her for two years.

Sometimes a coordinating conjunction connects ideas that are
not of equal importance. When you revise, correct this type of
error by changing the less important idea into a phrase or a
subordinate clause.

FAULTY COORDINATION   Jaime Garcia quickly left the house,
and he locked the doors.

IMPROVED   **After locking the doors**, Jaime
Garcia quickly left the house.
(gerund phrase)

FAULTY COORDINATION   The acrobat performed his daring
act, **and** the audience looked on
in amazement.

IMPROVED   **While the audience looked on in
amazement,** the acrobat performed
his daring act. (subordinate clause)

To avoid faulty subordination, make sure that the more important idea is expressed in the independent clause.

FAULTY SUBORDINATION	Elizabeth was the youngest on the team, **although she competed as well as the oldest players.**
IMPROVED	**Although Elizabeth was the youngest on the team,** she competed as well as the oldest players.

Correcting Faulty Coordination and Subordination

- Use a connecting word that clearly shows the relationship to your ideas (similarity, contrast, or result).

- Express unrelated ideas in separate sentences.

- If the ideas are not of equal importance, express the less important idea in a phrase or a subordinate clause.

- Express your more important idea in an independent clause.

PRACTICE YOUR SKILLS

● *Choosing the Best Connecting Word*

Complete each of the following sentences, using the list of words on the previous page.

1. Michael has ■ confidence ■ persistence, a combination that often brings him success.

2. They said their good-byes, ■ Sarah boarded the train.

3. I would like to go with you; ■ I must be home by 7:30.

4. Tina had a toothache, ■ she went to the dentist.

5. The movie lacked action; ■ it seemed very long.

● *Revising to Correct Sentence Faults*

Use the strategies above to improve the faulty sentences in the following paragraph. Remember to use commas where needed.

Eclipse

The moon glowed orange and it was hard to believe humans have actually stood on it. Hurrying to set up the telescope, we worried that the eclipse was about to begin. We watched for a long time, and nothing seemed to be happening. Finally, the earth's shadow took a bite out of the moon; consequently, the moon continued to glow. Little by little the shadow covered the moon, yet we watched intently. We understand what causes the eclipse, and to the ancients it must have been very frightening. The telescope magnified the moon so that we could see the craters, and it had been my grandfather's. The eclipse reached totality, and we could still see a faint, copperish, crescent-shaped glow. The moon finally reappeared, and the shadow passed into the darkness. The eclipse took more than three hours, although we enjoyed every minute of it.

Rambling Sentences

Sentences with long strings of phrases and clauses are hard to follow because they often clutter the main point. Break up rambling sentences into shorter sentences.

RAMBLING   Computers are used by some major-league baseball teams to help managers make decisions because baseball is a game that depends on statistics to judge a player's worth, and the computer can use these statistics to make suggestions about batting order and which player to send in as a designated hitter or runner under a variety of circumstances, including number of outs, number of men on base, weather conditions, and opposing pitcher.

IMPROVED	Some major-league baseball teams use computers to help their managers make decisions. Since statistics are often used to measure a player's worth, the computer can use these figures to choose the right player for a specific situation. It can recommend batting order and designated hitters or runners. It can also weigh such variables as number of outs, number of men on base, weather conditions, and the opposing pitcher.

PRACTICE YOUR SKILLS

Revising a Rambling Sentence

Revise the following sentence by breaking it into shorter sentences. Remember to capitalize and punctuate the new sentences correctly.

Back to the Future

Your grandparents were probably happy when grocery stores did away with food in barrels and started selling food in small packages on the shelves, but grocery stores are now stocking food in barrels as well as on shelves, and you can choose prepackaged food from the regular shopping aisles, or you can help yourself to foods like flour, rice, dried fruit, and peanut butter from large vats, from which you can scoop up as much or as little as you like, and your grandparents may like being reminded of the good old days.

Faulty Parallelism

Parallelism give a sentence balance. **Faulty parallelism** occurs when two or more similar ideas are expressed in different grammatical constructions joined by *and, but* or *or*. The following sentences show several ways to correct faulty parallelism.

FAULTY	Rosie's favorite sports are **swimming, water-skiing,** and **to go horseback riding.** (two gerunds and an infinitive phrase)
PARALLEL	Rosie's favorite sports are **swimming, water-skiing,** and **horseback riding.** (three gerunds)
FAULTY	The athletes were not only **energetic,** but also **they had a great deal of enthusiasm.** (predicate adjective and an independent clause)
PARALLEL	The athletes were not only **energetic** but also **enthusiastic.** (two adjectives)
FAULTY	**Silent, watchful,** and **having an owlish quality,** the woman slowly turned her head. (two adjectives and a participial phrase)
PARALLEL	**Silent, watchful,** and **owlish,** the woman slowly turned her head. (three adjectives)
FAULTY	The child demanded a **bottle of juice** or **that his mother buy him a toy car.** (a noun and a noun clause)
PARALLEL	The child demanded a **bottle of juice** or a **toy car.** (compound predicate)

PRACTICE YOUR SKILLS

● *Correcting Faulty Parallelism*

Revise each of the following sentences to eliminate faulty parallelism. Use the strategies shown in the sentences above.

1. Joanne was determined to find a car with air-conditioning, with an AM/FM radio, and one that had an automatic transmission.

2. The student who won the lead in the school play was tall, handsome, and with style.

3. Going to a school dance is much more fun than to go to a movie.

4. Carla walked onstage slowly, confidently, and with pride.

5. The president of the sophomore class is athletic, friendly, and a good student.

6. Chester's guidance counselor recently told him that laughter and to cry is good for the soul.

7. The whisper of leaves, the gurgle of water, and that the birds were chirping made me feel peaceful.

8. Penniless, friendless, and having no home, the man limped toward the open door.

9. Benjamin asked us either to come for a picnic or that we stay for supper.

10. Summer is the smell of mowed grass, the sound of outdoor concerts, and the way grilled hamburgers taste.

11. Succeeding at team sports requires conscientiousness, discipline, and having a cooperative attitude.

12. The next year brought new construction and that our playing in the vacant lot was ended.

13. Jim's job is taking tickets for the games and to run the concession stand.

14. The striking workers demanded higher pay and that the working conditions be made safer.

15. The coach remarked that the young gymnast was powerful yet like a graceful dancer.

16. The bewildered tourists inquired about a restaurant and where to shop for records and souvenirs.

17. Driving safely means obeying all traffic laws and to watch out for the other person.

18. Tired but with elation, the winner of the cross-country ski marathon spoke to reporters.

19. The piano teacher was a taskmaster, a perfectionist, and inspired his students.

20. The invitation asked that we bring a dish for the main course and to dress very casually.

Writing Tip

When you revise, eliminate **faulty coordination, faulty subordination, rambling sentences,** and **faulty parallelism.**

Time Out to Reflect

"Read and revise, reread and revise, keep reading and revising until your text seems adequate to your thought."
—*Jacques Barzun*

Having studied various techniques for improving your writing style, take a moment to think about the quotation above. What do you think Barzun means by "adequate to your thought"? Can changes in word choice and sentence structure reveal your thoughts more clearly? How so? Is your writing beginning to reflect more closely what you want to say?

Prewriting Workshop
Drafting Workshop
Revising Workshop
Editing Workshop ▶
Publishing Workshop

Nouns

When you speak, your words come out once and they are gone. When you write, you have many chances to check your spelling and punctuation. As you look over your writing, keep in mind that your choice of words and the correct spelling and punctuation of those words is important for communicating effectively to your reader.

Capitalization of Proper Nouns

Previously in this chapter, you learned that specific nouns are better than general nouns. One way to make nouns more specific is to use proper nouns where possible. A **common noun** is any person, place, or thing; a **proper noun** is a particular person, place, or thing. All proper nouns, as you may recall, begin with a capital letter.

COMMON NOUNS	The **team** is sponsored by a **store** in **town**.
PROPER NOUNS	The **Strikers** is sponsored by **Mullen's Hardware** in **Newington**.

Punctuation with Possessive Nouns

A noun that shows possession or ownership is written with an apostrophe. To form the possessive of a singular noun, simply add *'s*. To form the possessive of a plural noun, however, you need to do one of two things: add only an apostrophe to a plural noun that ends in *s* or add *'s* to a plural noun that does not end in *s*.

SINGULAR POSSESSIVE	No one could find the **catcher's** mitt.
PLURAL POSSESSIVE	The **coaches'** friends and the **children's** parents attend most of the at-home games.

Punctuation of a Series

Three or more similar items together form a **series.** You will often have the occasion to write a series of nouns. Keep in mind, however, that other words, phrases, and clauses can also be written in a series. Without commas to separate the items in a series, the items would run into one another and cause confusion and misunderstanding.

INCORRECT	All new team members need a catcher's mitt a uniform and a book of rules
CORRECT	All new team members need a catcher's mitt, a uniform, and a book of rules.

Spelling the Plurals of Nouns

Most of the time you simply have to add an *s* to make a singular noun plural. In a few cases, however, you must change the ending of a noun before adding *s*. For example, if a word ends in a consonant and a *y*, you must change the *y* to *i* and add *es;* therefore, *salary* becomes *salaries.*

SINGULAR	My **family** enjoys softball.
PLURAL	Many of the **families** enjoy softball.

Editing Checklist

✔ Are all proper nouns capitalized?
✔ Is an apostrophe used correctly with possessive nouns?
✔ Do commas separate any series of words?
✔ Are plural nouns spelled correctly?

Your Writing Style Checklist

Style is like a writer's unique fingerprint, which is created through the careful drafting of sentences and words. Use the following checklist to review some of the many ways you can develop your writing style. The numbers in parentheses refer to pages where you can get help with your writing.

WRITING CONCISE SENTENCES

- Keep your sentences concise by eliminating redundancy, empty expressions, wordiness, and wordy phrases and clauses. *(pages C67–C70)*

CREATING SENTENCE VARIETY

- Vary the length and structure of sentences by combining short, choppy sentences into longer ones that read more smoothly. *(pages C73–C76)*
- Vary your sentence structures. Strive for a mixture of the four basic sentence types: simple, compound, complex, and compound-complex. *(pages C77–C78)*
- Vary sentence beginnings to avoid monotony. *(pages C79-C80)*

CORRECTING FAULTY SENTENCES

- Avoid faulty coordination by expressing ideas in separate sentences or by changing less important ideas into a phrase or clause. *(pages C81–C83)*
- Avoid faulty subordination by expressing the more important idea in an independent clause. *(page C83)*
- Break up rambling sentences by expressing separate ideas in separate sentences. *(pages C84–C85)*
- Avoid faulty parallelism by using the same grammatical construction to express similar ideas. *(page C86)*

CHOOSING VIVID WORDS

- Use specific nouns, verbs, adjectives, and adverbs to make your writing clear and vivid. *(page C62)*
- Use figurative language, such as similes and metaphors, to create strong mental images. *(page C64)*
- Avoid clichés. *(page C64)*

Representing in Different Ways

Treatment for "Small Town Big Tops"

The sun begins to break over the treetops as the circus workers emerge from their trailers and tents. They begin to dismantle the circus tents. Men and women work together, lowering the tents and folding the canvas material. The sounds of elephants and lions fill the morning air as they are led from their pens and loaded onto the wooden paneled railway cars. Dust clouds swirl and trail the speeding forklifts as they carry long wooden beams that support the big top. Flags and strings of colored light are packed away. Jugglers, sword swallowers, and clowns pack their equipment and board the train that will lead them to the next town.

. . . to Visuals

The director of a documentary video called "Small Town Big Tops" asks you to create a storyboard for this segment of the video. Using the information in the passage above, draw a storyboard with three cells. Be sure to reflect the style of the passage in the storyboard.

From Visuals . . .

. . . to Print

Using the storyboard above, write a passage for the narrator of "Small Town Big Tops" to read. Write in the style of a circus ringmaster who uses flowery and vivid language to interest the crowd.

- Which strategies can be used for creating both written and visual representations? Which strategies apply to one, not both? Which type of representation is more effective?
- Draw a conclusion, and write briefly about the differences between written ideas and visual representations.

Writing for Oral Communication
Descriptive Oral Presentation

It is "Hobbies and Pastimes Week" at your school. Each student must present a speech to the class about a hobby that is interesting and fun. You believe you have a unique hobby, and you wish to reveal it to your classmates.

Prepare an oral presentation describing your favorite hobby to your classmates. Include vivid words and figurative language. Create sentence variety by using phrases, coordination, or subordination to vary the length of your sentences. Eliminate rambling sentences by separating your ideas into a variety of short and long sentences.

What strategies did you use to describe your hobby to the class?

You can find information on oral presentation on pages C592–C601.

Writing in Everyday Life
Persuasive Informal E-mail

Your friend Barney is trying desperately to win the attention of Juliet, a girl in his class. He wishes to send her an E-mail, asking her to this weekend's 9th Annual Marathon Dance Contest. Unfortunately Barney needs help using colorful and vivid language to describe how good a dancer he is. He has come to you for help!

Compose an E-mail for Barney in which you ask Juliet to the Marathon Dance and describe how good a dancer Barney is. Employ vivid comparisons by using at least five examples of fresh similes and metaphors, and be careful to avoid clichés.

What strategies did you use to write an E-mail to Juliet?

You can find information on writing E-mail on pages C736–C738.

Writing in the Workplace

Note to Employees

You are ready for your much-needed vacation from your job at the Rookie Cookie Factory. In your absence Tamara and Nicholas will take over your duties of making the cookies. Tamara and Nicholas are known throughout the company for their lack of interest in making cookies. You think it is a good idea to make the task sound more exciting than it really is.

> Write a note to Tamara and Nicholas telling them that they have to bake cookies while you are on vacation. Write in a style that will convince them that baking cookies will be fun and exciting.

> What strategies did you use to write the note to Tamara and Nicholas?

Writing in Everyday Life

Letter to Your Cousin

Your older cousin who is studying abroad wants to stay informed about the latest rock bands. When you last talked to her on the telephone, she asked you to write a letter to her describing your favorite new band. This week your favorite band is Sam Glam and the Retro-Actives, and you think it may be difficult to describe them without using slang expressions.

> Write a letter to your cousin telling her about Sam Glam and the Retro-Actives. Try to make the writing style of your letter vivid and clear so your cousin can visualize an image of the band.

> What strategies did you use to tell your cousin about Sam Glam and the Retro-Actives?

Assess Your Learning

Your professor at Coaster University is offering a particularly interesting course titled, "Amuse Me, Amuse You: Theme Park Rides of the Twentieth Century." Unfortunately, the title of the course is not exciting enough to attract the interest of students who normally would be thrilled to take a class about roller coasters.

▶ **Rewrite the following text for the flyer that advertises the course in a style that you think would spark students' interest:**

> **Do you find it agreeable to your senses to ride roller coasters? Do you enjoy being frightened by the velocity and motion of a car running on tracks? If so, "Amuse Me, Amuse You: Theme Park Rides in the Twentieth Century" is a course that may interest you very much. This introductory course offers a retrospective of the past century's most famous theme park ride, the roller coaster.**

▶ **Begin the flyer's text with an intriguing and vivid opening and provide a clear and concise introduction to the course that will spark students' interest. Vary the sentence beginnings and revise by streamlining sentences to reduce empty expressions and wordy phrases. Organize your ideas to ensure coherence and logical progression. Replace general words with more vivid and specific ones in a style that will spark the interest of the reader.**

Before You Write **Consider the following questions:**
What is the **subject?**
What is the **occasion?**
Who is the **audience?**
What is the **purpose?**

After You Write **Evaluate your work using the following criteria:**
- Have you begun the text with an intriguing and vivid opening?
- Have you varied your sentence beginnings?
- Have you streamlined sentences to reduce empty expressions and wordy phrases?
- Have you organized your ideas to ensure coherence and logical progression?
- Have you replaced general words with more vivid and specific ones to create a style that will spark interest of the reader?

Write briefly on how well you did. Point out your strengths and areas for improvement.

CHAPTER 3

Writing Informative Paragraphs

Informative paragraphs inform or explain. Reports, summaries, letters, essay test answers, directions— informative writing is probably the type of writing you do most often. An informative paragraph can be brief and simple, as when you write instructions for getting to your house. Or an informative paragraph might need to be complex to explain a theory in science or an idea in history.

What is the most effective way to organize an informative paragraph? No single answer fits every topic. The order you use depends on the material itself and on your purpose for writing. When you are using informative writing, your goal should be to present ideas and facts in as logical an order as you can. In so doing, you help the reader to see the relationship between each sentence you write and the overall topic of the paragraph. This chapter will show you different types of informative paragraphs and sharpen your skills at writing these important paragraphs.

Reading with a Writer's Eye

The following excerpt from *In Suspect Terrain* is about a topic you most likely know little about— where diamonds come from. As you read this piece of informative writing for the first time, notice how writer John McPhee uses specific details to help us understand how diamonds are formed. Then when you go back and read for a second time, try to identify some techniques McPhee uses to engage his readers.

FROM

IN SUSPECT TERRAIN

John McPhee

The source of a diamond is a kimberlite[1] pipe, a form of
diatreme—a relatively small hole bored through the crust of the
earth by an expanding combination of carbon dioxide and water
which rises from within the earth's mantle and moves so fast
driving magma to the surface that it breaks into the atmosphere
at supersonic speeds. Such events have occurred at random
through the history of the earth, and a kimberlite pipe could
explode in any number of places next year. Rising so rapidly
and from so deep a source, a kimberlite pipe brings up exotic
materials the like of which could never appear in the shallow
slow explosion of a Mt. St. Helens or the flows of Kilauea.
Among the materials are diamonds. Evidently, there are no
diamond pipes, as they are also called, in or near Indiana. Like
the huge red jasper boulders and the tiny flecks of gold,
Indiana's diamonds are glacial erratics.[2] They were transported
from Canada, and by reading the fabric of the till[3] and taking
bearings from striations[4] and grooves in the underlying rock—
and by noting the compass orientation of drumlin[5] hills, which
look like sculptured whales and face in the direction from
which their maker came—anybody can plainly see that the
direction from which the ice arrived in this region was something extremely close to 045°, northeast. At least one pipe
containing gem diamonds must exist somewhere near a line

---

[1] **kimberlite** *n.*: A kind of volcanic rock.
[2] **erratic** *n.*: A block of rock that has been moved by a glacier.
[3] **till** *n.*: Clay, sand, gravel, and boulders mixed together.
[4] **striations** (strī ā′shəns) *n.*: Minute grooves, scratches, or channels.
[5] **drumlin** *n.*: An oval hill of glacial drift.

between Indianapolis and the Otish Mountains of Quebec, because the ice that covered Indiana did not come from Kimberley—it formed and grew and, like an opening flower, spread out from the Otish Mountains. With rock it carried and on rock it traversed, it narrated its own journey, but it did not reveal where it got the diamonds.

There is a layer in the mantle, averaging about sixty miles below the earth's surface, through which seismic tremors pass slowly. The softer the rock, the slower the tremor—so it is inferred that the low-velocity zone, as it is called, is close to its melting point. In the otherwise rigid mantle, it is a level of lubricity upon which the plates of the earth can slide, interacting at their borders to produce the effects known as plate tectonics. The so-termed lithospheric plates, in other words, consist of crust and uppermost mantle and can be as much as ninety miles thick. Diamond pipes are believed to originate a good deal deeper than that—and in a manner which, as most geologists would put it, "is not well under-stood." After drawing fuel from surrounding mantle rock—compressed water from mica, in all likelihood, and carbon dioxide from other minerals—the material is thought to work slowly upward into the overlying plate. Slow it may be at the start, but a hundred and twenty miles later it comes out of the ground at Mach 2. The result is a modest crater, like a bullet hole between the eyes.

No one has ever drilled a hundred and twenty miles into the earth, or is likely to. Diamond pipes, meanwhile, have brought up samples of what is there. It is spewed all over the landscape, but it also remains stuck in the throat, like rich dense fruitcake. For the most part, it is peridotite, which is the lowest layer of the subcontinental package and is believed to be the essence of the mantle. There is high-pressure recrystallized basalt, full of garnets and jade. There are olivine[6] crystals of

---

[6] **olivine** (ŏl′ ə vēn) *n*.: A greenish mineral made of magnesium and iron.

incomparable size. The whole of it is known as kimberlite, the matrix rock of diamonds.

The odds against diamonds appearing in any given pipe are about a hundred to one. Carbon will crystallize in its densest form only under conditions of considerable heat and pressure—pressures of the sort that exist deep below the thickest parts of the plates, pressures of at least a hundred thousand pounds per square inch. The thickest parts of the plates are the continental cores, the cratons. All diamond-bearing kimberlites ever found have been in pipes that came up through cratons. Down where diamonds form, they are stable, but as they travel upward they pass through regions of lower pressure, where they will swiftly turn into graphite. Only by passing through such regions at tremendous speed can diamonds reach the earth's surface as diamonds, where they cool suddenly and enter a state of precarious preservation that somehow betokens to human beings a touching sense of "forever." Diamonds shoot like bullets through the earth's crust. Nonetheless, they are often found within rinds of graphite. Countless quantities turn into graphite altogether or disappear into the air as carbon dioxide. At room temperature and surface pressure, diamonds are in repose on an extremely narrow thermodynamic shelf. They want to be graphite, and with a relatively modest boost of heat graphite is what they would become, if atmospheric oxygen did not incinerate them first. They are, in this sense, unstable—these finger-flashing symbols of the eternity of vows, yearning to become fresh pencil lead. Except for particles that are sometimes found in meteorites, diamonds present themselves in nature in no other way.

Kimberlite is easily eroded. A boy playing jacks in South Africa in 1867 picked up an alluvial[7] diamond that led to the discovery of a number of pipes, one of which became the Kimberley Mine. From that pipe alone, fourteen million carats

[7] **alluvial** (ə loō′ vē əl) *adj.*: Found in soil deposited by flowing water.

followed. The rock source of diamonds had never before been known. The Regent, the Koh-i-noor, the Great Mogul had been eroded out by streams. As the ice walls of the Pleistocene[8] moved across Quebec, resculpting mountains, digging lakes, they apparently dozed through kimberlite pipes, scattering the contents southwest. The ice that plucked up the diamonds not only brought questions with it but also obscured the answers. How many pipes are there? Where are they? How rich are they in diamonds? If one ten-millionth of their content is gem diamond, they would be worth mining. They are somewhere northeast of Indiana. They are in all likelihood less than a quarter of a mile wide. They may be under glacial drift. They may be under lakes. A few have been discovered—none of value. Presumably, there are others, relatively studded with diamonds. Many people have searched. No one has found them.

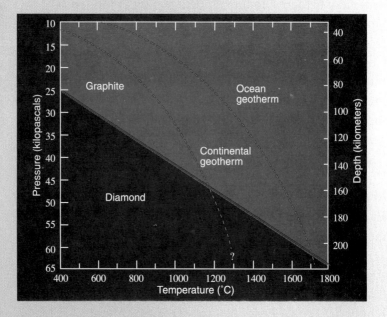

---

[8] **Pleistocene** (plī′ stə sēn′) *n.*: A geological era

Thinking as a Writer

Evaluating Informative Writing

- Look again at the exerpt from *In Suspect Terrain*, paragraph by paragraph. What does the author explain to the reader or give information about in each paragraph? Decide what the main idea or message of each paragraph seems to be. Then find the information that the author uses to support the main idea. Do you think there is enough supporting information in each paragraph? About which ideas would you like to know more?

Giving an Informative Talk

Oral Expression Suppose you wanted to tell a friend about where diamonds come from.

- Drawing upon information in *In Suspect Terrain*, think about what you might say. Then in a brief talk, sum up for a partner the most important information in the piece. After giving your talk, listen as your partner summarizes *your* points.

Relating Images to Text

Viewing • Look at the images on this and the previous page and think about what each of them tells you about diamonds. Which image do you think would more effectively accompany the piece on diamonds that you have just read? Why?

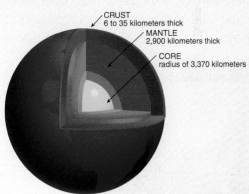

CRUST
6 to 35 kilometers thick

MANTLE
2,900 kilometers thick

CORE
radius of 3,370 kilometers

Developing Your Skills of Writing Paragraphs

"A sentence," wrote William Strunk, Jr., "should contain no unnecessary words, a paragraph no unnecessary sentences, for the same reason that a drawing should have no unnecessary lines and a machine no unnecessary parts."

Forming each paragraph with all the necessary sentences—but no unnecessary ones—is one of a writer's major challenges. The process of writing is similar to what an architect faces when designing a house. In a well-planned house, all the rooms and hallways work together to form a pleasing and useful space. There are no rooms without windows, stairways in the wrong place, or unreachable closets.

Similarly, all the sentences of a paragraph must work together to form a pleasing whole. At the same time, they must also develop a main idea. In this section, you will learn about writing well-planned paragraphs.

A **paragraph** is a group of related sentences that present and develop one main idea.

● Paragraph Structure

A well-written paragraph has three basic parts: a topic sentence, supporting sentences, and a concluding sentence. Notice how each part serves a purpose in the following informative paragraph.

MODEL: Paragraph Structure

Life in Caves

TOPIC SENTENCE:

STATES THE MAIN IDEA

Most large caves have three distinct zones, and each zone is home to a different kind of natural life. In the innermost part of the cave, the darkness is complete, and the temperature never varies.

Without light, green plants cannot live and animals
have no need for eyes. The next zone, although
still dark and moist, has a variable temperature.
Animals that otherwise live outside inhabit this
zone seasonally. The third zone, called the twilight
zone, begins wherever light from the cave entrance
can first be seen. A few green plants can grow in
this zone. Most of the animals in this zone use the
cave as shelter from the outdoors. In each zone
the plants and animals adapt to the meager
resources of their home.

CONCLUDING
SENTENCE:

ADDS A STRONG
ENDING

In some paragraphs the main idea is implied rather than stated
directly in a **topic sentence.** In others the main idea may be
expressed in two sentences instead of one. Most paragraphs that stand
alone, however, have a clearly stated topic sentence, a body of
supporting sentences, and a **concluding sentence** that adds the
finishing touch.

> **Guidelines for a One-Paragraph Composition**
> - Make your main idea clear.
> - Develop your main idea fully.
> - Provide a strong ending.

Topic Sentence

The topic sentence can come at the beginning, middle, or end
of a paragraph. Although its placement may vary, its purpose is
always the same.

A **topic sentence** states the main idea of the paragraph.

The main idea of a paragraph is like a summary of its details.
The topic sentence is, therefore, more general than the other
sentences in the paragraph. It is also specific enough to focus the
subject to one main point that can be covered in a paragraph.

Use the following guidelines to identify and write good topic sentences.

> **A Topic Sentence**
> - states the main idea.
> - focuses the limited subject to one main point that can be adequately covered in the paragraph.
> - is more general than the sentences that develop it.

The topic sentence in the following paragraph is suitably specific.

MODEL: Topic Sentence

TOPIC
SENTENCE

SUPPORTING
SENTENCES

CONCLUDING
SENTENCE

On my recent trip to Sea World, I learned a great deal about the amazing dolphin. Dolphins, like other higher animals, show many signs of caring for their fellow creatures. Mother and child are closely attached. Some dolphins become close friends and stay close friends. When a friend or mate dies, a dolphin shows signs of sorrow. It may circle the body, making a whistling noise. It may even refuse to eat. These signs have convinced scientists that dolphins are intelligent, feeling creatures.

–Patricia Lauber, The Friendly Dolphins

The following topic sentences are too general. The reader would not have known what to expect in the rest of the paragraph.

TOO GENERAL Dolphins are interesting creatures.

TOO GENERAL Dolphins behave in an interesting way.

The sentences above need to be focused in order to provide a topic that is narrow enough to be covered adequately in one paragraph.

PRACTICE YOUR SKILLS

● *Identifying Topic Sentences*

Write the topic sentence of each of the following paragraphs.

1. A Doozie

Have you ever heard someone say, "It's a doozie!" when they were describing an item that was really special or of extra high quality? This expression is not used much today, but in the 1930s it was quite common. It originated in connection with the fabulous Duesenberg, the finest automobile ever produced in the United States. Something that was considered as good as a Duesenberg was very good indeed!

—*Richard L. Knudson,* Fabulous Cars of the 1920s and 1930s

2. Remnants of Pompeii

Archaeologists working on the ruins of Pompeii have discovered an ingenious way of reconstructing some of their finds. When the lava from the eruption of A.D. 79 cooled, it solidified around all the objects which had been unable to escape. Over the centuries many of these objects decayed, leaving hollows in the solid lava. Archaeologists refill these with liquid plaster. The plaster is allowed to set. The lava can then be chipped away, leaving an accurate plaster cast of whatever was trapped by the lava flow nearly 2,000 years ago.

—*Ian Andrews,* Pompeii

3. Arctic Etymology

Once a large flightless bird called the giant auk lived in the cold Arctic regions. It had strong wings adapted for swimming, a big beak, and a dark brown head with white patches around the eyes. Fishermen from Brittany called it by the ancient Welsh name *pen-gwyn*, meaning "white head." That reminded scholars of the Latin word *pinguis*, meaning "fat." Since the giant auk was plump, they called it pinguin, "fat bird." The Latin *pinguis* blended with the *pen-gwyn* of the fishermen led to our modern word for the auk, *penguin*.

—*Robert Silverberg,* Forgotten by Time

4. Silken Status Symbols

To settlers in early New England, clothes were often a measure of a person's wealth, and people were supposed to dress according to their station in life. The wealthy dressed themselves in expensive clothes imported from London, while poorer people wore clothes made from rough home-spun. Dressing above one's station was actually against the law. In 1678, 68 young people were fined for wearing silken clothes. In a strange new world, settlers tried to hold fast to laws and customs that made their society feel orderly.

—*Ann Palmer,* Growing Up in Colonial America

Supporting Sentences

A topic sentence on an interesting subject usually raises questions in a reader's mind. The supporting sentences, which form the body of the paragraph, answer these questions. They back up the main idea with specific information.

Supporting sentences explain the topic sentence with specific details, facts, examples, incidents, or reasons.

As you read the following topic sentence about the eclipse of the sun, think about the questions you would want answered in the rest of the paragraph.

> TOPIC SENTENCE
>
> About every 18 months, the moon passes directly between Earth and the sun, and somewhere in the world a brilliant drama unfolds in the sky.

If you are like most readers, you expect the rest of the paragraph to answer questions about the appearance of Earth and the sun when the moon travels between them. The supporting sentences provide specific details that answer those questions.

MODEL: Supporting Sentences

> The silhouetted moon begins to eat into the sun's disk, producing an ever-narrowing solar crescent. At first nothing particularly remarkable occurs on the earth below. Shadows gradually sharpen, colors soften, the landscape and sky darken. Then, as the moon's shadow arrives, racing over the countryside at 1,000 miles an hour, there is a descent into darkness. The sun, giver of warmth and life, is suddenly gone. All that remains is a black hole in the sky, fringed by flamelike tongues and the pearly glow of the corona. It is a sight that has left its mark on mythology, art, and history. In 585 B.C., an eclipse so unnerved a battlefield of Lydians and Medes that they threw down their weapons on the spot.
>
> —*Dennis Overbye*, Discover

PRACTICE YOUR SKILLS

● *Writing Supporting Sentences*

For each of the following topic sentences, use brainstorming or clustering to develop a list of specific details, facts, examples, incidents, or reasons to support the topic sentence. Then write three supporting sentences from each list.

1. Our high school offers excellent extracurricular activities.

2. We need to take seriously the threat of drug abuse to our society.

3. Teenagers can benefit from participating in community service.

Concluding Sentence

A televised sporting event usually ends with a wrap-up of the highlights and outcome. In the same way, good paragraphs end with a sentence that wraps up the main idea.

A **concluding sentence** recalls the main idea and adds a strong ending to a paragraph.

Good concluding sentences are not dull summaries or repetitions of the topic sentence. They offer, instead, a fresh insight that locks the main idea in the reader's mind. These sentences are called *clinchers*.

The following paragraph has a weak concluding sentence.

MODEL: Concluding Sentence

Prey and Predator Asleep

Whether a mammal dreams or not depends in part on whether it is predator or prey. In a dream state, sleep is very deep, and an animal does not know what is going on around it. The dream state is safer for predator than for prey because a predator does not have to worry about sudden attack. A prey animal, in contrast, needs to be able **CONCLUDING** to make a quick getaway. As you can see, dreams **SENTENCE** depend on whether a mammal is predator or prey.

The following concluding sentence is stronger. It clinches the main idea by adding new information.

CLINCHER   Experiments show that predators dream but prey sleep in a shallow, dreamless state.

PRACTICE YOUR SKILLS

🔵 *Identifying Strong Concluding Sentences*

In the following pairs of concluding sentences, one sentence is better than the other. Write the letter of the clincher from each pair.

EXAMPLE   **a.** That is the way some rock bands have made it big.

b. For some, rock music has been a profitable business.

1. a. In conclusion, opening the right kind of bank account will allow your money to earn interest.

   b. With the right kind of bank account, a penny saved is more than a penny earned.

2. a. As you can see, Newton was indeed a great scientist.

   b. Newton's inventive work led to a whole new way of seeing the world.

3. a. Despite the headaches, owning a car is often an adventure in freedom.

   b. Owning a car certainly has both a good side and a bad side.

4. a. In a nutshell, becoming a veterinarian takes hard work.

   b. A lasting love for animals sustains many veterinary students through the years of hard work.

5. a. To creators of television comedies, the phrase *a laugh a minute* is no joke.

   b. As I've said, creators of television comedies plan the laugh lines to come at regular intervals.

Time Out to Reflect

As you have worked to improve your skills in writing topic, supporting, and concluding sentences, what have you noticed about your writing? What are your particular strengths? Perhaps you have a knack for writing a strong concluding sentence. What areas do you notice yourself spending extra time on? Perhaps you sometimes forget to address certain details in your supporting sentences. Take stock of your recurring errors and note strategies for correcting them in the Learning Log section of your **journal.**

Process of Writing an Informative Paragraph

"We write to expose the unexposed," notes author Anne Lamott. Whenever you want to provide information or explain something to your readers, you will be using informative writing. Learning how to write an informative paragraph will help you analyze, define, and compare and contrast the subjects you want to write about. If you are writing to explain a process, you may want to use a how-to or how-it-works paragraph. These and other types of informative paragraphs are explained in detail in **A Writer's Guide to Presenting Information**, which follows this chapter on pages C150–C161.

Informative writing explains or informs.

Your Writer's Journal

In your journal, list some topics that you know about and would like to share with others. You might be interested in major events of the day or miniature golf, rock music, or just rocks. Automobiles, archaeology, computers, ecology, martial arts—there is no end to the possibilities. Add a few new items to your journal list, jotting down some details or information you might include if you were to write about these topics.

Prewriting Writing Process

A good informative paragraph offers a stimulating idea on a subject of interest. Subjects for informative writing are everywhere—on television, in books, and even in your own experiences. In fact, *choosing* a subject from among the many possibilities poses a real challenge.

Discovering Subjects to Write About

The search for subjects calls for a free mind and an active pen. Asking the right questions and jotting down answers through freewriting, brainstorming, clustering, and other prewriting techniques will unlock a storehouse of ideas.

Personal Experience   One way to find subjects is to think about your interests, hobbies, skills, and special knowledge. Another way is to ask, "What do I know that my classmates probably do not know?" Then jot down answers, which may give you ideas.

Drawing on Outside Sources   Books, magazines, television, radio, and conversations with people also provide a wealth of information. Asking questions about what you read or hear is another way to discover interesting subjects for informative writing. Critical readers and listeners question much of what they read or hear by asking *How? Why? What?* and *Do I agree?*

Writing Tip

Draw on **personal experience** and **outside sources** to find subjects for writing.

PRACTICE YOUR SKILLS

● *Finding Subjects from Personal Experience*

Brainstorm with a classmate or group answers to the following questions. Save your work.

1. Of the subjects you take in school, which is your favorite? What are two ideas concerning this subject that you could write about?

2. What are your interests outside school? Name two you could write a paragraph about.

3. Have you ever taken any lessons? If so, what did you learn that you could explain to others?

4. What is your position in the family—youngest child? oldest? only child? only girl? What general truth can you state about people in your position?

5. What careers are you interested in? What kind of personality do you think would be best suited to each of the careers you named?

● *Finding Subjects from Reading*

Read the paragraph below. Then write five questions that occur to you as you read it.

Seaweed for Sale

The possibility exists that seaweed algae could have commercial value in this country. Dried, it could be fed to livestock. Collected in quantity and decomposed, it could give off sufficient methane gas to be used as fuel. So far, however, no one has succeeded in producing a crop that is commercially usable. Scientists are testing a system, however, that may produce vast quantities of algae at very low cost. One scientist, Walter Adley, has discovered that algae will grow extremely rapidly under the proper conditions: sunlight, wave action, and harvesting at an early age. In the waters off the West Indies, he has tested a scheme to build platforms covered with a heavy plastic screen. Kept wet by the waves, algae grow rapidly on the screens. Adley has successfully harvested the algae. Adley's technique may make it possible to put algae to many good uses.

—L. E. *Taylor,* Measuring the Pulse of Life on Maine's Coast

Choosing and Limiting a Subject

After you find several possible subjects, the next step is to choose one subject and refine it until it is suitable for a one-paragraph explanation. Use the following guidelines to choose a good subject for an informative paragraph that clearly introduces and expands on one subject.

Exploring a Subject   One way to decide which subject to choose is to use freewriting or brainstorming to see how much you know about a subject. The following questions will help you assess your knowledge.

> ### Exploratory Questions
> - What do I already know that would help me explain my subject clearly to my audience?
> - What further information do I need to find out?
> - Where can I find this information?

If you can think of only one or two answers to these questions and cannot think of sources for finding more, you probably should choose another subject. If, on the other hand, your paper becomes crowded with scattered ideas, your subject is probably too broad for one paragraph. Of the subjects that are left, choose one and explore it. You may find that the subject you have chosen is too broad to cover adequately in one paragraph.

Limiting a Subject   To limit a broad subject so that it is manageable, ask questions that lead to specific answers. Continue the process until you can express in one phrase what your paragraph will be about.

The chart on the following page demonstrates the steps to follow as you limit your subject. Note that the question words **which** and **what about** can be asked of almost any topic you need to limit.

STEPS IN LIMITING A SUBJECT

BROAD SUBJECT
- Ask yourself

careers
Which career?

MORE LIMITED
- Ask yourself

computer programming
What about computer programming?

SUITABLY LIMITED

how to prepare for a career in computer programming

PRACTICE YOUR SKILLS

● *Limiting Subjects for an Informative Paragraph*

Choose five of the following subjects. Then, using the steps above as a guide, limit each subject for one paragraph.

1. music

6. modern heroes

2. sports

7. food

3. part-time jobs

8. machines

4. clothes

9. space travel

5. foreign lands

10. fads

Communicate Your Ideas

PREWRITING *Limited Subjects*

Review the **journal** entries you have written. Freewrite about any questions or ideas you wish to explore about these topics. Think of three subjects for an informative paragraph. Limit each subject, writing the limited subject beside the original broad subject. Finally, circle the subject you think has the most promise for development into an informative paragraph. Save your work.

SAVE YOUR WORK

Using an online search engine is a great way to find supporting details for your paragraph. If you type in a topic that is too broad, however, you will get far too many sites to cope with. Be as specific as you can when you enter the topic for a search, and try placing quotation marks around your topic.

Determining Your Audience

When your purpose is to explain, think carefully about who will be reading your work. To suit your writing to your audience, ask yourself the following questions.

Audience Questions

- What do my readers already know about my subject? What else might they need to know as background information?

- What are my readers' attitudes toward my subject? If these attitudes differ substantially from mine, how can I address those differences?

- Why are my readers reading my writing? How can I address their needs?

The more information you have about your audience, the more effectively you will be able to communicate through your writing. Knowing your audience can actually spark your imagination, giving you ideas about what to say when.

Communicate Your Ideas

PREWRITING *Audience*

 Determine who will be reading the informative paragraph you will write. Then ask yourself the audience questions above. With a classmate, brainstorm answers to the questions and write suggestions for tailoring your essay to the background and needs of your audience. Save your notes.

Developing Supporting Details

Supporting details include any specific information that will help explain your subject. The following chart shows some of the different types of details you can use to support the main idea in an informative paragraph.

TYPES OF SUPPORTING DETAILS		
examples	incidents	facts/statistics
reasons	directions	steps in a process
causes	definitions	comparisons/contrasts
effects	analogies	classifications

When you choose the type of supporting details to use, keep in mind the purpose of the paragraph and the kinds of questions a reader may have about the subject.

Writing Tip

List **details** that suit the main idea of your paragraph and that explain the subject clearly to the reader.

If you are familiar with the subject you are writing about, you may already have many supporting details on hand. Most likely, though, you will have to do research by reading and talking to knowledgeable people.

You can learn more about research techniques on pages C520–C534.

PRACTICE YOUR SKILLS

● *Listing Supporting Details*

For each of the following subjects, list four supporting details that would help you explain it. The following example and the questions on page C113 will help you with this activity.

SUBJECT   the value of team athletics

SUPPORTING   • staying in shape helps you feel good
DETAILS   • being part of a team builds understanding
             • a team is like a family
             • the time when the star player had to sacrifice
               to help the team win in the play-offs

1. the pleasures of listening to music

2. the importance of Martin Luther King, Jr., Day

3. how to be a good student

4. how to lose ten pounds

5. ways that every citizen can help protect the environment

6. the importance of a part-time job

7. making a vegetable garden

8. how to wash a car

9. a winning streak

10. caring for an animal

● *Identifying Supporting Details*

**Copy and complete the word web below. In the center, write your
main idea. Use the surrounding ovals for supporting details and
specific examples.**

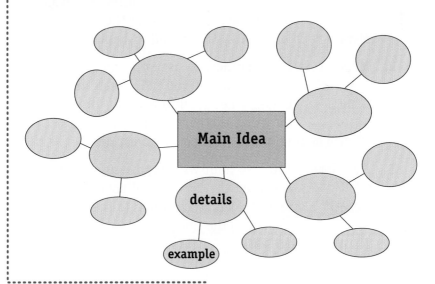

PREWRITING *Supporting Details*

 Review the subject you choose for your informative paragraph. Then look at the types of supporting details in the list on page C116. Which one would be useful in explaining your subject? Brainstorm, research, or use a **word web** to develop other details that you could use. Save your notes for later use.

Classifying Supporting Details

After listing details about your subject, classify them to find the best way to develop your paragraph. When you **classify,** you group specific details into general categories. The following examples show different ways to classify supporting details in an informative paragraph. Notice that each way of classifying is appropriate to the main idea.

You can learn more about classifying on pages C31–C32.

1. MAIN IDEA   Computers can perform certain tasks very fast.

      DETAILS   **Classify** details according to facts about the tasks computers perform and examples of how fast they perform the tasks.

      METHOD OF DEVELOPMENT   Facts and examples

2. MAIN IDEA   Learning how to use your computer is fun and easy if you follow certain steps.

      DETAILS   **Classify** details into a set of directions for using the computer.

      METHOD OF DEVELOPMENT   A set of directions

3. MAIN IDEA   After an hour with my friend's computer, I learned the meaning of *user-friendly*.

      DETAILS   **Classify** details according to the incidents leading to the understanding of *user-friendly*.

      METHOD OF DEVELOPMENT   Incident

4. **MAIN IDEA**   A program instructs the computer to perform tasks.
   DETAILS   **Classify** details according to the characteristics of a program.
   METHOD OF DEVELOPMENT   Definition

5. **MAIN IDEA**   The process of writing a software program involves many steps.
   DETAILS   **Classify** details according to the steps in the process of writing a software program.
   METHOD OF DEVELOPMENT   Steps in a process

6. **MAIN IDEA**   To understand the inside of a computer, imagine that the chip is a railroad switch.
   DETAILS   **Classify** details according to the similar characteristics of a chip and a railroad switch.
   METHOD OF DEVELOPMENT   Analogy

7. **MAIN IDEA**   The typical computer has five basic parts.
   DETAILS   **Classify** details according to the function each part performs.
   METHOD OF DEVELOPMENT   Analysis

8. **MAIN IDEA**   The microchip is responsible for the computer revolution.
   DETAILS   **Classify** details about the microchip (cause) and the computer revolution (effect).
   METHOD OF DEVELOPMENT   Cause and effect

9. **MAIN IDEA**   Computers and calculators share certain features, but they differ in major ways.
   DETAILS   **Classify** details according to the similarities and differences between a calculator and a computer.
   METHOD OF DEVELOPMENT   Comparison/contrast

10. **MAIN IDEA**   There are many different types of computers.
   DETAILS   **Classify** computers according to their types.
   METHOD OF DEVELOPMENT   Grouping into types

Two techniques you can use to classify supporting details are charting and outlining.

The following model shows how charting can be used to classify the supporting details from example number 7 on C119.

You can learn more about outlining on pages C397–C399.

MODEL: Charting to Classify Details

Basic Parts of the Computer

Parts	Function Performed
keyboard (input device)	user enters information and instructions by typing
storage disk	receives information and permanently stores it
monitor	displays information that user is working on
central processing unit (CPU)	holds information being used and directs the computer functions
printer	prints the processed information on paper

The following model shows the informative paragraph that resulted from the charting above.

MODEL: Informative Paragraph

The Parts of a Computer

TOPIC SENTENCE

SUPPORTING DETAILS
ANALYZE PARTS
OF THE WHOLE

Before I attended computer camp, I was very confused about this complicated monster that would rule my life. After a few days, though, I began to understand how it works. Regardless of its size or type, the computer has five basic parts. First, there is a keyboard on which the user types information and instructions. Second, there is a storage disk, usually referred to as the computer's memory, which receives the information and permanently stores it. Third, a monitor, or screen, displays the information the user is working on. Fourth is a central processing unit (CPU) where the computer functions take place. The CPU holds the

CONCLUDING
SENTENCE

information while it is being worked on and directs the computer to perform functions. Finally, a printer prints the processed information on paper. This astonishing combination of parts produces a machine that has an enormous impact on our lives.

PRACTICE YOUR SKILLS

● Identifying Methods of Development

Write the method of developing supporting details used in each paragraph. Use the examples on pages C118–C119 as a guide.

1. Miller Race Cars

Harry Miller was an automotive genius who dominated American racing for many years. His front-wheel-drive (fwd) cars were well-suited to American oval-track racing because of their superior cornering. Miller's first fwd racer was built in 1924. Two years later 9 out of the first 10 finishers at Indy were Miller cars. In the 1929 race, 27 of the 33 cars on the Indy track had Miller engines, and 7 Millers were among the first 10 cars to cross the finish line.

—*Richard L. Knudson,* Fabulous Cars of the 1920s and 1930s

2. Mining for Gold

Gold set free from rocks and mixed with streambed sand and gravel is called placer gold. Placer mining was the only kind practiced in California in the first two years of the gold rush. It was brutal work. The prospector squatted beside a stream and dipped a washbowl into the water, scooping up a panful of dirt. Then he performed the delicate task of panning for gold by swirling the contents of the washbowl. The trick was to let the surplus sand and gravel spill over the edge of the pan. At the same time, any gold that might have been scooped up had to be kept inside. Since the gold was much heavier than the gravel, it would settle to the bottom of the basin.

—*Robert Silverberg,* Ghost Towns of the American West

3. Basic Training
Operant conditioning is often used to train porpoises. In this kind of training, the animal makes something happen. He starts it; he is the operator. When he does something, a reward appears. It is the same sort of training you use when you ask your dog to sit up and speak and then reward him with a snack.

—*Margery Packlam,* Wild Animals, Gentle Women

4. A Balancing Act
Deep-sea divers are in balance between the internal pressure of their bodies and the pressure of the sea. This state may fairly well be illustrated by comparison with that of a tire on a loaded truck. So long as the tire is inflated with sufficient air, it stays rounded and supports the load pressing down on it. If the tire "blows out," down comes the weight of the truck upon it and flattens it. In the same way, if the diver's suit by any chance loses its air pressure, down comes the weight of the sea, instantly crushing the diver as flat as any blown-out tire.

—*Captain Edward Ellsberg,* The Bends

5. Something Deeply Hidden
I experienced a wonder of nature as a child of four or five years, when my father showed me a compass. That this needle behaved in such a determined way did not at all fit into the nature of events. I can remember—or at least I believe I can remember—that this experience made a deep and lasting impression on me. Something deeply hidden had to be behind things.

—*Albert Einstein*

Choosing a Method of Development

Write the method of development that would be most suitable for the following main ideas. Refer to the examples and the chart on pages C118–C119.

1. There are about 250 different kinds of sharks in the world's oceans today.

2. To understand how astronomers measure the distance between stars, try this simple experiment.

3. My first day as a hospital volunteer taught me the value of teamwork.

4. The harpsichord and clavichord, although similar, produce sound in very different ways.

5. Advancements in the fields of transportation and communication have brought the far countries of the world closer together.

6. If you can picture the ripples around a pebble thrown into a pond, you can begin to understand how radio waves travel.

7. People are living longer now than ever before.

8. Imprinting is nature's way of assuring that young ducks and geese will be cared for.

9. There are many different types of computers.

10. The slash-and-burn process is one widely used method of clearing trees.

Classifying Supporting Details

Choose one of the following main ideas and brainstorm with someone a list of details. Then decide on a method of development and make a chart like the one on page C120 to show the classification of your supporting details. You may wish to save these notes for a future composition.

1. I use several steps to prepare for a competitive event. (For your answer, choose an athletic or academic event or an event where you compete with a special talent.)

2. Here are the directions for this game. (Choose any game of skill.)

3. I believe that there are several causes of pollution in my community.

4. Our community offers many different cultural events throughout the year.

5. This year's candidates certainly have their similarities and differences. (Choose any two candidates.)

Communicate Your Ideas

PREWRITING *Method of Development*

Review the list of supporting details that you developed for your topic. Then look again at the classifying examples on pages C118-C119. Choose a method of development for your paragraph and make a chart similar to the one on page C120 to classify your details. Save your work.

Organizing Details in Logical Order

The final step in prewriting is to arrange your supporting details in a logical order. Well-organized details will help you write a clear explanation. Look for relationships among your supporting details and use one of the following methods of organization to arrange them.

Order of Importance, Interest, or Degree   Arrange details in the order of least to most or most to least. Either way, the reader can take in ideas in a logical progression.

Developmental Order   When your ideas are of equal importance, use developmental order. Arrange your supporting details in a logical order in which one idea grows out of another.

Chronological Order   In chronological order, arrange details in the order in which they occur over time. When chronological order is used to organize the steps in a process or in a set of directions, it is sometimes called sequential order.

Spatial Order   Spatial order places details in the order of near to far, top to bottom, inside to outside, left to right, and so on. Use this method to describe a scene or physical structure.

Writing Tip

Choose the **method of organization** best suited to your supporting details.

PRACTICE YOUR SKILLS

● *Identifying Methods of Organization*

Identify the method of organization in each paragraph as *order of importance, developmental order, chronological order,* **or** *spatial order.*

1. The Birth of a Car
    The Packard was born around the turn of the century, brought into existence by one man's dissatisfaction with another automobile. In 1898, James Ward Packard, an engineer in Warren, Ohio, bought a brand-new Winton motorcar in nearby Cleveland. On the drive home, he had several breakdowns. When he complained to the manufacturer of the car, Alexander Winton, he got no results. In fact, Winton told Packard that if he didn't like the car, he should go out and build a better one himself. Packard accepted the challenge, and on November 6, 1899, the first Packard automobile rolled down the streets of Warren. It *was* a better product, and the newly formed company quickly established itself as a manufacturer of quality automobiles.

    —*Richard L. Knudson,* Fabulous Cars of the 1920s and 1930s

2. Four-Legged Remedies

Animals are helping people come out of their shells or recover from illnesses. Troubled young people who are given a pet to care for often develop a sense of responsibility. More important, people whose leg and back muscles have been seriously injured can get a therapeutic massage from riding a horse. Most important, people with heart disease or high blood pressure can actually lower their blood pressure by petting a dog. For these reasons pets are becoming just what the doctor ordered.

3. Defensive Architecture

The center of a medieval castle was the massive stone tower, which all the rest of the structures were designed to protect. Adjacent to the tower were lean-to sheds and surrounding these was a walled courtyard. Another courtyard, the outer bailey, surrounded the inner space. The outer bailey wall was built of stone and fortified with lookout towers. In addition to all these layers of protection, most castles also had a moat that encircled the outer wall. In an age when enemy attacks were commonplace, defense was the guiding principle in architecture.

4. The Mighty Queen

The queen is a key piece in a chess game. When it is on the board, it has great firepower because it can move in all directions to capture the opponent's pieces. Making the most of the queen's power also determines the way a player will move the other pieces. When both queens are out of play after having been captured or traded, the nature of the game changes. Without the queens, attacking and defending strategies must be tighter and more precise. The change is so drastic that this stage of the game has its own name: *endgame*.

● *Arranging Details in Logical Order*

Arrange the details for each subject in *order of importance, developmental order, chronological order,* or *spatial order.*

1. SUBJECT   how the days of the week got their names

DETAILS
- Friday—from Germanic goddess Freya
- Monday—moon's day
- Thursday—from Germanic god Thor
- Tuesday—from Germanic god Tiw
- Saturday—Saturn's day
- Wednesday—from Germanic god Woden
- Sunday—sun's day

METHOD OF DEVELOPMENT   Facts and examples

2. SUBJECT   negative effects of daylight saving time

DETAILS
- people feel generally confused
- increase in automobile accidents
- people sometimes arrive late

METHOD OF DEVELOPMENT   Cause and effect

3. SUBJECT   the first photograph

DETAILS
- by 1780, scientists had discovered how to retain an image made by light
- *camera obscura,* invented in 1500, projected an image onto a screen
- in 1826, used metal plates to take the very first photograph
- scientists needed to find a way to make the image permanent

METHOD OF DEVELOPMENT   Incident

Communicate Your Ideas

PREWRITING *Logical Order of Details*

Look over the supporting details you classified for your informative writing paragraph. Decide which logical order would best suit these details. Arrange them accordingly. Save your work for later use.

Newspaper Graphics

One of the main challenges of all media is to compete for our attention. Television does it with dazzling, eye-catching visuals. More and more, Websites are adding animation to catch our eyes. Visuals—especially with motion—almost always pull our eyes in their direction.

In part to compete with TV and Websites, some newspapers are adding graphics and color, and presenting information graphically instead of in writing.

Most major newspapers today include graphics features. These features, sometimes called *snapshots*, present statistics in a colorful, creative way. Look at the following chart. With few words and a clearly presented graphic, the information is conveyed in an appealing way.

In some ways, this chart is like a visual informative paragraph. The topic sentence might be: *The vast majority of Americans have earned a high school diploma.* The supporting sentences are the statistics themselves, which might be stated as follows: In 2000, seventy-seven percent of Americans 15 years of age or older have completed high school. An additional 20.9% have earned B.A.'s or better at universities. Only 1.5% of Americans have not earned high school diplomas.*

Educational Levels of Americans 15 Years and Older	
77.6% high school diploma	
20.9% college degree	1.5% no educational degree

If this information were presented in a written paragraph, readers might not notice it. However, in a colorful graphic, people are drawn to it.

Media Activity

Use the information below to create a graphic. Use few words, bare statistics, and good graphics with symbols. Then rewrite your graphic as an informative paragraph.

WORKING HIGH SCHOOL STUDENTS
72% don't work
25% work part-time
3% work full-time

Once you have developed your subject, you are ready to write the first draft by transforming your notes into a topic sentence, supporting sentences, and a concluding sentence.

Drafting the Topic Sentence

A topic sentence can come anywhere in a paragraph, but drafting it before your paragraph will help clarify your ideas.

 Steps for Writing a Topic Sentence
- Look over your prewriting notes.
- Express your main idea in one sentence.
- Revise to clarify your main idea and control all details.

Suppose you had written the following prewriting notes.

SUBJECT	the new high-speed train (MLV)
DETAILS	• engineers developed magnetic levitation train (MLV)
	• magnets on train motor and rail hold train four to six inches above single rail
	• magnetic force also drives train forward
	• may travel up to 300 miles per hour

You might start by writing a topic sentence like the following.

WEAK TOPIC SENTENCE	The magnetic levitation vehicle can travel at up to 300 miles per hour.

This topic sentence, however, does not control all the supporting details; it focuses on only one aspect—speed. The following topic sentence is better because it also refers to the force that propels the train.

REVISED TOPIC SENTENCE	A new type of train uses magnetic force to achieve high speeds.

PRACTICE YOUR SKILLS

● *Revising Topic Sentences*

Revise each topic sentence until it accounts for all of the details.

1. Life in a big city offers many rewarding advantages.
- music, ballet, theater, art museums
- wide variety of other entertainment
- exposure to many different people and lifestyles
- not much chance to experience natural beauty
- need for added security measures
- feeling of congestion

2. The eye is amazing.
- every person's eye has a unique pattern of blood vessels
- new machine has been invented to identify people by taking an eyeprint
- machine scans a person's eye and matches it with a previously recorded image stored in its memory
- forgery-proof method of identification

3. As amateurs, today's Olympic stars cannot be paid for their athletic performances.
- to earn money, some take jobs making commercials
- some receive gifts that do not affect their amateur status
- ancient Greeks also gave gifts to their Olympic winners
- prizes and gifts made athletes in ancient Greece wealthy

Communicate Your Ideas

DRAFTING *Topic Sentences*

After reviewing your prewriting notes, follow the guidelines on page C129 to develop a strong topic sentence. Continue reworking your sentence until you think it ties together all the details you will use. Save your work.

Is ▸ Thinking

Generalizing

To write a topic sentence, you often use the thinking skill of **generalizing.** In other words, you look at specific details, facts, and examples to form a general observation or principle.

Not all generalizations are true. To persuade your parents to buy you a car, you might pose this unsound generalization: *All parents of teenagers buy them cars when they turn sixteen!*

Making a chart like the one below can help you examine the soundness of your generalizations. Start by listing a preliminary generalization. List additional details based on research or experience and rewrite your limited generalization to reflect the new information by using words such as *some, many,* or *most.*

REVISING A GENERALIZATION

Preliminary Generalization	All students who do not attend sports events lack school spirit.
Additional Research Details	Poll results: 10 students do not care to attend any school events but like the school; 15 students do not attend sports but belong to clubs; 10 students attend no school events and admit to having no school spirit.
Qualifying Words	some, many, most
Revised Generalization	Some students who do not attend sports events lack school spirit.

THINKING PRACTICE

Write a generalization using one of the following topics. Then use a chart like the one above to test and revise it.

1. how watching television can affect grades
2. why people show off at parties
3. how malicious rumors get started

Drafting the Body

If you planned your paragraph well, drafting the body should proceed smoothly. You are simply changing your list of details into sentences that clearly state your ideas. At this point you should not concern yourself about correct usage and mechanics since you will have opportunities for editing later.

> ### Strategies for Drafting the Paragraph Body
> - Draft quickly, focusing on getting your ideas down on paper.
> - Combine sentences that seem to go together.
> - To keep your ideas developing logically, pause now and then to reread what you have just written.
> - Where necessary, add words and phrases to help one sentence lead smoothly into the next.

While drafting, try to develop the habit of showing the relationship among your ideas. You can use words and phrases called transitions to join sentences.

A **transition** is a word or phrase that shows how ideas are related to one another.

The following chart shows some commonly used transitions that you can use to maintain the organization of your ideas.

TRANSITIONS FOR FOUR TYPES OF LOGICAL ORDER			
Importance	**Chronological**	**Spatial**	**Development**
even more	after	above	also
finally	as soon as	ahead	besides
first	first	behind	despite
more important	at last	below	for example
most important	second	higher	however
one reason	later	inside	therefore
to begin with	meanwhile	outside	while

DRAFTING *Body*

Use your notes and the strategies you have learned to draft the body of your informative paragraph. Include your topic sentence and remember to link sentences with transitions. Save your work for later use.

Drafting a Concluding Sentence

To complete your first draft, read over your topic sentence and paragraph body. Then think of a concluding sentence that will serve one or more of the following functions.

> **Functions of a Concluding Sentence**
>
> A concluding sentence
> - restates the main idea in fresh words.
> - summarizes the paragraph.
> - evaluates the supporting details.
> - adds an insight that emphasizes the main point.

Reread the paragraph "The Birth of a Car" on page C125. The concluding sentence restates the main idea in new words, but the writer might have written any of the following concluding sentences instead.

With one offhand comment, Alexander Winton had planted the seeds for a thriving competitor. (summarizes)

It would have been better for Winton if he had dealt more fairly with Packard's complaint. (evaluates details)

Many product improvements may result from a person's dissatisfaction with the old product. (adds an insight)

PRACTICE YOUR SKILLS

● *Concluding a Paragraph*

Look at the last paragraph of "In Suspect Terrain" on pages C99–C100. Find and read the concluding sentence. Then reread the items in Functions of a Concluding Sentence on the preceding page. Which of these functions does the concluding sentence of the article serve?

Communicate Your Ideas

DRAFTING *Concluding Sentence*

Write three possible concluding sentences for the informative paragraph you have just drafted. Then read the draft aloud with each concluding sentence to choose the one that sounds the best. Save your work.

Time Out to Reflect

Think about informative writing you have done in the past. Most of the answers you have written for essay tests, for example, are informative writing. What difficulties have you had in the past writing these informative paragraphs? Describe some of these problems. Now think about what you learned in this chapter. Which of the skills you have learned about will help you most when you use informative writing in the future? Record your thoughts in the Learning Log section of your **journal.**

Revising — Writing Process

As you revise your paragraph, look for wording that might confuse a reader or leave the reader in doubt about your meaning.

Checking for Adequate Development

A common fault in informative writing is lack of adequate development. Readers of informative writing are looking for information and clear explanations, and you must meet their expectations by providing an ample number of specific details to support your ideas.

Writing Tip

Achieve **adequate development** by adding any specific information that the reader will need to understand your subject.

In the first model below, not enough details are included. In the second, the writer provides specific information, allowing the reader to understand the subject more completely.

MODEL: Inadequately Developed Paragraph

> The Empire State Building in New York City is one of the most impressive buildings in the world. It once was the world's tallest building, and it still ranks as one of the tallest. Every year many people visit it. On a clear day, you can see far away. Besides its height the Empire State Building is impressive in other ways, for it has many windows and other things. People who are visiting New York City should be sure to see the Empire State Building.

MODEL: Adequately Developed Paragraph

> The Empire State Building in New York City is one of the most impressive buildings in the world. Completed in 1931, it was the world's tallest building until 1972. At 1,250 feet it is now the eighth tallest building in the world. The two observation decks, which are on the 86th and 102nd stories, are visited by 1.5 million people every year. From the higher

deck on a clear day, observers can see as far as 80 miles away. Besides its height, the Empire State Building is impressive in other ways. It has 6,500 windows, 7 miles of elevator shafts, and 60 miles of water pipes. People who are visiting New York City should be sure to see the Empire State Building.

PRACTICE YOUR SKILLS

● *Checking for Adequate Development*

The following paragraph lacks adequate development. Use your own knowledge or do some research to find specific supporting details that will strengthen the paragraph. Then revise the paragraph accordingly.

Memory Tricks

Memory tricks, called *mnemonics*, often succeed when unaided memory fails. For example, some people use a memory trick to remember the names of the Great Lakes. Others use a trick so they will remember the lines on a musical staff. Whenever you have to remember a series of items, make up a sentence with words that begin with the same letters as the items.

Checking for Unity

A paragraph that lacks unity can confuse readers. This problem occurs when one or more supporting sentences stray from the main point.

Writing Tip

Achieve **unity** by making sure all the supporting sentences relate to the topic sentence.

The sentences that stray from the subject in the following paragraph are crossed out. Read the paragraph first with the crossed-out sentences. Then read it without them to see how the paragraph gains unity once the sentences that stray from the subject are eliminated.

MODEL: Paragraph That Lacks Unity

Predicting Earthquakes

Scientists face a difficult yet important task in trying to predict earthquakes. ~~Scientists are usually successful in the end, however.~~ Each year earthquakes take 10,000 to 15,000 lives and cause billions of dollars in damage. Many cities have been totally destroyed. In 1811 and 1812, a series of earthquakes in Missouri changed the course of the Mississippi River, shaking the earth enough to stop clocks in Boston. ~~Boston is also sometimes struck by tornadoes.~~ Recent efforts to predict earthquakes have met with only limited success. Chinese scientists predicted an earthquake in Haicheng in 1975, and Soviet scientists predicted an earthquake in 1978. To control destruction from earthquakes, scientists must find a way to predict them more consistently.

PRACTICE YOUR SKILLS

● *Checking for Unity*

Decide which of the following paragraphs lacks unity, then revise it by writing it without the two sentences that stray from the subject.

1. Inventing Names

Many products are named after their inventors. The saxophone, for example, was named after Antoine Sax, a Belgian musical-instrument maker. The Geiger counter, used to detect radiation, was named for Hans Geiger, the German physicist who invented it. The macadam pavement that covers so many roadways is named for John McAdam, a

British engineer. As long as these inventions are used, their creators' names will be remembered.

2. Pointed Toes

A fifteenth-century nobleman often tripped over his own feet. His shoes were long and pointed, and the toes extended as much as 24 inches beyond his feet. At the same time in history, noblemen's hats were also pointed. The points on the shoes became so inconvenient that they were sometimes attached with a decorative chain to the tops of the boots. Many of today's shoes have points, but they are not as long as those of the fifteenth century. After a law limited toe length, the style gradually died out and noblemen could again walk without tripping.

Checking for Coherence

Another confusing problem in a paragraph can be a lack of coherence. **Coherence** is the glue of the paragraph, the quality that makes each sentence seem connected to the one before and after it. Following are some tips for achieving coherence.

Strategies for Achieving Coherence

- Double-check your organization to make sure each detail fits logically into your method of organization.
- Use transitional words and phrases. You may want to review the chart with transitions on page C132.
- Every now and then repeat key words.
- Use similar words or phrases in place of key words.
- Use pronouns in place of key words.

In the following paragraph, the words and phrases that aid coherence are in **boldface** type. The paragraph is in chronological order.

People are often slow to recognize good ideas. **For years** Tommy Rice, sportswriter for the *Brooklyn Eagle*, wrote about the need to have numbers on baseball players' shirts. **Without numbers** fans had a hard time identifying players. **Although** he wrote many columns, Rice always got the same reply from club owners—"Ridiculous!" Rice **finally** gave up. In **1929**, the Yankees **suddenly** announced that they would assign their players numbers. Other teams **soon** followed. **Although** baseball managers were slow to see it, Tommy Rice's idea made good sense.

PRACTICE YOUR SKILLS

● *Checking for Unity and Coherence*

After you read this paragraph, answer the questions that follow. Then rewrite the paragraph according to your answers.

(1) Tsunamis, unlike all other sea waves, are created by a sudden and drastic change in the seafloor. (2) *Tsunami* is a Japanese word meaning "harbor wave." (3) In some cases tsunamis are created by an undersea landslide. (4) In other cases tsunamis occur as a result of an earthquake or a volcanic eruption. (5) The force of these earthquakes and volcanic eruptions disturbs and displaces the seafloor, sending gigantic tsunamis to far shores. (6) Tsunamis have occurred throughout history. (7) Understanding how tsunamis are formed has helped scientists develop a way to warn people living in the tsunamis' paths. (8) In May of 1983, 13 people on the coast of Honshu were killed by a tsunami. (9) Until better warnings are devised, the casualties from these tsunamis will continue to mount.

1. Which two sentences in the paragraph stray from the main point?

2. Which pronoun could replace the word *tsunamis* in sentence 4?

3. Which one word could replace the words *earthquakes* and *volcanic eruptions* in sentence 5?

4. Which term could replace the word *tsunamis* in sentence 5?

5. What transitional word is needed in sentence 8?

6. What words could replace the word *tsunamis* in sentence 9?

> ## Evaluation Checklist for Revising

Checking Your Paragraph

✓ Do you have a strong topic sentence?
(pages C103–C104 and C129)

✓ Does your paragraph have adequate supporting sentences?
(pages C106–C107)

✓ Is your paragraph logically organized? (pages C124–C125)

✓ Does your paragraph have unity? (pages C136–C137)

✓ Does your paragraph have coherence? (page C138)

✓ Did you use transitions? (page C132)

✓ Do you have a strong concluding sentence?
(pages C107–C108)

Checking Your Sentences

✓ Do your sentences have variety? (pages C73–C80)

✓ Did you combine related sentences? (pages C73–C76)

✓ Are your sentences concise? (pages C67–C70)

✓ Have you avoided faulty parallelism? (page C86)

Checking Your Words

✓ Did you use specific, vivid words? (page C62)

✓ Did you use figurative language where appropriate?
(page C64)

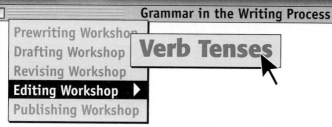

Prewriting Workshop
Drafting Workshop
Revising Workshop
Editing Workshop ▶
Publishing Workshop

Verb Tenses

When you write paragraphs, you will use verbs in different tenses to show whether events occurred in the past, the present, or the future.

> From that pipe alone, fourteen million carats *followed*.
>
> Down where diamonds form, they *are* stable, but as they travel upward they *pass* through regions of lower pressure, where they *will* swiftly *turn* into graphite.

In the first sentence above, *followed* is a past tense verb. In the second sentence, the verbs *are* and *pass* are in the present tense and *will turn* is a future tense verb.

Shifts in Tenses

When you edit, look for improper shifts in tenses. Do not shift tenses within or between sentences unless such a change is needed to clarify meaning.

IMPROPER SHIFT IN TENSE	A boy playing jacks in South Africa in 1867 **picked up** an alluvial diamond that led to the discovery of a number of pipes, one of which **becomes** the Kimberly Mine.
CORRECT TENSE	A boy playing jacks in South Africa in 1867 **picked up** an alluvial diamond that led to the discovery of a number of pipes, one of which **became** the Kimberly Mine.

Principal Parts of Verbs

The present tense and past tense of a verb are two of its principal parts. The present participle and past participle are the two other principal parts of a verb. The present participle of a regular verb is formed by adding *-ing* to the present tense. The past participle of a regular verb is formed by adding *-ed* to the present tense. The present participle of *occur*, for example, is *occurring*. The past participle is *(have) occurred*.

Many English verbs are irregular. That means they do not use *-ed* to form their past participles. When editing your paragraphs, make sure you have used the correct part of verbs.

IRREGULAR VERBS			
Present	Present Participle	Past	Past Participle
put	putting	put	(have) put
lose	losing	lost	(have) lost
break	breaking	broke	(have) broken
see	seeing	saw	(have) seen
ring	ringing	rang	(have) rung
go	going	went	(have) gone

Active and Passive Voice

Besides tense, some verbs have voice. *Active voice* indicates that the subject is performing the action. *Passive voice* indicates that the subject receives the action of the verb.

ACTIVE VOICE	Castles and huge statues **attracted** customers to the golf courses.
PASSIVE VOICE	Customers **were attracted** to the golf courses by castles and huge statues.

Use the active voice whenever possible. Verbs in the active voice will make your writing forceful and concise.

Editing Checklist

✔ Have you used correct tenses?

✔ Are there any shifts in tense?

✔ Have you used the correct principal parts of verbs?

✔ Have you used the active voice wherever possible?

REVISING *Paragraph Development, Unity, Coherence*

Look over the informative paragraph you have finished drafting. Check it carefully for adequate development, unity, and coherence. Revise as necessary to improve your draft, using the checklist on page C140. Save this revision for editing.

Editing | Writing Process

After revising your paragraph it is a good idea to put it aside long enough to give you a little distance. When you edit, you reread your paragraph looking for mistakes in language. It is a good idea to refer to your Personalized Editing Checklist. That way, you will not repeat errors that you have made in the past. The checklist on the previous page and on page C46 will also help you check your work.

EDITING *Verb Tense*

Using the checklist on the previous page, look at the verbs in your informative paragraph. Also review the **Editing Checklist** on page C46 and your Personalized Editing Checklist to find any other errors.

PORTFOLIO

Process of Writing an Informative Paragraph

Remember that the writing process is recursive—you can move back and forth among the stages of the process to achieve your purpose. For example, after revising, you may wish to return to the drafting stage and try a different approach to your subject. The numbers in parentheses refer to pages where you can get help with your writing.

PREWRITING

- Find ideas from your experiences or reading. *(pages C110–C112)*
- Choose and limit your subject. *(pages C112–C114)*
- Determine your audience. *(page C115)*
- Develop a list of supporting details by reading and talking to knowledgeable people. *(page C116)*
- Classify supporting details. *(pages C118–C120)*
- Organize your details in a logical order. *(pages C124–C125)*

DRAFTING

- Draft a topic sentence. *(page C129)*
- Change your organized list of details into sentences for the body of your paragraph. *(page C132)*
- Add a concluding sentence. *(page C133)*

REVISING

- Using the <u>Evaluation Checklist for Revising</u> on page C140, check paragraph structure, adequate development, unity, coherence, transitions, sentences, and words. *(pages C132–C138)*

EDITING

- Using the <u>Editing Checklists</u>, check your grammar, usage, spelling, and mechanics. *(pages C46 and C142)*

PUBLISHING

- Prepare a neat final copy of your work and present it to an interested reader.

A Writer Writes

A Paragraph to Inform

Purpose: **to use incidents and examples to support a generalization**

Audience: **your classmates and teacher**

Prewriting

Plan an informative paragraph that uses incidents and examples from your life to support a quotation. As you read the following quotation, think about what it means.

> Try to play easy pieces well; it is better than to play difficult ones poorly.
>
> —*Robert Schumann*

These questions may help you focus your ideas about the meaning of the quotation. Freewrite answers to the questions.

1. Even though Schumann was advising young musicians when he made this statement, do you think it is *just* about music? What makes you believe as you do?

2. What generalization does this quotation seem to be making?

3. To what other areas of life could this quotation apply? Why might it apply to these areas?

4. What famous personalities or historical figures lived by this generalization? How do they show that they lived by this general truth?

Read over your freewriting. Using ideas from your freewriting, write a one-sentence generalization that clearly states the meaning of the quotation.

Then brainstorm incidents or examples from you life that support the generalization. List your ideas. When your list is complete, choose the incidents and examples that best support the generalization.

Organize these incidents, using a graphic organizer or an outline. You might find some ideas on pages C32 and C124 to help you make an effective plan to organize you material.

Drafting

Write a first draft of your paragraph. Include the quotation very early in the paragraph and then use your supporting incidents and examples to develop your paragraph.

Revising

As you read your first draft aloud, listen to it as if you had never heard it before. Is the broad meaning of the generalization clearly explained? Have you included enough examples and details to support the generalization, and are they arranged in a logical order? Make whatever changes are needed.

Editing

Use the Editing Checklists on pages C46 and C142 as guides to correct any errors in your writing. You may also wish to refer to the Personalized Editing Checklist in your **journal**.

Publishing

After you make a final copy, be prepared to read it aloud to classmates and to discuss various ideas that students developed in their paragraphs. Then form small committees to brainstorm ideas about the best way to collectively publish your paragraphs.

Connection Collection

Representing in Different Ways

. . . to Visuals

From the text, create a flowchart demonstrating the incidents leading J. T. Millson to demand a refund. Be sure to include every event mentioned in the letter—from the time J. T. ordered the tape to the time she wrote the letter.

From Visuals . . .

Received "How to Play the Oboe" CD. No refund.

Sent letter requesting full refund.

Received "How to Play the Tuba" CD. No refund.

Received "How to Play the Oboe" CD. No refund.

Sent letter requesting full refund.

2632 Carelton Lane
Byram, CT 06830
December 7, 2000

Daniel Knight
Learn Anything, Inc.
179 Chilton Road
Berkeley, CA 94740

Dear Mr. Knight:

On December 1, I purchased your set of instructional CDs, "How to Play the Harpsichord in Three Days." Citing your money-back guarantee, I wish to return the CDs for a full refund. The CDs do not work.

This is a continuation of problems I have had with your company's instructional products. Prior to this incident, I was shipped a set of incorrect instructional CDs. I ordered "How to Play the Xylophone in Three Days," but I received a set for building model airplanes. Despite constant phone calls, I received no action on the part of your company to rectify the situation.

I demand a full refund for the ordered products and have enclosed my receipt.

Yours truly,

J. T. Millson

J. T. Millson

. . . to Print

Using the flowchart above, write a letter to Learn Anything, Inc., describing the sequence of events since you last wrote to request a full refund.

- **Which strategies can be used for creating both written and visual representations? Which strategies apply to one, not both? Which type of representation is more effective?**
- **Draw a conclusion, and write briefly about the differences between written ideas and visual representations.**

Writing in the Workplace

Informative E-mail

You work for Hevi Starch and Sons, a very prestigious law firm. Like most modern businesses, your office has a "casual Friday" dress policy. Instead of wearing coats and ties and other office dress, employees are allowed to wear less formal clothing. Unfortunately some of the employees have begun to abuse the policy. Some have started coming to work dressed in torn blue jeans, frayed sneakers, and T-shirts.

> Write an E-mail message informing the other employees of the importance of adhering to office policy. Make sure you end your message with a strong concluding sentence.

> What strategies did you use to inform the employees?

> *You can find information on writing E-mails on pages C736–C739.*

Writing in Everyday Life

Informative Note

You discover in the newspaper that your favorite poet is giving her last public performance at a used bookstore near your house. You wish to take a friend to the reading. Your friend recently expressed to you an interest in poetry, but he is not familiar with poetry and has never attended a poetry reading. You are excited about attending and wish to invite your friend.

> Write a note informing your friend about the poetry reading. Consider what your friend knows about the subject and what else he or she might need to know as background information.

> What strategies did you use to inform your friend?

Assess Your Learning

Your best friend disagrees with you on the impact and importance of the Internet. He has used the Internet only once, and he felt overwhelmed by the amount of available information and options for topics. He felt confused by the technicalities involved in using the Internet as a tool for research. Your friend claims the Internet is "just a fad" and within a few more years no one will use it. In response to your friend's feelings, you decide to write an article for the local newspaper.

▶ **Write an article for the newspaper informing the public that the Internet is an enjoyable and useful resource. Begin your article with a strong topic sentence, and use supporting sentences that expand on the topic sentence by giving specific details, facts, examples, or reasons. Organize your article so that your supporting details are in order of importance from least important to most important. Check your paragraph structure for clarity and coherence.**

⊳ *Before You Write* **Consider the following questions:**
What is the *subject*?
What is the *occasion*?
Who is the *audience*?
What is the *purpose*?

⊳ *After You Write* **Evaluate your work using the following criteria:**
- Does your article have a strong topic sentence?
- Have you used supporting sentences that expand on the topic sentence by giving specific details, facts, examples, or reasons?
- Have you organized your article so that the supporting details are in order of importance from least important to most important?
- Have you presented your information in a clear and organized way?
- Have you checked your paragraph structure for unity and coherence?
- Have you revised your paragraph to add transitions between ideas?
- Does your entry show accurate spelling and correct use of punctuation and capitalization?

> **Write briefly on how well you did. Point out your strengths and areas for improvement.**

A Writer's Guide to Presenting Information

The world is bursting with information. There is so much to absorb that you may at times find yourself overwhelmed by it all. Whether it is nutrition information on a cereal box, directions to your school, or an article in a magazine about your favorite band, information comes at you in a barrage from all directions.

The most basic function of writing is to convey information. In fact, when you have information you want to convey to others, often writing is the best means to organize and present it clearly. It is helpful to choose the organizational model and method of development best suited to what you want to write.

Information can be categorized in several ways, depending on its type. If, for example, you need to explain how to assemble a piece of furniture, you would write a how-to paragraph. A how-it-works paragraph might explain how data is sent over the Internet, while a cause-and-effect paragraph might explain what makes your heart beat faster when you exercise. You could write a compare-and-contrast paragraph to compare one kind of tree to another, but a definitions paragraph to tell what a cyborg is. This guide offers you information that will help you decide how best to gather and present the information you want to convey.

How-to Paragraphs

A **process** is a sequence of steps by which something is made or done. There are several kinds of processes; one common type is the how-to process. Use this kind of paragraph to describe the sequence of steps in the process of making or doing something.

A **how-to paragraph** gives step-by-step instructions for doing or making something.

Generally these paragraphs describe simple tasks or processes that almost anyone could do. No matter what process you write about, your goal is to provide a clear and simple explanation for your readers. The following is an example of a how-to paragraph.

MODEL: How-to Paragraph

A Simple Silk-Screen Print

Stenciled prints made on a silk screen can be simple and fun to do. Gather the following supplies available from a craft store: the screen—a piece of polyester net (not silk) stretched tightly across a wood frame; a squeegee—a rubber blade attached to a piece of wood; some art paper; small jars of paint; a roll of stencil film; a stencil or utility knife; and some mineral spirits. First draw a simple design of the size you want your print to be. Next lay a piece of stencil film over the design, and use the knife to trace and cut out the shapes from the film. This cutout is the stencil from which you print. Adhere the film to the underside of the silk screen by rubbing it lightly through the fabric with a piece of cloth dipped in mineral spirits. Then tape a sheet of art paper to an old table or a similar surface and place the stencil over it. Next pour some paint on the screen just above your design, and use the squeegee to pull it slowly over the paper. Finally lift the stencil carefully and admire your print.

 Writing a How-to Paragraph

The following activities will help you write your own how-to paragraph that explains how to do something.

Prewriting

To choose a topic for a how-to paragraph, think about your favorite hobbies, sports, and crafts. You've probably learned many skills while pursuing these activities. For example, you may know how to bunt a baseball, do a double somersault dive, make delicious chili, or tune up a car. Chances are you will be better able to describe a process if you are already familiar with it.

One idea for prewriting is to videotape the process you plan to describe and then take notes on each step or phase. Or you can draw pictures, a diagram, or a flowchart to help you order the steps in your own mind.

Drafting

Begin your paragraph in a way that will get your audience's attention. Be sure to present the steps in the order in which they occur or are performed. When possible, show how each step relates to the whole process. Include all the important details, and don't forget to define any unfamiliar terms. Transition words that show time order—*first, next, before, after, now, later,* and *finally*—will help your audience follow the steps.

Revising

After you have finished your draft, ask someone to read it and comment. If possible, the reader might try following the steps or explain the process in his or her own words. This is a good way to find out if any of the steps are confusing, missing, or out of order. Think about word changes that might make your writing more precise. Also decide whether you need to add transition words to clarify the order. Use the <u>Evaluation Checklist for Revising</u> on page C140 to help you revise too. Then save your work in your writing folder in case you want to polish it to share with someone later.

How-It-Works Paragraphs

When you are describing how something forms, happens, or is put together, you are explaining the stages in a process or an operation. The information is usually arranged in chronological order.

A **how-it-works paragraph** describes how something happens, forms, or is put together.

This type of paragraph usually explains a technical or abstract process, rather than something readers could do themselves, as in a how-to paragraph. A how-it-works paragraph often resembles narrative writing. The following is an example of a how-it-works paragraph.

MODEL: How-It-Works Paragraph

The Blink of an Eye

In the blink of an eye, your eyes, nervous system, and brain will see and process the words in this paragraph. The complex process begins when light reflected from the page enters your eye through your pupil, the black dot at the center of your eye. Controlling how much light enters the pupil is the iris, a colored ring of brown, blue, or green, that acts like a muscular curtain. After passing the pupil and iris, the light reaches the lens of your eye, where the light rays are focused. The lens flips the light pattern upside down and projects an inverted image onto the retina. The retina, a soft, transparent layer of nervous tissue inside the eyeball, is connected to the optic nerve. The long optic nerve transmits the image (still upside down) to your brain, which performs a complex analysis of the light patterns so that you can read and understand these words—and it all occurs in the blink of an eye.

Writing a How-It-Works Paragraph

The following activities will help you write a paragraph that explains how something happens or works.

Prewriting

Your everyday life is filled with countless topics for how-it-works paragraphs. Dark thunderclouds fill the sky and pour down rain. Lasers in supermarkets scan each product you buy. Cars convert the energy in gasoline into motion. Since you will have to do some research for your how-it-works paragraph, choose a topic that you really do want to find out more about. Avoid choosing a topic that is too broad or complicated to cover in a paragraph.

You will probably want to use encyclopedias, nonfiction books, and the Internet to find details for your paragraph. Make sure you find enough details to explain the whole process; don't leave any steps out. Since order is crucial whenever you describe a process, you may want to number the details you plan to use in order to put them in the correct order. Don't hesitate to draw a simple sketch or diagram to show the process you will write about.

Drafting

Working from your numbered notes and/or a diagram, draft your paragraph. Strive for a simple, straightforward tone; you don't want to baffle your readers with difficult scientific terms, unless they really are necessary. Some readers may have decided beforehand that a how-it-works paragraph is boring. Surprise them! Do whatever you can to make your writing lively and interesting. A sketch, diagram, or other visual might complement your paragraph nicely and help readers better understand the process.

Revising

As you revise your draft, focus on whether your paragraph is complete. You may need to add additional details if your audience is to get a clear picture. Also decide whether terms in your paragraph need definitions. As you revise, check to make sure that the steps are in order. You may need to add transition words to make the progression of steps clearer. Don't forget to use the Evaluation Checklist for Revising on page C140 for additional revising hints. When you are finished, place your paragraph in your folder in case you want to polish it to share with someone later.

Compare-and-Contrast Paragraphs

To understand a concept, you might find it helpful to compare it to another that is similar or contrast it with one that is dissimilar. A compare-and-contrast paragraph is a good way to do that.

A **compare-and-contrast paragraph** examines the similarities and differences between two subjects.

This type of paragraph will help you interpret, understand, and explain two related subjects or events. One way to do this is to explain all the characteristics of Subject A and then, in the same order, all the characteristics of Subject B. Another way is to take the characteristics one at a time, describing them alternately as they appear in Subject A and then in Subject B until all the characteristics are covered. The following paragraph is an example of the second approach.

MODEL: Compare-and-Contrast Paragraph

Two Dragons

Although the dragon appears often in the myths and early legends of Europe and Asia, the creatures have always played a more positive role in Asian cultures. Both Europeans and Asians describe dragons as large, lizard-like animals that breathe fire and have long, scaly tails. In Europe, dragons were ferocious beasts that terrorized human communities; they seemed to represent the evils that people fought. In Asia, by contrast, dragons were magical animals and usually good luck, a cross between a lion and an angel. The European dragon lived in dark mountainous caves. In Asia, however, they were associated with rivers, clouds, and much-needed rainfall. In later time, the European dragon became a ridiculous figure, something to poke fun at. This has not occurred in Asia, where the dragon remains a much-revered symbol.

Writing a Compare-and-Contrast Paragraph

The following activities will help you write a paragraph that compares a concept or object to another that is similar and/or contrasts it with one that is dissimilar.

Prewriting

When choosing topics to compare and contrast, think of two things that have enough common features to make a comparison sensible but enough differences to make the contrast interesting.

Brainstorm suitable topics. You might want to write about two baseball teams, for example, or two important figures from history. Two similar products that you have bought and used—such as running shoes or breakfast foods—might lend themselves to a compare-and-contrast paragraph too.

Once you have chosen your subjects, make a list or chart of the features you plan to compare. Note how your subjects compare in relation to each of these features. These will be the supporting details of your paragraph.

Drafting

Using your list or chart of features, draft your paragraph. Begin with a topic sentence that states the main point you want to make. You can organize your draft by subject or feature. In a subject-by-subject comparison, you discuss each subject in turn. In a feature-by-feature comparison, you go back and forth between the two subjects as you discuss each feature. The model paragraph about dragons is a feature-by-feature comparison.

Revising

Read over your paragraph. Have you begun with a topic sentence that states your main idea? Have you found both similarities to compare and differences to contrast? Have you organized your paragraph in either a subject-by-subject or a feature-by-feature fashion? If you answered *no* to any of these questions, fix the problems you found. Share your paragraph with a test reader to see if he or she understands the similarities and differences you describe. Then check your work against the <u>Evaluation Checklist for Revising</u> on page C140. Save your paragraph in your writing folder in case you want to polish it to share with someone later.

Cause-and-Effect Paragraphs

When your informative subject requires you to explain *why* something happened, very often the best type of writing to use is a cause-and-effect paragraph.

A **cause-and-effect** paragraph explains why actions or situations (causes) produce certain results (effects).

A simple cause-and-effect paragraph deals with a single cause, such as an icy sidewalk, and a single effect, such as a fall. A more complex paragraph describes a series of causes and effects, each one dependent on the one before—a chain of events. The explanation given in a cause-and-effect paragraph is supported with specific evidence that is presented in a well-organized and logical sequence. The following is an example of a cause-and-effect paragraph.

MODEL: Cause-and-Effect Paragraph

The Fall of the Soviet Union

Although the world was shocked by the collapse of the Soviet Union, the causes for this upheaval are easy to trace. For decades, Soviet citizens had been impatient with Communism, frustrated by low living standards and a lack of individual liberties. The key cause for the downfall of the Soviet Union, however, was Mikhail Gorbachev's rise to power in 1985. Promising to restructure the Soviet Union (*perestroika*) in a spirit of openness (*glasnost*), Gorbachev urged a series of democratic reforms. Taking Gorbachev at his word, the Soviet Union's satellite countries in Eastern Europe—Poland, East Germany, Czechoslovakia, and Hungary—began to "restructure" themselves by overthrowing their Communist governments. This greatly weakened the Soviet Union politically. Finally, when an August 1991 attempt by the Soviet military to get rid of Gorbachev failed, Gorbachev quit the Communist Party and the Soviet Union began to fall apart.

Writing a Cause-and-Effect Paragraph

The following activities will help you write a paragraph that explains why something happened or happens.

Prewriting

Anything that arouses your curiosity is possible material for a cause-and-effect paragraph. To find a topic, you might check the daily news for intriguing questions in newspaper stories and TV broadcasts. Or think of a key event in history and consider why it turned out the way it did. The human dramas going on around you—people's behavior and the reasons they act the way they do—might also provide you with topics.

You will want to focus and organize your paragraph in a way that suits your topic. For some topics, you may describe a series of events in which each cause has an effect that in turn causes another effect—a cause-and-effect chain. For other topics, you may begin with a single cause and present several of its effects. Alternately, you might describe one effect that was brought about by several causes. The paragraph on the previous page, for example, presents several different causes that all led to one effect—the collapse of the Soviet Union.

Drafting

When drafting a cause-and-effect paragraph, make sure your readers will be able to follow the connections you make between one situation or event and another. One good way to do this is to use cause-and-effect transitional words such as *because, therefore, consequently, as a result,* and *so.* These words let a reader know that a cause or an effect is about to follow.

Revising

As your revise your cause-and-effect paragraph, ask yourself questions such as: Have I given my readers enough information to understand what I am saying? Are the relationships between the causes and effects I discuss clear? Should I add more transitional words to clarify the causes and effects I describe?

Ask a peer reader for suggestions about how to make your writing clearer. Take those suggestions into account as you revise. Also check your work against the **Evaluation Checklist for Revising** on page C140. Save your paragraph in your writing folder in case you want to polish it to share with someone later.

Definition Paragraphs

One of the most basic functions of informative writing is to explain what something means. If you suspect your audience may be unfamiliar with a term you will be using, or if a concept you are discussing might be misinterpreted, use a definition paragraph to explain the meaning of the term or concept.

A **definition paragraph** explains the nature and characteristics of a word, an object, a concept, or a phenomenon.

Sometimes a word will be unfamiliar to most readers, even though it represents something that affects their everyday experience. The following is an example of a definition paragraph.

MODEL: Definition Paragraph

Cookie

A cookie is a set of data that a Website sends to a browser the first time the user visits the site. The data are updated with each return visit. The Website saves the information the cookie contains about the user, and the user's browser does the same. Not all browsers support cookies, meaning they don't store them. Cookies store information such as user name and password and the parts of the site that were visited. This information can be updated with each visit. The browser shares each cookie only with the server that originated it; other servers can read only their own cookies. Your browser's preferences can be set up to alert the user when a cookie is being sent so the user can choose to accept it or not.

 Writing a Definition Paragraph

The following activities will help you write a paragraph that explains or defines a word, a concept, an object, or a phenomenon.

Prewriting

For your definition paragraph, think about the subject areas that interest you. Perhaps, for example, there is a term used in baseball or football, such as *balk* or *sudden death,* that you would like to define. Maybe you have strong feelings about a political, societal, or environmental goal. The term for this goal can be an interesting subject for a definition paragraph. Maybe you would like to write about an unusual word, expression, or idiom that you have heard recently.

Search for details about your subject in dictionaries, encyclopedias, nonfiction books, or magazines and newspapers. Incorporate your personal experiences and observations, too, if they are relevant. A cluster diagram might be a useful way to generate and record the details you will use.

Drafting

When deciding which information to include in your definition paragraph, select the details that will most help your readers understand the concept. Start with a definition of the term you are defining, either quoted or paraphrased from a dictionary or reference source. Then organize the rest of your definition in a logical order that presents your ideas clearly.

Revising

When revising your paragraph, ask yourself whether your definition gives a full picture of your subject. Check to make sure that you have opened with a definition that will be clear to readers. Decide whether the details in your paragraph might be clearer if they were ordered in a different way. Finally, check your paragraph using the **Evaluation Checklist for Revising** on page C140. Save your work in your writing folder in case you want to polish it to share with someone later. You may also want to consider compiling your paragraph with those of your classmates into a class dictionary.

▶ Your Checklist for Presenting Information

When you are writing to inform, you will probably find that the information you want to express falls into one of the categories below. Use the following checklist to review some of the guidelines for developing the information in each category. The numbers in parentheses refer to pages where you can get additional help with your writing.

HOW TO
- The process should be clear. *(page C151)*
- Give step-by-step instructions. *(page C151)*

HOW IT WORKS
- Arrange your paragraph in chronological order. *(page C153)*
- Always describe a process or operation clearly. *(page C153)*

COMPARE AND CONTRAST
- Clearly identify two subjects. *(page C155)*
- Discuss the two subjects in the same order in which they were presented. *(page C155)*

CAUSE AND EFFECT
- Place your causes and effects in logical sequence. *(page C157)*
- Use cause-and-effect transitional words. *(page C158)*

DEFINITION
- Open with a clear, simple definition. *(page C160)*
- Follow with details in a logical order. *(page C160)*

CHAPTER 4

Writing Other Kinds of Paragraphs

Every day, you read, learn from, and enjoy many different kinds of writing. When you follow written directions for setting up a computer, for example, you are reading informative writing, which you explored in Chapter 3. When you get caught up in an exciting novel, you are reading and reflecting on narrative and descriptive writing. When you agree or disagree with an editorial in your school newspaper, you are reading and reacting to persuasive writing.

Narrative writing tells, or narrates, a real or imaginary story. Descriptive writing portrays an object, person, or scene in a vivid or memorable way. Persuasive writing expresses an opinion and often uses reason and facts to influence others. As you learn more about narrative, descriptive, and persuasive writing in this chapter, you will learn how you can affect others through the power of the written word.

Reading with a Writer's Eye

Beryl Markham (1902–1986) was the first person to fly solo westward across the Atlantic from England to North America. As you read about Markham's September 1936 flight in *West with the Night,* imagine yourself aboard her tiny airplane, the *Gull.* Notice how Markham uses narrative and descriptive writing to create a suspenseful and vivid account of one dangerous episode in her record-setting journey.

FROM

WEST WITH THE NIGHT

Beryl Markham

At ten o'clock P.M., I am flying along the Great Circle Course[1] for Harbour Grace, Newfoundland, into a forty-mile headwind at a speed of one hundred and thirty miles an hour. Because of the weather, I cannot be sure of how many more hours I have to fly, but I think it must be between sixteen and eighteen.

At ten-thirty I am still flying on the large cabin tank of petrol,[2] hoping to use it up and put an end to the liquid swirl that has rocked the plane since my take-off. The tank has no gauge, but written on its side is the assurance: "This tank is good for four hours."

There is nothing ambiguous about such a guaranty. I believe it, but at twenty-five minutes to eleven, my motor coughs and dies, and the Gull is powerless above the sea.

I realize that the heavy drone of the plane has been, until this moment, complete and comforting silence. It is the actual silence following the last splutter of the engine that stuns me. I can't feel any fear; I can't feel anything. I can only observe with a kind of stupid disinterest that my hands are violently active and know that, while they move, I am being hypnotized by the needle of my altimeter.[3]

I suppose that the denial of natural impulse is what is meant by "keeping calm," but impulse has reason in it. If it is night and you are sitting in an aeroplane with a stalled motor, and there are two thousand feet between you and the sea, nothing

---

[1] **Great Circle Course:** The shortest distance between any two points on the earth.
[2] **petrol** (pĕt′ rəl) *n.:* Gasoline.
[3] **altimeter** (ăl tĭm′ĭ tər) *n.:* An instrument for measuring altitude.

can be more reasonable than the impulse to pull back your stick in the hope of adding to that two thousand, if only by a little. The thought, the knowledge, the law that tells you that your hope lies not in this, but in a contrary act—the act of directing your impotent craft toward the water—seems a terrifying abandonment, not only of reason, but of sanity. Your mind and your heart reject it. It is your hands—your stranger's hands—that follow with unfeeling precision the letter of the law.

I sit there and watch my hands push forward on the stick and feel the Gull respond and begin its dive to the sea. Of course it is a simple thing; surely the cabin tank has run dry too soon. I need only to turn another petcock[4] . . .

But it is dark in the cabin. It is easy to see the luminous dial of the altimeter and to note that my height is now eleven hundred feet, but it is not easy to see a petcock that is somewhere near the floor of the plane. A hand gropes and reappears with an electric torch, and fingers, moving with agonizing composure, find the petcock and turn it; and I wait.

At three hundred feet the motor is still dead, and I am conscious that the needle of my altimeter seems to whirl like the spoke of a spindle winding up the remaining distance between the plane and the water. There is some lightning, but the quick flash only serves to emphasize the darkness. How high can waves reach—twenty feet, perhaps? Thirty?

It is impossible to avoid the thought that this is the end of my flight, but my reactions are not orthodox; the various incidents of my entire life do not run through my mind like a motion-picture film gone mad. I only feel that all this has happened before—and it has. It has all happened a hundred times in my mind, in my sleep, so that now I am not really caught in terror; I recognize a familiar scene, a familiar story with its climax dulled by too much telling.

---

[4] **petcock:** A small valve for letting out air, releasing compression, or draining.

I do not know how close to the waves I am when the motor explodes to life again. But the sound is almost meaningless. I see my hand easing back on the stick, and I feel the Gull climb up into the storm, and I see the altimeter whirl like a spindle again, paying out the distance between myself and the sea.

The storm is strong. It is comforting. It is like a friend shaking me and saying, "Wake up! You were only dreaming."

A few hours later, as Markham was approaching Canada, the Gull's *engine failed again. That time, the pioneering pilot wasn't so lucky. Unable to coax her plane back to life, Markham crash-landed in a rocky bog. Dazed and wounded, the Englishwoman still made her way to safety and was eventually hailed worldwide for her accomplishment.*

Thinking as a Writer

NARRATION Evaluating Effectiveness of Narration

- Imagine that you are running a publishing company and Beryl Markham has submitted her narrative to you for publication. Does her writing make you feel you are with her in her plane? Why or why not? Identify details that support your evaluation.
- Discuss what Markham might have done differently to increase the effectiveness of her writing.
- Finally, decide whether to publish the narrative as written. Explain your decision.

DESCRIPTION Describing a Person

Viewing The photograph on the previous page shows Beryl Markham soon after her flight.

- Work with a partner. Close your book and have your partner describe Markham as you sketch what you hear. Then change roles.
- Compare both sketches to the photograph. Did you give each other accurate descriptions? What additional details might have been helpful?

PERSUASION Using Arguments to Convince

Oral Expression Beryl Markham believed the progress of aviation was worth the personal risk she took. Others might disagree.

- With a partner, role-play a discussion between Beryl Markham and a friend on the day before the flight. If you are playing Markham, try to persuade your friend that your decision to fly solo to New York is a sound one. If you are playing Markham's friend, try to persuade her not to go. As you listen to your partner, decide which words and arguments are most persuasive.

Developing the Skills of Narration

If you want to tell about a series of events—in a letter, on a history test, or in a short story—you will be writing narration. You can develop the skills required for narrative writing by creating paragraphs that grab and hold your reader's attention.

Narrative writing tells a real or an imaginary story with a clear beginning, middle, and ending.

 Your Writer's Journal

Firsts are risk-taking experiences. Your first performance in a play, your first steps as a child: in each of these experiences you took some risk. In your journal, brainstorm a list of your first experiences, such as the first time you expressed an unpopular opinion with a group of friends. You will find this list to be useful in your later writing.

Narrative Paragraph Structure

A narrative paragraph has three main parts. Each part performs a specific function.

 Structure of a Narrative Paragraph

- The **topic sentence** captures the reader's attention and makes a general statement that sets the scene.
- The **supporting sentences** tell the story event by event.
- The **concluding sentence** shows the outcome, summarizes the story, or adds an insight.

The following narrative paragraph describes the experience of a deep-sea diver who took a foolish risk.

A Narrow Escape

TOPIC SENTENCE:

MAKES A GENERAL STATEMENT

SUPPORTING SENTENCES:

RELATE EVENTS ONE BY ONE

CONCLUDING SENTENCE:

GIVES OUTCOME

We were young and sometimes we went beyond the limits of common sense. Once, my comrade Philippe Tailliez was diving alone in December, with his dog Soika guarding his clothes. The water was 52 degrees Fahrenheit. Philippe was trying to spear some big sea bass but had to break off the chase when he could no longer stand the cold. He found himself several hundred yards from the deserted shore. The return swim was a harrowing, benumbed struggle. He dragged himself out on a rock and fainted. A bitter wind swept him. He had small chance of surviving such an exposure. The wolfhound, moved by an extraordinary instinct, covered him with its body and breathed hot air on his face. Tailliez awoke with near paralyzed hands and feet and stumbled to a shelter.

—*Jacques Cousteau, "Menfish"*

PRACTICE YOUR SKILLS

● *Writing Topic Sentences*

Imagine how each event listed below would take place. Then write a topic sentence for each one. Be sure each sentence captures the reader's attention and makes a general statement or sets the scene.

1. struggling with your conscience

2. beginning a new friendship

3. meeting your favorite movie star

4. witnessing a street-corner drama

5. moving to a new neighborhood

6. disagreeing with a friend

7. meeting a new classmate

8. learning a new skill

Communicate Your Ideas

PREWRITING *Topic Sentences*

Reread the list of first experiences you wrote in your **journal**. Choose one of them to develop into a narrative paragraph. Write freely about that experience on a separate sheet of paper. When you have finished, you may want to record how another person might remember that same experience. You might also express how your feelings are different today from what they were during the time of the experience. Then write a topic sentence for your narrative paragraph. Save your work for later use.

SAVE YOUR WORK

Chronological Order and Transitions

A narrative paragraph tells about an event that occurs within a certain time period. For this reason the most common organization for a narrative paragraph is **chronological order**. Words and phrases called **transitions** are used to show the relationship of events. The following chart lists transitions that are commonly used in narrative writing.

TRANSITIONS FOR CHRONOLOGICAL ORDER			
after	meanwhile	during	last night
before	next	at last	on Monday
suddenly	then	at noon	the next day
just as	immediately	while	by evening

PRACTICE YOUR SKILLS

● *Using Chronological Order*

Arrange the following events in chronological order. Then save your work.

- The passengers cheered when the engines started up again.
- The takeoff of Flight 81 from Los Angeles to Denver was normal.
- We flew into a thunderstorm above the Rocky Mountains.
- Passengers were relaxing and enjoying a snack after the captain turned off the seat belt sign.
- We heard a loud thump followed by a frightening silence.
- There was an even bigger cheer as the plane touched down safely.
- The pilots restarted the engines at 15,000 feet.
- The flight attendants said to prepare for an emergency landing.
- The plane began to descend without power at 20,000 feet.

● *Using Transitions*

Now write a narrative paragraph based on these events. Use transitions to show how these events are related in time.

Communicate Your Ideas

PREWRITING *Chronological Order*

Review the freewriting you did about a first in your life. After you have selected details about the event to include in a narrative paragraph, list those details in chronological order. Save your work for later use.

● Point of View

Every story has a **narrator**, the person whose voice is telling the story. If you tell a story about yourself and refer to yourself with first person pronouns—such as *I, we, us,* and *our*—you are using **first person narration**. If you use a narrator who does not participate in the events and refers to the characters with third person pronouns—such as *he, she,* and *they*—you are using **third person narration**. These different voices are called **point of view**, because they indicate through whose eyes the story is being told.

FIRST PERSON   **I** held **my** breath as the judge prepared to announce the winners. (narrator is participant)

THIRD PERSON   **She** held **her** breath as the judge prepared to announce the winners. (narrator is observer)

Once you have chosen a point of view for a narrative, maintain it throughout the story.

> ### Writing Tip
>
> Use **first person point of view** if you are describing your own actions in the story.
> Use **third person point of view** if you are reporting what happened to others.

PRACTICE YOUR SKILLS

● *Recognizing Point of View*

Write *first person* or *third person* to indicate the point of view of each of the following quotations.

1. Yes, he had practically saved my life. He had also practically lost it for me.

—John Knowles, A Separate Peace

2. His lips curled in a smile and then opened with a short triumphant laugh.

—George Eliot, Middlemarch

3. No scheme could have been more agreeable to Elizabeth, and her acceptance to the invitation was most ready and grateful.

—Jane Austen, Pride and Prejudice

4. The grocer opened later than usual this Saturday morning, but still it was early enough to make him one of the first walkers in the neighborhood.

—James Alan McPherson, "A Loaf of Bread"

5. I think my honesty is the only sort in the world, and he thinks his is the only sort in the world as well.

—Alan Sillitoe, The Loneliness of the Long-Distance Runner

Experimenting with Point of View

The following paragraph is written in third person. After you read it carefully, rewrite it in first person from Angela's point of view.

Angela Gets a Computer

Angela had wanted a new computer for a long time. One day she went into a computer store and found the computer of her dreams. Every day of the following week, she stopped in at the store to look at it and gently press its keys. Then she headed straight home to convince her parents that they should buy it for her. Her parents finally agreed, and they all went back to the store the following Saturday. The salesperson helped them pack it in its box, and off they drove with the computer jiggling around in the trunk. When they returned home, Angela and her father set up the machine and plugged it in. Immediately Angela inserted the training software and, following its directions, typed in her name. The computer called her by name as she progressed step-by-step through the lesson. The words "Good job, Angela" appeared on the screen every time she completed a step. Angela stayed up long past her usual bedtime that night, getting acquainted with her new friend.

Using a Creative Point of View

Rewrite the story from the point of view of the computer. Use the first person point of view as if you are the computer. Try to imagine how the computer might describe the events in the story above if it could.

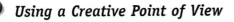

Communicate Your Ideas

DRAFTING, REVISING *Point of View, Transitions*

Choose the best point of view for your narrative about a first in your life. Then draft your paragraph, using transitions where appropriate to make the chronological order of details clear. Revise and polish your paragraph using the <u>Process of Writing a Narrative Paragraph</u> on page C176.

COMPUTER TIP

If you are working on a computer to draft your paragraph, you can use the Cut and Paste functions from the Edit menu to speed up the process of rearranging and organizing details in a chronological order. You can also use Cut and Paste to find the best place to position your topic sentence. Remember to save your original draft and later versions with your changes.

Process of Writing a Narrative Paragraph

"When someone writes a story," says author Natalia Ginzburg, "he should throw the best of everything into it, the best of whatever he possesses and has seen, all the best things that he has accumulated throughout his life." As you look for ideas for narrative paragraphs, think about ways that you can add some of the best things in your life.

Writing a First Person Narrative Paragraph

Prewriting

Like most people, you probably have memories of times when you felt great about something you did. Recall some of those times when you did your very best. Perhaps it was a time that you won a trophy in a competition. Maybe you made a perfect dive at the pool, played a solo at a recital, or helped a friend in trouble. Write a narrative paragraph about one of those times from your point of view.

- Use freewriting or clustering to list as many incidents as come to mind. Choose the one idea that would make the most interesting narrative.

- Use brainstorming to develop a list of details you might include in the narrative.

- Choose the details you will use and arrange them in chronological order.

Oral Expression   Tell a partner about the narrative that you plan to write. Include as many details as you can. Notice which parts of the story seem to make an impact on your partner. After you've told the story, ask your partner for feedback. What are the strong and weak points of your narrative? Make notes recording your partner's comments and suggestions.

Drafting

Use your notes from the Oral Expression activity and from your **journal** to write a first draft of your paragraph.

Revising Conferencing

Exchange papers with a classmate, and give each other helpful comments and suggestions about your paragraphs. Concentrate on features such as word choice, sentence variety, clarity of the details, and the impact they make on you as a reader. Use your classmate's comments and the guidelines for writing a narrative paragraph on the next page to revise your work.

PORTFOLIO

● Writing a Third Person Narrative Paragraph

Think of an incident in the life of a friend or relative that you feel reveals a unique aspect of that person's character. For example, you might feel that the way a cousin dealt with a serious illness showed special courage. You might say that the way a parent or an ancestor overcame a difficult obstacle showed a unique kind of determination. Write a narrative paragraph about the incident and what you feel it reveals about the person. For help, use the checklist on the following page.

PORTFOLIO

● Writing a Narrative Paragraph of Your Choice

Write a paragraph about a funny or serious incident that happened while you were with your family. Decide whether it would be more effective to tell about the event from the first person or third person point of view. If you would like, try writing a version from each point of view. Use the **Process of Writing a Narrative Paragraph** on the following page for help. Share your paragraph or paragraphs with the family members with whom you had the experience.

PORTFOLIO

Process of Writing a Narrative Paragraph

PREWRITING

- Use brainstorming, clustering, freewriting, or any other technique to remember incidents that will make a good subject for a narrative paragraph. *(pages C10–C19)*
- Determine your audience by asking yourself questions about your readers' interests and level of knowledge. *(pages C22 and C15)*
- Think back to the first incident that set the event in motion. Then list all the details about the event, including details of time and place. *(pages C25–C30)*
- Arrange your notes in chronological order, use appropriate transitional words to link ideas together, and eliminate any unnecessary details. *(pages C169 and C30–C34)*

DRAFTING

- Decide what point of view you will be using in your writing and be sure to maintain it throughout the narrative. *(page C171)*
- Write a topic sentence that captures the reader's attention and that makes a general statement about the story or sets the scene. *(pages C167–C168)*
- Use your prewriting notes to write the supporting sentences, which tell the story event by event. *(pages C167–C168)*
- Add a concluding sentence that summarizes the story or makes a point about the meaning of the event. *(pages C167–C168)*

REVISING

- Does your paragraph have all the elements shown in the <u>Structure of a Narrative Paragraph</u> chart? *(page C167)*
- Should you delete anything to strengthen the unity of the story? *(pages C136–C137)*
- Should you add anything to strengthen the development? *(pages C135–C136)*
- Should you rearrange anything to strengthen the coherence? *(pages C138–C139)*
- Do your sentences have variety? *(pages C73–C80)*
- Did you avoid rambling sentences? *(pages C84–C85)*
- Can you substitute any specific, vivid words for general ones? *(page C62)*

EDITING

- Check for errors in grammar and usage.
- Check spelling, capitalization, and punctuation.
- Did you indent correctly? Are your margins even? *(pages C49–C52)*

PUBLISHING

- Present a neat final copy to a reader.

Developing the Skills of Description

When you want your reader to picture a person, an object, or a place clearly, you need to write a good description. Good descriptive writing helps your reader see, hear, smell, taste, and feel all the details you are describing.

Descriptive writing paints a vivid picture of a person, an object, or a scene by stimulating the reader's senses.

Your Writer's Journal

Write down memorable sensory impressions you experience every day. You can use these impressions when looking for an idea for descriptive writing.

Descriptive Paragraph Structure

Like a narrative paragraph, a descriptive paragraph has three main parts. In a good descriptive paragraph, all these parts work together to create a clear image of the subject.

Structure of a Descriptive Paragraph

- The **topic sentence** makes a general statement about the subject, often suggesting an overall impression.
- The **supporting sentences** supply specific details that help readers use their five senses to bring the picture to life.
- The **concluding sentence** summarizes the overall impression of the subject.

The following paragraph describes a unique and popular place in the middle of a busy city.

The Riverwalk

TOPIC
SENTENCE

BODY OF
SUPPORTING
SENTENCES:

PROVIDES

SENSORY

DETAILS

CONCLUDING
SENTENCE

The Riverwalk in San Antonio, Texas, is a favorite noon-hour getaway for workers in nearby offices. Below street level the green river winds leisurely between the promenades on either side, carrying occasional boatloads of sightseers in brightly colored gondolas. Lining the river are bakeries, art and handicraft stores, ice-cream stands, and restaurants, where lunchtime shoppers and idlers under the hot sun browse and sample the goods. As the lazy hour draws to a close, the relaxed workers slowly climb the stone stairs to the busy streets of the city.

Notice that the topic sentence creates a positive overall impression by using the words *favorite* and *getaway* to suggest that it is a special place.

PRACTICE YOUR SKILLS

● *Recognizing the Overall Impression*

Write *positive* or *negative* to indicate the type of overall impression suggested by each topic sentence.

1. Davis Street was like a well-tended garden in the middle of a war zone.

2. The house was a remarkable mixture of inspiration and boldness.

3. The team members dragged themselves off the field as if they wore iron shoes.

4. The litter-strewn park was a slap in the face of decency.

5. The kite festival turned the pale blue sky into a colorful, modern painting.

Write a topic sentence for a descriptive paragraph about each of the following subjects. Make each topic sentence suggest the overall impression indicated in parentheses.

1. a dog (positive)   **6.** an oil slick (negative)

2. a gymnasium (negative)   **7.** walking (positive)

3. a parade (positive)   **8.** trash (negative)

4. a subway station (negative) **9.** books (positive)

5. a friend's face (positive) **10.** dancing (positive)

Communicate Your Ideas

PREWRITING *Overall Impression*

Because first experiences involve risk, they usually are memorable. Can you remember, for example, where your first job interview took place? Was your interview in an office, in a store, or in a barn? Do you remember where you sat and what was on the wall behind the person interviewing you? Choose an indoor location where one of your most unforgettable first experiences occurred. Then close your eyes and picture that place in your mind. Once you see it clearly, jot down every detail you can remember. When you have finished, read over your notes and summarize the overall impression of that place. For example, was it gloomy or bright? Formal or friendly? Save your work for later use.

SAVE YOUR WORK

● Specific Details and Sensory Words

Often the topic sentence indicates the overall impression you wish to create. The body of a descriptive paragraph then fleshes out that overall impression by providing specific details and sensory words—words that appeal to the reader's five senses. If you choose your details well, your paragraph will *show* the person, place, or thing being described—rather than merely telling about it.

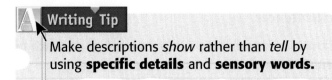

Make descriptions *show* rather than *tell* by using **specific details** and **sensory words.**

The specific details and sensory words in the following paragraph are in **bold** type.

MODEL: Paragraph with Specific Details and Sensory Words

He was a **stout tallish** young man. The **high color** of his **cheeks pushed** upwards even to his **forehead** where it **scattered** itself in a few **formless patches of pale red;** and on his **hairless face** there **scintillated restlessly** the **polished lenses** and the **bright gilt rims** of the **glasses** which **screened** his **delicate** and **restless** eyes. His **glossy black hair** was parted in the middle and brushed in a **long curve behind his ears** where it **curled slightly** beneath the **groove** left by his hat.

—*James Joyce,* The Dead

PRACTICE YOUR SKILLS

● *Recognizing Specific Details and Sensory Words*

Write at least ten specific details or sensory words from the following paragraph.

Then in the evening he stood in the doorway of his house and looked across the land, his own land, lying loose and fresh from the winter's freezing, and ready for planting. It was full spring and in the shallow pool the frogs croaked drowsily. The bamboos at the corner of the house swayed slowly under a gentle night wind and through the twilight he could see dimly the fringe of trees at the border of the near field. They were peach trees, budded most delicately pink, and willow trees thrusting forth tender green leaves. Up from the quiescent, waiting land a faint mist rose, silver as moonlight, and clung about the tree trunks.

—*Pearl S. Buck,* The Good Earth

● *Developing Sensory Details*

To help you develop rich sensory details for a description, you might use a web like the following one to organize your notes.

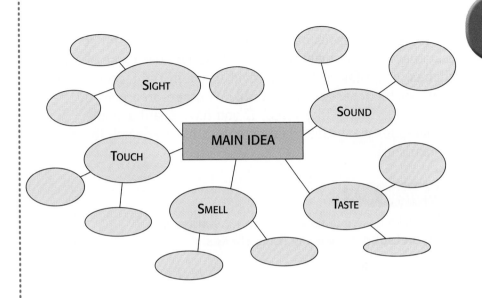

Copy the web. Then look back at the excerpt from *West with the Night* (pages C163–C165) and find several examples of sensory words and details for the headings in the web. Are there any senses that do not have corresponding sensory words or details in the selection? If so, why do you think that is the case? Which senses are most important for writing about this subject? Which ones are least important?

Figurative Language   Sometimes the best way to help readers see a subject is to compare it to something else, using figurative language. The two most common figures of speech are the **simile** and the **metaphor**. Both invite the reader to see similarities between two things that are essentially different. The simile uses the words *like* or *as* to compare one thing to another, while the metaphor implies a comparison without using *like* or *as*.

SIMILE	**Like illumined pearls** the lamps shone from the summits of their tall poles.
	—James Joyce
METAPHOR	The **soft rope** of her hair tossed from side to side.
	—James Joyce

Some comparisons have been used so often and for so long that they have become worn-out. These familiar expressions, called **clichés**, often fail to create a vivid image in the reader's mind. Avoid such clichés as "they are like two peas in a pod" or "her eyes twinkled like stars." If you have heard a simile or metaphor many times before, do not use it. Search for fresh comparisons.

Writing Tip

Make descriptions vivid by using **similes** and **metaphors**. Avoiding using **clichés**.

PRACTICE YOUR SKILLS

● *Using Figurative Language*

Write a sentence containing an original simile or metaphor to describe each subject.

EXAMPLE	a foggy day
CLICHÉ	The fog was as thick as pea soup.
POSSIBLE ANSWER	With a velvet touch, the fog draped itself over the sleeping city.

1. the starry sky

2. a wild colt

3. a snowfall

4. twilight in the city

5. an older person's face

6. an athlete's body

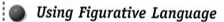

● Spatial Order and Transitions

A well-organized description leads the reader from point to point until the picture is complete. This method of organization is called spatial order.

Spatial order arranges details according to their location.

In a descriptive paragraph, transitions show where each item fits into the larger picture. In this way, the reader can begin to see clearly the object or scene that is being described. Transition words help orient the reader. The following chart shows transitions commonly used for different kinds of spatial order.

TRANSITIONS FOR SPATIAL ORDER	
Spatial Order	**Transitions**
top to bottom (or the reverse)	higher, lower, above, below, at the base (top), in the middle, halfway
side to side	at the left (right), in the middle, next to, beside, at one end, at the other end
inside to outside (or the reverse)	within, in the center, on the outside, innermost, in the middle
near to far (or the reverse)	in front of, nearby, farther, beyond, across, to the north (etc.), in the distance

Many descriptive paragraphs use a special spatial order that is different from those shown in the chart. In this special type of order, writers describe details in the order in which the details strike them rather than in a set pattern such as top to bottom. Transitions make this order clear.

PRACTICE YOUR SKILLS

● *Recognizing Spatial Order and Transitions*

Write all the transitional words and phrases in the following paragraph. Then write *top to bottom* **(or the reverse),** *side to side, inside out* **(or the reverse),** *near to far* **(or the reverse), or** *special* **to indicate the type of spatial order.**

From my window here in Bellaggio, Italy, I have a view of the other side of the lake, which is as beautiful as a picture. A scarred and wrinkled precipice rises to a height of eighteen hundred feet. On a tiny bench halfway up its vast wall sits a little snowflake of a church, no bigger than a martin box apparently. Skirting the base of the cliff are a hundred orange groves and gardens, flecked with glimpses of the white dwellings that are buried in them. In front, three or four gondolas lie idle upon the water. In the burnished mirror of the lake, mountain, chapel, houses, groves, and boats are counterfeited so brightly and so clearly that one scarce knows where reality leaves off and the reflection begins!

—*Mark Twain,* The Innocents Abroad

Communicate Your Ideas

DRAFTING, REVISING *Spatial Order and Transitions*

Review your notes about the location of one of your first experiences. Then arrange your descriptive details in a logical order, including only those that support the overall impression you wish to leave in the reader's mind. After you are satisfied that your topic sentence gives a general impression, draft your descriptive paragraph. Use any necessary transitions. When you have finished, revise your paragraph, using the <u>Process of Writing a Descriptive Paragraph</u> on page C189 for assistance. Save your work; you may wish to polish it later.

Photography

Through whose eyes am I seeing? That is the question you ask yourself when you read critically and determine point of view. The same question is worth asking when you respond to a photograph or other work in a visual medium. Where is the camera? Why? What does the camera position add to the meaning of the photograph or visual work?

The point of view in the photograph below helps to clarify the relationships among the player, the hoop, and the ball.

Aerial shot emphasizes height.

Contrasting colors and textures increase visual appeal.

Ball appears bigger than boy; too big to handle.

Media Activity

Look closely at the photograph above. Write a paragraph identifying the point of view and explaining how the point of view conveys meaning. Also consider how lines, shapes, colors, and textures contribute to the meaning of the photograph.

If you have access to a camera, take some photographs from different points of view, using the information above to guide your choices. Share the photographs with classmates and invite discussion about how point of view affects the impact of each photo.

Process of Writing a Descriptive Paragraph

"Don't describe it, show it. That's what I try to teach all young writers," said author James Baldwin. "Don't describe a purple sunset, make me see that it is purple." Now it is time to sharpen your senses and use your imagination so that your readers will see—and hear and smell and taste and touch—the scene you want to show.

Writing a Paragraph That Describes a Scene

Prewriting

Describe a scene in nature with a focal point, such as a mountain, a lake, a splendid garden, or a specific object. Through freewriting or clustering, develop a list of descriptive details and arrange them in spatial order.

Drafting

Write a first draft of your paragraph, revealing details one by one.

Revising

Using the chart on page C189, revise your paragraph. Substitute vivid words for general ones. Save your work.   **PORTFOLIO**

Writing a Paragraph That Describes a Person

Write a detailed description of someone who has played a special role in your life. For example, if you participate in sports, you might write about a favorite coach. If music is your main interest, you might describe a teacher or professional musician who has influenced you. Use the guidelines in the Process of Writing a Descriptive Paragraph on page C189 for help with prewriting, drafting, revising, and editing.   **PORTFOLIO**

Prewriting Workshop
Drafting Workshop
Revising Workshop
Editing Workshop ▶
Publishing Workshop

Adjectives

Throughout the selection from *West with the Night,* Beryl Markham describes what she saw so vividly, you almost feel as if you are there beside her.

> It is <u>dark</u> already and I am over the south of Ireland. There are the lights of Cork and the lights are <u>wet</u>; they are drenched in <u>Irish</u> rain, and I am above them and <u>dry</u>. I am above them and the plane roars in a <u>sobbing</u> world . . .

The underlined words in the description above are **adjectives**—words that describe nouns and pronouns and add color and exactness to the narrative.

Comparison of Adjectives

When you compare two people or things, add *–er* to most one- and two-syllable adjectives. Add *more* to those two-syllable adjectives that sound awkward with *–er* and to all adjectives with three or more syllables.

ONE OR TWO SYLLABLES	The *Gull* was **swifter** than other planes Markham had flown.
	Markham experienced many risks in **earlier** trips.
	She felt **more alone** on this flight than on others.
THREE OR MORE SYLLABLES	A blind flight was **more dangerous** at night than during the day.

When you compare three or more people or things, add *–est* to most one- and two-syllable adjectives. Add *most* to two-syllable adjectives that sound awkward with *–est* and to all adjectives with three or more syllables.

ONE OR TWO SYLLABLES	Her plane was the **newest** model available.
	This was the **riskiest** flight she had ever made.
THREE OR MORE SYLLABLES	The *Gull* had the **most accurate** instruments for a small craft.

Capitalization of Proper Adjectives

Like the proper nouns from which they are formed, proper adjectives begin with a capital letter.

PROPER NOUNS	Ireland	Canada
PROPER ADJECTIVES	**Irish** rain	**Canadian** coast

Punctuation with Adjectives

When a conjunction does not connect two adjectives before a noun, a comma is sometimes used to separate them. To decide if you should use a comma, read the sentence with *and* between the adjectives. If the sentence sounds natural, a comma is needed. If it doesn't sound natural, a comma is not needed.

COMMA NEEDED	I felt the strong, wet wind inside the cabin. (*Strong and wet* sounds natural.)
COMMA NOT NEEDED	I felt the strong October wind inside the cabin. (*Strong and October* does not sound natural.)

Editing Checklist

✔ Have you used the correct form when writing comparisons with adjectives?

✔ Are proper adjectives capitalized?

✔ Have you correctly punctuated two adjectives before a noun?

Process of Writing a Descriptive Paragraph

PREWRITING

- Use brainstorming, clustering, freewriting, or any other technique that works for you to record memories of persons, scenes, or objects that lend themselves to vivid description. *(pages C10–C19)*
- Ask yourself whether your audience is likely to be familiar with the person, place, or thing you are going to describe. If yes, what can you add to make your approach new and interesting? If no, what can you do to create a clear image and impression? *(pages C22 and C115)*
- Form an overall positive or negative impression of your subject. Then list all the specific details and sensory words you can use to create that overall impression. *(pages C179–C182)*
- Arrange your details in an appropriate form of spatial order and eliminate any details that do not support your overall impression. *(pages C183–C184 and C30–C34)*

DRAFTING

- Write a clear topic sentence that states an overall impression. *(pages C177–C178)*
- Use your prewriting notes to draft the supporting sentences, which reveal the details one by one. *(pages C179–C180)*
- Add a concluding sentence that summarizes your description. *(pages C177–C179)*

REVISING

- Does your paragraph have all the elements shown in the <u>Structure of a Descriptive Paragraph?</u> *(page C177)*
- Should you delete anything to strengthen unity? *(pages C136–C137)*
- Should you add anything to strengthen the paragraph's development? *(pages C135–C136)*
- Should you rearrange anything to strengthen coherence? *(pages C138–C139)*
- Do your sentences have variety? *(pages C73–C80)*
- Did you avoid rambling sentences? *(pages C84–C85)*
- Can you substitute any vivid words for general ones? *(page C62)*

EDITING

- Using the <u>Editing Checklist</u> on the previous page, check for errors in grammar and usage.
- Check for spelling, capitalization, and punctuation.
- Did you indent correctly? Are your margins even? *(pages C49–C52)*

Developing the Skills of Persuasion

If your purpose is to express an opinion—whether in a letter to your mayor, in a newspaper editorial, or in a letter of complaint about a faulty product—you will be writing **persuasion**. Audience is an important consideration in persuasive writing since many of your readers may hold different views from yours.

Persuasive writing asserts an opinion and uses facts, examples, and reasons to convince readers.

Your Writer's Journal

In your journal, record any social or political issues that come up in your everyday life and any opinions you have about them. You may be able to use these notes when you need new ideas for writing persuasive paragraphs or compositions.

Persuasive Paragraph Structure

A persuasive paragraph has three main parts. The following chart shows how each element in a persuasive paragraph functions and is connected to the others.

Structure of a Persuasive Paragraph
- The **topic sentence** asserts an opinion.
- The **supporting sentences** back up the opinion with facts, examples, reasons, and if necessary citations from experts.
- The **concluding sentence** restates the opinion and often makes a final appeal to the reader.

The following model shows how each sentence in a persuasive paragraph functions. Notice how the supporting sentences are used to back up the opinion in the topic sentence.

MODEL: Persuasive Paragraph

Pennies from Heaven?

TOPIC
SENTENCE:
ASSERTS AN OPINION

The millions of dollars spent by NASA in recent years to search for life in outer space has been a waste of taxpayers' money. Since 1959, when the first organized search for extraterrestrial life began, not one single piece of evidence has been found that life exists anywhere but on Earth. Frank J. Tipler, a physicist at Tulane University,

SUPPORTING
SENTENCES:
BACK UP OPINIONS

points out that if intelligent beings existed, they would already have contacted us. So convincing were these arguments that in 1978 Congress withdrew its support of the search for life in outer space. A movement led by Carl Sagan, however, gained wide popular support, based largely on the emotional appeal of finding life in outer space. As a result Congress again appropriated money that could have been better spent on much-needed social programs. While the expensive radio

CONCLUDING
SENTENCE:
MAKES A FINAL
APPEAL

telescopes continue to detect nothing, people right here on Earth continue worrying about housing and medical care—problems that government should be solving.

PRACTICE YOUR SKILLS

● *Recognizing Opinions and Facts*

Some of the following topic sentences assert an opinion and are suitable for a persuasive paragraph. Others state a fact and are better suited for an informative paragraph. Identify each sentence by writing *P* for *persuasive* and *I* for *informative*.

1. The best way to protest against bad television programs is to boycott the products of the sponsors.
2. Advertising jingles sometimes become a deep-rooted part of a nation's popular culture.
3. Movie theaters should bring back ushers to keep the noise down during a movie.
4. A trained dog is a happy dog.
5. Some trees are actually giant weeds.
6. Carpooling helps conserve natural resources.
7. To encourage carpooling, toll roads should offer reduced rates to cars with two or more passengers.
8. Public buses should be equipped with automatic lifts for people in wheelchairs.
9. In recent years, the nursing profession has attracted an increasing number of men.
10. Praise and rewards are effective ways to encourage good behavior.
11. The economy is stronger now than it used to be.
12. Professional sports players earn far too much money these days.
13. Hip-hop is the most innovative genre of music to emerge in the twentieth century.
14. Young people today have more access to popular music than they did in the past.

Communicate Your Ideas

PREWRITING *Topic Sentence*

Look over the various notes and issues you have recorded in your **journal** and choose one that you have a strong opinion about. Once you have chosen a topic, begin to develop it as the subject of a persuasive paragraph. Write a topic sentence that clearly states your opinion. Save your work for later use.

Solving Problems

When writing persuasion, you often have to approach issues as if you are solving problems. The best solution then serves as the main idea of your persuasive writing. To solve problems, follow these steps.

1. State the problem.
2. Think of several possible solutions.
3. List the reasons for (pros) and reasons against (cons) each solution.
4. Decide on the solution with the most pros.

The following chart shows how these steps can be applied to evaluating the search for life in outer space.

SOLVING A PROBLEM

1. *State the problem.*
How can money be found to search for life in outer space?

2. *List several possible solutions.*
Solution 1: Raise taxes
Solution 2: Find backers in the private sector

3. *Evaluate solutions.*
Solution 1: **Pro:** would raise money
Con: unpopular with people and lawmakers
Solution 2: **Pro 1:** would not be taxpayers' money
Pro 2: corporations manage very large projects
Con: might take longer to raise money

4. *Make a decision.*
Raise money through private sector

The final decision can be a topic sentence: Raising money in the private sector is the best way to fund a search for life in outer space.

THINKING PRACTICE

Make a similar chart to propose a solution to one of the problems listed below or to one of your choice.

1. the amount of violence in movies
2. the dangers of fad diets

Techniques of Persuasion

To establish your believability, as a persuasive writer, use the following techniques for making an argument persuasive.

> ## Tools of Persuasion
>
> - Use reasonable language rather than highly charged words.
> - If the opposition has a good point, admit it, but then show why it failed to convince you.
> - Refer to experts who agree with your position.

PRACTICE YOUR SKILLS

● Analyzing Persuasive Techniques

Answer the questions that follow this draft of a persuasive paragraph. Refer to the numbered sentences in your responses.

(1) The search for extraterrestrial life is well worth the money the government has granted NASA for this purpose. (2) In the first place, if the giant radio telescopes did pick up a signal from an intelligent civilization, the practical benefits would be enormous. (3) In order to send the signals, such a civilization would have to be highly advanced. (4) Our own planet could benefit from the knowledge of how another advanced civilization manages its precious resources and avoids destroying itself. (5) Shortsighted and unimaginative opponents argue that the chances of finding intelligent life are very slim. (6) As physicists Philip Morrison and Giuseppe Cocconi point out, however, "If we never search, the chance of success is zero." (7) Furthermore, while it is true that life has not yet been found, the search for it has led to other discoveries, including the detection of pulsars in 1967. (8) The annual cost per taxpayer of this program is only a few pennies. (9) Whether or not life is found, the knowledge gained along the way makes this program a great bargain.

1. List all facts that support the writer's opinion.

2. Revise sentence 5 to eliminate the emotional language.

3. Write the sentence where the writer shows why an opposing point is not convincing.

4. How does the writer use other sources?

5. Reread the model paragraph on page C191. Which side of the issue are you on? Did the evidence in the argument change your mind? Explain your position in a paragraph.

Order of Importance and Transitions

Another important tool of persuasion is logical organization. The most common way to organize supporting details in a persuasive paragraph is to use the order of importance, either from most to least important or from least to most. In both paragraphs about the value of the search for life in outer space, the details are arranged in the order of most to least important.

Order of importance arranges supporting points in the order of least to most important or the reverse.

Writers use transitions to show the relative importance of ideas. That is, these transitions show the relationship among the supporting points. Some of the most common transitions used with order of importance are listed in the following chart.

TRANSITIONS FOR ORDER OF IMPORTANCE		
also	moreover	for this reason
another	furthermore	more important
besides	in addition	most important
finally	similarly	in the first place
first	likewise	to begin with

When you want to show that another argument is not persuasive, you must point out contrasting ideas. Doing so is called giving a **rebuttal**. The following transitions are useful for showing contrast.

TRANSITIONS SHOWING CONTRAST

but	however	nevertheless
yet	instead	in contrast
or, nor	still	on the other hand

| EXAMPLE OF A REBUTTAL | You say that compact cars are less than safe in collisions, **but** designers have already corrected many of these problems. |

PRACTICE YOUR SKILLS

● **Using Transitions**

In the following paragraph, the ideas are arranged in order of importance, but the transitions are missing. Using examples from the charts above and on the previous page, add a transition for each blank. Write the transitions on a separate piece of paper. Use commas as needed.

Relieving Congestion

As convenient as automobiles are, all privately owned automobiles should be banned from the downtown sections of congested cities such as New York and Chicago. ■ automobiles create air pollution, especially smog. Such conditions are dangerous for everyone, particularly children and the elderly. ■ banning automobiles would force people to use public transportation such as buses and trains. Such means of transportation create less pollution than cars do. ■ cities would be much less congested without automobiles. Police cars, fire trucks, and ambulances could all move more freely. People may claim that automobiles are more convenient than public transportation. ■ the inconvenience of a few people is a small price to pay for making cities cleaner, more livable places.

PREWRITING, DRAFTING *Techniques of Persuasion*

Think again about the issue or opinion you chose for your topic sentence. Use freewriting to develop a list of facts, examples, and illustrations you could use to convince someone that your opinion on this issue is correct.
Then you may want to gather supporting evidence from the library to add to your notes. Once you have enough material to create a convincing argument for your persuasive paragraph, make a first draft.

Time Out to Reflect

Once you have completed your first draft, pause for a moment to think about what you have written. Have you truly considered all sides of the issue? Can you acknowledge or come up with valid arguments on the other side of the issue? Being able to do so will strengthen your own position and enable you to anticipate opposing arguments and articulate meaningful rebuttals.

Process of Writing a Persuasive Paragraph

"Good columns are written by people with opinions, with a point of view on life," writes Ellen Goodman, the Pulitzer Prize-winning columnist. "And the most important thing, you have to care." Goodman's advice about writing newspaper columns can be applied to all forms of persuasive writing. To write persuasively, you need to believe deeply in the opinions that you hold.

Writing an Editorial

Prewriting

Through freewriting, explore opinions you have about different aspects of school, such as the effects of part-time jobs on grades. Choose one opinion you think worthy of developing into an editorial for the school newspaper. Brainstorm a list of supporting facts and examples you could use to make your point. Arrange your details in logical order.

Drafting

Write a quick first draft of your editorial.

Revising Conferencing

Exchange papers with a classmate. Offer each other suggestions for making your arguments more convincing. Using your partner's comments and the chart on page C200, revise your editorial.

Editing

Use the guidelines in the **Process of Writing a Persuasive Paragraph** on page C200 to edit your work.

Publishing

Make a neat final copy of your editorial and submit it to your school newspaper for possible publication.

⦿ Writing a Product Review

Think of a product you use regularly. Then write a review of it for a consumer magazine. Include an overall evaluation of the product and identify the specific features of the product that have influenced your evaluation. Use the guidelines from the <u>Process of Writing a Persuasive Paragraph</u> chart on the next page for assistance.

PORTFOLIO

⦿ Writing an Advertisement

Artist David Strickland arranged tractor parts to create this whimsical and humorous assemblage. Write an advertisement to convince people that they should have this object in their home.

PORTFOLIO

David Strickland, *Case Alien,* 1991. Metal machinery parts and glass, 104 by 46 by 63 inches. Private collection.

Time Out to Reflect

In the course of this chapter, you have written at least three different kinds of paragraphs. Reread each one. Which paragraph did you find easiest to write? Why? What did you learn from this writing experience that you can apply to the writing you will do in the future?

▶ Process of Writing a Persuasive Paragraph

Remember, as you work through the writing it is never too late to go back to the drafting stage and try a different approach to your subject. In the summary below, the numbers in parentheses refer to pages where you can get specific help with your writing.

PREWRITING

- Use brainstorming, clustering, freewriting, or any other prewriting strategy to explore opinions that you hold on a variety of subjects. Choose an opinion and limit it. *(pages C10–C19)*
- Determine your audience by asking yourself questions about their attitudes, beliefs, and opinions. *(pages C22 and C115)*
- Gather whatever information you need to convince people that your opinion is worthwhile. *(pages C25–C30)* As you gather evidence, note opposing views.
- Arrange your ideas in a logical order. *(pages C195–C196)*

DRAFTING

- Write a topic sentence stating your opinion. *(pages C190–C192)*
- Use your prewriting notes to provide facts, examples, and reasons to back up your claim. *(pages C190–C192)*
- Add a concluding sentence that makes a final appeal to readers. *(pages C190–C192)*

REVISING

- Does your paragraph have all the elements shown in the <u>Structure of a Persuasive Paragraph</u>? *(page C190)*
- Should you delete anything to clarify your opinion? *(pages C136–C137)*
- Should you add anything to strengthen the argument? *(pages C135–C136)*
- Should you rearrange anything to strengthen coherence? *(pages C138–C139)*
- Do your sentences have variety? *(pages C73–C80)*
- Did you avoid rambling sentences? *(pages C84–C85)*
- Can you make any general descriptions more vivid? *(page C62)*

EDITING

- Using the <u>Editing Checklists</u>, check for errors in grammar and usage, spelling, capitalization, and punctuation. *(pages C44, C90, C142, and C188)*
- Did you indent correctly?

PUBLISHING

- Is your handwriting clear, or your typing clean?
- Are your margins even?
- Present a neat final copy to a reader and check the chart on page C49 for other publishing ideas.

A Writer Writes

A News Story

Using different writing purposes, explore the subject of people who take risks—not for their own sake but to benefit others.

Narrative

Purpose: to relate an experience of a modern-day risk taker—either someone you know or someone you have read or heard about—whose action has affected others positively

Audience: general

Use the guidelines on page C176 to tell a third person story of a risk taker. Remember, the risk taker does not have to be a great explorer. He or she could be a friend or neighbor whose action benefited others, or your subject could be anyone you have read or heard about who took a risk.

Descriptive

Purpose: to describe a scene associated with the risk taker's experience

Audience: general

Review the third person narrative you wrote. Then refer to the guidelines on page C189 to create a vivid scene that describes a key aspect of the risk taker's experience. If necessary, do some research to find interesting supporting details.

Persuasive

Purpose: to assert and support an opinion

Audience: general

Using the guidelines on page C200, develop a paragraph on a risk worth taking. Then persuade someone to take that risk.

Connection Collection

Representing in Different Ways

14 Freedom Parkway
Funkytown, TX 12345
February 16, 2001

Jyoti Singh
Chief Executive Officer
Prestige Auto Dealerships
Funkytown, TX 12345

Dear Mr. Singh,

As you may know, our recent sales campaign has not been a smashing success. I admit that the idea for a "Buy One Car, Get One Free" sale was mine alone. I take full responsibility for this financial misstep. Quite frankly, Mr. Singh, I am more than a little embarrassed to acknowledge that our dealership is losing money at an alarming rate. Since February 1, when the sale began, our losses have been running at exactly $50,000 per day. As of February 15 our losses totaled $750,000. Therefore, I recommend that we discontinue our "Buy One Car, Get One Free" sale immediately.

Regretfully yours,

Nino Naive

Nino Naive
Marketing Director
Prestige Auto Dealership

. . . to Visuals

Create a line graph from the letter on the right indicating the losses suffered by Prestige Auto Dealerships since the beginning of their ill-fated "Buy One Car, Get One Free" sale.

Connection Collection

Transportation to High School

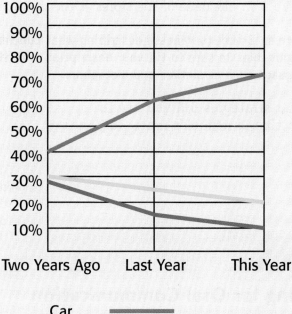

Car ━━━━━
Bus ━━━━━
Bicycle ━━━━━

. . . to Print

Write a letter to your boss at Prestige Auto Dealerships using the information from the line graphs above to persuade him to spend more money creating TV and radio advertisements directed at teenagers.

- **Which strategies can be used for creating both written and visual representations? Which strategies apply to one, not both? Which type of representation is more effective?**
- **Draw a conclusion, and write briefly about the differences between written ideas and visual representations.**

Writing in Everyday Life
Descriptive E-Mail

Vanessa is a friend of yours who lives across the country and shares your taste in music. Vanessa has never heard your favorite local band, Lunchbox. You want to send Vanessa a copy of Lunchbox's latest CD, *Everyday P.B.J.,* but none of the stores at the mall has it in stock.

Write an E-mail to Vanessa describing what Lunchbox's music sounds like. Be sure to fill your description with figurative language such as similes and metaphors.

What strategies did you use to describe Lunchbox's music to Vanessa?

> *You can find information on writing E-mail messages on pages C736–C739.*

Writing for Oral Communication
Persuasive Oral Speech

In your family you are in charge of assigning chores to your younger brothers and sisters. They usually obey you, but this autumn your brothers and sisters refuse to rake the leaves in the front and backyards. They say that it is only natural that the leaves remain close to the trees where they grew up.

Prepare an oral presentation persuading your brothers and sisters of the benefits of raking leaves. Be sure to include a topic sentence that asserts an opinion; supporting sentences that back up the opinion with facts, examples, and reasons; and a concluding sentence that restates the opinion and makes a final appeal to the reader. Deliver your speech to classmates or family members.

What strategies did you use to persuade your brothers and sisters to rake the yards?

> *You can find information on writing persuasive oral speeches on pages C592–C601.*

Assess Your Learning

The birth of your baby sister was the most exciting experience of your life. Since the day she was born you have adored her and felt very protective of her. For her first birthday, you have decided to give her something she can cherish her entire life.

▶ Write a narrative essay for your baby sister describing the day she was born. For example, you can describe a mad dash to the hospital, the tense time spent waiting, and the feeling of joy you had when she finally came into the world.

▶ In each paragraph remember to use a topic sentence to capture the reader's attention and make a general statement that sets the scene, supporting sentences to tell the story event by event, and a concluding sentence that shows the outcome, summarizes the story, or adds an insight. Organize your essay in chronological order and use appropriate transition words.

Before You Write **Consider the following questions:**
What is the *subject?*
What is the *occasion?*
Who is the *audience?*
What is the *purpose?*

After You Write **Evaluate your work using the following criteria:**
- Have you written in a voice and style appropriate to your audience and purpose?
- Have you included topic sentences in each paragraph to capture the reader's attention and make a general statement that sets the scene?
- Have you included supporting sentences in each paragraph to tell the story event by event?
- Have you included a concluding sentence in each paragraph to show the outcome, summarize the story, or add an insight?
- Have you organized your paragraph in chronological order and used appropriate transition words and phrases?
- Did you use transitions for persuasive writing such as *although, on the other hand, nevertheless,* and *however?*

Write briefly on how well you did. Point out your strengths and areas for improvement.

CHAPTER 5

Writing Effective Compositions

Artists in different fields create compositions using different elements. Musical composers use sound to convey ideas and feelings. Painters use color, line, and shape as the basic symbols to construct ideas. Writers produce compositions as well, and the elements they use are paragraphs made up of words and sentences.

Ideally the notes of a song or symphony have an order that pleases the listener. Colors and shapes are placed on a canvas to delight or inform the viewer. Similarly the paragraphs of a composition are organized to engage and satisfy the reader.

Beyond this basic organization, effective compositions are as varied as the CDs you will find in the music store or the paintings you will discover in a museum. Each has its own "personality." As you develop and refine your skills of writing effective compositions, remember that your writing can be as unique as your fingerprint.

Reading with a Writer's Eye

In "Darkness at Noon," Harold Krents deals with people's misconceptions about blindness. As you read "Darkness at Noon," pay attention to the way Krents uses the basic building blocks of effective compositions to express his ideas about blindness through his own writing personality.

Darkness at Noon

Harold Krents

Blind from birth, I have never had the opportunity to see myself and have been completely dependent on the image I create in the eye of the observer. To date it has not been narcissistic.[1]

There are those who assume that since I can't see, I obviously cannot hear. Very often people will converse with me at the top of their lungs, enunciating each word very carefully. Conversely, people will also often whisper, assuming that since my eyes don't work, my ears don't either.

For example, when I go to the airport and ask the ticket agent for assistance to the plane, he or she will invariably pick up the phone, call a ground hostess and whisper: "Hi, Jane, we've got a 76 here." I have concluded that the word "blind" is not used for one of two reasons: Either they fear that if the dread word is spoken, the ticket agent's retina will immediately detach, or they are reluctant to inform me of my condition of which I may not have been previously aware.

On the other hand, others know that of course I can hear, but believe that I can't talk. Often, therefore, when my wife and I go out to dinner, a waiter or waitress will ask Kit if "*he* would like a drink" to which I respond that "indeed *he* would."

This point was graphically driven home to me while we were in England. I had been given a year's leave of absence from my Washington law firm to study for a diploma in law degree at Oxford University. During the year I became ill and was hospitalized. Immediately after admission, I was wheeled down to the X-ray room. Just at the door sat an elderly woman—elderly I would judge from the sound of her voice. "What is his name?" the woman asked the orderly who had been wheeling me.

"What's your name?" the orderly repeated to me.

"Harold Krents," I replied.

"Harold Krents," he repeated.

"When was he born?"

"When were you born?"

"November 5, 1944," I responded.

---

[1] **narcissistic:** Contributing to feelings of self-love or self-confidence.

"November 5, 1944," the orderly intoned.

This procedure continued for approximately five minutes at which point even my saint-like disposition deserted me. "Look," I finally blurted out, "this is absolutely ridiculous. Okay, granted I can't see, but it's got to have become pretty clear to both of you that I don't need an interpreter."

"He says he doesn't need an interpreter," the orderly reported to the woman.

The toughest misconception of all is the view that because I can't see, I can't work. I was turned down by over forty law firms because of my blindness, even though my qualifications included a cum laude[2] degree from Harvard College and a good ranking in my Harvard Law School class.

The attempt to find employment, the continuous frustration of being told that it was impossible for a blind person to practice law, the rejection letters, not based on my lack of ability but rather on my disability, will always remain one of the most disillusioning experiences of my life.

I therefore look forward to the day, with the expectation that it is certain to come, when employers will view their handicapped workers as a little child did me years ago when my family still lived in Scarsdale.[3]

I was playing basketball with my father in our backyard according to procedures we had developed. My father would stand beneath the hoop, shout, and I would shoot over his head at the basket attached to our garage. Our next-door neighbor, aged five, wandered over into our yard with a playmate. "He's blind," our neighbor whispered to her friend in a voice that could be heard distinctly by Dad and me. Dad shot and missed; I did the same. Dad hit the rim; I missed entirely; Dad shot and missed the garage entirely. "Which one is blind?" whispered back the little friend.

I would hope that in the near future when a plant manager is touring the factory with the foreman and comes upon a handicapped and nonhandicapped person working together, his comment after watching them work will be, "Which one is disabled?"

---

[2] **cum laude** (kŭm loûd′ā): With distinction.
[3] **Scarsdale:** A city in New York.

Thinking as a Writer

Analyzing the Author's Voice

- How would you describe Harold Krents's voice—his attitude toward his subject and audience—in "Darkness at Noon"? What other voice might he have used? Would another voice have made the piece more effective? Why or why not?

Experimenting with a Humorous Tone

Oral Expression As the title suggests, "Darkness at Noon" deals with a serious subject. Nevertheless, Harold Krents uses humor to make his points about people's misconceptions about his blindness.

- Read aloud one of the humorous incidents that contains dialogue. Use your voice to experiment with pitch, tone, and emotion—as if you were rehearsing for a play. Does that incident seem more or less funny when spoken aloud? Why?

Examining Photographs for Objective and Subjective Responses

Viewing • Study the photograph below. What objective information do you observe in it? What subjective thoughts and feelings come into your mind as you view it? Do you think others would have the same responses you did? Why or why not?

The Power of Composing

You have just read an example of an effective composition—Harold Krents's moving plea against the stereotyping of the disabled. Everywhere in your world, you will find various kinds of compositions addressing a wide variety of topics, appearing in many different publications and formats. You are likely to find effective compositions written about whatever issues matter to people.

Uses of Composition Writing

Here are just a few examples of situations where you will encounter compositions.

- ▶ **Your local newspaper describes a fire** that destroyed three buildings in your community.

- ▶ **An artist explains her creative goals** in the catalog for an exhibit of her sculpture.

- ▶ **The cover story of a sports magazine** describes the basketball play-off games.

- ▶ **You write a review of your favorite music group's new CD** for your school newspaper.

- ▶ **You speak at a community meeting,** urging your neighbors to save a nearby forest from development.

- ▶ **You hear a television reporter describe the lasting legacy** of a powerful politician who has just died.

- ▶ **The new president delivers an inaugural speech** outlining his or her plans for the country.

Developing Your Composition Writing Skills

"I like to stand and stare at things, to talk with people, and to read a lot. From this, I'm always learning something I didn't know before. Some time later, when I've had a chance to think things over, I write down what I heard, saw, felt, and thought." That's how award-winning author Patricia Lauber describes her writing. There probably isn't a better description in so few words of how to write an effective composition.

Taking an interest in the people and things around you is the first step toward finding the right subject for a composition. Talking, reading, and thinking about a subject come next.

A **composition** presents and develops one main idea in three or more paragraphs.

Your Writer's Journal

In your journal, freewrite whatever ideas have been on your mind recently. You might have been thinking about trends in American culture, for example, and how they affect you and the people around you. Perhaps you are interested in the impact of movies, rock music, or television. You don't have to write about American culture, though. You can jot down ideas about history, literature, and science—whatever you feel strongly about. When it is time to write a composition, these entries will be a good source of topics.

Structure of a Composition

Carefully constructed compositions have three main parts: an introduction, a body, and a conclusion. These three parts of a composition parallel the three-part structure of a paragraph.

PARAGRAPH STRUCTURE	COMPOSITION STRUCTURE
Introduction	
topic sentence that introduces the subject and expresses the main idea	introductory paragraph that introduces the subject and states the main idea in a thesis statement
Body	
supporting sentences	supporting paragraphs
Conclusion	
concluding sentence	concluding paragraph

As you read the following composition, notice how the three main parts and the thesis statement work together to present a unified subject.

MODEL: Composition

Cryptanalysis: Breaking Codes

INTRODUCTION

THESIS STATEMENT

There are no easy ways to crack a code. In fact, no one has yet discovered a shortcut that will bypass the hard work. Breaking a code requires certain qualities on the part of the cryptanalyst.

BODY

The first quality is the ability to study. Before anyone can hope to break a code, he or she must know how codes are put together. There may be a similarity between a system one has studied and the system one has to break. Therefore, the wider one's knowledge of various code systems, the more likely it is that one will begin to recognize messages at a first or second look.

The second quality required is patience. Consider the story of the patience of the Arab cryptanalyst who studied an intercepted message to the Sultan of Morocco for 15 years before success was achieved! A particular code may reveal nothing, even after precious hours of searching for a clue. That's because good codes can be uncrackable. Short cryptograms with only a few letters or words often fall into this category. The only hope of breaking short coded messages sometimes is to know something about the sender and the intended recipient and to accumulate a collection of messages from the sender.

The third quality required by the cryptanalyst is a vivid imagination. When breaking codes, one has to be prepared for almost anything. A good imagination helps when the time has come to make wild or calculated guesses and when nothing but imagination can hope to get answers.

CONCLUSION With all this, the cryptanalyst still needs luck. A little luck can bring answers that all the logical thinking in the world could never achieve.

–*Julian A. Bielewicz*, Secret Languages

PRACTICE YOUR SKILLS

● *Analyzing a Composition*

Use the composition "Cryptanalysis" above to answer the following questions.

1. What is the main idea of the composition?

2. How do the paragraphs in the body support the main idea?

3. What is the conclusion of the composition?

4. How does the conclusion recall the introduction?

PREWRITING *Subject*

Review your **journal** entries. You may have jotted down some ideas about American culture. You may have listed ideas on other topics, too. Choose one of your ideas as the subject for a composition. If necessary, limit the topic to one you can cover in a short composition. Save your work to use later.

SAVE YOUR WORK

Introduction of a Composition

The introduction of a composition has several functions. You should keep these in mind as you plan the approach to your subject and develop your opening paragraph.

Functions of the Introduction

- It introduces the subject.
- It captures the reader's attention and prepares the reader for what is to follow.
- It establishes the tone—the writer's attitude toward both the subject and the audience.
- It presents the main idea in a thesis statement.
- It states or implies the purpose for writing.

When beginning the introduction, you might use any of a number of strategies to capture the reader's attention. For example, you could use a lively quotation, cite a little-known statistic or fact, provide an anecdote, quote from a conversation you heard, or just relate an arresting bit of information.

Tone

In the introduction of a composition, writers often reveal the attitude they have taken toward their subject and audience. This attitude is called tone.

Tone is the writer's attitude toward the subject and audience.

In setting the tone of a composition, consider your positive or negative feelings about your subject. For example, your tone may be serious or comical, admiring or critical, scary or reassuring, sympathetic or mocking, joyful or sad.

The following paragraph, from a composition by Woody Allen, sets a humorous tone about a subject many people take seriously—the existence of UFOs.

MODEL: Humorous Tone

> All UFOs may not prove to be of extraterrestrial origin. Experts do agree, however, that any glowing, cigar-shaped aircraft capable of rising straight up at 12,000 miles per second would require the kind of maintenance and spark plugs available only on Pluto. If these objects are indeed from another planet, then the civilization that designed them must be millions of years more advanced than our own. Either that, or they are very lucky. Professor Leon Speciman theorizes a civilization in outer space that is more advanced than ours by approximately 15 minutes. This, he feels, gives them a great advantage over us, since they needn't rush to appointments.
>
> —*Woody Allen,* "The UFO Menace"

The tone of Harold Krents's "Darkness at Noon" is friendly and serious. Notice how both Allen and Krents set the tone of their compositions through their choice of language. The next paragraph —which is taken from "The Great American Game"—has an enthusiastic, admiring tone.

Baseball is a truly American game. . . . In its speed, skill, and brevity, it seems particularly adapted to our high nervous tension. It lasts about as long as a theater play and resembles that form of entertainment in more ways than one. The mystery of hero and villain is discovered in about two hours, sometimes at the rate of a thrill a minute. Frequently the unexpected happens. Victory suddenly emerges from the very core of defeat.

—*William Phelps,* "The Great American Game"

PRACTICE YOUR SKILLS

● *Identifying Tone*

Read each opening sentence for a composition about cars. Then write an adjective—such as *reflective, humorous,* or *enthusiastic*—to describe the tone of each one.

1. I regard driving a car as a responsibility, not a right.

2. My first car was a used-parts shop on wheels.

3. I was thrilled when I got my first car.

4. My new car was a symbol of my deep desire for freedom.

Communicate Your Ideas

PREWRITING *Tone*

Review the subject you have chosen for a composition. Think about your attitude toward your subject and audience. Decide what the appropriate tone would be for this composition and write a few words describing that tone. Save your work for later use.

Thesis Statement

In addition to introducing the subject and setting the tone, the introduction also contains the thesis statement.

The **thesis statement** states the main idea and makes the purpose of the composition clear.

Notice how each of the following thesis statements makes the main idea and purpose of the composition clear.

MODEL: Thesis Statements

The first time I drove a car I was a jumble of nerves and fear. (expresses a feeling about an experience)
The Japanese Tea Ceremony reveals the beauty in everyday routine. (explains a factual subject)
A healthy society depends on a high degree of citizen participation in the government. (states an opinion)

The thesis statement is the controlling idea of the composition. It should be broad enough to include the main points in the composition yet limited enough to allow you to cover your subject adequately in the number of paragraphs you plan to write. When you write your thesis statement, you might state an idea that is too vague or general for a composition. It will then be necessary to refine your thesis. Refining and revising your thesis statement guarantees that it will fit your subject perfectly.

The thesis statement usually creates the strongest impression when it is the first or last sentence of the introduction.

PRACTICE YOUR SKILLS

● *Identifying Thesis Statements*

Write the thesis statement from each of the following introductory paragraphs. Then indicate the writer's purpose: *to explain a factual subject, to express a feeling about a personal experience, to describe,* or *to persuade.*

1. San Juan, Puerto Rico, is really two cities in one. Old San Juan is rich in Spanish history. It has walled forts and stunning cathedrals dating back hundreds of years. The new city has skyscrapers, international banks and businesses, and the bustling atmosphere of modern cities everywhere. For tourists as well as residents, the two-in-one city provides a seemingly endless variety of enjoyable activities.

2. A single knoll rises out of the plain in Oklahoma, north and west of the Wichita Range. For my people, the Kiowas, it is an old landmark, and they gave it the name Rainy Mountain. I returned to Rainy Mountain in July. My grandmother had died in the spring, and I wanted to be at her grave. Although my grandmother lived out her long life in the shadow of Rainy Mountain, the immense landscape of the continental interior lay like memory in her blood. She could tell of the Crows, whom she had never seen, and of the Black Hills, where she had never been. I wanted to see in reality what she had seen more perfectly in the mind's eye, and traveled 1,500 miles to begin my pilgrimage.

—N. Scott Momaday, The Way to Rainy Mountain

3. It is hard to find a movie theater these days where a comedy is playing. In the days of the silent films, it was equally hard to find a theater which was not showing one. The laughs today are pitifully few, far between, shallow, quiet, and short. They almost never build, as they used to, into something combining the jabbering frequency of a machine gun with the delirious momentum of a roller coaster. Saddest of all, there are few comedians now below middle age, and there are none who seem to learn much from picture to picture, or to try anything new.

—James Agee, "Comedy's Greatest Era"

4. Millions of years before people walked the surface of the earth, moles were tunneling beneath it. Today, the meandering surface runways made by these animals in their constant search for food are a familiar sight to many Americans. Few people, however, have more than a vague understanding of the creatures that inhabit them. Of the many mole species living today, none is more bizarre than the semiaquatic, star-nosed mole.

—*Terry L. Yates,* "The Mole That Keeps Its Nose Clean"

Writing a Thesis Statement

For each of the following subjects and lists of details, write a thesis statement.

1. SUBJECT   energy consumption

   DETAILS   • Early people used fuel for light and heat.

   • The use of fuel for mechanical power was a big change.

   • The present rate of energy consumption is the greatest in all of history.

   • The world's resources are being depleted.

   • People must change the way they use energy.

2. SUBJECT   transportation in America in the 1830s

   DETAILS   • People liked fast horses.

   • Harnessed pairs of horses pulled wagons.

   • Hackney coaches were available for hire.

   • Omnibuses were used in cities.

   • Horse-drawn stagecoaches carried nine passengers.

   • Steamboats were popular for river travel.

   • Railroad trains traveled at 14 to 16 miles per hour.

DRAFTING *Thesis Statement, Introduction, Tone*

Draft a working thesis statement for your composition. Then build on that thesis statement by drafting two or three possible introductions for your composition. Place your thesis statement at the beginning and the end of your introduction to see which position has more impact. As you write, consider ways to establish the tone appropriate for your audience and purpose. After you select your most effective introduction, save it for later use.

COMPUTER TIP

When using a word-processing program, you can use the Save As function to save more than one version of your work. Save your original draft with its own title. Then, as you draft and revise, go to File and select Save As to give each version a new name. Then you will have all the versions of your work for reference through all the writing stages.

Body of a Composition

After you have written the introduction, your next task is to develop your preliminary working thesis statement, idea by idea, in the body of your composition.

Supporting Paragraphs

The paragraphs that make up the body of a composition develop the main idea presented in the thesis statement. Although all the supporting paragraphs relate to the thesis, each one deals with one aspect of that thesis. Like any good paragraph, each has its own topic sentence and supporting sentences.

The **supporting paragraphs** in the body of a composition develop the thesis statement.

Across the Media: Representing Culture

On page C218 you read one paragraph about Puerto Rico and another about Rainy Mountain and the Kiowa people. Unless you are Puerto Rican or Kiowa yourself, you probably do not have much personal knowledge of these cultures. Yet no doubt you were able to call to mind vivid images about each. Where did these images come from?

Chances are that some of them—maybe even most— came from the media. Television and movies leave powerful, lasting, and highly selective impressions. The way a culture is portrayed in media presentations is always incomplete. Cultures are far too rich and complex to be reduced to a few images or well-worn stereotypes. Nonetheless, the power of the media can shape the way we see and think about other cultures.

Media Activity

To see how your own views about a culture have been shaped by the media, choose a culture to focus on and write answers to the questions that follow.

- In what television shows has this culture been portrayed? How was it portrayed? What generalizations did the shows suggest about this culture? Give specific examples.

- In what movies has this culture been portrayed? How was it portrayed? Was the overall portrayal positive or negative? Were the characters from this culture presented respectfully and with complexity, or were they oversimplified? Explain your answer.

- What do you know about these cultures beyond what you have seen in the media? Where did you learn these things? How does your knowledge compare or contrast with the impressions created by the media about this culture?

Discuss your responses with your classmates.

Following is the introduction and body of a composition. Notice how each of the supporting paragraphs develops the thesis statement.

MODEL: Introduction and Body of a Composition

Why I Like Going to the Movies

When the windchill factor is 62 degrees below zero and most people are keeping warm indoors, I am likely to be standing in a line to buy movie tickets, determined to see the latest release. On a warmer day, when the lines circle around the block, I will be waiting patiently, planning my purchases at the refreshment counter to help the time pass. To me going to the movies is worth any amount of hardship. The experience of seeing a movie satisfies me in a way few other experiences can match.

Once I purchase a ticket, I feel a thrill of anticipation. In the darkened theater, leaning back and settling low into my seat, I am transported from the real world into another world. The sound wraps me in a shield that deflects the noises of the outside world. Eyes riveted to the screen, I float comfortably into a world of sheer imagination. For two hours I can escape the cares of life beyond the theater walls.

During a good movie, the isolated feeling is so complete that I lose the sense of viewing the movie and begin to feel that I am actually in it. In one scene I am the romantic hero; in another, the tortured villain. I am all of the characters: comic and tragic, noble and selfish, aging and youthful. As I identify with the characters, my personality stretches and bends. I feel what they feel and experience what they experience.

Even a mediocre movie is worth the price of admission. The track and zoom of the camera, the light and darkness and colors, the settings and scenery and costumes—all of these are enjoyable to see. Although the familiar sights of school, home, and neighborhood are pleasant to me, I hunger for new colors and images as well. Movies serve up a feast for my eyes and my mind.

TOPIC SENTENCE

The body of "Why I Like Going to the Movies" can be presented in a simple outline that shows how the main idea of each paragraph supports the thesis statement of the entire composition.

THESIS STATEMENT   The experience of the movies satisfies me in a way few other experiences can match.

    I. Transports me into another world

   II. Allows me to identify with the major and minor characters

  III. Offers a feast for my eyes and mind

PRACTICE YOUR SKILLS

● *Analyzing Supporting Paragraphs*

Reread the thesis statement and the paragraphs that make up the body in the composition "Cryptanalysis" on pages C212–C213. After you see how each paragraph supports the thesis of the composition, develop an outline like the one above. In your outline use Roman numerals to show the main idea of each paragraph and how each supports the thesis statement.

● *Developing Supporting Ideas*

Under each of the following thesis statements, write three ideas that could be developed into three supporting paragraphs for the body of a composition. Write them in the form of the preceding outline.

1. I have some advice for incoming ninth graders on the art of adjusting to high school.

2. Judging others by their appearance may lead to big mistakes.

3. Three of my favorite songs have different moods.

4. People need to learn early in life the importance of saying no.

5. Becoming an accomplished musician takes special training.

6. There are three things you should always do before going to bed at night.

7. The desktop computer will soon be replaced by the laptop computer.

8. All students should spend some time traveling in another country.

Time Out to Reflect

The passage of time—and reflection—can bring about changes in our attitudes toward the subjects we write about. In a first draft, for example, you may be upset or annoyed by a topic and so adopt an angry tone. If you put the draft of your composition aside and think over the events you describe, your attitude may change. Your tone might become more matter-of-fact or objective, for example. Sometimes the passage of time even lets us see the humor and sadness in situations that at first left us angry. Try putting the draft of your composition aside while you explore your attitude toward your subject further. Might a change in tone help you express your attitude more accurately?

Is **Thinking**

Classifying

Once you generate details that support your thesis statement, your next step is to group, or **classify**, those details into meaningful categories that you can use to organize the body of your composition. When you classify, you group details together on the basis of shared features or characteristics. The following chart shows one way that details for a composition on your favorite recreational activities might be classified.

CLASSIFICATION CHART

Thesis: Although my favorite recreations are an odd assortment, together they give me year-round pleasure.

Details	Classification
Climbing rocks	I. Done by myself
Recording music	A. Making kites
Making kites	B. Collecting comic books
Bowling	C. Recording music
Watching videos	II. Done indoors with friends
Collecting comic books	A. Bowling
Playing soccer	B. Watching videos
	III. Done outdoors with friends
	A. Climbing rocks
	B. Playing soccer

THINKING PRACTICE

Choose one of the following subjects. Through freewriting or clustering, list as many details as you can that relate to the subject. Then classify your details by making a chart like the one above.

1. the contents of your closet

2. the range of television programming available

3. the ideal collection of CDs

4. part-time jobs available for teenagers

Unity, Coherence, and Emphasis

A composition has **unity** when all the supporting paragraphs relate to the main idea in the thesis statement. As a result, readers are not distracted by sentences or paragraphs that seem to wander off the main point.

Compositions should also have **coherence**—the quality that makes the ideas in the paragraphs flow logically and naturally from one to the next. When your composition has a coherent organization, readers can easily follow the sequence of your ideas. You can create coherence in your compositions by using transitional words and phrases to connect supporting paragraphs. You can also achieve coherence by repeating key words or by using pronouns and synonyms to refer to key words.

Emphasis, another important quality of a composition, helps readers recognize your most important ideas. You can show your emphasis by writing more about one idea, by discussing it first, or by using transitional words and phrases to highlight it.

> ### Writing Tip
>
> Check your compositions for the qualities of **unity**, **coherence**, and **emphasis**.

Julian Bielewicz's composition "Cryptanalysis" on pages C212–C213 shows all three of these qualities. It has unity because all the supporting paragraphs describe what qualities a cryptanalyst needs to break a code. It has coherence because in each of the supporting paragraphs, the author uses introductory transitions such as *the first quality*, *the second quality*, and *the third quality* to make the organization clear. Finally he reveals his emphasis by placing his most important idea in his first supporting paragraph.

PRACTICE YOUR SKILLS

● *Analyzing Unity, Coherence, and Emphasis*

Reread the introduction and the body of the composition "Why I Like Going to the Movies" on pages C222–C223. Then write answers to each of the following questions.

1. What characteristic of the three supporting paragraphs gives this composition unity?

2. What transitional phrase in the second supporting paragraph links it to the first supporting paragraph?

3. What aspect of the experience of going to the movies is probably most important to this writer? How do you know this author's emphasis?

4. How do transitions from each paragraph to the next give the composition coherence?

5. What three transitional phrases give coherence to the second paragraph of the body of the composition?

Communicate Your Ideas

DRAFTING *Body*

 Return to the outline that you made to classify the supporting ideas and details in your composition. Using those ideas and details to support your thesis statement, draft the body of your composition. As you write, follow the organization you decided on for your supporting paragraphs. Make sure you have a clear idea of the structure and flow of your composition.

Looping Back to Prewriting

Additional Details

As you write your paragraph, you may discover you need more supporting details. If so, go back and freewrite new details or research additional information to support your thesis statement. Your writing process is flexible. You can go back and forth between the various stages as necessary to create your very best work.

● Conclusion of a Composition

No composition is complete without a conclusion that sums up the ideas in the body and reminds readers of the thesis statement. A good conclusion often ends with a clincher statement that rings in the reader's memory.

> The **conclusion** completes the composition and reinforces the thesis statement.

The following paragraph is the conclusion to "Why I Like Going to the Movies" on pages C222–C223. It reinforces the thesis stated in the introduction, restates the ideas in the supporting paragraphs, and has an excellent clincher statement.

MODEL: Conclusion of a Composition

As I see more and more movies, I recognize the acting and filmmaking techniques that mark a great movie. Still, all my new critical skills are nothing compared to the fundamental pleasure I experience at the movies. Although the images disappear with the last click of the projector, they find a lasting home in me. As I leave the theater, I feel as if I have discovered a great treasure, or captained a starship, or danced to a driving rock beat. I like living in my everyday world, but movies give me exciting new worlds to enjoy.

CLINCHER STATEMENT

Writing Tip

Remember that the **concluding paragraph** completes the composition and reinforces the main idea.

PRACTICE YOUR SKILLS

● *Analyzing Structure and Flow*

Copy and complete the following composition circle to analyze the structure and flow of Harold Krents's "Darkness at Noon." (pages C207–C208)

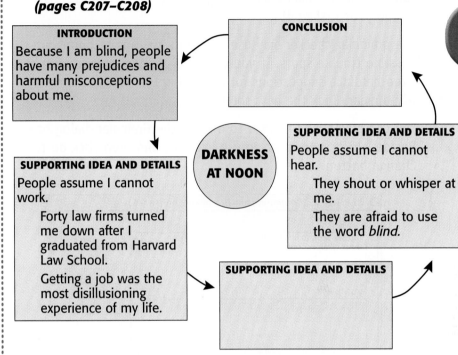

INTRODUCTION
Because I am blind, people have many prejudices and harmful misconceptions about me.

CONCLUSION

DARKNESS AT NOON

SUPPORTING IDEA AND DETAILS
People assume I cannot work.
Forty law firms turned me down after I graduated from Harvard Law School.
Getting a job was the most disillusioning experience of my life.

SUPPORTING IDEA AND DETAILS
People assume I cannot hear.
They shout or whisper at me.
They are afraid to use the word *blind*.

SUPPORTING IDEA AND DETAILS

Communicate Your Ideas

DRAFTING, REVISING *Conclusion*

Add a strong conclusion to your composition. Then, when you have finished drafting, check your work for the qualities of unity, coherence, and emphasis. If some of your paragraphs do not support your thesis statement, think of what you could delete or add to provide unity. If some paragraphs do not follow clearly from one to another, add transitional words or phrases for coherence. If your readers could misunderstand what your most important idea is, think of a way to add emphasis. Revise your conclusion, if necessary, and save your work for later use.

The grammar checker of your computer will analyze your composition for sentence fragments and run-on sentences. It's a quick way to correct these errors in your composition. You can use the grammar checker as you write or after you finish typing your first draft.

The grammar checker may use a green wavy line to point out possible trouble spots. If you click the problem area, one or more boldface suggestions for correcting the sentence error will appear. Click the best solution.

You can also click Grammar to display the Grammar dialog box. Decide which suggestion to use, click it, and then click on the Change button.

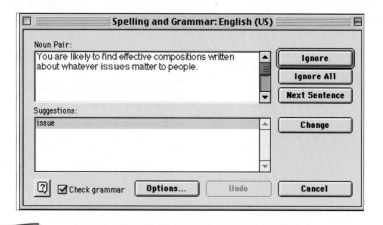

Communicate Your Ideas

EDITING, PUBLISHING

Using the **Editing Checklists** on pages C46 and C232, correct any mistakes in your composition. Then make a neat final copy. Explore different publishing options with your classmates. For example, if a number of students have written compositions about American culture, you might bind these together in a class magazine entitled *Our American Culture*.

PORTFOLIO

Prewriting Workshop
Drafting Workshop
Revising Workshop
Editing Workshop ▶
Publishing Workshop

Sentence Fragments and Run-on Sentences

Just as paragraphs are the building blocks of compositions, sentences are the building blocks of paragraphs. To create effective paragraphs, you must write sentences that work together clearly and well. Sentence fragments and run-on sentences are two common errors that make paragraphs less effective.

Sentence Fragments

A **sentence fragment** is a group of words that does not work as a complete sentence. On page C43, you reviewed sentence fragments that were missing either a subject or a verb. The most common type of sentence fragment, however, is a phrase that does not have either a subject or a verb.

SENTENCE FRAGMENTS	The toughest misconception of all.
	To study for a diploma in law degree at Oxford University.

If you read aloud as you edit, you will be able to detect most sentence fragments. When you finish reading most sentence fragments, your voice is still up—expecting more information to follow. If you read the first example above, for instance, you end on a note of anticipation. You think you will find out what the toughest misconception is, but you never do. Therefore, to correct most fragments, add whatever information you anticipated would be there.

SENTENCES	The toughest misconception of all **is the view that because I can't see, I can't work.**
	I had been given a year's leave of absence from my Washington law firm to study for a diploma in law degree at Oxford University.

Run-on Sentences

A **run-on sentence** is a mistake that happens when there are no words or punctuation to stop one sentence from running into another sentence. To correct a run-on sentence, you have to separate the two sentences. You can do this (1) with a period and a capital letter, (2) with a comma and a conjunction, or (3) with a semicolon.

RUN-ON SENTENCE   Dad shot and missed I did the same.

CORRECTED SENTENCE   Dad shot and missed**.** I did the same.

CORRECTED SENTENCE   Dad shot and missed**, and** I did the same.

CORRECTED SENTENCE   Dad shot and missed**;** I did the same.

Another way to correct a run-on sentence is to make one of the sentences into a subordinate clause.

RUN-ON SENTENCE   My father would stand beneath the hoop and shout I would shoot over his head at the basket attached to our garage.

CORRECTED SENTENCE   **When my father would stand beneath the hoop and shout,** I would shoot over his head at the basket attached to our garage.

Using either a coordinating or a subordinating conjunction to correct a run-on sentence helps show the relationship between the two sentences.

Editing Checklist

✔ Are there any sentence fragments?
✔ Are there any run-on sentences?

▶ Process of Writing an Effective Composition

Remember that the writing process is recursive—you can move freely among the stages to achieve your writing purpose. For example, you may decide in revising to loop back to prewriting to generate more details. The page numbers indicate where you can find help with your writing.

PREWRITING

- Find subjects by drawing on your personal experiences and insights and choose one to develop into a composition. *(pages C10–C17)*
- Limit your subject. Focus your ideas by asking yourself questions about your writing purpose, your audience, and the tone you have decided to use. *(pages C18–C19, C21–C22, and C215–C216)*
- Brainstorm, freewrite, or cluster to develop supporting details. *(pages C25–C30)*
- Sort through your details and classify them in meaningful groups or supporting ideas for your thesis statement. Organize your groups into a simple outline. *(pages C30–C34 and C220–C223)*

DRAFTING

- Write a working thesis statement that expresses your main idea and states or implies your writing purpose. *(page C217)*
- Write an introduction that catches the attention of your audience, establishes your tone, and includes your thesis statement. *(pages C214–C217)*
- Write the supporting paragraphs of the body. *(pages C220, C222–C223)*
- Use transitional words and phrases to link your supporting paragraphs. *(page C226)*
- Add a concluding paragraph with a clincher statement. *(page C228)*
- Add a title that engages your audience's attention. *(page C36)*

REVISING

- Revise your composition for structure and well-developed paragraphs. *(pages C221–C223)*
- Maintain unity, coherence, and emphasis. *(page C226)*
- Vary your choice of words to keep your sentences lively. *(pages C62–C64)*

EDITING

- Use your <u>Editing Checklists</u> to check your grammar, usage, mechanics, and spelling. *(pages C232 and C46)*
- Correct any sentence fragments or run-on sentences. *(pages C231–C232)*

PUBLISHING

- Make a neat final copy in standard manuscript form. Present your finished composition to a reader. *(pages C48–C52)*

▷ A Writer Writes

A Composition About a Shared Experience

Purpose: to relate an incident involving you and someone from a culture different from your own

Audience: your classmates and teacher

Prewriting

Brainstorm or talk to friends and family members to help you recall any experiences throughout your life that you have shared with someone whose cultural background was different from your own. As you remember various incidents, focus on any revelation, or new understanding, you may have gained as a result. (If you have never had such an experience, choose a different culture and imagine what the incident would be like.)

Through freewriting or brainstorming, recall details about your shared experiences. For instance, perhaps you tasted some new foods, heard a different kind of music, or observed a previously unknown custom or tradition. Then concentrate on one particularly meaningful incident that you could develop into a composition.

After writing a preliminary working thesis statement, list all the facts and details you can recall about your experience. If possible, gather additional information by reviewing the experience with someone who shared it with you. Then, after you group your details and ideas into meaningful categories, use a simple outline to arrange your categories into a logical order.

Drafting

As you begin the first draft of your composition, write an introduction that will capture your readers' attention. Your introduction should also establish your tone and include a thesis statement that states your main idea and makes your purpose clear. Then, after you use your outline to write your supporting paragraphs, end with a strong conclusion. Choose a title that captures the significance of the experience described in your composition.

Revising

In addition to checking your draft for unity, coherence, and emphasis, examine the vividness of your word choice and the variety of your sentence structure. Wherever necessary, add, substitute, delete, or rearrange to improve the clarity and forcefulness of your work.

Editing

Use the **Editing Checklists** on pages C46 and C232 as guides to editing your draft.

Publishing

Make a neat final copy of your composition using standard manuscript form. You may wish to plan and videotape a cultural festival in which students dress in the native costumes of their cultures, play appropriate music, serve ethnic food, and share their compositions. If this publishing idea is impossible, consult the **Ways to Publish Your Writing** chart on page C49 for publishing ideas.

Connection Collection

Representing in Different Ways

. . . to Visuals

You are employed by the Abacus Advertising Agency. Your boss has assigned you to the Tough Guy Vitamins account. Find a picture from a magazine or the Internet based on the memo on the right that shows a dog you feel will be most effective for their ad campaign.

To: Abacus Advertising Agency
From: Paul Paulsen, Tough Guy Vitamins
Date: 6-30-00
Subject: New animal for label

We at Tough Guy are committed to excellence. We are currently preparing to market a new line of vitamins designed to appeal to bodybuilding men. For the labels on our vitamin bottles, we want to show a picture of a dog that will appeal to strong men and make them interested in our product. That's why we are asking you for help. We feel that you at Abacus will guide us to finding just the right animal for our vitamins.

Thank you.

From Visuals . . .

. . . to Print

Today you received another memo from Paul Paulsen. He wants to use the dog on the right for his Tough Guy vitamins campaign! You think you have a better idea. Prepare a detailed letter to Mr. Paulsen, explaining your reasons. Provide a thesis statement with supporting evidence, and argue why your initial choice is right for their product.

- **Which strategies can be used for creating both written and visual representations? Which strategies apply to one, not both? Which type of representation is more effective?**
- **Draw a conclusion, and write briefly about the differences between written ideas and visual representations.**

Writing in Academic Areas
Descriptive Proposal

You work in the corporate health club at Templeton Plastics. After years of study, you have concluded that jumping rope is one of the most beneficial ways to stay healthy and build strong muscles. You believe that further study on this activity with various subjects will allow you to complete your groundbreaking research in this area of physical fitness.

Write a descriptive proposal to the Department of Health and Physical Education in which you ask for a grant to finance the rest of your research. Explain your idea in clear and concise terms, keep the purpose of your composition clear, and use vivid and personal details to support your points. Be sure to avoid sentence fragments and run-on sentences.

What strategies did you use to inform your department head?

You can find information on descriptive writing on pages C177–C189.

Writing for Oral Communication
Problem/Solution Speech

Your local city council officers are currently voting on ways to improve your city. They are strongly considering a curfew measure that would require everyone under the age of eighteen to be at home before 8:00 P.M. on school nights. You feel very strongly about this issue, and would like to present your opinion at a public forum next week.

Prepare your speech for your school to be presented at the public forum. Decide on your thesis statement, and use prewriting to develop your ideas. Begin your speech with an intriguing quote or personal detail. Then practice the speech on your classmates.

What strategies did you use to state a strong opinion at the public forum?

You can find information on writing speeches on pages C592–C601.

Writing in Everyday Life

Informative E-Mail

Congratulations! You have won the lottery. The total prize is $10,000. Your friend Vanessa just heard the news over her radio and has written you an E-mail to offer her congratulations. She also wants to know what you plan to do with your money.

> Write an E-mail message to Vanessa in which you explain how you will spend your money. Consider things you might buy for yourself, as well as plans you might have for your family or charity. Use a reflective tone for your composition. Be sure to use clear and smooth transitions in the text of your E-mail.

> What strategies did you use to compose the E-mail to Vanessa?

> *You can find information on writing E-mail in* A Writer's Guide to Using the Internet, *pages C722–C768.*

Writing in the Workplace

Persuasive Note

You work as a publicist for a leading publishing company. Your assistant, Miranda, prides herself on the speediness of her work— she consistently submits the promotional materials on a book to magazines, newspapers, and television stations early enough for success! In recent months, however, you have noticed a decline in Miranda's proofreading skills. Some possible publicity opportunities for books have been missed because of her sloppy spelling and mechanics.

> Write a note to Miranda that will persuade her to be more careful with her work. Support the thesis of your note with strong supporting details, and supply an effective conclusion that will persuade Miranda to improve her skills.

> What strategies did you use to persuade Miranda to improve her job performance?

Assess Your Learning

This summer, there has been a problem with poisonous beetles in your area. The city has had to cut down a number of trees, and nearly fifty people have fallen ill after receiving beetle bites. Your city council has decided to start spraying the area to kill the bugs—but the spray they are using, you have discovered, is toxic to most animals and could even cause more sickness in humans!

▶ **Write an essay for your local paper that will argue your point about the city council's decision to spray your town to kill the beetles. Prewrite to generate ideas about your thesis statement, and use supporting details and evidence to back up your thesis. Be sure to use appropriate transitions, and do not forget to vary the types of sentences you use. Finally, end your composition for the paper with an effective and detailed conclusion.**

Before You Write **Consider the following questions:**
What is the *subject?*
What is the *occasion?*
Who is the *audience?*
What is the *purpose?*

After You Write **Evaluate your work using the following criteria:**
- Have you used a topic sentence that expresses the main idea of your composition for the newspaper?
- Do the supporting paragraphs in the body of your composition develop the thesis statement?
- Have you correctly used transitional words in the body of the essay?
- Does your composition have unity, coherence, and emphasis?
- Have you avoided sentence fragments and run-on sentences?
- Does your composition effectively persuade the city council to consider your point that spraying for beetles may be a bad idea?
- Have you checked for appropriateness of organization, content, style, and conventions?

Write briefly on how well you did. Point out your strengths and areas for improvement.

CHAPTER 6

Personal Writing: Self-Expression and Reflection

Personal stories are a part of your day-to-day life. Every day, friends and family recount to you what has happened to them. Participants on talk shows publicly relate the most trivial and the most profound personal experiences. Newspaper reporters interview participants in and witnesses to newsworthy events. In a school hallway, on a bus, or at the mall, you may often overhear tantalizing bits and pieces of the stories strangers tell their friends.

Writing a personal narrative can be a profound experience for the storyteller. Carefully choosing details and words that best express what happened may lead to a deeper understanding of the event. You may even end up with a greater knowledge of yourself.

Reading with a Writer's Eye

In "The Jacket," Gary Soto recalls a time in his youth when he had no choice but to wear an ugly green plastic jacket. As you read this personal story, think about how Soto expresses his ideas and feelings about the jacket. Also consider how he reflects on the meaning this experience had for him.

THE JACKET

Gary Soto

My clothes have failed me. I remember the green coat that I wore in fifth and sixth grades when you either danced like a champ or pressed yourself against a greasy wall, bitter as a penny toward the happy couples.

When I needed a new jacket and my mother asked what kind I wanted, I described something like bikers wear: black leather and silver studs with enough belts to hold down a small town. We were in the kitchen, steam on the windows from her cooking. She listened so long while stirring dinner that I thought she understood for sure the kind I wanted. The next day when I got home from school, I discovered draped on my bedpost a jacket the color of day-old guacamole. I threw my books on the bed and approached the jacket slowly, as if it were a stranger whose hand I had to shake. I touched the vinyl sleeve, the collar, and peeked at the mustard-colored lining.

From the kitchen mother yelled that my jacket was in the closet. I closed the door to her voice and pulled at the rack of clothes in the closet, hoping the jacket on the bedpost wasn't for me but my mean brother. No luck. I gave up. From my bed, I stared at the jacket. I wanted to cry because it was so ugly and so big that I knew I'd have to wear it a long time. I was a small kid, thin as a young tree, and it would be years before I'd have a new one. I stared at the jacket, like an enemy, thinking bad things before I took off my old jacket whose sleeves climbed halfway to my elbow.

I put the big jacket on. I zipped it up and down several times, and rolled the cuffs up so they didn't cover my hands.

I put my hands in the pockets and flapped the jacket like a bird's wings. I stood in front of the mirror, full face, then profile, and then looked over my shoulder as if someone had called me. I sat on the bed, stood against the bed, and combed my hair to see what I would look like doing something natural. I looked ugly. I threw it on my brother's bed and looked at it for a long time before I slipped it on and went out to the backyard, smiling a "thank you" to my mom as I passed her in the kitchen. With my hands in my pockets I kicked a ball against the fence, and then climbed it to sit looking into the alley. I hurled orange peels at the mouth of an open garbage can and when the peels were gone I watched the white puffs of my breath thin to nothing.

I jumped down, hands in my pockets, and in the backyard on my knees I teased my dog, Brownie, by swooping my arms while making bird calls. He jumped again and again, until a tooth sunk deep, ripping an L-shaped tear on my left sleeve. I pushed Brownie away to study the tear as I would a cut on my arm. There was no blood, only a few loose pieces of fuzz. Damn dog, I thought, and pushed him away hard when he tried to bite again. I got up from my knees and went to my bedroom to sit with my jacket on my lap, with the lights out.

That was the first afternoon with my new jacket. The next day I wore it to sixth grade and got a D on a math quiz. During the morning recess Frankie T., the playground terrorist, pushed me to the ground and told me to stay there until recess was over. My best friend, Steve Negrete, ate an apple while looking at me, and the girls turned away to whisper on the monkey bars. The teachers were no help: they looked my way and talked about how foolish I looked in my new jacket. I saw their heads bob with laughter, their hands half-covering their mouths.

Even though it was cold, I took off the jacket during lunch and played kickball in a thin shirt, my arms feeling like braille from goose bumps. But when I returned to class I slipped the jacket on and shivered until I was warm. I sat on my hands, heating them up, while my teeth chattered like a cup of crooked dice. Finally warm, I slid out of the jacket but a few minutes later put it back on when the fire bell rang. We paraded out into the yard where we, the sixth graders, walked past all the other grades to stand against the back fence. Everybody saw me. Although they didn't say out loud, "Man, that's ugly," I heard the buzz-buzz of gossip and even laughter that I knew was meant for me.

And so I went, in my guacamole jacket. So embarrassed, so hurt, I couldn't even do my homework. I received Cs on quizzes, and forgot the state capitals and the rivers of South America, our friendly neighbor. Even the girls who had been friendly blew away like loose flowers to follow the boys in neat jackets.

I wore that thing for three years until the sleeves grew short and my forearms stuck out like the necks of turtles. All during that time no love came to me—no little dark girl in a Sunday dress she wore on Monday. At lunchtime I stayed with the ugly boys who leaned against the chainlink fence and looked around with propellers of grass spinning in our mouths. We saw girls walk by alone, saw couples, hand in hand, their heads like bookends pressing air together. We saw them and spun our propellers so fast our faces were blurs.

I blame that jacket for those bad years. It was a sad time for the heart. With a friend I spent my sixth-grade year in a tree in the alley waiting for something good to happen to me in that jacket, which had become the ugly brother who tagged along wherever I went. And it was about that time that I began to grow. My chest puffed up with muscle and, strangely, a few more ribs. Even my hands, those fleshy hammers, showed bravely through the cuffs, the fingers already hardening for the coming fights. But that L-shaped rip on the left sleeve got bigger; bits of stuffing coughed out from its wound after a hard day of play. I finally scotch-taped it closed, but in rain or cold weather the tape peeled off like a scab and more stuffing fell out until that sleeve shriveled into a palsied arm. That winter the elbows began to crack and whole chunks of green began to fall off. I showed the cracks to my mother, who always seemed to be at the stove with steamed-up glasses, and she said that there were children in Mexico who would love that jacket. I told her that this was America and yelled that Debbie, my sister, didn't have a jacket like mine. I ran outside, ready to cry, and climbed the tree by the alley to think bad thoughts and watch my breath puff white and disappear.

But whole pieces still casually flew off my jacket when I played hard, read quietly, or took vicious spelling tests at school. When it became so spotted that my brother began to call me "camouflage," I flung it over the fence into the alley. Later, however, I swiped the jacket off the ground and went inside to drape it across my lap and mope.

I was called to dinner: steam silvered my mother's glasses as she said grace; my brother and sister with their heads bowed made ugly faces at their glasses of powdered milk. I gagged too, but eagerly ate big rips of buttered tortilla that held scooped up beans. Finished, I went outside with my jacket across my arm. It was a cold sky. The faces of clouds were piled up, hurting. I climbed the fence, jumping down with a grunt. I started up the alley and soon slipped into my jacket, that green ugly brother who breathed over my shoulder that day and ever since.

Thinking as a Writer

Discussing Style of Self-Expression

Oral Expression "The Jacket" is a lively and humorous account of one boy's hate affair with some outerwear.

- With a group of classmates, talk about the views and feelings that Gary Soto expresses. How does he turn an ordinary situation into a lively, humorous account?

Reflecting on an Event

- Suppose you had been forced to wear the jacket described in the narrative when you were in sixth grade. For a moment, put yourself in the jacket. Imagine what you're thinking and feeling about the "green ugly brother" lying on your shoulders. What would your feelings have been? How would you have reacted to having to wear the jacket or a similarly ugly item of clothing?
- Would you have recounted the event using humor, as Soto does, or another style?

Connecting Appearance with Self-Expression

Viewing How cool Gary Soto would have felt if he had gotten a black leather biker's jacket with "enough belts to hold down a small town"! Instead he spent years being mortified in a vinyl monstrosity "the color of day-old guacamole." Often our description of an object reflects feelings about it. Look at these jackets. What words come to mind as you look at these jackets? How might you feel wearing each one? Explain.

The Power of Personal Writing

"If I had to give a young writer some advice," remarked the Nobel Prize winner Gabriel García Márquez, "I would say to write about something that has happened to him." The things that happen in your life—and your reflections on them—are important. As you saw in Gary Soto's story, these experiences can be central to who you are as a person. Writing narratives is a way to remember and understand those significant events. It is also a way to share who you are with others.

Uses of Personal Writing

People use personal narrative whenever they tell what happened. The following examples show that narratives play a regular part in our everyday lives.

- **You explain to friends** how you broke your leg on a skiing trip.

- **A newcomer to your school relates** how war and political unrest forced her to leave her homeland.

- **You read Marco Polo's account** of his trip to China in order to write a history report.

- **You write an E-mail message** to your cousin in another state recounting an amusing anecdote you overheard.

- **Your mother tells** how at age three you gave yourself a haircut and ended up half bald.

- **You stay up late reading a thriller** to make sure the hero escapes from the kidnappers.

Process of Writing a Personal Narrative

In "The Jacket" Gary Soto has written about a personal experience in which a green jacket played a major role. This experience, of course, is only one of thousands of experiences that he might have chosen as the topic for a personal narrative. You, too, have had countless experiences that you might narrate. Choosing the right one will depend on what you wish to express in your personal narrative. Your choice will also depend on your feelings and reflections on the event since it has happened. You should write from the first-person point of view, using the pronoun *I*. In addition, you should write in a natural, personal style and follow a less formal structure than in most of the other writing you do.

A **personal narrative** expresses the writer's personal point of view on a subject drawn from the writer's own experience.

Your Writer's Journal

In your journal, list and freewrite about possessions that have been important to you over the years. Perhaps, for example, you absolutely had to have a certain toy, article of clothing, or piece of sports equipment. Perhaps you received a gift you came to treasure. Reflect on why these objects were so important. In all likelihood, you associate certain memories with them. You don't have to write only about possessions in your journal though. Now is the time to record any major—or minor—stories of your life. Include whatever details or ideas that come to mind in order to help fill out the story. These notes will be a rich source of ideas when it comes time to write your personal narrative.

The starting point for thinking of a subject for a personal narrative is your own experience, reflections, and observations. Writers have penned essays about a tremendous variety of personal subjects—everything from taking driving lessons to expressing the importance of a friendship. In the following excerpt from a personal narrative, writer Annie Dillard writes about a childhood experience that had personal significance for her.

MODEL: Personal Narrative

When I was six or seven years old, growing up in Pittsburgh, I used to take a precious penny of my own and hide it for someone else to find. It was a curious compulsion; sadly, I've never been seized by it since. For some reason I always "hid" the penny along the same stretch of sidewalk up the street. I would cradle it at the roots of a sycamore, say, or in a hole left by a chipped-off piece of sidewalk. Then I would take a piece of chalk, and, starting at the other end of the block, draw huge arrows leading up to the penny from both directions. After I learned to write I labeled the arrows: SURPRISE AHEAD or MONEY THIS WAY. I was greatly excited, during all this arrow-drawing, at the thought of the first lucky passerby who would receive in this way, regardless of merit, a free gift from the universe. But I never lurked about. I would go straight home and not give the matter another thought, until, some months later, I would be gripped again by the impulse to hide another penny.

—*Annie Dillard,* Pilgrim at Tinker Creek

Drawing on Personal Experience

To think of a subject for a personal narrative, look through your **journal** entries and try clustering or freewriting to recall experiences, people, places, and objects that have personal significance for you. For instance, you might recall a coach or a teacher who has had a strong influence on you. You might visualize a special place that has always provided you pleasure. Even a simple object, such as an old baseball mitt or a pair of sneakers, can be the starting point for a personal narrative. The following sources can all lead to appropriate subjects.

SOURCES OF SUBJECTS FOR PERSONAL NARRATIVES

photograph albums	school yearbooks
letters from friends	newspapers and magazines
family stories	souvenirs from vacations
scrapbooks	items in your desk
diaries	favorite places
clothing or jewelry	old toys or games

Communicate Your Ideas

PREWRITING *Subject Related to Personal Experience*

Using your **journal** and the sources suggested above, create a list of five possible subjects for a personal narrative. Your list might include possessions and the experiences you associate with them. It might also include memorable occurrences and events. Then, from your list, choose the one subject that appeals to you most. It should be something that you remember vividly and is meaningful to you. Save your subject for later use.

SAVE YOUR WORK

Exploring the Meaning of an Experience

While a personal narrative may not have a thesis statement, it does communicate a main idea to the audience. This main idea usually grows out of the meaning that the experience had for you. For instance, suppose that you acted in a school play in your freshman year in high school, and you want to write about that experience. In the resulting personal narrative, you could turn any of the following interpretations of that experience into the main idea of your narrative.

- The experience helped you build self-confidence and self-esteem.

- The experience stimulated an interest in theater as a career.

- The experience introduced you to a group of talented people.

In the following excerpt, notice how Annie Dillard explains the meaning of her childhood experience of hiding pennies.

MODEL: Personal Narrative

> The world is fairly studded and strewn with pennies cast broadside from a generous hand. But—and this is the point—who gets excited by a mere penny? If you follow one arrow, if you crouch motionless on a bank to watch a tremendous ripple thrill on the water and are rewarded by the sight of a muskrat kit paddling from its den, will you count that sight a chip of copper only, and go on your rueful way? It is dire poverty indeed when a man is so malnourished and fatigued that he won't stop to pick up a penny. But if you cultivate a healthy poverty and simplicity, so that finding a penny will literally make your day, then, since the world is in fact planted in pennies, you have with your poverty bought a lifetime of days. It is that simple. What you see is what you get.
>
> —*Annie Dillard,* Pilgrim at Tinker Creek

As Dillard makes clear, her experience of hiding pennies for strangers to find taught her a lesson about the importance of noticing the small things in life. The pennies symbolize for her all of the details that fill our lives: more valuable, perhaps, than the monetary value of one cent. As a result, that lesson serves as the main idea of her personal narrative.

Interpreting Experience

When you are in the middle of an experience, you are often too caught up in it to understand fully its impact on your life. When planning a personal narrative, you need to interpret the experience in order to decide what makes it worth writing about. A checklist, like the one below, may help you explore the experience.

CHECKLIST FOR INTERPRETING EXPERIENCE

Experience: We moved to a new town between seventh and eighth grades.

This experience is important to me now because it
- ❏ helped me see something in a new way.
- ☑ changed the way I feel about myself.

I will always remember this experience because it
- ☑ strongly affected my attitudes.
- ❏ had important consequences.

This experience is worth writing about because it
- ❏ will be familiar to many readers.
- ☑ gave me an insight that may help other people.

Interpretation: This experience helped me become more outgoing with people. I had to make an effort to make friends, and it worked!

THINKING PRACTICE

Choose one of the following experiences or one of your own choice. Then interpret that experience by developing a checklist like the one above.

- a humorous episode you had while on vacation
- an insight you had about someone you know
- an incident that gave you an insight into your neighborhood

PREWRITING *Meaning of Experience*

 Think about the possession or experience that you chose as your subject for a personal narrative. In a sentence or two, write what the object or experience means to you—what has made it important. Save your work for later use.

Determining Purpose and Audience

Once you have decided on the meaning of an experience, you need to think about the purpose and audience of your narrative. Usually you will write a personal narrative for the general purpose of entertaining your readers. However, you can combine this general purpose with specific purposes, which you achieve by including different kinds of paragraphs. For example, listed in the following box are possible specific aims for a composition about being in the freshman class play.

PURPOSE IN PERSONAL WRITING

OVERALL PURPOSE: to express thoughts and feelings about being in a class play

Specific Aims	Kinds of Paragraphs
to explain the challenges of playing a particular role	informative
to tell an anecdote about a humorous person in the cast	narrative
to describe the director of the play	descriptive

Considering Your Audience When writing personal narratives, you need to give special attention to making the subject as appealing and significant for your audience as it is for you. Suppose, for instance, that you are writing about white-water rafting on the

Colorado River. Since most readers have not had this experience, you should describe the river and the process of rafting in sufficient detail so that your readers will be able to understand and visualize the experience.

PRACTICE YOUR SKILLS

● *Determining Purpose and Audience*

Choose three of the following subjects for personal narratives, and write an appropriate purpose and audience for each one.

- helping a close friend achieve a goal
- watching a younger brother or sister do well in a special activity
- getting on a varsity team
- moving to a new home
- starting a new part-time job

Communicate Your Ideas

PREWRITING *Purpose and Audience*

Review the main idea sentence or sentences that you wrote about the subject of your personal narrative. Do those sentences fully explain what this experience meant to you? If not, revise them to reflect your feelings more accurately. Also make notes on the purpose of your narrative and the intended audience. Save your notes for later use.

Developing and Selecting Details

An important part of developing a personal narrative is using details that will flesh out your experience and give it life. After deciding on your purpose and audience, you should think of and write down details that make readers feel they are at the scene of the experience with you. If you are writing about a person, think about the look on the person's face or in his or her eyes. If you are writing about a place, think of details about the smell in the air, the feel of the ground—all that you saw, heard, touched, tasted, and smelled.

After making a list of details, you should select those details you want to include when you draft your narrative. Weed out details that, while interesting, are not relevant to the main idea. The following additional guidelines will help you select the most effective details.

> ### Guidelines for Selecting Details

- Choose specific details that are appropriate for your purpose and audience.
- Use factual details to provide background information.
- Use vivid descriptive and sensory details to bring your experience to life.

In the following excerpt from a personal narrative, the writer E. B. White describes his return to a favorite childhood haunt—a camp at a lake in Maine. Notice how he has selected details that develop the main idea—that the week at the camp was memorable.

MODEL: Sensory Details in a Personal Narrative

> We had a good week at the camp. The bass were biting well and the sun shone endlessly, day after day. We would be tired at night and lie down in the accumulated heat of the little bedrooms after the long hot day and the breeze would stir almost imperceptibly outside and the smell of the swamp drift in through rusty screens.
>
> —E. B. White, "Once More to the Lake"

Now look at how another writer, Eudora Welty, introduces her long selection "Listening" with details that you can almost hear. The details develop the main idea, which is that listening was important in her family when she was young.

When I was young enough to still spend a long time buttoning my shoes in the morning, I'd listen toward the hall: Daddy upstairs was shaving in the bathroom and Mother downstairs was frying the bacon. They would begin whistling back and forth to each other up and down the stairwell. My father would whistle his phrase, my mother would try to whistle, then hum hers back. It was their duet.

—*Eudora Welty,* One Writer's Beginnings

PRACTICE YOUR SKILLS

● *Identifying Effective Details*

Review "The Jacket" by Gary Soto. Find details in the narrative that the author uses to give life to the experience he wrote about. Then write at least ten details under the title "Examples of Effective Details."

Communicate Your Ideas

PREWRITING *Effective Details*

List details that you want to include in your personal narrative. Pay particular attention to details that will assist the reader in understanding and visualizing the experience. Save your list of details for later use.

Organizing Details

The overall organization of your personal narrative will probably be developmental order. That is, ideas will be arranged in a progression so that one idea grows out of the previous idea and leads to the next idea. However, within this overall pattern of organization, you will usually use individual paragraphs that are narrative, descriptive, or informative. Within each paragraph, you should use an appropriate method of organizing your details, as the following chart shows.

TYPES OF ORDER		
Kind of Writing	**Kind of Details**	**Type of Order**
Narrative	events in a story, narrated from beginning to end	chronological order
Descriptive	details to help readers visualize from top to bottom, right to left, or vice versa	spatial order
Informative	background details and details explaining the meaning of an experience	order of importance

Writing Tip

Organize details in each paragraph of your personal narrative depending on the type of paragraph you are using.

Communicate Your Ideas

PREWRITING *Types of Order*

Organize the details that you listed for your personal narrative into groups for specific paragraphs and order them, using the preceding chart to assist you. In ordering details, you may find it helpful to write organized notes consisting of phrases or sentences. Save your notes for later use.

Across the Media: People in the News

Personal narratives are often the heart of what is presented on the news, but their treatment in newspapers, on television, and on the Internet can vary considerably. Following is an example of how the story was treated when a famous writer was hit by a car.

- The newspapers reported the basic facts.
- The television news added film clips of the accident and the hospital, and from movies based on his books.
- On the Internet, there was an online chat room and links to related information. Fans E-mailed their get-well wishes to the author. Months later, there was information on his recovery.
- A television newsmagazine interviewed the author, who discussed how the accident affected his life.

Media Activity

Study the coverage a personal story gets in various media. Choose a personal story that is making headlines today and complete the following activities on your own or with a partner or small group.

- Clip articles from the newspaper about the story. Write a sentence evaluating the impact of each article and how effectively it conveyed information.
- Watch television news to see how the story is covered. Make a video recording or take detailed notes that you can review later. Evaluate the impact of the story in a sentence or two.
- Search the Internet to see how the story is being covered online. In addition to general searches, search for discussions of the story at http://www.deja.com. Evaluate the online coverage.

Finally, write a brief essay comparing the coverage in different media. Also include a critique of each medium: What can other media do better?

Even though a personal narrative is less formal in structure than other types of essays, it should still have all the parts of any good piece of writing: an interesting introduction, an effective body, and a memorable conclusion.

Drafting the Introduction

You should introduce your personal narrative in a way that convinces your readers that this experience, person, place, or thing had a strong impact on you. To achieve this goal, your introduction should not only tell readers what your narrative is about but also give them a clue as to how you feel about your subject. Consequently your introduction should set the tone of your narrative.

> **Introduction of a Personal Narrative**
>
> • It introduces the subject and purpose of the essay.
> • It makes clear the main idea of the essay.
> • It sets the tone to reveal the writer's point of view.
> • It captures the reader's interest.

Creating a Tone The **tone** of an essay expresses the writer's attitude toward the subject. To choose an appropriate tone for your narrative, think about the effect that you want to have on your readers. Do you want them to laugh with you, cry with you, or share the pleasure of a special time or place? Notice how the writer of the three paragraphs on the next page has used three different tones—humorous, angry, and reflective—to deal with the same subject.

COMPUTER TIP ↖

Tone is largely determined by word choice. To help you find words that create the right tone, use the Thesaurus feature of your computer.

Who knew what lurked in those pale waters? All around me happy snorkelers surfaced, crowing with glee about the rainbow of fish that had nibbled at their fingertips. I looked at my own fingers with a sense of doom, absolutely certain that a razor-toothed barracuda was preparing to greet me when *I* went below. Grimly I locked my bloodless lips over the mouthpiece, ducked my head, breathed in water, and came up choking. *Why* in the world was I doing this?

Model: Angry Tone

It was a raw, windy day, and I was furious. I hate swimming! Since I'm too skinny to look good in a bathing suit, I never go to the beach if I can help it. Here I was, though, all signed up for a free lesson in snorkeling— a sport I'd never wanted to try. Ow! Was that a sea urchin I stepped on?

Model: Reflective Tone

This little bay is my favorite spot in the world. When I go out very early in the morning before the crowds, it is like paradise. I never grow tired of the magic in that clear and silent world as I am surrounded by bright blue and yellow fish. In their world I cannot help feeling at peace.

PRACTICE YOUR SKILLS

● *Analyzing Tone*

Look once again at "The Jacket" by Gary Soto. What do you think is the author's tone? In other words, what attitude does he have about the events he describes? Is he happy? nostalgic?

sad? bitter? Write a paragraph in which you explain what you think the tone is. Be sure to support your opinion by including examples—including specific quotations—from the selection.

Communicate Your Ideas

DRAFTING *Introduction and Tone*

 Draft three possible introductions to the personal narrative that you have been planning. Select a different tone for each introduction and use that tone consistently. Save your work for later use.

Drafting the Body

Once you have introduced the subject and set a tone that is appropriate for your purpose, you are ready to draft the body of your narrative. As you write, make your interpretation of the experience clear, and use sensory details to add richness, interest, and individuality to your writing. The following guidelines will also help you draft the body of your personal narrative.

Guidelines for Drafting the Body

- Make sure that each supporting paragraph has a topic sentence that supports the main idea.
- Follow a logical order of ideas and details.
- Use transitions between sentences and paragraphs to give your narrative coherence.
- If you discover new ideas and details as you write, go back and make changes in those sections of the narrative that are affected by the new insights or details.

In personal essays, you may use different types of writing, such as narrative, descriptive, or informative, to accomplish your purpose. For instance, throughout his essay "The Jacket," Gary Soto uses description and narration to express his feelings about the jacket. Early in the essay, he uses description to imply his initial feelings about it.

> The next day when I got home from school, I discovered draped on my bedpost a jacket the color of day-old guacamole. I threw my books on the bed and approached the jacket slowly, as if it were a stranger whose hand I had to shake. I touched the vinyl sleeve, the collar, and peeked at the mustard-colored lining.

A few paragraphs later, Soto uses narration to tell what he did when he was alone with the jacket.

> I put the big jacket on. I zipped it up and down several times, and rolled the cuffs up so they didn't cover my hands. I put my hands in the pockets and flapped the jacket like a bird's wings. I stood in front of the mirror, full face, then profile, and then looked over my shoulder as if someone had called me. I sat on the bed, stood against the bed, and combed my hair to see what I would look like doing something natural. I looked ugly.
>
> —*Gary Soto,* "The Jacket"

Communicate Your Ideas

DRAFTING *Body*

Select one of the three introductions that you wrote for your personal narrative. Now draft the body, continuing in the same tone that you established in your introduction. Be sure to use the details that you collected. In the course

of drafting, stop occasionally and read over what you have
written to see whether you are using a consistent tone
in your writing.

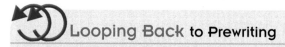

Looping Back **to Prewriting**

Effective Details

As you draft your personal narrative, you may find you need
more or richer details to assist the reader in understanding
and visualizing your experience. To gather those details, it
may be helpful to talk with family members or friends who
are familiar with your subject or experienced it with you.
Include these additional descriptive details in your draft.

Drafting the Conclusion

The conclusion of a personal narrative should give readers a
sense of completion and a lasting impression of the personal experience or insight that you have written about. Following are
several appropriate ways to end a personal narrative.

Ways to End a Personal Narrative

- Summarize the body or restate the main idea in new words.
- Add an insight that shows a new or deeper understanding
  of the experience.
- Add a striking new detail or memorable image.
- Refer to ideas in the introduction to bring your narrative
  full circle.
- Appeal to your reader's emotions.

The following paragraph concludes the narrative that was introduced in the last model paragraph on page C259. The narrative was
given the title "Early Morning Magic." This conclusion both summarizes the experience of swimming in the morning and restates
the main idea.

After an early morning swim like this, I come out of the water and spread out on the sand to dry off. The sound of the waves soothes me, and I continue to picture the fish I have seen and the reef that I have explored. Days and even weeks later, I'm able to reflect back on that time and feel a moment of peace in the middle of a hectic day.

Time Out to Reflect

Writing a personal narrative is likely to bring you some deeper insight or understanding about the meaning of an experience. If this insight or understanding is not apparent right away, don't worry. Give yourself time. Think about what you have written in your draft. Be open to any new feelings or ideas that come to mind as a result of your writing experience. Jot them down and decide whether they might be effective in the conclusion of your essay.

Communicate Your Ideas

DRAFTING *Conclusion*

Reread the introduction and body of your personal narrative. Decide what kind of conclusion would be most appropriate. Is there an additional insight or perception that would make an effective conclusion? Should you summarize the experience you have shared? After you draft at least two possible conclusions for your personal narrative, choose the one that seems to work better. Save your work for later use.

At this point you have turned the raw materials of your personal perceptions and reflections into a rough draft. Your draft is far from a polished piece of writing, though. As Donald M. Murray, a well-known teacher of writing, wrote, "When a draft is completed, the real job of writing can begin." In a personal narrative, this job involves the important task of adding details for adequate development and checking unity, coherence, and clarity.

Checking for Adequate Development

An effective personal narrative should touch the reader in some way. For instance, if you have narrated a personal experience, your narrative should make the reader feel the way you did during that experience. The reader should be able to hear and see and touch everything as you did. To evaluate whether you have achieved this effect, check your essay for vivid and interesting details. The following strategies will help you think of additional details as you revise your personal narrative.

STRATEGIES FOR CHECKING FOR ADEQUATE DEVELOPMENT	
EVENTS	Close your eyes and slowly visualize the experience that you are writing about. Write details as you "see" them in your mind's eye.
PLACES	Visualize the place you are describing. Start at the left side and visualize slowly to the right. Then visualize the place from top to bottom or vice versa.
PEOPLE	Visualize each person that you are writing about. Start by visualizing the head and face and slowly move down to the feet. Write details as you "see" them.
FEELINGS	Imagine yourself once again undergoing the experience that you are writing about. This time focus on your feelings, thoughts, and impressions as you move through the experience.

PRACTICE YOUR SKILLS

● *Revising for Adequate Development*

What details are missing from the following paragraph that would help a reader truly understand the experience? After considering these questions, revise the paragraph.

> As I walked home from school yesterday, I decided this had been one of the worst days of my life. Not one thing had gone right. I looked at the book in my hand. I didn't understand the homework assignment, so tomorrow was going to be bad too. Just then it started to rain, and that made me feel worse.

● *Reflecting on Events*

Copy the reflection chart below for use with your own writing. In the left column, note the main events as you have addressed them in your draft. In the right column, note your personal reflection as it corresponds to that event. If necessary, revise your essay to incorporate new ideas.

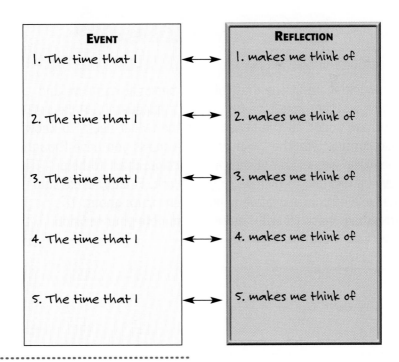

EVENT		REFLECTION
1. The time that I	←→	1. makes me think of
2. The time that I	←→	2. makes me think of
3. The time that I	←→	3. makes me think of
4. The time that I	←→	4. makes me think of
5. The time that I	←→	5. makes me think of

Checking for Unity, Coherence, and Clarity

You will also want to revise the style of your personal narrative. Specifically, supply any needed transitions to help your writing flow more smoothly. The following checklist will help you identify a few other areas for improving when you revise.

Evaluation Checklist for Revising

✓ Does your introduction capture the reader's interest? If not, what might make a better beginning? *(page C258)*

✓ Have you held the reader's interest to the end? If not, how can you add to the interest level of your narrative? *(pages C253–C255)*

✓ Does your feeling about your subject come through? If not, how can you make the point more clearly? *(page C258)*

✓ Does your ending give the reader a sense of completion? If not, how might you make it more effective? *(page C262)*

✓ Write a title for your personal narrative.

Communicate Your Ideas

REVISING *Adequate Development, Reflection, and Tone*

Look again at the draft of your personal narrative and decide whether you have developed it adequately. Make sure you have added all the details that the reader needs to know. Also consider whether your narrative shows you have thought about the events. If not, use a **reflection chart** to help develop insights to include in your work. Finally, make sure the tone of your narrative is consistent throughout. The preceding checklist will help you complete your revision. Save your work for later use.

Prewriting Workshop
Drafting Workshop
Revising Workshop
Editing Workshop ▶
Publishing Workshop

Verbal Phrases

In "The Jacket" Gary Soto wrote, "I stared at the jacket, like an enemy, thinking bad things . . . " The words *thinking bad things* make the sentence dramatic because they emphasize what the writer's feelings were. Notice how much less dramatic the sentence would be if it were phrased differently.

I thought bad things about the jacket.

The words *thinking bad things* form a phrase. Like all phrases it has no subject or verb. However, this is a special kind of phrase called a **verbal phrase**. A **verbal**, which is a verb form that is used as an adjective or a noun, is often combined with modifiers or complements to form a verbal phrase. Writers use verbal phrases frequently to create lively and dramatic sentences, as Gary Soto did in the example above. By using verbal phrases to combine sentences, you can also vary your sentences and eliminate a choppy writing style.

Participial Phrases

One kind of verbal phrase is a participial phrase. A **participle** is a verb form used as an adjective to describe nouns or pronouns. Present participles end in *-ing*, and past participles end in *-ed*, *-n*, *-t*, or *-en*. A **participial phrase**, therefore, is a participle plus its modifiers and complements. In the following examples, the participial phrases not only add liveliness to each sentence but also supply important additional information.

PARTICIPIAL PHRASES	**Smiling a "thank you" to my mother,** I went outside.
	I saw their hands **covering their mouths** and their heads **bobbing with laughter.**

Punctuation with Participial Phrases

When a participial phrase comes at the beginning of the sentence, as in the first example above, place a comma after it. In addition, set off a nonessential participial phrase from the rest of the sentence with commas. A participial phrase is nonessential when you can remove it from a sentence without changing the meaning of the sentence.

NONESSENTIAL PHRASE	The ugly boys, **leaning against the fence**, watched the couples walk by. (The participial phrase *leaning against the fence* is nonessential because it can be removed without changing the meaning of the sentence.)

Combining Sentences by Using Participial Phrases

You can use participial phrases to combine sentences, thus eliminating wordiness from your writing.

TWO SENTENCES	I spent my sixth-grade year in a tree. I was waiting for something good to happen.
COMBINED	I spent my sixth-grade year in a tree **waiting for something good to happen**.

Editing Checklist

✔ Have participial phrases been used to add liveliness to sentences and to incorporate additional information?

✔ Are all participial phrases punctuated correctly?

✔ Could participial phrases be used to combine any sentences?

Remember that when you edit, you carefully reread your revised draft for the conventions of language—grammar, punctuation, spelling, and usage. Sometimes it is useful to allow time to put your writing aside. When you review it again, you may be better able to see areas in which you can make improvements and corrections.

Communicate Your Ideas

EDITING

Refer to your Personalized Editing Checklist to make sure you are not repeating errors you have made in the past. The checklist on the previous page will also help you in editing your work. Save your work.

You may decide to complete the writing process by sharing your writing with someone who was part of the experience you wrote about or with someone who may have an interest in it.

Communicate Your Ideas

PUBLISHING

After you have prepared a neat final copy using correct manuscript form, give your narrative to your teacher, who may choose several to be read aloud in class.

PORTFOLIO

Process of Writing a Personal Narrative

As a writer, you are not locked into the order of the stages of the writing process—prewriting, drafting, revising, editing, and publishing. Feel free to move back and forth among the stages, as you see fit. For example, it is never too late to go back to the drafting stage to come up with new details or additional reflections for your narrative.

PREWRITING

- Sift through your memories for experiences, reflections, and observations about which you would like to express your thoughts and feelings. *(pages C248–C249)*
- Decide on the meaning that a particular subject has for you. *(pages C249–C250)*
- Determine your purpose and audience. *(pages C22 and C252–C253)*
- Choose the most suitable means of developing your subject: narration, description, exposition, or perhaps a combination of all three. *(page C252)*
- List the details that will best develop your main idea and share the meaning of the experience. *(pages C253–C255)*

DRAFTING

- Introduce your subject in a way that catches the reader's interest and sets the tone of the essay. *(pages C258–C259)*
- Build the body of your essay from the details you have chosen so that you make the point you wish to share. *(pages C260–C261)*
- Add a conclusion that leaves your reader with the idea or feeling that you wish to convey. *(page C262)*

REVISING

- Revise your essay for adequate development. *(page C264)*
- Revise your essay for unity, coherence, emphasis, and transitions that make your writing flow smoothly. *(page C266)*
- Choose a title that is true to the tone of your essay. *(page C266)*

EDITING

- Use the <u>Editing Checklist</u> to polish your grammar, spelling, usage, and mechanics. *(pages C46 and C268)*

PUBLISHING

- Refer to <u>Ways to Publish Your Writing</u> for ideas on how to present your personal essay. *(pages C48–C49)*

A Writer Writes

A Personal Experience Essay

Purpose: to express your thoughts and feelings about a personal experience

Audience: your classmates and teacher

Prewriting

In "The Jacket" Gary Soto wants a black leather jacket, the kind that many of the other boys are wearing. Without that kind of a jacket, he does not feel confident or attractive. In school, students often place great importance on looking alike and wearing the same things.

Think about an experience you have had during your school years in which a trend or a fashion played a part. Perhaps you wore a type of clothing in order to follow a trend. On the other hand, there may have been a time when you resisted a fad because you wanted to express your independence. As you explore ideas by reading over your **journal** and freewriting, think about how each experience was meaningful to you. What did you learn about yourself or others as a result of each experience?

After you have a list of several possible subjects, choose the best, most meaningful experience. Then freewrite or cluster to gather all of the details you will need to include in a retelling of your experience.

Drafting

Write a first draft of your personal essay, including an introduction that states or implies your main idea, a body of supporting paragraphs, and a conclusion.

Revising

Have you left out any details that will make your essay clearer? Have you stated or implied a main idea about your experience?

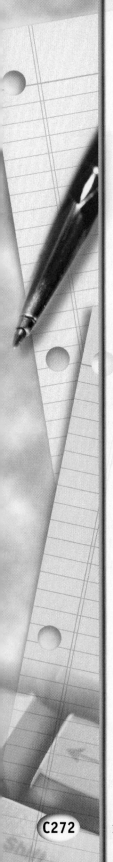

Will the reader's interest be maintained throughout the essay? Have you developed the essay with adequate details regarding the events, people, places, and things that are included in your essay? Finally, is the tone of the essay consistent from beginning to end? Make revisions and add transitions that will make your essay flow more smoothly.

Editing

Use the checklists on pages C46 and C268 to edit your personal experience essay. Remember to check for the conventions of language—grammar, punctuation, spelling, and usage.

Publishing

Reproduce your corrected essay so that all your class-mates can read a copy. You may wish to include a photo-graph collage for added interest.

Connection Collection

Representing in Different Ways

From Print . . .

. . . to Visuals

Maurizio's account of his vacation to Hollywood gives you a good verbal picture of what he saw while he was there. Find a photograph of Hollywood in a magazine or on the Internet that vis Maurizio's vacation.

Dear Rosanna,

Hollywood is a blast! There are so many movie stars that I'm too starstruck to visit other parts of Los Angeles! Yesterday I spent eight hours at the Chinese Theatre making charcoal rubbings on paper of all the stars' handprints and footprints on the sidewalk. If I work for another eight hours today, I might have a complete collection before I fly back to Fayetteville. I feel like I know Tom Hanks personally now that I have a copy of his footprints! I see a long black limousine and a cell-phone in my future. Maybe you'll see me soon in the movies!

Sincerely,
Maurizio

Rosanna Bruno
2 Hampton Court
Overland Park, KS 62204

From Visuals . . .

. . . to Print

Because you live in a big city, you have always dreamed of a vacation in the countryside. Using the photo above, write a postcard to your best friend explaining what you have done on your vacation. Pay attention to tone in the postcard, making it as humorous as possible.

- **Which strategies can be used for creating both written and visual representations? Which strategies apply to one, not both? Which type of representation is more effective?**
- **Draw a conclusion, and write briefly about the differences between written ideas and visual representations.**

Writing in Everyday Life

Narrative Journal Entry

You are Dr. X. J. Morris, a scientist who has spent the last ten years studying the ant populations in Brazil. Yesterday you returned to your hometown high school to be honored at the graduation ceremony. You were surprised, however, at all the changes your hometown has gone through in the last ten years.

Write a journal entry that details your first day returning to your hometown. Give specific details about your experiences, reflections, and observations. Be sure to include a discussion of what has made the experience of returning important.

What strategies did you use to reach a deeper insight about the return to your hometown?

You can find information on writing journal entries on page C14.

Writing for Oral Communication

Oral Personal Narrative

You have been asked to be a guest on a local public television show, "Adventure Time," hosted by world-renowned adventurer Sir Edmund Brackenback. Sir Edmund has asked you to prepare a talk for the television audience that will enlighten them on the most exciting adventure you have taken in your lifetime.

Prepare an oral presentation to give on "Adventure Time." Choose details that will be appropriate for your television audience. Use factual details to provide background information, and bring your speech to life with descriptive and sensory details. Then deliver your speech to your classmates.

What strategies did you use to describe your adventure to the television audience?

You can find information on oral presentations on pages C592–C601.

Assess Your Learning

Many people have taken a very long journey in a car, bus, train, or airplane with a well-liked friend or relative. Such a journey can be an unforgettable and rewarding experience. Wanting to share this insight, you have decided to start a magazine that features only personal narratives about people's journeys to faraway places. The magazine is called *Getting There*.

▶ **Write a personal narrative for the first issue of *Getting There* about a long and enjoyable journey you have taken with a friend or family member.**

▶ **Be sure to introduce your subject in a way that catches your reader's interest and sets the tone for the personal narrative. Try to interweave the narration of events with the expression of your thoughts. Add a memorable conclusion that leaves your reader with the idea or feeling that you wish to convey.**

Before You Write **Consider the following questions:**
What is the *subject?*
What is the *occasion?*
Who is the *audience?*
What is the *purpose?*

After You Write **Evaluate your work using the following criteria:**
- Have you developed the body of your personal narrative from the details you have chosen so you make the point you wish to share?
- Is your content organized logically? Have you included appropriate information to support your ideas? Do your ideas hold together throughout the paper?
- Have you refined your style to suit your occasion, audience, and purpose for the personal narrative?
- Have you demonstrated control over grammatical elements, such as subject-verb agreement, verb forms, and parallelism?
- Have you chosen a title that is true to the tone of your personal narrative and catches the reader's attention?

Write briefly on how well you did. Point out your strengths and areas for improvement.

CHAPTER 7

Using Description: Observation

Seeing is without limit," said Robert Henri, a painter, writer, and teacher who influenced many American artists of the early twentieth century. He was talking about the seeing that an artist does: seeing not only with the eyes but with the mind and the heart.

When we see (or hear, or touch, or taste), we interpret—and when we interpret, we understand. The more closely we observe, the more we comprehend. The artist notices that the model's elbow is bent at a certain angle, and this angle tells him something about the model's personality. The doctor hears a patient's heartbeat and this pulsation tells her something about the patient's health.

Being observant involves not only the eyes (and the ears, the nose, the taste buds, the skin) but also the mind. In this chapter you will exercise your powers of observation.

Reading with a Writer's Eye

In the following piece, noted Native American author N. Scott Momaday describes an old arrow-maker who used to visit his house when Momaday's father was a boy. Think about why the author has chosen to describe this particular individual. Notice that this is not simply a description of what Cheney, the arrow-maker, looks like. It is a description of who he is.

A Vision Beyond Time and Place

N. Scott Momaday

When my father was a boy, an old man used to come to [my grandfather] Mammedaty's house and pay his respects. He was a lean old man in braids and was impressive in his age and bearing. His name was Cheney, and he was an arrowmaker. Every morning, my father tells me, Cheney would paint his wrinkled face, go out, and pray aloud to the rising sun. In my mind I can see that man as if he were there now. I like to watch him as he makes his prayer. I know where he stands and where his voice goes on the rolling grasses and where the sun comes up on the land. There, at dawn, you can feel the silence. It is cold and clear and deep like water. It takes hold of you and will not let you go.

I often think of old man Cheney, and of his daily devotion to the sun. He died before I was born, and I never knew where he came from or what of good and bad entered into his life. But I think I know who he was, essentially, and what his view of the world meant to him and to me. He was a man who saw very deeply into the distance, I believe, one whose vision extended far beyond the physical boundaries of his time and place. He perceived the wonder and meaning of Creation itself. In his mind's eye he could integrate all the realities and illusions of the earth and sky; they became for him profoundly intelligible and whole.

Once, in the first light, I stood where Cheney had stood, next to the house which my grandfather Mammedaty had built on a rise of land near Rainy Mountain Creek, and watched the sun come out of the black horizon of the world. It was an irresistible and awesome emergence, as waters gather to the flood, of weather and of light. I could not have been more sensitive to the cold, nor than to the heat which came upon it. And I could not have *foreseen* the break of day. The shadows on the rolling plains became large and luminous in a moment, impalpable, then faceted, dark and distinct again as they were run through with splinters of light. And the sun itself, when it appeared, was pale and immense, original in the deepest sense of the word. It is no wonder, I thought, that an old man should pray to it. It is no wonder . . . and yet, of course, wonder is the principal part of such a vision. Cheney's prayer was an affirmation of his wonder and regard, a testament to the realization of a quest for vision.

This native vision, this gift of seeing truly, with wonder and delight, into the natural world, is informed by a certain attitude of reverence and self-respect. It is a matter of extrasensory as well as sensory perception, I believe. In addition to the eye, it involves the intelligence, the instinct, and the imagination. It is the perception not only of objects and forms but also of essences and ideals, as in this Chippewa song:

> as my eyes
> search
> the prairie
> I feel the summer
> in the spring

Even as the singer sees into the immediate landscape, he perceives a now and future dimension that is altogether remote, yet nonetheless real and inherent within it, a quality of evanescence and evolution, a state at once of being and of becoming. He beholds what is there; nothing of the scene is lost upon him. In the integrity of his vision he is wholly in possession of himself and of the world around him; he is quintessentially alive.

Most Indian people are able to see in these terms. Their view of the world is peculiarly native and distinct, and it determines who and what they are to a great extent. It is indeed the basis upon which they identify themselves as individuals and as a race. There is something of genetic significance in such a thing, perhaps, an element of being which resides in the blood and which is, after all, the very nucleus of the self. When old man Cheney looked into the sunrise, he saw as far into himself, I suspect, as he saw into the distance. He knew certainly of his existence and of his place in the scheme of things.

In contrast, most of us in this society are afflicted with a kind of cultural nearsightedness. Our eyes, it may be, have been trained too long upon the superficial, and *artificial*, aspects of our environment;

we do not see beyond the buildings and billboards that seem at times to be the monuments of our civilization, and consequently we fail to see into the nature and meaning of our own humanity. Now, more than ever, we might do well to enter upon a vision quest of our own, that is, a quest after vision itself. And in this the Indian stands to lead by his example. For with respect to such things as a sense of heritage, of a vital continuity in terms of origin and of destiny, a profound investment of the mind and spirit in the oral traditions of literature, philosophy, and religion —those things, in short, which constitute his vision of the world— the Indian is perhaps the most culturally secure of all Americans.

As I see him, that old man, he walks very slowly to the place where he will make his prayer, and it is always the same place, a small mound where the grass is sparse and the hard red earth shows through. He limps a little, with age, but when he plants his feet he is tall and straight and hard. The bones are fine and prominent in his face and hands. And his face is painted. There are red and yellow bars under his eyes, neither bright nor sharply defined on the dark, furrowed skin, but soft and organic, the colors of sandstone and of pollen. His long braids are wrapped with blood-red cloth. His eyes are deep and open to the wide world. At sunrise, precisely, they catch fire and close, having seen. The low light descends upon him. And when he lifts his voice, it centers upon the silence and carries there, like the call of a bird.

William Hart. *The Last Gleam, an American Landscape,* 1860.
Fine Art Photographic Library/PNI.

Thinking as a Writer

Describing a Character

- Who is Cheney? Describe him in your own words, not as N. Scott Momaday perceives him but as you perceive him.
- Look again at Momaday's writing. What words has he used that influence your perception of Cheney? List these words.

Inventing a Description of the Narrator

Oral Expression   N. Scott Momaday was not alive at the same time as Cheney, and yet he describes Cheney in detail. Nor does he describe himself, but his presence as the first-person narrator runs throughout "A Vision Beyond Time and Place." Who do you think the narrator is?

- With a partner, collaborate to discuss and interpret your personal visions of this narrator. Together, exchange descriptive details, offer responses, and focus your vision until you have described the narrator so thoroughly that you can almost see him standing right in front of you. What does he look like? How does he stand? What does his voice sound like?

Analyzing Artistic Vision

Viewing   • In "A Vision Beyond Time and Place," Momaday describes the sunrise. Look at the artwork on the preceding page. How would you describe the artist's personal vision of the sunset?

- How is that vision conveyed through the artist's style and technical choices? How is it conveyed through the elements of art, such as line, shape, color, and texture? How is it conveyed through the principles of design, such as pattern, rhythm, unity, emphasis, and variety?

The Power of Description

You have now read an essay rich in sensory detail about a subject for which the author has fond feelings. The descriptions in "A Vision Beyond Time and Place" help us as readers see, hear, and touch the place that is being described. You can find more examples of descriptive writing in personal narratives, informative essays, persuasive essays, poems, short stories, and novels.

Uses of Description

Here are a few ways that writers use description.

- **Novelists and story writers describe characters, settings, and scenes** so that readers can enter a lifelike fictional reality.

- **Poets describe objects and feelings in ways that we often don't expect** so that we will look at the world from a new perspective.

- **Scientists include an "Observations" section in professional papers,** reporting the results of experiments.

- **Local and national activists, in speeches, articles, and books, describe social or environmental problems** so vividly that readers want to take action.

- **Nature writers create word-pictures** of animals, plants, and geological or oceanic formations.

- **Restaurant reviewers describe dishes in precise detail** so that a newspaper or magazine reader can almost taste the cuisine.

Refining Your Skills of Description

"It is harder to see than it is to express. The whole value of art rests in the artist's ability to see well into what is before him," wrote Robert Henri. Notice those little words "well into." Henri did not merely write "see what is before him." Those two extra words imply that artistic vision is not simply a matter of looking at surfaces. It involves seeing beneath the surface too. This is as true for writers as it is for visual artists. For that matter, it is equally true for doctors, business people, teachers, and anyone else who wishes to achieve excellence. Mastery of any skill requires observing thoughtfully and deeply, and practicing the skill often.

Descriptive writing creates a well-developed verbal picture of a person, an object, or a scene by stimulating the reader's senses.

Your Writer's Journal

Momaday describes a person whose approach to life has influenced his own. Think of someone who has been an influence in your life. Write down as many details as you can about this person. If you wish, use freewriting, clustering, or brainstorming techniques to help you recall details. Try to go beneath the surface of the character: describe not only what he or she looks like and what he or she has done, but also describe the deeper impressions this person has made on you. You will be able to consult this entry when searching for subjects for a descriptive essay.

Descriptive Essay Structure

As with a descriptive paragraph (*pages C177–C178*), a descriptive essay has three major sections.

Structure of a Descriptive Essay

- The **introduction** captures the reader's interest, introduces the subject, and often suggests or implies the writer's overall impression of the subject.
- The **body of supporting paragraphs** presents vivid details, especially details that appeal to the five senses.
- The **conclusion** reinforces the overall impression and ties the essay together as a whole.

PRACTICE YOUR SKILLS

● *Analyzing a Descriptive Essay*

Answer the following questions about "A Vision Beyond Time and Place."

1. What passages in the essay make up the introduction?
2. What passages in the essay make up the body of the work?
3. What passages in the essay make up the conclusion?
4. What do you think is the subject of the essay?
5. What overall impression of the subject did you get from the essay?
6. List five or more details that convey the overall impression you received.
7. Find two or more examples in which the writer uses a comparison to enhance or clarify a description.
8. How would you describe the organizational pattern of this essay? What is the logical progression from one paragraph to the next?
9. The physical description of Cheney is more detailed in the conclusion than in other parts of the essay. Why do you think Momaday chose this strategy? What impression does the last paragraph make?

⬤ Specific Details and Sensory Words

When you show a description rather than merely tell it, you use vivid, specific details and words that appeal to the senses. When reading a good description, the reader almost feels as if he or she is actually seeing, hearing, and feeling the things described.

> ### Ⓐ Writing Tip
>
> Use **specific details** and **sensory words** to bring your description to life.

The great American naturalist John Muir, as a young man in 1869, took a job herding sheep in California. The experience allowed him to explore the Sierra Nevada, a mountain range in California. The following is his description of a moment of rest on the trail.

MODEL: Sensory Details

> The sheep are lying down on a bare rocky spot such as they like, chewing the cud in grassy peace. Cooking is going on, appetites growing keener every day. No lowlander can appreciate the mountain appetite, and the facility with which heavy food called "grub" is disposed of. Eating, walking, resting, seem alike delightful, and one feels inclined to shout lustily on rising in the morning. . . . Sleep and digestion as clear as the air. Fine spicy plush boughs for bedding we shall have to–night, and a glorious lullaby from this cascading creek.
>
> —*John Muir*, My First Summer in the Sierra

This passage describes both physical sensations and the personal responses of the narrator. In a single short paragraph, it involves all five senses. Muir uses specific, vivid, accurate, and imaginative word choices to describe his subject. These sensory images are listed in the chart on the next page.

SPECIFIC SENSORY DETAILS	DESCRIPTIONS
SIGHT	sheep lying on bare rock; clear air
SOUND	"lullaby from this cascading creek," sheep that are "chewing the cud"
SMELL	"spicy" aroma of the branches used for bedding
TASTE	heavy "grub"
EXTERNAL FEELING	"plush" feel of the bedding branches
INTERNAL FEELING	keen appetite

Figurative Language

In Muir's description, his sleep is "clear as the air." He describes one sensation—the feeling of being asleep—in terms of another—the clarity of the air. Also, he compares the scent of branches to that of spice.

Writers often use imaginative comparisons to make their description simultaneously clearer and more interesting. Perhaps the most familiar types of **figurative comparison** are **simile,** which uses *like* or *as* to compare two dissimilar things, and **metaphor,** which makes an explicit comparison of two dissimilar things without using *like* or *as*. Comparisons can also be made between similar things. For example, in a passage near the one quoted on the preceding page, Muir compares the falls of Tamarack Creek with the falls of the Yosemite, without using figurative language. He merely reports, "These falls almost rival some of the far-famed Yosemite falls." That statement is a **literal comparison,** since it is a comparison of one waterfall with another.

You can find out more about types of figurative comparisons on pages C366–C367.

Use **figurative language** and **comparisons** to add color and depth to your description.

PRACTICE YOUR SKILLS

● *Generating Similes and Metaphors*

You can make general observations into strong figurative comparisons by using a **chart**. Here, a comparison found in "A Vision Beyond Time and Place" is used as the base for a simile and a metaphor.

Comparison	Simile	Metaphor
"When old man Cheney looked into the sunrise, he saw as far into himself, I suspect, as he saw into the distance" (page C278).	Cheney's self was as vast as the landscape, as bright as the sunrise.	Cheney's self-insight is the rising sun, spreading its light into the darkest corners of the human mind.

Copy and complete the chart, using other comparisons you find in Momaday's essay to create similes and metaphors.

Process of Writing a Description

Writing vivid descriptions will not only help you write a descriptive essay but also aid you in writing vivid stories, poems, persuasive essays, informational essays, and explanatory essays. Description plays a part in all those types of writing. It would be very difficult to inform readers about a part of the world, or to convince them to hold a certain opinion on an issue, or to express your personal experience and feelings, without using your powers of description.

Prewriting — Writing Process

If necessary, your writing process can be adjusted to fit your needs. The one-two-three order of prewriting, drafting, and revising is probably the most common process, but the stages of writing often overlap and intermingle. Sometimes you may want to continue freewriting throughout your writing process. Other times you may choose to set your writing aside for a while before revising so that you can evaluate your draft with fresh eyes.

Choosing a Subject

Cheney the arrowmaker was important to N. Scott Momaday, and the Sierra Nevada was important to John Muir (so important, in fact, that he founded the Sierra Club in 1892 to help preserve that natural region). Both authors cared deeply about their subjects, and this caring helped them observe their subjects very closely and learn from them. This knowledge of and esteem for their subjects come across in their descriptive writing. It is important that you choose a topic that you care about.

The following guidelines can help you choose a subject for your descriptive essay.

Guidelines for Choosing a Subject

- Choose a subject that is important to you—something that really matters. If you are genuinely interested in your subject, your reader will be too.
- Choose a subject you know well and in detail.
- Choose a subject that, by its very nature, offers good opportunities for description: a subject that has sensory impact.

Identifying Your Audience

N. Scott Momaday was writing for a general audience that includes people of all ages. If he were writing a book for small children, he might have taken a different approach; for instance, he probably would have used simpler comparisons and shorter sentences. If he were writing for a newsletter that chronicles Native American spiritual practices and rituals, he might have gone into even more detail about Cheney's daily devotions.

Whom you are writing for influences how you write. It affects the kinds of details you put in and the ones you choose to leave out. It also affects your choice of vocabulary, sentence structure, and language.

The following questions can help you aim your descriptive writing at a specific intended audience.

Questions for Analyzing an Audience

- How much, if anything, does my audience already know about my subject?
- What background information, if any, should I include in order to explain the basics of this subject to this audience and to make my description clear, concise, and meaningful?
- How does my audience feel about my subject? Should I expect to encounter any biases, and if so, how can I organize my essay in order to neutralize or disarm them?
- Do I share the audience's opinion, and if not, how can I address their opinion respectfully while expressing my own?

PRACTICE YOUR SKILLS

● *Identifying Your Audience*

Identify four appropriate audiences for each of the following descriptive subjects. Explain how the way you address these audiences affects your descriptions.

SUBJECT   a polar bear

AUDIENCES   zoologists, hunters, artists, people on a tropical island who have never seen a polar bear

1. a computer

2. a prehistoric cave painting

3. a coral reef

4. a newborn baby

5. the night sky

6. an anthill

7. a telephone

8. a mountain

9. an Internet Website

10. an automobile

Communicate Your Ideas

PREWRITING *Subject and Audience*

Look through your **journal** entries for possible subjects for a descriptive essay. Follow the suggestions for thinking of subjects on the previous page. Use brainstorming, freewriting, clustering, and any other prewriting techniques you have found helpful. Visualize your audience and write answers to the Questions for Analyzing an Audience on the previous page. Save your work for later use.

SAVE YOUR WORK

Developing an Overall Impression

"A Vision Beyond Time and Place" does not tell everything a reader would like to know about Cheney; it probably does not even tell everything the author knows. Selecting, or filtering, details—knowing what to put in and what to leave out—is extremely important when writing descriptions. The goal is to give the reader a clear impression without overwhelming the reader with minor details.

In order to know which details should pass through your filter and which should be barred by it, you should have in mind an overall impression—a feeling about the subject that you want to transmit to your reader. You can then leave in the material that contributes to the desired impression and take out the material that does not.

PRACTICE YOUR SKILLS

● *Determining Overall Impressions*

1. What is the overall impression Momaday is trying to convey in "A Vision Beyond Time and Place"?

2. What phrases or passages work toward establishing this overall impression in the introduction to the essay?

3. What phrases or passages continue expressing this overall impression in the body of the essay?

4. What phrases or passages carry this overall impression into the conclusion of the essay?

5. Did you derive any different or conflicting impressions from the essay? If so, what were those impressions and how did you get them?

Communicate Your Ideas

PREWRITING *Overall Impression*

Review your prewriting notes on a descriptive subject. What overall impression of your subject do you wish to communicate? State that impression briefly, in as little as one word or, at most, one sentence. Save your work.

Home Pages

First impressions can be critical in any relationship. This is why businesses and other organizations put so much effort into creating their home pages. A successful Website will have enough detail that even an impatient Internet surfer will stay at the site. An overall impression that is inviting, positive, and exciting will make visitors want to explore the site and learn more about what it offers.

The illustration gives the impression that the Website is like a classroom, with desks, a window, some bookshelves, as well as a large chalkboard, which is the focal point of the page.

The links give the variety of options available for exploration. The major subject areas are covered along with additional links to related topics.

The books are the universal symbol of learning.

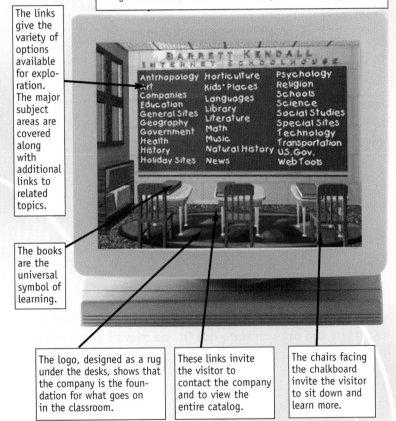

The logo, designed as a rug under the desks, shows that the company is the foundation for what goes on in the classroom.

These links invite the visitor to contact the company and to view the entire catalog.

The chairs facing the chalkboard invite the visitor to sit down and learn more.

Media Activity

On your own, explore three other home pages for businesses, universities, sports teams or leagues, or other organizations. Identify the overall impression that each home page is trying to make and the details that contribute to it.

Developing a Description

With your intended audience and desired overall impression in mind, you can begin to fill out the details of your description. Use one or more of the strategies below.

Strategies for Developing a Description

- List as many sensory details as you can about your subject. If you wish, make a chart like the one on page C285.
- Freewrite to come up with figurative comparisons you can use to help readers understand your description. Use metaphors and similes.
- Find any background information or factual details you might need to describe the subject to your audience. Compile outside information if necessary.
- If you are describing a scene, draw a picture; if you are describing a location, draw a map.
- Filter some details into your writing and filter some out, depending on whether they fit with your desired overall impression.

PRACTICE YOUR SKILLS

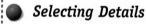

● *Selecting Details*

Look at the following list of details for a description about a hospital. Write the ones that do not fit the overall impression. Explain why you think they do not fit.

OVERALL
IMPRESSION: a busy, welcoming, well-run place where people are healed

DETAILS:
- A quiet stream of visitors enters the lobby carrying flowers and other gifts for patients.

- An ambulance drives up to the emergency entrance. Orderlies await with a gurney bed.

- In a corridor, a surgeon reassuringly explains a procedure to a patient's relatives.

- A security guard grapples with a patient's relative who loudly insists on being allowed into the operating room.

- In the children's wing, young patients draw with crayons.

- A nurse sprints down a long corridor to answer a patient's call.

- In an overcrowded emergency room, sick and injured people watch the hours tick away before being seen by a busy, curt doctor.

- A patient tastes his dinner, makes a sour face, and throws it on the floor.

- An orderly smiles as he brings a tray of food to a bedridden patient.

- An intern runs down the hallway, stumbles into a stretcher bed, and calls out, "Nurse Maxwell, where is that chart?"

- New parents and siblings proudly look at the swaddled, sleeping babies in the nursery.

Communicate Your Ideas

PREWRITING *Development of Details*
Use the strategies on page C292 to help you develop details for your description. You may want to use a **figurative language chart** like the one on page C286. Check your sensory details and figurative comparisons against the overall impression you hope to convey so that you can delete any details that do not belong. Save your work for later use.

Observing

If a spaceship landed on Mars, and a video camera began automatically recording images, those images would be **objective:** not based on an individual's opinions or judgments. If, however, an astronaut picked up the camera, the images would become **subjective:** based on the astronaut's opinion of what was interesting enough to record. Subjectivity is what makes a description interesting because it bears the stamp of a human being.

Examples of both kinds of details in N. Scott Momaday's essay are shown on the following chart. Notice how the objective details supply the most basic information and how subjective details are added to this information in order to make a more vivid description.

OBJECTIVE DETAILS	SUBJECTIVE DETAILS
A man came to a house.	"When my father was a boy, an old man used to come to Mammedaty's house and pay his respects."
Dawn arrives.	". . . at dawn, you can feel the silence. It is cold and clear and deep like water."
A man prays.	"He was a man who saw very deeply into the distance . . ."
A man's eyes open.	"His eyes are deep and open to the wide world."

Momaday's objective details can be verified by any impartial onlooker. The subjective observations and inferences, in contrast, can vary. Unique, subjective details are the ones that say, "This is what the world looks like to me."

THINKING PRACTICE

Make a chart like the one above to record objective and subjective observations of your classroom. Compare your work to that of your classmates.

Organizing a Description

Your organizational plan for a descriptive essay should depend on your aim and on the nature of your details. The following chart shows some possible ways to organize your thoughts.

WRITING AIM	KINDS OF DETAILS	TYPE OF ORDER
to **describe** a person, place, object, or scene	sensory details	spatial *(page C183)*
to **recreate** an event	sensory details events	chronological *(page C169)*
to **explain** a process or show how something works	sensory and factual details, steps in a process, how parts work together	sequential *(pages C151–C152)*
to **persuade**	sensory and factual details, examples, reasons	order of importance *(pages C195–C196)*
to **reflect**	sensory and memory details, factual details, interpretations	developmental *(page C124)*

PRACTICE YOUR SKILLS

● *Organizing Descriptive Details*

Review the list of details describing a hospital on pages C292–C293. Decide on an appropriate organizational pattern for them. Then make a rough outline showing the order in which you would present them. Exclude any details that would work against your desired overall impression or that you think would not fit for other reasons. Then briefly explain the reasons for each of your choices.

PREWRITING *Organization of Details*

 Look over your details for your descriptive essay. Then use the chart on page C295 to help you choose an appropriate order in which to present your supporting points. Make an outline of your descriptive essay. Save your work for later use.

Drafting Writing Process

If you have done extensive prewriting, you are already well on your way toward the creation of a good descriptive essay. You probably have a fairly clear, but flexible, idea of what you want to describe, what light you wish to show it in, and what general shape your description will be. During the drafting stage, let your words flow freely as they follow the path set down in your organizational plan. Keep your audience and intended impression in mind as you follow this path.

When drafting a descriptive essay, also remember the following points.

> **Tips for Drafting a Description**

- Create reader interest with a catchy introduction. Try out several possible beginnings if necessary.
- Suggest your overall impression early on to unify the essay.
- Follow your outline, but be willing to improvise if you come up with new ideas as you go along.
- Use fresh, vivid language. Employ descriptive, sensory words and images.
- Use transitions that are appropriate for the type of order you have chosen *(pages C132, C169, C183, and C195–C196)*.
- Conclude in a way that ties the description together and leaves the reader with a satisfying feeling of closure.

Prewriting Workshop
Drafting Workshop
Revising Workshop
Editing Workshop
Publishing Workshop

Choice of Adjectives

Nouns as Adjectives

In the following examples, the boldfaced words switch from being nouns to being adjectives, depending on whether they are the word that modifies or the word that is modified.

NOUNS	light **cotton;** good **dog;** winter **cold**
ADJECTIVES	**cotton** dress; **dog** food; **cold** winter

Pronouns as Adjectives

Many common pronouns become adjectives when they are used in front of a noun or pronoun that they modify. The following examples show the different kinds and ways they are used.

DEMONSTRATIVE	that, these, this, those
INTERROGATIVE	what, which, whose
INDEFINITE	all, another, any, both, each, either, few, many, more, most, neither, other, several, some

PRONOUN	**This** is yours.
ADJECTIVE	**This** book is yours.
PRONOUN	**Which** is her car?
ADJECTIVE	**Which** car is hers?

Understanding that words can change their parts of speech gives you an additional tool for finding the right word, whether it is an adjective, pronoun, or noun. As you write, ask yourself whether you have used well-chosen adjectives.

DRAFTING *Observations*

 Write a first draft of your description, using the details you developed, your outline, and the tips on page C296. Save your work for later use.

Revising Writing Process

Revising is an opportunity to mold and shape your essay, just as if you were molding and shaping clay. At times it may be hard to tell where drafting ends and revising begins. While dashing off your first draft, you might slow down to alter some wordings, and while revising, you might think of a whole new passage.

> ### Evaluation Checklist for Revising
>
> **Checking Your Introduction**
>
> ✓ Does your introduction grab your reader's attention and make him or her want to keep reading? *(page C283)*
>
> ✓ Have you suggested an overall impression of the subject? *(page C290)*
>
> ✓ Have you set a tone for the essay as a whole, one that is appropriate for your subject and audience? *(pages C287–C288)*
>
> ✓ Are you providing all the background information your audience may need? *(page C292)*
>
> **Checking Your Body Paragraphs**
>
> ✓ Are you supporting the overall impression with enough details? *(page C295)*
>
> ✓ Are you using specific sensory words and details to bring the description to life? *(pages C284–C285)*
>
> ✓ Are you using comparisons and figurative language to enhance details? *(pages C285–C286)*
>
> ✓ Do your paragraphs have clear topics with relevant supporting details that develop the topics?

✓ Do your paragraphs proceed in a logical order, with suitable transitions from paragraph to paragraph? *(page C296)*

Checking Your Conclusion

✓ Have you elaborated on the overall impression you set out to establish?

✓ Have you referred back to an idea in the introduction?

✓ Have you ended with a memorable phrase or image that lingers in the reader's mind?

Checking Your Words and Sentences

✓ Is your word choice specific and lively?

✓ Do your sentences involve the reader through the five senses?

✓ Have you varied your word choice and sentence structure?

Communicate Your Ideas

REVISING *Specific Language*
Conferencing

Return to your descriptive essay and check for content. Is your essay rich in details and sensory words? What senses are you using? Have you written about sound? taste? touch? smell? Continue revising your essay, as necessary. Use the <u>Evaluation Checklist for Revising</u> to help you in your revision. When you feel that your revision meets all the criteria of the checklist, form small groups with your classsmates to share your descriptions. Listen open-mindedly to your peers' comments, and make appropriate changes. Save your work.

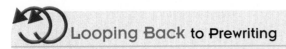

Looping Back to Prewriting

Additional Details

Suppose you are describing a hospital and have planned to include five details, but during the revising stage you think of three more. Can you include them or not? Yes, if they support your desired overall impression. Return to the prewriting skill of using your mental filter to decide whether these new details belong. Then find a place in your organizational plan for the details you decide to keep.

Editing ≡ Writing Process

At this stage, you polish your essay by catching any errors that remain after revising. Even famous writers make errors of spelling, grammar, usage, or mechanics, so don't feel bad if you've made some too.

Communicate Your Ideas

EDITING

 Use the Editing Checklist on page C46 and your Personalized Editing Checklist to edit your description. Also keep an eye out for excessive or stale use of modifiers.

Publishing ≡ Writing Process

Seek out ways to make your description available to readers. Think about who would be interested in your subject, or in good student writing, or in you as an expressive person. Consider the following possible ways to publish a descriptive essay.

- Create a class anthology of descriptive writings, including your own. Supply illustrations.

- Submit your descriptive piece to a magazine that publishes student writing.

- Conduct an oral reading in your classroom.

- Send your descriptive essay as an E-mail or traditional letter to a friend or family member.

- Add your descriptive essay to your personal Web page.

Communicate Your Ideas

PUBLISHING

Prepare a neat final copy of your edited essay. Then use one of the ideas on the preceding page, or any other idea you may have, to share it.

PORTFOLIO

COMPUTER TIP

Before printing your final manuscript, check it in the Print Preview format. This format shows how your manuscript will appear when printed. Use it to check that spacing, margins, headers, and page numbers are as you wish them to be.

Time Out to Reflect

Have your skills observing and describing changed as a result of this chapter? If so, how does your work from this chapter differ from your earlier descriptions? Why do you think one description is better than another? Record your thoughts in the Learning Log section of your **journal**.

▶ Process of Writing Descriptive Essays

Remember that writing is a recursive process. At any point in the process, you may get a new idea that you wish to incorporate into your essay. Be open to these new ideas, even as you write your draft and revise.

PREWRITING
- Use brainstorming, freewriting, clustering, and any other techniques that you enjoy in order to find potential subjects. *(pages C10–C19)*
- Select a subject that is meaningful and interesting to you. *(pages C287–C288)*
- Identify your writing purpose and intended audience. *(page C288)*
- Identify and jot down an overall impression you intend to convey through your description of the subject. *(page C290)*
- Filter details in or out, according to how much they contribute to the overall impression. *(page C292)*
- Make a plan or outline for writing your essay. *(page C295)*

DRAFTING
- Draft an introduction that will grab readers' attention while suggesting your purpose and your desired overall impression. *(page C283)*
- Refer to your plan or outline when drafting the body. *(page C295)*
- Use transitions and other connecting devices to help your ideas and words flow logically from one to the next. *(page C295)*
- Provide a concluding paragraph that strengthens the overall impression and ties the essay together. *(page C296)*
- Add a title.

REVISING
- Use all your senses to engage the reader. *(pages C284–C285)*
- Make sure your word choices are vivid, specific, and fresh. *(page C262)*
- Use peer conferencing to get an outside perspective on your essay and to hear suggestions for improvement. *(page C41)*
- Revise for adequate development, logical progression, coherence, and emphasis. *(pages C226 and C264–C266)*
- Use the <u>Evaluation Checklist for Revising.</u> *(pages C298–C299)*

EDITING
- Use the <u>Editing Checklist</u> and your Personalized Editing Checklist to eliminate errors in grammar, usage, spelling, and mechanics. *(page C46)*

PUBLISHING
- Make a neat final copy of your essay using standard manuscript form. *(pages C49–C52)*
- Search for appropriate ways to reach your intended audience in print, online, or orally. *(pages C48–C49)*

A Writer Writes
Text for a Portrait Gallery

Purpose: **to describe objective and subjective details of faces in a photography exhibit**

Audience: **viewers attending an exhibit**

If you have ever strolled through an art museum or gallery, you have probably noticed the printed cards that hang near the artwork. These cards identify pictures by title, artist, medium, size, and date, and in many cases, they provide descriptive details for the viewer.

Paul Cézanne. *APPLES AND ORANGES,* **ca. 1900.**
Oil on canvas, 29⅛ by 36⅝ inches. Musée d'Orsay, Paris.

These texts may include objective details about aspects of the artwork that many people might overlook. For example, "Heavy brushwork gives a mottled texture to the face," or, "The photographer uses a process called *photogravure,* in which a photographic plate is run through a printing press."

Other portions of the text may contain subjective observations or interpretations, such as "This mottled texture gives a sickly appearance to the face of the fishmonger, who seems ready to chastise the little boy," or, "This rare photographic process produces dreamy images that seem to occupy some other misty time in history."

Prewriting

Find an interesting photograph of a person, either in a magazine or newspaper or in your own photo collection. Prepare a text to accompany the portrait, as if the photograph were hanging on a gallery wall. Look at the portrait and allow it to communicate meaning to you. Jot down notes about the visual details you observe. Use any

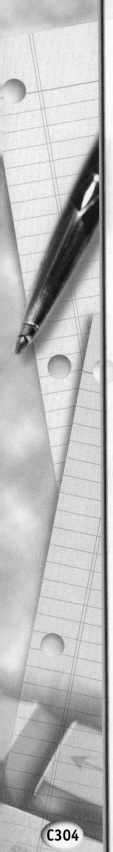

techniques that will help you respond to the portrait, such as clustering or freewriting.

Drafting

Draft a text of one or two concise paragraphs. At the top, provide a title for the work (usually the name of the person portrayed or a description such as, *Young Man Holding Broom*). If you know the name of the photographer and date of the photo, write this information under the title. If you are guessing at this information, use a question mark for the artist and the notation *ca.* (an abbreviation of *circa*, which means "approximately") for the date—for example: "John Johnson? ca. 1999." If you have no idea about the information, write, "Photographer unknown, n.d."

Your text should expand viewers' perceptions. For instance, do not simply say, "This is a portrait of a baby in a stroller." Instead, write, "The shadows of the passers-by point to the sleeping infant, guiding the viewers' eyes to the tiny subject of the portrait."

Revising

Look again, pretending you have never seen the photograph. Does your text provide insights beyond what the viewer could imagine from a casual glance? Does it help the viewer see what you see? Be clear in your writing. Don't use unnecessary words or phrases.

Editing

Use the checklist on page C46 to edit your descriptive text for spelling, grammar, usage, and mechanics.

Publishing

Create a class exhibit by mounting the portraits with descriptive texts on a bulletin board.

Using Description: Observation

Connection Collection

Representing in Different Ways

From Print . . .

. . . to Visuals

Design and draw "before" and "after" pictures of a teddy bear for an advertisement for Red D. Freddy's Teddy Bear Repair Service.

Red D. Freddy's Teddy Bear Repair Service

How is your teddy bear looking these days? Is his fur still furry, or is your bear now bare? Are his eyes sparkling glass beads, or are they dull, black buttons? Are his little legs still stitched tightly, or are they loosely attached and leaking sawdust?

Red D. Freddy's Teddy Bear Repair Service can make any weathered teddy bear look like new!

From Visuals . . .

Doozy Shoe Repair: Old to New!

Before

After

. . . to Print

Doozy Shoe Repair has hired you to create a radio advertisement based on their magazine advertisement above. Prepare a script for the advertisement describing what Doozy can do to old shoes.

- Which strategies can be used for creating both written and visual representations? Which strategies apply to one, not both? Which type of representation is more effective?
- Draw a conclusion and write briefly about the differences between written ideas and visual representations.

Writing in the Workplace
Descriptive E-Mail

It is the first day of spring. You overslept, and to make up for lost time you decide to take a shortcut on your drive to work. Your shortcut takes you through the outskirts of the city, through a part you have never seen before. The landscape is so breathtaking that you feel compelled to slow down and observe every flower, tree, rock, and pond. Luckily you have a laptop computer so that you can E-mail your boss and tell him why you are going to be late.

> Write an E-mail message to your boss describing the beautiful landscape. Paint a vivid picture of the landscape by stimulating the reader's senses. Make your description show rather than tell by using specific details and sensory words. Make your description vivid by using similes and metaphors. Avoid using clichés.

> What strategies did you use to describe your location to your boss?

You can find information on writing E-mail in on pages C736–C738.

Writing in Academic Areas
Descriptive Oral Presentation

You are a scientist who has just returned home after spending the last two years in northern Argentina observing the behavior of ocelots. The principal of the local elementary school invites you to speak to a class of second graders. During your presentation you spend an hour describing your theory of how ocelots communicate. Finally one of the students raises her hand. She wants to know what ocelots look like.

> Prepare an oral presentation describing to an audience of second graders what ocelots look like. Use specific details and sensory words to bring your description to life.

> What strategies did you use to describe the ocelots to the group?

You can find information on oral presentations on pages C592–C601.

Assess Your Learning

Your English teacher, Dr. Swelter, is preparing a book of essays for a publisher in Kotzebue, Alaska, entitled *Sweltering*. She has asked you to write an essay describing the hottest day you can remember. She would like to know important details, such as what it felt like to step outside into the sun, what you did to cool down, and how much you sweated. Each writer who contributes an essay will receive a free ice machine.

▶ **Write a brief essay for Dr. Swelter describing the hottest day that you can remember.**

▶ **Be sure to use vivid descriptions that appeal to the senses and to enhance and clarify your descriptions with similes and metaphors.**

Before You Write **Consider the following questions:**
What is the *subject?*
What is the *occasion?*
Who is the *audience?*
What is the *purpose?*

After You Write **Evaluate your work using the following criteria:**
- Have you identified an audience?
- Have you written in a voice and style that is appropriate to your audience and your purpose?
- Have you used specific details and vivid sensory words to bring your description to life?
- Have you included similes and metaphors to add color to your descriptions?
- Have you revised for specific language?
- Have you produced a legible work that shows accurate spelling and correct use of the conventions of punctuation and capitalization?
- Have you written in complete sentences, varying the types, such as compound and complex sentences, and used appropriately punctuated independent and dependent clauses?

Write briefly on how well you did. Point out your strengths and areas for improvement.

CHAPTER 8

Creative Writing: Stories, Plays, and Poems

Most of the writing that you do throughout your life will have a very practical purpose: to explain or pass along information. From time to time, however, you may want to kick off your shoes, lean back, and let your imagination loose. You may want to create imaginary people who accomplish amazing feats in uncharted places. Your purpose for writing such imaginary stories, poems, or plays will be simply to create a work and to entertain your reader.

Coming up with ideas for successful fiction is not always easy. Sitting and waiting for inspiration may work occasionally, but you cannot count on it. Instead, as Jack London once said, "You have to go after it [inspiration] with a club." This chapter will supply you with the "club" you need to explore your imagination and shape your ideas into a short story, play, or poem.

Reading with a Writer's Eye

In the following excerpt from May Swenson's *Made with Words*, the poet describes the genesis of her poems. Read the excerpt first to acquaint yourself with the poet's thoughts and her writing. Then as you read the excerpt again, think about what makes May Swenson's writing poetic as well as what makes a poem poetic. What can a poem offer that a story or play cannot?

FROM

MADE WITH WORDS

May Swenson

I do not know why I write poems or what makes me write them. Often, when I want *to write a poem,* I cannot—or, if I stubbornly sit down and write something anyway, I discover sooner or later that it is *not* a poem. I suspect this may be because, by concerning oneself with making a poem, one is so conscious of going through the correct motions of doing so, that the spirit of the creation refuses to enter the hard, premeditated clay, and, when it is finished, all the physical parts may have been admirably fashioned, but no passion is there to animate the figure.

It does not breathe.

It is like making a wonderful violin complete in every way, except that one can't get music from it.

On the other hand, it sometimes happens that I am unwilling to write the poem but that it forces itself from me without permission. A poem that happens in this way will often be inexplicable to myself, as to source, content, or significance. Months later, or years later, such a poem may "dawn on me," and I know for the first time what it is I have written. Sometimes I agree with my own observation, and sometimes I think it absurd.

These detached instances of creation seem not to be mystic, trancelike, or extrasensory—I think they are common to most artists in whatever medium.

Thinking as a Writer

Evaluating a Poem

May Swenson asserts that going through the "correct motions" in writing a poem does not necessarily give the poem its "life."

- Select a poem, short story, or play that you particularly like, and note in the Response Log section of your **journal** what gives this literary work its "life."

Creating Images

Viewing May Swenson suggests in her essay that one cannot "force" a poem—it just seems to happen.

- Look at the photograph below. Freewrite words or phrases that create vivid, poetic images based on what you observe.
- Was the image helpful to you as you tried to come up with poetic language? If so, how?

Interpreting a Story, Play, or Poem

Oral Expression May Swenson says that she often does not know what makes her write a poem.

- After your class has divided into groups, choose a story, poem, or scene from a play that you find intriguing, and take turns presenting it to the other groups. Discuss what might have motivated the author—and you might be the author—to write it.

The Power of Creative Writing

Creative writing gives power to the imagination and its infinite possibilities. It can explore the unexplored, and it can enable thoughts and feelings to be expressed in unusual ways. Creative writing's unique window on the world has the ability to change the way we look at and think about things.

Uses of Creative Writing

Here are some examples of the ways that creative writing has had impact in real life.

- **Stories, poems, and plays have been written in response to political turmoil.**

- **A play can be adapted for different contexts,** and thus bring new meaning to the issues in it. For example, a play by Shakespeare could be set in modern times.

- **Poets participate in poetry slams,** providing a different way of experiencing a poem and an opportunity for developing their craft.

- **Role-play is used in conflict-resolution training,** a method to curtail violence in schools, across the country.

Writing a Story

The main purpose of writing a short story is to create a piece of fiction that will entertain. When writing your short story, you will be using both your narrative skills and your descriptive skills to express yourself. In a short story, you tell what happens to a character or characters who try to resolve a conflict or problem. As the narrative unfolds, you describe the characters, places, events, and objects in order to give the reader a clear picture of what happens.

You can learn more about narrative and descriptive writing on pages C174–C175 and C276.

A **short story** is a well-developed fictional account of characters resolving a conflict or problem.

As you read "A Worn Path" by Eudora Welty, think about whether it is an effective story or not and why.

A Worn Path

It was December—a bright frozen day in the early morning. Far out in the country there was an old Negro woman with her head tied in a red rag, coming along a path through the pinewoods. Her name was Phoenix Jackson. She was very old and small and she walked slowly in the dark pine shadows, moving a little from side to side in her steps, with the balanced heaviness and lightness of a pendulum in a grandfather clock. She carried a thin, small cane made from an umbrella, and with this she kept tapping the frozen earth in front of her. This made a grave and persistent noise in the still air, that seemed meditative like the chirping of a solitary little bird.

She wore a dark striped dress reaching down to her shoe tops, and an equally long apron of bleached sugar sacks, with a full pocket: all neat and tidy, but every time she took a step she might have fallen over her shoelaces, which dragged from her unlaced shoes. She looked straight ahead. Her eyes were blue with age. Her skin had a pattern all its own of numberless branching wrinkles and as though a whole little tree stood in the middle of her forehead, but a golden color ran underneath, and the two knobs of her cheeks were illumined by a yellow burning under the dark. Under the red rag her hair came down on her neck in the frailest of ringlets, still black, and with an odor like copper.

Now and then there was a quivering in the thicket. Old Phoenix said, "Out of my way, all you foxes, owls, beetles, jack rabbits, coons and wild animals! . . . Keep out from under these feet, little bob-whites. . . . Keep the big wild hogs out of my path. Don't let none of those come running my direction. I got a long way." Under her small black-freckled hand her cane, limber as a buggy whip, would switch at the brush as if to rouse up any hiding things.

On she went. The woods were deep and still. The sun made the pine needles almost too bright to look at, up where the wind rocked. The cones dropped as light as feathers. Down in the hollow was the mourning dove—it was not too late for him.

The path ran up a hill. "Seem like there is chains about my feet, time I get this far," she said, in the voice of argument old people keep to use with themselves. "Something always take a hold of me on this hill—pleads I should stay."

After she got to the top she turned and gave a full, severe look behind her where she had come. "Up through pines," she said at length. "Now down through oaks."

Her eyes opened their widest, and she started down gently. But before she got to the bottom of the hill a bush caught her dress.

Her fingers were busy and intent, but her skirts were full and long, so that before she could pull them free in one place they were caught in another. It was not possible to allow the dress to tear. "I in the thorny bush," she said. "Thorns, you doing your appointed work. Never want to let folks pass, no sir. Old eyes thought you was a pretty little *green* bush."

Finally, trembling all over, she stood free, and after a moment dared to stoop for her cane.

"Sun so high!" she cried, leaning back and looking, while the thick tears went over her eyes. "The time getting all gone here."

At the foot of this hill was a place where a log was laid across the creek.

"Now comes the trial," said Phoenix.

Putting her right foot out, she mounted the log and shut her eyes. Lifting her skirt, leveling her cane fiercely before her, like a festival figure in some parade, she began to march across. Then she opened her eyes and she was safe on the other side.

"I wasn't as old as I thought," she said.

But she sat down to rest. She spread her skirts on the bank around her and folded her hands over her knees. Up above her was a tree in a pearly cloud of mistletoe. She did not dare to close her eyes, and when a little boy brought her a plate with a slice of marble-cake on it she spoke to him. "That would be acceptable," she said. But when she went to take it there was just her own hand in the air.

So she left that tree, and had to go through a barbed-wire fence. There she had to creep and crawl, spreading her knees and stretching her fingers like a baby trying to climb the steps. But she talked loudly to herself: she could not let her dress be torn now, so late in the day, and she could not pay for having her arm or her leg sawed off if she got caught fast where she was.

At last she was safe through the fence and risen up out in the clearing. Big dead trees, like black men with one arm, were standing in the purple stalks of the withered cotton field. There sat a buzzard.

"Who you watching?"

In the furrow she made her way along.

"Glad this not the season for bulls," she said, looking sideways, "and the good Lord made his snakes to curl up and sleep in the winter. A pleasure I don't see no two-headed snake coming around that tree, where it come once. It took a while to get by him, back in the summer."

She passed through the old cotton and went into a field of dead corn. It whispered and shook and was taller than her head. "Through the maze now," she said, for there was no path.

Then there was something tall, black, and skinny there, moving before her.

At first she took it for a man. It could have been a man

dancing in the field. But she stood still and listened, and it did not make a sound. It was as silent as a ghost.

"Ghost," she said sharply, "who be you the ghost of? For I have heard of nary death close by."

But there was no answer—only the ragged dancing in the wind.

She shut her eyes, reached out her hand, and touched a sleeve. She found a coat and inside that an emptiness, cold as ice.

"You scarecrow," she said. Her face lighted. "I ought to be shut up for good," she said with laughter. "My senses is gone. I too old. I the oldest people I ever know. Dance, old scarecrow," she said, "while I dancing with you."

She kicked her foot over the furrow, and with mouth drawn down, shook her head once or twice in a little strutting way. Some husks blew down and whirled in streamers about her skirts.

Then she went on, parting her way from side to side with the cane, through the whispering field. At last she came to the end, to a wagon track where the silver grass blew between the red ruts. The quail were walking around like pullets, seeming all dainty and unseen.

"Walk pretty," she said. "This the easy place. This the easy going."

She followed the track, swaying through the quiet bare fields, through the little strings of trees silver in their dead leaves, past cabins silver from weather, with the doors and windows boarded shut, all like old women under a spell sitting there. "I walking in their sleep," she said, nodding her head vigorously.

In a ravine she went where a spring was silently flowing through a hollow log. Old Phoenix bent and drank. "Sweetgum makes the water sweet," she said, and drank more. "Nobody know who made this well, for it was here when I was born."

The track crossed a swampy part where the moss hung as white as lace from every limb. "Sleep on, alligators, and blow your bubbles." Then the track went into the road.

Deep, deep the road went down between the high green-colored banks. Overhead the live-oaks met, and it was as dark as a cave.

A black dog with a lolling tongue came up out of the weeds by the ditch. She was meditating, and not ready, and when he came at her she only hit him a little with her cane. Over she went in the ditch, like a little puff of milkweed.

Down there, her senses drifted away. A dream visited her, and she reached her hand up, but nothing reached down and gave her a pull. So she lay there and presently went to talking. "Old woman," she said to herself, "that black dog come up out of the weeds to stall you off, and now there he sitting on his fine tail, smiling at you."

A white man finally came along and found her—a hunter, a young man, with his dog on a chain.

"Well, Granny!" he laughed. "What are you doing there?"

"Lying on my back like a June-bug waiting to be turned over, mister," she said, reaching up her hand.

He lifted her up, gave her a swing in the air, and set her down. "Anything broken, Granny?"

"No sir, them old dead weeds is springy enough," said Phoenix, when she had got her breath. "I thank you for your trouble."

"Where do you live, Granny?" he asked, while the two dogs were growling at each other.

"Away back yonder, sir, behind the ridge. You can't even see it from here."

"On your way home?"

"No sir, I going to town."

"Why, that's too far! That's as far as I walk when I come out myself, and I get something for my trouble." He patted the stuffed bag he carried, and there hung down a little closed claw. It was one of the bob-whites, with its beak hooked bitterly to show it was dead. "Now you go on home, Granny!"

"I bound to go to town, mister," said Phoenix. "The time come around."

He gave her another laugh, filling the whole landscape. "I know you old colored people! Wouldn't miss going to town to see Santa Claus!"

But something held old Phoenix very still. The deep lines in her face went into a fierce and different radiation. Without warning, she had seen with her own eyes a flashing nickel fall out of the man's pocket onto the ground.

"How old are you, Granny?" he was saying.

"There's no telling, mister," she said, "no telling."

Then she gave a little cry and clapped her hands and said, "Git on away from here, dog! Look! Look at that dog!" She laughed as if in admiration. "He ain't scared of nobody. He a big black dog." She whispered, "Sic him!"

"Watch me get rid of that cur," said the man. "Sic him, Pete! Sic him!"

Phoenix heard the dogs fighting, and heard the man running and throwing sticks. She even heard a gunshot. But she was slowly bending forward by that time, further and further forward, the lid stretched down over her eyes, as if she were doing this in her sleep. Her chin was lowered almost to her knees. The yellow palm of her hand came out from the fold of her apron. Her fingers slid down and along the ground under the piece of money with the grace and care they would have in lifting an egg from under a setting hen. Then she slowly straightened up, she stood erect, and the nickel was in her apron pocket. A bird flew by. Her lips moved. "God watching me the whole time. I come to stealing."

The man came back, and his own dog panted about them. "Well, I scared him off that time," he said, and then he laughed and lifted his gun and pointed it at Phoenix.

She stood straight and faced him.

"Doesn't the gun scare you?" he said, still pointing it.

"No, sir, I seen plenty go off closer by, in my day, and for less than what I done," she said, holding utterly still.

He smiled, and shouldered the gun. "Well, Granny," he said, "you must be a hundred years old, and scared of nothing. I'd give you a dime if I had any money with me. But you take my advice and stay home, and nothing will happen to you."

"I bound to go on my way, mister," said Phoenix. She inclined her head in the red rag. Then they went in different directions, but she could hear the gun shooting again and again over the hill.

She walked on. The shadows hung from the oak trees to the road like curtains. Then she smelled wood-smoke, and smelled the river, and she saw a steeple and the cabins on their steep steps. Dozens of little black children whirled around her. There ahead was Natchez shining. Bells were ringing. She walked on.

In the paved city it was Christmas time. There were red and green electric lights strung and crisscrossed everywhere, and all turned on in the daytime. Old Phoenix would have been lost if she had not distrusted her eyesight and depended on her feet to know where to take her.

She paused quietly on the sidewalk where people were passing by. A lady came along in the crowd, carrying an armful of red-, green- and silver-wrapped presents; she gave off perfume like the red roses in hot summer, and Phoenix stopped her.

"Please, missy, will you lace up my shoe?" She held up her foot.

"What do you want, Grandma?"

"See my shoe," said Phoenix. "Do all right for out in the country, but wouldn't look right to go in a big building."

"Stand still then, Grandma," said the lady. She put her packages down on the sidewalk beside her and laced and tied both shoes tightly.

"Can't lace 'em with a cane," said Phoenix. "Thank you, missy. I doesn't mind asking a nice lady to tie up my shoe, when I gets out on the street."

Moving slowly and from side to side, she went into the big building, and into a tower of steps, where she walked up and around and around until her feet knew to stop.

She entered a door, and there she saw nailed up on the wall the document that had been stamped with the gold seal and framed in the gold frame, which matched the dream that was hung up in her head.

"Here I be," she said. There was a fixed and ceremonial stiffness over her body.

"A charity case, I suppose," said an attendant who sat at the desk before her.

But Phoenix only looked above her head. There was sweat on her face, the wrinkles in her skin shone like a bright net.

"Speak up, Grandma," the woman said. "What's your name? We must have your history, you know. Have you been here before? What seems to be the trouble with you?"

Old Phoenix only gave a twitch to her face as if a fly were bothering her.

"Are you deaf?" cried the attendant.

But then the nurse came in.

"Oh, that's just old Aunt Phoenix," she said. "She doesn't come for herself—she has a little grandson. She makes these trips just as regular as clockwork. She lives away back off the Old Natchez Trace." She bent down. "Well, Aunt Phoenix, why don't you just take a seat? We won't keep you standing after your long trip." She pointed.

The old woman sat down, bolt upright in the chair.

"Now, how is the boy?" asked the nurse.

Old Phoenix did not speak.

"I said, how is the boy?"

But Phoenix only waited and stared straight ahead, her face very solemn and withdrawn into rigidity.

"Is his throat any better?" asked the nurse. "Aunt Phoenix, don't you hear me? Is your grandson's throat any better since the last time you came for the medicine?"

With her hands on her knees, the old woman waited, silent, erect and motionless, just as if she were in armor.

"You mustn't take up our time this way, Aunt Phoenix," the nurse said. "Tell us quickly about your grandson, and get it over. He isn't dead, is he?"

At last there came a flicker and then a flame of comprehension across her face, and she spoke.

"My grandson. It was my memory had left me. There I sat and forgot why I made my long trip."

"Forgot?" The nurse frowned. "After you came so far?"

Then Phoenix was like an old woman begging a dignified forgiveness for waking up frightened in the night. "I never did go to school, I was too old at the Surrender,"[1] she said in a soft voice. "I'm an old woman without an education. It was my memory fail me. My little grandson, he is just the same, and I forgot it in the coming."

"Throat never heals, does it?" said the nurse, speaking in a loud, sure voice to old Phoenix. By now she had a card with something written on it, a little list. "Yes. Swallowed lye. When was it?—January—two, three years ago—"

Phoenix spoke unasked now. "No, missy, he not dead, he just the same. Every little while his throat begin to close up again, and he not able to swallow. He not get his breath. He not able to help himself. So the time come around, and I go on another trip for the soothing medicine."

"All right. The doctor said as long as you came to get it, you could have it," said the nurse. "But it's an obstinate case."

"My little grandson, he sit up there in the house all wrapped up, waiting by himself," Phoenix went on. "We is the only two left in the world. He suffer and it don't seem to put him back at all. He got a sweet look. He going to last. He wear a little patch quilt and peep out holding his mouth open like a little bird. I remembers so plain now. I not going to forget him again, no, the whole enduring time. I could tell him from all the others in creation."

"All right." The nurse was trying to hush her now. She brought her a bottle of medicine. "Charity," she said, making a check mark in a book.

Old Phoenix held the bottle close to her eyes, and then carefully put it into her pocket.

"I thank you," she said.

"It's Christmas time, Grandma," said the attendant. "Could I give you a few pennies out of my purse?"

"Five pennies is a nickel," said Phoenix stiffly.

"Here's a nickel," said the attendant.

Phoenix rose carefully and held out her hand. She received the nickel and then fished the other nickel out of her pocket and laid it beside the new one. She stared at her palm closely, with her head on one side.

Then she gave a tap with her cane on the floor.

---

[1] The surrender of General Robert E. Lee (1807-1870) of the Confederacy on April 9, 1865, to General Ulysses S. Grant (1822-1885) of the Union, which ended the Civil War.

"This is what come to me to do," she said. "I going to the store and buy my child a little windmill they sells, made out of paper. He going to find it hard to believe there such a thing in the world. I'll march myself back where he waiting, holding it straight up in this hand."

She lifted her free hand, gave a little nod, turned around, and walked out of the doctor's office. Then her slow step began on the stairs, going down.

Your Writer's Journal

In "A Worn Path," Eudora Welty gives a moving portrayal of an elderly woman whose determination and resolve carry her through an arduous journey on a cold winter day. In your journal, note your responses to the story. Has there been anyone in your life whom Phoenix Jackson brings to mind? Through the week, continue noting thoughts and ideas that the story brings up for you.

At the end of the week, reread your journal entries and think about how you could use your imagination to turn some of your ideas into short stories. Next to each idea, add an imaginative twist to lend creative angles to ordinary situations. You may be able to use these notes later.

Elements of a Short Story

A short story has three major sections: a beginning, a middle, and an end. The beginning identifies the person telling the story, describes the place and time when the story takes place, and gradually introduces the major and minor characters. In addition, the writer creates a problem or obstacle that the main character must overcome. The middle of the story relates a chain of events that results as the characters try to resolve the problem. The ending of the story usually explains how everything turns out.

Plot and the Central Conflict

The **plot** of a short story is like a play-by-play account of a sporting event. It tells who does what as the story unfolds. It also tells how the characters behave in the face of a **conflict**—the struggle or major problem—around which the story is built. In a sporting event, the conflict is between two opponents, and it usually boils down to the simple question of who will win. In a short story, the conflict is rarely so simple. It usually grows between the main character or a natural force, like a storm or a drought. On the other hand, the conflict could center around a force within the main character—such as a driving, unmet desire or a bitter struggle with his or her conscience. This central conflict drives the plot, from which all the action and dialogue of the story flow. The plot, therefore, usually begins with an event that triggers the conflict. Once the central conflict is revealed, the plot moves briskly on to the greatest part of the conflict—the climax. Finally the plot resolves the conflict or presents another outcome.

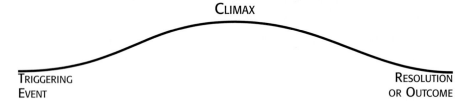

CLIMAX

TRIGGERING
EVENT

RESOLUTION
OR OUTCOME

Characters

Believable characters struggling through the twists of a plot are the hallmarks of an effective short story. In most stories the spotlight is on one character who is trying to resolve the conflict. Other characters either help or hinder the main character. Well-written short stories present believable characters so that readers can identify with them and become involved in the story.

To create lifelike, memorable characters, base your characters on yourself or people you know but give each one a separate, unique identity. Short-story writer Shirley Jackson cautions, " . . . I want to emphasize that people in stories are called characters because that is what they are. They are not real people." The challenge for you is to make the characters as believable as possible. You must create lifelike qualities for the characters through narration, description, and dialogue.

Setting

The setting of a story is the environment in which the action takes place but it is more than a simple location. It includes the time and the historical or cultural context in which the story occurs. The setting also establishes a mood or atmosphere that reflects the events of the story. **Mood** is the overall feeling that the story conveys.

Writers rely on vivid sensory details to establish their setting and often to reflect the characters' thoughts and feelings. For example, a brooding, angry character may spend a lot of time sitting in a dark room listening to the wailing winds and thunder of a violent storm and contemplating an unpleasant encounter with an enemy. As the story progresses, some elements of the setting may change to match the changes in action and in the characters' feelings. A frightening story, for example, may begin at the stroke of midnight on a rainy night. By the end of the story—if it has a happy ending—dawn might be breaking on a clear new day.

Narrator

The narrator is the storyteller—the "voice" that tells what happens. The reader follows the events of the story through the eyes or **point of view** of that narrator. The following chart represents the different points of view a narrator may assume to tell a story.

POINT OF VIEW	NARRATOR'S ROLE IN THE STORY
FIRST-PERSON	Observes or participates in the story's action; uses *I, we,* and other first-person pronouns.
EXAMPLE	Before breaking the wishbone, **I** phrased **my** wish carefully in my mind, for never before had a wish been so important to **me.**
THIRD-PERSON OBJECTIVE	Observes but does not participate in the story's action; relates the words and actions of the characters but not their thoughts and feelings; uses *he, she, him, her, his, hers, they, them, their,* and *theirs.*

EXAMPLE	Before breaking the wishbone, **the contenders** were silent for a moment, **their** brows knit.
THIRD-PERSON OMNISCIENT ("ALL-KNOWING")	Observes but does not participate in the story's action; relates the thoughts and feelings as well as the words and actions of all the characters.
EXAMPLE	Before breaking the wishbone, **Alexis** repeated her wish silently to **herself,** while her sister **Connie, with equal fervor, hoped** that **her sister's wish** would come true.

Each point of view has certain advantages. The first-person narrator not only narrates as a participant in the story but also responds to the other characters. With a first-person narrator, the reader experiences all of the story through that narrator's observations, thoughts, and feelings. The third-person objective narrator can relate two events happening simultaneously in two different places. This technique permits the reader to see the connections between those events. The third-person omniscient narrator can relate not only simultaneous events but also all the characters' inner thoughts and outer actions at the same time. This technique gives the reader a broader opportunity to identify with all the characters and see the connections among the events of the story.

Theme

Most stories have a **theme,** or main idea, of some kind. For instance, a story may be about hope or despair, love or hate, courage or fear, peace or war, life or death. Its outcome may also imply some lesson or moral or make some meaningful observation or conclusion about life. Still other stories present a twist or surprise that is a lesson or moral in itself.

PRACTICE YOUR SKILLS

● *Understanding Elements of a Short Story*

Write answers to the following questions about *A Worn Path* on pages C312–C321.

1. What event triggers the action of the story?

2. What is the central conflict and what event brings about that conflict?

3. At what point does the story reach its climax?

4. How does the boy's grandmother resolve her problem?

5. What is the outcome of the story? Does the outcome suggest a theme, or message, about life? If so, what is it?

6. Who are the characters in the story?

7. Who is the main character?

8. What is the setting of the story? Describe it in a few sentences.

9. How do you think the setting contributes to the overall effect of the story?

10. What point of view does the writer use?

Prewriting Writing Process

Writers approach the task of beginning a short story in different ways. For many the process begins with an urge to write. William Faulkner followed a different process. "With me, a story usually begins with a single idea or memory or mental picture. The writing of the story is simply a matter of working up to that moment, to explain why it happened or what caused it to follow." The following prewriting strategies will help you discover the best approach for getting your story started.

Developing Story Ideas

"What will my story be about?" Many people waste too much time worrying about subjects for their stories. Famous short story writer Shirley Jackson offers the following explanation.

> People are always asking me—and every other writer I know—where story ideas come from. Where *do* you get your ideas, they ask; how do you ever manage to think them up? It's certainly the hardest question in the world to answer, since stories originate in everyday happenings and emotions, and any writer who tried to answer such a question would find himself telling over, in some detail, the story of his life. Fiction uses so many small items, so many little gestures and remembered incidents and unforgettable faces, that trying to isolate any one inspiration is incredibly difficult, but basically, of course, the genesis of any fictional work has to be human experience. . . . A bald description of an incident is hardly fiction, but the same incident, carefully taken apart, examined as to emotional and balanced structure, and then as carefully reassembled in the most effective form, slanted and polished and weighed, may very well be a short story.
>
> —*Shirley Jackson,* Experience and Fiction

Short stories, then, may be based on real-life happenings or forged in a writer's imagination. Whatever the source, a good story will hold a reader in suspense until the problem or conflict that the characters face is finally resolved. The following strategies provide possible sources for story ideas and may even directly stimulate a few ideas.

Strategies for Developing Story Ideas

- Review your **journal** writings for conflicts or turning points in your life that may be worth developing into a story.
- Whenever you think of a story idea, write it in your **journal.**

- If possible, form a small discussion group to generate story ideas.
- Scan newspaper headlines and news items for an event you could build into a fictional story. Some pieces of information, for example, might suggest a mystery, a romance, an adventure, or a comic tale.
- Observe people in your daily life. Sometimes even small events or snatches of conversation, such as an incident that you noticed in a shopping mall or a conversation you overheard in a pizza parlor, will suggest a conflict around which you can build a plot.

Whatever approach you take, concentrate on finding an event that triggers a conflict for you or for someone else. Do not discard events that seem ordinary or humdrum. Well told, stories about the simple pains or pleasures of daily life can be effective and moving.

Communicate Your Ideas

PREWRITING *Developing Story Ideas*

Reread the above <u>Strategies for Developing Story Ideas</u> and apply them to developing your own ideas for a story. Start by reading over all the ideas that you have written in your **journal.** You may also want to scan newspapers for story ideas or use ordinary situations as the basis for imagining unexpected happenings.

Once you have used the above strategies to generate several ideas, think about each one to see if any can trigger a conflict. After you evaluate each idea and its potential, select the one you like best—the one you think you can use to create the most imaginative story. Then save your work in your writing folder for later use.

SAVE YOUR WORK

Developing a Plot

After you have settled on an event related to a conflict, you can begin building the plot. Because a plot usually unfolds from the event that triggers the conflict to the event that resolves the conflict, you need to arrange the details of your plot so that they unfold *naturally* as your tale progresses. The following chart shows several strategies for developing the events of a plot—along with a few examples.

Strategies for Unfolding a Plot

1. Introduce the event or circumstance that triggers the action.

FROM WITHIN A CHARACTER	• a decision to try something new
	• an uncomfortable or painful feeling
FROM THE OUTSIDE WORLD	• an accident
	• a meeting with a stranger

2. Develop details that describe the nature of the conflict.

CONFLICT WITH SELF	• a struggle with conscience or desires
	• a struggle against old ways
CONFLICT WITH OTHERS	• friends, family members
	• authority figures, enemies, strangers
CONFLICT WITH NATURE	• storms and floods
	• fire, pollution, or famine

3. Develop details about the obstacles the characters will struggle against or overcome to resolve the conflict.

WITHIN A CHARACTER	• fears or habits of the past
	• illness
IN THE OUTSIDE WORLD	• misfortunes
	• challenges from nature

4. Develop details concerned with how the main character will overcome obstacles.

BY THE CHARACTER	• strength of character or growth
	• perseverance and new skills
THROUGH OUTSIDE EVENTS	• luck or change of circumstances
	• others' decisions

5. Develop details concerned with the resolution, or solution to the problem, and the outcome.

OVERCOMING OBSTACLES	• new wisdom
	• success, feeling at peace
FAILING TO OVERCOME	• acceptance of shortcomings
	• decision to try again

PRACTICE YOUR SKILLS

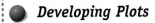 **Developing Plots**

Each of the following sentences can serve as an event that triggers the action of a story. After the appropriate number, briefly describe a possible plot for each triggering event. Use the chart on pages C328–C329.

1. Amy is stranded on her way home from school when a winter storm closes all roads and knocks out power lines.

2. A teenager walking the dog hears a human voice coming from it.

3. Both Mike and his best friend Mario want the lead in the play.

4. Sarah and Ramona vow that nothing will ever come between them, and then Jason moves to town.

5. Dennis discovers Alicia won the scholarship he hoped was his.

Communicate Your Ideas

PREWRITING *Plot*

Review your prewriting work from the previous activity on developing a story idea. Refer to <u>Strategies for Unfolding a Plot</u> on pages C328–C329 and then sketch out the steps in the development of your plot. Let your imagination range freely to create possibilities. When you are satisfied that you have some good ideas for your plot, save your notes in your writing folder for later use.

Sketching Characters

In her autobiography, famous mystery writer Agatha Christie explained that she often used real people she saw on the bus as the basis for many of her characters. She knew that to be believable, characters in a story must ring true to a reader. In other words they must look and walk and talk like real people.

To create such imaginary "real" people you should always visualize your characters in your mind—or on paper—until you have added enough details to turn the characters into flesh and blood. For example, you would want to consider such aspects as a character's name, age, physical appearance, voice, mannerisms, background, personality traits, and eccentricities. The following description shows how the specific details of physical features contribute to a characterization.

MODEL: Characterization

> Elisa Allen, working in her flower garden, looked down across the yard. . . . She was thirty-five. Her face was lean and strong and her eyes were as clear as water. Her figure looked blocked and heavy in her gardening costume, a man's black hat pulled down over her eyes, clod-hopper shoes, a figured print dress almost completely covered by a big corduroy apron with four big pockets and the knife she worked with. She wore heavy leather gloves to protect her hands while she worked.
>
> —*John Steinbeck, "The Chrysanthemums"*

The following model will help you create a preliminary sketch of your characters so that they will be realistic and believable to your reader.

MODEL: Character Sketch

Name:
Age:
Role in story:

Physical appearance:
Most important personality traits:
Mannerisms:
Background information:
Strengths:
Weaknesses:

PRACTICE YOUR SKILLS

● *Sketching Characters*

Complete the Character Sketch chart for each of the following imaginary characters. Save your work for possible stories.

1. a practical joker

2. a banker who always behaves very properly

3. an attractive but self-centered teenage girl or boy

Communicate Your Ideas

PREWRITING *Character Sketch*

Review your prewriting notes from previous activities for developing your short-story idea. Using the model above, create a preliminary character sketch for each of the characters that will appear in your story. Then, referring to the chart on page C333, elaborate on each of your main characters. Save your character sketches to use when drafting your story.

Creating a Setting

When planning the setting of your story, remember that the most effective settings are those that establish a mood that mirrors the characters' feelings and the action.

Elaborating

One way to reveal character is through precise description. To help your readers see characters exactly as you see them, you may need to call on the skill of elaborating. When you **elaborate** on a character, you work out the details of that character.

To assist in the elaborating of your characters, construct a chart like the one below. Visualize an aspect of the character for each heading on the chart. Then list as many details as you can to reveal your character's age, physical traits, and mannerisms. When you write your story, you can select the details from the chart that contribute to the impression you want to create.

CHARACTER ELABORATION CHART

Character	teenager Mark Stevens
Appearance (face, age, eyes, hair, face, physical build)	sixteen, lean but muscular, strong features, brilliant blue eyes, gleaming white teeth; long, blond, curly hair; unusually long arms with huge hands
Clothing	baseball cap, basketball shoes, cutoff jeans, baggy T-shirt with neon colors
Mannerisms, actions (ways of walking, talking, voice)	chews gum, squints, and looks at training track; shoulders hunched, hands jammed in pockets; speaks in rapid half-sentences with low voice
Possessions	camera around neck

THINKING PRACTICE

Select a character from your **journal** or originate a new one and then elaborate about him or her with as many details as possible. Construct a chart like the one above to help you visualize the character more completely.

Match the **setting** of your story to the
characters' feelings and the action.

Notice the mood of fear that the author develops in his story
about the taboos and beliefs of people in a primitive hunting society.

MODEL: Details of Mood in a Setting

My father is a priest; I am the son of a priest. I have been
in the Dead Places near us, with my father—at first, I was
afraid. When my father went into the house to search for the
metal, I stood by the door and my heart felt small and weak.
It was a dead man's house; a spirit house. It did not have the
smell of man, though there were old bones in a corner. But it
is not fitting that a priest's son should show fear. I looked at
the bones in the shadow and kept my voice still.

—*Stephen Vincent Benét,* "By the Waters of Babylon."

Also strive for as much realistic detail in your setting as
possible to help the action unfold believably. As English writer
Ford Madox Ford said, "Unless I know what sort of doorknob his
fingers closed on, how shall I—satisfactorily to myself—get my
character out-of-doors?"

MODEL: Realistic Details in a Setting

It was a narrow, little shop, not very well lit, and the
doorbell pinged again with a plaintive note as we closed it
behind us. For a moment or so we were alone and could
glance about us. There was a tiger in *papier-mâché* on the
glass case that covered the low counter—a grave, kind-eyed
tiger that waggled his head in a methodical manner. There
were several crystal spheres, a china hand holding magic
cards, a stock of magic fishbowls in various sizes, and an
immodest magic bat that shamelessly displayed its springs.

On the floor were magic mirrors; one to draw you out long and thin, one to swell your head and vanish your legs, and one to make you short and fat like a draught; and while we were laughing at these the shopman, as I suppose, came in.

—H. G. Wells, "The Magic Shop"

PRACTICE YOUR SKILLS

● *Choosing Settings*

Write the letter of the setting that is best suited to each character and explain your choice.

Characters

1. a shy boy who is afraid to come out of his shell

2. a girl who tests her strength against nature

3. a boy who does not feel a sense of belonging in his family

4. a girl who dreams of going places and making it big in show business

5. a miser who values riches above friendship

Settings

a. a room added onto the main house

b. a room with closed windows and doors

c. a small town on a river near a bridge leading to the big city

d. a room decorated in black and gold

e. the mountains of Montana

● *Sketching Settings*

Visualize interesting and appropriate settings for three of the following imaginary situations. Then write a brief sketch of each setting that reflects the situation or relates to the character's mood.

1. While waiting for the coach to call her into the game, Lottie felt panic rising in her throat.

2. Rob's wondering eyes saw the great expanse of ocean and horizon ahead.

3. Pushing her pen tensely against the examination paper, Marge struggled to concentrate.

4. Jeff, his heart pounding, approached Manuela for a dance.

5. Mrs. Lacongo frowned as she entered the subway station.

Communicate Your Ideas

PREWRITING *Settings*

Review your prewriting work on your short-story idea. Then create an appropriate setting for your characters and the events you have developed for your plot. Remember to establish a mood. Freewrite, brainstorm, or cluster to include as many details as possible. Then save your notes in your writing folder to refer to later when you draft your story.

Choosing a Point of View

The power you have as a writer is both fun and challenging. You can make anything happen that you want, such as changing the characters, the mood, and the setting. You also have complete control over the point of view you choose for your story. As you learned on pages C323-C324, you can choose one of three points of view when telling your stories: first person, third person objective, or third person omniscient. Even if the story is about an experience you have had, for example, you could tell it from the third person objective or omniscient point of view, referring to yourself as *he* or *she*. In a similar way, if your story is actually about your best friend, you could tell it in the first person, referring to the main character as *I*. Choose whatever point of view is most suitable for your story, but be sure to use it consistently throughout the story, without switching back and forth.

If you choose a point of view that does not allow you to enter the minds of all your characters, remember that a character's actions and dialogue can reveal what he or she is feeling.

Action	Anna gripped the wood armrests tightly as she awaited the news. (Anna's actions show that she feels nervous.)
Dialogue	"I won!" Loren shouted triumphantly as he approached his mother in the kitchen. (The dialogue shows that Loren feels proud and happy.)

PRACTICE YOUR SKILLS

● *Revealing Feeling Through Actions*

Imagine that you have just come upon a friend of yours sitting under a tree. Write five sentences that describe the person's actions. Choose actions that reveal the following feelings.

Example	surprise
Possible Answer	My friend's huge eyes became still larger when he noticed me.

1. surprise   **4.** excitement

2. discouragement   **5.** anger

3. fear

● *Choosing Point of View*

While riding her new bicycle, Rhoda collides with Mrs. Schneider, who is carrying a large bag of groceries. Choose two of the following points of view to relate the incident, writing a paragraph for each.

1. first person as Rhoda

2. first person as Mrs. Schneider

3. third person objective as a witness

PREWRITING *Point of View*

Review all your prewriting notes for the story that you have been developing. Imagine how your story would read if it were told from the point of view of your main character, or from the third-person objective or omniscient point of view. Review the chart on pages C323-C324 and then choose the most appropriate point of view for your story. Make a note of your choice and save it.

Ordering Events

When you sketched out the events in the unfolding of your plot, you probably placed them in chronological order, the order in which they happen. If you plan to tell your story in chronological order, look over your list of events to make sure each happening progresses logically from the one before it. Also consider all the events you wish to include in your story and add any new events to your list, in proper sequence. Your final list might look like the one below.

MODEL: Events in Chronological Order

- At the breakfast table, Anthony's father teases him about the bandage on his face and says he's too young to shave.
- Anthony leaves the table and slams the door on his way out.
- Hurrying angrily to school, Anthony crosses the street without noticing an approaching car.
- The car slams on its brakes but knocks Anthony down.
- Police come and take Anthony to the hospital, where his broken arm is put in a cast.
- Police call Anthony's father at work and report the accident.
- Anthony's father heads straight for the hospital with a gift.
- Anthony's father gives him the gift: an electric razor.

Understanding Flashback Sometimes when drafting your story, you may want a variation from chronological order. You may, for example, begin at the end of the story and use flashbacks to show the events leading up to your ending. A **flashback** is a memory sequence that interrupts the chronological order of events for the purpose of telling what happened at some time in the past. You could also begin your story at the moment of highest tension, use flashbacks to tell what came before that moment, and then continue in chronological order—on through the resolution and outcome.

PRACTICE YOUR SKILLS

● *Using Flashbacks*

Reorder the events of the story about Anthony on page C337 by beginning with either the final detail or a detail that shows the moment of highest tension. Then tell the rest of the story with flashbacks or a combination of flashbacks and chronological order.

Communicate Your Ideas

PREWRITING *Order of Events*

Make a complete list of all the events you want to include in your story. If you decide to present your story in strict chronological order, be sure your details are arranged accordingly. If you decide to use flashbacks, make a list showing where you will start in the story and in what order you will present the other events. Save your work in your writing folder.

Drafting ← Writing Process

Most writers have their own special strategy and style of drafting. Some, for example, use their prewriting work rigorously, referring often to their list of organized details as a guide. Others find that they have a clear enough idea of their story to sit down and write it from start to finish without once looking back at their notes. Experiment until you find a drafting style that is effective for you.

Drafting the Beginning

As you draft your story, keep your audience and purpose in mind. While your basic writing purpose is to create and be inventive, you may have another more specific goal. For example, you may want to have your audience strongly identify with a particular character. On the other hand, your goal may be to influence your reader by providing an insight about life. To reach your audience successfully, use the following strategies to begin your story.

 Strategies for Beginning a Story

- Be inventive and capture the reader's attention by using sensory details to describe the setting and to create a mood.

- Establish the narrator's point of view and use it consistently.

- Use vivid language and interesting details to introduce the characters and the central conflict.

- Provide any background information about the time and place of the story that the reader may need.

- If you are using strict chronological order, include the triggering event that starts the story in motion. If you are using flashbacks, however, begin with an incident in the story that reflects the central conflict.

Drafting the Middle

A good beginning will help you write the middle of your story as well. Once the plot is set in motion in well-written stories, the events seem to unfold somewhat naturally. As you draft the middle of your story, present those events as smoothly as possible and make your characters live and breathe. The following strategies will help you draft the middle of your story.

Connecting the Events in the Story   When you draft the middle of your story, you simply pick up where you left off and show how each event follows from the triggering event at the beginning of your story. Keep in mind that the story's events should not just follow each other but should build on each other, with each event adding to the tension until the plot reaches its climax. Use transitions to show the passage of time between events as well as the buildup of tension as your story approaches its climax. The transitions will also keep your story flowing smoothly from one event to another.

For a list of common transitions used in chronological order, turn to page C169.

Using Flashbacks   If you are using flashbacks, how do you accomplish the same smooth-flowing results? In movies or on television, directors sometimes indicate that a flashback is about to start by playing dreamlike music and making the screen look dim, fuzzy, and wavy. When you write, you have several options. You can simply skip a line or use a row of stars or asterisks to indicate a break in the chronology.

> Anthony was still thinking about his father's teasing as he charged across the street. He didn't even see the car at first—he just heard a heart-stopping screech of brakes. Without thinking, he was in the middle of the street himself, feeling the crunch of the car's fender.
>
> * * *
>
> Anthony had come down to breakfast—feeling good and ready and eager for the day ahead, which he knew included a chance to sit next to Julie at lunch. . . .

With an appropriate point of view, you can make the connections even smoother by using narration to introduce the flashback so that the events will be smoothly connected.

> Anthony was still thinking about his father's teasing as he charged across the street. He didn't even see the car at first—he just heard a heart-stopping screech of brakes. Without thinking, he was in the middle of the street himself, feeling the crunch of the car's fender. For a while all was a blur of pain. Little by little, Anthony began to remember how the day had begun.
>
> He had come down to breakfast—feeling good and ready and eager for the day ahead, which he knew included a chance to sit next to Julie at lunch. . . .

Notice that in both cases the verb tense changes from simple past to past perfect when the flashback begins. This change in tense indicates to the reader that the events in the flashback have occurred earlier.

Using Dialogue   Besides using narration to tell your story, you can also use dialogue to show how the plot unfolds. Using natural-sounding dialogue is also one of the best ways to bring your characters to life and to let your reader "hear" as well as visualize the people in your story. As you read the following two versions of an event, notice how much livelier the one with the dialogue is.

NARRATIVE He shyly handed her a tiny white package tied with a narrow gold ribbon, explaining that he was sorry he had missed her birthday and hoped she liked it. She beamed with pleasure.

DIALOGUE "Here," he said shyly as he thrust the slim white package at her. "I'm real sorry I didn't come around last night for your birthday, but I had to work."

"Oh Josh," she breathed. "What's this?"

"Not much, actually," he gulped. "Hope you like it."

"Cool, it's just the charm I wanted! How could you have known?"

PRACTICE YOUR SKILLS

● **Writing Dialogue**

After imagining each of the following situations, select one and write a dialogue of about fifteen lines between the characters.

1. a confrontation between a sales clerk and a dissatisfied customer

2. an offer to assist a young child across a busy intersection

3. a discussion of a major news story

4. a dinner-table discussion about curfews

5. an argument about a play on the sports field

Drafting the Ending

The mystery writer Mickey Spillane wrote, "I write the ending first. Nobody reads a book to get to the middle." The ending of a story is, after all, the payoff. Especially in a mystery story, it is where the conflicts are resolved and everything is explained. Keep in mind, though, that the ending of a short story does not have to be upbeat, with all the characters living happily ever after. In any kind of story, however, the ending must bring the events to a fitting close. To write an effective ending to your short story, you may want to use the following strategies.

Strategies for Ending a Story

- Resolve the conflict and complete the action of the story.
- If the conflict is not to be resolved, present an outcome that is logical and believable.
- Continue to use dialogue, action, or description to show, not just tell, what happens.
- Match the mood of the story.
- Leave the reader feeling satisfied.

Writing Tip

End your short story by showing how the **conflict** is resolved and by telling the final outcome of events. Remember to leave a strong emotional impression on your readers.

Drafting a Title   Once you are satisfied with your story, read it aloud and think of a title that will enliven your story and capture your reader's attention. A successful title will simultaneously invite and challenge the reader to set aside some time to read your story.

Communicate Your Ideas

DRAFTING

Use the strategies and skills above to draft your story. Save your work in your writing folder for revising and editing later.

When you revise a short story, spend some of your time checking for believability. Are your characters walking, talking people with whom your readers can identify? Does your setting seem real? Even extremely imaginative settings like another planet should have a ring of authenticity to them. As you revise, look for any missing details needed to make your story ring true to another reader.

COMPUTER TIP

If you are revising your draft on a computer, you can use the Save As function to save more than one version of your composition. Save your original draft with its own title. Then, after you have revised your composition, go to file and select Save As and give the revised version a new name. If you find that some of the revisions you have made don't work as well as your original material, you still have a complete copy of your original draft.

Sharpening Characterizations

When revising, take a good, hard look at each and every one of your characters. Does each convey a distinct, memorable personality? Have you fallen into the trap of presenting a "type" instead of a real person (a kindly grandmother, for example, rather than a living, breathing elderly person with unique characteristics)? Focus on sharpening your characterizations to make your story more memorable and believable. The following strategies will help you create lifelike characters.

> ### Strategies for Revealing Character
> - Avoid stereotypes.
> - Use dialogue with natural-sounding speech that reflects the personality of your characters.
> - Use descriptions rich in sensory details to help readers see your characters.

- Use narration to record significant actions—such as little gestures, particular turns of phrase, and automatic reactions of surprise, fear, or anger.
- With a third-person omniscient narrator, use narration to record thoughts and feelings.

PRACTICE YOUR SKILLS

● *Matching Dialogue to Character*

The statements below all express the same general meaning. Each one, however, creates a different image and would therefore be suitable to reveal a different kind of character. Choose one statement. Then, avoiding stereotypes, write a one-paragraph description of the character that the statement leads you to visualize. Save your work.

1. "Yup," I says again, "that was one fine meal you rustled up."

2. "Wow! That was like really dee-lish!"

3. "That was a wonderful dinner indeed."

4. "I am beholden to you for a fine meal."

5. "Please! I'd love the recipes. What a meal!"

● *Revealing Character*

Write one paragraph telling what goes on in Brenda's mind when she learns her family must move out of state by the end of the month. Use a third person omniscient narrator. The first sentence is provided for you.

Brenda grew steadily more angry at being wrenched from her friends, her new job, and—worst of all—her lifelong confidant, cousin Burt.

Tightening the Descriptions

When some people are learning how to write fiction, they tend to overwrite, or to use **purple prose.** In other words they use unnecessary or redundant words to describe a character or a setting. One function of revising, therefore, is to look for any purple prose and reduce it to clear, uncluttered description. Following is an example of how purple prose can call so much attention to itself that it distracts the reader from becoming involved with the character. Reread John Steinbeck's description of his character Elisa Allen on page C330. Contrast that effective description with the purple prose below and then consider the effects of the purple prose if it had appeared in Steinbeck's story.

> Elisa Allen worked in her flower garden. And what a garden it was! Fragrant roses blushed hot pink in the glimmering sunshine and sent their roots ever deeper and deeper into the fertile, life-giving mud beneath the surface. Lambent lilies arched their slender backs and reached toward the sunshine, drawn as if to a gigantic burning magnet in the cloudless, endless, brilliant blue sky. . . .

As you can see, purple-prose Elisa becomes lost as the focus in this rambling, self-conscious description. Although elaborating is useful to paint sharp, accurate pictures of your characters, limitless descriptive details that serve no purpose will only cloud the picture. Tighten your descriptions so that you say as much as possible in a few well-chosen words.

> In her flower garden, Elisa Allen poked the fertile soil around the hot-pink roses, yanked the weeds, and then stood, staring at the tall, brilliant lilies.

PRACTICE YOUR SKILLS

● *Tightening Descriptions*

Write a two-paragraph passage of purple prose about the character you described previously. Have fun. Try to make your description as overdone and rambling as possible. Then trim it back to an effective three- or four-sentence description. Select a partner and exchange papers. Revise your partner's description so that the writing is even tighter. Discuss your changes.

Using an Evaluation Checklist for Revising

After sharpening your characterizations and tightening your descriptions, you are ready to check over your whole story and look for ways to make it even better. The following checklist will help you revise your short stories.

 Evaluation Checklist for Revising

✓ Does the beginning of your story give the setting, capture attention, introduce the characters, and include the triggering event? *(page C321)*

✓ Does the middle present events directly related to the central conflict? Are the events arranged in strict chronological order, or a variation with flashbacks? Are they connected by smooth transitions? *(page C340)*

✓ Does your story build on the conflict until the action reaches a climax? *(page C343)*

✓ Did you use dialogue and description to bring your characters to life? *(pages C341–C342 and pages C344–C345)*

✓ Does the ending of your story show how the conflict was resolved or present an outcome and bring the story to a close? *(pages C342–C343)*

✓ Is the narrator's point of view consistent throughout the story? *(pages C335–C336)*

Communicate Your Ideas

REVISING *Conferencing*

After your class has divided into small discussion groups, take turns reading your stories aloud. Comment on what is especially strong about them and what could be improved, paying special attention to sharp characterizations and tight descriptions. Then return to your seat and use your listeners' comments and the checklist above to make a complete and thorough revision of your short story. If time permits, repeat the process of meeting in small groups or share your story with new test readers, including friends or family members. Different audiences can sometimes have different responses to your work that will help you approach your revisions with new insights. Then save your work in your writing folder for use later.

Editing
Writing Process

In the editing stage, the writer produces error-free writing that demonstrates control over grammatical elements as well as accurate spelling and correct use of capitalization and punctuation.

Communicate Your Ideas

EDITING

Use the checklist on page C350 and the one on page C46 to edit your story. Make sure you have punctuated, capitalized, and indented all dialogue correctly. When you are pleased enough with it, make a final copy.

Publishing
Writing Process

After editing your work, prepare a neat final draft. In the publishing stage, the writer makes a final copy for his or her intended audience.

Communicate Your Ideas

PUBLISHING

Make an audiotape of your story, if possible. You may wish to assume the different voices of your characters yourself. On the other hand, you could invite others to take on roles and give a dramatic reading. Give your tape to the school library.

Prewriting Workshop
Drafting Workshop
Revising Workshop
Editing Workshop ▶
Publishing Workshop

Pronouns and Punctuation with Dialogue

When you write fiction, an extremely useful tool is dialogue. You can use it to move the plot along, to reveal character traits, and to add realism to a story. However, you will need to know which pronouns to use and how to punctuate your dialogue correctly.

Cases of Pronouns

A **pronoun** is a word that takes the place of a noun. **Nominative case** pronouns, used as subjects and predicate nominatives, are *I, you, he, she, it, we,* and *they.* **Objective case** pronouns used as objects are *me, you, him, her, it, us,* and *them.* **Possessive case** pronouns, used to show ownership or possession, are *my, mine, your, yours, his, her, hers, its, our, ours, their,* and *theirs.*

> NOMINATIVE CASE **She** was very old and small, and **she** walked slowly.
>
> OBJECTIVE CASE The hunter lifted **her** up and set **her** down.
>
> POSSESSIVE CASE **Her** chin was lowered almost to **her** knees.

Quotation Marks with Dialogue

When you are writing dialogue, enclose a person's exact words—and nothing else—inside quotation marks. Put the opening quotation marks before the first word a person says and put the closing quotation marks after the last word a person says—even if the quotation is several sentences long.

> Old Phoenix said, "Out of my way, all you foxes, owls, beetles, jack rabbits, coons, and wild animals!"

Capital Letters with Dialogue

Begin each sentence of a direct quotation with a capital letter.

"**A**re you deaf?" cried the attendant.

Then the nurse came in and said, "**O**h, that's just old Aunt Phoenix."

Commas and End Marks with Dialogue

Use a comma to separate a direct quotation from a speaker tag, such as *he said*. Place the comma *inside* the closing quotation marks. Also an end mark should be placed inside the closing quotation marks when the end of the quotation comes at the end of the sentence.

"I thank you**,**" she said.

"It's Christmas time, Grandma**,**" said the attendant. "Could I give you a few pennies out of my purse**?**"

Indentation with Dialogue

Begin a new paragraph each time the speaker changes so that the reader will know who is speaking. For an example, look at the previous lines of dialogue.

Editing Checklist

✔ Has the correct case of each pronoun been used?
✔ Has all dialogue been punctuated, capitalized, and indented correctly?

Writing a Play

Since a play is written to be performed, its very nature brings its characters to life. No feeling or emotion can be truly hidden from the audience. There is a certain rhythm or flow to the work too—often driven by the emotional content of the story. In this sense, plays can be quite poetic as well as an animated form of a story.

A **play** is a piece of writing intended to be performed on stage by actors.

As you read an excerpt from *The Piano Lesson* by August Wilson, pay close attention to how emotions affect the rhythm or flow of the story when it is told in play form.

The Piano Lesson

ACT TWO
Scene One
(The lights come up on the kitchen. It is the following morning. DOAKER is ironing the pants to his uniform. He has a pot cooking on the stove at the same time. He is singing a song. The song provides him with the rhythm for his work and he moves about the kitchen with the ease born of many years as a railroad cook.)
Doaker: Gonna leave Jackson, Mississippi
    and go to Memphis
    and double back to Jackson
    Come on down to Hattiesburg
    Change cars on the Y.D.
    coming through the territory to
    Meridian
    And Meridian to Greenville
    And Greenville to Memphis
    I'm on my way and I know where

Change cars on the Katy
Leaving Jackson
and going through Clarksdale
Hello Winona!
Courtland!
Bateville!
Como!
Senitobia!
Lewisberg!
Sunflower!
Glendora!
Sharkey!
And double back to Jackson
Hello Greenwood
I'm on my way Memphis
Clarksdale
Moorhead
Indianola
Can a highball pass through?
Highball on through sir
Grand Carson!
Thirty First Street Depot
Fourth Street Depot
Memphis!

(**Wining Boy** *enters carrying a suit of clothes.*)

Doaker: I thought you took that suit to the pawnshop?

Wining Boy: I went down there and the man tell me the suit is too old. Look at this suit. This is one hundred percent silk! How a silk suit gonna get too old? I know what it was he just didn't want to give me five dollars for it. Best he wanna give me is three dollars. I figure a silk suit is worth five dollars all over the world. I wasn't gonna part with it for no three dollars so I brought it back.

Doaker: They got another pawnshop up on Wylie.

Wining Boy: I carried it up there. He say he don't take no clothes. Only thing he take is guns and radios. Maybe a guitar or two. Where's Berniece?

Doaker: Berniece still at work. Boy Willie went down there to meet Lymon this morning. I guess they got that truck fixed, they been out there all day and ain't come back yet. Maretha scared to sleep up there now. Berniece don't know, but I seen Sutter before she did.

Wining Boy: Say what?

Doaker: About three weeks ago. I had just come back from down there. Sutter couldn't have been dead more than three days. He was sitting over there at the piano. I come out to go to work . . . and he was sitting right there. Had his hand on top of his head just like Berniece said. I believe he broke his neck when he fell in the well. I kept quiet about it. I didn't see no reason to upset Berniece.

Wining Boy: Did he say anything? Did he say he was looking for Boy Willie?

Doaker: He was just sitting there. He ain't said nothing. I went on out the door and left him sitting there. I figure as long as he was on the other side of the room everything be alright. I don't know what I would have done if he had started walking toward me.

Wining Boy: Berniece say he was calling Boy Willie's name.

Doaker: I ain't heard him say nothing. He was just sitting there when I seen him. But I don't believe Boy Willie pushed him in the well. Sutter here cause of that piano. I heard him playing on it one time. I thought it was Berniece but then she don't play that kind of music. I come out here and ain't seen nobody, but them piano keys was moving a mile a minute. Berniece need to go on and get rid of it. It ain't done nothing but cause trouble.

Wining Boy: I agree with Berniece. Boy Charles ain't took it to give it back. He took it cause he figure he had more right to it than Sutter did. If Sutter can't understand that . . . then that's just the way that go. Sutter dead and in the ground . . . don't care where his ghost is. He can hover around and play on the piano all he want. I want to see him carry it out the house. That's what I want to see. What time Berniece get home? I don't see how I let her get away from me this morning.

Doaker: You up there sleep. Berniece leave out of here early in the morning. She out there in Squirrel Hill cleaning house for some bigshot down there at the steel mill. They don't like you to come late. You come late they won't give you your carfare. What kind of business you got with Berniece?

Wining Boy: My business. I ain't asked you what kind of business you got.

Doaker: Berniece ain't got no money. If that's why you was trying to catch her. She having a hard enough time trying to get by as it is. If she go ahead and marry Avery . . . he working every day . . . she go ahead and marry him they could do alright for themselves. But as it stands she ain't got no money.

Wining Boy: Well, let me have five dollars.

Your Writer's Journal

In this scene from *The Piano Lesson,* Doaker and Wining Boy have a conversation about the ghost of a character named Sutter. In your journal, note your responses to the scene. How vivid is the dialogue? Do the characters come to life through their words? Think about conversations you have been part of or witnessed recently on any similarly disturbing topic. Put yourself back in the scene to bring it back to life in your mind. What were the thoughts and feelings of the participants? Were they listening attentively to one another? What were they doing during the conversation? Note these observations and reflections in your journal. You may want to use them later as a source for a dramatic scene.

Finding Ideas For Plays

In some ways, plays are like stories. These forms of literature both have characters, settings, and plots, and both make use of many other literary devices. With plays, though, there's a big difference. Plays are meant to be performed by actors in front of an audience. So, when you write a play, you must give the cast and crew enough information to perform the play, along with writing something that is going to entertain an audience.

The plot of a play is driven by a problem or a conflict that needs to be resolved. Since plays are often about people and how they interact with each other, one of the easiest ways to think of a plot is to imagine a situation in which people experience something together, but react to it differently. Their different reactions create conflict. For instance, think about an incident that might occur with a group of students while they are riding the bus to school. Think about three students' reactions to this incident that could cause a conflict and then determine how this conflict is going to be resolved.

PRACTICE YOUR SKILLS

● *Finding Ideas for a Play Scene*

Here are some situations in which people experience the same thing but react differently. Write a brief description of what might be going on in each of these situations.

1. a family Thanksgiving meal

2. a class trip

3. students waiting for their teacher to arrive

4. people playing a game or a sport

5. people on a date

Characters

The same play can seem very different each time it is performed, in part because of what the actor brings to each performance. Watching an actor is very different from reading about a character in a book. Actors bring many of their own ideas about how a character is portrayed and they make many decisions with the director of the play about how a character should be represented. It's the playwright, though, who invents the characters and writes the dialogue. It's up to the playwright to create interesting characters with colorful personalities, so the actors can bring them to life.

PRACTICE YOUR SKILLS

● *Sketching Characters*

Look back to the situations that you described in the previous Practice Your Skills activity. Choose one situation and develop each of the characters involved in that situation. List the most apparent traits of each character's personality; explain how they know each other, and what they think of each other. How might each of these characters react to something surprising?

Setting

You can be as imaginative as you want when you are writing a play, but you have to keep in mind that someone is going to have to stage your play and build whatever sets you describe. **Setting** is where and when the action occurs in a play. In addition to creating a physical representation of place and time, the setting often contributes to the overall mood. Works of fiction have settings too; however, it is one thing to write about the Grand Canyon, and it is another very different thing to build the Grand Canyon on a stage. Many plays use simple sets so that they are easier to stage and also so that the audience pays more attention to the characters than the sets. A playwright who has something specific in mind for a setting must describe it, so that the set designer can build it. For instance, "a bedroom" is more specific than "a house" but if you have in mind a particular kind of bedroom, like the sloppy bedroom of a troubled teenager, then you must supply that information in your play.

PRACTICE YOUR SKILLS

● *Finding Settings*

Describe where and when the situation you have chosen from the previous Practice Your Skills activity takes place. Then provide instructions for building your set. As a playwright you need to give enough information for a set designer to build your set, but you don't need to account for every detail of the setting. Instead, concentrate on creating something interesting enough for an audience to look at and/or convincing enough for the characters to inhabit.

Dialogue

Dialogue is simply what your characters say to each other in your play. It is ultimately up to the playwright to develop the characters by giving them something revealing and interesting to say.

Dialogue is a major component of a play. The audience finds out about the characters primarily through dialogue, and it has to sound just right. Even dialogue that sounds very natural may not work. For example, imagine two characters sitting next to each other on a bus ride home after school. One asks the other, "What do you want to do today?" The other says "I don't know. What do you want to do?" And then the first character replies, "I don't know—whatever." This is a conversation that everyone has had. Yet, it obviously doesn't lend itself to drama. Entertain your audience by having your characters talk about something interesting without making their conversation sound too much like a series of unfocused speeches. Remember that the plot as well as its emotional content is almost always driven by dialogue in a play.

PRACTICE YOUR SKILLS

● *Writing Dialogue*

Write a conversation between two of your characters in the situation you have chosen to develop from the previous Practice Your Skills activities. For example, if your situation is a Thanksgiving meal, and two of your characters are an elderly mother and her adult son, then their conversation might involve sharing a memory of something that took place before the younger members of the family were born. Try and develop your characters' personalities by giving them dialogue that reveals how they think and feel.

Stage Directions

Stage directions tell the cast how to deliver their lines and what to do while they are onstage. They also inform the play's crew about what sort of effects—such as the sound of rain—they need to produce. As the playwright, you need to account for all of the important action that occurs during a performance: you must write in your stage directions when characters enter and leave the stage, how they will speak, any important gestures they will make, and even, if it is crucial to the scene, where they will stand on the stage. In fiction, this is handled by the narrator, who might say something like "Dirk gave me a long stare and then angrily told me to leave him alone." In a play, the long stare and the fact that Dirk is angry have to be written in the stage directions. "Dirk: [pausing and staring angrily at Jen] 'Leave me alone.'" The crew also uses your stage directions. For example, if your scene needs a ringing telephone, you must write "[the telephone rings three times]," so that the crew can follow the script and ring the phone at the correct time.

PRACTICE YOUR SKILLS

● *Writing Stage Directions*

Return to the dialogue that you wrote for the previous lesson. Rewrite it, adding stage directions that indicate how the characters are speaking and what they are doing onstage. Keep your stage directions brief, since complicated stage directions make the rest of the play difficult to understand.

SCENE FROM A PLAY

Try writing a scene from a play. You might want to use the material you've already written in previous Practice Your Skills activities for developing a plot and characters, or you might want to develop another idea. If you want, write a summary of the scenes that come before and/or after your scene. Stick with one setting if you can, since too many changes of setting can make a play very difficult to stage. Finally, you need to determine the tone of your play. Will it be serious, comic, light-hearted, friendly, angry, absurd, realistic, or what? Then, carefully draft your scene with dialogue and stage directions that will reveal the plot and the characters.

After you've written a draft of your play, share it with your peers for feedback. After you have listened to their commentary and revised it to your satisfaction, prepare a final copy. You may want to stage a production of it. One of the best parts of writing a play is to see it being performed.

Artistic Performances

Some works of literature are written to be performed. Sets, costumes, blocking, makeup, lights, and music are the elements that bring a play to life. Though the script may remain unchanged, no two performances will be alike.

If an artistic performance moved you and caused you to see things a little differently, it was effective. The following questions may help you evaluate an artistic performance on the stage or over the airwaves.

Questions for Evaluating Artistic Performances

1. Does the performance move you?
2. Does the performance help illuminate the work?
3. Are the performers confident and well prepared?
4. Did the performers establish a good rapport with the audience through eye contact and effective body language?
5. If it is an audio presentation, do the performers provide ample vocal variety to express the work's nuances and underlying meanings?
6. If it is a live stage presentation, does the performance use the stage effectively?
7. If it is a video presentation, are the video tools used effectively to make statements? For example, are there thoughtful uses of camera angles, lighting, sequencing, and music? How do they contribute to the overall effect?

- Review the scene on pages C351–C354. Practice reading it aloud and take turns performing it for the class. The rest of the class will use the above questions to evaluate your work.

- See a live play or recall a live performance you saw. Write a paragraph evaluating the performance against the criteria listed above.

- Find and view a video presentation of a literary work. As before, write a paragraph evaluating the work using the criteria above.

Writing a Poem

A great poem stops you in your tracks. Whether it stirs deep emotions or startles the mind, its impact is certain. Poetry is a way of using language that gets the most out of each word and syllable.

Poetry is a writing form that expresses powerful feelings through imaginative uses of language, such as sound and imagery.

As you read the following poem by May Swenson, think about what gives this poem its impact.

> Hold a dandelion and look at the sun,
> Two spheres are side by side.
> Each has a yellow ruff.
>
> Eye, you tell a lie,
> that Near is large, that Far is small
> There must be other deceits. . . .

Your Writer's Journal

Review your journal for entries that evoke strong emotions or vivid imagery. Choose one of these entries that also includes powerful words and phrases. You might want to use this entry as a starting point for developing your poem.

Finding Ideas For Poems

How do poets become inspired? How do they decide what to write about? Many poets do not begin with a clear picture of how their poems will look when they are finished writing. However, they do begin with a kernel of an idea from which their poem emerges. Some of these "seeds" for poems are strong emotions, striking images, and interesting phrases that the poet may have heard or seen.

Once you have thought of a "seed" for your poem, the rest of the poem will follow as you begin to collect memories, impressions, and new ideas about your subject.

You can write a poem about anything, whether you think your subject is very important, such as how you feel about someone close to you, or whether you think it is mundane, such as the description of a meal. Sometimes great poems delight their readers by helping them see something familiar in a fresh way. Look how the British poet Simon Armitage makes the familiar image of a doctor new in this excerpt from his poem "The Anaesthetist":

> Hard to believe him when he trundles in,
> scrubbed up and squeaky clean, manoeuvering
> a handcart of deep-sea diving gear.

Time Out to Reflect Think about how you have generated ideas for stories, plays, and poems. How are the strategies that you have used to generate these ideas for each form similar? How are they different? What kind of ideas, if any, are particularly well suited for a story? for a play? for a poem? Why?

PRACTICE YOUR SKILLS

● *Charting to Find Ideas for a Poem*

Create an Idea Chart by using the following sample topics as the left-hand entries. Imagine a brand-new way to think about the sample topic and write at least one new idea for each topic on the right-hand side.

Sample Topics

a telephone conversation
monkeys
a car ride
a field of sunflowers
a backpack

Using Sound Devices

Remember not only that words mean things, but also that they have sounds of their own. Some poets even make up words so that their audience will listen to the sound of their poems without trying to figure out what the words mean. You don't have to write nonsense to emphasize sound in your poem. Imagine writing a poem called "Snake" with a line like "She silently slips toward the songbird's eggs." The *s-* sounds most likely make you think of a slithering snake. Even the word *slithers* sounds snakelike. When a poet uses a certain kind of sound in a poem, it is called a **device,** and there are many types of devices. Here are a few definitions of sound devices, along with some examples:

SOUND DEVICES	
ONOMATOPOEIA	Use of words whose sounds suggest their meanings **splash, click, zoom, woof**
ALLITERATION	Repetition of a consonant sound or sounds at the beginning of a series of words "**B**ring me the **br**atty **b**aby"
CONSONANCE	Repetition of a consonant sound or sounds used with different vowel sounds, usually in the middle or at the end of words "The heavy li**mb**s cli**mb** into the **m**oonlight bearing feathers" *—W. S. Merwin, "December Night"*
ASSONANCE	Repetition of a vowel sound within words "The dr**ow**ned t**ow**ns of the Quabbin/ the pilfered burial m**ou**nds" *—Adrienne Rich, "North America"*

REPETITION	Repetition of an entire word or phrase
	"You do not do, you do not do/ Any more, black shoe"
	—Sylvia Plath, "Daddy"
RHYME	Repetition of accented syllables with the same vowel and consonant sounds
	"When I have utterly re**fined** The composition of my **mind**, Shaped language of my marrow **till** Its forms are instant to my **will**"
	—Stanley Kunitz, "Single Vision"

Rhythm and Meter

Rhythm is a sense of flow produced by the rise and fall of accented and unaccented syllables. In some poems, especially traditional poems, the rhythm follows a specific beat called a **meter.** Metered poems follow a regular, countable pattern like the beats of a piece of music. If you were to listen to a marching band play a song, you would hear the beats of the snare drum form the meter of that song. The beats or meter help the marchers know when to take a step. As a matter of fact, those beats that form a poem's meter are called **feet.** Here is an example of some lines from a poem written nearly 200 years ago that has a clear meter:

Tyger! Tyger! burning bright
In the forests of the night,
What immortal hand or eye
Could frame thy fearful symmetry?

—William Blake, "The Tyger"

Poetry that does not have a regular, clear meter is called **free verse.** Many contemporary poets write in free verse. A poem can have a rhythm even if it does not have a meter.

When people speak to each other, the rhythm of their speech depends on their accent, whether they repeat words, what kind of emphasis they place on words, and many other factors. Walt Whitman was an American poet who wrote most of his work in the middle of the nineteenth century. He tried to use the rhythm of conversational speech in his poems and helped make free verse popular. Here is an example of his work, written in free verse.

> I celebrate myself, and sing myself,
> And what I assume you shall assume,
> For every atom belonging to me as good belongs to you.
>
> —"Song of Myself"

PRACTICE YOUR SKILLS

● **Developing Sound Devices**

Write a sentence using each of the sound devices listed below. For instance, you could use the word *buzzed* for onomatopoeia in the sentence "The honeybee buzzed toward me."

1. onomatopoeia   **5.** repetition

2. alliteration   **6.** rhyme

3. consonance   **7.** meter

4. assonance

Using Figurative Language

There are many other devices a poet can use to make a poem rich and interesting besides sound devices. Many of these devices are types of figurative language. This is language that is not limited to a strict explanation of its topic, and using it allows a poet to write more exciting and inventive work. Here are some definitions of types of figurative language, along with examples.

FIGURATIVE LANGUAGE

IMAGERY   Use of visual details or details that appeal to other senses.

Valley Candle

My candle burned alone in an
    immense valley.
Beams of the huge night converged
    upon it,
Until the wind blew.
Then beams of the huge night
Converged upon its image,
Until the wind blew.

—Wallace Stevens

SIMILE   Comparison using the words *like* or *as*
"Darkness falls like a wet sponge"

– John Ashbery,
"The Picture of Little J.A. in a Prospect of Flowers"

METAPHOR   Implied comparison that does not use *like* or *as*
"The locker room of my skull is full
of panting egrets."

—James Tate, "Happy as the Day is Long"

PERSONIFICATION   Use of human qualities to describe something nonhuman

The bird would cease and be as other birds
But that he knows in singing not to sing.
The question that he frames in all but words
Is what to make of a diminished thing.

—Robert Frost, "The Oven Bird"

HYPERBOLE   Use of extreme exaggeration or overstatement

The Chinese say we live in the world of the
10,000 things,
Each of the 10,000 things
crying out to us
Precisely nothing

—Charles Wright, "Night Journal"

OXYMORON	Combination of opposite or incongruous terms
	"Fight fire with fire and water with water."
	—*William Matthews,* "Blue Notes"
SYMBOL	Use of an object or action to stand for another In this excerpt from May Swenson's "Strawberrying," the strawberries that stain the hands and that look like heads in a basket or bursting hearts stand for both the vitality (strength) of life and its fragility.

> My hands are murder-red. Many a plump head drops on the heap in the basket. Or, ripe to bursting, they might be hearts, matching the blackbird's wing-fleck.

PRACTICE YOUR SKILLS

● *Developing Figurative Language for Poems*

Now it's your turn to think of some figurative language. Write an example of your own for each of the following types of figurative language. You may write them in verse or prose, as long as your examples are imaginative.

1. image   **5.** hyperbole

2. simile   **6.** oxymoron

3. metaphor   **7.** symbol

4. personification

Choosing a Form

The form of a poem, is its shape. In the end, any poem you write will have a shape, but many of poetry's forms have names and use a variety of methods of rhyming and counting words to give poems special shapes. Some of these forms are simple, like a **couplet,** which is just two lines per stanza. Others are much more complicated, like sestinas and pantoums.

The most elemental unit of a poem is the word. One word hardly makes a poem, though. Words are like the bricks used to make a building: they must be solid and well built, and they must also be mortared together carefully with other words. In a poem, a sequence of words becomes a line, and then a sequence of lines becomes a **stanza.** Most types of poetry have lines, and each of these lines ends with a line break. Stanzas are separated by stanza breaks.

A line of poetry is something like a sentence of prose, but it does not need to follow the same grammatical rules as a sentence does. Lines can be any length, but they are typically no longer than the margins of a page. Lines usually express one thought or idea, just like short sentences.

In traditional poetry, lines are based on the poem's meter and often have a specific number of words or syllables. When the last word of a line rhymes with the last word of another line—not always the next line—the last words of the lines are called end **rhymes**. Here's an example of lines with end rhymes, from Robert Frost's poem, "Departmental."

> An ant on the table cloth
> Ran into a dormant moth
> of many times his size.
> He showed not the least surprise.

See how 'cloth' and 'moth' rhyme with each other, and likewise for 'size' and 'surprise'? Those are the end rhymes. Frost has also composed these lines using seven syllables per line (except for the third line—he wasn't trying to be perfect). This is called a syllable count and forms the poem's meter. Not every poem uses syllable counts and meters in its lines, though. In fact most contemporary poems do not follow the traditional verse structures.

William Carlos Williams's poem "This Is Just to Say" uses short, unrhymed lines and short stanzas:

> **This Is Just to Say**
> I have eaten
> the plums
> that were in
> the icebox

and which
you were probably
saving
for breakfast

Forgive me
they were delicious
so sweet
and so cold

This poem uses four-line stanzas, known as **quatrains,** as its structure. A stanza break is a stronger break in the flow of a poem than a line break, in the same way that a paragraph is a stronger break in the flow of a story than a break is after a sentence.

Poems can be written with or without stanzas and can contain any number of lines. Did you notice that there is no punctuation in Williams's poem? He uses line breaks and stanzas instead of punctuation.

Communicate Your Ideas

WRITE A POEM *Rhymed and Free Verse*

The key to writing a poem is to use your imagination. If you think you might enjoy following a pattern in writing a poem, then try writing it with a rhyme scheme. If you would rather let the poem decide what form it wants to take, try writing a free-verse poem. Writing poetry can be like taking a walk without knowing exactly where you are going. As you are writing, or just thinking, leave yourself open to surprises—the sights, sounds, tastes, and smells that you couldn't have anticipated before you "took your walk." These "surprises" that you didn't expect often become the most interesting images in a poem. You may also want to use figurative language and sound devices to enhance the imagery and impact of the poem. Once you've written a poem, share it with your peers for feedback. Write your final copy. Then put your class poems together into an anthology, and take turns reading them aloud to your classmates.

A Writer Writes

A Short Story

Purpose **to create and to entertain with a science-fiction or mystery story**

Audience **lovers of suspense**

Prewriting

Most everyone enjoys reading mysteries and science-fiction stories because they usually surprise and baffle readers with unexpected happenings and events. In fact, an entire science-fiction story may revolve around an unexpected creature or character. On the other hand, some of the best mysteries are based on ordinary people who are unexpectedly caught up in a situation that is out of the ordinary and often frightening.

To find a subject for a mystery or science-fiction story, review the <u>Strategies for Developing Story Ideas</u> on page C326-C327. You could also make a cluster with the word *unexpected* in the center of a page and see what possibilities you discover. Then choose one and decide whether it would work better in a science-fiction story or a mystery.

After you have established the theme and a point of view for your story, sketch the setting and characters, keeping the number of characters to a minimum. Decide on what conflict your characters will face and outline the steps of the plot: the triggering event, the buildup of tension to the climax, the resolution, and the outcome. In the case of a mystery, also be sure that before you begin to write your first draft, you carefully plan several clues to include in your story. Then decide whether you will tell the story in strict chronological order or use a flashback and list the events accordingly.

Drafting

Use your prewriting work to draft an effective beginning, middle, and end to your story. At all times make your characters behave in ways that match the personalities you established for them. Also remember to use dialogue, description, and narration to bring your characters and action to life.

Revising

Use the checklists on pages C39 and C347 and the following questions as guides to your revision. Is the sequence of events clear? If you are writing a mystery, have you given enough clues so that your reader can figure it out? Do all the events lead to the climax of the mystery? Where can you add figurative language and sensory words to help you tell the story? Where can you add sound devices to heighten the effect of a suspenseful moment? Now read your dialogue aloud. Does it sound like an everyday conversation between real people?

Editing

Using the checklists on pages C46 and C350 to edit your story.

Publishing

Make a final copy to read it to your classmates. If time permits, your teacher may hold a writing contest, in which everyone in your class votes on the best story.

Process of Writing Stories, Plays, and Poems

Remember that you can move back and forth among the stages of the writing process to achieve your purpose.

Writing a Short Story

PREWRITING

- Choose a conflict and a theme. *(pages C321–C324)*
- Sketch all the characters for your story. *(pages C330–C331)*
- Choose a point of view for your story. *(page C335)*
- Match the setting of your story to the action, mood, and characters' feelings. *(pages C331–C332)*
- Plan a plot with a high point and resolution. *(pages C328–C329)*
- Use chronological order except for flashbacks. *(pages C337–C338)*
- Prepare a story outline. *(page C337)*

DRAFTING

- Draft a beginning that interests the reader and introduces the setting, the main character, and the conflict. *(page C339)*
- Use transitions, dialogue, and descriptive details. *(pages C339–C342)*
- Draft an ending that resolves the conflict and completes the action of the plot. *(pages C342–C343)*

REVISING

- Revise plot, characterization, and style. *(pages C344–C346)*
- Use the <u>Evaluation Checklist for Revising</u> to improve your story. *(page C347)*

EDITING

- Use the <u>Editing Checklists</u> *(pages C46 and C350)* to check your story for errors in grammar, usage, spelling, and mechanics.
- Punctuate, capitalize, and indent dialogue. *(pages C349–C350)*

PUBLISHING

- Prepare a final copy and publish your work. *(page C348)*

Writing a Play

- Develop characters who are involved in dramatic conflicts. *(pages C355–C356)*
- Select a stage-specific setting. *(page C356)*
- Use dialogue to convey emotion and information. *(page C357)*
- Use stage directions at appropriate moments. *(page C358)*

Writing a Poem

- Use sound devices in your poem. *(pages C363–C365)*
- Use figurative language. *(pages C366–C367)*
- Write rhymed verse or free verse. *(pages C367–C369)*

Connection Collection

Representing in Different Ways

From Print . . .

. . . to Visuals

Read Emily Dickinson's poem carefully to yourself and then aloud with a partner. Draw a picture or find a picture in a book or magazine that you feel best represents the action and images in the poem.

> She sweeps with many colored
>   brooms,
> And leaves the shreds behind;
> Oh, housewife in the evening west,
> Come back, and dust the pond!
>
> You dropped a purple ravelling in,
> You dropped an amber thread;
> And now you've littered all the East
> With duds of Emerald!
>
> And still she plies her spotted Brooms,
> And still the aprons fly,
> Till Brooms fade softly into stars—
> And then I come away.
>
> —Emily Dickinson

From Visuals . . .

Vincent van Gogh, *Enclosed Field with Rising Sun,* 1889. Oil on canvas, $27^2/_3$ by $35^1/_3$ inches. Private collection.

. . . to Print

Write a poem based on the imagery in the above painting by Vincent van Gogh. Consider how the painting makes you feel. Choose your figures of speech and sound devices carefully to match the mood of his picture.

- Which strategies can be used for creating both written and visual representations? Which strategies apply to one, not both? Which type of representation is more effective?
- Draw a conclusion and write briefly about the differences between written ideas and visual representations.

Writing in the Workplace
Scene for a Commercial

You work as a writer for a company that produces television commercials. Your client, the Uneeda Burrito Company, wants you to write a commercial script for their new line of frozen burritos, the Burrito Inferno. They have given you freedom to write what you want, with the following restrictions: the commercial's setting must be a kitchen; the characters must include a mother, father, daughter, son, and dog; and the characters must love the burritos.

Write a scene for the Uneeda Burrito Company commercial. Develop the characters' personalities by giving them dialogue that reveals how they think and feel. Include stage directions to indicate how the characters are speaking and what they are doing.

What strategies did you use to write a scene for the Uneeda Burrito Company commercial?

> *You can find information on writing plays on pages C351–C359.*

Writing for Oral Communication
Story for a Radio Broadcast

You have been selected to write a story for the weekly radio broadcast on WIAM-AM of *The Life I Never Lived.* Each week an author is selected to read a story on the air about a life he or she would like to have lived. The author last week read a story titled, "I Was a Teenage Crooner in King Arthur's Court."

Prepare the story to read for the radio broadcast. Maintain a consistent point of view throughout your story, and list your events in a logical, dramatic order. Use your descriptions, dialogue, and action to advance the plot of the past year of your imagined life. Perform your story for your classmates.

What strategies did you use to write your story for the radio?

> *You can find information on writing stories on pages C312–C348.*

Assess Your Learning

Morgan McGraw was walking home from his sousaphone lesson with his sousaphone wrapped around his shoulders like a brass boa constrictor. Just as he turned the corner onto his street, he heard a crashing sound that he recognized from the band room. He turned and saw Carol Merrill, the shy girl from the percussion section. She was carrying a pair of cymbals. As Morgan took a step toward her, it began to rain.

▶ Write a short story that builds on the scene above. Introduce at least two other characters, and make certain the plot is driven by a conflict that needs to be resolved.

▶ Use vivid language and interesting details to introduce the characters and the central conflict. Include background details to set the time and place of the story and to capture your reader's interest. Write the story in the third person, and keep it clear and consistent throughout. End the story in a way that makes the outcome clear and leaves a strong emotional impression on your readers.

⊙ *Before You Write* Consider the following questions:
What is the *subject?*
What is the *occasion?*
Who is the *audience?*
What is the *purpose?*

⊙ *After You Write* Evaluate your work using the following criteria:
- Have you used vivid language and interesting details to introduce the characters and the central conflict?
- Have you used background details to set the time and place of the story?
- Have you written the story in the third person, and does this point of view stay clear and consistent throughout the story?
- Have you ended your story in a way that makes the outcome clear and leaves a strong emotional impression on your readers?
- Have you proofread your story for spelling, capitalization, and punctuation errors?

Write briefly on how well you did. Point out your strengths and areas for improvement.

CHAPTER 9

Writing to Inform and Explain

If you have ever had a long conversation about the meaning of true love or friendship, then you have sought after definitions. If you have ever discussed changes in fashions, debated the respective merits of men's and women's basketball, compared an Elizabethan sonnet to a contemporary rap lyric, or likened a domestic cat to an untamed tiger, then you have used techniques of analysis as well as contrast and comparison. You draw upon the same skills that you use in everyday life when you write to inform and explain. In an informative essay, you use analysis, classification, definition, and comparison and contrast. When writing to explain, you may also describe sequences in a process, note how something works, explain how to do something, or tell why something happens. In this chapter you will learn to write essays to inform. During the process, you will develop strategies for sharing with others your understanding of the world and the way it works.

Reading with a Writer's Eye

The selection that you are about to read shows how a natural scientist observes and analyzes animal behavior, makes comparisons, and draws innovative conclusions from the patterns she discovers. Read the selection once or twice to appreciate how the author has presented new information. What techniques does the author use to support her point of view?

The Mind of The CHIMPANZEE

Jane Goodall

When I began my study at Gombe[1] in 1960 it was not permissible—at least not in ethological circles—to talk about an animal's mind. Only humans had minds. Nor was it quite proper to talk about animal personality. Of course everyone knew that they *did* have their own unique characters—everyone who had ever owned a dog or other pet was aware of that. But ethologists,[2] striving to make theirs a "hard" science, shied away from the task of trying to explain such things objectively. One respected ethologist, while acknowledging that there was "variability between individual animals," wrote that it was best that this fact be "swept under the carpet." At that time ethological carpets fairly bulged with all that was hidden beneath them.

How naive I was. As I had not had an undergraduate science education, I didn't realize that animals were not supposed to have personalities, or to think, or to feel emotions or pain. I had no idea that it would have been more appropriate to assign each of the chimpanzees a number rather than a name when I got to know him or her. I didn't realize that it was not scientific to discuss behavior in terms of motivation or purpose.

---

[1] **Gombe:** Gombe Stream Reserve (National Park) in the northwest of Tanzania.
[2] **ethologist** (ĭ thŏl′ə jĭst): One who engages in the scientific study of animal behavior, especially as it occurs in a natural environment.

And no one had told me that terms such as *childhood* and *adolescence* were uniquely human phases of the life cycle, culturally determined, not to be used when referring to young chimpanzees. Not knowing, I freely made use of all those forbidden terms and concepts in my initial attempt to describe, to the best of my ability, the amazing things I had observed at Gombe. . . .

The editorial comments on the first paper I wrote for publication demanded that every *he* or *she* be replaced with *it,* and every *who* be replaced with *which.* Incensed, I, in my turn, crossed out the *its* and *whichs* and scrawled back the original pronouns. As I had no desire to carve a niche for myself in the world of science, but simply wanted to go on living among and learning about chimpanzees, the possible reaction of the editor of the learned journal did not trouble me. In fact I won that round: The paper when finally published did confer upon the chimpanzees the dignity of their appropriate genders and properly upgraded them from the status of mere "things" to essential Being-ness. . . .

It is not easy to study emotions even when the subjects are human. I know how I feel if I am sad or happy or angry, and if a friend tells me that he is feeling sad, happy or angry, I assume that his feelings are similar to mine. But of course I cannot know. As we try to come to grips with the emotions of beings progressively more different from ourselves, the task, obviously, becomes increasingly difficult. If we ascribe human emotions to non-human animals we are accused of being anthropomorphic[3]—a cardinal sin in ethology. But is it so terrible? If we test the effect of drugs on chimpanzees because they are biologically so similar to ourselves, if we accept that there are dramatic similarities in chimpanzee and human brain and nervous system, is it not logical to assume that there will be similarities also in at

---

[3] **anthropomorphic** (ăn'thrə pə môr'fĭk) *adj.*: Having ascribed human characteristics to things not human.

least the more basic feelings, emotions, moods of the two species?

In fact, all those who have worked long and closely with chimpanzees have no hesitation in asserting that chimps experience emotions similar to those which in ourselves we label pleasure, joy, sorrow, anger, boredom, and so on. Some of the emotional states of the chimpanzee are so obviously similar to ours that even an inexperienced observer can understand what is going on. An infant who hurls himself screaming to the ground, face contorted, hitting out with his arms at any nearby object, banging his head, is clearly having a tantrum. Another youngster, who gambols[4] around his mother, turning somersaults, pirouetting[5] and, every so often, rushing up to her and tumbling into her lap, patting her or pulling her hand towards him in a request for tickling, is obviously filled with *joie de vivre*.[6] There are few observers who would not unhesitatingly ascribe his behavior to a happy, carefree state of well-being. And one cannot watch chimpanzee infants for long without realizing that they have the same emotional need for affection and reassurance as human children. An adult male, reclining in the shade after a good meal, reaching benignly to play with an infant or idly groom an adult female, is clearly in a good mood. When he sits with bristling hair, glaring at his subordinates and threatening them, with irritated gestures, if they come too close, he is clearly feeling cross and grumpy. We make these judgments because the similarity of so much of a chimpanzee's behavior to our own permits us to empathize.[7]

---

[4] **gambols** (găm′bəl) *intr. v.*: Leaps about playfully.

[5] **pirouetting** *intr. v.*, **pirouette** (pĭr′o͞o ĕt′) *n.*: A turn on the point of the toe or on the ball of the foot in ballet.

[6] *joie de vivre* (zhwä′ də vē′vre) *n.*: Hearty or carefree enjoyment of life.

[7] **empathize** (ĕm′pə thīz′) *intr. v.*: To identify with and understand another's situation, feelings, and motives.

Thinking as a Writer

Evaluating Informative Strategies

Jane Goodall challenges long-standing scientific views about animal emotion and intelligence.

- What particular prejudices does the author address?
- What stand does the author take on the issue of animal intelligence?
- How does the author make use of comparisons to support her argument?
- Do you think the author gives a balanced analysis of the facts?

Debating the Facts

Oral Expression • Using information from the article and other sources you find, organize a debate with a classmate on the differences between primate and human intelligence. Take turns arguing each side.

Interpreting Visual Information

Viewing Examine the photograph below that shows a chimpanzee mother with her young.

- What details strike you as characteristically *animal*?
- Are there details that seem to indicate the kind of primate intelligence Goodall describes? What are these details?

The Power of Informative Writing

Informative writing provides readers with needed facts. The article you just read was a magazine article, one common type of informative writing. Following are some other typical uses of writing that informs.

Uses of Informative Writing

Here are some examples of informative writing.

- **An investigative journalist writes a hard-hitting exposé** that reveals wrongdoing among elected officials.

- **Computer manufacturers write documentation** to support their latest software applications.

- **An architect draws a blueprint** showing the plan for a new fine arts center.

- **A writer for a consumer magazine compares and contrasts this year's new automobiles,** listing the pros and cons of each.

- **A group of scientists explains the results** of their latest experiments in a scientific journal.

- **High school students write answers to essay questions** on history tests explaining the causes and effects of World War II.

- **Corporations publish annual reports** explaining why they made or lost money during the year.

- **A chef demonstrates the intricacies** of gourmet cooking on a television show.

Process of Writing an Informative Essay

When writing an informative essay, you set out ideas, information, or explanations for your readers.

An **informative essay** presents information or offers an explanation.

In writing an essay for the purpose of explaining or informing, you will be able to use several types of writing that you have already learned about, including narrative writing and descriptive writing *(pages C167–C189)*. In addition, you will be able to use classification *(pages C31–C32)*, and you may be able to use evaluation *(page C39)*.

Your Writer's Journal

Some informative essays can be written "out of your head" since you already know a great deal about some topics. Other informative essays will send you on a hunt to the library, the Internet, or other information sources. In your journal, begin to keep two lists of topics for possible essays. The "out of your head" list might include such topics as baseball television commercials, mountain bikes, Chinese food—whatever you know a lot about. The "hunt" list will describe informational topics that you would like to learn more about. Add to your list each day. Also jot down some facts and ideas you might want to include about a topic.

Prewriting Writing Process

Planning an informative essay is a very important step, which may also be an enlightening and enjoyable step. As you explore a subject, you undoubtedly will learn some new, fascinating facts and details. First, though, you must choose a subject.

Discovering Subjects

The first step in discovering subjects for informative essays is to take an inventory of subjects you already know from your own experience and study. For example, in science class you may have learned enough about the hole in the ozone layer to write about its effects on the environment. If you are a musician, you might want to explain how your favorite instrument works. The following strategies may also serve as springboards for discovering subjects.

Strategies for Discovering Subjects for an Informative Essay

- Use the clustering technique, starting with the phrase *things I could explain.*
- Freewrite to discover what is on your mind.
- Ask yourself questions about your interests and skills and write them down.
- Review your **journal**—particularly your Learning Log—for subjects suitable for explaining or informing. *(pages C16–C17)*
- Browse through the library and skim books, newspapers, or magazines for subjects that interest you.
- Consider your favorite subjects in school and read your notes to find possible subjects.
- View educational television programs—such as documentaries—for issues or events you would like to explore in writing.

Communicate Your Ideas

PREWRITING *Topics*

Review your **journal** for topics that interest you. Using the strategies above and the techniques of clustering and brainstorming, explore possible subject ideas for an informative essay.

SAVE YOUR WORK

Choosing and Limiting a Subject

After you think about possible subjects, the next step is to choose the one that interests you the most and limit it until it is manageable. To make your choice, use the following guidelines.

> ## Guidelines for Choosing a Subject for an Informative Essay
> - Choose a subject that you will enjoy writing about.
> - Choose a subject that will interest your readers.
> - Choose a subject that you know about or can readily find information about.
> - Choose a subject that you can develop in a short essay.
> - Choose a subject about which you have achieved some insight.

A broad subject is like a lump of clay that needs to be shaped before it takes on clearly defined features. To shape, or narrow, a subject for an informative essay so that it is manageable, answer the following questions.

> ## Questions for Limiting a Subject
> - What about my subject do I want to explain?
> - What possible approaches can I choose to explain my subject?
> - What insight or understanding can I draw from my subject?

Suppose your broad subject is the Big Dipper. Using the questions above, you might limit your subject as follows.

What about my subject . . . ? I want to explain the importance of the Big Dipper to travelers and stargazers.

What possible approaches . . . ? I could tell how people viewed the Big Dipper throughout history or how people use it today, or I could compare it with other constellations.

What insight or understanding . . . ? Constellations like the Big Dipper help people feel less overwhelmed by space.

The example below shows how the broad subject has been limited to a more manageable one.

BROAD SUBJECT	the Big Dipper
LIMITED SUBJECT	the importance of the Big Dipper to travelers and stargazers

PRACTICE YOUR SKILLS

● **Limiting a Subject**

For each of the following subjects, suggest possible answers to the three Questions for Limiting a Subject. Use the examples above as a guide. Then save your work for later use.

1. the exploration of space

2. fads

3. country and western music

4. recycling

5. the Bill of Rights

6. educational television

7. cost of health care

8. nutritional food

9. motorcycles

10. national parks

Communicate Your Ideas

PREWRITING *Topics*

Using your **journal** as well as fresh ideas, make a list of ten possible subjects for an informative essay. Put a check next to the subject that comes closest to following the Guidelines for Choosing a Subject for an Informative Essay on the previous page. Then narrow the subject you chose by answering the Questions for Limiting a Subject. Save your work for later use.

Determining Your Audience

Before going further, think about who will be reading your essay. Ask yourself the following questions about your readers.

- What do my readers already know about my subject? What questions might they ask about the subject?

- What are my readers' attitudes toward my subject? If their attitudes differ from mine, how can I address those differences?

For example, who will read your essay about the Big Dipper? Will your audience be a class of fifth graders at the elementary school or the members of the astronomy club that you belong to? If the fifth graders are your audience, you can assume that they do not know too much about the Big Dipper. Therefore, your explanations should be simple, basic, and straightforward. If, however, your audience is made up of members of the astronomy club, you can assume that they already know quite a bit about the Big Dipper. Therefore, you would need to look for a new or different focus for your essay.

Communicate Your Ideas

PREWRITING *Audience*

Write a brief paragraph in which you profile your audience. Determine as best you can your readers' knowledge, attitudes, and needs regarding the subject you have chosen and narrowed. Save your work for later use.

Gathering Information

Once you have a limited subject, you should gather information for an essay of three or more paragraphs. Using brainstorming, freewriting, charting, or clustering to explore your subject, collect as much information as possible. The chart on the next page shows some of the most common types of supporting details used in informative essays.

You can learn more about gathering information on page C525.

TYPES OF SUPPORTING DETAILS		
facts	incidents	analogies
examples	comparisons	causes and effects
reasons	contrasts	steps in a process

As you collect your information, jot down any details you think of or come upon—without concerning yourself about the order of your ideas. The following prewriting notes list facts and examples for an essay about the Big Dipper.

MODEL: Gathering Information

LIMITED SUBJECT

The importance of the Big Dipper to travelers and stargazers

FACTS AND EXAMPLES AS DETAILS

- Stars pointing to the North Star and the last star on the handle are moving away from each other; the Big Dipper will lose its shape in 50,000 years.
- In ancient times shepherds along the Tigris and Euphrates Rivers and Iroquois Indians along Lake Ontario saw the dipper as a bear.
- The seven stars in Ursa Major are seen as a dipper or a plow.
- Two stars opposite the handle at the front of the dipper point to the North Star.
- The constellation helps stargazers get oriented in the night skies.
- The handle points to Arcturus—a bright star in the constellation Boötes.
- From Arcturus you can find the bright star Spica in the constellation Virgo.
- Virgo contains the double star (Mizar and Alcor) which ancient Arabs saw as a horse and rider and American Indians saw as a woman carrying a baby.

- The stars at the top of the dipper, near the handle, point to Vega in the constellation Lyra (the harp).
- In the 1800s, slaves escaping from the South to the North were told to follow the drinking gourd.
- Navigators in northern seas use the Big Dipper to find the North Star.
- The Big Dipper is bright enough to be seen from cities, where lights brighten the sky too much to see many stars.
- On winter evenings the Big Dipper's handle points down, but its position is reversed on summer evenings.

Communicate Your Ideas

PREWRITING *Information Gathering*

Review the topic that you have chosen for an informative essay. Now use any of the prewriting techniques you have learned to gather information for your essay. If you do not have all the information you think you need, use the library or media center, the Internet, or other resources. Save all your information for later use.

Developing a Working Thesis

As you gather information, you will begin to see connections between the facts and examples. At this point you should focus your thoughts more precisely by drafting a **working thesis**—a preliminary statement that announces your subject and expresses a main idea. For example, notice that several facts on pages C387–C388 indicate that the Big Dipper has been an important marker in the sky for a long time. With this idea in mind, you could write the following working thesis.

| LIMITED SUBJECT | the importance of the Big Dipper to travelers and stargazers |
| WORKING THESIS | For centuries the Big Dipper has served as an important beacon to travelers and stargazers. |

The working thesis will guide you in selecting information to use in your essay. That is, you would select from the list only those facts, examples, and incidents that explain the historical importance of the Big Dipper. If you decide later to include other information or refine your ideas, you will have to revise your working thesis. Formulating a working thesis now, however, helps you keep your purpose and ideas on track as you develop your essay.

You may find the following steps helpful in developing a working thesis.

Steps for Developing a Working Thesis

- Look over the information you have gathered.
- Express the main idea you plan to convey.
- Select the details you will use to support your main idea.
- Check that the working thesis takes into account all of the information you selected to include in your essay.

Communicate Your Ideas

PREWRITING *Working Thesis*

 Review the information you collected on your limited subject. Then focus your thoughts more precisely by formulating a working thesis that is a complete statement expressing the main idea about your subject. Save your working thesis for later use.

Constructing Analogies

When writing an informative essay, you may need to explain something unfamiliar to your audience. It may help to make a comparison, or an **analogy,** between an unfamiliar process or situation and facts or concepts more familiar to your reader. Suppose you want to explain the process of running for office. Suppose, too, that you have experience as a runner in track-and-field events. You might focus on the similarities and build an analogy between running in track and running for office. Remember, an analogy is never exact. Running for office is not running in track but is similar enough to be helpful to your readers.

When you are comparing familiar and unfamiliar ideas, a chart like the one below will help you develop the analogy.

ANALOGY CHART

Essay subject: running for office

Familiar situation: running in track

Runner's needs	Candidate's needs
proper training and equipment	background and job skills, a campaign staff, and funds
physical and mental stamina for the race	competitive spirit, stamina
sense of timing and pacing in the race	well-planned schedule of speeches and media events

THINKING PRACTICE

Choose a subject from the left column below. Then use the knowledge or skill from the right column to make an analogy chart that would help you explain the subject to your reader.

Essay Subjects

1. writing a poem

2. building a friendship

Familiar Knowledge/Skills

1. repairing cars

2. cooking or baking

Organizing Your Essay

Once you have gathered your information and have a working thesis statement, you will use the thinking skills of classifying and ordering to organize the information.

You can learn more about organizing information on pages C124–C125.

Grouping Supporting Details into Categories   To group your list of supporting details into categories, ask yourself what one item has in common with another. The groupings that follow show three categories that can be made from the list of supporting details about the Big Dipper.

MODEL: Classifying Details

CATEGORY 1:   Interpretations of the Big Dipper's star pattern
- Ancient shepherds along the Tigris and Euphrates rivers and Iroquois Indians along Lake Ontario saw the shape of a bear.
- When just the seven stars are included in the constellation, people see a dipper or a plow.

CATEGORY 2:   Use of the Big Dipper in locating the North Star
- Navigators in northern seas use the Big Dipper to find the North Star.
- In the 1800s, slaves escaping from the South to the North were told to follow the drinking gourd in the sky.
- Two stars at the front of the dipper point to the North Star.

CATEGORY 3:   Use of the Big Dipper in locating other stars
- It helps stargazers get oriented in the night sky.
- You can follow the handle to Arcturus, a bright star in the constellation Boötes.
- If you continue following the handle from Arcturus, you can find the bright star Spica in the constellation Virgo.
- The stars at the top of the dipper, closest to the handle, point to Vega in the constellation Lyra (the harp).

Some of the details from the original list were not placed in any category. Keep such leftover details because you might be able to use them in the introduction or conclusion of the essay.

A classification cluster is one way you can organize information. Often this type of cluster will help you see whether you need more information for one or more of your categories.

Here is a classification cluster for an essay about grizzly bears. Notice the types of categories and information the writer has included.

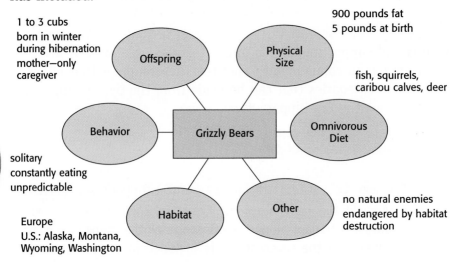

1 to 3 cubs
born in winter
during hibernation
mother—only
caregiver

900 pounds fat
5 pounds at birth

fish, squirrels,
caribou calves, deer

solitary
constantly eating
unpredictable

Europe
U.S.: Alaska, Montana,
Wyoming, Washington

no natural enemies
endangered by habitat
destruction

PRACTICE YOUR SKILLS

● *Organizing Information*

Create three categories into which you can group the following details on the subject of why people enjoy amusement parks. Then, using a classification cluster, list the details that fit in each category.

SUBJECT: People enjoy amusement parks for many reasons.

- The roller coaster gives a thrill without any real danger.
- Special wide-screen films make you feel like you're riding in an airplane without ever leaving the ground.
- Tilt-a-whirl seems to defy gravity.
- Some games let you test your skill and strength.
- Singers and musicians perform in special areas.
- Games of chance with good prizes are challenging.
- Water rides are cooling because of the spray.

Arranging Categories in a Logical Order

After creating categories, you need to decide on the order in which to present them. The chart that follows lists five commonly used types of logical order.

TYPES OF LOGICAL ORDER	
CHRONOLOGICAL ORDER	Items are arranged according to when they happened in time.
ORDER OF IMPORTANCE	Items are arranged according to location.
SPATIAL ORDER	Items are arranged in order of importance, interest, or degree.
DEVELOPMENTAL ORDER	Items of equal importance are arranged in an order made clear to the reader.
COMPARISON AND CONTRAST	Items are arranged according to similarities (comparisons) and differences (contrasts).

Organizing Comparison and Contrast

A common type of informative essay is one of **comparison and contrast.** When you **compare,** you explain how two items are similar. For example, you might explain how an orange is like a grapefruit. When you **contrast,** on the other hand, you emphasize differences rather than similarities. For example, you might explain how an orange differs from a grapefruit. In an informative essay of comparison and contrast, you include *both* similarities and differences between two items.

If you have chosen to write an essay of comparison and contrast, you have two ways to organize your information. One way is to write about one subject first and then to write about the other subject. For example, if you were comparing outdoor camping (subject A) to vacationing in motels (subject B), you would first write all your information about subject A (camping) and then all your information about subject B (motel stays). For convenience this is called the **AABB pattern** of comparison and contrast.

You can use the AABB pattern in two ways. You can organize the pattern within one paragraph by discussing **A** in the first half of the paragraph and **B** in the second half. You can also use an alternative organization in two paragraphs by discussing **A** in one paragraph and **B** in the second paragraph. The following portion of an essay about vacation options shows the AABB pattern, which starts after the essay's introduction.

MODEL: AABB Pattern of Organization

Vacation Options

After World War II, dramatic new options for family vacations appeared on the American scene. Two of these options—**(A)**the family outdoor camping vacation and **(B)**the on-the-spot motel vacation—show the contrasting tastes of vacationers.

Suddenly, in the 1950s, shoppers began to see a variety of goods available for a new way to vacation—outdoor camping for the whole family. **(A)**The camping trailer and the motor home equipped with sleeping and cooking accommodations showed up in car dealers' lots and on the television screen. Hundreds of varieties of **(A)**camping gear—such as sleeping bags, cookers, tents, backpacks, and hiking boots—flooded the marketplace. People became aware of the **(A)**National Park Service and the development of private land into **(A)**camping facilities. American families were on the move out into the fresh air to enjoy the peace and pleasure of the country's wilderness, lakes, and seashores. "Let's go, America!" became the battle cry of **(A)**camping vacationers by the millions.

On the other hand, there loomed a whole population of **(B)**noncampers, who were allergic to campsites, to bugs, and perhaps to exertion. Their attention was soon captured by a new kind of vacation possibility. Road signs and neon lights and paper flyers in mailboxes announced the arrival of the **(B)**roadside motel. **(B)**Beautiful air-conditioned rooms with television and—wonder of wonders—a door leading directly to one's automobile beckoned the curious. Forget all that camping gear! **(B)**After a long drive, conveniences such as a swimming pool, a restaurant, a dance floor, miniature golf, and shuffleboard were within immediate reach. Moreover, these **(B)**complexes were available at all the pleasure spots of America! Such a splendid vacation option had never before existed.

The second way to organize comparison and contrast is called the **ABAB pattern.** In this pattern you discuss your two subjects together instead of separately. That is, first you compare both **A** and **B** in terms of one similarity or one difference. Then you compare both of them in terms of another similarity or difference. The following portion of the essay on vacation options switches to the ABAB pattern.

MODEL: ABAB Pattern of Organization

Even today families planning a trip often face the decision whether to go **(A)**camping or to stay in **(B)**motels along the way. Families would do well to weigh the advantages and disadvantages of each option by considering three major items. The first item, expense, is an important one, for **(A)**a camping vacation is much less expensive than **(B)**a vacation using motels. **(A)**Overnight camping accommodations will probably average a tenth of the expense of **(B)**motel accommodations. The second item is convenience. Although fortunate **(A)**campers may bathe in a quiet lake at sunset, many people prefer a hot shower in **(B)**a motel at the end of a long day of sightseeing. The third item to consider is accessibility to beautiful scenery. **(A)**Campers can pitch tents on wooded mountain slopes, near cool streams, in pine forests, or on the seashore. Most **(B)**motel sites are situated on crowded, noisy highways. After weighing the pros and cons, most families must make an intelligent compromise for a successful vacation for all.

Television News

There's no escaping it: television has changed the way people get their information *and* form their opinions. Politicians and their messages are often reduced to sound bites or brief quotes on the evening news. Images sometimes seem to have a bigger impact than the people creating them.

However, some sources in the media have the potential to probe deeper. Notice in the chart below how the format of newsmagazines and documentaries allows for substantial, in-depth looks at political issues.

Nightly News	Newsmagazines	Documentaries
very brief (two to three minutes)	usually twenty-minute segments	usually fifty minutes or longer
intro by anchor	intro by anchor	often beginning with a dramatic visual before introduction
brief videotape shots	lengthy videos	video with much attention to camera style and technique
brief interview or quote from person involved	lengthy interviews/ multiple quotes and sources	multiple quotes and sources, real-life conversations
editing to achieve maximum effect and stay within time limit; balanced presentation	editing with much concern for effect and balance	editing to enhance overall effect—music and voice-over narration often added to heighten emotions
closing from anchor or reporter	closing from anchor or reporter	often concludes with strong emotional effect
often put together on same day news happens	requires preparation time (weeks at least)	requires longest preparation time (even years)

Media Activity

To understand the characteristics of each of these types of visual media, view each one critically and describe how each might present a politician. Write at least a paragraph for each medium sketching out what the presentation might include.

PRACTICE YOUR SKILLS

● *Organizing Comparison and Contrast*

Choose one of the following pairs of subjects and list three similarities and three differences. Then organize the information according to the AABB or the ABAB pattern.

1. an analog and a digital clock

2. two popular television comedians

3. a halogen bulb and a conventional lightbulb

4. a book and a film based on the book

5. two means of transportation

6. college basketball and professional basketball

Making an Outline

As a final step before writing a first draft, consider making an outline. An **outline** is a helpful plan for drafting the body of your essay. The form of an outline allows you to use a numbering and lettering system to show the order of your ideas. Each large category of information becomes the main topic of a supporting paragraph in the body of the essay and is assigned a Roman numeral. For example, the beginnings of an outline for an essay on the Big Dipper might look like this.

FIRST MAIN TOPIC	**I.** People's interpretations of star pattern in the Big Dipper
SECOND MAIN TOPIC	**II.** Use of Big Dipper to locate North Star
THIRD MAIN TOPIC	**III.** Use of Big Dipper to locate other stars

The supporting details for each category become the subtopics and supporting points of the outline. As you add subtopics and supporting points under each main topic, order them logically within each category of thought.

You can review types of logical order on page C393.

The following outline for the body of an essay on the Big Dipper shows logical developmental order.

MODEL: Outline of the Body of an Essay

MAIN TOPIC

SUBTOPIC
SUPPORTING
POINTS

I. People's interpretations of star pattern in Big Dipper
   A. Largest shape—Great Bear
      1. Shepherds in the Tigris-Euphrates area
      2. Iroquois Indians near Lake Ontario
   B. Seven stars only
      1. Dipper
      2. Plow
   C. Double star within dipper
      1. Horse and rider to Arabs
      2. Mother and baby to Indians

II. Use of Big Dipper in locating North Star
   A. Pointers at front of dipper
   B. Use by navigators
   C. Use by land travelers—importance to slaves

III. Use of Big Dipper in locating other stars
   A. Arcturus
   B. Spica
   C. Vega

Notice that when you write a formal outline for the body of an essay, you use Roman numerals for each idea that supports your thesis. Each idea becomes the **main idea** of a supporting paragraph. You then use capital letters for each category of information that comes under a topic. Then, under each subtopic, you use Arabic numerals to list the supporting details or points. When you draft the body of your essay, the information below each Roman numeral in the outline will correspond with a separate paragraph. After finishing an outline, check its form. The following questions will help you see if you have consistency and balance in each part.

> ## Checking an Outline
> - Did you use Roman numerals for main topics?
> - Did you use capital letters for subtopics?
> - Did you use Arabic numerals for supporting points?
> - If you included subtopics under topics, did you have at least two of them for each topic?
> - If you included supporting points under subtopics, did you have at least two of them for each subtopic?
> - Did you indent the outline as shown in the model?

PRACTICE YOUR SKILLS

● *Creating an Outline*

Write an outline using the categories about an amusement park that you created in the exercise on page C392. The outline should show three main topics, each with a Roman numeral, and at least three subtopics.

Communicate Your Ideas

PREWRITING *Logical Order and Outlines*

Review all the prewriting you have done for an informative essay. Sort out your details into meaningful categories. Then arrange those categories in a logical order, using one of the types of order listed on page C393. Create an outline for the body of your essay, using the checklist above. Save your outline for later use.

Time Out to Reflect
Discuss with four or five classmates your insights into your own writing processes. Use the discussion to learn from previous writing activities and other members of the group.

When you draft, you convert the items in your outline into sentences and paragraphs. If you discover some new ideas you would like to include, keep your original purpose in mind so that any new ideas relate clearly to your main idea. When writing a first draft, focus on getting your ideas on paper without worrying about spelling and punctuation.

As you write your first draft, you are likely to think of new ideas. You may incorporate them into your draft as long as they relate to your main idea and help to develop it. Remember, your first draft should include all the parts of an essay: an introduction with a thesis statement, a body of supporting paragraphs, and a conclusion.

Drafting Your Thesis Statement

In drafting your thesis statement, you may have to refine your working thesis to take into account any new ideas you wish to include in your essay. Use the following guidelines to help you.

Drafting a Thesis Statement

- Review your prewriting notes and your working thesis.
- Revise your thesis until it covers all your supporting ideas.
- Avoid such expressions as "In this paper I will . . ." or "This paper will be about . . ."

Review the information about the Big Dipper on pages C387–C388 and C391 and the working thesis on page C389, which does not cover the various shapes people see in the Big Dipper's star pattern. If you want to include these details, you could expand the thesis statement as follows.

REFINED THESIS STATEMENT | The stars in and near the Big Dipper are a distinguishing feature of the northern skies and a beacon for travelers and stargazers.

Prewriting Workshop
Drafting Workshop
Revising Workshop
Editing Workshop
Publishing Workshop

Phrases

For impact, you will want your refined thesis statement to be a single sentence that covers all your ideas fully. Prepositional phrases and appositive phrases will help you express your ideas in smooth, well-turned sentences. This, of course, is the type of sentence you want for your thesis statement.

Prepositional Phrases

A **prepositional phrase** is a group of words that begins with a preposition and ends with noun or a pronoun and is used to describe another word in the sentence. Prepositional phrases can be added to transform a vague, unmodified sentence into a precise and particularized thesis statement.

VAGUE THESIS STATEMENT	The natural balance is seriously threatened.
PRECISE THESIS STATEMENT	The natural balance **of Florida's** ecosystem is seriously threatened **by nonnative plants from Australia, America, and Asia.**

Appositive Phrases

An **appositive phrase** is a group of words that identifies or explains a word in the sentence. Appositive phrases are often used in informative writing to define an unfamiliar term or give identifying information.

Combining Sentences with Phrases

Once you understand prepositional phrases and appositive phrases, you can use them to combine two short sentences into one fluid, mature sentence.

PRACTICE YOUR SKILLS

 Evaluating Thesis Statements

Reread the prewriting notes for the essay on the Big Dipper on pages C387–C388 and C391. Then explain why each of the following thesis statements is inadequate.

1. This essay will be about the Big Dipper.

2. The Big Dipper can be used to locate missing stars.

3. People have seen many shapes in the stars near the Big Dipper.

Drafting the Introduction

In an informative essay the introduction captures the reader's attention, sets the tone, and states the thesis. A direct and matter-of-fact tone is appropriate for an informative essay. The following suggestions will help you draft your introduction.

> **Ways to Begin an Essay**
> - Give some background information or relate an incident that shows how you became interested in your subject.
> - Cite an example or incident that catches the reader's attention.
> - Give one or two of the original details that did not fit into your outline.
> - Always include your thesis statement, preferably as the last sentence of the introduction.

In the following introduction to the essay on the Big Dipper, the writer sets the tone, captures attention, and includes a slightly altered version of the thesis statement.

THESIS STATEMENT

On a clear night in the country, the sky blazes with countless points of light. An earthbound observer like me feels small and lost until I find the Big Dipper, the familiar, easy-to-spot shape that was for most of us our first-known constellation. Even in a city sky illuminated by the bright lights below, the seven stars that form the Big Dipper are easy to see. Their pattern is a distinguishing mark of the northern skies and a centuries-old beacon for travelers and stargazers.

Communicate Your Ideas

DRAFTING *Introduction*

Read over the working thesis and outline that you developed for your informative essay. If necessary, revise the working thesis. Then draft an introduction, using one of the suggestions for beginning an essay. Save your work for later use.

Drafting the Body

When you draft the body of your essay, follow the order of your outline and include all the points you have listed. Each main topic (Roman numeral) in your outline becomes one paragraph in the body of your essay. If covering all the points under a main topic makes an extremely long paragraph, use two or more paragraphs to cover the points. Be sure, however, that all the paragraphs in the body relate to the thesis statement.

Guidelines for Adequately Developing an Essay

- Include enough supporting points or ideas to explain your thesis statement fully.
- Leave no question that readers might ask unanswered.
- Include enough information to explain each topic and subtopic fully.
- Use specific details and precise language to explain each piece of information fully.

As you draft your essay you will want to provide smooth transitions from sentence to sentence and paragraph to paragraph. Seamless transitions will keep your reader from becoming confused, frustrated, and disoriented. Above all, coherence in your essay will ensure that your reader continues to read. Use the following strategies to connect your thoughts and to achieve coherence.

You can learn more about coherence on page C138.

Strategies for Achieving Coherence

- Use transitional words and phrases.
- Repeat a key word from an earlier sentence.
- Use synonyms for key words from an earlier sentence.
- Repeat an idea from an earlier sentence, using new words.
- Use a pronoun in place of a word used earlier.

You can find a list of transitions on page C132.

Compare the outline on page C398 with the body of the essay on the Big Dipper, which follows. As you read, you will see how the words and phrases in **boldface** type make the ideas flow smoothly. Notice how the repetition of key words—such as *shape, pattern, stars,* and *constellation*—is also used as a connecting device. Also notice how transitional words, such as *therefore* and *also,* help the writer achieve coherence.

**FROM I
IN OUTLINE**

People have made different interpretations of **this pattern** of lights near the North Star. Many observers, including the ancient shepherds along the Tigris and Euphrates Rivers and the Iroquois near Lake Ontario, saw the seven stars as part of a larger **shape,** a great bear. In **this shape,** called Ursa Major, the handle of the dipper forms the tail of the bear. The **smaller** form made by the seven stars **alone** has been seen both as a dipper, or drinking ground, and as a plow. **Inside the dipper** is a double star, including the bright star Mizar and the tiny star Alcor. Ancient Arabs saw **this pair** as horse and rider. Early American Indians saw **it** as a woman with her baby. **All** the various interpretations, **from** the strong Great Bear **to** the nurturing woman, are positive images.

**FROM II
IN OUTLINE**

Aside from stirring people's imagination, the Big Dipper **also** serves a practical guide for travelers. Navigators in northern waters have long used **it** to locate the North Star. The **stars** that form the front of the dipper point directly to the North Star. Travelers on land can **also** find north by tracing a line from the Dipper to the North Star. Historians note that slaves escaping from the South on the Underground Railroad were told to "follow the drinking gourd."

**FROM III
IN OUTLINE**

The Big Dipper can **also** be used as a guidepost for finding **other stars** and **constellations.** If you trace a line extending from the handle of the dipper, you can easily find the bright star Arcturus in the constellation Boötes (the shepherd). Extend **that** line **even farther** in the **same** direction and you can see Spica, the bright star in the constellation Virgo (the maiden). A stargazer, **therefore,** can rely on the Big Dipper **throughout** the year for help in finding **other patterns** in the sky.

● *Identifying Connecting Devices*

Identify each connecting device as a *repeated word*, an *earlier idea in new words*, a *pronoun*, or a *transitional word or phrase*.

The Flying Disk

From **(1)** <u>its</u> earliest days, the sport of Frisbee has symbolized fun, individual skill, and the dream of flight.
The **(2)** <u>flying disk</u> is believed to have originated in the early 1900s, when students at Yale University treated themselves to the bakery goods of the Frisbee Pie Company. All over campus students tossed both pie tins and the lids of cookie tins. The thrower would always yell "Frisbee!" to alert the catcher that the **(3)** <u>metal disk</u> was on its way. The game was played purely for **(4)** <u>fun</u>, which is still true of Frisbee.

(5) <u>In the 1940s</u>, designers came out with a much more flyable disk made of plastic. Continued improvements in design made the **(6)** <u>disk</u> a marvel of aeronautics. Throwers began developing intricate techniques to control the flight pattern of this amazing **(7)** <u>saucer</u>. **(8)** <u>Unlike requirements for athletes in other sports</u>, the size and strength of the thrower are unimportant. A Frisbee is easy to throw, and its flight can be mastered through skill instead of muscle power.

(9) <u>Perhaps the greatest appeal of the Frisbee</u> is its link with flight itself. Although the thrower is earthbound, the well-controlled Frisbee soars, glides, and arcs with all the beauty of a bird. Its flight is powered not by a battery or an engine but by a human hand. For many players the thrill of creating and controlling flight is the main pleasure of the game.

The fun and art of Frisbee helped to make it a respected sport. National tournaments offer Frisbee fans a chance to match their skills with those of others. People who have grown tired of other sports and are looking for both fun and a challenge should pick up a **(10)** <u>flying disk</u> and toss it around for a while. They may find, as so many others have, one of the most refreshing games in town.

DRAFTING *Body*

 Working from the outline you developed, draft the body of your informative essay. Make sure you write one paragraph for each main topic in your outline. As you write, refer to the <u>Strategies for Achieving Coherence</u> on page C404. Then save your work for later use.

Drafting the Conclusion

The conclusion to an informative essay should be strong and leave a lasting impression with your audience. A good conclusion sums up the idea in the body of the essay and reminds the reader of the thesis statement. It should also end with a **clincher sentence** that echoes in the reader's mind. The conclusion provides an excellent opportunity to express whatever insights you have gained from writing about your subject. Following is a list of ways to end an essay.

> ### Strategies for Writing a Conclusion
> - Summarize the body of the essay.
> - Restate the thesis statement in new words.
> - Draw a conclusion based on the body of the essay.
> - Add an insight about the thesis.
> - Refer to details from your prewriting notes that were not used in the body or introduction but that support your thesis.
> - Refer to ideas in the introduction to bring the essay full circle.
> - Write a memorable clincher statement that will echo in the minds of your readers.

In the following example, the basis for the conclusion of the essay on the Big Dipper was a detail that was not used anywhere else.

CONCLUSION

Although they appear stationary, the stars above are really speeding through space at the rate of one million miles a day. Five stars in the Big Dipper are moving in the same direction, so they will keep their positions relative to one another. Two of the stars, however—the star nearest the North Star and the last star in the handle—are speeding away from each other in opposite directions. Stargazers 50,000 years from now will no longer be able to see a dipper shape. No doubt they will find meaningful shapes in

CLINCHER SENTENCE

the new pattern of stars. They must find a new and equally important compass and guide at night as they try to understand the distant heavens and their own small place within them.

The clincher sentence brings the essay full circle by referring to an idea in the introduction. It also fixes in the reader's mind the main idea that the Big Dipper is a familiar sight and practical guide.

Drafting a Title   When you are satisfied with your conclusion, think of a title for your essay. Read over each paragraph, looking for words and phrases you could use as a title. A good title should make your readers curious enough to want to read your essay.

MODEL: Creating a Title

Clear Skies (boring)

Star Dust (?? doesn't really fit)

Stargazers (a detail)

Clear Nights (not on the mark)

On a Clear Night (pretty good)

When You Can See Forever (I like it!)

● *Writing a Conclusion*

Reread the essay about the Big Dipper—the introduction on page C403, the body on page C405, and the conclusion on page C408. Then write a different conclusion, using one of the other ways to end an essay listed on page C407.

● *Thinking of Titles*

Make a list of five titles for the essay about the Big Dipper. Think of catchy titles that would make *you* want to read the essay.

Communicate Your Ideas

DRAFTING *Conclusions*

Look over the first draft of your introduction and body for your essay. Using the chart on page C407 as a guide, draft a suitable conclusion and then read the entire essay aloud. More than likely you wrote your first draft quickly without too much concern for minor problems. Now keep your first draft at your side as you write a second draft of your essay. Line by line look for ways to expand, delete, rearrange, or substitute to improve the quality of your second draft. Take the time to think about the best possible ways to express your ideas. Now that your thoughts are securely on paper, you can concentrate on clarifying and refining them. If necessary, experiment with several different introductions and conclusions, and then choose those that you think make the greatest impact. You can use your outline to evaluate whether your ideas are presented in the most effective order. Perhaps the impact of your argument could benefit by a slight adjustment of details. When you are satisfied that you have an acceptable second draft, think of a catchy title for your essay and write it at the top. Save your paper for revising at a later time.

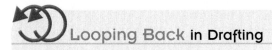
Looping Back in Drafting

Capturing Readers' Interest

"What is written without effort," Samuel Johnson once remarked, "is in general read without pleasure." In other words, producing an essay that will capture your readers' interest is hard work. In your desire to finish drafting, did you keep your audience and purpose in mind? Rework your draft as necessary, maintaining a direct, matter-of-fact tone. At the same time, consider whether you have presented interesting examples and incidents that will hold your readers' attention.

Revising | Writing Process

Many writers put away their first or second draft for a few hours or overnight before they revise it. In this way they have a fresh outlook and can more easily see what needs to be improved. In this stage you may decide that some ideas are out of order and must be moved, or that your essay requires cuts in some places. You may also have new insights to add. This is your opportunity to make these changes and to adjust the overall structure of your essay. As you revise your essay, think of your readers and find ways to make your messages as clear as possible.

Checking for Unity, Coherence, and Emphasis

If your essay has **unity,** all the supporting paragraphs relate to the main idea and the thesis. As a result, your readers will not be distracted by paragraphs or sentences that stray from your main idea. If your essay has **coherence,** the ideas in the paragraphs flow logically and naturally from one to the next. When your essay has coherence, your readers can easily follow the sequence of your well-connected ideas. If your essay has **emphasis,** your readers will understand which points are the most important. The following questions will help you check your essay for unity, coherence, and emphasis.

Checking for Unity, Coherence, and Emphasis

Checking for Unity

✓ Does every idea and detail relate to the subject?

✓ Does every paragraph in the essay support the thesis statement?

✓ Does every sentence in each paragraph support its topic sentence?

Checking for Coherence

✓ Did you write the paragraphs in the body of your essay in a logical order?

✓ Did you use transitions between paragraphs?

✓ Did you write the sentences within each of the paragraphs in a logical order?

✓ Did you use transitions between the sentences within each paragraph?

Checking for Emphasis

✓ Do your transitional words show the relative importance of your ideas?

✓ Did you give an adequate amount of space to important and complex ideas?

Communicate Your Ideas

REVISING *Unity, Coherence, and Emphasis*

Carefully read over the second draft of your essay, using the checklist above to evaluate the unity, coherence, and emphasis of your work. Revise your work as necessary. Then exchange essays with a classmate and provide each other with suggestions for improvements, keeping in mind the purpose and intended audience of your essay. When your paper is returned, use your partner's comments to make further refinements. Save your paper for editing later.

In addition to checking for unity, coherence, and emphasis, you should use a revision checklist to help you revise your essay.

> ### Evaluation Checklist for Revising
>
> **Checking Your Essay**
> - ✓ Do you have a strong introduction that sets the tone and captures attention? *(pages C402–C403)*
> - ✓ Does the thesis statement express the main idea clearly? *(page C400)*
> - ✓ Does your essay have unity, coherence, and emphasis? *(pages C410–C411)*
> - ✓ Do you have a strong conclusion? *(page C407–C408)*
> - ✓ Did you add a title? *(page C408)*
>
> **Checking Your Paragraphs**
> - ✓ Does each paragraph have a topic sentence? *(pages C103–C104)*
> - ✓ Does every sentence in each paragraph support the topic sentence? *(pages C106–C107)*
> - ✓ Is each paragraph unified and coherent? *(pages C136–C138)*
>
> **Checking Your Sentences and Words**
> - ✓ Are your sentences varied? *(pages C73–C80)*
> - ✓ Did you combine sentences that go together? *(page C74)*
> - ✓ Are your sentences clear and concise? *(pages C67–C70)*
> - ✓ Have you avoided faulty sentences? *(pages C81–C88)*
> - ✓ Did you use figurative language? *(page C64)*

Editing
Writing Process

Now you are ready to edit your essay by checking for errors in grammar, spelling, capitalization, and punctuation. You may want to put your writing aside for a while, and then go back to it. A little distance will help you see mistakes.

EDITING

 Reread your essay one more time, looking for errors. Using your Personalized Editing Checklist will help you avoid the types of errors you are prone to make. After editing your essay, prepare a neat final copy in the standard manuscript form shown on page C49–C52.

Publishing · Writing Process

Writing an essay should not be like shooting an arrow into the dark. Every writer needs an audience. When you have an audience that reacts and responds to your work, you will get a much better sense of your work. Audience reaction will even stimulate you to write better next time.

PUBLISHING

Recall the audience you profiled during prewriting on page C386. Now think of someone you know who is like the reader you imagined. Ask this person to read and respond to your essay. You can find more ideas for publishing your essay on pages C48–C49. Place a copy of your essay in your portfolio.

PORTFOLIO

Time Out to Reflect How is the essay that you have just finished different from previous work you have done in other classes? How have the skills taught in this chapter improved your ability to write an informative essay? After comparing the two pieces of writing, record your reactions to them in the Learning Log section of your **journal**.

Process of Writing an Informative Essay

The chart below shows the overall process for writing an informative essay. Remember, though, that the writing process is recursive: good writers move back and forth among the different stages to achieve the best possible result. The numbers in parentheses on this chart refer to pages where you can find help with your writing.

PREWRITING
- Find subjects by drawing on your experiences and reading. *(page C383)*
- From a list of possible subjects, choose one to develop into an essay. *(page C384)*
- Limit your subject. Focus your ideas by asking yourself questions about your purpose, audience, and tone. *(pages C384–C386)*
- Develop a list of supporting ideas. *(pages C386–C388)*
- Develop a working thesis. *(pages C388–C389)*
- Organize your list of ideas into categories and an outline. *(pages C391–C399)*

DRAFTING
- Refine your thesis statement. *(page C400)*
- Write an introduction that includes your thesis statement. *(page C402)*
- Use your outline to write the paragraphs of the body. *(pages C403–C405)*
- Use connecting devices to link your thoughts. *(pages C404–C405)*
- Add a concluding paragraph. *(pages C407–C408)*
- Add a title. *(page C408)*

REVISING
- Using the <u>Evaluation Checklist for Revising</u>, revise your essay for structure, well-developed paragraphs, unity, coherence, emphasis, and varied, lively sentences and words. *(page C412)*

EDITING
- Using your Personalized Editing Checklist, check your grammar, spelling, and mechanics. *(pages C412–C413)*

PUBLISHING
- Make a neat final copy of your essay in standard manuscript form.
- Present your finished work to a reader. *(page C413)*

▶ A Writer Writes

An Informative Essay About Scientific Research

Purpose: **to explain how the use of animals in medical research has both positive and negative outcomes**

Audience: **your classmates**

In "The Mind of the Chimpanzee," Jane Goodall uses the strategies of comparison and contrast as well as analogy to challenge the long-standing scientific belief that chimpanzees are incapable of thought or feeling. Adopting similar strategies, write an informative essay about the use of live animals in scientific research. Consider both their contribution to the advancement of scientific knowledge and the concern about their treatment.

Prewriting

Think about your purpose and audience and be sure to limit your subject so it is manageable. If necessary, use reference books and electronic sources in the library or media center to find additional facts to use in your essay. To develop a working thesis, concentrate on the benefits and drawbacks of research using animals. Then group your details into categories and choose AABB or ABAB pattern to arrange them in a logical order. Finally use your categories as the basis of an outline.

Drafting

Refine your thesis statement to cover all your ideas and details. As you draft your essay, make sure that your introduction includes your thesis statement, captures your reader's interest, and sets the tone. For the body of your essay, draft a supporting paragraph for each main category of details.

Strive to incorporate the strategy of analogy along with comparison and contrast as you develop your ideas. Then, after you draft a concluding paragraph, think of an interesting title to capture your audience's interest.

Revising

Put your draft aside for a time. When you are ready to revise it, you can read it again with fresh eyes. During your revision read through your essay several times, using the Evaluation Checklist for Revising on page C412 as a guide. If possible, also get a friend's comments. Then make whatever changes or adjustments you think will make your essay more effective.

Editing

When you are pleased with your essay, check it for grammar, spelling, punctuation, and neatness. Use the checklist on page C46 to help you put the finishing touches on your work.

Publishing

You may want to share your essay with your classmates by reading it aloud. You may also choose to address a larger audience by submitting it for for publication in your school newspaper. If your school has a local Intranet, you can convert the text and post it there as a Web page.

Connection Collection

Representing in Different Ways

From Print . . . **FLOPPY'S CLOWN COLLEGE**

offers a variety of classes, including character development, miming, improvisation, makeup, pie-throwing, and balloon sculpture, just to name a few. Clowns who complete Floppy's training are often invited to perform in professional circuses.

Floppy's graduates do not walk in caps and gowns to receive diplomas. They are more likely to play leapfrog, soak one another with trick flowers, or wear white makeup, red noses, and oversized shoes.

. . . to Visuals

Using this excerpt from Floppy's Clown College brochure, draw a series of frames for a documentary film about the school and its graduates. You may also find photographs in magazines or on the Internet that you can paste together in chronological order. Try to match the visual information in your pictures to what is explained in the text of the brochure.

from Visuals . . .

. . . to Print

Based on the pictures, write a treatment for a documentary on clown colleges. Develop a working thesis and express your main idea clearly and concisely.

- **Which strategies can be used for creating both written and visual representations? Which strategies apply to one, not both? Which type of representation is more effective?**
- **Draw a conclusion, and write briefly about the differences between written ideas and visual representations.**

Writing in the Workplace
Informative E-mail

Ann E. Droyd has been promoted as your new boss. She is a robot and struggles to understand the human behavior of her co-workers. She seems confused when employees gather around the water cooler to talk, or when they leave the office to go home. She does not understand why people do not work nights, weekends, or holidays.

Write an informative E-mail to your boss explaining why people need to have friendly talks and take breaks from their work. Start with a strong introduction that clearly sets the tone. Limit your subject so Ann Droyd does not overheat trying to compute the information.

What strategies did you use to explain human behavior to your boss?

You can find information on writing E-mail letters on pages C736–C739.

Writing in Academic Areas
Informative Note

You are a geologist working in the town of Meltaway. The city council has asked you to survey the land on which it plans to build an ice rink. Unfortunately, your tests indicate heavy volcanic activity in this area.

Write a note to explain to the Meltaway city council why the rink should not be built. While informing it of your red-hot discovery, keep your note cohesive by using transitional words and phrases. You might want to set the tone with figurative language to ease the city council's concerns.

What strategies did you use to inform the city council of your observations?

You can find information on writing business letters on pages C569–C575.

Assess Your Learning

You are a time traveler who has just returned from the year 3000. The objective of your trip was to study the people of 3000, observing the technology they use and the culture they have created. Since the government funded this top-secret mission, you have been asked to prepare a brief report with details from your trip. You are required to submit this report to the Secret Government Agency, or SGA.

▶ **Write a brief report to the SGA informing them about the civilization of the future.**

▶ **Gather information and start with a working thesis and an outline. Include enough supporting details to develop your thesis fully. Leave no question unanswered. Keep your audience in mind as you organize your ideas. Organize your writing in the report to ensure coherence, logical progression, and support for your ideas.**

▶ *Before You Write* **Consider the following questions:**
What is the *subject?*
What is the *occasion?*
Who is the *audience?*
What is the *purpose?*

▶ *After You Write* **Evaluate your work using the following criteria:**
- Have you used specific details and precise language?
- Have you limited the focus of your report?
- Does each paragraph have a clear and concise topic sentence?
- Have you used conjunctions to connect ideas meaningfully?
- Have you organized your writing in the report to ensure coherence, logical progression, and support for your ideas?
- Have you varied the types of details you used to support your topic sentences?
- Add two criteria of your own.

Write briefly on how well you did. Point out your strengths and areas for improvement.

CHAPTER 10

Writing to Persuade

No doubt at some time you have had the experience of being "moved" by something you have read. Perhaps it was the ending of a much-loved book. Maybe it was the heartfelt letter of a child to Santa or a parent's loving words in a birthday card. Writing does indeed have the power to move, to stir strong feelings.

Persuasive essays take the word *move* to a new level. Some persuasion may attempt to move your way of thinking about a subject from one point of view to another. Some may try to move you literally—to get you up out of your chair to act, to do something. As a longer form than the paragraph, the persuasive essay invites the reader into an extended mental debate on the subject of a controversy. Whether the reader is moved by that debate depends in large part on how well the writer uses the tools of persuasion. This chapter will help you deepen your persuasive skills and your ability to move readers—maybe even mountains.

Reading with a Writer's Eye

The following selection appeared in the *Chicago Tribune* during the height of the winter holiday season. Read it through once or twice just to understand it well. Then look back over it as if you were the newspaper editor, deciding whether to print the article as written. What persuasive tools has the writer used? Which are most effective? least effective?

Giving Intelligently to WORTHY CAUSES

One group, for example, reported it spends 90 percent of its donations on telemarketing to keep the gifts coming

Joan Beck

Along with the forest of mail-order catalogs and a blizzard of holiday cards, the pre-holiday mail brings burdens of cleverly crafted guilt. How can you toss away those appeals for money—when people are homeless, hungry, afflicted with catastrophe, disabled, aging, suffering from every disease known to humanity? When the environment needs protecting, victims of discrimination lack aid, your alma mater is short of scholarship money. . . .

To rub in the guilt, some of the appeals include a clutch of inexpensive greeting cards (typically Monet lilies), or a set of address labels, or a calendar, or a good luck token from an Indian tribe. Dump them in the trash and you feel like you're stealing from sick kids or taking nickels from a blind man's cup. Send a check and you can't be sure you aren't a sucker for a familiar holiday scam or that the money won't be used simply to send out more fundraising letters.

You get lavish invitations to pay $10,000 for a table at a holiday ball for a charity you didn't even realize existed. There are intimate notes from "friends" you don't remember asking that you join them in sending a check to help their favorite good cause. An apparently "personal" note from a celebrity wants you to join him in a favorite appeal.

The holiday season is the peak time for charity solicitations. The experts who craft the pleas know that you are most open to goodwill-toward-men feelings this time of year, that your resistance to sales pitches is lower, that you're too busy to check out the soliciting organizations carefully, that you are feeling slightly guilty because your family has so much and others are so needy. Americans gave more than $143 billion last year to charitable organizations, up 7.5 percent from the year before. More money than you'd like to think did not go to further the cause itself, but for more fundraising.

If you have more time, you could check out the appeals with a national ratings service for charities (there are three major ones). Or send for an annual report or IRS tax filing. Or look for data on the Internet (double-check the source of information). But there are more than 650,000 non-profits out there and all of them seem to have your name and address.

There are a few guidelines to help. Be sure you at least know the identity of the organization that wants your check. Some unscrupulous groups—in the cancer research field, for example—use names that sound like familiar established charities, assuming you won't pay close attention and dash off a check.

Find out how much of your money will actually go for the purpose you intend. It's a rule of thumb in charity fundraising that at least 60 percent to 65 percent of donations should actually be used for the good cause; the best non-profits make it 80 percent or more. The rest is spent on more fundraising and administration or the vague-sounding "education." That means an unscrupulous organization can tuck a message about cancer's warning signs into its fundraising letters and count them as "programs."

Abuses can be blatant, indeed. One group, for example, reported it spends 90 percent of its donations on telemarketing to keep the gifts coming. It's not considered unusual for an organization to send out 100,000 appeals in hopes of generating 1,000 responses from first-time contributors.

You should make sure the group you are considering helping has the same purpose you have in mind. If you're giving to combat a disease, for example, you should know whether your money is going largely for research, prevention or treating patients. The Nature Conservancy has a much different approach to environmental concerns than, say, Greenpeace.

There is an easier way. You can share your holiday blessings with the Chicago Tribune Holiday Fund. Every cent and more that you give will go to help children have a happy holiday and a better future, to relieve hunger and homelessness, aid the abused, and support programs for the developmentally disabled. Not only does the Tribune pay all of the expenses of the fund, it matches every dollar you contribute with 60 cents from the McCormick Tribune Foundation. Instead of hoping 60 to 65 percent of your gift is going for the work you intend, you can be sure that 160 percent will.

Thinking as a Writer

Evaluating Persuasive Evidence

- Try to boil down the author's main points into a single, clearly worded statement.
- What kinds of evidence does she use to "prove" her points? List all the points she uses to support her position.
- Are the supporting facts and examples effective? In other words, does this essay move you out of your chair into action? If so, what action will you take? If not, why not?

Analyzing Persuasive Appeals

Viewing
- The poster shown below was used by the American Red Cross to raise funds. What details in the poster catch your eye? Is the poster effective? Explain your response.

Using a Persuasive Tone

Oral Expression
- What is the tone of the introduction to this essay? Does the tone change in other parts of the essay? If so, how?
- Read the essay aloud, trying to match your style of reading to the tone. Listen carefully when others do the same, and evaluate whether their reading expresses the tone that comes through in the writing.

The Power of Persuasion

You have already seen one real-world example of a persuasive essay—the appeal in the *Chicago Tribune* for sensible holiday gift giving. This is an example of an editorial, one of the most common uses of the persuasive essay.

Uses of Persuasion

Here are just a few examples of the ways in which persuasive writing is guiding important decisions in our lives.

- **Elected officials develop "position papers"** to explain, defend, and promote their stands on the tough issues of the day.

- **Medical researchers write articles** for popular magazines explaining recent scientific findings in health and medicine and urging healthful behaviors for prevention of serious disease.

- **High school students submit essays** with their college admission applications trying to persuade the reviewers to accept them into their programs.

- **Employees write a proposal** based on an idea for a new product and try to persuade the company decision makers to put up the money to develop it.

- **Attorneys draw up their closing arguments** to bring together all the facts and other evidence in a case and persuade the jury to decide a certain way.

- **Movie reviewers and book critics assess a work** and use persuasion to convince readers of their point of view.

Refining Your Skills of Persuasion

"If you can't annoy somebody," wrote Kingsley Amis, "there is little point in writing." That quip may apply especially well to persuasive writing. If everybody already agreed with your point of view, there would be no need to argue in favor of it. A good persuasive subject is one that is likely to stir some strong opposition.

The ability to cast a net into a controversial subject area, draw back and evaluate the ideas you have "caught," and shape them into a reasonable and forceful statement of opinion is among the most valuable skills you can develop. Writing persuasive essays will help you develop and refine this skill.

A **persuasive essay** states an opinion on a subject and uses facts, reasons, and examples to convince readers.

 Your Writer's Journal

In your journal, write about times when you have disagreed strongly with others on matters of public, not personal, interest. What events in the news have stirred up strong opinions among your family members and friends? As you look around you, where do you see injustice? Whom would you "annoy" if you proposed a solution to ease that injustice, and why? What annoys you? Take these starting points and expand them into journal entries. Try to explain as much as possible in your journal about why you feel as you do.

Persuasive Essay Structure

Like all essays, a persuasive essay has three main parts: an introduction, a body, and a conclusion. The chart on the next page shows how each of these parts contributes to the essay.

Structure of a Persuasive Essay

- The **introduction** captures the audience's attention, presents the issue, and expresses the writer's opinion in a thesis statement.

- In an effective persuasive essay, the **body of supporting paragraphs** presents reasons, facts, examples, and expert opinions to support the writer's opinions.

- The **conclusion** presents a summary or strong conclusive evidence—logically drawn from the arguments—that drives home the writer's opinion.

As you read the following persuasive essay, notice how each part carries out the purpose of persuading the reader.

MODEL: Persuasive Essay

Talking Chimps

INTRODUCTION:
PROVIDES
BACKGROUND
INFORMATION ON
THE ISSUE

In the past several decades, a number of chimps have been taught the gestures of American Sign Language (Ameslan). The results of these studies are hotly debated. A recent survey asked scientists to name the most significant discovery in recent years. Many replied that it was the failure of chimps to acquire language. About an equal number, however, believed the most significant discovery was the *success* of chimps in learning and using language. These opinions arise from differing definitions of language use. The first group of scientists see too much simple imitation or reward seeking in chimp language to

THESIS STATEMENT
call it true language learning. The success of chimps in mastering sign language, however, indicates that they have indeed learned a simple language.

FIRST BODY
PARAGRAPH:
USES FACTS,
EXAMPLES, AND
REASONS

To use language, it is first necessary to understand that a word—or a sign—is a symbol. It is a symbol of the thing it names, not the thing itself. Humans know, for example, that the word *cup* is a symbol for the thing they drink from. The five chimpanzees, Washoe, Moja, Pili, Tatu, and Dar, reared by Professors R. A. and B. T. Gardner at the University of Nevada, acquired between 100 and 200 signs by age five. They were able to name things in pictures, showing another level of understanding. In addition to learning the names of things, such as *cat, hat,* and *tree,* they also learned the names of actions, such as *chase, hug,* and *tickle,* and of qualities, such as *dirty* and *hot.*

SECOND BODY
PARAGRAPH:
ANSWERS
OPPONENTS'
OBJECTION

Critics of the early experiments argued that since chimps did not understand the concept of negating, they were not really using language. (Negating is adding a negative, such as *no* or *not,* to a thought.) Sarah, a chimp trained at the University of California, Santa Barbara, showed an understanding not only of negating but also of compound and complex sentences. Sarah learned to compose and read sentences by placing metal symbols on a metallic board. She once asked herself, "What is an apple not?" and correctly— and creatively—replied, "Bread."

THIRD BODY
PARAGRAPH:
ANSWERS
OPPONENTS'
OBJECTION

Many critics also doubt the use of language by chimps. They think the animals are cued by their trainers. Sarah's trainers decided to test the chimp's ability to use language without the help of cues. They sent an inexperienced person in to "converse" with Sarah—a person who did not know Sarah's language. That person was unable to cue Sarah to do something that she could then imitate. Sarah did not do as well as she usually did, probably because she was confused by the appearance of a new human partner. Still she scored high enough on her test to convince her

CONCLUSION:

DRIVES HOME
THE MAIN POINT

trainers that she could use language without being cued.

Those who doubt that chimps have successfully learned a simple language place too much emphasis on comparing chimps to humans. Our language has developed over a long period of time, while chimps have only recently been exposed to language learning. Given their short exposure to language, chimps have demonstrated remarkable mastery. Any creature who can sign to himself, "Cry me; me cry" after his trainer has left him for the day surely can handle simple language.

PRACTICE YOUR SKILLS

● *Analyzing a Persuasive Essay*

The following essay takes the opposite position on the question of a chimp's ability to use language from that presented in the model essay, "Talking Chimps." Read the next essay carefully and write answers to the questions that follow it. The paragraphs are numbered for easy reference.

Monkey See, Monkey Do, Monkey Get

(1) The language experiments with chimps are fascinating and thought provoking. They do not, however, convince all experts that chimps have acquired a humanlike grasp of language. While the chimps have learned more than one hundred words, they do not use these words well enough to be called true language users.

(2) Dr. Herbert S. Terrace conducted an experiment for almost four years with a chimp named Nim. At first, Nim's seeming success delighted him. Nim readily gestured many Ameslan signs. Then Dr. Terrace studied the videotapes of Nim and his trainers. He made several discoveries that led him to question Nim's use of language. One was that only 10 percent of Nim's utterances were uncued, whereas 40 percent were imitations of gestures the trainer had just used. Another discovery was that Nim, unlike human children, did not take turns in a conversation. He frequently interrupted his trainer to express his needs and desires. Dr. Terrace also discovered as he examined Nim's progress that the number of words in Nim's "sentences" did not increase with time. Children build increasingly longer sentences as they learn more words. Nim's sentences stayed at an average level of about 2.5 words per sentence.

(3) The combining of words into one utterance is often viewed as a real use of language. Many experts point to clever word combinations in chimps as signs of their mastery of language. Washoe, for example, gave a sign meaning "water bird" when she saw a swan for the first time in a pond. To the trainers this expression seemed like one word. Another explanation, however, is that Washoe was simply naming two things she saw, and the trainers, not Washoe, combined the two symbols into one.

(4) Finally, many of the language experiments with chimps involve the use of rewards—a banana, a piece of chocolate, a tickle—for correct answers. At the Yerkes Primate Center in Atlanta, Georgia, a chimp named Lana was taught a computer language called Yerkish. If she used the correct word order for requests, the machine would give her the item she requested. Sarah, a chimp at the University of California, was also rewarded with a treat if she "composed" a proper sentence on her magnetic board. The link between communication and reward is too strong in these cases to prove mastery over language. Until chimps can convey information instead of seeking a reward, they cannot be said to be language users.

(5) Nonetheless, the chimp experiments revealed much to delight even those who doubt. The chimps' engaging personalities and intelligence suggest that future studies will be fruitful. For now, however, despite the dramatic use of individual signs, the evidence does not prove that chimps can truly use language.

1. What is the thesis statement?
2. Explain the controversy expressed in paragraph 1.
3. What three facts about the chimp named Nim are offered as support in paragraph 2?
4. What chimp in the first essay is a counter-example to Nim?
5. What example is used in paragraph 3 to support the point about word combinations?
6. Both essays report the use of tickling in the chimp experiments. In the first essay, what does the detail about tickling suggest? How is it used to make a different point in the second essay?
7. How many specific chimps are used as examples in the second essay?
8. How does paragraph 4 support the thesis?
9. What is the author's conclusion in the second essay?

▶ Facts and Opinions

Persuasive essays are primarily made up of two types of statements: facts and opinions. When you write a persuasive essay, you should be aware of the difference. Facts are statements that can be proved. Opinions, on the other hand, are beliefs or judgments that can be supported but not proved.

A **fact** is a statement that can be proved. An **opinion** is a belief or judgment that cannot be proved.

You can test whether a statement is factual in two ways. One way is to ask yourself whether you would be able to prove the statement through your own observation and experience.

FACT   There are three chimpanzees at our local zoo.
          (You could go to the zoo and observe this.)

The second way is to ask yourself whether you could prove it by consulting accepted authorities.

FACT	The chimpanzee is an anthropoid ape with a high degree of intelligence. (You cannot use your experience to test this statement, but you can verify it by consulting a recognized expert or an encyclopedia.)

Unlike facts, opinions cannot be proved. They are personal judgments, interpretations, preferences, and predictions that differ from person to person. Here are some examples.

War movies are **too violent.**

Mr. Ling is the **best** candidate for mayor.

I believe that nuclear energy plants are a **terrible** threat to the atmosphere.

Computer programming is our school's **most valuable** course.

Sometimes you can recognize opinions in what you hear, read, and write by listening and watching for some of the following words that are often used in statements of opinion.

OPINION WORDS		
should	good, better, best	probably
ought	bad, worse, worst	might
can	beautiful	perhaps
may	terrible	maybe

In persuasive essays the soundest opinions are those supported by factual evidence, logical arguments, or both.

UNSUPPORTED OPINION	Chimps can be taught to speak English. (No supporting facts back up this statement.)
SUPPORTED OPINION	Chimps are an endangered species. (African environmentalists support this statement.)

Writing Tip

Support your opinions with convincing factual evidence from your own experience and observation as well as from reliable authorities.

PRACTICE YOUR SKILLS

● *Identifying Facts and Opinions*

State whether each sentence below is a *fact* or an *opinion*. If you are in doubt about a statement, verify it by checking its validity in the library or media center or with a reliable authority.

1. Recycling is not worth the expense.

2. The bald eagle is no longer on the list of endangered species.

3. The United States expects major fuel shortages in the future.

4. Toxic wastes have often been disposed of in populated areas.

5. Cutting down forests diminishes the oxygen supply in the air.

● *Supporting Opinions*

Write one fact that could be used to back up each of the following opinions. If necessary, use library or media center resources to find supporting evidence.

EXAMPLE   Teenagers benefit from employment.
POSSIBLE ANSWER   Some jobs teach many useful skills.

1. Nutrition should be a required course in elementary school.

2. Using illegal drugs is self-destructive.

3. Many citizens are careless about energy consumption.

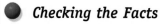

Checking the Facts

Think of one strong opinion you have about your city, town, school, or favorite pastime. List three facts you could use to back up your opinion. Check your supporting facts by asking the following two questions. Then rework any statements that cannot be verified.

- Can I verify each supporting fact?
- Can each fact be verified by my own experience, or do I need to consult a reliable source?

Reasoning

When you write a persuasive essay, your ability to win over your reader usually depends on your reasoning skills. Facts and opinions cannot argue by themselves. Instead, you must create a logical argument by fitting the facts together so they lead to a reasonable conclusion.

Generalizations   When you state a rule or a principle based on fact and experience, you are **generalizing**. For example, suppose you have visited Washington, D.C., three times in July and August, and each time the weather was hot and muggy. From these experiences you could generalize that Washington, D.C., is hot and muggy in the summer.

Generalizing is an important reasoning skill that will help you develop a strong thesis statement for your essay. However, you must use it carefully so that you do not overlook those important exceptions that will make a generalization false.

Hasty Generalizations   When you reason, beware of the pitfall of **hasty generalizations**—broad generalizations based on insufficient evidence. Such hasty generalizations often lead to misleading or false conclusions. To avoid this fallacy, you must examine *enough* particular experiences so that you can draw a sound conclusion.

Hasty Generalization	All professional athletes are healthy. (Has the writer examined enough athletes to conclude that they *all* are healthy?)
Hasty Generalization	Chlorine in swimming pools causes earaches. (Does *everyone* who swims in chlorinated pools have earaches?)

You can make the previous hasty generalizations more sound if you limit them to *some, many,* or *most* cases instead of *all* cases.

Sound Generalization	**Most** professional athletes are healthy.
Sound Generalization	**Some** people experience earaches from swimming in pools that are chlorinated.

Avoiding Hasty Generalizations

- Examine several facts or examples.
- Be sure your examples represent the whole group.
- Check reliable authorities to confirm your generalization.
- Be able to explain any exceptions.
- Avoid words like *all, complete, always, never,* and *none,* because they suggest that there are no exceptions.
- Limit your generalization by using words like *some, many, most, probably, often,* and *sometimes.*

Writing Tip

Avoid **hasty generalizations** by limiting generalizations to *some, many,* or *most* cases.

PRACTICE YOUR SKILLS

● *Writing Sound Generalizations*

Choose one of the following hasty generalizations. Limit the statement to an opinion with which you agree.

1. Any rural area is less polluted than a city.
2. Chimps are more intelligent than any other animal.
3. Adults are responsible for more litter than teenagers.
4. Education is the only avenue to success.
5. Television shows are too violent.
6. Two boys from Webster High School crossed Mr. Kim's lawn and trampled a shrub. Students from that school are destructive.
7. An Italian friend made pizza. Italians are terrific cooks.
8. Lying in the sun causes skin cancer.
9. Boys are not interested in baby-sitting.
10. Politicians have the greatest impact on life in the United States.

Glittering Generalities   Careless thinking about general ideas can lead to another reasoning problem called **glittering generalities,** words and phrases most people associate with virtue and goodness. These words and phrases are used intentionally to trick people into feeling positive about a subject.

Here are some words that almost always stir positive feelings in people.

democracy	family	motherhood
values	moral	education

However, what one person means by any of these words can be very different from what another person means. When one of these virtue words is attached to a controversial idea, chances are the speaker or writer is trying to influence you to associate a positive attitude with the idea.

For example, suppose a politician says, "We must change this law to preserve our democracy." Since the politician rightly assumes you support—even love—our democracy, she or he hopes to convince you that our democracy will come tumbling down if the law does not get changed and that you would not want to see that happen.

Watch for glittering generalities in persuasive appeals made by public figures, in newspapers and magazines, and in television advertisements and programs. A convincing argument should be supported by facts, examples, and sound reasoning, not just by words that make us feel good about the subject.

When you recognize a glittering generality, slash through it by asking yourself these questions, recommended by the Institute for Propaganda Analysis.

- What does the virtue word really mean?

- Does the idea in question have a legitimate connection with the real meaning of the word?

- Is an idea that does not serve my best interests being "sold" to me merely through its being given a name I like?

- Leaving the virtue word out of consideration, what are the merits of the idea itself?

PRACTICE YOUR SKILLS

Dimming a Glittering Generality

Analyze the following glittering generality by writing answers to the four questions above.

"Nothing is more important to our ideal of motherhood than the repeal of Amendment 19, the right of women to vote."

Print Advertisement

A good way to develop the habit of careful reasoning is to examine careless reasoning with a critical eye. Advertisements are usually geared more toward emotion than reason; they often contain careless thinking in their messages. Consider the following example:

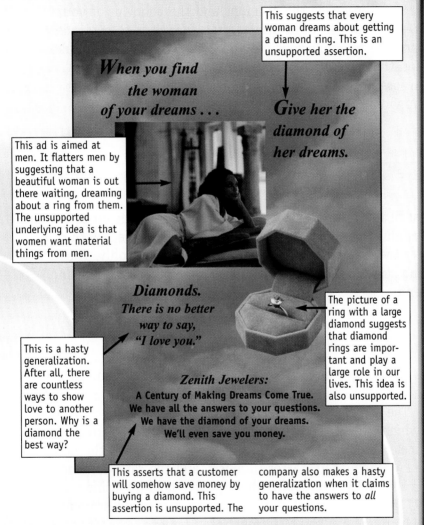

This suggests that every woman dreams about getting a diamond ring. This is an unsupported assertion.

When you find the woman of your dreams . . .

Give her the diamond of her dreams.

This ad is aimed at men. It flatters men by suggesting that a beautiful woman is out there waiting, dreaming about a ring from them. The unsupported underlying idea is that women want material things from men.

Diamonds.
There is no better way to say,
"I love you."

The picture of a ring with a large diamond suggests that diamond rings are important and play a large role in our lives. This idea is also unsupported.

This is a hasty generalization. After all, there are countless ways to show love to another person. Why is a diamond the best way?

Zenith Jewelers:
A Century of Making Dreams Come True.
We have all the answers to your questions.
We have the diamond of your dreams.
We'll even save you money.

This asserts that a customer will somehow save money by buying a diamond. This assertion is unsupported. The company also makes a hasty generalization when it claims to have the answers to *all* your questions.

Oral Expression Find a dramatic, illustrated ad from a newspaper or magazine and take turns reading your ads aloud to the class. The listeners should identify facts, supported or unsupported opinions, and hasty or sound generalizations in each advertisement.

Process of Writing a Persuasive Essay

As you write a persuasive essay, keep in mind that your purpose is to influence the opinions and the behavior of your readers—your audience. In other words, you want to persuade your audience to adopt your point of view and perhaps to take an action that you suggest. Your first step in accomplishing this purpose is to develop a logical and reasonable argument that supports your opinion.

Most of the success of a persuasive essay depends on careful planning during the prewriting stage. Choose a subject with care and take the time to prepare your argument thoroughly. The following strategies will help you plan a logical and convincing argument.

Choosing a Subject

The subject you choose should be meaningful to you. The stronger your interest, the more convincing your persuasive essay will be. The subject you choose should also be controversial—one about which people tend to disagree. For instance, the treatment of the homeless in American society, the effectiveness of the new welfare laws, teenagers' tastes in music, and the care of American seashores are all issues about which people hold opposing points of view. Brainstorm for a list of issues you care about strongly— about which you can say, "I think," or "I believe." Next narrow your choices by brainstorming, freewriting, or clustering on each of the issues under consideration. Then use the following guidelines to choose the best subject for your persuasive essay.

Guidelines for Choosing a Subject

- Choose a subject about an issue that is important to you.
- Choose a subject about an issue on which people hold very different opinions.
- Choose a subject that you can support with examples, reasons, and facts from your own experiences or from other reliable sources.
- Choose a subject for which there is an audience whose beliefs or behavior you would like to influence.

Identifying Your Audience

Sometimes when you write a persuasive essay, you may have to address an audience outside of the classroom. Learn as much as possible about that audience in advance in order to decide whether you can successfully persuade them or move them to action. Knowing your audience well also helps you choose the best material to support your argument.

Questions for Analyzing an Audience

- What does my audience already know about my subject?
- What is my audience's point of view about my subject?
- Do they already agree or disagree with my position?
- What are the chances of changing the opinions and behavior of my audience?
- Are there any sensitive issues I should be aware of?

Writing Tip

If your audience disagrees with your position, make sure you know exactly why they disagree. That way you will be better able to develop a strong argument that directly or cleverly counters their specific point or points of opposition.

● *Identifying Your Audience*

Form a small group and identify five possible audiences for each of the following subjects.

EXAMPLE   establishing a large green space in town

AUDIENCE   joggers, day-care helpers, landscape architects, senior citizens, gardeners

1. establishing a clean-up committee for riverbanks

2. establishing bird sanctuaries

3. establishing walking trails on conservation land

Communicate Your Ideas

PREWRITING *Subject and Audience*

Review your **journal** notes about the subjects that stir strong opinions in you. Then brainstorm for other ideas for a persuasive essay. As you consider different subjects, list those that have two sides and will permit you to recommend some type of action or resolution to the problem. Use the guidelines on page C439 to make your final choice. Then place a star beside your choice and save your work for later use.

SAVE YOUR WORK

Developing a Thesis Statement

Once you have chosen a subject and identified your audience, you are ready to develop a **thesis statement.** This is a statement of the point of view you will argue for in your essay. Avoid a statement of fact or of personal preference, for these do not make suitable thesis statements for a persuasive essay. Look carefully at the opinion you have about your subject; it should be a supportable opinion and worth the consideration of others. Also avoid hasty generalizations by limiting your thesis statement. Keep in mind that often the thesis statement will take the form of a recommendation for action.

FACT	Throughout history, some companies have polluted water resources in the United States.
OPINION	I think my town should form a watchdog committee to protect the reservoir.
THESIS STATEMENT	Although cleaning up water resources will be a long, costly process, this town should start at once.

Guidelines for Developing a Thesis Statement

- Choose a debatable opinion—one that has two sides.
- State the thesis simply and directly in one sentence.
- Avoid hasty generalizations by limiting your statement.
- Give a supportable opinion or a recommendation for action.
- As you collect more information, continue to revise the thesis statement until it is clear-cut and defensible and covers all the evidence.

If your thesis does not meet all of these guidelines, you need to rethink your position or look for a more appropriate issue.

PRACTICE YOUR SKILLS

● *Choosing a Suitable Thesis Statement*

Write whether each of the following statements would be suitable as a thesis statement for a persuasive essay. Use the guidelines above.

1. It really makes me angry and discouraged to see so much trash on the city's streets.

2. The United Nations should provide funds for research in global warming trends.

3. Our science club should volunteer to plant 1,000 tree saplings around the town dump.

Prewriting Workshop ▶
Drafting Workshop
Revising Workshop
Editing Workshop
Publishing Workshop

Clauses

Strong topics for persuasive writing have at least two sides. Good persuasive writing usually acknowledges other viewpoints and, in fact, often builds arguments around them. If you can show in your argument that your opponents' views are flawed, you strengthen your own case.

Two Independent Clauses

When you write your thesis statement, you can express your opponents' views in an independent clause (printed in **bold** type), coupled with another independent clause expressing your viewpoint. This construction, however, puts your opponents' viewpoint on an equal footing with yours.

> **The United States Air Force has dismissed UFOs,** but there is so much evidence of their existence that UFOs are worth taking seriously.

One Subordinate Clause, One Independent Clause

A better way to express the same idea is to use a subordinate, or dependent, clause for your opponents' views. This construction allows you to present opposing views without taking away from the emphasis on your own beliefs. In the following example, the subordinate clause is in **boldface** type.

> **Although the United States Air Force has dismissed UFOs,** there is so much evidence of their existence that they are worth taking seriously.

This statement lets readers know that the writer has taken into consideration the efforts of the Air Force but has rejected its conclusion. By making this statement in a subordinate clause, the writer acknowledges opposing views and *still* keeps the focus on the writer's viewpoint, expressed in the main clause.

PREWRITING *Thesis Statement*

Return to your subject for a persuasive essay. Identify your audience by using **Questions for Analyzing an Audience** on page C439. Then use the guidelines on page C441 to write a clear thesis statement, experimenting with a subordinate clause to show an opposite view. Save your work for later use.

Developing an Argument

After you have defined your position in a thesis statement, you are ready to develop the argument that will defend your thesis. You should first consider your audience. You will want to use evidence—facts, examples, and expert opinions—that your audience will find convincing. Be sure to select factual evidence that supports your opinion (pro) and also evidence that refutes it (con) so that you can address opposing views in your essay. Keep in mind that as you collect this evidence and your argument develops, you may have to revise your thesis statement. Once you have collected your evidence, use the following guidelines to help you develop your argument.

Guidelines for Developing an Argument

- List pros and cons in separate columns in your notes. Be prepared to address the opposing views point by point.

- Use facts and examples rather than more opinions to support your opinions.

- If those with the opposing view have a good point, admit it. Then show why the point is not enough to sway your opinion. Such an admission is called *conceding a point,* and it will strengthen your credibility.

- Use polite and reasonable language rather than words that show bias or overcharged emotions.

- Refer to respected authorities who agree with your position.

Is Thinking

Evaluating Evidence

In order to make an argument in a persuasive essay as convincing as possible, use evidence consisting of facts, examples, statistics, anecdotes, incidents, and opinions of qualified experts. Before you decide to include a piece of evidence, however, you should **evaluate** (critically judge) it. To do so, use the following criteria to decide whether the piece of evidence will truly support your argument.

- Is this evidence clearly related to my thesis?
- Is this a fact or an expert opinion?
- Is my source reliable?
- Is my evidence up-to-date?
- Is the evidence unbiased and objective?
- Is this a fact my audience will readily grasp?

Suppose, for example, that you are arguing for longer hours at your public library or media center. Here is how you could evaluate evidence on this issue.

EVIDENCE	EVALUATION
Students and workers need access to information.	Supports thesis—shows need for longer hours.
Some taxpayers object to homeless people using libraries for sanctuaries.	Does not support thesis—evidence is not related to the thesis.
Some librarians need longer hours to supplement earnings.	Does not support thesis—evidence is not related to the thesis.

THINKING PRACTICE

Choose one of the following arguable opinions or one based on an issue that is important to you. Make a chart like the one above to evaluate the evidence for your position.

1. Skateboarding is not a public menace.
2. Safer working environments for teenagers are needed.
3. Biodegradables cost little more than other paperware.

● *Listing Pros and Cons*

For each of the following thesis statements, list three facts, examples, incidents, reasons, or authoritative opinions that support the thesis (pros) and three that oppose it (cons). Save your work for later use.

1. Everyone should attend college for at least two years.

2. Retail stores should replace plastic shopping bags with paper bags.

3. The price of gasoline should be raised dramatically to force people to conserve energy.

4. Every taxpaying citizen should elect to have one dollar from tax returns contributed to environmental controls.

5. Homemade gifts are better than those bought in stores.

Organizing an Argument

After gathering and evaluating the evidence for your argument, you should organize your material in a logical way. The most common organization for persuasive essays is **order of importance**—beginning with the least important point and working up to the most important point at the end. With this emphasis your audience is likely to remember the last, most convincing point of your argument.

As you develop your argument, also remember to use transitional words and phrases to guide the reader from one point to the next. The following transitions are especially strong when conceding a point or showing contrasting ideas.

TRANSITIONS FOR PERSUASIVE WRITING		
although	instead	on the other hand
admittedly	nevertheless	still
however	nonetheless	while it is true that

You can learn more about transitions on pages C132 and C195–C196.

PRACTICE YOUR SKILLS

● *Organizing Persuasive Evidence*

Choose one of the thesis statements from the previous activity and decide which side of the issue you wish to support. Then follow the instructions below.

1. Revise the thesis statement, if necessary, to express your view. (If you agree with the thesis statement given in the practice activity, you may use it.)

2. Review the supporting evidence you prepared. Then list the three points that support your position in the order of least to most important. Leave two blank lines under each point.

3. Assign each of your three points a Roman numeral, as in an outline.

4. Add at least two supporting points under each Roman numeral.

5. Your outline should look like this.

I. (Least important point)

   A. (Supporting point)

   B. (Supporting point)

II. (More important point)

   A. (Supporting point)

   B. (Supporting point)

III. (Most important point)

   A. (Supporting point)

   B. (Supporting point)

Using a Reasoning Pillar

A good way to picture a solidly built persuasive essay is to see it as a pillar, with each block strengthening the whole.

Thesis Statement

Without support, the thesis statement would topple.

Least Important Point —supporting point —supporting point

More Important Point —supporting point —supporting point

Supporting points are presented so that each one rests on an even stronger one.

Most Important Point —supporting point —supporting point

Strong restatement of thesis, now with evidence to support it

A thesis with compelling evidence is the foundation for an effective essay.

Make a reasoning pillar using the thesis statement you chose for the previous activity.

Communicate Your Ideas

PREWRITING *Organization of Ideas*

Return to the thesis statement you wrote. Using the guidelines on pages C443 and C444, gather and evaluate evidence to develop your argument. Then organize your ideas into an outline like the one on page C446 or in a **reasoning pillar** like the one above. Save your work for later use.

As you write your first draft, remember that you will have an opportunity to review and revise it later. Use your outline and prewriting notes to express your ideas as quickly as possible and note any place where your information seems weak and where new facts may be required.

An effective way to capture your audience's attention is to begin with a startling fact or a probing question. You can give the reader a sense of how important the issue is by making sure that your thesis is a strong statement of your position. Experiment with emphasis, for example, by placing the thesis statement at different places in the introduction for the most dramatic effect.

As you draft the body of your essay, devote one paragraph to each main point in your outline. In addition to presenting your own supporting evidence, include the opposition's position where appropriate and show why this position has not changed yours. Remember to use transitional words *(page C445)* to guide the reader through your argument.

Finally, draft a conclusion that summarizes your position and restates your thesis. If you want to persuade the readers to take some action, make a recommendation. Then add a title that is lively and challenging.

Using Persuasive Language

The strong, emotional words used in high-pressure advertising get attention; but if those words are offensive, they will never convince people to buy the product. Keep this in mind as you write your persuasive essay. If you use sincere, straightforward language, you will more likely convince your audience.

EMOTIONAL LANGUAGE	The oily lake is full of **dead** fish, and **dirty little kids dump junk** all over the beach.

Once the lake was **blue** and **sparkling**. Now fish **die** in its oily waves, and **youngsters litter** the beach with **trash**.

PRACTICE YOUR SKILLS

● *Identifying Emotional Language*

Read each pair of sentences. Write the sentence that relies on emotional language. After you write the sentence, circle the words that are emotional.

1. The new houses were thrown up on top of an old garbage dump.

The development was built on the site of a former landfill.

2. The builder never told the home buyers that the site had been a landfill.

The builder hoodwinked the home buyers, never mentioning that their neighborhood was once a trash heap.

3. Now the rotting waste is spewing poison into the soil and water.

Higher-than-average levels of toxic substances have been found in the soil and water.

4. If I lived there, I'd demand that the city take action.

If I lived there, I'd be raising a ruckus down at city hall.

5. A mob of bureaucrats has finally begun to nose around at the site.

Environmental officials are beginning to monitor the situation.

6. The mayor will publish a report with suggestions for resolving the problem.

The mayor will throw together a flyer with some half-baked ideas for taking care of this shocking mess.

DRAFTING *Persuasive Language*

Write a first draft of your persuasive essay. Use sincere but reasonable language to present your argument. Save your work for later use.

Revising
Writing Process

One purpose for revising your persuasive essay is to make each point as clear and persuasive as possible. You will be most successful if you read your essay several times, each time addressing a different aspect of the writing.

- Does your introduction challenge your audience?
- Is your thesis statement a strong and clear statement of your position on the issue?
- Can your facts be strengthened by better examples?
- Have you overlooked any important points?
- Have you conceded a point? In other words, have you admitted that an opposing point has validity but is not strong enough to sway you?
- Are there words you might use that have more impact?
- Does your conclusion work?

COMPUTER TIP

If you are working at your computer and have an Internet connection, you can quickly find other word choices to use in persuasive writing by going to an online version of *Roget's Thesaurus*. All you have to do is type a word and press Enter. A whole list of options for synonyms is returned to you. You may want to bookmark this page as a tool you can return to time and again.

www.thesaurus.com

Once you have refined your language and strengthened your argument, read your essay again to check your logic and eliminate any of the following logical fallacies.

Eliminating Logical Fallacies

A **fallacy** is an error in logic. You have already seen how to avoid hasty generalizations on pages C433–C434. Following are several other fallacies that can creep into your reasoning and weaken your argument.

Writing Tip

Eliminate **logical fallacies** in your writing.

Attacking the Person Instead of the Issue   In Latin this fallacy is called *argumentum ad hominem* ("argument against the man"). Writers who fall into this trap criticize the character of their opponent instead of concentrating on the issue.

Ad Hominem Fallacy	The clean-water study was doomed to failure because Mayor Reed is always out of town.
	(Unless the mayor is personally conducting the study, his absence had very little to do with its doom.)

It is just as illogical for a writer to use positive aspects of a person's personality as a basis of the argument.

Ad Hominem Fallacy	The clean-water study should have been a great success because Mayor Reed is interested in everything— especially Little League.
	(In this case the mayor's interests had little to do with the study's success.)

PRACTICE YOUR SKILLS

● *Recognizing an* Ad Hominem *Fallacy*

Identify which of the following sentences contain an
***ad hominem* fallacy.**

1. Tim Lee drives a big car, so he isn't concerned about energy conservation.

2. Because Ron is always tardy, he should not be given the Most Friendly Class Member award.

3. Anna White is a good choice for chairperson of the Halloween party committee.

4. The senator is so dignified that he should give a wonderful persuasive speech.

5. I don't see how Tia's proposal for a class budget can work.

Either-Or Fallacy   Sometimes a writer of a persuasive essay assumes that there are only two sides to an argument. In fact, there may be many alternative opinions situated between the two extremes.

EITHER-OR FALLACY   Senator Wing must be willing to risk disastrous oil spills because she is against the use of atomic energy. (Senator Wing may actually support other alternative sources of energy.)

PRACTICE YOUR SKILLS

● *Avoiding the Either-Or Fallacy*

Write a sentence that offers a third alternative to the extreme opinions of each of the following either-or fallacies.

1. If you care about the environment, you will not own a car.

2. If we are to help farm animals, we must all become vegetarians.

3. Either we stop using oil, coal, and gas for fuel, or we will never breathe clean air again.

Confusing Chronology with Cause-Effect   Writers fall into this trap when they assume that whatever happens after an event was caused by that event. In many cases the relationship between the two events is merely coincidental.

| CAUSE-EFFECT FALLACY | Every time Chris and his family go on vacation it rains, so they must plan poorly. (Chris and his family are unlikely to plan for the rain. They may be victims of unlucky coincidence, or they may unknowingly vacation in the rainy season of particular areas.) |

PRACTICE YOUR SKILLS

● *Supplying Logical Causes*

In each of the following sets of circumstances, chronology is confused with cause-effect. Write a more likely cause of the second event in each case.

1. Every time I try to grow corn in our backyard, it fails. I must be doing something wrong.

2. Tina found a big black rock in her yard. Since it wasn't there yesterday, it must have been a meteorite.

3. Immediately after the new computers were installed, we had a big power failure. We must have bought the wrong computers for this building.

4. Our government class discussed federal taxes yesterday, and today the news broadcaster announced the passage of a new tax law. Someone in Washington, D.C., must have alerted my teacher.

5. Martin and Justine had an argument before school. That's why Martin fell off his bike on the way to school.

False Analogies An **analogy** is a comparison between two things that are alike in some important ways. A writer or speaker can use an analogy to communicate an unfamiliar idea by showing how it is very much like a more familiar one. You could, for example, explain the effect of acid rain to a small child by using the following analogy.

> ANALOGY Acid rain hurts trees the way the salt on the road last winter hurt my bicycle.
> (The unfamiliar idea—*acid rain hurts trees*— is compared to the quite familiar idea—*salt on the road hurt my bicycle last winter.*)

A **false analogy** is an attempt to compare two things that are alike in some ways but too far apart in others to be logically compared.

> FALSE ANALOGY Since this desert wilderness is just a great big sandbox, environmentalists should stop worrying about preserving it.
> (Both a desert and a sandbox contain sand, but a desert is a complex ecosystem that is home to many forms of life. A person's concept of a desert, based on one's knowledge of the contents of a sandbox, would have nothing to do with reality.)

> FALSE ANALOGY José García owns a new skateboard. I should have one too.
> (José García may have a different level of ability on a skateboard and may also have more money to buy a new one.)

Symbols

Often, especially in advertising, the analogy will be made through the use of a symbol. Consider the following advertisement:

The purpose of this ad is to represent a feeling and attitude through the use of a visual symbol, and then to attach that feeling to the product. The symbol is the cowboy hat and spurs, bringing to mind feelings of rugged individualism, bravery, strength. By analogy, the bottled water begins to pick up those characteristics too. This isn't ordinary bottled water that *females* might drink: this is *cowboy* water. Obviously, unexamined symbolic analogies are as unreliable as other false analogies.

Media Activity

Imagine that you, too, are designing an advertisement for a bottled water company. You have been told to use a visual symbol to help customers associate the bottled water with youth, health, and happiness. You have also been asked to think of a name for the water. Design an ad that uses a visual symbol and explain your symbolic analogy in a paragraph.

PRACTICE YOUR SKILLS

● *Finding the Flaws in False Analogies*

Write a sentence that explains the logical flaw in each of the following false analogies.

1. If a chimp can learn sign language, I should be able to teach my dog to do the same.

2. Long Beach High School has a water-skiing club. We should have one too.

3. Since driving a car is just like riding a bicycle, a driver's license should not be required.

4. I enjoyed reading *A Tale of Two Cities*. I will probably enjoy any book written in the nineteenth century.

5. The word-processing software I have is easy to use. I'm sure they are all the same.

Communicate Your Ideas

REVISING *Logical Fallacies*
Conferencing

Return to your persuasive essay and check it for logical fallacies. If you find any, revise as necessary. Then exchange essays with a classmate and provide each other with suggested improvements. When your paper is returned, use your partner's comments and the checklist on the next page to revise your essay.

Time Out to Reflect

In what ways have your persuasive skills deepened as a result of this chapter? If you have written a persuasive essay earlier in the year, take it out and read it again. How does it differ from the work you just completed? What did you do better in your most recent work? Is there anything you did better before? Record your thoughts in the Learning Log section of your **journal**.

Evaluation Checklist for Revising

Checking Your Introduction

✓ Does the thesis statement present your opinion effectively? *(pages C440–C441)*

✓ Will your introduction convince the readers that your topic is important? *(page C448)*

✓ Is the language you use both persuasive and objective? *(pages C448–C449)*

Checking Your Body Paragraphs

✓ Does each paragraph have a topic sentence? *(page C103–C104 and C397–398)*

✓ Have you supported your main points with verified facts, examples, and authoritative opinions? *(pages C430–C432)*

✓ Have you developed arguments and organized them in the most appropriate way? *(pages C443–C447)*

✓ Have you dealt with opposing views effectively? *(page C443)*

✓ Have you used sound reasoning and avoided logical fallacies? *(pages C433–C436, C443, and C451–C454)*

✓ Have you used transitions to help your reader follow your argument from point to point? *(page C445)*

Checking Your Conclusion

✓ Does your conclusion summarize your main points? *(page C426)*

✓ Did you restate your thesis? *(page C440)*

✓ Is your conclusion logically drawn from your arguments? *(pages C433–C436)*

Checking Your Words and Sentences

✓ Are your sentences varied? *(pages C73–C80)*

✓ Have you avoided biased, emotionally charged words? *(pages C435–C436 and C448–C449)*

When you edit, you carefully reread your revised draft for the conventions of language. Often, however, you are so familiar with what you intended to say that you miss errors. Allow time to put your writing aside. A little distance will help you see mistakes.

Communicate Your Ideas

EDITING

As you carefully edit your paper, refer to your Personalized Editing Checklist to make sure you are not repeating errors you have made before. Asking a classmate or family member to help you catch errors is another good choice.

Voltaire wrote, "To hold a pen is to be at war." Through persuasive writing you can make a difference in the world— triumph over injustice or bring about positive changes.

You may want to complete the writing process by sharing your writing with a reader who has a clear interest in your subject, someone who can help you make the difference you argue for.

Communicate Your Ideas

PUBLISHING

Think back to the prewriting work when you analyzed your audience. What specific people did you have in mind? Choose one person and write a letter explaining that you wrote this essay with him or her in mind. Attach the essay to the letter and send it off.

Process of Writing a Persuasive Essay

Remember that the writing process is recursive—you can move back and forth among the stages of the process to achieve your purpose. For example, during editing, you may wish to return to the revising stage to add details that have occurred to you while editing. The numbers in parentheses refer to pages where you can get help with your writing.

PREWRITING

- Use brainstorming, freewriting, or clustering to identify issues about which you have strong opinions. *(page C438)*
- Choose one subject and identify the audience you want to persuade. *(page C439)*
- Avoiding hasty generalizations, write a thesis statement that accurately presents your opinion. *(pages C433–C436 and C440–C441)*
- Gather evidence that will convince your audience. *(page C443)*
- Evaluate your evidence. *(page C443)*
- Develop a defensible argument by considering pros and cons, by supporting the thesis with facts and examples, and by acknowledging any weak points in your opinion. *(pages C443–C445)*
- Organize the details of your argument in an outline in order of importance. *(pages C445–C447)*

DRAFTING

- If necessary, refine the thesis statement and write an introduction that includes your thesis statement. *(page C448)*
- Use your outline to write the body of your essay. *(pages C445–C447)*
- Use transitional words to link your thoughts. *(page C445)*
- Avoid highly charged, emotional language. *(pages C448–C449)*
- Add a concluding paragraph and a title. *(page C426)*

REVISING

- Revise your essay to eliminate highly charged, emotional language and these logical fallacies: hasty generalizations, personal attacks, either–or fallacies, false analogies, or any confusion of chronology with cause and effect. *(pages C450–C454)*
- Use the <u>Evaluation Checklist for Revising</u>. *(page C457)*

EDITING

- Use the <u>Editing Checklist</u> to check your grammar, usage, spelling, and mechanics. *(page C46)*

PUBLISHING

- Make a neat, final copy of your essay in standard manuscript form, and consult <u>Ways to Publish Your Writing</u> chart for ideas about publishing. *(page C49)*

A Writer Writes

A Newspaper Editorial

Purpose: to persuade people in your community to follow your recommendation for a holiday project

Audience: readers of your local newspaper

Prewriting

Joan Beck's editorial *(pages C421–C422)* points out that people are more inclined to "goodwill" feelings during the holiday season. What does your community do to help others at this time of year? Does the local government sponsor events? How do store-owners and other businesspeople contribute to the community's welfare in this season? How do churches, synagogues, and other organizations try to do good deeds? Is enough being done? What are some of the glaring needs that are not being met? What gifts could your community offer to ease these problems?

Think of a way in which community residents, despite their diverse backgrounds or the ways in which they do or do not celebrate winter holidays, could come together for a community project. Maybe it could be using less money for decorations on lampposts and more money for feeding hungry children. Maybe it could be a partnership between the police department and a youth organization to go door to door with information on preventing gun violence. The possibilities are limited only by your imagination.

Before you formulate a recommendation, read some magazine and newspaper articles that describe what people in your community have already accomplished to help those in need or to make more positive changes. After your research, develop a plan that would be likely to work as a project in your community. Think through who would need to be persuaded for your plan to succeed. Then write a working thesis statement that makes clear the purpose of your editorial and establishes your main idea. Gather more information if necessary—listing both the pros and the cons of your position. When you have enough information, if necessary revise your thesis statement to cover all the facts. Then choose an organizing scheme and outline the body of your editorial.

Drafting

Write the first draft of your editorial, beginning by capturing your readers' attention perhaps with a startling fact or illustration. Then, after you write a strong introduction around your thesis statement, follow your outline to develop the arguments that support your opinion in the body paragraphs. Your arguments may take the form of examples and illustrations of successful or unsuccessful efforts that individuals or small local groups have made locally or nationally. Remember to confront opposing arguments and show why your arguments are more reasonable. In your conclusion reaffirm your position and suggest ways that convinced readers could take action.

Revising

Set your editorial aside for a day or so and then reread it carefully. Following the <u>Evaluation Checklist for Revising</u> on page C457, evaluate and revise your editorial to make it as persuasive as possible.

Editing

Use the checklist on page C46 to polish your editorial.

Publishing

Prepare a final copy of your editorial and add a cover letter to it, explaining how and why you wrote it. Then send both to the editor of your local newspaper.

Connection Collection

Representing in Different Ways

12 Bank Street
Bogalusa, LA 70427
August 22, 2000

Mr. B. Cheese
Ye Olde Pizza Barn
47 Mozzarella Lane
Bogalusa, LA 70427

Dear Mr. Cheese:

This summer, we employees at Ye Olde Pizza Barn have worked hard. We sold an average of 122 pizzas a day in June, 184 pizzas a day in July, and 246 pizzas a day in August. Because of the increased business, we had to work more hours as the summer progressed. All employees worked overtime; thus, we had less leisure time. On average, each employee had six daytime leisure hours in June, three daytime leisure hours in July, and only one daytime leisure hour in August. Your business has been a big success.

We would like to suggest a pool party, which could be held at your house. Please be in touch with me so that I can help organize the event.

Sincerely,

Tess Smith

Tess Smith

. . . to Visuals

From the information in the letter, draw two pie charts demonstrating 1) pizzas sold each month and 2) daily leisure hours each month.

To illustrate your point clearly, shade the charts with three different colors. Each month should have the same color in both graphs.

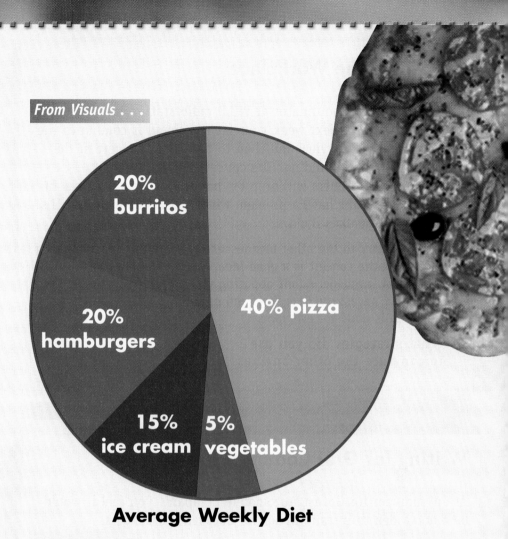

20%
burritos

40% pizza

20%
hamburgers

15%
ice cream

5%
vegetables

Average Weekly Diet

. . . to Print

The pie chart above demonstrates the average weekly diet for workers at Ye Olde Pizza Barn during the summer. Based on the chart, write a persuasive letter concerning what food should be served at the Employee Pool Party.

- Which strategies can be used for creating both written and visual representations? Which strategies apply to one, but not both? Which type of repre-sentation is more effective?
- Draw a conclusion and write briefly about the differences between written ideas and visual representations.

Writing in the Workplace
Persuasive Business Letter

Your job as Talent Coordinator at WILD radio station has put you in an odd position. Next week your favorite band is coming to the station to do an interview and then to perform a concert in the lobby of your office building. The concert will be great for business. Many listeners will drop by, but the other businesses in your building might have a problem with Mad Man Morris and His All Drum and Cymbals Band.

> Write a letter to the other businesses in your building, convincing them that the concert is a good idea. Avoid highly charged, emotional language. Admit opposing viewpoints ("concede a point") if necessary. Give facts and opinions pointing out why this idea is good for everyone.

What strategies did you use to convince the other businesses?

You can find information on writing business letters on pages C569–C575.

Writing for Oral Communication
Oral Business Proposal

As an engineer for GoFast Automobile Company, you feel it would be a good idea to install airbags for backseat passengers.

> Prepare an oral presentation for the CEO, President, and members of the Board of Directors. Explain that the seats will cost extra, but argue that people are willing to pay for the added safety. Mention necessary time and production delays, extra factory workers needed, advertising, increased sales due to this unique feature, and other pertinent factors. Use a thesis statement and connecting devices in developing a strong and persuasive argument. Deliver your proposal to classmates or family members who will listen as the company's executives.

What strategies did you use to persuade the company's executives?

You can find information on preparing presentations on pages C592–C601.

Assess Your Learning

The mayor, council members, and businesspeople in your community have decided to construct a 100-foot statue of a muskrat in your downtown city plaza. The statue will be gold-plated. Designed and built by a local muskrat lover, it will cost $5 million, to be paid for with added tax on food sales. The town leaders seem certain that tourists from all over the world will want to come to your town to see The Golden Muskrat.

▶ Think of a way that you would prefer the money be spent. Write a letter to the political and business leaders aimed at persuading them to spend the money the way you think is best.

▶ In trying to convince others of your ideas, be sure to identify your audience. Know the difference between fact and opinion, and use these in a way that supports your ideas about the topic. Avoid highly charged, emotional language that might alienate your audience. Present pros and cons, and be sure your argument is organized to ensure coherence, logical progression, and support.

Before You Write **Consider the following questions:**
What is the *subject?*
What is the *occasion?*
Who is the *audience?*
What is the *purpose?*

After You Write **Evaluate your work using the following criteria:**
- Is there a thesis statement?
- Have you identified your audience and geared your argument in order to influence them?
- Are pros and cons included?
- Have you acknowledged opposing viewpoints and conceded a point, if appropriate?
- Are facts and opinions presented clearly?
- Have you developed your arguments in a coherent manner that supports your ideas?
- Have you used connecting devices so that your thinking progresses logically?
- Have you checked for grammatical, spelling, and punctuation errors that might weaken your authority in the eyes of your audience?

Write briefly on how well you did. Point out your strengths and areas for improvement.

CHAPTER 11

Writing About Literature

When you read a story, poem, or play for entertainment, your response can be as simple as the initial "That was great!" or "That was really bad." In the classroom, however, you are almost always asked to think beyond that initial response to a work of literature. You answer critical thinking questions about a story, discuss a poem's meaning with classmates, and write papers dealing with the characters in a play. In order to answer, discuss, and write, you must understand the work.

Analyzing the work—breaking it down into small parts and examining each part—helps you understand the meaning: what the writer of the story, poem, or play is saying. Once you understand the work's meaning, you can evaluate the work—decide how well the writer has communicated the message and judge how significant that message is. As you analyze and evaluate the poems in this chapter, you will learn to move from an initial response to a more thoughtful statement about the meaning of the work for you and for other readers.

Reading with a Writer's Eye

What is your idea of courage? When have you been courageous? What examples of courage have you seen? In Anne Sexton's "Courage" and Edna St. Vincent Millay's "The Courage That My Mother Had," we see different portraits of courage. As you read the poems, think about how your idea of courage is similar to or different from the kinds of courage presented in the poems.

COURAGE

Anne Sexton

It is in the small things we see it.
The child's first step,
as awesome as an earthquake.
The first time you rode a bike,
5   wallowing up the sidewalk.
The first spanking when your heart
went on a journey all alone.
When they called you crybaby
or poor or fatty or crazy
10   and made you into an alien,
you drank their acid
and concealed it.

Later,
if you faced the death of bombs and bullets
15   you did not do it with a banner,
you did it with only a hat to
cover your heart.
You did not fondle the weakness inside you
though it was there.
20   Your courage was a small coal
that you kept swallowing.
If your buddy saved you
and died himself in so doing,
then his courage was not courage,
25   it was love; love as simple as shaving soap.

Later,
if you have endured a great despair,
then you did it alone,
getting a transfusion from the fire,
30   picking the scabs off your heart,
then wringing it out like a sock.
Next, my kinsman, you powdered your
        sorrow,
you gave it a back rub
and then you covered it with a blanket
35   and after it had slept a while
it woke to the wings of the roses
and was transformed.

Later,
when you face old age and its natural
        conclusion
40   your courage will still be shown in the
        little ways,
each spring will be a sword you'll sharpen,
those you love will live in a fever of love,
and you'll bargain with the calendar
and at the last moment
45   when death opens the back door
you'll put on your carpet slippers
and stride out.

The Courage That My Mother Had

Edna St. Vincent Millay

The courage that my mother had
Went with her, and is with her still:
Rock from New England quarried;
Now granite in a granite hill.

5   The golden brooch my mother wore
She left behind for me to wear;
I have no thing I treasure more:
Yet, it is something I could spare.

Oh, if instead she'd left to me
10   The thing she took into the grave!—
That courage like a rock, which she
has no more need of, and I have.

Thinking as a Writer

Responding to a Work of Literature

Although both Anne Sexton's "Courage" and Edna St. Vincent Millay's "The Courage That My Mother Had" deal with the subject of courage, the poems are very different.

- Which poem do you prefer? Why? Give at least three reasons for your preference.

Listening for Rhythm

Oral Expression
- The rhythm of a poem is essential to its meaning. Think of your favorite song. How would the song change if it were performed as a country song? a rap? a jazz piece?
- Just as altering the rhythm of a song changes the impact of the song, altering the rhythm of a poem changes the impact of the poem. In a small group, experiment with the rhythm of "The Courage That My Mother Had." Each group member should read the poem aloud, using a different rhythm. Which rhythm sounds most natural and expressive?

Understanding Character and Theme

Viewing Although many of us think of courage in terms of glorious and dangerous deeds that make history, both poets present quieter, everyday portraits of courage.

- In the last stanza of "Courage," Anne Sexton describes the courage of an elderly man. Using the photograph to the right, find examples of this man's everyday courage.

The Power of Literary Analysis

You have just read two works of literature—two poems—and without realizing it, you have begun thinking critically about them. Supporting your personal preference with evidence from the poem, reading with meaningful rhythm, and understanding a character are all ways of responding to the work.

Uses of Literary Analysis

Here are some examples of how the skills of thinking, writing, and speaking about literature are used both in school and in life.

- **Members of a "Mystery Lovers" book group read a new writer's work and discuss** how the mystery compares to favorites by Agatha Christie, Patricia Cornwell, and Sir Arthur Conan Doyle.

- **An Internet magazine publishes poems** that express the experience of living in our society. Readers are invited to post responses to the poems on a message board.

- **High school drama students select a play** to act in, direct, produce, and present to the school as a final project.

- **The weekly entertainment section of the newspaper prints a review of a new movie.** The reviewer shares a personal reaction to the film, as well as insights about the characters, plot, and dialogue.

Process of Writing a Literary Analysis

"I can't remember right now what the moral is, but I shall remember it in a bit."

"Perhaps it hasn't one," Alice ventured to remark.

"Tut, tut child," said the Duchess. "Everything's got a moral, if only you can find it."

As the Duchess points out in Lewis Carroll's *Alice's Adventures in Wonderland,* everything has a moral—a meaning. The job of the reader is to find it. The critical thinking skills that you will use to write a literary analysis in this chapter will help you find meaning in works of literature.

A **literary analysis** presents an interpretation of a work of literature and supports that interpretation with appropriate responses, details, and quotations.

STRUCTURE OF A LITERARY ANALYSIS	
TITLE	identifies which aspect of the work the writer will focus on
INTRODUCTION	names the author and the work, and contains a thesis statement expressing an interpretation of some aspect of the work
BODY	supports the thesis statement with details and direct quotations from the work. In some instances the body contains quotations from other respected sources, such as literary critics and biographers. It may also include the author's personal comments and letters.
CONCLUSION	summarizes, clarifies, or adds an insight to the thesis statement

In your journal write the names of three favorite songs, three favorite movies, and three favorite stories. Then write in a few words what each one says to you—its meaning. Chances are you enjoy those songs, movies, and stories for their meanings and for the way they communicate those meanings to you. As you write a literary analysis in this chapter, you will be writing about the meaning of a work— deciding how well the writer communicates a message and how meaningful that message is to you. Your journal notes will help you think about how you respond to a work and the reasons you respond as you do.

Prewriting — Writing Process

Reading literature is a creative process in which you, the reader, interact with a literary work. Before you can write formally about a work, you need to experience this creative process by responding openly to what you read. Furthermore, it is important to understand that your response comes from several sources.

Sources of a Reader's Response to Literature

- individual characteristics—such as age, sex, and personality
- cultural or ethnic origins, attitudes, and customs
- personal opinions, beliefs, and values
- life experiences and general knowledge
- knowledge of literature and literary genres
- knowledge of the historical and social climate in which an author has written a work
- reading and language skills

All of these sources contribute to your ability to identify with the characters and understand the theme, setting, and message of a piece of literature. Who you are, what you know, what you

believe, and where, when, and how you live all help you to understand the content of the story, novel, play, or poem you are
reading. The more you identify with a work, the greater your
enjoyment will be in reading it.

Responding from Personal Experience

A writer once commented, "You will not find poetry anywhere
unless you bring some of it with you." To understand the meaning
of this statement, think back to poems you have read that have
had a lasting impact on you. Chances are that each of those poems
calls something to mind—an experience, dream, mood, hope—of
personal importance to you. Your willingness to let yourself go and
personally respond to a poem is the way you can "bring poetry
with you." The poet contributes the words and structure of the
poem; you and your memories contribute to what the poem's
special meaning and its structure will convey to you.

A similar interaction occurs with any literary work you are
reading: a story, play, or novel—as well as a poem. Your ability to
identify with characters, to let the work serve as a mirror to your
own world, makes you an integral part of each literary work you
read. As a result your reactions to literature may not always be
positive; sometimes a work will irritate, disturb, or even bore you.
A negative response, however, is just as important as a positive
one, and it also deserves to be explored.

All of the following techniques will help you respond and will
help you make sense out of those responses to literature.

> ### Personal Response Strategies
> **1.** Freewrite answers to the following questions:
>
> **a.** When you approached this reading, did you have any
> expectations of the text? In other words, did you expect
> to be bored? to experience pleasure? to be stimulated? to
> have difficulty? Were your expectations met? How? Were
> you surprised? If so, explain why.

b. Where in the poem, story, novel, or play do you see yourself? In other words, with what character or characters do you most closely identify? Why? Do your feelings about the character or characters stay the same? Do they change? If so, when and why do they change?

c. What characters remind you of other people you know? In what ways are they like those real people? In what ways are they different? How has your experience with those real people influenced your reactions to the characters in the work?

d. If you were a character in the work, would you have behaved any differently? Why or why not? What actions or behaviors puzzle you?

e. What experiences from your own life come to mind as you read this work? How are they similar to the events portrayed? How are they different? What feelings do you associate with the experiences? Are those feelings in any way represented in the work?

f. What moved you in the work? How and why did it affect you?

2. Write a personal response statement explaining what the work means to you.

3. In small discussion groups, share your personal response statement and your various reactions to the questions above. Listen carefully to your classmates' reactions and, if appropriate, contrast them with your own. Be open to changing your responses if you find other points of view convincing. Afterward write freely about whether your ideas changed and why.

The model on page C477 shows how a reader used the strategies above to write a personal response statement about the following two poems. Notice how the reader explores feelings in depth, relates the poems to life experiences, and makes distinctions in responses to the different poems.

The Explorer

Somehow to find a still spot in the noise
Was the frayed inner want, the winding, the frayed
   hope
Whose tatters he kept hunting through the din.
A satin peace somewhere.
5 A room of wily hush somewhere within.

So tipping down the scrambled halls he set
Vague hands on throbbing knobs. There were behind
Only spiraling, high human voices,
The scream of nervous affairs,
10 Wee griefs,
Grand griefs. And choices.

He feared most of all the choices, that cried to be
   taken.

There were no bourns.
There were no quiet rooms.

—Gwendolyn Brooks

The Road Not Taken

Two roads diverged in a yellow wood,
And sorry I could not travel both
And be one traveler, long I stood
And looked down one as far as I could
5 To where it bent in the undergrowth;

Then took the other, as just as fair,
And having perhaps the better claim,
Because it was grassy and wanted wear;
Though as for that, the passing there
10 Had worn them really about the same,

And both that morning equally lay
In leaves no step had trodden black.

Oh, I kept the first for another day!
Yet knowing how way leads on to way,
15   I doubted if I should ever come back.

I shall be telling this with a sigh
Somewhere ages and ages hence;
Two roads diverged in a wood, and I—
I took the one less traveled by.
20   And that has made all the difference.

—Robert Frost

MODEL: Personal Response

    I had just read Gwendolyn Brooks' poem "The Explorer" twice and felt really depressed and anxious. The poem makes life sound so scary and grim. After a while I read Robert Frost's "The Road Not Taken" and must admit I felt calmer, yet a bit let down. That poem makes life sound ho-hum and very business-like without any enthusiasm or fun. The traveler speaks as though all you have to do is "case" things and then make up your mind. Everything will work out. Then I decided to read both poems aloud. After that I had a few different feelings and thoughts.

    I can't say I strongly prefer the Frost poem; it's just that I like its message better. The view of life and choice seem more helpful to anyone who's wondering what life's all about or needs direction.

    Both poems talk about choices. As a sophomore in high school, I have a lot of choices I have to make soon. I must decide what college to go to—if I do go—and what to study. If I don't go to college, I have to decide what else to do with my life. Besides worrying about these practical matters, I guess I'm in the process of deciding just who I am. My choice of friends and my choice of clothes and pastimes tell who I am. I guess everything we do one way or another is a choice, which is a little scary to think of. However, I don't feel as fearful about the choices as the explorer does in the first poem. Still, I wish I knew as much about choice as the traveler in the Frost poem does. That person already knows the consequences of choice and isn't afraid to grab the one "less traveled by." This poem means more to me because I realize, too, that the choices I make now will have a lasting effect on my life. As I read the poem, I kept saying to myself, "Yeah, that's how it is!"

PRACTICE YOUR SKILLS

● *Responding from Personal Experience*

Review the poems "The Explorer" and "The Road Not Taken" on pages C476–C477. Then answer the following questions.

1. Do you like "The Explorer"? Why or why not?

2. What in your life comes to mind when you read this poem?

3. Do you like "The Road Not Taken"? Why or why not?

4. What in your life comes to mind as you read this poem?

5. Can you identify with either character? If so, how?

Communicate Your Ideas

PREWRITING *Personal Experience*

Review the poems "Courage" and "The Courage That My Mother Had" on pages C467–C469. Then, using the Personal Response Strategies chart on pages C474–C475, freewrite a personal response to the poems. Save your work for later use.

SAVE YOUR WORK

Time Out to Reflect Think back to the reflections you recorded in your **journal** about favorite songs, stories, and movies. Have you found that one of the poems in this chapter shares any characteristics with your favorites? After reading these poems, jot down more elements that your favorites have in common.

Movie Criticism

Movies and literature have many common elements. In fact, most of the criteria presented in this chapter for finding meaning in and evaluating literature hold true for movies as well. In addition, movies have their own "language" that expresses meaning. Good movie critics evaluate how the camera work, lighting, soundtrack, special effects, and editing enhance the basic narrative elements of plot, character, and theme.

The following excerpt is from a review of David Lynch's *Straight Story* (1999), a true-story movie about a 73-year-old man traveling by lawn mower to see his brother.

> Through the slow breath of his editing, ever-shifting camera placement and supersaturated colors, Lynch sets his mid-American landscape at a fine aesthetic remove. . . . When the camera is distant from the actors, their voices aren't amplified. We strain to overhear them. An early, rule-breaking shot pans up from Alvin's puttering road progress, lingers on a sky full of clouds, then pans back down to measure his inching advance. The message is: Unfasten your seat belts for once. Start looking at the world around you. . . .
>
> —*Bob Campbell*

Media Activity

Challenge your abilities to find meaning in visual elements by writing your own movie review. Choose a movie you know well and that you can rent or borrow to watch at home. Using all you have learned in this chapter about writing a critical essay, write a review that examines the movie's impact on you and analyzes the features in the movie that created that impact.

When you are satisfied with your review, search movie review sites on the Internet. Create a Web version of your movie review and, if your school has a site, publish your review online.

You can find information on how to create a Website on pages C717–C721.

Responding from Literary Knowledge

Each story, poem, and novel that you have read has probably taught you something about literary traditions and literary elements—the parts and characteristics of a literary work. For example, when you were just a child and were read your first fairy tale, you probably were nervous about how it would come out in the end. Because you had never heard a fairy tale before, you had no way of knowing that the good characters in fairy tales always live "happily ever after." The more fairy tales you heard or read, the more you learned about that literary tradition, and the more you came to expect happy endings!

The same process has taken place over the years as you have read other types of literature, including poems, novels, and plays. You have learned more about what you can expect in the various genres of literature and about how literary elements work.

The chart below shows the main elements of fiction, poetry, and drama. The elements listed under drama show only the features that differ from those of other kinds of literature.

ELEMENTS OF LITERATURE	
FICTION	
PLOT	the events in a story that lead to a **climax** (high point) and to an outcome that resolves a central **conflict**
SETTING	when and where the story takes place
MOOD	prevalent feeling or atmosphere in the work
CHARACTERS	the people in the story who advance the plot through their thoughts and actions
DIALOGUE	the conversations among characters that reveal their personalities, actions, and motivations, or reasons for behaving as they do
TONE	the writer's attitude toward her or his characters
POINT OF VIEW	the "voice" telling the story—**first person** *(I)* or **third person** *(he* or *she)*
THEME	the main idea or message of the story

POETRY

PERSONA	the person whose "voice" is saying the poem, revealing the character the poet is assuming
METER	the pattern of stressed and unstressed syllables in each line
RHYME SCHEME	the pattern of rhymed sounds, usually at the ends of lines
SOUND DEVICES	techniques for playing with sounds to create certain effects, such as **alliteration** and **onomatopoeia**
FIGURES OF SPEECH	imaginative language, such as **similes** and **metaphors**, which creates images by making comparisons
SHAPE	the way a poem looks on the printed page, which may contribute to the underlying meaning of the poet's thoughts and feelings
THEME	the underlying meaning of the poem

DRAMA

SETTING	the time and place of the action; lighting and stage sets, as described in the stage directions
CHARACTERS	the people who participate in the action of the play
PLOT	the story of the play divided into acts and scenes and developed through the characters' words and actions
THEME	the meaning of a play, as revealed through the setting and the characters' words and actions.

How Literary Elements Contribute to Meaning   The elements of each genre of literature contribute to the meaning of a work. In poetry, for example, a poet may use figurative language, sound devices, meter, and sometimes rhyme. On the other hand, a poet may use free verse—which has no regular meter or rhyme—to reveal his or her message to readers. To find meaning in a work of literature, therefore, you can analyze how the author has used such elements in writing. Ask yourself the following questions as you explore the meaning of a literary work.

> ## Questions for Finding Meaning in Poetry
> - Who is the poet's persona? How does the persona relate to the subject, mood, and theme of the poem?
> - How does the meter affect the rhythm of the poem? How does that rhythm express the mood?
> - How does the rhyme scheme, if any, affect the expression of thoughts and feelings?
> - What sounds do alliteration and onomatopoeia create? What images do those sound devices suggest?
> - What images do the figures of speech create? What feelings do those images suggest?
> - How does the shape of the poem relate to the subject, mood, or theme?
> - What feeling, theme, or message does the poem express?
> - What meaning does the poem have for me?

> ## Questions for Finding Meaning in Drama
> - What details of setting and character do the stage directions emphasize? How do those details contribute to the meaning of the play?
> - What are the key relationships among the characters? How do those relationships reveal the central conflict? What changes in the relationships help resolve the conflict?
> - How does the dialogue advance the plot? What plot developments occur with each change of act and scene?
> - What is the subject and theme of the play? What meaning does the play have for me?

> ## Questions for Finding Meaning in Fiction

Plot

- How does each event in the plot affect the characters?
- What do details in the plot reveal about the central conflict?
- What do the climax and the ending reveal about the theme?

Setting

- How does the setting contribute to the tone or mood of the story? How does the setting help define the characters?
- Which details of the setting are most important in the development of the plot?

Characters

- How do the characters relate to their setting?
- How does each character contribute to the development of the plot? Who or what does each character represent? How do the details of characterization reveal personalities?
- What does the dialogue reveal about the characters' personalities and motivations?
- How does the point of view of the story affect the characterizations?

Theme

- What passages and details in the story best express the main theme? Are there other recurring ideas that contribute to the meaning?
- How does the author communicate the theme through the development of setting, characters, and plot? Does this theme have meaning for me? What else have I read that has a similar theme?

Evaluating a Literary Work Analyzing the elements of literature helps you make judgments about the work. You set standards for each element and judge how well those standards are met. You evaluate the work as a whole, its meaning for you and for others, based on those individual standards. However, your personal judgment and the judgment of others may not agree. Following are some criteria by which great literature is judged.

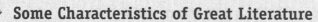

Some Characteristics of Great Literature

- Explores great themes in human nature and the human experience that many people can identify with—such as growing up, family life, love, the courageous individual's struggle against oppression, and war
- Expresses universal meanings—such as truth or hope—that people from many different backgrounds and cultures can appreciate
- Conveys a timeless message that remains true for many generations of readers
- Creates vivid impressions of characters, situations, and settings that many generations of readers can treasure

The literary work you are reading may or may not meet the criteria for great literature, but you can still apply other standards of evaluation. When you are making judgments about a work, ask yourself the following questions.

Questions for Evaluating Literature

- How original and inventive is the work?
- How effectively does the writing achieve the author's purpose?
- How vividly and believably are characters, settings, dialogue, actions, and feelings portrayed? In fiction and drama, is the plot well structured? Is there a satisfying resolution of the central conflict?
- How strongly did I react to the work? Did I identify with a character, situation, or feeling? Did the work stir my memories and emotions?
- Does the message of the work have meaning for me? What do I think I will remember about this work in the future?

PRACTICE YOUR SKILLS

● *Responding from Literary Knowledge*

Answer these questions about "The Explorer" and "The Road Not Taken" on pages C476–C477. Refer to the chart on pages C481 to help you understand any unfamiliar terms.

1. What can you infer about the persona in "The Explorer"?

2. What are some of the images the poet uses in "The Explorer"? What does the imagery contribute to the poem?

3. What figures of speech does the poet use in "The Explorer"? What do they add to the poem?

4. What is being said about life in this poem? In other words, what is the theme of the poem?

5. What can you infer about the persona in "The Road Not Taken"?

6. Identify the rhyme scheme of "The Road Not Taken" by noting the final sound in each line. How does the rhyme scheme affect the feeling of the poem?

7. Around what metaphor is "The Road Not Taken" built? Is it a convincing metaphor? Why or why not?

8. What is the theme of "The Road Not Taken"? How is it like or unlike the theme of "The Explorer"?

Communicate Your Ideas

PREWRITING *Literary Response*

In your **journal** freewrite a literary response to "Courage" and "The Courage That My Mother Had." Using the chart on page C481, identify the literary elements the poets use to evoke your individual response. How do the figures of speech, rhyme scheme, or imagery influence how you respond to the poems? Save your work for later use.

Choosing a Subject

The prewriting work you have completed so far has helped you explore your responses—both personal and literary—to the work or works you are reading. You can now use these responses to help you focus on a subject for your literary analysis.

Although your teacher may assign you a subject, most often he or she will expect you to think of your own. The following questions will help you think of subjects that are personally important to you and appropriate for a literary analysis.

> **Questions for Choosing a Subject**
> - What parts of the work puzzle me? What would I like to understand better?
> - What parts of the work move me especially? Why do they have an effect on me?
> - What images or details make a strong impression on me?
> - What do they contribute to the overall work?
> - With which character do I identify and why?
> - What message does the work convey to me? What new insight or understanding have I gained from this work?
> - How do the characters in the work differ? What motivates each one?
> - What other works am I reading (or have I read) that are similar to this work? What elements of these works might I compare in some meaningful way?

For subjects you might like to develop further, search through all the responses you have recorded thus far in your **journal** and that you might have saved in your writing folder. See if any ideas come up repeatedly. If they do, these ideas undoubtedly intrigue you in some way. Developing a literary analysis around such intriguing ideas would probably be a satisfying writing challenge.

Before you choose a subject, be sure to consider your audience. In this chapter you usually will be writing for your teacher and classmates. Therefore, you can assume that your audience is familiar with the literature you are analyzing.

Synthesizing

When choosing a subject for your literary analysis, remember that while your subject should reflect your personal response to the literary work, it cannot ignore the literary elements in the work. By **synthesizing**— combining or bringing together—you can include both responses in your subject.

Suppose you have decided to write about "The Explorer" and "The Road Not Taken." Make a chart like the one below to track your personal response to both poems. Then look for a focus. In the chart below, the idea of choices clearly intrigues the reader.

Now you must synthesize your personal responses with a literary element. You may decide on the element of theme, since the theme of both poems deals with choices. Then take brief notes on the right side of the chart about the theme of each poem.

PERSONAL RESPONSE	LITERARY ELEMENT
Choices are so important in life. Can be scary. Career? Friends? My future life? I'm not as afraid as the explorer. I'm more like the person in "Road." I know that my choices, like college, could lead to lots of other choices. Some I might regret later.	*Theme of "Explorer":* Life is a journey with choices that bring conflict, depriving us of peace and quiet. *Theme of "Road":* We stumble upon choices, try to see consequences, but can see only so far. We must make the choice, or never know how it might have been.

Synthesis: The subject is the theme of choice in two modern poems.

THINKING PRACTICE

In your journal make a chart like the one above to combine your personal responses with the literary elements of the poems "Courage" and "The Courage That My Mother Had." Synthesize your responses to the subject of courage in each poem.

PRACTICE YOUR SKILLS

● *Choosing Subjects*

Review the Elements of Poetry on page C481. Then, for each of the following literary elements, think of a possible subject for a literary analysis of "The Explorer," "The Road Not Taken," or both poems.

EXAMPLE	persona
POSSIBLE SUBJECT	how the character in "The Explorer" differs from the character in "The Road Not Taken"

1. figures of speech   **3.** rhyme and meter

2. theme   **4.** imagery

Communicate Your Ideas

PREWRITING *Subject*

For your literary analysis, you will be comparing and contrasting "Courage" and "The Courage That My Mother Had." However, it is up to you to determine the subject. You may choose, for example, to compare and contrast elements of both poems—such as the personae, the themes, or the uses of figurative language. Review your personal and literary responses to the poems, and synthesize your responses to identify the element that interests you most. Save your subject for later use.

Limiting a Subject

Before you have thought of a subject for your literary analysis, you may sometimes feel as if you have nothing at all to say about a work of literature. Once you have focused on a subject, however, ideas often begin to flood your mind. To be sure your main idea does not drown in the flood, take the time to limit your subject appropriately.

One good way to limit your subject is to try to express it in a phrase instead of a single word. To develop a single-word subject into a phrase-length subject, ask yourself, "What do I plan to say about my subject?" When you can express the answer to that question in a phrase, you probably have a suitably limited subject.

If you were writing about "The Explorer" and "The Road Not Taken," you might go through the following thought process.

MODEL: Limiting a Subject

TOO GENERAL	theme
ASK YOURSELF	What do I plan to say about the theme?
POSSIBLE ANSWER	In both poems the theme has to do with choice, but the poems seem to have different attitudes toward choice.
LIMITED SUBJECT	the differing attitudes toward choice in the two poems

PRACTICE YOUR SKILLS

● *Limiting Subjects*

Each of the following subjects is too unfocused for a literary analysis comparing and contrasting "The Explorer" and "The Road Not Taken." Write a suitably limited subject for each one.

EXAMPLE   choice
LIMITED SUBJECT   differing attitudes toward choice

1. regret   **3.** fear   **5.** peacefulness
2. hope   **4.** views of life   versus chaos

Communicate Your Ideas

PREWRITING *Limited Subject*

Review the subject you chose for your literary analysis of "Courage" and "The Courage That My Mother Had." Ask yourself, "What do I want to say about my subject?" until you have a clearly focused phrase. Then save your limited subject for later use.

Developing Your Thesis

Every good literary analysis has a thesis at its core. This **thesis**, or proposition, is the main point the writer is making about some part of a literary work. Since interpretations of literary works do differ from one reader to another, your task in a literary analysis is to convince your audience that your thesis is valid and that your interpretation makes good sense based on the evidence you have found in the work to support that thesis. The foundation of a literary analysis is, therefore, a soundly reasoned thesis.

As you have been limiting your subject, you have also been slowly homing in on your thesis. In fact, your limited subject is just a step away from your thesis statement. To develop your limited subject into a clear thesis statement, you simply have to express your main idea in a complete sentence instead of in a phrase.

In the following example about "The Explorer" and "The Road Not Taken," the thesis statement makes a definite proposition that was only hinted at in the limited subject.

FOCUSED, LIMITED SUBJECT	the differing attitudes toward choice in the two poems
THESIS STATEMENT OR PROPOSITION	"The Explorer" presents a fearful attitude toward choice, while "The Road Not Taken" presents a calmer, more resigned attitude toward choice.

To convert your limited subject into a clear thesis statement, you can repeat the technique of asking yourself, "What exactly do I want to say about my subject?" The thesis statement at this stage should be precise enough to guide you through the rest of your planning. However, you should regard it as a working thesis statement only. As a result, you can change or adjust it as you continue to develop your essay.

Writing Tip

After you have focused and limited your subject, express it in a complete sentence as a **thesis statement.**

PREWRITING *Thesis*

 Review your focused, limited subject. If you are satisfied that your subject homes in on your thesis, you are ready to proceed. To develop your working thesis statement, write your limited subject in the form of a sentence. Keep in mind that you can change or adjust it as needed. Save your work for later use.

Gathering Evidence

What happens when you read a poem or some other work of literature? If you are like most readers, you probably pay little conscious attention to such elements as character, theme, imagery style, or form. Instead you probably lose yourself in the work and let it speak to you on an emotional level.

Even though you may not be aware of it, the only way a work can succeed in moving you is through the details it uses. These details form an overall impression, touching off memories and surges of emotion. This overall impression helps you formulate your ideas about a literary work and express them in a thesis statement.

Once you have a clear thesis statement, however, you can go back over the work and take a closer, more conscious look at what exactly in the poem or story created the overall impression. Ask yourself, "Why did the work make me feel this way?" and then review the work to find the quotations and details to back up what you want to say about your feelings and reactions. For example, the student who wrote the personal response on page C477 to "The Explorer" and "The Road Not Taken" decided to write about the different attitudes toward choice in the two poems and looked for all the references to choice in each work. The student also looked for ways in which the other elements of the poems reinforce the attitudes toward choice.

The summary on the next page explains basic steps to follow when you are gathering evidence for a critical essay on a literary work.

Gathering Details for a Literary Analysis

- As you scan the work, look for quotations and other details that support your interpretation.
- Write each detail on a commentary card or piece of paper. If it is a quotation, indicate who said it and write the page number on which it appears. If it is a quotation from a poem, write the number of the line from which it comes.
- Tell how a particular detail supports your interpretation.
- Use a separate card or piece of paper for each detail.

The model cards below show how one writer gathered evidence to support the thesis that "The Explorer" and "The Road Not Taken" express sharply contrasting views toward choice.

MODEL: Gathering Evidence for "The Road Not Taken"

Two roads diverged in a yellow wood,
And sorry I could not travel both
And be one traveler, long I stood
And looked down one as far as I could
5   To where it bent in the undergrowth;

> 1. Seems to welcome choices, only wishes he could take both roads and still "be one traveler." Looks down road, thinks through consequences of choices.

Then took the other, as just as fair,
And having perhaps the better claim,
Because it was grassy and wanted wear;
Though as for that, the passing there
10   Had worn them really about the same,

> 2. 2nd stanza confusing. Says one road has "the better claim," but then they're "really about the same." Suggests how hard choice is.

And both that morning equally lay
In leaves no step had trodden black.
Oh, I kept the first for another day!
Yet knowing how way leads on to way,
15   I doubted if I should ever come back.

> 3. Sigh "oh" in line 13 is important—suggests traveler feels regret at not traveling both roads. Lines 14 and 15 accept that "way leads on to way."

I shall be telling this with a sigh
Somewhere ages and ages hence;
Two roads diverged in a woods, and I—
I took the one less traveled by.
20 And that has made all the difference.

> 4. Last stanza mentions sigh. Dash at end of line 18 suggests another sigh—more regret. Yet he expects to tell his story someday.

MODEL: Gathering Evidence for "The Explorer"

> 1. word somehow suggests how impossible a task it's going to be; reinforced in lines 4 and 5 with word somewhere.

Somehow to find a still spot in the
noise
Was the frayed inner want, the
winding, the frayed hope
Whose tatters he kept hunting
through the din.
A satin peace somewhere.
5 A room of wily hush somewhere within.

> 2. Explorer is low on hope—hope is "frayed" (line 2) and in "tatters." (line 3)

So tipping down the scrambled halls
he set
Vague hands on throbbing knobs.
There were behind
Only spiraling, high human voices,
The scream of nervous affairs,
10 Wee griefs,
Grand griefs. And choices.

> 3. Images seem nightmarish in 2nd stanza; explorer "tips" down "scrambled halls." (line 6) "Vague hands" make explorer uncertain. (line 7)

He feared most of all the choices,
that cried to be taken.
There were no bourns.
There were no quiet rooms.

> 4. Line 12 presents statement about choice. Explorer fears choice. Also it "cried to be taken." Choice is frightening and insistent.

> 5. Last two lines suggest explorer will never find peace.
>
> Bourns means "gentle streams" or "limits."

PREWRITING *Evidence*

Gather evidence to support your thesis by skimming the poems "Courage" and "The Courage That My Mother Had." On separate pieces of paper or commentary cards, jot down each supporting detail you find, and write a brief note explaining the significance of each detail. Save your work for later use.

Organizing Details into an Outline

When gathering your evidence, you probably will jot down supporting details in the order in which they appeared in the literary work. In most cases you may wish to keep your evidence in that order when writing your literary analysis. For example, when writing about a single poem, you may wish to present your evidence line by line. If you are writing about fiction and you are showing how a character changed over time, following the chronology of the story would be the best way to show the changes.

On the other hand, if you give reasons why a character behaves in a certain way, using cause and effect or order of importance would be a more effective way to organize your details. With some other subjects you might have to use comparison and contrast—one of the best ways to support an interpretation of two works. In all cases you need to reorder your supporting details so that they are arranged in the most effective way possible to support your thesis.

Comparison and Contrast   A common type of literary analysis is one that discusses the similarities and differences between two works of literature. In this type of essay, comparison and contrast is the most appropriate way to organize your supporting evidence.

You can organize details in a comparison and contrast essay in two different ways. To understand how these methods work, assume that you are comparing and contrasting "The Explorer" and "The Road Not Taken." The first pattern of organization is called **AABB.** In this pattern you would make all your points about "The Explorer" (poem A). Then you would make all your points about

"The Road Not Taken" (poem B). As you discuss the second work, you would explain how it is similar to and different from the first work. Such an approach is called **whole by whole** because you examine the whole of one work before moving on to the other work.

Another way to organize comparison and contrast is called **ABAB** or **point by point**. In this pattern, you make one point about both literary works. This point could be either a similarity or a difference. For instance, you might discuss how the tone of "The Explorer" (poem A) is similar to or different from that of "The Road Not Taken" (poem B). Then you move on to make another point about the two poems. You might compare and contrast the imagery in the two poems, for example.

Outlining   Once you organize your details, write an outline to guide you as you draft. The outline below shows the plan one writer used for a literary analysis about "The Explorer" and "The Road Not Taken."

MODEL: Outline

Introduction: includes thesis statement as well as points of similarity and difference between two poems

Body
  I. "The Explorer" shows hopeless feelings about choice.
      A. line 1: "somehow" = impossible task
      B. lines 2–3: "frayed inner want" and "frayed hope in tatters" = hopelessness
      C. line 5: "somewhere" = impossible place
  II. "The Explorer" shows fearfulness about choice.
      A. lines 6–7: "scrambled halls" and "vague hands on throbbing knobs" = desperation
      B. line 12: "choices . . . cried to be taken" = fear
  III. "The Road Not Taken" shows acceptance of difficulties of choice.
      A. lines 2–3: "travel both and be one traveler" = wants both choices
      B. line 4: "looked down as far as I could" = thinks about choices

IV. "The Road Not Taken" shows awareness of choice and need for action.
  A. line 6: "as just as fair" = options are very similar
  B. line 8: "it was grassy and wanted wear" = second choice is less traveled
V. "The Road Not Taken" shows acceptance of all the consequences of choice.
  A. line 14: "how way leads on to way, / I doubted if I should ever come back"
  B. line 16: "telling this with a sigh" = regret and resignation

Conclusion: ties both poems together, emphasizing differences in their attitude toward choice

Writing Tip

Use an **outline** to help organize the details for your literary analysis.

Communicate Your Ideas

PREWRITING *Outline*

Review your notes on "Courage" and "The Courage That My Mother Had." After deciding on a whole by whole or point by point pattern for your supporting details, create an outline showing a plan for your literary analysis. Save your work for later use.

Drafting Writing Process

Your outline will prove to be a valuable guide as you draft your literary analysis. The suggestions on the next page may also help.

Guidelines for Drafting a Literary Analysis

- Use present-tense verbs throughout your essay.
- In the introduction be sure to identify the author and the title of the work you are discussing.
- Include your thesis statement somewhere in the introduction. Refine it as needed and work it in as smoothly as possible.
- In the body of your essay, include your clearly organized supporting details, using transitions to show how one detail relates to another. Throughout your essay use direct quotations from the work if they strengthen the points you are tying to make. (Always enclose direct quotations in quotation marks.)
- In the conclusion draw together the details you have included to reinforce the main idea of your essay. Then add a title that suggests the focus of your essay.

Using Quotations

The best supporting evidence for a critical essay about literature comes from the work itself. You should plan to have your essay full of references to the literature, with plenty of quotations. To give strong support to your thesis statement, however, be sure your quotations make a strong point rather than just fill space. The following guidelines will help you.

You can learn more about citing sources on pages C542–C549.

Guidelines for Writing Direct Quotations

- Follow the examples below when writing quotations in different positions in a sentence. Notice that quotations in the middle of a sentence are not usually capitalized.

BEGINS SENTENCE   "Two roads diverged in a yellow wood," observes the persona in Robert Frost's poem.

INTERRUPTS SENTENCE	Since one road in the Frost poem is "just as fair" and worn "really about the same," the persona suggests that the options themselves are not that different.
ENDS SENTENCE	The road Frost chose "made all the difference."

- If you need to show that words have been left out of a quotation, use an **ellipsis**—a series of three dots—for the missing words.

> "Oh . . . I doubted if I should ever come back."

- If the quotation is two lines or longer, set it off by itself without quotation marks. Indent it and leave space above and below.

> The persona in "The Road Not Taken" shows resignation and perhaps regret in the final stanza.

> > I shall be telling this with a sigh
> > Somewhere ages and ages hence;
> > Two roads diverged in a wood, and I—
> > I took the one less traveled by,
> > And that has made all the difference.

- After each quotation, cite the page number of the source in parentheses. The citation should precede punctuation marks such as periods, commas, colons, and semicolons. For plays or long poems, also give the act and scene of the play or part of the poem, plus line numbers.

PRACTICE YOUR SKILLS

● *Using Direct Quotations*

Use direct quotations from "The Explorer" to complete the following practice items.

1. Write a sentence about the theme of choices in "The Explorer." Begin the sentence with a quotation.

2. Write a sentence about the theme of choices in "The Explorer." Interrupt the sentence with two quotations.

3. Write a sentence about the theme of choices in "The Explorer." Use a quotation with ellipses.

4. Write a sentence about the theme of choices in "The Explorer." Use a quotation that is two lines or longer.

The following literary analysis, which has already been revised and edited, will give you an idea of how to create a convincing presentation of your interpretation. Notice that this model uses the AABB pattern of organization.

MODEL: Literary Analysis

TITLE:
IDENTIFIES FOCUS

INTRODUCTION:
PRESENTS POINTS OF SIMILARITY BETWEEN BOTH POEMS

THESIS STATEMENT

MAIN TOPIC I:
FROM OUTLINE (POEM A)

MAIN TOPIC II:
FROM OUTLINE (POEM A)

Choice in "The Explorer" and "The Road Not Taken"

"The Explorer," by Gwendolyn Brooks, and "The Road Not Taken," by Robert Frost, are both poems that express the confusion people often face when confronted with choice. Both poems focus on a person traveling through life. One is searching for peace and quiet, and the other for all the richness that life can offer. Both poems also suggest that what the travelers seek can never be found. Despite these similarities the two poems are starkly different in their attitude toward choice. "The Explorer" represents a fearful, desperate attitude, while "The Road Not Taken" presents a calmer, more resigned attitude toward choice and its consequences.

From the very first word in "The Explorer," the reader senses that hopelessness and fear lie ahead. The word *somehow* suggests a virtually impossible task, just as *somewhere,* repeated in lines 4 and 5, suggests an impossible place. The explorer's hope for a quiet spot amid the noise and chaos of life is far from strong. In fact, it has worn so thin that it is "frayed" and in "tatters."

The desperation increases in the second stanza of the poem. In lines 6 and 7, for example, the explorer unsteadily tips down "scrambled halls" as if in a nightmare of tilted, frightening reality. His "vague hands" make him seem almost random in his efforts to find his way through the chaos. At each turn he finds only more of the same: "high human voices, Wee griefs, Grand griefs. And choices." In line 12 the poem makes its strongest, clearest point about choice; the explorer fears the choices. The choices do not beckon temptingly; instead they "cried to be taken." To the explorer any choice would be painful, since it would lead again only to grief, "wee" or "grand." No matter how hard he searches or what choices he makes, the explorer will not find his peace. This fact is clearly stated in the final lines of the poem.

MAIN TOPIC II:
FROM OUTLINE
(POEM B)

In sharp contrast to "The Explorer," Robert Frost's famous poem presents a calm, accepting attitude toward the choices life offers. The persona in "The Road Not Taken" does not fear each choice before him; instead he wishes he could take both roads and still "be one traveler." He thinks long and hard about which road to take, trying to follow each as far as his eye will take him. He acts like many people who, before they act, think through all the consequences of a choice they have to make.

MAIN TOPIC IV:
FROM OUTLINE
(POEM B)

The second and third stanzas raise a question familiar to anyone who has ever faced a choice. How different, really, are the options? The poem never clearly resolves this question. First the traveler says the second road is "just as fair." Then he suggests in lines 7 and 8 that the second road is less traveled; "it was grassy and wanted wear." Just as quickly he turns around and admits in lines 9–11 that the two roads are "really about the same" and "both that morning equally lay." The traveler's inability to tell for sure how different the roads are reinforces the theme of the poem. Unless one actually makes a choice and follows it through, one can never know for sure how the choice would have come out.

MAIN TOPIC V:
FROM OUTLINE
(POEM B)

As stanza 3 continues, the traveler makes his choice but also recognizes that he will probably never come back to try the other road. He knows— and seems to accept—"how way leads on to way." Frost's language and style suggest regret but resignation. The sigh "Oh" at the beginning of line 13 is the first of several to come. Indeed the word *sigh* appears in the first line of stanza 4, and the dash at the end of line 18 signals another sigh. All the sighs add up to a sense of resigned regret.

CONCLUSION:
TIES BOTH POEMS
TOGETHER AND
CONTRASTS THE
TRAVELERS'
ATTITUDES TOWARD
CHOICE

How different, though, is the traveler's sigh in "The Road Not Taken" from the explorer's fear and misery in the poem by Gwendolyn Brooks? In "The Road Not Taken," the persona realizes that little by little, through the choices he makes, he gradually limits his options and defines his life in narrower terms. Although he accepts this inevitability, he regrets that he cannot follow several different choices at once. The traveler in "The Road Not Taken" is left at least with the mixed pleasure and regret of telling his tale "ages and ages hence." The explorer, in contrast, is left with nothing—neither "bourns" nor "quiet rooms," where a weary wanderer could tell his tale.

Notice how the writer has seamlessly incorporated quotations from the poems in the literary analysis. Also notice how the topics, as well as the conclusion, support the thesis statement.

Communicate Your Ideas

DRAFTING *Literary Analysis*

Using the guidelines on page C497 and the work you have saved in your writing folder, write a first draft of your literary analysis of "Courage" and "The Courage That My Mother Had." Save your work for later use.

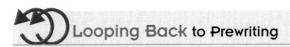

Looping Back to Prewriting

Reworking Your Thesis

After writing your first draft, reread your thesis statement. You may find you have taken a different direction. If so, you need to rewrite your thesis to reflect your new point.

Revising   Writing Process

When you are satisfied with your first draft, you may want to share your essay with a peer reader to find out whether your points are clearly expressed.

> ### Evaluation Checklist for Revising
>
> **Checking Your Essay**
>
> ✓ Do you have a strong introduction that identifies the author and work you will discuss? *(page C472)*
>
> ✓ Does your introduction contain a clear thesis? *(page C472)*
>
> ✓ In the body of your essay, have you provided ample details from the work to support your thesis? *(pages C491–C493)*
>
> ✓ Did you quote the work to strengthen your points? *(pages C497–C498)*
>
> ✓ Does your conclusion summarize the details in the body of your essay and reinforce your thesis statement? *(page C472)*
>
> ✓ Does your whole essay have unity and coherence? *(pages C136–C138)*
>
> ✓ Did you add a title showing the focus of your essay? *(page C497)*
>
> **Checking Your Paragraphs**
>
> ✓ Does each paragraph have a topic sentence? *(pages C103–C104)*
>
> ✓ Is each paragraph unified and coherent? *(pages C136–C138)*
>
> **Checking Your Sentences and Words**
>
> ✓ Are your sentences varied and concise? *(pages C67–C80)*
>
> ✓ Did you use lively, specific language? *(pages C62–C64)*

Prewriting Workshop
Drafting Workshop
Revising Workshop ▶
Editing Workshop
Publishing Workshop

Clauses

Your writing can be transformed once you know and understand clauses. An **independent clause** can stand alone as a sentence, but a **subordinate clause** cannot stand alone as a sentence. It must be attached to an independent clause. In addition to adding information to sentences, subordinate clauses also can transform your writing if you use them to combine short, choppy sentences into smooth-flowing, mature sentences.

Adverb Clauses

An **adverb clause** is a subordinate clause used as an adverb to describe mainly a verb. Adverb clauses add information to sentences by answering questions such as *Where? When? How?* and *Why?* An adverb clause at the beginning of a sentence also provides sentence variety.

WHY?	**If she knew the answer to the contest question,** her team would win first prize.
WHEN?	He paused but went on **when nothing happened.**

Adjective Clauses

An **adjective clause** is a subordinate clause that is used as an adjective to describe a noun or a pronoun. Adjective clauses add information to sentences by answering questions, such as *Which one? What kind?* and *How many?*

WHICH ONE?	Upon the shelf they saw the book **that he had written.**
WHAT KIND?	They opened a door, **which was made of brightly colored glass.**

Punctuation with Clauses

Place a comma after an introductory adverb clause—like the first example on the previous page. Also use commas to set off a nonessential adjective clause from the rest of the sentence. A **nonessential adjective clause** could be removed from the sentence without changing its meaning.

NONESSENTIAL CLAUSE	The intersection, **where two main highways crossed the town,** stood silent. (The nonessential clause can be removed without changing the meaning: *The intersection stood silent.*)
ESSENTIAL CLAUSE	They saw the book **that he had written.** (Without the clause *that he had written*, we do not know which book.)

Combining Sentences with Clauses

Once you understand clauses and how they work in a sentence, you can use them to improve your writing style. When revising or editing, you can show the relationship between two short sentences by combining them into one sentence.

TWO SENTENCES	He overslept by ten minutes. He missed the bus.
COMBINED	**Because he overslept by ten minutes,** he missed the bus.
TWO SENTENCES	The boys were covered in dirt from head to toe. The boys were nine years old.
COMBINED	The boys, **who were nine years old,** were covered in dirt from head to toe.

REVISING Conferencing

Exchange the draft of your literary analysis with a partner. Comment on the strengths and weaknesses of your partner's paper. Consider your partner's comments as you use the preceding Evaluation Checklist for Revising to improve your draft. Save your work for later use.

Time Out to Reflect

With the comments from your peer fresh in your mind, think back to responses to other essays you have written. Are your reviewers and teachers making similar remarks each time? Record your findings, as well as strategies for improving, in the Learning Log section of your **journal.**

COMPUTER TIP

If you are revising your draft on a computer, you can use the Save As function to save more than one version of your essay. Save your original draft with its own title. Then, after you have revised your essay, click the Save As key and give the revised version a new name.

If you want to go back to any of your original material, you will have a saved copy.

Editing ☰ Writing Process

You are now ready to edit your literary analysis for errors in grammar, usage, spelling, capitalization, and punctuation. As you check for mistakes, look especially for problems with clauses. The workshop on pages C503–C504 will help you transform your writing with correct and effective use of clauses.

EDITING

Edit your revised draft for grammar errors. Try reading your draft aloud to hear sentences that simply sound odd. Pay close attention to the clauses you have written. Use the checklist on page C83 to help you use clauses correctly and effectively in your writing. When you are satisfied with your changes and corrections, save your work in your writing folder.

Publishing — Writing Process

You can complete the writing process by connecting your literary analysis with a reader who would have an interest in it. You can also submit your literary analysis to your school's literary magazine for publication or enter your work in a literary competition.

PUBLISHING

Entering your literary analysis in a competition is a great way to share your work with others. For information on literary contests, write to the National Council of Teachers of English, 1111 Kenyon Road, Urbana, IL 61801. Be sure to follow standard manuscript form and follow any specific entry rules for the competition.

PORTFOLIO

Process of Writing a Literary Analysis

Remember that the writing process is recursive—you can move back and forth among the stages of the process to achieve your purpose. For example, during editing you may wish to return to the revising stage to add fresh details that have occurred to you while editing. The numbers in parentheses refer to pages where you can get help with your writing.

PREWRITING

- Read the work carefully and respond to it from both personal experience and your literary knowledge. *(pages C473–C484)*
- By synthesizing your personal and literary responses, choose and limit a subject for your composition. *(pages C486–C489)*
- Shape your limited subject into a working thesis statement that will guide you as you write. *(page C490)*
- Skim the work again, looking for details from it that will support your thesis statement. On a commentary card or separate paper, jot down each detail with a page reference after it. If you are writing about poetry, cite the number of the line of the poem. *(pages C491–C493)*
- Organize your supporting details into an informal outline. *(pages C494–C496)*

DRAFTING

- Use present-tense verbs throughout your essay. *(page C497)*
- In the introduction be sure to identify the author and the title of the work you are discussing. *(page C497)*
- Include your thesis statement somewhere in the introduction. *(page C497)*
- In the body include supporting details, using transitions to show how one detail relates to another. Use direct quotation if they strengthen the points you are trying to make. (Always enclose direct quotation in quotation marks.) *(pages C497–C498)*
- In the conclusion draw together the details you have included to reinforce the main idea of your essay. Then add an interesting title that suggests the focus of your essay. *(page C497)*

REVISING

- Use the <u>Evaluation Checklist for Revising</u> to help you make a thorough revision of your essay. *(page C502)*

EDITING

- Remember to check your grammar, spelling, usage, and mechanics.
- Pay special attention to the punctuation of direct quotations.

PUBLISHING

- Prepare a neat final copy of your work and present it to an interested reader in an appropriate way. *(page C506)*

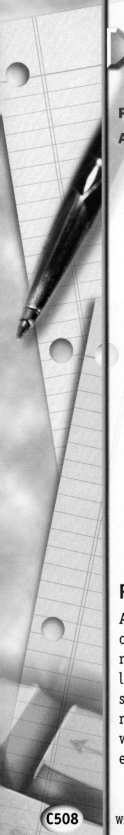

A Writer Writes

A Literary Analysis

Purpose: to explain your understanding of a poem

Audience: your teacher and classmates

The Coach of Life

Though often somewhat heavy-freighted,
The coach rolls at an easy pace;
And Time, the coachman, grizzly-pated,
But smart, alert—is in his place.

5 We board it lightly in the morning
And on our way at once proceed.
Repose and slothful comfort scorning,
We shout: "Hey, there! Get on! Full speed!"

Noon finds us done with reckless daring,
10 And shaken up. Now care's the rule.
Down hills, through gulleys roughly faring,
We sulk, and cry: "Hey, easy fool!"

The coach rolls on, no pitfalls dodging.
At dusk, to pains more wonted grown,
15 We drowse, while to the night's dark lodging
Old coachman Time drives on, drives on.

—Aleksandr Pushkin

Prewriting

After reading "The Coach of Life" by Alexander Pushkin, one of Russia's greatest poets, write your personal and literary responses to the poem. Consider discussing the metaphor of life as a coach, as well as the theme, imagery, and rhyme scheme Pushkin uses. Synthesize your personal and literary responses. Then choose a subject and focus it. When you have written a thesis statement for your literary analysis, gather evidence to support it.

Drafting

Using your outline as a guide, draft your literary analysis. As you write, you also may find it helpful to refer to the <u>Process of Writing a Literary Analysis</u> summary on page C507.

Revising

Exchange papers with a partner and share responses to the poem, commenting on both the strengths and weaknesses of your partner's paper. Pay special attention to how effectively the supporting details strengthen the ideas in the thesis statement. After your discussion, make any changes to your essay that you think are appropriate. Then use the <u>Evaluation Checklist for Revising</u> on page C502 to revise your composition.

Editing

Use the <u>Editing Checklist</u> on page C46 as a guide to polishing your literary analysis. Also make sure that you have consistently used present-tense verbs throughout your essay and check for the correct punctuation of quotations.

Publishing

When you are pleased with your composition, write a neat final copy. Then give it to an interested reader who is familiar with the poem.

Connection Collection

Representing in Different Ways

Acquainted with the Night

Read the poem by
Robert Frost aloud.
Consider the different
images Frost uses to
evoke his mood and
describe his feelings.
Then search through
magazines to find
pictures that best
illustrate the poem
for you. Create a
collage of these
images to accompany
the text of the poem.

I have been one acquainted with the night.
I have walked out in rain—and back in rain.
I have outwalked the furthest city light.

I have looked down the saddest city lane.
I have passed by the watchman on his beat
And dropped my eyes, unwilling to explain.

I have stood still and stopped the sound of feet
When far away an interrupted cry
Came over houses from another street,

But not to call me back or say good-by;
And further still at an unearthly height,
One luminary clock against the sky

Proclaimed the time was neither wrong nor right.
I have been one acquainted with the night.

—Robert Frost

René Magritte. *The Mysteries of the Horizon,* 1955.
Oil on canvas, 19½ by 25⅓ inches. Private collection.

. . . to Print

Write a poem that you think
represents the subject, mood,
and theme of *The Mysteries of the
Horizon* by René Magritte. Consider
how the rhythm you use in the
poem can express the mood of
the painting.

- **Which strategies can be
  used for creating both
  written and visual
  representations? Which
  strategies apply to one,
  not both? Which type of
  representation is more
  effective?**
- **Draw a conclusion and
  write briefly about the
  differences between
  written ideas and visual
  representations.**

Writing in Everyday Life

E-mail to a Friend

Next Tuesday will be the birthday of your best friend Laura. Unfortunately, Laura is on vacation in Morocco and will not be able to spend the day with you. You have decided to make your friend feel special by writing an E-mail to tell her about a song you especially like and analyzing how the lyrics remind you of your friendship.

> Write an E-mail to your friend analyzing how the lyrics are significant to your friendship. Describe the experiences from your own life that come to mind when you hear the song or read its lyrics. Also describe what aspects of the song move you and why.
>
> What strategies did you use to analyze the lyrics for your friend?

You can find information on writing E-mail on pages C736–C739.

Writing in the Workplace

Analytical Essay

You have just been promoted to the position of Assistant Editor at *Image Journal*, an important literary magazine. This month's issue will be devoted to poetry. Babs Johnson, the head editor, has asked you to find a haiku to reprint in the magazine. As a test for your skills as an editor, Ms. Johnson also wants you to write an essay that analyzes the meaning of the poem.

> Find a haiku that you like and write an essay analyzing its meaning. Analyze the attitude of the persona of the poem to the subject, mood, and theme of the poem. Also analyze what images the figures of speech create and what feelings those images suggest.
>
> What strategies did you use to analyze the haiku you chose?

You can find information on responding to poetry on pages C473–C484.

Assess Your Learning

You are trying to get into Poison Ivy Paradise, an exclusive summer camp in a remote forest setting that explores the value of the arts . You are currently compiling your application materials for the camp's tough admissions board. One of the required items for applying is a personal essay. This year's essay topic: "The Character from Literature with Whom I Most Identify."

▶ **Write the essay for the admissions board of Poison Ivy Paradise. First, think about a character from a book, play, or even poem who has made a strong impression on you. Consider reasons why the character may have been vivid and important. Did the character help to express some meaning in life that was influential to you specifically? Are there ways you have lived your life differently because of this specific figure from literature? Be sure your essay for Poison Ivy Paradise contains a strong introduction, body, and conclusion, and cite specific examples from the chosen text to support your points.**

🔘 *Before You Write* **Consider the following questions:**
What is the *subject?*
What is the *occasion?*
Who is the *audience?*
What is the *purpose?*

🔘 *After You Write* **Evaluate your work using the following criteria:**
- Does the introduction to your essay identify the author and title of the work from which you have chosen your character?
- Have you decided on a title that reflects the focus of your essay?
- Have you used present-tense verbs when discussing the character from literature?
- Have you used direct quotations from the work that strengthen the points you are making about the character?
- Have you organized your ideas to ensure coherence, logical progression, and support for ideas?

Write briefly on how well you did. Point out your strengths and areas for improvement.

CHAPTER 12

Research Reports

The best research reports begin with curiosity about a subject. You might be curious about something practical, such as which running shoes are the best buy for your money. You may wonder about who makes the best pizza in your town. Magazines and newspapers often publish research reports on topics like these.

Your curiosity might also lead you in less practical directions. For example, you might want to explore why so many people are afraid of mice. You might research how top rock bands choose their names or some of the ways slang originates and spreads.

Countless things will interest you if you take time to be curious. Research reports are a way to explore these interests and satisfy your curiosity. In this chapter, you will learn the skills you need to research topics that interest you. You will also learn how to plan, organize, and write research papers so that you can effectively share what you learn with others.

Reading with a Writer's Eye

In "The Diverse Creatures of the Deep May Be Dying," newspaper science reporter William J. Broad reports on an environmental problem in the deepest waters of the ocean. As you read this research report, what are your first reactions to the title and to the news in the article? As a writer, think about how the author might have researched the information included in the report. What else could he have added to inform his readers?

FROM *THE NEW YORK TIMES*

The Diverse Creatures of the Deep
MAY BE DYING

William J. Broad

Hordes of creatures living in the hidden depths of the deep sea are in danger of starving to death, scientists report. This remote part of the planet is believed to harbor millions of undiscovered species, an unknown number of which may be in crisis.

A study of food supply and demand miles down in the North Pacific between 1989 and 1996 found that creatures of the seabed suffered from growing food shortages. A likely culprit, scientists say, is a documented increase in sea surface temperatures during the same period.

"If the food deficit continues, it is going to change the configuration of the deep-sea communities," said Kenneth L. Smith Jr., a biologist at the Scripps Institution of Oceanography in San Diego and a co-author of the report, which was published recently in Science. "Some species will die out while those that can survive on a very low food supply will still be able to maintain themselves."

Little is known about the creatures of the darkness, much less about fluctuations in their diets and fortunes.

The sea's inky depths, which dwarf the planet's land masses in overall size, have been found to support fish, snails, worms, slugs, barnacles, corals, crabs, prawns, sponges, sea anemones, brittle stars, sea cucumbers, sea urchins, feather stars and sea lilies. Scientists estimate up to 10 million species—far more than

the 1.4 million types of land dwellers.

Most animals of the deep rely on a food chain that begins in the sea's lighted realms, where sunlight is captured by the microscopic plants known as phytoplankton. The plants in turn nourish a riot of sea life. Leftovers from the feast, including dead plants and animals, as well as fecal droppings, produce a constant rain of organic matter that feeds the bottom dwellers.

Dr. Smith and Ronald S. Kaufmann, a former Scripps postdoctoral researcher now at the University of San Diego, found that the rainfall of food in the North Pacific had declined over seven years. About 135 miles off the central California coast, in a region more than two and a half miles deep, they measured the rain in sediment traps, cone-shaped devices that catch falling particles. The traps were suspended off the bottom at elevations of roughly 150 and 2,000 feet. Trapped particles were collected periodically over the seven-year study period and analyzed to determine organic carbon content.

The amount of sinking particulate matter (a measure of food supply) was compared with oxygen consumption by marine creatures in the seabed (a measure of food demand). The scientists reported that between 1989 and 1996 the ratio decreased by more than 50 percent.

"The findings of Smith and Kaufmann will have far-reaching implications," Ellen R. M. Druffel of the University of California at Irvine and Bruce H. Robison of the Monterey Bay Aquarium Research Institute, in Moss Landing, Calif., said of the research in a Science commentary. "We used to think of the deep sea as a highly stable, steady-state system."

Dr. Smith and Dr. Kaufmann said the decline in the food supply might be related to an increase in surface temperatures during the same period. The ocean warming, they said, may have prompted a decline in zooplankton—tiny creatures that eat the tiny plants of the sea and in turn become food for a vast web of life. And their diminishment in turn may have cut the total amount of food that falls into the depths.

"A long-term reduction in surface productivity," Dr. Kaufmann said in a Scripps statement, "could severely impact the amount of food delivered to the deep ocean."

Trouble Below

A study of food supply and demand shows that deep-sea creatures are suffering from growing food shortages.

DEPTH
IN MILES

SUNLIGHT AND INCREASED TEMPERATURE

Higher sea-surface temperatures depleted the plankton available

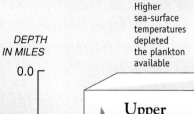

Upper Ocean

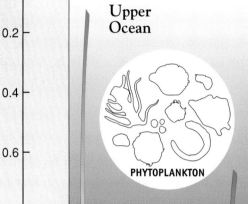

PHYTOPLANKTON

◄ Photosynthesis driven by sunlight supports microscopic plant life called phytoplankton near the surface.

◄ Phytoplankton, in turn, support the rich surrounding ecosystem of sea life.

The falling food supply to the deep-sea ecosystem is decreasing

Leftovers from this process, including dead plants and animals, fecal droppings, etc., produce a constant rain of organic matter that falls into the depths and feeds the deep-sea
◄ creatures.

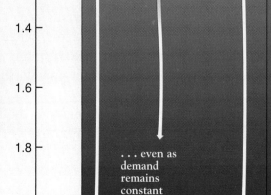

... even as demand remains constant

Sediment traps show a steady decrease of nutrients reaching the
◄ deep ocean.

0.0
0.2
0.4
0.6
0.8
1.0
1.2
1.4
1.6
1.8
2.0

Thinking as a Writer

Journalist William J. Broad is not convinced that the creatures of the deep are starving. Since the long-term effects of this environmental change are still unknown, the title of his report states only that they "may be" dying.

- Go back over the report and look for the evidence that Broad supplies. Where does his evidence come from? Do you think there is enough evidence to conclude that the creatures are, indeed, starving to death?
- Is Broad correct to suggest this is only a possibility? Be prepared to cite evidence in the research report to support your conclusion.

Summarizing a Research Report

Oral Expression

- If you had to sum up the main ideas of William J. Broad's report for someone who has not read it, what main points would you include?
- Briefly, summarize the research report for some classmates. Take turns and listen carefully while others do the same.
- Decide which ideas are most important for a summary of the report, and share your decisions and ideas with your classmates.

Analyzing a Diagram

Viewing

- Study the illustration on the previous page that accompanied William J. Broad's report. What details in the report are also represented in the diagram? What additional information does the diagram provide that the report cannot?
- How does the diagram help you to understand the main points of Broad's report? In one paragraph, explain your response.

The Power of Research Reports

"The Diverse Creatures of the Deep May Be Dying" is a newspaper report on recent scientific findings. Reports in newspapers, either in print or online, can alert a large audience to a recent event or problem quickly. Reports in other media such as books or magazines take longer to produce but are good sources for more in-depth information.

Uses of Research Reports

In many professions and occupations, reports are used to gather information, reach conclusions, and make important recommendations. The following examples are only a few uses of research reports:

- **A historian finds documents that shed new light on the life of a famous poet** and writes a paper to report on the discovery.

- **Doctors in a university hospital release the results of a new study on blood pressure** and write a report to share their findings.

- **A television news reporter investigates how some companies in one city are cheating customers.** The televised report alerts viewers to the problem.

- **Two journalists spend a year traveling with farm workers.** Afterward, they write a book that details the difficulties that these workers face.

- **A political consultant researches voter polling data** and reports on issues that are likely to be important for a new candidate.

Process of Writing Research Reports

"The absolute first thing to do when you launch a writing project is to resist the impulse to start writing. You need to relax, to settle down, and above all *you need to think*. Don't worry about wasting time; it's never a waste of time to get your thoughts in order."

This advice from Herbert and Jill Meyer is important to consider whenever you start to write a research report.

> A **research report** is an essay based on information drawn from sources such as books, periodicals, the media, and interviews with experts.

Before you begin, ask yourself: What subject really interests me? What points do I want to make about my subject? What is the best way to convey these points to my readers? Once you answer these questions, you can begin your work with confidence and purpose. When they begin writing, some students forget to use the basic writing skills that they learned in other writing tasks. Remember, a research paper, first and foremost, is an informative essay that should present information clearly and effectively.

Your Writer's Journal

In your writer's journal, keep a list of topics that you are curious about. The goal is to find a topic that interests you— one you want to research and write about. Maybe recent events in the news have caught your eye, or there is some historical figure you want to know more about. As you list ideas in your journal, identify the ones that might make possible topics for a research paper. Jot down any thoughts you have about the points you might make in the report.

Since you will be collecting information from a variety of different sources for your report, keep your notes organized from the beginning. Use a folder with pockets to store index cards, paper clips, rubber bands, and pens.

Discovering Subjects

Browsing through the stacks of the library or media center, skimming through magazines, taking ideas from television shows, and surfing the Internet are all good ways to discover subjects for a research report. You can also refer to the Learning Log in your **journal** for ideas. If these strategies do not produce a subject, use freewriting or brainstorming to complete the following statement: *I've always wondered why. . . .* The best research reports usually grow out of a genuine desire to learn more about a subject.

Choosing and Limiting a Research Subject

When you have five to ten possible subjects, choose one that you think best suits your purpose and audience. The following guidelines will help.

> ### Guidelines for Choosing a Subject
> - Choose a subject you would like to know more about.
> - Consider your audience by choosing a subject your readers would like to know more about.
> - Consider your purpose by choosing a limited subject that can be covered thoroughly in a short paper of three to five pages.
> - Choose a subject for which there is sufficient information from a variety of sources in the library or media center, including online sources.

Limiting a Subject   Find a clear, specific focus with which to approach the subject. One good way to limit your subject is by using a **cluster diagram**. In the following cluster, the general subject is families, and each offshoot from the center is a more limited version of that subject. To limit the subject even further, you can create another cluster, using one of the offshoots as the middle of the cluster.

MODEL: Limiting a Subject by Clustering

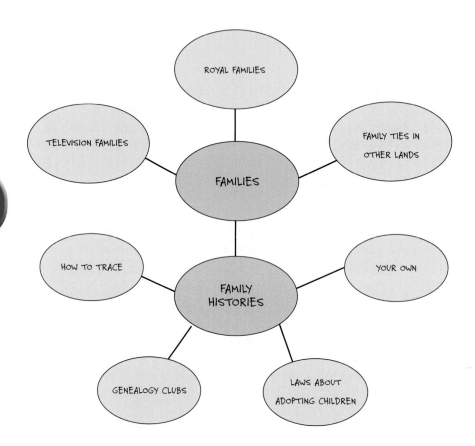

Any of the offshoots in the second cluster is a suitably limited subject for a report. Each has a specific enough focus to provide the writer an angle on the subject.

Practice Your Skills

● *Evaluating Subjects*

Decide which of the following subjects are suitable for a short research report and which are too broad. Indicate your answer by writing *suitable* or *too broad*.

1. the Industrial Revolution
2. how computers are used in airplane cockpits
3. how Oscar®-winning movies are chosen
4. space exploration
5. the impact of television on presidential campaigns
6. ecology
7. effect of Trans-Alaska Pipeline on animal life
8. the music industry
9. how U.S. Olympic athletes are chosen
10. bowling

● *Limiting a Subject*

For each subject above that is too broad, use a cluster to limit it. Then choose an offshoot in the first cluster to create a second cluster with at least four new offshoots. Each of these offshoots should be a suitably limited subject for a report.

Communicate Your Ideas

PREWRITING *Limited Subject*

After you review the list of possible research subjects that you recorded in your **journal**, use the guidelines on page C521 to help you choose one for further research. Then, use clustering or any other prewriting strategy you prefer to limit your subject. Write the subject in your notes, and save your work for later use.

SAVE YOUR WORK

Gathering Information

Once you have limited your subject, the next step is to jot down a few questions that you want to answer in your research. These questions will serve as a guide for gathering information and therefore eliminate the possibility of wasting time. As you develop these questions, keep in mind the purpose of your research report and the audience you intend to reach so that the direction of your research is appropriate and on the mark. On the subject of family histories, for example, the questions that you might consider are as follows.

MODEL: Questions

- What basic information does a family researcher need to know to start tracing his or her ancestry?

- What kinds of documents are needed in the search for family roots?

- Which libraries around the country have special aids for family researchers?

- What problems might an inexperienced family researcher encounter?

- Who are some experts in family history I might be able to interview?

As you begin the research process, keep in mind that not all sources of information you discover will be equally useful to you. Before using a source, you need to evaluate it with some basic guidelines in mind. Regardless of your specific topic, all of your sources should be relevant, reliable, up-to-date, and unbiased. The information should relate directly to your topic; the author should be a respected, trusted expert; the material should be current; and if your subject is controversial, your report should represent different points of view on the topic.

With your preparatory questions clearly in mind, you can begin to find the information you need by using the following steps.

Steps for Gathering Information

- Use a general reference work such as an encyclopedia, either in print or online, to get an overview of your subject. *(pages C680–C685)*

- Use a computer-based card catalog or other database in the library or media center to find books on your subject. *(pages C664–C673)*

- Use a variety of primary sources (firsthand accounts), and secondary sources (information about primary sources) to explore your topic, especially if the subject is about a historical figure or event. *(pages C676–C687)*

- Consult the *Readers' Guide to Periodical Literature*, either in print or online, to find magazine articles on your subject. *(pages C676–C678)*

- Use a search engine to do a keyword search on the Internet for your topic. Make note of any Websites you find that you think would be useful. *(pages C742–C768)*

- Make a list of all sources available on your subject. Include the author, title, copyright year, publisher and location, and call number, or Internet address if there is one, for each source.

- Assign each source on your list a number that will easily identify it when you take notes.

Writing Tip

Remember, not all sources on the Internet are reliable. Many sites may contain information that is either outdated or inaccurate. Be sure to **evaluate your sources** before you use them in your report. These guidelines are true for both print and electronic sources.

For more information on evaluating online sources refer to pages C733–C734.

PRACTICE YOUR SKILLS

● *Gathering Information*

Use the library or media center to locate five sources for each of the following subjects. If possible, include at least one magazine article for each subject and one online source. Remember to record author, title, copyright year, publisher and location, and call number or Internet address for each source.

1. solar energy

2. new features of laptop computers

3. gorillas as an endangered species

4. earthquakes along the San Andreas fault

5. the most recent World Series

Communicate Your Ideas

PREWRITING *Library or Media Center Research*

Use the library or media center to find at least eight sources for the subject of your research report. If possible, at least two of the sources should be magazine articles in print, and one should be an online source. Follow all the guidelines in the **Steps for Gathering Information** listed on the previous page. Save your work for later use.

Taking Notes and Summarizing

Before you take any notes from your library or media center sources, review your research questions. Check to see if your source contains the information you need. When you are looking for information in a book, check the index to see if your topic, or related ones, are listed. If you are using articles, skim the contents to see what topics are covered. If you decide to use the source, keep in mind that the goals of note taking are to summarize the main points in your own words and to record quotations that you might use in your research report.

Notice how the following information about tracing a family tree is summarized on the note card below.

"Genealogy, like charity, begins at home," says Dr. Kenn Stryker-Rodda of the New York Genealogical and Biological Society in New York City. "Begin by digging into the memories of all your living relatives and by checking family records—letters in an old trunk in the attic, for instance, or entries in a family Bible—for records of births, marriages, and deaths. This information will be the skeleton of your family tree."

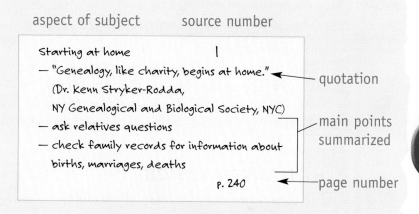

aspect of subject   source number

Starting at home   1
— "Genealogy, like charity, begins at home." ←——— quotation
  (Dr. Kenn Stryker-Rodda,
  NY Genealogical and Biological Society, NYC)
— ask relatives questions   main points
— check family records for information about summarized
  births, marriages, deaths
                              p. 240 ←——— page number

Clip together the note cards from each source and keep them in your folder. Make sure, however, that the source is identified on each card. Later you will re-sort your note cards.

COMPUTER TIP

If you are working on a computer as you prepare your notes, you can store this information in an easily accessible place by using the Note Pad feature of computers.

Summarizing

When you research a report, summarize key ideas and details from your sources onto note cards. **Summarizing** means restating the main idea concisely in your own words using several important thinking processes. First, you **translate**, or make sense of, what you have read. Then, you **analyze**, or identify, the passage and **evaluate**, or decide, which points are important. Finally, in your own words, you **synthesize**, or put back together, these important points in a concise summary—often no longer than a phrase or a sentence.

If you look back at the sample note card on the previous page, you will see a clear, simple summary of a paragraph. The writer decided that there were two main points—to question relatives, and to check family records. The writer then reworded the main points concisely.

THINKING PRACTICE

Write a one-sentence summary of the following paragraph. First read the paragraph to make sure you understand it. Then include the most important points in your sentence, omitting unnecessary details.

Though most people would name the wood or the fruit of a tree as its most useful part, a surprising number of trees are valued chiefly for their bark. The bark of the cork oak, for example, provides the world with cork. Another tree, the cinnamon tree, which grows in Sri Lanka and India, has bark that curls as it dries. The curled bark becomes cinnamon sticks and can be ground for use as a spice. The aroma and flavor of cinnamon are savored around the world. In addition, the cinchona tree, related to the poplar tree, has bark that contains the chemical quinine. This chemical protects the tree from pests and is used in the treatment of malaria.

PRACTICE YOUR SKILLS

● *Taking Notes and Summarizing*

Take notes on the following article for a report called "Esperanto: The Universal Language." On your note card, identify the aspect of the subject being discussed. Then summarize the main points in your own words and record any useful quotations. Use the note card on page C527 as a model.

A Language of Hope

Bialystok is a city that has been part of several countries, held at first by one and then by another warring nation. When Ludwig Zamenhof (1859–1917) was growing up there, it was in Poland, although the Russians occupied the area. Throughout Zamenhof's upbringing, people of different backgrounds—Russians, Poles, and Germans—were in political and social conflict all around him. He believed strongly that their language differences were causing a division among them.

One reason for his belief was the rising tide of nationalism in world affairs. Nationalism is the belief that the good of one's country surpasses all other values, including peaceful coexistence with neighbors. Nationalism stresses the ties that bind a nation's people together: native music, literature, folk traditions, and—most importantly— language. Zamenhof believed that if language differences were done away with, humanity instead of nationality would become the tie that binds.

Under the pen name Doktoro Esperanto, Zamenhof published a book outlining an international language he had carefully worked out. The name he chose for himself means "one who hopes." The language itself is known by that name. For the thousands who have learned Zamenhof's language, it still speaks of hope for a peaceful future.

Review the sources that you have compiled for your research subject. Using the information that you have learned about note taking and summarizing, prepare some useful notes on the sources that you will use for your report. Save your note cards for later use.

Developing a Working Thesis

Your subject is probably already limited enough to permit you to begin your research, but focusing your thoughts even further will save you time and effort as you organize your research. The best way to focus your thoughts at this stage is to develop a **working thesis** that expresses the main ideas your research revealed. A working thesis is a tentative proposition; you can revise it as needed if you discover more information that you want to include in your research report.

To develop your working thesis, think carefully about what you know about your subject. For example, after gathering information about tracing family histories, the writer of that report learned that there are some basic sources and documents each genealogist should consult and also discovered that there are a number of common mistakes beginners make. Consequently, she developed a working thesis statement that accounts for this information.

MODEL: Developing a Working Thesis Statement

LIMITED SUBJECT	How to trace a family history
WORKING THESIS STATEMENT	The best way to study one's family history is to know the sources of genealogy and to avoid some common mistakes.

PREWRITING *Working Thesis*

Formulate a working thesis from the limited subject you have selected for your research report. Review your note cards and summarize the main points of the information you have gathered. Taking these points into account, express your thesis in the form of a complete sentence. Save your work for later use.

Outlining

After you have answered all of the preresearch questions on page C524 and written a working thesis statement, you can begin to organize your notes and plan the structure of your research report. Then you can use your notes to develop an outline.

Organizing Your Notes The first step in organizing your notes is to group your note cards into categories. Notice how the following categories for the subject of family histories come from the preresearch questions on page C524.

CATEGORY 1   general information: popularity of genealogy, events that made genealogy popular

CATEGORY 2   kinds of public documents needed

CATEGORY 3   famous library collections of genealogies

CATEGORY 4   problems to avoid from the start

CATEGORY 5   the family itself as a starting point

After grouping your note cards into three or more main categories of information, clip together the cards in each category and bind each set with a rubber band. Cards that do not fit into any of your categories should be clipped separately. You may be able to use some of those notes in the introduction or conclusion of your report.

PRACTICE YOUR SKILLS

● *Creating Categories*

Write three main categories into which the following tips for staying healthy can be grouped. Then write each item under the appropriate category. Save your work for later use.

Tips for Staying Healthy

1. Eat fresh fruits and vegetables.
2. Do cardiovascular exercise to strengthen the heart and lungs.
3. Avoid foods high in fat.
4. Follow a regular sleeping schedule.
5. Exercise for twenty minutes, three times a week.
6. Avoid foods that are high in sugar (empty calories).
7. Clear your mind before sleeping.
8. Stretch your muscles before and after exercise to avoid injury.
9. Get plenty of sleep to maintain your resistance to viruses.
10. Eat a variety of foods from all of the four basic food groups.

Structuring Your Outline   The categories you created when organizing your notes will be the basis for your outline. You can begin structuring your outline by deciding which type of logical order suits your subject: chronological order, spatial order, order of importance, or developmental order.

Then, after you assign each category a Roman numeral, arrange the categories according to the type of order you have chosen.

You may want to read more about types of logical order on pages C124–C125.

The list on the following page is the beginning of an outline for a research report about family history. As you will see, the main categories are arranged in developmental order.

I. Collecting family data
II. Using library collections
III. Using public documents
IV. Avoiding common mistakes

The next step is to go back over your notes and add subtopics (indicated by capital letters), and supporting points (indicated by Arabic numerals) to fill out the outline. The following list is the final outline for the research report on tracing a family history.

MODEL: Outline

MAIN TOPIC
SUBTOPIC
SUPPORTING
POINTS

I. Collecting family data
   A. Asking the right questions
      1. Basic facts
      2. Family stories
   B. Interpreting family photographs
II. Using library collections
   A. Library of the Church of Jesus Christ of Latter-Day Saints
      1. Size
      2. Scope of information available
   B. Other good libraries
      1. Newberry Library, Chicago
      2. Fort Wayne Public Library, Indiana
      3. Free Library of Philadelphia
      4. New Orleans Public Library
III. Using public documents
   A. Types of documents
      1. Local records
      2. Federal records
      3. Online sources
   B. How to request information
IV. Avoiding common mistakes
   A. Lack of organization
   B. Lack of focus
   C. Lack of critical approach to documents

PRACTICE YOUR SKILLS

● **Outlining**

> **Write a simple outline, using the categories you wrote on the subject about staying healthy. You should have three main topics (indicated by Roman numerals) with at least three subtopics (indicated by capital letters) under each one. Remember that each entry in the outline should be a phrase rather than a complete sentence.**

Communicate Your Ideas

PREWRITING *Categories, Outline*

Look back over all your research notes. Organize your note cards into categories, and select a logical order that suits your subject. Then use those categories to write an outline for the body of your research report, identifying main topics and subtopics with the appropriate numerals. Save your outline for later use.

Drafting ▸ Writing Process

A well-written research paper, like any good piece of writing, has a lively and engaging style. As you draft your research report from your notes and outline, you should also strive for sentence variety, precise words, and fresh comparisons to make your report more interesting.

You may wish to read more about developing style on pages C62–C88.

Writing a Thesis Statement

Now that you have an outline with clear categories of information, check your working thesis once again to make sure it is broad enough to cover the categories in your outline but also limited enough to express the main idea of the research report.

The following guidelines will help you refine your working thesis into an appropriate thesis statement.

> **Guidelines for Refining a Thesis Statement**
>
> - A thesis statement should make the main point of your research report clear to a reader.
> - A thesis statement should cover all the main topics listed in your outline.
> - A thesis statement should fit smoothly into the introduction of your research report.

The writer of the research report on studying a family history wanted to point out that the inexperienced person studying a family history is a "budding genealogist." She also wanted to use wording that was smoother than the wording she used in her working thesis. The model below shows how she accomplished these goals.

MODEL: Refining a Working Thesis

WORKING THESIS	The best way to study one's family history is to know the sources of genealogy and to avoid some common mistakes.
THESIS STATEMENT	Before becoming a family detective, a budding genealogist should become familiar with the basic sources of genealogy and the common mistakes beginners make.

PRACTICE YOUR SKILLS

Refining Thesis Statements

Rewrite each of the following thesis statements so that it covers all the main topics listed in the outline accompanying it.

1. The construction of a building begins with the substructure, or foundation.

    I. Substructure—construction below ground

    II. Superstructure—construction above ground

2. The sun may be the main source of energy in the future.

    I. Fossil fuels

    II. Solar energy

    III. Nuclear energy

3. Watching a solar eclipse can be very hazardous to the eyes unless it is done in the proper way.

    I. Dangers

    II. Proper way to watch

    III. Watching a lunar eclipse

4. Jazz trumpeter Miles Davis played music that blended jazz and rock styles.

    I. Early years—bebop style

    II. Middle years—cool style

    III. Final years—jazz/rock style

5. The trumpet and bugle are very similar instruments.

    I. Tubing

    II. How sound is produced

    III. Differences

6. Gardening is a healthful pastime.

    I. Exercise

    II. Stress reduction

    III. Fresh air

Communicate Your Ideas

DRAFTING *Outline, Thesis Statement*

    Look again at the outline and thesis statement you have developed for your report. Does your thesis statement cover all the main points in your outline? If not, decide how you might refine your thesis statement to cover all the main points clearly. Save your work for later use.

Structuring the Research Report

The following chart will help you structure your research report as you write your first draft. Notice that a research report contains special features.

THE STRUCTURE OF A RESEARCH REPORT	
Parts	**Purpose**
TITLE	• suggests the subject of the research report
INTRODUCTION	• captures attention • provides background information • contains the thesis statement
BODY	• supports the thesis statement with information drawn from research • contains well-developed paragraphs
CONCLUSION	• brings the report to a close by restating the thesis or by referring to earlier ideas with fresh emphasis
Special Features	
CITATIONS	• give credit to other authors for ideas
WORKS CITED	• lists sources used in preparing the research report • appears at the end of the report on a separate page

The following model report was written from the outline on page C533. Although it is more polished than your first draft will be, it shows you how each part in the report contributes to the whole. Notice that whenever words or ideas are borrowed, a citation in parentheses refers the reader to the proper source on the works-cited page, about which you will learn more on page C548.

TITLE

INTRODUCTION

BACKGROUND
INFORMATION

THESIS
STATEMENT

MAIN TOPIC I

MAIN TOPIC II

Climbing a Family Tree

Since the United States celebrated its 200th birthday in 1976, the study of family history, called genealogy, has gained many devoted followers. According to John H. Tennent of the National Genealogical Society in Washington, D.C., "tracing your ancestry is like eating peanuts—once you get started, it's hard to stop." ("Trace Your Family Tree" 240). Before becoming a family detective, become familiar with the basic sources of genealogy and the traps that could leave you dangling from a branch in someone else's tree.

The first basic source of information for your family tree is your family. Useful questions to ask family members include these: "Who were my ancestors? Where and when were they born? Where and when did they die? What was their relationship to one another?" (Croom 12). The Smithsonian Institution in Washington, D.C., also recommends a good question for family reunions: "Are there any stories about how a great fortune was lost or almost, but not quite, made? Do you believe them?" (Shenker 27). Family photographs are another excellent source. To learn as much as you can, ask yourself, "What conclusions about the past can explain why the picture looks the way it does?" (Croom 37). Tracing a family history, of course, is more than filling in a chart. You must learn as much as you can about how life really was for people in the past.

After you have explored family sources, consult the genealogical library of the Church of Jesus Christ of Latter-Day Saints in Salt Lake City, Utah. This collection is considered the greatest in the world. It has the equivalent of "more than 1.5 billion book pages" on over a million rolls of microfilm (Westin 60). If you cannot go to Salt Lake City, you can use one of the more than 200 branch libraries around the country. The library of Latter-Day Saints is open to all people and includes records on more than 60 million people from 126 different countries (Westin 60). Other libraries with excellent family-history collections are the Newberry Library in Chicago, the Fort Wayne (Indiana) Public Library, the Free Library of Philadelphia, and the New Orleans Public Library (Westin 71–77).

MAIN TOPIC III

If these family records do not include your ancestors, you should search through local and federal records to track down your forebears. Birth, marriage, and death certificates are the biggest group of records people use for genealogy, but other documents—wills and deeds—often answer crucial questions (Nottle 2). Census records, which have been kept in the U.S. since 1790, are a useful resource ("Genealogy"). Other useful records are wills, church records, census reports, military records, ships' passenger lists, and immigration files. Your local library or media center will have the addresses of public offices you can write to for information. "In writing for records," Gilbert H. Doane and James B. Bell suggest, "you should always offer to pay any fee that the clerk may charge. It is also a good policy to enclose a stamped, self-addressed envelope for a reply." (Doane and Bell 82) If you state your questions clearly, you will be more likely to receive the information you need to add a missing piece to the family puzzle. Online services and the Internet provide access to genealogical information that might take months to locate using traditional methods. An impressive array of computer bulletin boards, networks, and newsgroups now help genealogists find missing ancestors more rapidly than ever (Crowe 49).

To beginning family detectives, the great number and variety of sources can seem overwhelming. David Thackery, Librarian of Local and Family History at the Newberry Library, points out three common mistakes that people often make. The first is "not having a good system of organizing" research. With so many sources, keeping well-organized and accurate notes is critical to putting the pieces together later. The second problem is "a lack of focus." It is best not to attempt everything at once. Thackery suggests that researchers should "focus on one particular branch for a month or two" before moving on to the next. The third problem is "the lack of a critical approach" to the documents. Many documents have errors, omissions, or exaggerations. For example, one writer has observed that female ancestors may be harder to locate in most civic archives because they were often barred from owning land and writing their own wills (Przecha 1). These obstacles require careful researching to overcome. A careful researcher will learn to question the accuracy of every source until it can be verified by another (Thackery, telephone interview).

Despite the pitfalls, Thackery is enthusiastic about family research. In his mid-teens he began to trace his roots. He has found all of his great-great-great-grandparents on his father's side and 12 of his great-great-great-great-great-grandparents on his mother's side, as far back as the early 1700s. "We're all part of hundreds of families," says Thackery, and tracing one's roots is a "means of self-discovery." With the help of family memories, library collections, and the expert guidance of librarians, anyone with the patience and motivation can discover the pleasures of climbing the family tree.

Works Cited

Croom, Emily Anne. <u>Unpuzzling Your Past: A Basic Guide to Genealogy</u>. Cincinnati: Betterway Books, 1995.

Crowe, Elizabeth Powell. <u>Genealogy Online</u>. New York: McGraw-Hill, 1996.

Doane, Gilbert H., and James B. Bell. <u>Searching for Your Ancestors</u>. Minneapolis: University of Minnesota Press, 1980.

"Genealogy." <u>Compton's Encyclopedia Online</u>. 1997. Nov. 2, 1999. <http://www.comptons.com/ceo99–cgi/article?fastweb?getdoc+viewcomptons+A+3230+0++genealogy'>.

Nottle, Diane. "Wanted, Dead or Alive: Family Members Found Through Genealogy." <u>New York Times</u> 20 July 1997, late ed.:sec. 13: 6+.

Przecha, Donna. "Finding Female Ancestors." Apr. 4, 1999, <http:www.genealogy.com/50_donna.html>.

Shenker, Israel. "Smithsonian Urges Public to Dig at the Family Tree." <u>New York Times</u> 17 June 1976, sec. 1: 27+

Thackery, David. Telephone interview. 23 Nov. 1993.

"Trace Your Family Tree." <u>Good Housekeeping</u>. Oct. 1976: 240.

Westin, Jeanne Eddy. <u>Finding Your Roots</u>. Los Angeles: J. P. Tarcher, Inc., 1977.

Notice that only sources consulted and actually cited in the research report can be included on the works-cited page.

DRAFTING *Introduction, Body, Conclusion*

Using your outline and refined thesis statement, draft
the introduction to your research report. As in the model,
your thesis statement should fit in smoothly with the rest
of the introduction. Then follow your outline to draft the
body of your research report. For this first draft, do not
worry about using the correct form for your citations. Every
time you include a direct quotation or a specific piece of
information from a source you wish to credit, clearly
identify the source in parentheses with the page number so
that you know which source you mean. Later you will go
back over these citations and write them in proper form.
At that time, you can also put together your works-cited
page. When you have finished, save your work for
later use.

Using and Citing Sources

The model research report on pages C538–C541 shows the
different kinds of references that need to be credited to the
original authors. Failure to give proper credit for direct quotations
and borrowed facts and statistics is called **plagiarism**, a serious
and unlawful offense. In some cases you may want to **paraphrase**
an author's idea, or rewrite an author's idea in your own words.
Even if you paraphrase, however, you must credit the author for
the idea.

Using Sources   When you borrow material from sources, work it
smoothly into your research report. The following suggestions will
help you improve the flow of your presentation.

> ### Quoting and Paraphrasing Information
>
> • Use a quotation to finish a sentence you have started.
>
> EXAMPLE   Tracing your family history is a "means of
> self-discovery."

- Quote a whole sentence.

    EXAMPLE   "We're all part of hundreds of families," says Thackery.

- Quote just a few words.

    EXAMPLE   Many researchers lack a "critical approach" to their sources.

- Paraphrase information from a source.

    EXAMPLE   According to Thackery, all of us are part of many families.

PRACTICE YOUR SKILLS

● *Using Sources*

Read the following excerpt about the geyser Old Faithful. Then use it as a source to complete the assignment that follows it.

Every day of the year, at intervals that average a little over an hour, a plume of steam and boiling water bursts out of the ground. For two to five minutes, it thrusts straight upward, a total of 8,000 gallons forming a tower 180 feet high. Then it subsides, waiting for pressure to rebuild and a fresh crowd of tourists to gather. It has recurred without fail for the more than 110 recorded years and, geologists say, for thousands of years before that.

Although it is a metaphor for punctuality and power, Old Faithful is neither the most regular nor the most spectacular of the geysers in Yellowstone National Park. Steamboat Geyser, the most powerful in the world, can explode to a height of 300 feet. Some small geysers—squirting only a foot or two in the air—erupt every minute or so, like clockwork; Old Faithful's rest periods vary from three minutes to two hours.

Reprinted by permission from SCIENCE DIGEST. Copyright © 1983, The Hearst Corporation.

1. Write a sentence that ends with a quotation.
2. Write three sentences about geysers of different sizes. One of the sentences should be a direct quotation.
3. Write a sentence about Steamboat Geyser that quotes just a few words from the source.
4. Write a sentence paraphrasing part of the passage.

Citing Sources

Notes that tell the original source of words or ideas you have used in your research report are called **citations.** Although several formats for citing sources are available, this textbook uses the guidelines established by the Modern Language Association (MLA) for parenthetical citations—the preferred way to give credit to your sources. **Parenthetical citations** identify the source briefly in parentheses immediately after the borrowed material. **Footnotes** are another type of citation. Instead of identifying sources within the report in parentheses, footnotes use a number next to the borrowed material that refers to a source listed at the bottom, or foot, of the page. A similar type of citation is the **endnote.** Instead of identifying sources at the foot of the page, endnotes come at the end of the research report, after the conclusion but before the works-cited page.

Writing Tip

Cite the sources of information you include in your research paper by using **parenthetical citations, footnotes,** or **endnotes.** Your teacher will tell you which type of citation to use in your research papers.

Parenthetical Citations

When you use parenthetical citations, you give readers only enough information to identify the source of the borrowed material. Readers then refer to your works-cited page for complete information on each source. The examples on the following page show the correct form for using parenthetical citations.

BOOKS BY ONE AUTHOR	Give author's last name and page number(s): (Croom 12).
BOOKS WITH MORE THAN ONE AUTHOR	Give both authors' names and page number(s): (Doane and Bell 82).
ARTICLE WITH AUTHOR NAMED	Give author's last name and page number(s): (Shenker 27–30).
ARTICLE WITH AUTHOR UNNAMED	Give a shortened form of the title of the article (unless title is short to begin with) and page number(s): ("Trace Your Family Tree" 240).
ARTICLE FROM GENERAL REFERENCE WORK/ AUTHOR UNNAMED	Give title (or shortened form of title); no page number(s) needed if article is single page or from an encyclopedia arranged alphabetically: ("Genealogy").
ARTICLE FROM A CD-ROM	Give author's last name, if available, and page number. If no author is named, give a short article title and page numbers.
ARTICLE FROM AN ONLINE DATABASE WITH OR WITHOUT A PRINT VERSION	Give author's last name and page number: (Wallace 1–2). If no author is given, give title of material and page numbers. No page number is needed if the reference is a single page from an encyclopedia: ("Genealogy").

A parenthetical citation placed at the end of a sentence goes after a closing quotation mark and before the period. Titles of works should be enclosed in quotation marks within the parentheses.

See the model research paper on page C538 for examples.

Footnotes and Endnotes   If your teacher tells you to use footnotes or endnotes, you need to follow a different form for citing sources than you would use in parenthetical citations. With either footnotes or endnotes, place a small number, called a superscript, halfway above the line and immediately after the borrowed material.

| EXAMPLE | The collection in Salt Lake City has the equivalent of "more than 1.5 billion book pages"[1] on over a million rolls of microfilm. |

The small raised number refers readers to the proper footnote or endnote. The following examples show the correct form for footnotes and endnotes. If the author is given, list the first name first.

REFERENCE WORKS	[1] "Genealogy," <u>World Book Encyclopedia</u>; 1998 ed.
BOOKS BY ONE AUTHOR	[2] Elizabeth Powell Crowe, <u>Genealogy Online</u> (New York: McGraw-Hill, 1996) 49.
BOOKS BY TWO OR MORE AUTHORS	[3] Gilbert H. Doane and James B. Bell, <u>Searching for Your Ancestors</u> (Minneapolis: University of Minnesota Press, 1980) 82.
ARTICLES IN MAGAZINE (NO AUTHOR)	[4] "Trace Your Family Tree," <u>Good Housekeeping</u> Oct. 1976: 240.
ARTICLES IN NEWSPAPER	[5] Israel Shenker, "Smithsonian Urges Public to Dig at the Family Tree," <u>New York Times</u> 17 June 1976: late ed., sec. 1: 27+. (Note: plus sign shows that article continues on another page.)
INTERVIEWS	[6] David Thackery, telephone interview, 23 Nov. 1993.
ARTICLE FROM AN ONLINE DATABASE WITHOUT A PRINT VERSION	[7] "Genealogy," <u>Compton's Encyclopedia Online</u>. 1997. Nov. 1999 <http://www.comptons.com/ceo99-cgi/article?/fastweb?getdoc+view comptons+A+3230+0++genealogy/>.

| ARTICLE FROM AN
ONLINE DATABASE
WITH A PRINT VERSION | [8] Erin Wallace, "Locating Your Female Ancestor," 13 May 1999. 2 Nov. 1999. <www.expressnews.com/genealogy/archives/wallace/0217g.shtml>. |

For repeated references to a work already cited, you can use a shortened form of footnote.

| REPEATED REFERENCES | 1 Crowe 58.
2 Doane and Bell 36. |

COMPUTER TIP

If you are working with word processing software, adding footnotes or endnotes to a research report is easy. To add a footnote, move the cursor and click to show where to place the note in the text. Click on Footnote in the Insert menu to enter a footnote. Then click the Options-button to show whether you want a footnote or an endnote. Most software automatically numbers and renumbers footnotes and endnotes when they are added or removed from the text.

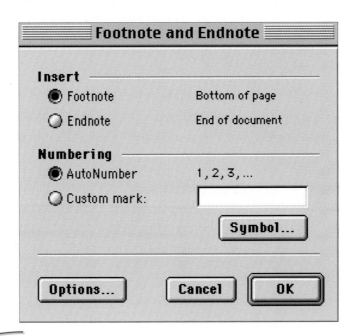

Preparing a Works-Cited Page   Sources cited in the research paper must also be listed on a separate works-cited page at the end of the report. The author's last name comes first and the indentation and punctuation are different. On a works-cited page, the entries are listed in alphabetical order by the author's last name. If no author is given for a work, the entry is alphabetized by first letter of the title.

MODEL: Form for the Works-Cited Page

BOOKS WITH
SINGLE AUTHOR

Croom, Emily Anne. <u>Unpuzzling Your Past: A Basic Guide to Genealogy</u>. Cincinnati: Betterway Books, 1995.

Crowe, Elizabeth Powell. <u>Genealogy Online</u>. New York: McGraw-Hill, 1996.

BOOKS WITH MORE
THAN ONE AUTHOR

Doane, Gilbert H., and James B. Bell. <u>Searching for Your Ancestors</u>. Minneapolis: University of Minnesota Press, 1980.

ARTICLE FROM AN
ONLINE DATABASE
WITHOUT A PRINT
VERSION

"Genealogy" <u>Compton's Encyclopedia Online</u>. 1997. 2 Nov. 1999. <http://www.comptons.com/ ceo99–cgi/article?/fastweb?getdoc+ viewcomptons+A+3230++genealogy/>.

NEWSPAPER ARTICLE

Nottle, Diane. "Wanted, Dead or Alive: Family Members Found Through Genealogy." <u>New York Times</u> 20 July 1997, late ed., sec. 13:6.+

Shenker, Israel. "Smithsonian Urges Public to Dig at the Family Tree." <u>New York Times</u> 17 June 1976, sec. 1: 27+.

INTERVIEWS

Thackery, David. Telephone interview. 23 Nov. 1993.

MAGAZINE ARTICLES

"Trace Your Family Tree." <u>Good Housekeeping</u> Oct. 1976: 240.

ARTICLE FROM AN ON-
LINE DATABASE WITH
A PRINT VERSION

Wallace, Erin. "Locating Your Female Ancestor" 13 May 1999. 2 Nov. 1999.<www.expressnews.com /genealogy/archives/wallace/0217g.shtml>.

BOOKS WITH
SINGLE AUTHOR

Westin, Jeanne Eddy. <u>Finding Your Roots</u>. Los Angeles: J.P. Tarcher, Inc., 1997.

REFERENCE WORKS

"Genealogy," <u>World Book Encyclopedia</u>. 1998 ed.

Your teacher may require a works-consulted page—often called a **bibliography**—in which you include all works you consulted whether or not you cited them in the actual report. A works-consulted list uses the same manuscript form as the works-cited page.

PRACTICE YOUR SKILLS

● *Preparing a Works Cited Page*

The following sources were used for a research report on sharks. Using the model on the previous page, write a works-cited page that includes all the sources.

1. Jacques Y. Cousteau, <u>The Shark: Splendid Savage of the Sea</u> (Garden City: Doubleday, 1970).

2. "Sharks Slay Half of Those Attacked," <u>New York Times</u>, 10 Aug. 1975, sec. 1, page 42.

3. Paul Budker, <u>The Life of Sharks</u> (New York: Columbia University Press, 1971).

4. "A Bum Rap for Sharks," <u>Changing Times</u>, Jan. 1982, page 6.

5. Sharon Begley, "Giving Sharks a Good Name," <u>Newsweek</u>, 2 Aug. 1982, pages 64–65.

● *Using Parenthetical Citations*

Write a parenthetical citation for each of the following references to the works-cited page you just developed.

EXAMPLE   A description by Jacques Cousteau

ANSWER   (Cousteau 72)

1. an example of a shark attack from the *New York Times* article

2. a little-known fact about sharks from the article in *Newsweek*

3. a choice quote from the article in *Changing Times*

4. information from *The Life of Sharks*

DRAFTING *Sources*

  Review what you have learned about using and citing sources correctly. Then read over the first draft of your research report, looking for ways to improve the flow of your paper and your use of cited material. Next, prepare your works-cited page. Save your work for later use.

Looping Back to Prewriting

Citing Sources

"When you steal from one author, it's plagiarism," remarked the humorist Wilson Mizner. "When you steal from many, it's research." Mizner's wisecrack need not apply to your research, of course, as long as you adequately cite all the sources you have used for your report. While citing sources in the drafting stage of your research report, you may have forgotten one or two. Take time now to go back and add any missing citations.

Revising Writing Process

Writing a research report can be a messy process, with piles of books in one corner, note cards fanned out in another, and the outline taped to the wall. When you begin, much of your time is spent organizing your sources. While pulling together the pieces of your research into a first draft, you may not have composed the smoothest-flowing piece of writing you can produce. In the revising stage, you should clear your desk and read over your report with a fresh eye and a keen sense of concentration. Your first concern is whether you have achieved the purpose of your research paper. Then ask yourself: Does the report inform the audience as fully and accurately as possible?

Prewriting Workshop
Drafting Workshop
Revising Workshop ▶
Editing Workshop
Publishing Workshop

Sentence Structure and Variety

When you write a research report about a complicated topic, as William J. Broad did in his article on the creatures of the deep, you will naturally tend to have longer, more complicated sentences. You can add variety to a report like this by using short, simple sentences to state main points or emphasize conclusions. Your goal is to avoid a monotonous style.

Kinds of Sentence Structure

Sentences are classified according to the numbers and kinds of clauses within each of them. The four basic kinds of sentences are simple, compound, complex, and compound-complex. A **simple sentence** consists of one independent clause. A **compound sentence** consists of two or more independent clauses. A **complex** sentence consists of one independent clause and one or more subordinate clauses, and a **compound-complex sentence** consists of two or more independent clauses and one or more subordinate clauses. When you revise, always include a variety of sentence structures so that your writing will flow at a lively and interesting pace.

SIMPLE SENTENCE	Hordes of creatures live in the hidden depths of the deep sea.
COMPOUND SENTENCE	Little is known about the creatures of the darkness, and much less is known about fluctuations in their diets and fortunes.
COMPLEX SENTENCE	Most animals of the deep rely on a food chain that begins in the sea's lighted realms.
COMPOUND-COMPLEX SENTENCE	Organic matter falls to the lower depths, and this sediment has been caught and measured in traps that are suspended off the ocean's bottom.

Punctuation with Compound Sentences

When you join two independent clauses in a compound sentence, you can use either a comma and a conjunction, or a semicolon.

COMMA AND CONJUNCTION	Some species will die out, but those with low food needs will survive.
SEMICOLON	The sea's inky depths harbor millions of undiscovered species; an unknown number of them may be in crisis.

Capitalization and Punctuation of Titles

In a research report, the following rules apply to the titles in your citations and in your list of works cited.

- **Capitalize** the first word, the last word, and all important words in the titles of books, newspapers, magazines, stories, poems, movies, plays, and other works of art.

- **Underline** (or, if you are using word processing software, italicize) the titles of long written or musical works that are published as a single unit, such as books, newspapers, magazines, full-length plays, and long poems.

- **Use quotation marks** to enclose the titles of chapters, articles, stories, one-act plays, short poems, and songs.

Checking for Adequate Development

One especially important feature to look for in your draft is adequate development. A good research report will have ample supporting material, enough to document the thesis statement thoroughly. If certain sections seem thin and weak, analyze them to determine what the problem is.

You may find that the addition of a detail here and there will do the trick. In other cases, you may need to return to the library or media center and do additional research to bolster these sagging parts of your report.

Checking for Accuracy

Another important feature of a research report is accuracy. Whenever you borrow material from another source, you need to take special care that you are accurately representing the views of the author of that source. In your zeal to support your thesis, make sure that you have not quoted an authority out of context or failed to include some important information that would cast your thesis in doubt.

Communicate Your Ideas

REVISING *Adequate Development, Coherence, and Accuracy*
Share the first draft of your research report with a classmate and ask for advice on where your report may need more supporting material. If necessary, complete any additional needed research and add this information to your report. Then take a careful, objective look at the sources you quoted. Have you quoted the material accurately? Furthermore, have you been accurate in representing the information you obtained while researching? If not, provide the citations and information that may be missing. Save your work for later use.

The checklist on the following page will help you identify the parts of your research report that need improvement. The first section of the checklist will help you improve the most important aspect of your report—the content. The second section will help you refine each paragraph within your report to make it as sharp and concise as it can be. The final section will help you weave words and sentence rhythms into your writing that are sure to hold your reader's attention.

Evaluation Checklist for Revising

Checking Your Research Paper

✓ Does your introduction contain a thesis statement that makes the main point of your research report clear? *(pages C534–C535)*

✓ Does the body of your research report support the thesis statement? *(page C537)*

✓ Does your research report have unity? *(page C226)*

✓ Does your research report have coherence? *(page C226)*

✓ Is your emphasis clear? *(page C226)*

✓ Does your conclusion have a strong ending? *(page C228)*

✓ Does your research report have parenthetical citations and a list of sources on a works-cited page? *(pages C544–C548)*

✓ Does your research report have a title that suggests the subject of the report?

Checking Your Paragraphs

✓ Does each paragraph have a topic sentence? *(pages C103–C104)*

✓ Is each paragraph unified and coherent? *(pages C136–C139)*

✓ Did you use transitions so that one paragraph leads smoothly into the next? *(page C132)*

Checking Your Sentences and Words

✓ Are your sentences varied? *(pages C73–C80)*

✓ Are your sentences concise? *(page C67–C70)*

✓ Did you avoid faulty sentences? *(pages C81–C88)*

✓ Did you use specific rather than general words? *(page C62)*

Communicate Your Ideas

REVISING *Introduction, Body, Conclusion*

Using the guidelines in the **Evaluation Checklist for Revising**, as well as any comments and suggestions from your classmates, evaluate and revise the first draft of your report. Save your work for later use.

Short Documentary

Documentaries are visual research reports. They "document" a slice of reality through images, interviews, sound, and narration that are artfully pieced together.

With a good idea and access to video tools, almost anyone can create a short documentary. The following steps will guide you through that process. They require you to work in groups of about six students each.

Watch as many documentaries as you can. Write a brief evaluation of each one using the criteria above. Include a sentence or two about its effect on you. Then use what you have learned to create your own documentary.

Steps in Making a Short Documentary

- Work with your group to choose a concept for your documentary. Perhaps it will relate to the subject of one of your team member's written research reports; perhaps it will be on a completely separate matter. You will probably have the best chance of success if you choose a local matter to document, since you will then have access to videotaping opportunities and interviews. When you have decided on a concept, write it up in a paragraph.

- When you are clear on your concept, define your audience. Who do you expect will see the documentary? Write a paragraph describing what you think your audience's knowledge of or attitudes toward your subject are.

- Next, begin your research. Whom do you need to interview? What are the basic facts of the situation? What background information may be necessary for your viewers? Keep good notes as each team member gathers the necessary information. Assign each group member a job, including writer, director, interviewer, camera operator, editor, and still photographer.

- The resources in **A Writer's Guide to Electronic Publishing** on pages C707–C717 provide details on the nuts and bolts of video production. Use those as you follow the process sketched out below to complete your documentary.

- Prepare a "treatment." Identify people to interview and list live-action and background footage to shoot. Explain the film's organization. Plan out how you will spend the 5-6 minutes you have for your documentary.

- Shoot your video footage, including live interviews, background footages, and live-action shots. Shoot more than you think you will need, because you will edit out much of what you shoot. Keep "log sheets" to record everything you have shot. Also take any still photographs that may be needed and record any additional sounds. Review your work so far. Do you have what you need to support your concept? If not, shoot more.

- Next, do a rough edit of your footage using your treatment as a guide. Once you see your shots in the order your treatment calls for, you can decide if your plan is working well or if it needs changing. Make a fine cut, a more polished editing. Be sure that your shots are ordered and connected the way you want and that they clarify or enhance the message of your documentary. Determine what else you still need to weave the shots together and make your points effectively. Music? Narration? Titles? Add in any of these elements to complete your film.

Showing and Evaluating

Show your documentary to your intended audience and invite feedback. After the showing, discuss the responses with your group. Also discuss what you learned in the process and what you would do differently next time to improve your documentary.

Editing
Writing Process

The final draft of your research report should be a document that readers can learn from and use as a reference. Check for any mechanical errors that can weaken your presentation.

Communicate Your Ideas

EDITING

Edit your work by using the **Editing Checklist** on page C46 and the **Evaluation Checklist for Revising** on page C554. Correct any mistakes in your report, and save your work.

Publishing
Writing Process

The final draft of your report should be a document that others can learn from. For example, if a number of your classmates have reported on the environment or related issues, you might want to hold an environmental awareness seminar in which students can present their reports and answer questions.

Communicate Your Ideas

PUBLISHING

Prepare a neat final copy of your report using the guidelines for correct manuscript form on page C50. You may want to share printed copies of your report with experts whom you interviewed as part of your research. You may also want to post your writing to a Website specifically for people interested in your topic. Save a copy of your report in your portfolio.

PORTFOLIO

For more information on publishing on the Internet, see A Writer's Guide to Electronic Publishing, *pages C717–C721.*

Process of Writing a Research Report

Remember that the writing process is recursive. This means that you are free to move back and forth among the stages as you see fit to accomplish your writing goals. For example, during the revising stage, you may need to return to prewriting to gather more details that will better support your thesis.

PREWRITING

- Use a variety of strategies including brainstorming, freewriting, and clustering to develop ideas that will lead to further research. *(page C521)*
- Make a list of possible subjects, and choose one as the topic for a research report. Then limit your subject. *(pages C521–C522)*
- Use note cards to gather information from references (in print and on-line), including books, magazines, and newspapers. *(pages C524–C527)*
- Develop a working thesis. *(page C530)*
- Organize your notes into categories. Decide on a logical order and create an outline for your report. *(pages C531–C533)*

DRAFTING

- If necessary, refine your working thesis. Write an introduction that includes your thesis statement, and then draft the body and conclusion for your research report. *(pages C534–C541)*
- Avoid plagiarism by using and citing sources accurately. *(page C542)*
- Use parenthetical citations in the body of your research report, and prepare a works-cited page. *(pages C544–C549)*
- Add an appropriate title.

REVISING

- Check your research report for adequate development and accuracy. *(pages C552–C553)*
- Using the **Evaluation Checklist for Revising** on page C554, check for well-developed paragraphs, unity, coherence, emphasis, and varied and lively sentences and words.

EDITING

- Using the guidelines from the **Editing Checklist** on page C46, check for errors in grammar, spelling, usage, and mechanics.
- Use the proper manuscript form for citations and the works-cited page. *(pages C544 and C548)*

PUBLISHING

- Make a neat final copy in standard manuscript form. Share your finished work with an interested reader, either in print or online form. *(page C557)*

A Writer Writes

An I-Search Paper

Purpose: to inform and explain

Audience: your teacher and classmates

Imagine yourself searching diligently in your community for information on a subject that you absolutely must know more about. Think of yourself as a camcorder, recording every sight and sound leading you toward the information you need. This is the sort of high-energy motivation you will feel if you explore a subject that is really important to you.

You may want to learn more about the exploration of the ocean floor, a favorite writer of science fiction, or some event in the lives of your ancestors. Only you can decide the topic of your I-Search report. The most important thing to remember is that the topic you choose should matter to you.

Prewriting

Once you decide what to search for, talk to your friends, classmates, teachers, and librarians, and ask them if they have any suggestions for resources—books, organizations, names of experts, phone numbers, or Websites—that may help you find what you want to know. As background research to your personal interviews and detective work, read books and newspaper and magazine articles to find out more about your topic. Locate and talk to experts on your topic, being careful not to waste their time with unproductive questions. Try to know as much about the topic as possible before you talk with them. Have your questions ready when you meet. Take good notes, and keep careful track of your sources. As you look for resources in the library or media center, be sure to research both firsthand, or primary, sources like the interviews above, and secondhand, or secondary, sources (such as books and magazines that tell you about what others have done). Using the information you find,

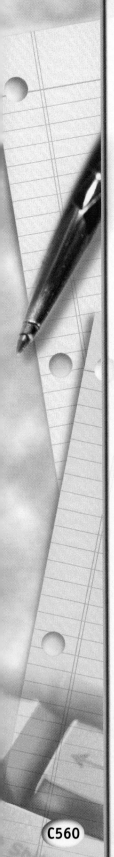

make an outline of your report. A good way to organize your paper is to tell what you did in the order that everything happened. You might divide your report into four parts: what you knew (and did not know) about your subject; why you chose the subject; how you went about the search; and what you learned (or did not learn) about the subject. You'll also need a thesis statement that covers the main points of your outline.

Drafting

Now it's time to draft an introduction, body, and conclusion to your report. Cite sources wherever necessary to give proper credit to any borrowed ideas or information. When you have completed your draft, add a title and prepare a works-cited page.

Revising

Use the guidelines from the <u>Evaluation Checklist for Revising</u> on page C554 to help you revise your paper.

Editing

Then using the <u>Editing Checklists</u> on page C46, check your work for errors in spelling, punctuation, grammar, usage, and mechanics.

Publishing

Share a copy of your report with your teacher and classmates. If your I-Search report is on a topic of general interest to your community, you might send a copy to the local newspaper, or share it with one of the experts that you interviewed. You may also want to post it to a Website specifically about your topic so that other people who are interested in the topic can learn more about it.

For more information about electronic publishing, see pages C717–C721.

Connection Collection

Representing in Different Ways

From Print . . .

. . . to Visuals

Mr. Malamorte did not quite specify where he has been. Use the clues in his descriptions to research what countries he has visited and draw postcards to represent each destination.

From Visuals . . .

Okefenokee

January 11, 2001

Dear Class,

    As you probably know by now, I decided to use up my sick days and take a trip around the world. I am having a wonderful time. Here are some highlights of my trip: watching sharks cruising along the Great Barrier Reef off the northeast coast of Australia; walking down the Champs Elysées and admiring the view of the Eiffel Tower in Paris; strolling along the canals and visiting the van Gogh Museum in Amsterdam; and climbing the ziggurats of Chichén Itzá.

    Have a great year, class! You may never see me again!

Sincerely,

Mr. Malamorte

Mr. Malamorte

. . . to Print

You have brought back a postcard from your vacation to Florida, and you wish to include it in a letter you will write to Mr. Malamorte. Research the place depicted on the postcard, and include the information to support the main idea of your letter—that you are an experienced and educated traveler too!

- Which strategies can be used for creating both written and visual representations? Which strategies apply to one, not both? Which type of representation is more effective?
- Draw a conclusion, and write briefly about the differences between written ideas and visual representations.

Writing in the Workplace

Works-Cited Page

You have been working for five years for Dotcomdotcom.com, an Internet design firm. This year the company announces it is going to offer stock options to all of its employees, and you have been chosen to write a brochure for the employees titled "Everything You Wanted to Know About Stock Options." There is only one catch—you don't know what stock options are!

Research corporate stock options, and write a works-cited page for the brochure. Use five real sources in the works-cited page and make sure they include sources from a Web page, a magazine article, and a reference book.

What strategies did you use to write a works-cited page?

You can find information on writing works-cited pages on page C548.

Writing for Oral Communication

Acceptance Speech

You are the bass guitar player in the wildly popular band Two Front Teeth. Your recent single, "That's Not My Dog," has been nominated for a prestigious award. All the critics are praising its refreshing mix of rap and country-western music. In case you win the award, the rest of your band has appointed you to prepare an acceptance speech to read at the ceremony.

Prepare a short speech that you will give if you win the award. Besides thanking the people who have helped you along the way, also summarize the history of the rap and country-western genres. Research important performers and highlights of these types of music, and make notes that will support the points of your speech. Then practice the speech by giving it to your classmates.

What strategies did you use to research and compose your speech?

You can find information on giving speeches on pages C592–C601.

Assess Your Learning

You are an encyclopedia editor. One of your writers has submitted the following article. You suspect that the writer has made a few mistakes:

John Edgar Kennedy (1961–1973), the 35th President of the United States of America, was one of the country's most popular leaders. In 1973 he was assassinated and was succeeded by Gerald Ford. During his administration, Kennedy defused the Vietnam missile crisis and supported the Civilian Rights Movement. During the Korean War, his boat, the *Andrea Doria*, was sunk in the Bay of Pigs. While he waited for rescue, he wrote the book *Profiles in Courage* on a coconut, for which he won a Pulitzer Prize.

▶ **Research the life of President Kennedy and use the information you discover to revise the encyclopedia entry above so that it is clear and the information is correct.**

▶ **Consult reference sources such as online databases, books, and documentaries in your library. Make sure that the facts in the entry are clear and concise. Take care to avoid plagiarizing in the rewording of the material from your research.**

▶ *Before You Write* **Consider the following questions:**
What is the *subject?*
What is the *occasion?*
Who is the *audience?*
What is the *purpose?*

▶ *After You Write* **Evaluate your work using the following criteria:**
- Have you used writing to discover information and support what needs to be learned about President Kennedy?
- Have you researched the material in the entry from reliable sources?
- Have you evaluated the entry for both mechanics and content?
- Have you researched the facts in the entry so that they are correct and concise?

Write briefly on how well you did. Point out your strengths and areas for improvement.

CHAPTER 13

Letters and Applications

Perhaps some time in the future, people in business will communicate exclusively through the Internet. Until that time, however, the business letter will remain an effective way to communicate. For the price of stationery and a stamp, you can request information, order merchandise, register a complaint, apply for a job, or apply to college.

Writing letters for these and other purposes will become increasingly important to you as you move closer to graduation from high school and make plans for your future. This chapter will show you how to write business letters that follow the correct form and are clear, to the point, and convincing. You will also wee how to compose effective résumés and fill out application forms.

Reading with a Writer's Eye

The following letter was written in May 1986 by a farmer facing bankruptcy. Although the writer uses the approach of a business communication, her narrative style creates a strong impact on the reader. Read the letter once to grasp the plight of the situation. Then reread the letter and notice how she both informs and persuades.

Mr. William L. Yaeger
Durham, N. C.
Re: Case No. B-86-00887C-7

Dear Mr. Yaeger,

   I suppose that bankruptcy is intended to be a "cut and dried"
business decision, and in the final analysis perhaps that is the
end result. However, with first-hand knowledge, I do know there is
far greater involvement, especially the emotional traumas of
seeing the upheaval and disposal of a lifetime of very hard work.

   My husband and I are from farm families of many generations.
Except for brief periods of our lives, we have always farmed and
know little of any other ways of life. Ernie, at 69 years of age,
was off the farm during the years of 1939–1945 while he was in
service during World War II with 30 months overseas. When he
returned in 1945, we were promptly married, having known each
other for many years. In early 1946 we bargained for a very run-
down piece of land on which we spent $800 to build a two-room
cottage without the amenities of plumbing or electricity on a rural
unpaved road. Conditions eventually improved—the road was
paved and we did get electricity and running water, but no bath
facility for 16 years.

   Our two daughters were born while we lived in that little
house—one was nine years old and the other three when we moved
into our modest FHA-financed home. The intervening years were
good because we loved the work of clearing those rolling hills and
turning red clay into beautiful green pastures and fields—grabbing
up roots and stumps and hauling off endless rocks. It should have
mattered that we never had any money at the end of the year, but
we always felt the promise and the hope of a better year next year.
I worked off the farm at a local bank, an insurance company, a
truck line (some of the time at two jobs) along with canning and
freezing fruits and vegetables to make ends meet. I sewed for the
children and if I needed new curtains or a bedspread, I made them.
So much of what we made from the farm went back into the farm,

but we didn't require a lot for family living and we simply plowed everything back to the farm.

Out of it all, we raised two very special girls—not extremely beautiful or extremely intellectual, but attractive and smart—pretty stable and altogether satisfactory. Through work-study programs, loans, and scholarships, they both acquired a fairly good basic education. One teaches, the other is a health educator with our local health department. Both have apparently solid and satisfactory marriages. The older one has two little girls, the younger has a new little daughter.

I am not sure why I am writing you this except that perhaps I need to reaffirm to myself that our dilemma is not the result of high and riotous living—that we are and have always been a plain, hard-working farm family. We've had a few health problems, none of which were very expensive, three or four really bad drought years that really set us back, perhaps some bad business decisions and maybe some management weakness. Actually we were not in bad shape until the years with the terrible interest rates and the grain embargo—it seems in retrospect that was the real beginning of a long, painful decline to this sorry state of affairs.

I think I want to tell you that, faced with the certainty of Federal land bank and Farmers Home foreclosure, we came to the conclusion that Chapter 7, with its inherent finality, seemed the preferred route out the morass of worry and debt. We are trying to maintain our self-respect and a degree of dignity (all honor and pride have gone by the way), trying to get through this most difficult of times with our sanity intact and see what we can do to maintain a livelihood so that we need not resort to public assistance or dependence on our children. At Ernie's age, it will be difficult to find work; his knees are worn out, too; but his Social Security of $296 monthly will help. I was able to get work at a nearby hospital at $4.10 hourly as a ward clerk—completely out of my past experience of book-keeping and accounting but it will pay routine bills, if we are very, very frugal.

Mr. Yaeger, we are very ignorant about bankruptcy, never having had anyone in either of our families or any of our associates involved in bankruptcy. We believe that when this is over, we will be relieved of all our holdings and of all our debts in their entirety and we will be left with our household goods and clothing. I would like to know if it would be possible for me to get a new pair of glasses (mine have not been changed in four or five years and the bifocal is no longer right for my vision). This would probably cost one half of a cow or about $130. I also have two teeth badly in need of repair—one needs a cap in order to save it and the other is in pretty bad shape also—will probably cost two cows or about $500. Also electric bills are continuing for the poultry house and will need to be paid soon. How will the auctioneer be paid? How will you be paid? Is there any way we can come out of this with even a few hundred dollars? We have nothing. We have acquired and accumulated nothing—with the 40 productive years of our life down the drain. How long can we remain in our house?

Our oldest daughter and her husband own a mobile home into which we will move. This has to be relocated since it now is located on a part of the bankruptcy property. Would it be possible or reasonable to request that we be allowed to live in our house perhaps as long as 60 days from probable discharge or until late September or October?

If you do not have the time to dictate a letter answering these questions, perhaps you can call me. Thank you for your time in reading this rather long letter. Perhaps it will establish that we are real flesh and blood people with very real problems and not merely a case number. I pray that the agonizing we have done in order to accept the inevitability of this decision has been the worst part of it, and we will greatly appreciate anything you can do to ease the finalizing technicalities and to enable us to pick up the fragments of our lives.

Sincerely,

Margie M. Brauer

Margie M. Brauer

Thinking as a Writer

Evaluating the Effectiveness of a Letter

- What does the writer accomplish with this letter? Are the language and style appropriate for its purpose?
- Is the letter clear? Does the writer use too many words? not enough words?
- How would you describe the tone of the letter? What specifically indicates that tone to you?

Comparing Written and Oral Language

Oral Expression
- Read part of the letter aloud. What do you learn about the writer?
- How similar is the writer's language to ordinary speech?
- Are there ideas that would be expressed differently in a telephone call?

Comparing Different Ways to Convey Emotion

Viewing The photograph below was taken during the Great Depression. Based on what you see as well as what you just read, think about what the woman in this photograph has in common with Margie Brauer, the farmer facing bankruptcy.

- What feelings does the photograph bring about in you? How are these feelings similar to those you experienced while reading Margie Brauer's letter?

- What does a photograph like this one tell you that you can't learn from words alone?

Dorthea Lange. *A Family Between Dallas and Austin, Texas,* August 1936. Library of Congress, Prints & Photographs Division, FSA-OWI Collection.

Developing Your Everyday Writing Skills

Whether you want a question or complaint answered, or a product sent to you, or an employer to hire you, the art of letter writing will be a useful one to acquire.

Writing Business Letters

Business letters often call for some action on the part of the recipient. To ensure that your purpose or request is clear, make your letters neat and easy to read.

MODEL: Business Letter

HEADING	2220 Peachtree Drive Atlanta, GA 30314
DATE	November 13, 2000
INSIDE ADDRESS	Customer Service P & W Video Productions 1252 N. Harvard Los Angeles, CA 90029
SALUTATION	Dear Sir or Madam:
BODY	
CLOSING	Yours truly,
SIGNATURE	*Leroy Washington* Leroy Washington

When writing a business letter, use white paper, preferably 8½ by 11 inches in size. Leave margins at least one inch wide. Whenever possible, use a word processor or typewriter. The parts of a letter are the heading, inside address, salutation, body, closing, and signature. The following guidelines will help you with each part.

PARTS OF A BUSINESS LETTER	
HEADING	Write your full address, including your ZIP code. Use the correct two-letter postal abbreviation for your state. Write the date beneath your address.
INSIDE ADDRESS	Write the receiver's address two lines below the heading. Include the person's name if you know it, using *Mr., Mrs., Ms., Dr.,* or some other appropriate title. If the person has a business title, such as *Sales Manager,* write it on the next line. Use the correct two-letter abbreviation for the state.
SALUTATION	Start the salutation two lines below the inside address. Use *Sir* or *Madam* if you do not know the person's name. Otherwise, use the person's last name preceded by *Mr., Ms., Mrs., Dr.,* or other title. Use a colon after the salutation.
BODY	Start two lines below the salutation. Double-space and indent if the letter is only a single paragraph. For longer letters, single-space each paragraph, skipping a line between paragraphs and indenting each new one.
CLOSING	Start two lines below the body. Align the closing with the left-hand edge of the heading. Use a formal closing such as *Sincerely,* or *Yours truly.* Capitalize only the first word. The closing is followed by a comma.
SIGNATURE	Type (or print, if your letter is handwritten) your full name four or five lines below the closing. Sign your name in the space between the closing and your typed name.

Keep a record of every business letter you write. If you use a computer, save your file and/or a printed copy. If your letter is handwritten, use a photocopier. If you use a word processor or typewriter, you should also print out or type the envelope. Finally, fold your letter neatly in thirds to fit into the envelope.

Envelope

Use the form shown below for your business letter envelopes.

MODEL: Business Envelope

YOUR NAME
AND ADDRESS

Leroy Washington
2220 Peachtree Drive
Atlanta, GA 30314

Customer Service
P & W Video Productions
1252 N. Harvard
Los Angeles, CA 90029

RECIPIENT'S
ADDRESS

COMPUTER TIP

Many word-processing programs will automatically set up and print envelopes directly from your business letters. Check your software manual for specific instructions.

Prewriting Workshop
Drafting Workshop
Revising Workshop
Editing Workshop ▶
Publishing Workshop

Capitalization

Follow these rules for capitalizing words in the different parts of your business letters. As you write the business letters in this chapter, proofread each one for capital letters.

Heading and Inside Address

Capitalize all names of people, companies, streets, cities, states, and months. Also capitalize titles such as *Mr.* and *Ms.*

> 2119 Spring Street
> Skokie, IL 60025
> April 24, 2000
>
> Mr. Neil Saperstein
> Movie Memories, Inc.
> 521 Maple Grove Road
> Lawrence, KS 66044

Salutation

Capitalize the first word, titles, and names.

> Dear Dr. Garcia:
>
> Dear Director of Human Resources:

Closing

Capitalize only the first word. In the signature, capitalize your name.

> Sincerely yours,
>
> *Tim Wong*
>
> Tim Wong

Letters of Request

A common type of business letter is the **letter of request**, in which you ask for information or for a specific item such as a pamphlet, brochure, or application. In such letters, make your purpose for writing apparent as soon as possible and state your request clearly. Be sure to include all six parts of the business letter.

MODEL: Letter of Request

2719 Lincoln Avenue
Chicago, IL 60657
May 11, 2000

Director
Tourist Information
State of Wisconsin
Box 7921
Madison, WI 53707

Dear Sir or Madam:

Our club, the Chicago Backpackers, is planning a hiking trip for the first week in July. We are interested in the Tuscobia Trail and would like to have more information about it. Would you please send me a pamphlet describing the trail and the stopping points along the way?

I would also be interested in learning the rules and regulations about backpacking on Wisconsin state lands. Please send this information so we can plan accordingly.

Thank you for your assistance.

Sincerely yours,

Salvatore Cabasino

Salvatore Cabasino

Order Letters

When ordering merchandise from a catalog or an advertisement, be sure to include the order number, price, quantity, and size for each item. If you are enclosing a check or money order, identify that enclosure in your letter. Remember to add any shipping and handling charges to the total cost of the merchandise.

MODEL: Order Letter

1015 Brookside
San Anselmo, CA 94960
January 7, 2000

Pacific Publishing Company
Box 9998
Centralia, WA 98531

Dear Sir or Madam:

Please send me the following books from your 2000 winter catalog:

1	*Basic CGI Scripting*, #777-B	$19.95
1	*Handbook for Web Animators*, #787-C	$10.95

Shipping and handling $4.00
                                              $34.90

A money order for $34.90 is enclosed.

Sincerely,

Maureen O'Connor

Maureen O'Connor

Letters of Complaint

Reputable companies stand behind their merchandise and services and are prepared to make amends if a mistake has been made. Express yourself courteously if you are registering a complaint and recommend a reasonable solution. Notice how clearly the following letter describes the problem and offers a remedy.

MODEL: Letter of Complaint

603 Paine Hill Road
Sleepy Eye, MN 56085
February 11, 2001

Customer Service
Northern Electronics
3278 Elson Avenue
St. Paul, MN 55109

Dear Sir or Madam:

On January 5 of this year, I ordered a set of speakers from your catalog (#AA-573). A check for $122.75 to cover $115.00 for the merchandise and $7.75 for shipping and handling was enclosed with the order. I received the speakers on January 19, but a bill was enclosed in the package.

As you can see from the enclosed photocopy of my canceled check, I have paid in full for the merchandise I ordered. Please adjust your records to show my payment and request your billing department to remove my name from the billing list.

Thank you for your cooperation.

Sincerely,

Edward Swanson

Edward Swanson

Video Letter

Letters are one of the richest primary sources in the study of history. Presented in a visual medium, with sounds, still photos, narration, and music, they can be even more powerful. The script on the following page shows how one letter was presented in a television documentary on the Civil War.

As the scene opens, still pictures from the Civil War era (of young soldiers and couples) are shown slowly, one after the other. Drums and the voices of marching soldiers in the distance fade in and out. During the second paragraph of the letter, a solo violin comes up, playing the sad melody "Ashokan Farewell," and continues playing throughout the reading of the letter.

Media Activity

To make your own historical video letter, find a letter you wrote or received and collect or create still photographs or live-action footage that you might use to illustrate ideas or feelings conveyed in the letter. Decide whether you want a narrator to introduce the letter. Choose music that fits the mood and meaning. Prepare a script like the one on the next page that shows how the music, narrator, and actor reading the letter would overlap.

For help in creating your video, use the information on adding soundtracks on pages C716–C717. When you have completed your video letter, share it with your classmates or friends. Ask them how well your video conveyed the feelings expressed in the letter.

NARRATOR: A week before Manassas, Major
Sullivan Ballou of the 2nd Rhode
Island Volunteers wrote home to
his wife in Smithfield.

ACTOR'S
VOICEOVER: (reading the following letter)

July 14, 1861
Washington, D.C.

Dear Sarah,

The indications are very strong that we shall move in a few days, if not tomorrow. Lest I should not be able to write again, I feel impelled to write a few lines that may fall under your eye when I shall be no more. . . .

I have no misgivings about or lack of confidence in the cause in which I am engaged, and my courage does not halt or falter. I know how strongly American Civilization now leans on the triumph of the Government, and how great a debt we owe to those who went before us through the blood and sufferings of the Revolution. And I am willing—perfectly willing—to lay down all my joys in this life, to help maintain this Government, and to pay this debt. . . .

Sarah, my love for you is deathless, it seems to bind me with mighty cables that nothing but Omnipotence could break; and yet my love of Country comes over me like a strong wind and bears me unresistable on with all these chains to the battle field. . . .

If I do not return my dear Sarah, never forget how much I love you, and when my last breath escapes me on the battle field, it will whisper your name. . . . O Sarah! if the dead can come back to this earth and flit unseen around those they loved, I shall always be near you; in the gladdest days and in the darkest nights . . . always, always, and if there be a soft breeze upon your cheek, it shall be my breath, and the cool air on your throbbing temple shall be my spirit passing by. Sarah, do not mourn me dead; think I am gone and wait for me, for we shall meet again. . . .

NARRATOR: Sullivan Ballou was killed a week
later at the first battle of Bull Run.

Application Letters

Often an application letter is your first contact with someone when you apply for a job or for admission to a school. Try to make as good an impression as possible by being neat, correct, and specific about your qualifications. Use the following model as a guide when you are writing to apply for a job.

MODEL: Letter of Application for Employment

145 Gila Terrace
Nogales, AZ 85621
May 15, 2000

Ms. Helen Carter
Desktop Productions
2112 Ronstadt Road
Tucson, AZ 85707

Dear Ms. Carter:

I am writing to apply for the full-time summer intern position advertised in the *Arizona Daily Star.* The enclosed résumé will give you an overview of my background and previous experience. Since my goals include studying to become a commercial artist, I am very interested in finding a job at a graphic studio.

I will be available to start work on June 7, when school will be out for the summer. Until then, I will be available for an interview after four o'clock on weekdays and anytime on Saturday. I look forward to hearing from you.

Sincerely,

Maya Chavez

Maya Chavez

If you are applying for admission to a college, a university, or a special program, your application letter should resemble a letter of request. Be specific about the information you are seeking. For instance, you may want to request a list of courses or information about financial aid. Since schools require you to fill out applications, be sure to request an application form in your letter.

MODEL: Letter of Application to a School

312 Lake Avenue
Lake Forest, IL 60045
May 23, 2000

Director
Cherub Program
Drama Department
Northwestern University
Evanston, IL 60201

Dear Sir or Madam:

I am interested in applying for admission to your summer program for high school students. I have acted in two drama productions at Lake Forest High School and intend to major in theater in college.

Please send me information about the program, including schedules, available classes, costs, and financial aid. I would also like an application form.

Thank you very much.

Sincerely,

Janet Chen

Janet Chen

● Writing a Résumé

A **résumé** is a written summary of your work experience, education, and interests. The purpose of a résumé is to give a potential employer a brief but positive overview of your qualifications for a job. The following guidelines and model will help you write your own résumé. You should update your résumé on a regular basis to include information about recent educational or work experiences.

HOW TO WRITE A RÉSUMÉ

FORM	• Use one sheet of white 8½- by 11-inch paper.
	• Use even margins and leave space between sections.
WORK EXPERIENCE	• List your most recent job first.
	• Include part-time, summer, and volunteer jobs.
	• For each job list the dates you worked, your employer's name, your title, and your primary responsibilities.
EDUCATION	• List the name and address of each school and the years you attended.
	• List any special courses you have taken that would help make you a valuable employee.
SKILLS, ACTIVITIES, AWARDS, AND INTERESTS	• List skills, such as word processing, computer literacy, or fluency in a foreign language, which relate to the position.
	• List school or community activities in which you have participated, such as tutoring or volunteer work.
	• List awards or certificates you have earned.
	• Include any relevant hobbies or special interests.
REFERENCES	• Give the names and addresses of people who have agreed to give you a recommendation.
	• List one previous employer, one teacher or school administrator, and one adult friend.

Use boldface, capital letters, or different fonts to make your résumé clear and easy to read.

MODEL: Résumé

JENNIFER CONN
314 South Madison Avenue
Cyrius, ME 04735
(207) 555-8642
E-mail: jenniferconn@isp.com

WORK EXPERIENCE

1999 to present	Craftmasters, 240 Moore Road Cyrius, ME 04735 Position: Freelance carver of miniature wooden animals Responsibilities: Supplied store with carvings on commission
1997–1999	Aroostook Forum, 3 Main Street Wiggins, ME 04730 Position: Delivery person Responsibilities: Delivered daily newspapers to 35 homes

EDUCATION

1998 to present	Hamlin High School, 170 High Street, Cyrius, ME 04735 Special Courses: graphic design, advanced photography
1996 to 1998	Blaine Middle School, Shays Lane, Cyrius, ME 04735

SPECIAL SKILLS	Speak French; proficient with most word-processing, spreadsheet, illustration and photographic editing applications on PC
ACTIVITIES	Tenth-grade class treasurer
AWARDS	Honorable Mention: Maine Young Photographers Awards, 1999
SPECIAL INTERESTS	Art, photography, graphic design

Completing a Job Application

When you apply for a job, you may be asked to fill out a job application form. Application forms vary, but most of them ask for similar kinds of information. You may wish to prepare your information ahead of time so that you will be ready to complete the form when you apply for a job. The following is a list of information you will most likely need to complete an application.

> ### Information Often Requested on Job Applications
>
> - The current date
> - Your complete name, address, and telephone number
> - Your date and place of birth
> - Your Social Security number
> - Names and addresses of schools you have attended, dates of attendance, and your year of graduation
> - Any special courses or advanced degrees
> - Names and addresses of employers for whom you have worked and the dates you were employed
> - Any part-time, summer, and volunteer jobs
> - Names and addresses of references (Obtain permission beforehand from each person you intend to list as a reference.)

Use the following general guidelines when completing a job application.

> ### Guidelines for Completing a Job Application
>
> - Print all information neatly, accurately, and completely.
> - Do not leave blanks. If a section does not apply to you, write *N/A* (not applicable).
> - List schools attended and work experience in order, giving the most recent first.
> - If you mail the application form, include a brief cover letter stating the job you are applying for.

The following sample shows a completed job application. Note that the applicant did not leave any blank spaces and supplied all the information required. Also notice that the applicant wrote neatly and legibly.

APPLICATION FOR EMPLOYMENT

Barton's Department Store

PERSONAL INFORMATION (Please print)

Name	Last	First	Middle	Social Security/Social Insurance Number	Date (M/D/Y)
	Samuels	Paula	Jane	181-78-0945	11/15/85

Other names you are known by _____ Are you less than 18 years of age? Yes ✔ No ____ (Barton's is required to comply with federal, state, or provincial law.)

U.S. Applicant Only:
Are you legally eligible for employment in the U.S.? Yes ✔ No ____
(proof of U.S. citizenship or immigration status will be required if hired for a position in the U.S.)

Have you been convicted of a felony in the last seven (7) years? Yes ____ No ✔
If Yes, list convictions that are a matter of public record (arrests are not convictions). A conviction will not necessarily disqualify you for employment.

Present Address	Street	City	State/Province	Zip Code/Postal Code
	414 Broad St.	Garfield	Pennsylvania	19015

Permanent Address	Street	City	State/Province	Zip Code/Postal Code

Phone Number	Daytime	Evening (215)555-3198	Referred By

EMPLOYMENT DESIRED (If you are applying for a retail hourly position, please keep in mind that the availability of hours may vary.)

Position *sales associate* Location/Department *women's apparel* Salary Desired *$7.50/hr* Date You Can Start *immediately*

	Sunday	Monday	Tuesday	Wednesday	Thursday	Friday	Saturday
Specify hours available for each day of the week	Any	4p.m.–8p.m.	4p.m.–8p.m.	4p.m.–8p.m.	4p.m.–8p.m.	4p.m.–8p.m.	Any

Are you able to work overtime? _____
Have you ever worked for Barton's Department Store? *no* If yes, when? _____ Which store/department? _____

EDUCATION

	Name and Address of School	Circle Last Years Completed	Did You Graduate?	Subjects Studied and Degrees Received
High School	Wilson High School	1 2 3 4	Y (N)	in first year
College		1 2 3 4	Y N	N/A
Post College		1 2 3 4	Y N	N/A
Trade, Business, or Correspondence School		1 2 3 4	Y N	N/A

List skills relevant to the position applied for _____

SKILLS *For Office/Administrative positions only* Typing WPM: _____ 10-Key: ☐ Yes ☐ No

Computer Proficiency: ☐ Word for Windows ☐ Excel ☐ Others: _____

Have you ever visited a Barton's Department Store? Where? Describe your experience.
I went to the Barton's in Pittsburgh and was impressed by the selection of merchandise and the courtesy of the sales associates.

What do you like about clothing? *I like to look nice and feel that I have a good fashion sense. I am good at helping people.*

Why would you like to work for Barton's Department Store? *It would be a convenient after-school location. I like working with people.*

Describe a specific situation where you have provided excellent customer service in your most recent position. Why was this effective? *When I worked at a bookstore I called around to all of our branches until I found a hard-to-find copy of a book a customer was looking for.*

FORMER EMPLOYERS

List below current and last three employers, starting with most recent one first. Please include any non-paid volunteer experience which is related to the job for which you are applying.

Date (M/D/Y): _11/15/01_

From: 10/10/01 **To:** 11/01/01	**Current Employer**(Name and Address—Type of Business): Della's Soup Kitchen 5 Gale Road, Garfield	**Salary or Hourly** Starting $4.25 Ending $4.75 If hourly, average # of hours per week 8 hrs.	**Position:** Waitress	**Reason for Leaving:** to gain more work experience

1. Duties Performed: serving soup & clearing & setting tables

Supervisor's Name: Della Nathan   Phone Number (215) 555-1234   May We Contact? yes

From: 6/5/01 **To:** 8/10/01	**Current Employer**(Name and Address—Type of Business): Reese's Candy Shop 55 Marsh Street, Garfield	**Salary or Hourly** Starting $4.00 Ending $4.00 If hourly, average # of hours per week 5 hrs.	**Position:** Cashier	**Reason for Leaving:** lack of hours

2. Duties Performed: working the register, opening the store

Supervisor's Name: Dana Reese   Phone Number (215) 774-2350   May We Contact?: yes

From: 12/7/00 **To:** 5/1/01	**Current Employer**(Name and Address—Type of Business): Garfield Grocery 125 Main Street, Garfield	**Salary or Hourly** Starting $3.00 Ending $3.25 If hourly, average # of hours per week	**Position:** Cashier	**Reason for Leaving:** insufficient wages

3. Duties Performed: working the register, straightening shelves, sweeping

Supervisor's Name: Lovey Gaber   Phone Number (215) 525-3725   May We Contact?: yes

---

REFERENCES   Give below the names of three professional references, whom you have known for at least one year.

Name	Address & Phone Number	Profession	Years Acquainted How Do You Know This Person?
1. Carl Smith	14 Main Street, Garfield (215) 705-2319	Principal	3
2. Jane Bart	211 Main Street, Garfield (215) 858-2672	Manager	5
3. Michael Reese	45 Dorand Road, Garfield (215) 646-2792	Accountant	7

Date _11/15/01_   Signature _Paula Samuels_

WE ARE AN EQUAL OPPORTUNITY EMPLOYER COMMITTED TO HIRING A DIVERSE WORKFORCE.

Barton's Department Store

ART FILE: BK_G09_C13_model
BKGSE

Writing Various Types of Letters

 Writing Business Letters

Requesting Needed Information   Write a letter to the Baseball Hall of Fame. Request information on the founding of the Hall of Fame and the people who have been honored there. Then prepare an envelope for your letter.

ADDRESS   Baseball Hall of Fame
Main Street
Cooperstown, NY 13326

Requesting Information of Interest   Think an interest of yours about which you would like more information. Use the media center or the Internet to determine which organization or business could best provide you with information. Then write a letter requesting the information and mail the letter. When you get a response, share it with your classmates.

To Place an Order   Use the following information to order merchandise from a catalog. Unscramble the information for the inside address and write it in the proper order. Use your own name and address and today's date for the heading. Add $3.00 for shipping and handling.

INSIDE
ADDRESS

Order Department, Medina, Olympic Sporting Goods, Ohio, 44256, 3237 Arlington Avenue

MERCHANDISE

1 sweat shirt, #45589, blue, size small, $14.95; 1 sweat pants, #45590, blue, size medium, $12.95; 3 pairs tube socks, #5667, $2.95 each

Applying for Employment   In the following letter, each line preceded by a numeral contains an error. Rewrite the letter, correcting each mistake.

1   Tanika Shaw
2   463 Powhatan street
    Richmond, VA 23240
3   August 19th, 2000

4 Mr. Alan Bishop.
The Charts Record Store
5 1396 Fairfax Avinue
Richmond, VA 23217

6 Dear Mr. Bishop,

    I am writing to apply for the part-time cashier's
7 position advertized in the *Richmond Times*. The enclosed résumé will inform you of my educational background and previous experience. Since my goal
8 is to pursue a career in retailing. I am especially interested in working in a store. I am good with numbers and throughout high school I have earned a B-plus average in my math courses.

    I can come to your store for an interview after 3:30 P.M. during the week and at any time during the
9 day on Saturdays. In addition, I am available to start workeing at any time. I look forward to hearing from you.

10   Yours Truly

      Tanika Shaw

      Tanika Shaw

Assess Your Learning

You are looking for a summer job and decide to flip through the yellow pages of your local town or city, or scan the classified ads of your newspaper. Find local businesses or job opportunities that sound interesting to you.

▶ **Choose a business to apply to, and write a letter of application. In your letter, explain that you are not writing in response to an advertisement for a specific position; rather, you are writing to inquire about the possibility of a part-time summer position at an entry level. If possible, call the business and ask for the name of the person who handles hiring. Use your own name and address and today's date. Prepare an envelope for your letter.**

▶ **Be certain to keep your letter concise, polite, and direct; in addition, try and give your prospective employer a good sense of your personality. Remember that this letter is the first evidence the employer will have of the kind of employee you will be.**

Before You Write **Consider the following questions:**
What is the *subject?*
What is the *occasion?*
Who is the *audience?*
What is the *purpose?*

After You Write **Evaluate your work using the following criteria:**
- Have you identified your prospective employer as your audience and geared your letter toward influencing the employer?
- Have you used a voice and style in the application letter that are appropriate to your audience?
- Does your letter give a good first impression?
- Have you organized your ideas in a coherent manner?
- Have you followed the rules for the structure of a business letter?
- Have you proofread your work for spelling, capitalization, and punctuation errors within the context of the application letter?

Write briefly on how well you did. Point out your strengths and areas for improvement.

CHAPTER 14

Speeches, Presentations, and Discussions

During his Inaugural Address in 1961, President John F. Kennedy spoke the famous words, ". . . ask not what your country can do for you—ask what you can do for your country." These words, communicated to the entire nation, inspired people to work for social causes and established a patriotic tone for Kennedy's presidency. They also sparked a new awareness of and respect for the power of artfully crafted and dramatically delivered eloquence. Through effective communication—a reciprocal process in which speakers speak clearly and forcefully and listeners hear and interpret what is being said—words can make people laugh or cry, move them from anger to joy, or inspire them to action. Spoken words are instruments that can bring about positive changes in people and in the world around them. This chapter will help you hone your speaking and critical listening skills so that you will be an effective speaker and listener whatever the audience or purpose may be.

Reading with a Writer's Eye

"I Have a Dream" by Dr. Martin Luther King, Jr. helped spur passage of the Civil Rights Act of 1964 and the Voting Rights Act of 1965. Read it through several times, imagining that you are one of the 250,000 people who attended the March on Washington for Jobs and Freedom on August 28, 1963. How does the speech personally affect you? Then read it again as if you were giving the speech. Why do you think it is so stirring?

I HAVE A DREAM

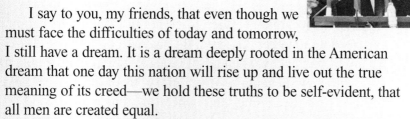

Dr. Martin Luther King, Jr.

I say to you, my friends, that even though we must face the difficulties of today and tomorrow, I still have a dream. It is a dream deeply rooted in the American dream that one day this nation will rise up and live out the true meaning of its creed—we hold these truths to be self-evident, that all men are created equal.

I have a dream that one day on the red hills of Georgia, sons of former slaves and sons of former slave-owners will be able to sit down together at the table of brotherhood.

I have a dream that one day, even the state of Mississippi, a state sweltering with the heat of injustice, sweltering with the heat of oppression, will be transformed into an oasis of freedom and justice.

I have a dream that my four little children will one day live in a nation where they will not be judged by the color of their skin but by the content of their character. I have a dream today!

I have a dream that one day, down in Alabama, with its vicious racists, with its governor having his lips dripping with the words of interposition and nullification, that one day right there in Alabama, little black boys and black girls will be able to join hands with little white boys and white girls as sisters and brothers. I have a dream today!

I have a dream that one day every valley shall be exalted, every hill and mountain shall be made low, the rough places shall be made plain, and the crooked places shall be made straight, and the glory of the Lord will be revealed and all flesh shall see it together.

This is our hope. This is the faith that I go back to the South with.

With this faith we will be able to hew out of the mountain of despair a stone of hope. With this faith we will be able to transform the jangling discords of our nation into a beautiful symphony of brotherhood.

With this faith we will be able to work together, to pray together, to struggle together, to go to jail together, to stand up for freedom together, knowing that we will be free one day. This will be the day when all of God's children will be able to sing with new meaning—"my country 'tis of thee; sweet land of liberty; of thee I sing; land where my fathers died, land of the pilgrim's pride; from every mountainside, let freedom ring"—and if America is to be a great nation, this must become true.

So let freedom ring from the prodigious hilltops of New Hampshire.

Let freedom ring from the mighty mountains of New York.

Let freedom ring from the heightening Alleghenies of Pennsylvania.

Let freedom ring from the snow-capped Rockies of Colorado.

Let freedom ring from the curvaceous slopes of California.

But not only that.

Let freedom ring from Stone Mountain of Georgia.

Let freedom ring from Lookout Mountain of Tennessee.

Let freedom ring from every hill and molehill of Mississippi. Fom every mountainside, let freedom ring.

And when we allow freedom to ring, when we let it ring from every village and hamlet, from every state and city, we will be able to speed up that day when all of God's children— black men and white men, Jews and Gentiles, Catholics and Protestants—will be able to join hands and to sing the words of the old Negro spiritual, "Free at last, free at last; thank God Almighty, we are free at last."

Thinking as a Writer

Analyzing the Effectiveness of a Speech

- Summarize Dr. King's message in a single, clearly worded statement.
- How does he capture your interest? What verbal techniques does he use to hold your attention?
- With what kinds of feelings does the speech leave you?

Delivering the Speech

Oral Expression
- Take turns with a partner reading aloud and listening to the speech. How does the language engage the listener? What special words or phrases does Dr. King use? What key words does he repeat? What impact do these words have?
- Try to convey the tone and rhythm of the speech in your reading. Do you think the speech allows for an expressive style to come through? How so?

Understanding Visual Impact

Viewing Below is a photo of a cross-section of the audience listening to Dr. King's speech in Washington, D.C.

- What do you think he saw that influenced the content of his speech?
- Why is knowing about your audience important in preparing and presenting a public speech?

Developing Public Speaking and Presentation Skills

You have just read an example of a speech written for a specific purpose—an appeal for freedom and brotherhood. This speech informs and persuades by appealing to the most profound ethical and moral interests of an entire nation.

▶ Preparing Your Speech

In school, as well as in your future career, you may be called upon to give a formal speech. In school, you may have to make a speech to a group of students, parents, or teachers. In your career, you may have to make a formal presentation to a group of coworkers at a small meeting or a large convention.

Preparing and delivering speeches for a variety of purposes is similar to preparing and writing a report, a persuasive essay, or a short story. In both speaking and writing, you choose and limit a subject, gather information, and organize your ideas. Instead of editing and publishing an essay, however, you will practice and deliver a speech to your audience.

Knowing Your Audience and Purpose

Sometimes you must choose a subject to suit the audience, and sometimes you must choose an audience for the subject. If, for example, you have been asked to give a humorous speech at a friend's birthday party, it would hardly do for you to give a lecture on the Invasion of the Huns. This subject and form would be inappropriate to the occasion, purpose, and audience of your speech.

Your audience may be a small group of friends or a large assembly of parents or voters. They may already know something about your subject or have particular views on it. It is important that you consider your audience when determining the purpose and choosing the subject of your speech. The following strategies will help you.

> **Strategies for Considering Audience and Purpose**
> - Find out the interests of your audience. Decide how you can limit your subject to match their interests.
> - Identify what your audience already knows about your subject. Consider what your audience may expect to hear.
> - Decide whether your purpose is to inform, to persuade, or to entertain by expressing your thoughts or by telling a story.

You can learn more about these specific purposes for written and oral essays on pages C252–C253 and C439.

The following examples illustrate three ways to address the subject of computers according to your purpose.

PURPOSES OF SPEECHES	
Purpose	**Example**
to inform	explaining how to save your work on the computer
to persuade	convincing computer users to save their work
to entertain	telling how the essay you forgot to save was lost when your computer crashed

PRACTICE YOUR SKILLS

● *Determining a Subject That Relates to Audience and Purpose*

Write an example of a subject for a speech you might give for each of three purposes—to inform, to persuade, and to entertain.

Choosing and Limiting a Subject

After choosing an interesting subject, you should limit it. Limiting the subject enables you to present it fully to a given audience within a limited period of time. As a rule of thumb, it takes about as long to deliver a ten-minute speech as it does to read aloud slowly four pages of a double-spaced written essay. The strategies for choosing and limiting a subject for a speech are the same as the strategies you would use to choose and limit a subject for an essay.

You can learn more about choosing and limiting the subject for an essay on pages C18–C19.

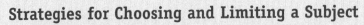

Strategies for Choosing and Limiting a Subject

- Choose a subject that interests you and is likely to interest your audience.
- Choose a subject that you know well or can research thoroughly.
- Limit the subject by choosing one aspect of it. For example, for a ten-minute speech on endangered species, you could limit the subject to the American bald eagle.

PRACTICE YOUR SKILLS

Determining a Subject

For each of the following items, write a subject for a speech.

1. personal experiences

2. experiences of others

3. current events or issues

4. past events or people

5. how to do something

6. how to make something

7. jobs or professions

8. school-related subjects

9. ideas for inventions

10. ideas about the future

Limit each subject so that it would be suitable for a ten-minute speech.

1. earthquakes
2. zoos
3. education
4. clean environment
5. computers/the Internet
6. songs/dances
7. space travel
8. weather
9. good health
10. fashion trends

Gathering and Organizing Information

After you have chosen and limited your subject, begin to gather information. List everything you already know about the subject. Then consult other useful sources of information, including encyclopedias, books, periodicals, CD-ROMs, and online materials in the library or media center. You might also consider interviewing people who are knowledgeable about the subject.

Taking Notes   Take notes on note cards throughout your research. Note cards are best for recording ideas because the information can be easily organized later as you prepare to make an outline of your speech. Use a separate card to summarize each important idea, and include facts and examples to support the idea. Record accurately any quotations you plan to use. If you conduct an interview, take notes or use a tape recorder, and then transfer the information to note cards. Your presentation should contain accurate and truthful information.

Collecting Audiovisual Aids   Audiovisual aids, such as maps, pictures, slides, CDs, CD-ROMs, and tapes, will add to the impact of your speech. Decide which of your main points to enhance with the use of audiovisual aids, and gather or create these materials as you prepare your speech.

Search the Internet for information that might help you make your points and capture the interest of your audience. It is also a good idea to cut and paste the address, or URL, of a site from your browser into a word-processing file. If your presentation software allows you to create links to the World Wide Web, you will need this address.

Strategies for Organizing a Speech

- Arrange your note cards by topics and subtopics. Then use the cards to make a detailed outline of your speech and draft an introduction and a conclusion. (*pages C531–C533*)

- To make your introduction interesting, begin with an anecdote, an unusual fact, a question, or an interesting quotation. Include a thesis statement that makes clear the main idea and the purpose of your speech. (*page C217*)

- Support your message in the body of your speech with logical points, claims, and arguments. Use appropriate appeals to support your claims and arguments. Choose valid proofs from reliable sources to support your claims.

- Arrange your ideas in a logical order and think of the transitions you will use to connect the ideas. (*pages C132, C169, C183, and C195*)

- Write a conclusion for your speech that summarizes your important ideas and signals to the audience that you have finished. Try to conclude your speech with a memorable sentence or phrase. (*page C228*)

PRACTICE YOUR SKILLS

● *Gathering and Organizing Information*

Choose and limit a subject for a ten-minute speech in which the purpose is to persuade. Write what you know about the subject on note cards. Next visit the library or media center and find additional information for ten more note cards. Then organize your cards, outline your speech, and draft an introduction and conclusion.

Practicing Your Speech

Although rehearsing your speech is important, in most cases you should not attempt to write it out or to memorize it. Instead, use your outline or convert your outline and note cards into cue cards. Cue cards include your main points along with key words, phrases, and quotations listed in the order you want to follow in your speech. While you are delivering your speech, your cue cards will help you to remember your important points and supporting details. Following are some strategies for practicing your speech.

> ### Strategies for Practicing a Speech

- Practice in front of a long mirror so that you will be aware of your gestures, facial expressions, and posture.
- Make effective use of volume, pitch, and tone of voice.
- As you practice, look around the room as if you were looking at your audience.
- Time your speech. If it is too long, cut some information. If it is too short, find additional information and add it to your speech. Keep to the main ideas.
- Practice using your cue cards and any visual aids or props that are part of your speech.
- Practice over a period of several days. Your confidence will grow each time you practice, and your nervousness will decrease as your confidence increases.

Revise your speech as you practice by experimenting with different wording, and adding or deleting information to make your main points clearer. You may find it helpful to practice your speech with a friend. Ask your friend to tell you if a point is not clear or if more information is needed to make a point. Listeners' comments may help you revise and improve your speech. As you deliver your speech, pay attention to the listeners' reactions. Make a mental note of their responses to help you revise your speech further and improve your delivery. Practice making your opening and closing sentences memorable.

You can create a folder to contain text, sound, and image files for a multimedia slide presentation. Interesting Websites should be saved, or bookmarked, as favorites. Bookmarks will enable you to return to the Website later. You can also store any material that you have downloaded from the Internet, and copy and paste information from these files directly into the slides of a multimedia presentation program.

PRACTICE YOUR SKILLS

● *Practicing and Revising Your Speech*

Make cue cards for the speech you have been preparing. Then, using the strategies on the next page, practice your speech before a relative, friend, or classmate.

● *Monitoring Audience Response*

Perform your speech once more for family or friends. Monitor their response. Are they laughing at the right places? Are they fidgeting in their seats or staring out the window? Are they nodding in agreement, or are they nodding off into dreamland? Try to be aware of your audience without distracting yourself from making the speech. Explore different ways of keeping their attention. Make a mental note of what works and what does not work.

● Delivering Your Speech

If you have researched your subject well, planned the content carefully, and rehearsed sufficiently, you will deliver your speech with confidence. When the time comes to give your speech, recall the following strategies for delivering a speech.

Strategies for Delivering a Speech

- Have ready all the materials you need, such as your outline or cue cards and audiovisual aids or props.
- Make sure that your computer equipment is assembled and running properly.
- Wait until your audience is quiet and settled.
- Relax and breathe deeply before you begin your introduction.
- Stand with good posture, your weight evenly divided between both feet. Avoid swaying back and forth.
- Look directly at the people in your audience, not over their heads. Try to make eye contact. Smile!
- Speak slowly, clearly, and loudly enough to be heard.
- Use good, clear diction.
- Adjust the volume, pitch, and tone of your voice to enhance communication of your message.
- Use correct grammar and well-formed sentences.
- Use informal, technical, or standard language appropriate to the purpose, audience, occasion, and task.
- Use rhetorical strategies appropriate to the message, whether your purpose is to inform or to persuade.
- Emphasize your main points with appropriate gestures and facial expressions.
- Remember to use your audiovisual aids, such as charts and overhead transparencies, making sure everyone in your audience can see them.
- After finishing your conclusion, take your seat without making comments to people in the audience.

COMPUTER TIP

Run your slide show by advancing each slide manually (pressing the Enter key on your keyboard), or set timing so that the slides advance automatically. Practice working with the slide show before you give your presentation. Make sure the projected images are large and clear enough for the audience to see.

Evaluating an Oral Presentation

The ability to evaluate and make judgments about an oral presentation will help you and your classmates improve your future speeches. The Oral Presentation Evaluation Form shown below may be useful. When evaluating a classmate's speech, remember to be honest while making positive and helpful comments. Make your comments specific in order to help the speaker understand your suggestions. Then complete an assessment form for speeches presented by your classmates. Each speaker should collect and read the listeners' evaluations of his or her speech. Use listener feedback to evaluate the effectiveness of your speech. Also use listener comments to help you set goals for future speeches.

ORAL PRESENTATION EVALUATION FORM

Subject:_____

Speaker:_____

Date:_____

Content
- Are the subject and purpose appropriate for the audience?
- Is the main point clear?
- Are there enough details and examples?
- Do all the ideas clearly relate to the subject?
- Is the length appropriate (not too long or too short)?

Organization
- Does the speech begin with an interesting introduction?
- Do the ideas in the body follow a logical order?
- Are transitions used between ideas?
- Does the conclusion summarize the main points?

Presentation
- Does the speaker choose appropriate words?
- Is the speech sufficiently loud and clear?
- Is the rate appropriate (not too fast or too slow)?
- Does the speaker make eye contact with the audience?
- Does the speaker use gestures and pauses effectively?

- Are audiovisual aids or other props used effectively?
- Are cue cards or an outline used effectively?

Comments: _____

_____

_____

_____

PRACTICE YOUR SKILLS

● *Delivering and Evaluating Your Speech*

Present the speech you practiced and revised. Afterward, complete the Oral Presentation Evaluation Form for your speech at the same time that your classmates are evaluating it. In addition, complete an evaluation form for any speeches presented by your classmates. Share your comments with the speakers you evaluated and read the comments your classmates wrote about your speech. Use the listeners' suggestions to note ways that you can improve your future speeches.

Developing Your Critical Listening Skills

A good listener engages in critical empathic, appreciative, and reflective listening. Skillful listening requires that you pay close attention to what you hear. When listening for information or ideas, you must be able to evaluate critically and reflect on what the speaker says. When you are listening to a persuasive speech, it is important that you evaluate the speaker's evidence, as well as the organization and logic of the argument. By recording the information in an organized way, you will be able to remember and use the information later. You should also monitor the emotional tone of the speech by putting yourself in the speaker's place. Empathic listening, or listening with feeling, will help you distinguish between reasonable and unreasonable emotional appeals. Skills that you have practiced while preparing and presenting a speech will be invaluable to you as you learn to develop your critical listening skills.

Listening Appreciatively to Presentations and Performances

Sometimes you may find yourself listening to a reading or dramatic performance of a work of literature, an essay, or a report. **Oral interpretation** is the performance or expressive reading of a written work. The oral interpreter emphasizes the message through judicious use of voice and gesture. Pauses, as well as changes of volume and variations of tone and pitch, can be employed to highlight important structural elements in the passage such as rhyme, imagery, and key words. As a listener, you must judge how successfully the reader has matched his or her voice to the intentions and style of the work performed. The following guidelines will help you listen appreciatively to oral presentations and performances.

- Be alert to the expressive power of a pause.
- Observe the use of gesture, voice, and facial expression to enhance the message.
- Listen for changes of volume, intonation, and pitch to emphasize important ideas.
- Listen for rhymes, repeated words, and alliteration.
- Listen for rhetorical strategies and other expressive features of the language.
- Take time to reflect upon the message and try to experience with empathy the thoughts and feelings being expressed.

You can find many opportunities to practice listening appreciatively. Perhaps your local bookstore hosts readings of original works of prose and poetry by well-known authors and poets. A nearby theater group might be performing a dramatic work that you have read for school, such as August Wilson's *The Piano Lesson*. You may also have occasion to evaluate original artistic performances by your peers. You will get the most out of the experience by developing a listening strategy suited to the speaker's subject and purpose.

PRACTICE YOUR SKILLS

● *Listening to Presentations and Performances*

Develop your own strategies for listening to and evaluating the following oral presentations. Identify what you would listen for in each case.

1. an actor reading a dramatic monologue from a play

2. a poet reading a collection of new poetry

3. an author reading a short story

4. a classmate delivering Martin Luther King, Jr.'s "I Have a Dream" speech

5. a celebrity delivering a humorous monologue

Oral Interpretation

Choose a poem, short story, or dramatic scene to perform for your class. Instruct your classmates to take notes and analyze the effect of the following artistic elements.

1. character development
2. rhyme
3. imagery
4. language style
5. gesture

Listening to Directions

Every day in school and elsewhere, you are given directions to follow. When listening to directions, always listen carefully from beginning to end, without assuming that you already know what to do. Then practice the following listening strategies.

Strategies for Listening to Directions

- Write down the directions while the speaker is presenting them.
- After listening to the directions, ask specific questions to help clarify the directions.
- When you finish an assignment, review the directions once more to make sure you have followed them correctly.

PRACTICE YOUR SKILLS

Following Directions

Have paper and pencil ready. As your teacher reads you a set of directions, follow them carefully.

1. Listen carefully as your partner gives you instructions on how to make something or how to perform a simple task. Perform the task or repeat the instructions aloud and have your partner assess their accuracy. Reverse roles.

2. Listen attentively as your partner gives you spoken directions to a special place. Draw a simple map as you listen to the directions and have your partner check it for accuracy. Reverse roles.

▶ Listening for Information

Much of your time as a student is spent listening, but you should not take this important skill for granted. Listening for the purpose of learning includes more than merely hearing words. You must be able to understand what you hear so that you can evaluate and apply the information. When listening to learn, you may find the following strategies helpful.

Strategies for Listening for Information

- Sit comfortably but stay alert. Try to focus your attention on what the speaker is saying without being distracted by people and noises.

- Determine whether the speaker's purpose is to inform, to persuade, or to entertain by expressing thoughts and feelings.

- Monitor the message for clarity and understanding. Listen for verbal clues to identify the speaker's main ideas. Often, for example, a speaker emphasizes important points by using such words as *first, finally, also consider, most important, remember that,* or *in conclusion.*

- Watch for nonverbal clues, such as gestures, pauses, or changes in the speaking pace. Such clues often signal important points.

- Determine the speaker's point of view about the subject. For example, is the speaker arguing for or against an issue?

- Take notes to organize your thoughts and to help you remember details. Your notes provide a basis for further discussion. You may also want to use your notes to outline the speech or write a summary of it. If the speech is a course lecture, notes will help you study for a test on the subject.
- Ask clear and relevant questions to clarify your understanding.
- Take time to reflect upon what you have heard.

PRACTICE YOUR SKILLS

● *Listening and Taking Notes*

As your teacher delivers a prepared lecture, listen carefully and take notes. After the lecture, form a small group with other students and compare notes. Try to explain why group members all recorded certain points and why in other cases everyone wrote different information. Then combine your notes to write a complete outline of the lecture. Compare your outline with the outlines other groups wrote.

▶ Recognizing Propaganda

People who listen with care and discernment know that words can sometimes be misleading. This is especially true when speakers use **propaganda** instead of facts and examples to get you to accept their point of view. A speaker may use propaganda to distort or misrepresent information or to disguise opinions as facts. Propaganda can also be used to appeal to listeners' emotions by using strongly biased language, stereotypes, and exaggerations. To evaluate the content or message of a speech and make judgments about what you hear, you must be able to recognize various kinds of propaganda devices.

Confusion Between Fact and Opinion

A **fact** is a statement that can be proved to be true or accurate, while an **opinion** is a personal feeling or judgment about something that cannot be proved. When opinions are stated as facts, misunderstanding or confusion often results for the listener. You can avoid confusion by listening critically to distinguish between facts and opinions.

| FACT | My sister is on the soccer team. |
| OPINION | Soccer players are the most talented athletes. |

PRACTICE YOUR SKILLS

● *Distinguishing Between Fact and Opinion*

Label each of the following statements *F* for *fact* or *O* for *opinion*.

1. Austin is the capital of Texas.

2. Animals in shelters should not be put to sleep, even if homes cannot be found for them.

3. My sister Shari made straight *A*'s in math throughout high school and college.

4. The longest day of the year occurs in June.

5. Miami is the best place to live in Florida.

6. Watching television is a waste of time.

7. Women are more sensitive, thoughtful, and considerate than men.

8. Men make better scientists than women.

9. My brother watches about two hours of television a day, usually after dinner.

10. Summer is the most carefree time of the year.

Bandwagon Appeals

The **bandwagon appeal** tries to get people to do or think the same thing as everyone else. Bandwagon appeals in advertising often try to make consumers feel inferior if they do not conform. Political parties and candidates use bandwagon appeals to win votes. Common slogans associated with this type of propaganda include *Get on board! Join the crowd! Everyone loves . . .* and *Don't be left out!*

> Everyone who is in the know wears Toe-Stomp'n Sneakers.
>
> Don't be an outsider; get your Toe-Stomp'ns today!

Testimonials

A famous person's endorsement, or support, of a product, candidate, or policy is called a **testimonial.** A testimonial can be misleading because it suggests that a famous person's opinions must be right or that a product must be good if a celebrity recommends it. Product placement, the subtle placement of products and logos in movies and television shows, is a variation of the testimonial appeal.

> Hi! I am Tiffany, star of the blockbuster film *Fire in the Desert.* You probably wonder how I can keep my hair so shiny while working under such harsh conditions. Well, it is easy with Shampoo Shazam. It works wonders on my hair, and it can do the same for your hair.

Unproved Generalizations

A **generalization** is a conclusion based on many facts and examples. Generalizations based on only one or two facts or examples are unproved, or unsound. Unproved generalizations can mislead you by suggesting that they are based on facts and examples that apply to all cases. Unproved generalizations usually contain words such as *always, never, all,* or *none.*

Public Presentations

The job of a citizen," wrote one observer, "is to keep his or her mouth open." Indeed, a healthy democracy depends on the active involvement of its citizens. One way citizens can participate in government is by providing testimony at public hearings. These may be neighborhood meetings, city council meetings, or state- or federal-level hearings. If a law or change in the law is being considered that has an impact on you, you have a right to make your views known.

Comments made at public hearings go into the public record, which is kept either by a court reporter or on videotape. Reporters and camera crews may also be present and you may end up on the news.

Media Activity

Work with your classmates to choose a subject on which the class has strong feelings and conduct a public forum. One at a time, address the class with your best arguments. The class can write a brief evaluation of each speaker touching on the following points.

Questions for Evaluating Public Presentations
• How impressive was each speaker?
• What really hit home in what she or he was saying?
• What fell flat?
• How strong was the evidence and other supporting information?
• How effective was she or he in using eye contact, posture, and variety in vocal pitch and tone?

When you receive your evaluation, use it to set goals in your Learning Log for how to improve your next presentation. As a follow-up, watch televised coverage of a city council meeting or other government body. Write a one-paragraph evaluation of the persuasive abilities of a public figure.

UNPROVED GENERALIZATIONS	All good lead guitarists have purple hair and use flat picks.
	Cats never get along with dogs.
	You are always at the computer with music blasting through the headphones.
ACCURATE GENERALIZATIONS	**Some** lead guitarists have purple hair and use flat picks.
	Cats **sometimes** do not get along with dogs.
	You are **often** at the computer with music playing through the headphones.

PRACTICE YOUR SKILLS

● *Identifying Propaganda Techniques*

Label each statement B for *bandwagon*, T for *testimonial*, or U for *unproved generalization*.

1. Glow Bright never lets you down! In one simple step you can wash, wax, and polish your kitchen floor. Glow Bright always leaves your kitchen floor as bright as the sun.

2. As the host of *Wheels of Wealth,* I need fresh breath when I talk to the contestants. That is why I use Mighty Mints. If I can depend on Mighty Mints, you can too.

3. Vote for Joe Barnes and join the crowd supporting a winner. Don't waste your ballot by casting your vote for the losing candidate. Get on the winning side!

4. For a short trip across town or a long trip across the world, use A-One Travel Service. We have the best service, the lowest prices, and the nicest travel agents in town.

5. You trusted me when I hosted the Olympic Games on television, so trust me now when I say that you need a lifetime membership in the Lifelong Health Club.

Participating in Group Discussions

Group discussion is a way of communicating ideas, exchanging opinions, solving problems, and reaching conclusions. Group discussions may be informal or formal. In informal discussions you can freely express your views and share your experiences. In formal discussions, on the other hand, you may have to present information you researched or use evidence to argue an issue.

You use group discussion skills in many learning contexts. In the writing process, group brainstorming may help you during the prewriting stage; and peer conferencing is an effective technique to help you evaluate your work. You may also use discussion and communication skills in preparing a speech or an oral report or in working with other students to prepare for a test. Group discussion skills will help you to present your ideas effectively and to listen thoughtfully to others' ideas. (*pages C27, C41, and C605*)

The following strategies will help facilitate group discussions in which you may take part.

Strategies for Participating in Group Discussions

- Listen carefully and respond respectfully to others' views.
- Ask clear and relevant questions to make sure you understand others' views or information.
- State or express your own ideas clearly. Present examples or evidence to support your ideas.
- Keep in mind that everyone in the group should have equal opportunity to speak.
- Make sure your contributions to the discussion are constructive and relevant to the subject.
- Give useful feedback to other members' comments and questions in the group discussion.
- Help your group draw a conclusion or reach a consensus.

 Directed Discussions

Sometimes your teacher will lead the discussion to make sure that it does not stray from the agenda. Sometimes a group appoints its own leader to focus the discussion and keep it on track. Such discussions are referred to as **directed discussions.** The leader, or moderator, of a directed discussion group has certain additional responsibilities. If you are chosen to lead a group discussion, use the following strategies for meeting these responsibilities.

> ## Strategies for Leading a Discussion
>
> - Introduce the topic, question, or problem. With the group's help, state the purpose or goal of the discussion.
> - Keep the discussion on track to help the group reach agreement and accomplish its goals.
> - Encourage everyone to participate.
> - Make sure that everyone has equal opportunity and equal time to speak.
> - Keep a record of the group's main points and decisions, or assign this task to a group member.
> - At the end of the discussion, summarize the main points and restate any conclusions or decisions the group reached.

PRACTICE YOUR SKILLS

● *Conducting a Directed Discussion*

Form small groups and have a directed discussion. Begin by choosing a current issue concerning your school, such as choice of subjects, security measures, dress codes, student privileges, extracurricular activities, or school improvement. Then choose a discussion leader and establish a goal. During the discussion, take turns assuming the responsibilities of a discussion leader. At the end of the discussion, review the main points and summarize your conclusions.

⊚ Cooperative Learning

In a **cooperative learning** group, members work together to achieve a goal. A subject is divided into manageable tasks and then the tasks are assigned to individuals in the group. For this reason, cooperative learning groups are sometimes called **task groups.** After the tasks are accomplished, members collect and organize the results of their individual efforts. For example, members of a task group in a biology class may cooperate to prepare an oral presentation on organisms that cause diseases. One member of the group may research viruses, another member may find information on bacteria, a third member may investigate fungi, and a fourth member may research parasites. Another member may use the computer to compile a database. As another option, the group may choose to share the work by assigning different types of diseases to be researched by individual members.

> ### Strategies for Cooperative Learning
>
> - Use the <u>Strategies for Participating in Group Discussions</u>. (*page C611*)
> - Participate in planning the project and in assigning roles.
> - If you have been assigned a task, do not let your group down by coming to meetings unprepared.
> - Cooperate with others in the group to resolve conflicts, solve problems, reach conclusions, and make decisions.
> - Help your group achieve its goals by taking your fair share of responsibility for the group's success.

PRACTICE YOUR SKILLS

⬤ *Organizing a Cooperative Learning Group*

Form a cooperative learning group of three to five members and plan a presentation on one of the following subjects or choose a subject of your own. Use the strategies above.

1. ways to become physically fit

2. music of the 1990s

3. innovations in technology

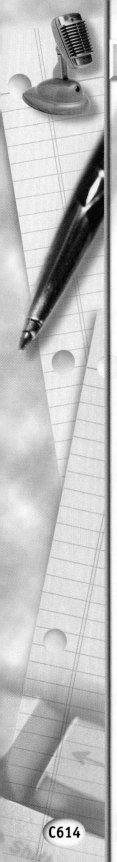

A Speaker Speaks

Oral Interpretation

Purpose: to express yourself artistically through a reading of a dramatic scene from *The Piano Lesson*

Audience: classmates and members of the local community

As a performer, you must understand the meaning of the work before you can convincingly express it to an audience. The oral interpreter conveys the meaning through expressive use of voice and gesture. When acting a speech from a dramatic work, for example, you must be able to convince your audience, through effective use of voice and body language, that you *are* the character. When reciting verse, you can employ pauses, changes of volume, and modulation of tone and pitch to emphasize important structural elements in the passage such as rhyme, imagery, and keywords. Take advantage of the expressive power of punctuation and grammar. Aim for clear and convincing communication of meaning to your listeners.

Preparing

Form a small group and choose a scene from August Wilson's *The Piano Lesson* (pages C351–C352) to perform as a reading for your classmates. Sit in a circle and read through the text. Look up unfamiliar words. Analyze the content and discuss the ideas that you think are most important in the scene. Identify rhymes, repeated words and sounds, imagery, and other language features that you wish to stress.

Using the five *W*s and *H*, analyze the scene for an understanding of character, purpose, and situation. **W**ho are you? **W**hat are you saying? **W**hy and **h**ow are you saying it? **W**hen are you saying it? **W**here are you saying it?

Prepare a printed passage from the play. Include a brief introduction to the passage. Highlight the lines that you are to perform. Mark keywords that you want to emphasize through gesture, voice, or facial expression.

Practicing

Rehearsing is revising. Every performance brings out different meanings in the text. When rehearsing, emphasize different words each time you read your part, until you arrive at the interpretation that you think is best. Listen to the other characters as they speak, and respond to them as though you were conducting a real conversation. Dramatic performance is a dynamic group effort. Use the techniques that you have learned to evaluate your performance and that of your peers. Give praise where it is due and make constructive suggestions for improvement.

Performing

Perform the reading for your classmates. When you have finished, ask them to critique your performance. Use their feedback to determine whether you successfully conveyed the meaning of the scene. Record your performance and send a copy of your tape to a local radio station. Give a performance at an elder-care center or at a day-care center for children. Share with members of your community the riches you have found in literature.

Connection Collection

Representing in Different Ways

To: Brenda Bramble
Editor, <u>In Scribe</u>

From: Chip Chindimple, Research
Department

Date: 12/03/00

Subject: Annual Haiku Contest

After weeks of reading poems, our judges chose a winner! A sizable 47 percent of the judges liked "Quiet Railroad" for first prize. Our second-place winner is "The Gridiron," which received 33 percent of the votes, and "Senses" came in third with 20 percent. Please notify the poets, whose names are on file. "Quiet Railroad" follows:

> Butterflies hover.
> A soft, still, starless night falls.
> The train's whistle weeps.

. . . to Visuals

Draw a pie chart based on the memo. Create a title for the chart, since you will refer to it in your presentation announcing the winners of the contest. What design style seems appropriate to the style of the winning poem? How can the chart help you in your presentation?

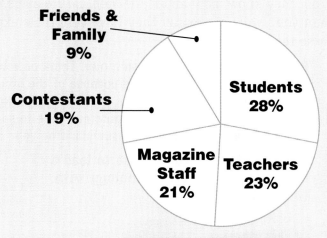

**Guests at *In Scribe's*
Annual Banquet**

Using the pie chart as a guide, prepare a short
speech to announce the winners of *In Scribe's*
haiku contest. Keep your entire audience in
mind as you acknowledge the presence of each
group of people attending the banquet.

- Which strategies can be used
  for creating both written and
  visual representations? Which
  strategies apply to one but not
  both? Which type of representation is more effective?
- Draw a conclusion and write
  briefly about the differences
  between written ideas and
  visual representations.

Speaking in the Workplace
Leading a Discussion Group
You work for SpiderWebsites, an Internet development company. Your job is to lead a discussion group with high school students, focusing on the role of technology in their lives. Some students claim they know more about the Web, DVD players, and 3-D games than you, while others say they have very little experience with these technologies.

> **Prepare to lead the discussion group. Think of how to introduce the topic. Be sure to state the purpose of the group—to explore the pros and cons of living in a technology age. Remember to keep the students on track, encouraging everyone to speak. Keep a record of the group's progress, summarizing your conclusions.**
>
> What strategies did you use to lead a discussion group on technology with the students?

You can find information on leading a discussion group on page C612.

Speaking in Academic Areas
Persuasive Speech
You are an experienced physical education professor at Winmore College. The principal of Count Jockula High School, Miranda Foxtrot, has asked you to give a speech to her students on the importance of exercise for good health. Ms. Foxtrot has told you that the students at Count Jockula prefer getting physically involved rather than sitting still during an assembly!

> **Prepare a speech to persuade your audience members to pursue an active exercise plan. Organize your notes, outline, and supporting details. Think of two ways to lead the students in physical activities without creating a big distraction.**
>
> What strategies did you use to persuade the students?

You can find information on persuasive speeches on page C593.

Assess Your Learning

At a recent assembly, a band called the Monkey Bars performed a short concert. Although they lip-synched to the music, the band provided free refreshments and made many new fans. Now, they are selling copies of their new CD, *Ride to the Playground*, during lunch hour. You think the music is terrible. This Friday, your class will hold an open forum, where any student can voice his or her opinion for five minutes.

▶ **Prepare a speech for your class expressing your viewpoint—that the Monkey Bars are not worthwhile. Suggest a different CD or an activity that you find enjoyable and rewarding. Mention the band's use of propaganda, such as bandwagon appeals, testimonials, and generalizations.**

▶ **In drafting your speech, anticipate any opposing arguments. Draw from your experience to lend support to your argument. What visual aids—posters, charts, or video clips—would make your presentation more vivid?**

Before You Write **Consider the following questions:**
What is the *subject?*
What is the *occasion?*
Who is the *audience?*
What is the *purpose?*

After You Write **Evaluate your work using the following criteria:**
- Have you arranged your notes logically to present pertinent information to your audience?
- Did you use an introduction, personal narratives, or specific examples to keep your audience's interest?
- Does your speech flow smoothly between ideas and make logical transitions?
- Have you included visual materials that will help catch the listener's attention?
- Have you developed drafts of your presentation, practicing them to suit your subject, occasion, and purpose?
- Have you remembered to speak slowly, use clear diction, relax, breathe deeply, and stand confidently?

Write briefly on how well you did. Point out your strengths and areas for improvement.

CHAPTER 15

Vocabulary

You have spent time studying sentences, paragraphs, and essays. None of those things could exist without words. To think about writing without also thinking about words is like trying to build a house without using wood, or brick, or cement. Words are the foundation for all of your writing and thinking. They allow you to vividly express your thoughts and feelings with precision and beauty, and they allow you to persuade with conviction. The more words you know, the more you will enjoy reading, and the better equipped you will be to write essays and speak clearly and convincingly.

There are many strategies for expanding your vocabulary. As you learn these strategies, you will also learn how English has developed into a language that is both rich and varied. Just as a historian looks at period documents in order to understand what is going on in the present day, it is helpful when building your vocabulary to look at the origins of the English language.

Reading with a Writer's Eye

You have no doubt heard of "freedom of speech." But where does the word *freedom* originate, and how are our perceptions of *freedom* influenced by the ancient meaning of the word? Allan Metcalf is a professor of English who has done extensive research on the origins of English. In the following selection you will see that the unique concept of *freedom* has a specific origin that can be traced to the creation of the word *freedom* itself.

FROM

The World in So Many Words

Allan Metcalf

Freedom

English had its beginnings about fifteen hundred years ago, when the "Angle-ish" spoken by Angles and Saxons separated from other Germanic languages as the Angles and Saxons themselves, crossing the water to settle in what they would call "Angle-land," separated from other Germanic tribes. Since that time, no word has been of more significance to English speakers than *freedom*. This word was not carried to England as part of the Angles' and Saxons' German language heritage, nor was it imported from another language. Instead, it seems to have been a homemade invention, put together from two existing Germanic words to form a distinctive concept.

The elements of *freedom* are *free* and *doom*, to use the modern spellings. *Free* originally meant "beloved" and is related to the word *friend*. By the time English came into being, *free* had evolved to take on its modern meaning, with the idea that one who is beloved is a friend, free from bondage. The development of *doom* is more complicated. Nowadays we think of *doom* as a judgment—and a harsh one at that—or as an unhappy fate. A thousand years ago, in the time of the early English language, *doom* had a different emphasis. It did indeed mean judgment, but it meant a considered judgment, related to the present-day *deem*.

Put *free* together with *doom* and you have the condition of being judged to be free. It involves being free and thinking about it, being free and accepting the responsibility for making the judgments that being free entails.

Appropriately, one of the earliest appearances of English *freedom,* in about the year 888, is in the best-known translation of a philosophical work ever to appear in English. The translation was made by King Alfred himself, the only English ruler ever to be called "the Great." Fate or free will? Necessity or freedom? That was the question Alfred answered in favor of the latter in his translation of the *Consolation of Philosophy* by the Roman Boethius. For the Latin *libertas,* our present-day *liberty,* Alfred uses the newly created *freedom.* To be governed by righteousness, he writes, is to be "on tham hehstan freodome," that is, in the highest freedom. He writes of the "fulne friodom" or "full freedom" attained by those who do not seek earthly gains. Through such language Alfred made a Platonic[1] work into a decidedly more Christian one. Alfred needed all the Platonic and Christian consolation he could find in the grim days of Viking invasions and the near anarchy of what we call the "Dark Ages" after the collapse of the Roman empire.

Freedom made itself thoroughly at home in English at an early date. In addition to Alfred's Boethius, about fifty other extant Old English texts use it, including English translations of St. Augustine's soliloquies,[2] Pope Gregory the Great's book on pastoral care, and the Venerable Bede's famous history of the English church and people.

---

[1] **Platonic** (plə tŏn′ik) Of or relating to the ancient Greek philosopher Plato.
[2] **Soliloquy** (sə lĭl′ə kwē) A dramatic discourse in which a character reveals his or her thoughts when alone.

There are a thousand or so words like *freedom* that appear to be truly English, that is, that do not seem to have existed in the ancestors of our language but were newly made after English developed from Proto-Indo-European and Germanic and that appear in the written records of the earliest period of English, about a thousand years ago.

The rest of English-speaking history might be said to be the development of the meaning of *freedom*. Much later, in the fourteenth century, we admitted the French *liberty* to our language in equal partnership, but *freedom* has remained fundamental. It has certainly been the watchword of the American experience. "Those who deny freedom to others," declared Abraham Lincoln, "deserve it not for themselves." In the darkest days of World War II, President Franklin Roosevelt spoke with hope of "a world founded upon four essential human freedoms": freedoms of speech and worship, freedoms from want and fear. And Martin Luther King Jr. concluded his most famous speech with the refrain, "Let freedom ring."

Thinking as a Writer

Exploring the History of a Word

- Make a list of what Metcalf says have been the events influential to our present understanding of *freedom*. Which of these influences was most impressive to you and why?

- What sorts of research tools did Metcalf use in his writing? Using your library or media center, list the possible sources of research into word origins.

Observing Changes in Language

Viewing • Pair up with a classmate and examine the excerpt from *Beowulf* below. What similarities and differences can you find between the Old English and the modern alphabet?

> ðæm eafera wæs æfter cenned,
> geong in geardum, þone god sende
> folce to frofre; fyrenðearfe ongeat
> þe hie ær drugon aldorlease
> lange hwile. Him þæs liffrea,
> wuldres wealdend, woroldare forgeaf.

- Then look at the translation and analyze how the spelling and vocabulary have changed.

To him an heir was afterward born,
a son in his halls, whom heaven sent
to favor the folk, feeling their woe
that erst they had lacked an earl for leader
so long a while; the Lord endowed him,
the Wielder of Wonder, with world's reknown.

Hearing Changes in Language

Oral Expression • Finally, read aloud the last line of each version. Discuss with your classmate what similarities and differences you hear in the language.

Understanding the Development of the English Language

Building a large and meaningful vocabulary in English means being sensitive to its texture. Under the influence of many other languages and cultures, English contains a range of expression that is unparalleled. In fact, the story of English and its varieties is the story of our culture. At the beginning of a new millennium, we can trace the roots of our language to the early part of another, nearly two thousand years ago.

Yesterday, Today, and Tomorrow

Our language has a long and rich history. English was born in England, of course, and its history follows the history of that northern European country.

Old English

In the early part of the fifth century, the Roman armies occupying Britain in order to attend to barbarian threats to Rome itself withdrew, exposing the island to invasions. As the Romans left, other groups poured into Britain. Up to this point, all educated Britons had spoken Latin. However, as with the languages of the Celts the Romans had displaced, Latin was largely forgotten. The most influential of the invading groups were Germanic tribes—the Angles, the Saxons, and the Jutes.

Anglo-Saxon, the language they brought with them, is the foundation of English. Although at first it may not seem to resemble English (as you may have discovered while reading the excerpt from *Beowulf*), this parent language contains many of our frequently used words, such as *home*, *friend*, and *brother*. Almost all of our pronouns, prepositions, conjunctions, articles, and auxiliary verbs are carryovers from the Anglo-Saxon language. **Old English** is the name most scholars have given to this period of the English language, which spanned from A.D. 410 to 1066.

Middle English

Middle English developed as a result of the Battle of Hastings in A.D. 1066. At that time, William the Conqueror, who came from northwestern France, won a decisive victory over the Anglo-Saxons. His Norman lords and followers, who became the ruling class, spoke only French at government meetings and in the courts. Nevertheless, the conquered English people and their language survived. Eventually French and English began to merge, and a richer, more expressive language was the result.

In 1362, English—with its many French words—became the official language of the courts, and later of the schools. Then Geoffrey Chaucer, the greatest poet in England at the time, began to write in English. This helped cement the permanence of the language. Another factor in the language's establishment was the introduction of William Caxton's printing machine in 1476. As a result of this invention, the rules for grammar and the spelling of words became standardized.

The following passage is from Chaucer's *The Canterbury Tales*, written in the fourteenth century.

MODEL: Middle English

A marchant was ther with a forked berd,
In mottelee, and hye on horse he sat;
Upon his heed a Flaundryssh bever hat,
His bootes clasped faire and fetisly.
His resons he spak ful solempnely,
Sownynge alwey th' encrees of his wynnyng.
He wolde the see were kept for any thyng
Bitwixe Middelburgh and Orewelle.
Wel koude he in eschaunge sheeldes selle.
This worthy man ful wel his wit bisette:
Ther wiste no wight that he was in dette,
So estatly was he of his governaunce
With his bargaynes and with his chevys-saunce.
For sothe he was a worthy man with alle,
But sooth to seyn, I noot how men hym calle.

—*Geoffrey Chaucer*, The Canterbury Tales

Here is the same passage, as translated over five hundred years later:

There was a merchant with forked beard,
In motley gown, and high on horse he sat,
Upon his head a Flemish beaver hat;
His boots were fastened rather elegantly.
His notions he spoke outright pompously,
Stressing the times when he had won, not lost.
He would the sea were held at any cost
Across from Middleburgh to Orwell town.
At money-changing he could make a crown.
This worthy man kept all his wits well set;
There was no way that he was in debt,
So well he governed all his trade affairs
With bargains and with borrowings and with shares.
Indeed, he was a worthy man withal,
But, sad to say, his name I can't recall.

—*Geoffrey Chaucer,* The Canterbury Tales

PRACTICE YOUR SKILLS

● *Analyzing Language*

With a partner, list the differences you discover in the two passages above. Be specific, citing particular words and phrases as needed. Also, describe what similarities you see. When it is your partner's turn to talk, listen carefully and attentively. Summarize what you discover and report your findings to the class. Support your findings with specific examples.

Modern English

The English spoken during the period from around 1500 to the present is often called Modern English. By the time playwrights Christopher Marlowe and William Shakespeare were writing and producing their plays, English had evolved to a language not much different from our own. This transformation was due in part to an influx of Greek and Latin words during the English Renaissance. Also during this period the first standardized grammar handbooks were printed, as well as the first dictionaries. These resources helped speakers agree on a uniform usage of the language.

The following is the first scene from the play *Hamlet* by William Shakespeare, as it appeared at the beginning of the 16th century. In this scene, the guards are meeting moments before the ghost of Hamlet's father appears. Compare the language with Old or Middle English, and notice how much closer this passage is to the English that you are used to speaking.

MODEL: Early Modern English

> *Enter Barnardo, and Francisco, two centinels*
>
> Bar. Whose there?
> Fran. Nay answere me. Stand and unfolde your selfe.
> Bar. Long live the King.
> Fran. *Barnardo.*
> Bar. Hee.
> Fran. You come most carefully upon your houre.
> Bar. Tis now strooke twelfe, get thee to bed *Francisco.*
> Fran. For this reliefe much thanks, tis bitter cold,
> And I am sick at hart.
> Bar. Have you had quiet guard?
> Fran. Not a mouse stirring.
> Bar. Well, good night:
> If you doe meete *Horatio* and *Marcellus;*
> The rivalls of my watch, bid them make hast.
> *Enter Horatio, and Marcellus*
> Fran. I thinke I heare them, stand ho, who is there?
> Hor. Friends to this ground.
> Mar. And Leedgemen to the Dane.
> Fran. Give you good night.
> Mar. O, farwell honest souldier, who hath reliev'd you?
> Fran. *Barnardo* hath my place; give you good night.
>
> —William Shakespear, The Tragedie of Hamlet

PRACTICE YOUR SKILLS

● *Analyzing Language*

With a partner, list the ways that Shakespeare's language is different from Old English and the English you speak today. Are there any words you do not know or letters that seem strange to you? Be specific, citing particular words and phrases as needed. Summarize what you discover, and report your findings to the class. Support your findings with specific examples.

American English

In 1937 the American linguist and critic H. L. Mencken discussed the origins of the word *raccoon* in an essay titled "The Beginnings of American." In a passage entitled "The First Loan Words," Mencken wrote:

> The earliest Americanisms were probably words borrowed bodily from the Indian languages—words, in the main, indicating natural objects that had no counterparts in England. Thus, in Captain John Smith's "True Relation," published in 1608, one finds mention of a strange beast described variously as a *rahaugcum* and a *raugroughcum*. Four years later, in William Strachey's "Historie of Trevaile Into Virginia Britannia," it became an *aracoune*, "much like a badger," and by 1624 Smith had made it a *rarowcun* in his "Virginia." It was not until 1672 that it emerged as the *raccoon* we know today.

The English language underwent a huge change when North America was settled. Separated from Europe, settlers began to develop a new kind of English, drawing on a variety of sources and influences. Settlers encountered people who had lived in North America for thousands of years, and other people from different cultures streamed into the continent. The English language reflected this influence.

The following two selections come from different periods in American history. As you read, think about how the language of each selection is different, and how it is similar. The first selection is from a letter written by Benjamin Banneker to Thomas Jefferson in 1791. Banneker was a well-respected inventor, mathematician, and social critic. In this letter Banneker, a black man, asks Jefferson to further consider the statement that "all men are created equal."

Maryland Baltimore County
Near Ellicotts' Lower Mills, August 19th, 1791

Thomas Jefferson, Secretary of State:

Sir: I am fully sensible of the greatness of that freedom, which I take with you on the present occasion, a liberty which seemed to me scarcely allowable, when I reflected on that distinguished and dignified station in which you stand, and the almost general prejudice and prepossession which is so prevalent in the world against those of my complexion.

I suppose it is a truth too well attested to you, to need a proof here, that we are a race of beings who have long laboured under the abuse and censure of the world, that we have long been considered rather as brutish than human, and scarcely capable of mental endowments.

Sir, I hope I may safely admit, in consequence of that report which hath reached me, that you are a man far less inflexible in sentiments of this nature than many others, that you are measurably friendly and well disposed towards us, and that you are willing and ready to lend your aid and assistance to our relief, from those many distresses and numerous calamities, to which we are reduced.

Now, sir, if this is founded in truth, I apprehend you will readily embrace every opportunity to eradicate that train of absurd and false ideas and opinions, which so generally prevails with respect to us, and that your sentiments are concurrent with mine, which are that one universal Father hath given Being to us all, and that he hath not only made us all of one flesh, but that he hath also without partiality afforded us all the same sensations, and endued us all with the same faculties, and that however variable we may be in society or religion, however diversified in situation or colour, we are all of the same family, and stand in the same relation to him.

—*Benjamin Banneker,* Letter to Thomas Jefferson

The next selection comes from a contemporary book written from the point of view of a little girl in an urban neighborhood. As you read, note how the language has changed and stayed the same.

MODEL: Contemporary American English

Mamacita is the big mama of the man across the street, third-floor front. Rachel says her name ought to be *Mamasota*, but I think that's mean.

The man saved his money to bring her here. He saved and saved because she was alone with the baby boy in that country. He worked two jobs. He came home late and he left early. Every day.

Then one day *Mamacita* and the baby boy arrived in a yellow taxi. The taxi door opened like a waiter's arm. Out stepped a tiny pink shoe, a foot soft as a rabbit's ear, then the thick ankle, a flutter of hips, fuchsia roses and green perfume. The man had to pull her, the taxicab driver had to push. Push, pull. Push, pull. Poof!

All at once she bloomed. Huge, enormous, beautiful to look at, from the salmon-pink feather on the tip of her hat down to the little rosebuds of her toes. I couldn't take my eyes off her tiny shoes.

Up, up, up the stairs she went with the baby boy in a blue blanket, the man carrying her suitcases, her lavender hatboxes, a dozen boxes of satin high heels. Then we didn't see her.

Somebody said because she's too fat, somebody because of the three flights of stairs, but I believe she doesn't come out because she is afraid to speak English, and maybe this is so since she only knows eight words. She knows to say: *He not here* for when the landlord comes, *No speak English* if anybody else comes, and *Holy smokes*. I don't know where she learned this, but I heard her say it one time and it surprised me.

My father says when he came to this country he ate hamandeggs for three months. Breakfast, lunch and dinner. Hamandeggs. That was the only word he knew. He doesn't eat hamandeggs anymore.

Whatever her reasons, whether she is fat, or can't climb the stairs, or is afraid of English, she won't come down. She sits all day by the window and plays the Spanish radio show and sings all the homesick songs about her country in a voice that sounds like a seagull.

Home. Home. Home is a house in a photograph, a pink house, pink as hollyhocks with lots of startled light. The man paints the walls of the apartment pink, but it's not the same, you know. She still sighs for her pink house, and then I think she cries. I would.

Sometimes the man gets disgusted. He starts screaming and you can hear it all the way down the street.

Ay, she says, she is sad.

Oh, he says. Not again.

¿Cuándo, cuándo, cuándo? she asks.

¡Ay, caray! We *are* home. This *is* home. Here I am and here I stay. Speak English. Speak English.

¡Ay! Mamacita, who does not belong, every once in a while lets out a cry, hysterical, high, as if he had torn the only skinny thread that kept her alive, the only road out to that country.

And then to break her heart forever, the baby boy, who has begun to talk, starts to sing the Pepsi commerical he heard on T.V.

No speak English, she says to the child who is singing in the language that sounds like tin. No speak English, no speak English, and bubbles into tears. No, no, no, as if she can't believe her ears.

—*Sandra Cisneros,* The House on Mango Street

PRACTICE YOUR SKILLS

● *Analyzing Language*

With a partner, describe the differences and similarities in language you observe between the two preceding selections. Be specific, citing particular words and phrases to support your findings. Write a brief summary of what you observe and report your findings to the class.

English in the New Millennium

English is the primary language of today's global economy. As trade becomes more and more universal, it is likely that English will continue to be spoken by ever greater numbers of people. Computers help drive the world economy, and their influence can be seen in the growing numbers of words that are derived from computer culture and innovation. Twenty years ago, if you mentioned the words *cell phone*, *E-commerce*, and *laptop* in a sentence, very few people would know what you were talking about. How exactly English will change in the coming millennium is impossible to know, but one thing is certain: the language will change. English is a wonderfully malleable creation, one that welcomes contributions from cultures all over the globe. As technology continues to erase borders, these contributions may become more frequent and more extensive.

 Computer Language

Many common computer terms are very old words.

Boot, as in *boot-up*, comes from the Middle English word *bote.*

Menu, as in *menu-bar*, can be traced to the Latin word *minutus.* *Minutus* became *menut* in Old French.

Disk is from the Latin *discus* and the Greek *diskos.*

Computer is derived from the Latin word *computus.*

 Your Writer's Journal

Build your vocabulary by reading challenging literature and participating in discussions. Use your writer's journal to record any unfamiliar words that you read or hear. Look up these unfamiliar words in a dictionary and note their origins. By looking at the words often, you will eventually make them a part of your everyday vocabulary. Then, as your vocabulary increases, you will have more words to choose from when you write.

Understanding the Varieties of English

The English language is made up of almost a million words. People in different countries—even different regions of the same country—have different ways of pronouncing certain words.

▶ American Dialects

You may have noticed that there is no one way of speaking English. People in different countries and sometimes even different neighborhoods often have their own way of pronouncing certain words. These different ways of speaking are called **dialects.** Dialects can differ from one another in vocabulary, pronunciation, and grammar. These differences are often what makes English such a vibrant, vital language.

▶ Standard American English

Writing in a dialect can be helpful in creative writing. The short story writer Flannery O'Connor was a master of the southern dialect. Toni Morrison has also used dialect in her novels. Neither of these writers, however, would use dialect in a formal speech or in informative writing. They would use Standard English. Standard English is the formal English taught in school and used in newspapers, scholarly works, and most books.

Writing Tip

Use **Standard English** when writing for school and for a large general audience.

● *Identifying Dialects*

With a small group, discuss the dialect that is spoken in your region of the country. Provide examples of the vocabulary, pronunciation, and grammar that characterize the dialect. What culture has influenced the dialect? Compare and contrast your examples with standard English. Make a chart, index, or dictionary of words to introduce your regional dialect to people from other parts of the country.

Colloquialisms, Idioms, Slang, and Jargon

Many words and phrases come into the English language through everyday conversation and usage. Such expressions include colloquialisms, slang, idioms, and jargon. These informal types of language are usually not appropriate for formal written English.

Colloquialisms

Colloquialisms are informal expressions that are used in conversation but usually not in formal writing. In writing dialogue in short stories or plays, however, you may want to use colloquialisms.

> Without her calculator she was **in a bind**. (had a problem)
>
> I **don't get** (don't understand) why we cannot use the gym today.

Idioms

An **idiom** is a phrase or expression that has a meaning different from the literal translation of the words. Idioms do not often make sense when taken literally, yet they are quite meaningful to most people who speak a particular language.

> Everyone **made the bus** (arrived at the bus) on time.

> Bao refused to **give in** (submit) to threats.

Slang

Slang consists of colorful or exaggerated expressions and phrases—usually in nonstandard English—that are used by a particular group, such as teenagers. Although slang constantly changes and quickly goes out of fashion, some slang expressions, such as those that follow, have become widely understood and used.

> That movie was a real **tearjerker.** (something sad, intended to make people cry)
> The guy (man) playing accordion was a real **cornball.** (sentimentalist)

Jargon

Jargon is the specialized vocabulary used in a technical, scientific, or professional field. Computer jargon, for example, includes *viruses, glitches, Zip drives, CD burners,* and *portals.* Although jargon allows professionals to share information with one another precisely and concisely, to the uninitiated it can be very confusing.

> EXAMPLE   My single-lens-reflex image maker has a light-leak because the aperture will not close.
>
> TRANSLATION   My camera will not work.

Your Writer's Journal

You encounter figurative language every day—in conversation, in magazines, on television, in books, and so on. In your journal, list any figurative language that you have encountered recently.

PRACTICE YOUR SKILLS

● *Using Standard English*

Substitute Standard English words or phrases for the underlined expressions.

1. Will you please <u>hit the light</u> on your way out?

2. It really <u>burns me up</u> that Victor would be so late and not bother to call.

3. The All-Pro running back decided to <u>hang up his cleats</u> after his best season.

4. Pauline and Marcia did not <u>hit it off</u> at first, but now they are close friends.

5. The final football game <u>was a real squeaker</u>, but our team won, 14–13.

6. The director asked the cast not to <u>goof off</u> during the rehearsals.

7. Maria <u>burned the midnight oil</u> to finish her science project in time for the beginning of the science fair on Friday.

8. Peter's <u>nose is out of joint</u> because he did not receive an invitation to the party.

9. Moving pianos is <u>back-breaking</u> work.

10. During the figure-skating finals, Laura <u>took a spill</u>.

Writing Tip

Idioms, colloquialisms, slang, and **jargon** can make your fiction and poetry convincing and lively. Usually, however, they are not appropriate for formal writing that you will do in school and at work.

Clichés, Tired Words, Euphemisms, and Loaded Words

Sometimes certain language gets used so often that it no longer has a precise meaning. The words themselves become **tired**, almost worn out. Similarly, expressions sometimes become so commonplace that their originality is lost; they become **clichés**. Avoid clichés and tired words, and your writing will be fresher, more precise, and more interesting to read.

Language that obscures the truth is often either euphemistic or loaded. A **euphemism** is a vague word or phrase that substitutes for something that is considered blunt or offensive. **Loaded words** are words with strong emotional connotations, often used by writers to get a reader to hold a certain opinion about a subject without saying directly what that opinion is.

PRACTICE YOUR SKILLS

● *Identifying Clichés, Tired Words, Euphemisms, and Loaded Words*

Read the following selection of sentences. Identify those words and phrases that are clichés, tired words, euphemisms, and loaded words.

1. If Maurice breaks the pole vault record, I will eat my hat.
2. "You are what you eat" is an old dietary maxim.
3. Angela served a really excellent dinner on Friday; the crabcakes were awesome.
4. Even though Reiko has been having a tough week, she can take comfort that all's well that ends well.
5. Judy was happy as a clam after she bought a lottery ticket and her ship came in.
6. Ten thousand peacekeepers have been sent overseas to protect civilians from terrorist activities.
7. Ms. Locks, who is alleged to have invaded the home of the well-respected Bear family, again insisted on her innocence.

8. When Marcus showed up wearing plaid pants and a polka-dot shirt, his grandmother smiled grimly and told him that his clothes fit him well and that he was very colorful.

9. During the thunderstorm it was raining cats and dogs.

10. Planet Jupiter is big.

Denotation and Connotation

When you search for precise, vivid words, keep in mind that most words have two levels of meaning. Their literal meaning is called *denotation*. On the other hand, most specific words also convey an emotional meaning, or *connotation*. Understanding connotations is important when you are choosing among words that have similar denotations but varying connotations. For example, when you are describing the mood and setting of a quiet library, your word choices can create different feelings in the reader.

Positive Connotation	The library was **silent** and **hushed** as people worked in the afternoon.
Negative Connotation	The library was **mute** and **tomblike** as people worked in the afternoon.

Good word choice involves choosing not only precise, specific words but also words with the appropriate connotation.

Writing Tip

Use **specific words** with **connotations** appropriate to your meaning.

PRACTICE YOUR SKILLS

● *Choosing Connotations*

Write the word in parentheses that has the connotation given in brackets.

> EXAMPLE The snow (buried, blanketed) the mountain town. (positive)
>
> ANSWER blanketed

1. After the storm (an adventurous, a foolhardy) boy set off on snowshoes for a hike. (negative)

2. As he climbed higher, he (drew in, gasped) deep breaths of the pure mountain air. (positive)

3. With each step he became more (self–satisfied, confident). (negative)

4. When he reached the top of the ridge, he (bellowed, proclaimed) for all to hear, "This mountain is mine!" (positive)

5. His echoing (boast, claim) was all that was needed to unlodge the new snow above him. (negative)

6. Within seconds a sheet of ice and snow came (moving, charging) down the slope toward him. (negative)

7. On the other side of the ridge, a group of experienced hikers heard the boy's shout and the (loud, thunderous) avalanche. (negative)

8. They trekked (determinedly, defiantly) across the ridge to search for the boy. (positive)

9. At last they found him when they heard a (low sound, moan). (negative)

10. The boy (survived, recovered) with prompt care, but he never again claimed a mountain on his own. (positive)

Advertising Slogans

Although good writing presents just the right word at the right time, some advertising writing is confusing on purpose. You have no doubt seen and heard such slogans as *More flavor!* or *Best tasting* or *Fun-filled adventure*. What exactly do these words and slogans mean? More flavor than what? Is *more* flavor really desirable? Who says the product is the *best tasting*? What exactly is a *fun-filled adventure*? What are the specifics behind these glittering generalities?

Advertisements are not designed to appeal to careful reasoning. They are designed, in fact, to short-circuit logic. They call out to your less rational, more emotional side. The words *More Flavor!* with a big exclamation point appeal to that irrational corner of your mind where *more* is good and excitement is everything.

Media Activity

Deliberately avoiding clear and accurate vocabulary, write an ad that parodies, or makes fun of, ads with slippery slogans. Appeal to the uncritical side of human nature that believes everything it hears and wants everything it sees. Draw an image or symbol to go along with your ad that also appeals to people's susceptibilities. Your aim is to conjure up a positive but unexamined response.

With your classmates, display around the classroom the advertisements you have created, as well as others that you have clipped from magazines.

Questions	for Analyzing Advertising Slogans

- What slogans were used?
- Are the slogans effective? Why or why not?
- What emotions do the slogans target?
- What images or symbols were used? How effective are they?
- How effective is the relationship between the text and the images in the ad?

Determining Word Meanings

Even a person with an excellent vocabulary knows only a small percentage of the over 600,000 words in the English language. When you come across an unfamiliar word, you can always look up its meaning in the dictionary. There are several other ways to discover and remember word meanings. These are methods upon which you can draw when you write, read, or speak.

🔘 Context Clues

Context clues can help you learn the meaning of a word. The **context** of a word is the sentence, surrounding words, or the situation in which the word appears. Notice how the following kinds of context clues can help you understand or discover the meanings of unfamiliar words.

DEFINITION OR RESTATEMENT	We read a collection of *fables,* **short tales that teach a lesson.** (*Fable* is defined in the sentence as a short tale that teaches a lesson.)
EXAMPLE	Bombay is a *populous* city; **one way the Indian government has tried to ease the overcrowding there is to build a second Bombay.** (The meaning of *populous* is made clear by the example of a way India has dealt with the overcrowding in Bombay.)
COMPARISON	Joseph Briggs has always been *amiable*— **almost as friendly as his older brother Stephen.** (*As* compares Joseph's disposition to that of his older brother Stephen.)
CONTRAST	Mayor Luzinski's popularity **soared to its highest point**, but the city council's **dropped** to its *nadir*. (A contrast is drawn between the highest point of Mayor Luzinski's popularity and the lowest point, the *nadir*, of the city council's.)

PRACTICE YOUR SKILLS

● *Using Context Clues*

Write the letter of the word that is closest in meaning to the underlined word. Then identify the type of context clue you used.

1. Using flattery, she tried to <u>cajole</u> him into singing "The Yellow Rose of Texas."

   (A) discourage   (B) persuade   (C) annoy
   (D) command   (E) mistreat

2. The leading actor's <u>vapid</u> performance sharply contrasted with the supporting actor's lively one.

   (A) fast   (B) sparkling   (C) ridiculous
   (D) dull   (E) vivid

3. Joan has won many awards for her <u>aquatic</u> ability, especially her diving and freestyle swimming.

   (A) hidden   (B) wasted   (C) water-related
   (D) flight-related (E) average

4. A <u>schism</u>, a separation caused by differences of opinion, split the group into two opposing factions.

   (A) division   (B) crystal   (C) treaty
   (D) scheme   (E) nightmare

5. Her gray hair was <u>lustrous</u>, like the glow of silver.

   (A) false   (B) important   (C) gleaming
   (D) foggy   (E) unattractive

6. The brothers were opposites; one was <u>wily</u>, while the other was honest and open in his dealings with others.

   (A) brilliant   (B) crafty   (C) innocent
   (D) funny   (E) stubborn

7. The day's <u>equestrian</u> event featured yearling colts and fillies.

   (A) gymnastic   (B) clown-related (C) soothing
   (D) amateur   (E) horse-related

8. They <u>gibed</u> him over his new haircut, mildy making fun of him in a joking way.

(A) amused   (B) disliked   (C) entertained
(D) teased   (E) protected

9. Her <u>hilarity</u> matched the laughter and good cheer of the other people at the party.

(A) merriment   (B) ambition   (C) outspokenness
(D) gloom   (E) honesty

10. Two <u>auxiliary</u> law enforcement officers were hired temporarily to help out whenever an emergency arose.

(A) full-time   (B) city   (C) assistant
(D) untrained   (E) unqualified

Your Writer's Journal

Choose five words from your journal. For each word, write a new sentence with a context clue to help you understand the word's meaning. Use all of the different types of context clues you have learned.

Prefixes, Roots, and Suffixes

If you know words and parts of words borrowed from Latin and Greek, you will understand the meanings of many English words. A **root** is the part of a word that carries the basic meaning. A **prefix** is one or more syllables placed in front of the root to modify the meaning of the root or to form a new word. A **suffix** is one or more syllables placed after the root to help shape its meaning and often to determine its part of speech. The following examples show how the meaning of word parts contribute to the meaning of a word.

USING WORD PARTS TO DETERMINE MEANINGS			
WORD	**PREFIX**	**ROOT**	**SUFFIX**
abnormality	ab- (away from)	-normal- (typical)	-ity (state of)

deodorize	de- (remove from)	-odor- (smell)	-ize (cause to be)
disagreement	dis- (not)	-agree- (get along together)	-ment (act or fact of doing)
nonfictional	non- (not)	-fiction- (invented story)	-al (characterized by)
postoperative	post- (later than)	-operate- (perform surgery)	-ive (that tends toward action)

Word parts usually only provide clues, not precise meanings. Following are the dictionary definitions of the words above.

abnormality: state of not being typical

deodorize: eliminate a smell

disagreement: the act of failing to agree

nonfictional: factual, realistic

postoperative: following a surgical procedure

Knowing the meanings of prefixes, roots, and suffixes can help you figure out the definitions of numerous words.

COMMON PREFIXES AND SUFFIXES		
Prefix	**Meaning**	**Example**
anti–	against, opposing	anti + freeze: protection against icing
de–	do opposite of, reduce, remove	de + vitalize: deprive of vigor or effectiveness
ex–	out of, outside	ex + clude: shut out
extra–	beyond, outside	extra + ordinary: going beyond what is usual

in–	not	in + tolerable: not bearable
mis–	badly, wrongly	mis + inform: give wrong or untrue information
pre–	before	pre + historic: occurring before written history
re–	again, back	re + enter: go in again

Suffix	Meaning	Example
–able, –ible	capable of	break + able: capable of being broken
–ate	cause to become	valid + ate: cause to become legal or official
–en	cause to be or to have	sharp + en: cause to be more pointed
–ion	act or process	construct + ion: act or process of building
–ist	one who does something	harp + ist: one who plays the harp
–ity	quality, state	equal + ity: state of being equal
–ize	cause to be formed into, conform to	visual + ize: form a mental image of
–ness	state, condition	neat + ness: state of being neat and orderly
–ous	full of	clamor + ous: full of noise

PRACTICE YOUR SKILLS

● *Combining Prefixes and Roots*

Write the prefix that has the same meaning as the underlined word. Combine the word parts and write the word.

EXAMPLE   badly + pronounce = say incorrectly
ANSWER   mis + pronounce = mispronounce

1. <u>beyond</u> + terrestrial = outside the earth's atmosphere

2. <u>again</u> + adjust = arrange or put in order again

3. <u>before</u> + determine = decide ahead of time

4. <u>remove</u> + hydrate = take water away from

5. <u>not</u> + compatible = not capable of existing in harmony

6. <u>again</u> + enact = repeat the actions of an event or incident

7. <u>badly</u> + interpret = understand or explain wrongly

8. <u>not</u> + variable = not changing or not capable of change

Using Prefixes, Roots, and Suffixes

Write the letter of the phrase that is closest in meaning to each word in capital letters. Use the word parts to help you determine the meaning.

1. HAUGHTINESS: (A) state of being proud and scornful (B) one who is arrogant (C) result of vanity

2. ACCESSIBLE: (A) cause to be reached (B) action of gaining entry (C) capable of being approached

3. RECONSIDER: (A) state of thinking (B) think carefully about again (C) deny responsibility

4. ANTAGONIST: (A) one who opposes another (B) state of competition (C) quality of dislike

5. UNTENABLE: (A) favoring defense (B) capable of defending (C) not able to be defended

6. SYSTEMIZE: (A) one who studies a plan (B) cause to conform to a definite plan (C) capable of a plan

7. BOISTEROUS: (A) crafty (B) full of noise (C) immature

8. DEVALUE: (A) reduce the worth of (B) be opposed to wealth (C) fill with something again

9. INCONSISTENT: (A) capable of regulating (B) state of being without (C) not regular or steady

10. DIFFERENTIATION: (A) act of finding differences (B) make similar (C) be capable of being unlike

Making New Words

Using the prefixes, roots, and suffixes below, form as many words as possible.

Prefix	Root	Suffix
anti–	turn	–able
de–	fortune	–ible
ex–	commune	–ate
extra–	harmony	–en
in–	military	–on
mis–	present	–ist
pre–	teen	–ity
re–	equal	–ize
	vocal	–ness
	climax	–ous
	scarce	
	regulate	
	change	
	threat	
	thunder	

Writing Tip

Knowledge of **prefixes, suffixes**, and **roots** will enable you to choose the most appropriate word for your situation, occasion, audience, and purpose.

Synonyms and Antonyms

A **synonym** is a word that has the same or nearly the same meaning as another word. An **antonym** is a word that has the opposite or nearly the opposite meaning of another word.

SYNONYMS	verbose : wordy	diminish : lessen
ANTONYMS	verbose : concise	diminish : increase

To find synonyms, use a book of synonyms or a specialized dictionary called a **thesaurus.** Both resources list words and their synonyms. The words in a book of synonyms usually appear in alphabetical order, as in a dictionary. A thesaurus, which is not alphabetical, provides a thorough index to make words easy to find. A thesaurus may also give you antonyms. One advantage of consulting a thesaurus is that you become aware of the many shades of meaning a word may have, and, therefore, of the complexity of the English language.

COMPUTER TIP

Although most word-processing programs include a thesaurus, the computer thesaurus is often not as extensive as what you will find in a book. If you wish to see a short list of alternatives to a word, highlight the word and look it up in the thesaurus. The computer thesaurus will give you a list of synonyms and antonyms.

● *Recognizing Synonyms*

Decide which word is the best synonym of the word in capitals.

1. EXTINCT: (A) brief   (B) clear   (C) inactive
             (D) imperfect (E) poor

2. THWART: (A) love   (B) frustrate (C) defend
            (D) grow   (E) advance

3. STIPEND: (A) plant   (B) financier (C) fluid
            (D) bank   (E) payment

4. PRECLUDE: (A) prevent (B) avoid   (C) promise
            (D) listen   (E) imagine

5. FOIBLE: (A) story   (B) flaw   (C) strength
            (D) tradition (E) good-bye

6. MEDITATE: (A) compromise (B) reject   (C) agree
            (D) ponder   (E) repair

7. PARADOX: (A) occurrence (B) heaven (C) approval
            (D) contradiction (E) example

8. SURMISE: (A) guess   (B) daybreak (C) provide
            (D) shock   (E) govern

9. PSEUDONYM: (A) falsehood (B) forgery (C) elephant
            (D) pen name (E) writer

10. ECCENTRIC: (A) trustworthy (B) truthful (C) prompt
            (D) earnest   (E) unusual

● *Recognizing Antonyms*

Write the letter of the word that is most nearly opposite in meaning to the word in capital letters.

1. OPAQUE: (A) heavy   (B) decorative (C) transparent
           (D) empty   (E) sensible

2. PLIABLE: (A) rigid   (B) honest   (C) flexible
           (D) loose   (E) mysterious

3. AMBIGUOUS: (A) friendly (B) generous (C) clear
           (D) lazy   (E) clever

4. DEJECTED: (A) joyous   (B) released (C) downcast
                    (D) satisfied (E) reckless

5. BENEVOLENT: (A) determined (B) unkind (C) foolish
                    (D) worthy   (E) informal

6. RECEDE: (A) advance   (B) retreat (C) proclaim
                    (D) unite   (E) offer

7. FASTIDIOUS: (A) sloppy   (B) precise (C) small
                    (D) cautious (E) restful

8. SURLY: (A) uncertain (B) amiable (C) doubting
                    (D) rude   (E) helpful

9. FRUGAL: (A) magnificent (B) friendly (C) wasteful
                    (D) doubtful (E) trivial

10. DEPLETE: (A) begin   (B) succeed (C) fold
                    (D) demonstrate (E) fill

Your Writer's Journal

Choose six words from the list in your journal. For three of the words, find synonyms. For the other three words, find antonyms. Be sure to list any antonym or synonym that helps you to understand the meaning of the unfamiliar word.

Analogies

Your ability to recognize synonyms and antonyms of words is sometimes tested in analogies on standardized tests. **Analogies** ask you to identify relationships between pairs of words. The following example shows the standard format for an analogy test item.

ARTIFICIAL : FAKE : :   (A) enormous : minute
                          (B) isolate : group
                          (C) drowsy : sleepy

Your first step in answering an analogy item is to identify the relationship between the first pair of words. In the example above, the words *artificial* and *fake* are synonyms. Next, look at the answer choices to find another pair of words with the same relationship. The first pair of words, *enormous* and *minute,* are antonyms. The next pair of words, *isolate* and *group,* are also antonyms. The final pair, *drowsy* and *sleepy,* is the correct answer. *Drowsy* and *sleepy* are synonyms.

Synonyms and antonyms are two types of relationships. There are many other ways that words can relate to one another.

Different Types of Analogies

Here are a few examples of the types of analogies you may encounter.

part to whole   grain : beach   : :   droplet : river
A grain of sand is part of a beach in the same way that a droplet of water is part of a river.

function   hand : carry   : :   shovel : dig
A hand can be used to carry something, and a shovel can be used to dig.

cause/effect   theft : incarceration   : :   tardiness : detention
Theft is punished with incarceration, and tardiness is punished with detention.

person/tool   singer : voice   : :   pianist : piano
A singer's instrument is his or her voice, and a pianist's instrument is the piano.

degree/intensity   talk : shout   : :   feel : experience
Talking is less intense than shouting, and feeling is less intense than experiencing.

PRACTICE YOUR SKILLS

● *Recognizing Analogies*

Write the letter of the pair of words that have the same relationship as the word pair in capital letters. Then identify the type of relationship.

1. ACCESSIBLE : REACHABLE :: (A) exotic : common
(B) expand : amplify   (C) lazy : industrious

2. DEPLETE : REPLENISH :: (A) foremost : primary
(B) affluent : wealthy   (C) optimist : pessimist

3. VERBOSE : WORDY :: (A) invisible : concealed
(B) fortunate : unlucky   (C) found : lost

4. CIRCLE : SPHERE :: (A) square : rectangle
(B) triangle : pyramid   (C) box : cube

5. MILK : CARTON :: (A) eggs : dozen   (B) ream : paper
(C) sandals : shoebox

6. DIMINISH : ENLARGE :: (A) musical : melodic
(B) stipulate : specify   (C) mute : noisy

7. EXCAVATE : DIG OUT :: (A) lucrative : unprofitable
(B) fallacy : truthfulness   (C) improvise : ad-lib

8. QUENCH : THIRST :: (A) satisfy : desire
(B) respond : reserve   (C) hear : reply

9. PERMANENT : JOB :: (A) full-time : part-time
(B) child : adult   (C) semi-gloss : paint

10. CAJOLE : COAX :: (A) reside : dwell
(B) dynamic : inactive   (C) increase : dwindle

● *Creating Your Own Analogies*

Select ten words from your writer's journal. Use a thesaurus or dictionary to come up with a synonym and antonym for each word. You will now have ten pairs of synonyms and ten pairs of antonyms. Use these pairs to create your own analogies. When you are finished, trade your analogies with a partner and answer each other's work.

A Writer Writes

A Survey of Informal Language

Purpose: to learn about informal language by interviewing adults

Audience: your peers and elders

Prewriting

Start by brainstorming with a partner a list of five expressions (idioms, colloquialisms, slang) from your everyday vocabulary. Next to each expression, note where you think these words came from and other meanings they may have. Are they appropriate only in certain circumstances? Collaborate with your partner to write a clear, precise, informative definition for each expression.

With your partner, decide on four people of various ages to interview to collect additional examples of informal language. You might want to interview a grandparent or an older neighbor in your area. Contact each person, tell him or her the nature of the interview, and schedule a time and place to conduct your interview. Ask your respondents to think about informal expressions they have used. Brainstorm a list of questions to ask each person. You may want to engage a person's interest by sharing your list of expressions to see if any mentioned are similar to yours. Consider making audio or video recordings of the interviews. Otherwise, take careful notes.

Avoid asking questions that can be answered with yes or no responses. Instead, try to ask questions that lead to new information, such as "How common was this expression?" or "How did your teachers and parents feel about the expression?"

Drafting

Review the tapes or notes of your interviews. Write down the expressions your interviewees discussed, and create definitions similar to the ones you and your partner created for your own expressions. Select the five most interesting expressions. Write a paragraph about each expression, discussing its meaning, uses, and origins. If possible, use your school's library or media center to conduct additional research into the origins of the expression. Conclude your examination of your elders' language by explaining what you have learned from your interviews.

Revising

Set your research and writing aside for a day or so. When you are ready to revise, read your draft aloud to a group of classmates and listen attentively to their feedback. Have you been clear? Are you missing any information? Evaluate the suggestions they give you and incorporate their advice into your draft.

Editing

Use the checklist on page C46 to polish your work.

Publishing

Consider the following ways to publish your work.
- Prepare a final copy of your work and read it to the class.
- Compile a class dictionary.
- Create a Website to share the expressions and invite others to E-mail you their words and phrases.
- Send a copy of your survey to the people you interviewed.

CHAPTER 16

Reference Skills

Reference skills allow you to find information in a variety of sources and turn unfamiliar subjects into familiar ones so you can write about them in interesting and informative ways. Of course you will need to use strong reference skills when you do research for a report, but you will need research skills for other types of writing, also.

For example, you may want to write a newspaper article persuading people to recycle newspapers, but you don't know enough hard facts. Research will make you an instant expert.

You will use research skills for fiction writing, too. Once you set a character in another country, another part of America, or another time, you will find yourself using reference works to fill in accurate details.

This chapter will take you further into the fascinating world of reference sources, both print and online.

Reading with a Writer's Eye

To write nonfiction articles, an author must use reference skills to gather facts and information. Then he or she must organize this information into a piece of writing that others can understand, learn from, and enjoy. The following selection is an excerpt from *The First Americans* by Joy Hakim. As you read the selection, think about what references the author might have explored to create this article.

FROM ___THE FIRST AMERICANS___

IN THE BEGINNING

Joy Hakim

Watch that band of people move across the plain. They look hungry and tired. The tribe is small, just twenty people in all, and only six are men of hunting age. But they are brave and their spears are sharp, so they will keep going. They follow the tracks of a mammoth.

If they can kill the mammoth—a huge, woolly elephant— they will feast for much of the winter.

The trail of the great animal leads them where no people have gone before. It leads them onto a wide, grassy earth bridge that stretches between two continents. They have come from Asia. When they cross that bridge they will be on land that someday will be called America. The trail of the mammoth leads them from Asia to a new world.

They don't realize what a big step they are taking. They don't know they are making history. All they know is that they have lost the mammoth. He has outsmarted them. But it doesn't matter; the new land is rich in animals and fish and berries. They will stay.

All that happened a long time ago, when families lived in huts and caves and the bow and arrow hadn't even been invented. It was a time when ice blankets—called *glaciers*— covered much of the northern land. We call it the Ice Age. Some of the glaciers were more than a mile high. Nothing man has built has been as tall.

If you look at a map, you will find the Bering Sea between Asia and Alaska. That is where the earth bridge used to be. It was quite a bridge. Today we call it Beringia, and it is under water. Back in the Ice Age, Beringia was a thousand miles wide. It had no trees, but was full of lakes and the kind of wild plants that drew animals. Men and women followed the animals: they settled on Beringia and lived there for generations. Not all the people were big-game hunters. Some were seagoers. They fished and caught small animals and lived near the beach. We think they were very good sailors. They had boats covered with animal skins, and they killed whales and explored and settled the coastline. Gradually these people—the land rovers and the seagoers—took that big step onto the new continent.

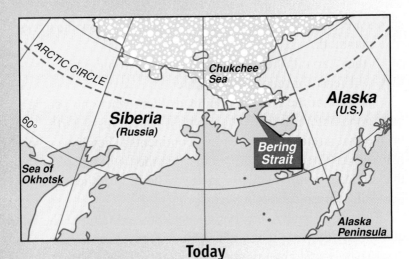

Today

Ice Age

Thinking as a Writer

Evaluating Information

- How would you describe the author's presentation of this information—is it like a story with characters and events, or does it present facts like a report? Write your ideas and explain why you think so.
- List a few facts that are presented. Speculate how the author might have gathered this information. Write a short paragraph to tell how you would find the information used to write this article.

Discussing the Use of Reference Materials

Oral Expression
- Talk with classmates about times when you've had to research a report. Describe what problems you encountered using reference materials. Then share your recollections of finding a source that led you to information that made your work a success.
- Think about how this article might have been different if it had not been researched. What would the article lack?

Comparing Visual and Print Information

Viewing
- Compare the two maps shown on the previous page. Both show part of the Northern Hemisphere.

If you had written this selection, which map would help you more? Explain your ideas. What information can you get from these maps that you didn't get from the selection? How does the information in the selection help you to better understand what you see in these maps? How do the maps help you to better understand the selection?

Developing Your Researching Skills

"They are ill discoverers that think there is no land, when they can see nothing but sea," wrote Francis Bacon in 1605 in his book *The Advancement of Learning*. Francis Bacon was an English philosopher who lived from 1561 to 1626. The quotation is a useful metaphor for the process of using reference skills to do research. Your topic is like the sea—a vast area waiting to be explored. At first it seems so challenging. There is no land in sight—no resources to guide your research. How do you start to explore this area? In what direction should you go? Eventually, with careful and dedicated searching, land appears in the form of reference materials—islands of knowledge, facts, and information that will be the foundation of your report.

This might sound like a dramatic way to think about using reference skills to do research, but the metaphor of exploration is a useful way to describe the research process. Researching the proper reference materials will help you discover, understand, and present information on topics that at first seemed so unfamiliar and challenging. *In the Beginning* shows how researching and becoming familiar with a topic enables a writer to produce an interesting and well-crafted article. With so many areas of information to explore, applying your reference skills should be considered an enjoyable part of the writing process, not an overwhelming challenge.

Your Writer's Journal

While visiting the library or media center or while reading newspapers and magazines during the week, you may come across new and interesting topics that stir your imagination. These topics can be anything you want to know more about—unique places, special people, moments in history, or scientific discoveries. Write each topic at the top of a separate page in your journal. As you go through this chapter, you'll be asked to use your new research skills to find references and information about some of your topics.

Using the Library or Media Center

In the past, when people thought about the library, they mostly thought of it as a place to find books. Today, however, most libraries operate as media centers where, in addition to books, you can find magazines, newspapers, and a wide range of reference materials in print, online, or in electronic formats. In addition to printed materials, libraries and media centers also carry nonprint materials, such as audio recordings, video documentaries, CD-ROM databases, photographic archives, and computers that provide access to the Internet and the World Wide Web. The library or media center is the best place to learn how to use reference materials and become a better researcher.

Most of the materials in a library or media center are arranged in four main sections: fiction, nonfiction, magazines and newspapers (or periodicals), and reference books.

Fiction

In many libraries or media centers, works of fiction, such as short stories and novels, are marked with the letters *FIC* or *F*. Books in the fiction section are arranged alphabetically by the authors' last names. In special cases, the following rules apply.

> **Guide for Finding Fiction**
>
> - Two-part names are alphabetized by the first part of the name. (**Mac**Donald, **O'**Connor, **Van** Dyke)
> - Names beginning with **Mc** or **St.** are alphabetized as if they began with **Mac** or **Saint**.
> - Books by authors with the same last name are alphabetized by the authors' first names.
> - Books by the same author are alphabetized by title, skipping the words *a, an,* or *the.*
> - Numbers in titles are alphabetized as if they were written out. (*50 = Fifty*)

Nonfiction

Nonfiction books are usually arranged according to the **Dewey decimal classification system,** developed by an American librarian named Melvil Dewey in the 1870s. In this system, each book is assigned a number known as a **call number** according to its subject. The same numbers apply to the same books in most libraries and media centers around the country. For example, a book on wolves by your favorite nature writer will carry almost the same call number in every library that owns it.

DEWEY DECIMAL SYSTEM

000–099 General Works (reference books)
100–199 Philosophy (psychology, ethics)
200–299 Religion
300–399 Social Science (law, education, economics)
400–499 Language
500–599 Natural Science (math, biology, chemistry)
600–699 Technology (engineering, business, health)
700–799 Fine Arts (painting, music, theater)
800–899 Literature (poetry, drama, essays)
900–999 History (biography, geography, travel)

Each main subject area has ten subdivisions. The subdivisions for science are as follows.

500–599 NATURAL SCIENCES

500–509	Pure Sciences	**550–559**	Earth Sciences
510–519	Mathematics	**560–569**	Paleontology
520–529	Astronomy	**570–579**	Anthropology
530–539	Physics	**580–589**	Botany
540–549	Chemistry	**590–599**	Zoology

The subdivisions of a main subject are further subdivided through the use of decimal numbers and letters. Together these numbers and letters form a book's **call number,** which is displayed on the book's spine. In addition to the call number, some works carry a special label to show the section of the library or media center in which they are shelved.

Biographies and Autobiographies

Biographies and autobiographies can usually be found in a separate section shelved in alphabetical order by the subject's last name rather than by the author's last name. Each book is labeled **B** for biography or **92** (a shortened form of the Dewey decimal subdivision 920), followed by the first letters of the subject's last name. A biography of Abraham Lincoln, for example, is labeled on the spine of the book in one of the following ways.

BIOGRAPHY	B	92
BEGINNING OF SUBJECT'S LAST NAME	Lin	Lin

The following chart lists other works that are often given special labels.

Categories	Special Labels
Biographies	B or 92
Juvenile Books	J or X
Reference Books	R or REF
Audiocassettes	AC

PRACTICE YOUR SKILLS

● *Using the Dewey Decimal System*

Using the list of classifications on page C662, write the subject numbers for each book. If the title is marked with an asterisk (*), also write the science subdivision.

EXAMPLE   *Chemistry Made Easy**

ANSWER   500–599, 540–549

1. *What to Listen For in Music*
2. *The Story of Speech and Language*
3. *Thinking Machines*
4. *Astronomy: The Cosmic Journey**
5. *Images of African Americans in Literature*
6. *Earth's Valuable Minerals**
7. *A Guide to Traveling Alone*
8. *Technology and the Future*
9. *Introduction to Geometry**
10. *Asimov on Physics**

Types of Catalogs

Even though most libraries or media centers have replaced their traditional card catalogs with online computer catalogs, many still have both types of card catalogs. The **traditional card catalog** is a cabinet of drawers filled with cards arranged in alphabetical order. Each drawer is labeled with several letters to show what part of the alphabet it contains. All books, fiction and nonfiction, have title and author cards. Nonfiction books, however, also have subject cards and sometimes cross-reference cards that tell you where additional information on the subject can be found.

All catalog entries give the same information: the book's title, author, and call number. Some may also give publication facts, indicate the book's page count, or show whether it contains illustrations or diagrams.

An **online catalog** is a computerized version of the card catalog, and it uses the same categories as the traditional card catalog. An online catalog, however, can locate information more quickly. Computer systems can vary from library to library, but generally the search methods are the same. To search the listings in an online catalog, you select a category to search—author, title, or subject. Authors' names are written last name first; for most titles, the words *A, An,* and *The* are omitted at the beginning of a title; and for subjects, searchers must enter the important words for each category.

On some systems, you can also do a keyword search, just as you would on an Internet search engine. A keyword search can search the library's collections by both title and subject headings at the same time. If the book you are looking for is not listed, or not available, the computer can tell you if it has been checked out and when it is due back. By using the Web to search other library databases, the librarian can also tell you if the book is available elsewhere.

If your book is available, the computer displays an entry similar to that in the following example:

ONLINE CATALOG RECORD	
Call Num.	KL 84-33
Author	Bradbury, Ray, 1920-
Title	The Martian Chronicles/by Ray Bradbury.
Imprint	Garden City, N.Y.: Doubleday & Company, c.1950
Location	Humanities–Rare Bks & Mss
Descript.	222 p.; 21 cm.
Series	[Doubleday science fiction]
Note	Printed at the Country Life Press, Garden City.
References	Tuck, D. H. Encyclopedia of Science Fiction, p. 62

While many libraries and media centers have computerized their traditional card catalogs, both cataloging systems are still used in most places.

For more information about searching online see <u>Strategies for Using an Online Catalog</u> on pages C672–C673.

Catalog Entries

A card in the card catalog will tell you where to find a book, but it cannot tell you if the book has been checked out. If a book is not on the shelf where it should be, you will need to ask the media specialist to help you locate it. Using the card catalog is a more time-consuming research method, but the cataloging system is still useful. Both computerized and traditional systems will give you the same information about a source, and both systems are equally precise. Most important, being familiar with the organization and categories of the card catalog will no doubt make you a better online researcher as well.

Each drawer in the card catalog is labeled to show what part of the alphabet it contains. Each nonfiction book has three cards listed in the following ways: by the author's last name, by the book's title, and by the subject.

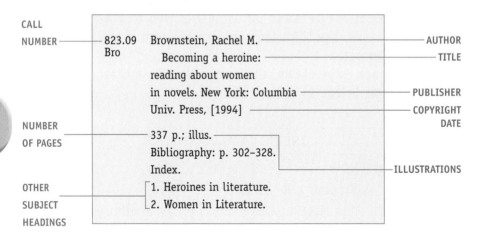

Author Cards   When you want to find books by a particular author, look under the author's last name in the card catalog.

If you searched for this author's name in an online catalog, you would probably get a list of several authors with the same last name. You might even get a list of several authors with the same first and last name. If the author wrote more than one book, you will see a full list of titles for that name. From that list, you would select the book you want, and you would see this information.
The following entry is from the Library of Congress online catalog. (The Library of Congress system is used by most colleges and universities. You do not need to know it in detail at this point, but you should be prepared to come across records that look like this.)

LC Control Number:	93042111
Type of Material:	Book (Print, Microform, Electronic, etc.)
Personal Name:	Brownstein, Rachel M.
Main Title:	Becoming a heroine: reading about women in novels/Rachel M. Brownstein.
Edition Information:	Columbia University Press Morningside ed.
Published/Created:	New York: Columbia University Press, c1994.
Description:	xxviii, 337 p. ; 23 cm.
ISBN:	0231100000 (acid-free paper)
Notes:	Includes bibliographical references (p. 302–328) and index.
Subjects:	Austen, Jane, 1775–1817—Characters—Women.
	English fiction—History and criticism.
	Heroines in literature.
	English fiction—Women authors—History and criticism.
	Women and literature—Great Britain—History.
	Women—Books and reading.
	Sex role in literature.

Series:	Women in literature. Gender and culture
LC Classification:	PR830.H4 B76 1994
Dewey Class No.:	823.009/352042 20
Geo. Area Code:	e=uk—
Call Number:	PR830.H4 B76 1994

Title Cards   When you know the title of the book, but not the author, you can find the book by looking up the title card. Title cards are alphabetized by the first word in the title, except for the words *A*, *An*, and *The*.

TITLE ——————————— ⌐Becoming a heroine

CALL
NUMBER —— 823.09   Brownstein, Rachel M. ————————— AUTHOR
           Bro   Becoming a heroine: reading ——————— TITLE
                  about women in novels.
PUBLISHER ——————— New York: Columbia Univ. Press, ——— COPYRIGHT
                  1994.   DATE

NUMBER
OF PAGES ———————— 332p.; illus. ———————————— ILLUSTRATIONS
                  Bibliography: p. 297–324.
                  Index.

If you searched for this book by title in an online catalog, you might get a list of several editions of the same book, depending on when it was first printed and how many times it was revised. If you knew the exact edition that you wanted, or if you wanted the most recent edition, this is what you would see. Note: some online catalogs often make one entry for each book. The same information is presented for every search category—author, title, or subject.

LC Control Number:	93042111
Type of material:	Book (Print, Microform, Electronic, etc.)
Personal name:	Brownstein, Rachel M.
Main Title:	Becoming a Heroine: Reading About Women in Novels/Rachel M. Brownstein.
Edition Information:	Columbia University Press Morningside ed.

Published/Created:	New York: Columbia University Press, c1994.
Description:	xxviii, 337 p.; 23 cm.
ISBN:	0231100000 (acid-free paper)
Notes:	Includes bibliographical references (p. 302–328) and index
Subjects:	Austen, Jane,1775–1817—Characters—Women.
	English fiction—History and criticism.
	Heroines in literature.
	English fiction—Women authors—History and criticism.
	Women and literature—Great Britain—History.
	Sex role in literature.
	Women in literature.
Series:	Gender and culture
LC Classification:	PR830.H4 B76 1994
Dewey Class No.:	823.009/352042 20
Geo. Area Code:	e=uk—
Call Number:	PR830.H4 B76 1994

Subject Cards   If you do not know the author of a book or its title, subject cards are particularly helpful. The subject is printed at the top of each card in capital letters. Subject cards are arranged alphabetically according to the first main word in the subject heading.

SUBJECT ———————————	WOMEN IN LITERATURE
CALL NUMBER ——— 823.09	Brownstein, Rachel M. ——————— AUTHOR
Bro	Becoming a heroine: reading ——— TITLE
	about women in novels.
PUBLISHER ——————— New York: Viking Press, 1982. ——— COPYRIGHT DATE
NUMBER OF PAGES ——— 332p.; illus. ——————————— ILLUSTRATIONS
	Bibliography: p.297–324
	Index.

Searching online by subject often produces more results than you actually need. The computer searches for keywords in the titles and descriptions of books simultaneously. If you searched for books on the subject *Women in Literature* as in the example above, you might get hundreds of titles. Limiting your search by year of publication or by more specific subject terms, such as *heroines in literature* or *English fiction—women authors,* will focus your search and produce results that may be more relevant and useful. A search of the Library of Congress's online catalog by *heroines in literature* produced 105 results, listed alphabetically, by the authors' last names. The three editions of Rachel Brownstein's book were listed along with others. If you selected the 1994 edition, you would see the same information that appears on pages C668–C669.

☐ 10	Heroines in literature	Batache-Watt, Émy.	Profils des héroïnes raciniennes / Émy Batache-Watt.	1976
☐ 11	Heroines in literature	Bedford, Herbert, 1867-1945.	Heroines of George Meredith.	1972
☐ 12	Heroines in literature	Bellman Nerozzi, Patrizia.	Virtù e malinconia : studi su Clarissa di Samuel Richardson / Patrizia Nerozzi Bellman.	1990
☐ 13	Heroines in literature	Bhatt¯ac¯arya, Dhruva.	Bhaktik¯al¯ina k¯avya mem n¯ayik¯a-bheda / Dhruva Bhattac¯arya.	1979
☐ 14	Heroines in literature	Botta, Gabriele.	Henry James' Heldinnen : fiktionale Gestaltung und pragmatische Ethik / Gabriele Botta.	1993
☐ 15	Heroines in literature	Brinsmead, Anne-Marie.	Strategies of resistance in Les liaisons dangereuses : heroines in search of "author-ity" / Anne-Marie Brinsmead.	1989
☐ 16	Heroines in literature	Brownstein, Rachel M.	Becoming a heroine : reading about women in novels / Rachel M. Brownstein.	1994
☐ 17	Heroines in literature	Brownstein, Rachel M.	Becoming a heroine : reading about women in novels / Rachel M. Brownstein.	1984
☐ 18	Heroines in literature	Brownstein, Rachel M.	Becoming a heroine : reading about women in novels / Rachel M. Brownstein.	1982
☐ 19	Heroines in literature	Cecil, Mirabel.	Heroines in love, 1750-1974 / Mirabel Cecil.	1974
☐ 20	Heroines in literature	Chance, Jane, 1945-	Woman as hero in Old English literature / Jane Chance.	1986
☐ 21	Heroines in literature	Chitnis, Bernice, 1942-	Reflecting on Nana / Bernice Chitnis.	1991
☐ 22	Heroines in literature	Chung, Ewha, 1966-	Samuel Richardson's new nation : paragons of the domestic sphere and "native" virtue / Ewha Chung.	1998
☐ 23	Heroines in literature	Clarke, Mary Cowden, 1809-1898.	Girlhood of Shakespeare's heroines: a series of fifteen tales. London, W. H. Smith, 1850-51.	1974
☐ 24	Heroines in literature	Coffin, Tristram Potter, 1922-	Female hero in folklore and legend / Tristram Potter Coffin.	1975

Cross-Reference Cards   In addition to three cards for each book, the catalog contains *See* and *See also* cards—also called **cross-reference cards**. A *See* card tells you that the subject you are looking for is under another heading. A *See also* card lists other subjects you could look up for additional titles.

Online versions of *See* and *See also* cards appear as text notes in the search results. When you enter a large category such as *literature*, the database will list several subcategories in alphabetical order. Cross-references appear when other search words are recommended.

Num	Mark	SUBJECTS (3218-3229 of 3411)	Entries 21166 Found
3218	☐	Literature Women Writers History And Criticism	1
3219	☐	Literature Woolf Virginia 1882-1941 Knowledge	10
3220	☐	Literature Wordsworth William 1770-1850 Knowledge	4
3221		Literature Work And Family -- see --Work And Family Literature	1
3222	☐	Literature Wuppertal Germany	1
3223		Literature Yearbooks -- see --Literature Periodicals	1
3224	☐	Literature Yeats W B William Butler 1865-1939 Knowledge	4
3225	☐	Literature Yeats W B William Butler 1865-1939 Knowledge Congresses	1
3226	☐	Literature Yevtushenko Yevgeny Aleksandrovich 1933- Knowledge	1
3227	☐	Literature Yugoslav 20th Century History And Criticism	1
3228	☐	Literature Yugoslav History And Criticism	1
3229	☐	Literature Yugoslavia	1

Strategies for Using a Traditional Card Catalog

- Think about the information you already have. Do you know the book's author? title? subject?
- Look for the book you want by finding the appropriate card.
- Read the card to determine if the book is likely to contain information that you need. Check the copyright to see how current the information is.
- In your **journal**, copy the call number, the title, the name of the author, (any information you don't already know), for each book you want to find.
- Use the call number located on the book's spine to find each book. The first line of the call number tells you which section of the library or media center to look in. Then find each book on a shelf by looking for its call number.

Strategies for Using an Online Catalog

- Think about what you already know that can limit your search. A title or author search will always give you more focused results than a subject search. If you are doing a subject search, find a way to limit the category, either by year or by subcategory.

Searching by Author's Name

- If the last name is common, type the author's complete last name followed by a comma and a space and the author's first initial or complete first name.
- Omit all accent marks and other punctuation in the author's name.
- For compound names, try variations in placement of the parts:

  von during klaus   or   **during klaus von**

Searching by Title

- If the title is long, type only the first few words. Omit capitalization, punctuation, accent marks, and article words such as *A*, *An*, and *The*.

  color pur (you need not include the full title)

  great gatsby (omit initial article words)

  going going gone (omit punctuation)

- If you are unsure of the correct form of a word, try variations such as spelling out or inserting spaces between initials and abbreviations; entering numbers as words; using an ampersand (&) for *and*; spelling hyphenated words as one or two words.

Searching by Subject

- Omit commas, parentheses, and capitalization.
- Broad categories can be divided into subcategories to make your search more specific.
- If you don't know the correct subject heading, find at least one source relevant to your topic by doing a title or keyword search. Use one or more of the subject headings listed there for additional searches.

Searching by Keyword

- Searching with a single word, such as *literature,* will find that word anywhere in the entry: in the title, author, subject, or descriptive notes.

- A phrase, such as *power plants*, finds entries containing the words *power* and *plants*. To search for *power plants* as a phrase, type *power and plants*, or *power adj plants* (adj = adjacent).

- An open search will look anywhere in the entry for your word. You can limit your keyword searches to specific search fields, such as author, title, or subject, by checking the key-word menu and selecting the appropriate field.

COMPUTER TIP

You can also limit your search by using the Boolean search terms (*and, or, not*):

and searches for several terms anywhere in the same entry

or searches for any or all of the terms in the same entry

not searches for the first term and will match the words only if the second word is NOT in the same entry

PRACTICE YOUR SKILLS

● *Using Catalog Cards*

Using the catalog card below, write the answers to the questions on the next page.

574.92	Cousteau, Jacques Yves
Cou	The ocean world. New York:
	H. N. Abrams [1985]
	44 p.; illus.
	1. Marine Biology 2. Ocean

1. Is the catalog card an author card, a subject card, or a title card?

2. Who is the author of this book?

3. What is the call number for this book?

4. Who is the publisher?

5. What is the copyright date?

6. How many pages does this book have?

7. Does the book contain illustrations?

8. Under what letter would you look to find the title card?

9. Would the title card *Dolphins: Playful Mammals of the Sea* be filed before or after the title card for this book?

10. Under what two subject headings is this book filed?

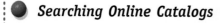 **Searching Online Catalogs**

Write the category you would select for a search on the following items. Then write the words that you would enter to find each item.

1. the life of Frank Lloyd Wright
2. the books of Charles Dickens
3. the art of sculpting
4. *The Sun Also Rises*
5. the fastest airplane
6. *The Best of Times*
7. the skill of public speaking
8. modern architecture
9. the works of Willa Cather
10. migration patterns of birds

Parts of a Book

The first step in the research process is to find sources that can help you with your project. Once you find several sources, you need to spend some time looking through them to see if they have any information that you can use. Books have features that can make finding this information easier if you know how to use the parts of a book effectively.

INFORMATION IN PARTS OF A BOOK

TITLE PAGE	shows the full title, author's name, publisher, and place of publication
COPYRIGHT PAGE	gives the date of first publication and dates of any revised editions
TABLE OF CONTENTS	lists chapter or section titles in the book and their starting page numbers
INTRODUCTION	gives an overview of the ideas in each chapter and to the work that other writers have done on the subject
APPENDIX	gives additional information on subjects in the book; charts, graphs, and maps are sometimes included here
GLOSSARY	lists, in alphabetical order, difficult or technical words found in the book and their definitions
BIBLIOGRAPHY	lists sources that the author used to write the book, including title and copyright information for works on related topics
INDEX	lists, in alphabetical order, topics that are mentioned in the book and gives the page numbers where these topics can be found

PRACTICE YOUR SKILLS

 *Using Parts of a Book*

Write the part of the book you would use to find each of the following items of information.

1. the year of publication

2. the author's explanation of the book's contents

3. the title of a specific chapter

4. the name and publication information for a source used by the author

5. a chart or graph with additional information

6. the name and location of the publisher

7. a specific topic or person mentioned in the book

8. definition of a difficult or technical word

 ## Using Print and Nonprint Reference Materials

Most libraries or media centers keep current reference materials in a separate section because these materials cannot be checked out. Following is a review of the kinds of reference materials you may find most helpful.

 Print and Electronic References

- encyclopedias and dictionaries
- atlases and almanacs
- specialized biographical and literary references
- online indexes to periodicals (including magazines, newspapers, and journals)
- CD-ROM versions of specialized encyclopedias, dictionaries, and almanacs
- microfilm and microfiche files of periodicals and government documents
- computer terminals with access to the Internet and World Wide Web
- audio recordings and video documentaries

Readers' Guide to Periodical Literature

Periodicals, including magazines and journals, are excellent sources for current information. The complete *Readers' Guide to Periodical Literature* is an index of articles, short stories, and poems published in more than 175 magazines and journals that is usually issued in paperback form twice a month. Many libraries and media centers subscribe to the abridged *Readers' Guide*, which indexes about 60 magazines. The guides are arranged by year and can be found in print or in an online database. Articles are listed in alphabetical order by subject and by author. Following are examples of entries from print and online versions of the *Readers' Guide*. Note: to include more information in an entry, abbreviations may be used. These abbreviations are explained at the front of each volume. In the entry below, *Bus Week* stands for *Business Week*; *il* stands for *illustrated*; and *Ag* stands for *August*.

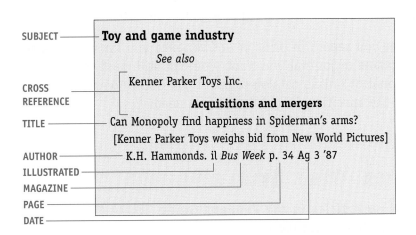

The *Readers' Guide* online is organized like a computer catalog. Searches can be done by author, title, or subject. If you entered the words *toy and game industry* for a subject search, a list of entries would appear. In each entry, the following information will appear.

NUMBER:	BRGA98064251
AUTHOR:	Morris, Kathleen.
TITLE:	The Pall Over Toyland.
SOURCE:	Business Week no. 3598 (Oct. 5 '98) p. 50 il.
STANDARD NO:	0007–7135
DATE:	1998
RECORD TYPE:	art
CONTENTS:	feature article
ABSTRACT:	Children's declining interest in toys, combined with a lack of top products, could make this a gloomy year for toy manufacturers. Arcadia Research analyst John Taylor observes that toy

companies have failed this year to come up with a sufficient number of exciting toys that are capable of bringing consumers into the stores. In addition, toy companies fear that kids are losing their interest in toys sooner than before, preferring Spice Girls CDs, clothes, and video games.

SUBJECT: Toy and game industry—Marketing.

Whether you search in print or online, once you know the name of the magazine or journal you want, you will still need to check the traditional or online catalog to see if the library or media center has the specific periodical that you need.

Practice Your Skills

⬤ *Locating Articles in the* Readers' Guide *to Periodical Literature*

Using the *Readers' Guide,* list two recent magazine articles on four of the following subjects. List the title of the article, the name of the magazine in which each article can be found, the date of publication, and the pages on which the article can be found.

1. architecture	**6.** land speed records
2. classical music	**7.** air travel
3. laptop computers	**8.** video games
4. solar energy	**9.** the North Pole
5. U.S. rivers	**10.** rain forests

Newspapers

Newspapers are valuable sources of current and historical information. The periodical reading room in the library or media center should have the most recent print issues of all the newspapers to which the library subscribes. To save space, most libraries store older issues of newspapers as photographic reproductions of print pages on rolls or sheets of film. These materials are located in another part of the library or media center and can be viewed on special projectors.

To learn more about using these microform archives, see <u>Microforms</u> on page C687.

Searching online gives you a few more options for finding newspaper articles. If a particular newspaper is available, a title search in the computer catalog will tell you where it is located— either in the reading room or on microform. Newspapers on photographic film are assigned call numbers that are listed in the catalog. A title search may also show you a hyperlink with an Internet address for the current newspaper's home page.

Most major newspapers now have Websites and electronic databases where you can view current issues and search for archived articles. The following examples are only a few of the many available online.

The Dallas Morning News	<u>http://www.dallasnews.com</u>
The Los Angeles Times	<u>http://www.latimes.com</u>
The Chicago Tribune	<u>http://www.chicago.tribune.com</u>
The New York Times	<u>http://www.nytimes.com</u>
The Miami Herald	<u>http://www.herald.com</u>

By going directly to the Web, you can also search databases that locate and access the home pages of newspapers from every state in the U.S. and many countries around the world.

Both of the following sites list hundreds of newspapers by location (country and state) and by subject (business, arts and entertainment, trade journals, or college papers).

THE INTERNET PUBLIC LIBRARY	<u>http://www.ipl.org/reading/news</u>
NEWSPAPERS ONLINE!	<u>http://www.newspapers.com</u>

By using a news service, you can search the databases of hundreds of newspapers, periodicals, and other documents at the same time. Check with the media specialist to see if your library or media center subscribes to these news services.

| LEXIS-NEXIS | http://www.lexis-nexis.com/lncc |
| PROQUEST | http://www.umi.com.au |

Remember: always read the guidelines at the home page for each newspaper or news service. Recent articles are usually available free of charge, but you may have to pay a fee to download and print an archived article.

Encyclopedias

Encyclopedias provide basic information on a wide variety of subjects. These subjects are arranged alphabetically in a number of volumes. An encyclopedia is a good reference to start with when you begin to collect information for a report. Two general encyclopedias are *Collier's Encyclopedia* and *Encyclopaedia Britannica*. Several general encyclopedias are also available on CD-ROM and online. These can be used to look up information just as you would with any other published encyclopedia.

PRINT	*Collier's Encyclopedia*
	Encyclopaedia Britannica
CD-ROM	*Encarta Encyclopedia Deluxe Edition*
	The World Book Multimedia
	Encyclopedia Deluxe Edition
	Compton's Interactive Encyclopedia
ONLINE	http://www.encyclopedia.com

Specialized Encyclopedias

Specialized encyclopedias are available on almost every subject. For example, most libraries or media centers have the *Encyclopedia of Mythology* and *The Baseball Encyclopedia*. Because a specialized encyclopedia concentrates on a specific subject area, it provides more detailed information on that subject than you will find in a general encyclopedia. Specialized encyclopedias online let you search for information by subject and connect to other Websites on your topic through hyperlinks. *The Encyclopedia Smithsonian* online, for example, covers topics in physical sciences, social sciences, and U.S. and natural history.

PRINT *Encyclopedia of Mythology*
The Baseball Encyclopedia
The Encyclopedia for American Facts and Dates
The International Encyclopedia of the
Social Sciences

ONLINE *Encyclopedia Smithsonian*
http://www.si.edu/resource/faq/start.htm
The World eText Library
http://www.netlibrary.net/WorldReferenceE. html
Includes: *Arts and Leisure Encyclopedia,*
Techweb/Technology Encyclopedia, and the
Britannica Internet Guide

Biographical References

Information about famous people of the past and of the present may be found in biographical reference books. Some biographical references contain only a paragraph of facts about each person, while others, such as *Current Biography*, contain long articles. The following excerpt about the American writer Maya Angelou is from *Who's Who in America* 1997.

ANGELOU, MAYA, author; b. St. Louis, Apr. 4, 1928: d. Bailey and Vivian (Baxter); 1 son, Guy Johnson. Studied dance with Pearl Primus, N.Y.C.; hon. Degrees, Smith Coll., 1975, Mills Coll., 1975, Lawrence U., 1976. Taught modern dance The Rome Opera House and Hambina Theatre, Tel Aviv; writer-in-residence U. Kans.-Lawrence, 1970: disting. vis. prof. Wake Forest U., 1974, Wichita State U., 1974, Calif. State U.-Sacramento, 1974: apptd. mem. Am. Revolution Bicentennial Council by Pres. Ford, 1975-76; 1st Reynolds prof. Am. Studies, Wake Forest U. since 1981, a lifetime appointment. Author: I Know Why the Caged Bird Sings, 1970. Just Give Me A Cool Drink of Water 'Fore I Die, 1971. Georgia, Georgia, 1972. Gather Together in My Name, 1974. Oh Pray My Wings are Gonna Fit Me Well, 1975. Singin' and Swingin' and Getting' Merry Like Christmas, 1976. And Still I Rise, 1978. The Heart of a Woman, 1981. Shaker, Why Don't You Sing?, 1983. All God's Children Need Traveling Shoes, 1986. Now Sheba Sings the Song, 1987. I Shall Not Be Moved, 1990. On the Pulse of Morning: The Inaugural Poem, 1992. Lessons in Living, 1993. Wouldn't Take Nothing for My Journey Now, 1993. My Painted House, My Friendly Chicken, and Me, 1994. The Complete Collected Poems of Maya Angelou, 1994 . . .

Other biographical references include important basic information, such as date of birth, education, occupation, and the person's accomplishments, and may have longer entries describing the person's life in more detail, depending on their focus. Several online and CD-ROM resources, in particular, document the lives of women and African Americans in U.S. history, and some multimedia versions contains film clips and audio recordings of important historical events.

PRINT	*Who's Who* and *Who's Who in America* *Current Biography* *Dictionary of American Biography* *Dictionary of National Biography* *Webster's Biographical Dictionary* *American Men and Women of Science*
MULTIMEDIA CD-ROM	*Her Heritage: A Biographical Encyclopedia of Famous American Women*
ONLINE	*Distinguished Women of Past and Present* http://www.netsrq.com *Encyclopaedia Britannica Guide to Black History* http://www.blackhistory.eb.com

References About Language and Literature

For your English class, you may need to consult reference books specifically about language and literature. Following are examples.

| SPECIALIZED DICTIONARIES | *Webster's New Dictionary of Synonyms*
Dictionary of Literary Terms |
| SPECIALIZED ENCYCLOPEDIAS | *Cassell's Encyclopedia of World Literature;*
Reader's Encyclopedia of American Literature |

Handbooks, or companions, are another kind of literary reference. Some handbooks give plot summaries or describe characters. Others explain literary terms or give information about authors. For example, most libraries or media centers have *The Oxford Companion to American Literature* and *The Oxford Companion to English Literature.*

Books of quotations, such as *Bartlett's Familiar Quotations*, tell you the source of a particular quotation. These books also list complete quotations as well as other quotations on the same subject.

Indexes are useful for finding a particular poem, short story, or play. An index such as *Granger's Index to Poetry* lists the books that contain the particular selection you are looking for.

On CD-ROM, *The Columbia Granger's World of Poetry* tells you where to find specific poems indexed by subject, title, and first line; and the *Gale Literary Index* contains information about authors and their major works.

Atlases

These books of maps present information about the regions of the world. Special-purpose maps and tables may show a region's physical geography, cities, population, climate, industries, natural resources, and systems of transportation. Historical atlases show maps of the world during different periods of history. In addition, some specialized atlases focus on the geography and history of a specific country or state. *Goode's World Atlas* and *The Times Atlas of the World* are found in most libraries. Some online resources from the U.S. Geological Survey incorporate satellite imagery to let you examine the geography of the U.S. by state and by region.

PRINT	*Goode's World Atlas*
	The Times Atlas of the World
	Rand McNally International World Atlas
	The National Geographic Atlas of the World
	Rand McNally Atlas of World History
ONLINE	*U.S. Geological Survey*
	http://www.nationalatlas.gov/mapit.html

Almanacs and Yearbooks

Because almanacs and yearbooks are published once a year, they are reliable sources for current information on a wide range of subjects, as well as for information about famous people, unusual achievements, and sports. *The Information Please Almanac* and the *Guinness Book of World Records* are two widely used almanacs. Almanacs also provide historical facts and geographic information. Some, such as *The Old Farmer's Almanac,* focus on weather-related and seasonal information.

PRINT	*Information Please Almanac*
	Guinness Book of World Records
	World Almanac and Book of Facts
ONLINE	*The Old Farmer's Almanac*
	http://www.almanac.com

Specialized Dictionaries

When you do research on topics that are new to you, you will often encounter words you do not know. A specialized dictionary, one that focuses on a particular field of study, will be of great help to you. You can find specialized dictionaries for many topics, such as music, medicine, science, and social sciences. Some online sites include dictionaries in several languages and excerpts from guidebooks on writing.

PRINT
Harvard Dictionary of Music
Concise Dictionary of American History
Webster's New Geographical Dictionary

ONLINE
English and foreign language dictionaries and excerpts from *MLA Handbook for Writers of Research Papers*
http://www.dictionary.com
Strunk's Elements of Style
http://www.bartleby.com/141/index.html

Books of Synonyms

Another type of dictionary, called a **thesaurus**, features synonyms (different words with the same meanings) and antonyms (words with opposite meanings). This resource is especially helpful if you are looking for a specific word or if you want to vary your word usage and build your vocabulary.

PRINT
Roget's Thesaurus in Dictionary Form
Webster's New Dictionary of Synonyms
Funk and Wagnall's Standard Handbook of Synonyms, Antonyms, & Prepositions

ONLINE
Roget's Thesaurus
http://www.thesaurus.com

PRACTICE YOUR SKILLS

● *Using Literary References*

Write one kind of reference work about language and literature that you could use to find the answer to each question.

EXAMPLE What collections of poetry contain Robert Frost's "The Road Not Taken"?

POSSIBLE ANSWER index to poetry

1. What does the term *unreliable narrator* mean?

2. Who defined a coward as "One who in a perilous emergency thinks with his legs"?

3. What was the real name of George Eliot, a British novelist?

4. Where could you find the short story "A Bottle of Milk for Mother" by Nelson Algren?

5. What is a synonym for *determine*?

6. Which play contains the line "Parting is such sweet sorrow"?

7. How many books did the American author Ralph Ellison write?

8. In what collections is the play *Pygmalion* published?

9. J. D. Salinger is a twentieth-century American author. What do the initials J. D. stand for?

10. What is the meaning of the term *denouement*?

Other Reference Materials

Most libraries and media centers have a variety of printed materials that are not found in bound form. They also have other nonprint resources such as audio recordings and video documentaries that contain information that cannot be conveyed in print form.

Vertical Files   Libraries often store pamphlets, catalogs, and newspaper clippings alphabetically in a filing cabinet called the **vertical file.** Materials are stored in folders in file cabinets and arranged alphabetically by subject.

Microforms   Many libraries and media centers save storage space by storing some documents and back issues of periodicals on **microfilm** and **microfiche**—photographic reproductions of printed material that are stored on rolls or sheets of film. References stored on microforms usually include past issues of newspapers, magazines, journals, and other periodicals; government documents from state and federal agencies; and original, historic records and papers.

These rolls and sheets of film are stored in filing cabinets in another part of the library or media center and can be viewed easily on special projectors. Newspapers, for example, are arranged in file drawers alphabetically by keywords in their titles. The holdings for each newspaper are then filed chronologically by date. For example, if you wanted to know what happened in Houston, Texas, on New Year's Eve in the year you were born, you could go to the file cabinets and get the roll of film for the *Houston Chronicle* on that day in that year.

Audio, Video, CD-ROM   Audiovisual materials and CD-ROMs can be valuable sources of information and are often available through your library or media center. Audiovisual materials may include recordings of interviews and speeches, and videotapes of documentaries and educational programs. If you cannot check out these materials to view in the classroom, listening and viewing equipment is usually available in the library. The CD-ROM format also makes it possible to include multimedia features like audio recordings and video clips on the disc itself. Many CD-ROMs also contain reliable hyperlinks and working Internet software that allow you to connect to Websites with more information about each subject. The CD-ROM collection of your library or media center may include specialized indexes and databases, as well as references such as *Encarta* and *Compton's* encyclopedias and specialized dictionaries such as the complete *Oxford English Dictionary*. Check with the media specialist to see which resources are available in these forms.

PRACTICE YOUR SKILLS

● *Using References*

Write one kind of reference work—other than a general encyclopedia—that would contain information about each subject.

1. magazine articles about the 1996 presidential election
2. famous young Americans
3. Olympic records in track and field events
4. location of active volcanoes in North America
5. college catalogs
6. the meaning of the term *allegro* in music
7. the name and location of the capital of Hawaii
8. pamphlets on museum exhibits
9. information about a scientific discovery this year
10. information about a Supreme Court justice

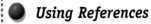

Time Out to Reflect

How does the Internet compare to some of the print resources you have used in terms of access, quality, and reliability? Why might one form—print or online—be better than another? What have you learned that will make researching easier later in print resources and online? What notes would you make to improve your reference skills for the future? Record your thoughts in the Learning Log section of your **journal.**

Across the Media: Advertisement or Not?

As you turn to reference sources, pay close attention to the kinds of articles you rely on for accurate information. Why were the articles created? Is their main purpose to inform, to entertain, or to persuade?

In print media such as encyclopedias or other reference books, the purpose is usually informative. Nonfiction books may have the dual purpose of informing and entertaining.

Sometimes, though, it is hard to tell for sure what the writing purpose is. Suppose, for example, that you are researching health fads. You find a book that argues that a certain herb will cure colds. You later find out that the author has a business interest in a company selling that herb. The writing purpose suddenly seems less clear. Is the book really one long commercial?

On the Internet, the distinctions among the different types of writing—and graphic presentations—are sometimes even harder to see. No one monitors the Internet to make sure only well-researched, accurate pieces are published. Almost anyone with a bit of coding skill and an Internet connection can publish something on the World Wide Web.

Using sources from the Internet, then, requires you to be very clear about their purposes. "Who wrote this, why, and when?" are the questions you should ask about every site from which you you plan to use information. There are many high-quality sites that will stand up well under this scrutiny.

Search the Internet for information on the subject of your research report or a related subject. Find and save (either electronically or by printing out) a piece of writing and one graphic in the following categories: informative, entertainment, and advertising.

Write a paragraph to a first-time Web user explaining how you knew the difference among these types.

Developing Your Word-Search Skills

Some of the most important elements of effective writing are proper spelling, word choice, and usage. The dictionary is your best resource if you need help in any of these areas.

Using the Dictionary

Most libraries have a large **unabridged** dictionary that sits on a stand in the reference section. Unabridged, or unshortened, dictionaries usually contain more than half a million words and have long, complete definitions. Smaller dictionaries are **abridged** (shortened), **college**, or **school dictionaries**.

Information in an Entry

You will probably use a dictionary most often to check the spelling, pronunciation, or meaning of a word. However, diction-aries contain much additional information. Through the use of symbols and abbreviations, dictionaries also tell the history of a word, its division into syllables, its part or parts of speech, its usage in idioms, and its synonyms or antonyms.

The word itself is called an **entry word**. All the information about each word entry is called a **main entry**. The following list shows the different kinds of entry words and how they would be listed in alphabetical order in the dictionary.

HYPHENATED WORD	ill-humored
COMPOUND WORD	ion exchange
SUFFIX	–ious
ABBREVIATION	IQ
PREFIX	ir–

| SINGLE WORD | iris |
| PROPER NOUN | Iron Age |

Writing Tip

The entries in this section came from the *American Heritage Dictionary* which is available on CD-ROM, and online at **http://www.ohiolink.edu/db/ahd.html**.

Preferred and Variant Spellings   The entry word, printed in heavy type at the beginning of each main entry, shows the correct spelling of a word. When words can be spelled in more than one way, the most commonly used spelling, called the **preferred spelling**, is listed first. Less common spellings, called **variants**, follow. In some cases a variant spelling may be listed as a separate entry that does not include a full definition. For the complete information, the entry refers you to the preferred spelling of the word. Always use the preferred spelling of words in your writing.

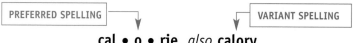

PREFERRED SPELLING   VARIANT SPELLING

cal • o • rie, *also* **calory**

PRACTICE YOUR SKILLS

● *Finding Preferred Spellings*

Using a dictionary, find the variant spelling of each word. Then write the preferred spelling.

1. theatre   **3.** moveable   **5.** chaperone
2. judgement   **4.** practise

Syllable Division of Words   The entry words in a dictionary show how to break words into syllables.

phe • nom • e • non   grad • u • ate   dy • nam • ic

Pronunciation   Following the entry word is the phonetic spelling of that word, which shows you how to pronounce the word.

com·put·er·ize (kəm-pyo͞o′tə-rīz′) *tr.v.* **-ized, -iz·ing, -iz· es.** *Usage Problem.* **1.** To furnish with a computer or computer system. **2.** To enter, process, or store (information) in a computer or system of computers. See Usage Note at **—ize. —com·put′- er·iz′a·ble** *adj.* **—com·put′er·i·za′tion** (-pyo͞o′tər-ĭ-zā′- shən) *n.*

A listing of phonetic symbols is at the beginning of a dictionary. Most dictionaries also provide a partial pronunciation key at the bottom of every other page.

PARTIAL PRONUNCIATION KEY

Symbols	Examples	Symbols	Examples
ă	pat	oi	boy
ā	pay	ou	out
âr	care	o͝o	took
ä	father	o͞o	boot
ĕ	pet	ŭ	cut
ē	be	ûr	urge
ĭ	pit	th	thin
ī	pie	*th*	this
îr	pier	hw	which
ŏ	pot	zh	vision
ō	toe	ə	about, item
ô	paw		

Stress Marks: ′(primary), ′(secondary) as in dĭk′ shənĕr′ ē

To find out how to pronounce the vowel in the second syllable of the word *computerize*, for example, look for the symbol o͞o in the pronunciation key. You can see that it is pronounced like the *oo* in *boot*.

To distinguish one vowel sound from another, phonetic spellings include diacritical marks above the vowels. The letter *u*, for instance, can be pronounced three different ways.

ŭ as in *cup*   o͝o as in *put*   o͞o as in *rule*

The letter *u* and other vowels are sometimes pronounced *uh*. This sound is represented by the symbol ə, called the *schwa*. In the word *computerize*, both the o and the first e are pronounced *uh*. A schwa is used in the phonetic spelling to represent this sound.

kəm pyo͞o′ tə rīz′

Phonetic spellings also have accent marks to show which syllables are stressed in pronunciation. A heavy accent mark, called a **primary stress**, shows which syllable in the word receives the most emphasis. **Secondary stresses** are marked with a lighter accent.

kəm pyo͞o′ tə rīz′

If a word can be pronounced more than one way, the dictionary will show both pronunciations. The first one shown, however, is preferred. In some dictionaries, only the parts of a word that differ in an alternate pronunciation are given.

da • ta (dā′ tə, dăt′ə, dä′tə)

pro • gram (prō′ grăm′, -grəm)

By permission. From *The American Heritage Dictionary*, Third Edition. © 1996 by Houghton Mifflin Company.

Phonetic symbols and the placement of accent marks differ from dictionary to dictionary. Check the front of your dictionary to see what symbols are used in pronunciation.

PRACTICE YOUR SKILLS

● *Using a Pronunciation Key*

Using the pronunciation key on page C692, write the word in Column B that matches each phonetic spelling in Column A.

Column A	Column B
1. ə māz´	subside
2. är´ jōō əs	caucus
3. ö dā´ shəs	quadrant
4. kö´ kəs	writhe
5. ek´ sə kyōōt	amaze
6. eg zil´ ə rāt´	arduous
7. in ö´ gyə rāt´	execute
8. kwod´ rənt	inaugurate
9. səb sīd´	audacious
10. rīth	exhilarate

Part-of-Speech Labels   Each word entry in a dictionary also contains an abbreviation that indicates what parts of speech the word can be. Because some words can function as more than one part of speech, some entries will contain several part-of-speech labels.

n. = noun		*tr. v.* = transitive verb
pron. = pronoun		*intr. v.* = intransitive verb
adj. = adjective		*prep.* = preposition
adv. = adverb		*conj.* = conjunction
v. = verb		*interj.* = interjection

Multiple Meanings   Many words have more than one meaning. Most dictionaries list the most common meaning first, although some list the meanings in historical order, showing the oldest meaning first.

Dictionaries use **restrictive labels** to help explain differences in meaning. These labels restrict a given definition to a particular subject area, dialect, or usage—such as *informal* or *slang*. The last part of an entry is often a list of synonyms—with an explanation of their different shades of meaning.

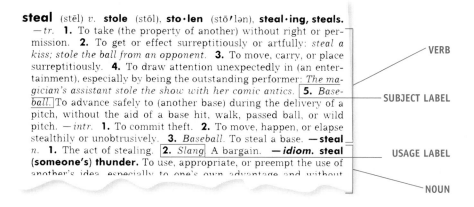

steal (stēl) *v.* **stole** (stōl), **sto·len** (stō′lən), **steal·ing, steals.**
— *tr.* **1.** To take (the property of another) without right or permission. **2.** To get or effect surreptitiously or artfully: *steal a kiss; stole the ball from an opponent.* **3.** To move, carry, or place surreptitiously. **4.** To draw attention unexpectedly in (an entertainment), especially by being the outstanding performer: *The magician's assistant stole the show with her comic antics.* **5.** *Baseball.* To advance safely to (another base) during the delivery of a pitch, without the aid of a base hit, walk, passed ball, or wild pitch. — *intr.* **1.** To commit theft. **2.** To move, happen, or elapse stealthily or unobtrusively. **3.** *Baseball.* To steal a base. — **steal** *n.* **1.** The act of stealing. **2.** *Slang.* A bargain. — *idiom.* **steal (someone's) thunder.** To use, appropriate, or preempt the use of another's idea, especially to one's own advantage and without

VERB

SUBJECT LABEL

USAGE LABEL

NOUN

By permission. From *The American Heritage Dictionary*, Third Edition. © 1996 by Houghton Mifflin Company.

Practice Your Skills

● *Recognizing Multiple Meanings*

Use the previous entry to write the part of speech of the word *steal* **as it is used in each sentence. Then write the number of the definition that matches that use of the word.**

EXAMPLE   Who stole the last piece of pie?

ANSWER   transitive verb, 2.

1. Do you think the runner on first will try to steal second base?

2. You bought that dress for 20 dollars? It was a steal!

3. The rock star, hoping that no one would recognize him, stole out of the store through a side exit.

4. Debra claimed that James stole her pen while she wasn't looking.

5. All the reviewers agreed that the new actress stole the show from her more experienced costars.

Inflected Forms and Derived Words The dictionary shows endings, or inflections, that change the form of the word but not its part of speech. Verbs, for example, can be inflected with *–ed* or *–ing* to change the principal part of the verb. Adjectives can be inflected with *–er* or *–est* to show comparative and superlative degrees. Nouns have plural forms, but most dictionaries show only those plural forms that are formed irregularly.

Derived words are made by adding endings that change the part of speech of a word. For example, by adding the suffix *–ment* to the verb *resent*, the noun *resentment* is formed. Most dictionaries list derived words at the end of a main entry.

en·vy (ĕn′vē) *n., pl.* **-vies.** **1.a.** A feeling of discontent and resentment aroused by and in conjunction with desire for the possessions or qualities of another. **b.** The object of such feeling: *Their new pool made them the envy of their neighbors.* **2.** Obsolete. Malevolence. **—envy** *tr.v.* **-vied, -vy·ing, -vies.** **1.** To feel envy toward. **2.** To regard with envy. [Middle English *envie*, from Old French, from Latin *invidia*, from *invidus*, envious, from *invidēre*, to look at with envy : *in-*, in, on; see EN–¹ + *vidēre*, to see; see **weid-** in Appendix. V., from Middle English *envien*, from Old French *envier*, from Latin *invidēre*.] **—en′vi·er** *n.* **—en′-vy·ing·ly** *adv.*

> IRREGULAR PLURAL
> INFLECTED FORMS
> DERIVED WORD

By permission. From *The American Heritage Dictionary*, Third Edition. © 1996 by Houghton Mifflin Company.

Etymologies A dictionary gives the etymology, or history, of a word. The etymology is usually explained in an entry through the use of abbreviations and symbols, or with the word *from*. The abbreviations stand for languages from which the word developed. The symbol <, or the word *from*, stands for such phrases as *derived from*, and = stands for *equivalent to*. A chart at the beginning of the dictionary lists all the abbreviations and symbols used in showing the etymology of a word. In an etymology, the most recent source of the word is listed first.

pa·tri·ot (pā′trē-ət, -ŏt′) *n.* One who loves, supports, and defends one's country. [French *patriote*, from Old French, compatriot, from Late Latin *patriōta*, from Greek *patriōtēs*, from *patrios*, of one's fathers, from *patēr, patr-*, father. See **peter-** in Appendix.]

> ETYMOLOGY

By permission. From *The American Heritage Dictionary*, Third Edition. © 1996 by Houghton Mifflin Company.

The etymology of *patriot* can be translated as follows: The modern word *patriot* comes from the Old French *patriote*, which meant *compatriot*. The Old French word was derived from the Late Latin *patriōta*, which came from the Greek *patriōtēs*. The Greek word *patriōtēs* was derived from *patris*, meaning *fatherland*, which in turn came from *pāter, meaning father*.

PRACTICE YOUR SKILLS

● *Tracing Word Origins*

Use the dictionary to find the etymology of each word. Write the etymology.

1.	brave	**6.**	comedy
2.	chariot	**7.**	mob
3.	infant	**8.**	rebel
4.	comet	**9.**	calisthenics
5.	eccentric	**10.**	shambles

Time Out to Reflect

Think about the different references you used in this chapter. Now that you have used different forms of the same references, including published and online versions of dictionaries and encyclopedias, how do they compare? Which do you feel was easier to use, and better organized? Which form had more of the information you needed? What notes would you make to yourself to make your researching easier in the future? Record your thoughts in the Learning Log section of your **journal.**

A Writer's Guide to Electronic Publishing

Using the Internet, your local media center, plus E-mail and other research sources, you can gather an abundant amount of data to help you create a well-developed article or an up-to-date report. Once all your material is written and organized, the question you will want to ask yourself is, How can I publish my information?

Years ago, your options might have been limited to using text from a typewriter, photos and glue, construction paper, and art materials. Today the world of electronic publishing has opened a world of options. Depending on the nature of your project, some of the choices open to you include desktop publishing, audio and video recordings, and online publishing on the World Wide Web.

Each of these communication methods has unique advantages and drawbacks. Some media are more suitable to certain types of projects. For example, a visual topic, such as information about bonsai trees, might be better expressed as a video. Reports with numerous facts, figures, and graphs might be better served in a document. An opinion poll in which many people are interviewed might lend itself well to an audio recording. And a subject that branches off into many different areas, such as a presentation about volunteer opportunities in your community, could be very effective as a Website.

Talk to your teacher to help you decide which publishing method is right for your project. Then let your imagination go and take advantage of all the creative possibilities electronic publishing has to offer.

Desktop Publishing

The computer is a powerful tool that gives you the ability to create everything from party invitations and banners to newsletters and illustrated reports. Many software programs deliver word-processing and graphic arts capabilities that once belonged only to professional printers and designers. Armed with the knowledge of how to operate your software, you simply need to add some sound research and a healthy helping of creativity to create an exciting product.

Word-Processing Magic

The written word is the basis of almost every project. Using a standard word-processing program, such as Microsoft Word, makes all aspects of the writing process easier. Use a word-processing program to:

- create an outline;
- save multiple versions of your work;
- revise your manuscript;
- proof your spelling, grammar, and punctuation;
- produce a polished final draft document.

Fascinating Fonts

Once your written material is revised and proofed, it's fun to experiment with type as a way to enhance the content of your written message. Different styles of type are called **fonts** or **typefaces**. Most word-processing programs feature more than 30 different choices. You'll find them listed in the Format menu under Font.

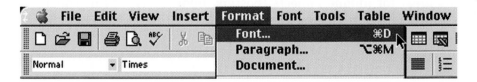

Or they may be located on the toolbar, which usually appears at the top left of your screen.

Although each typeface has its own distinguishing characteristics, most fonts fall into one of two categories: serif typefaces or sans serif typefaces. A serif is a small curve or line added to the end of some of the letter strokes. A typeface that includes these small added curves is called a **serif** typeface. A font without them is referred to as **sans serif,** or in other words, *without* serifs.

> Times New Roman is a serif typeface.
>
> Arial is a sans serif typeface.

In general, sans serif fonts have a sharp look and are better for shorter pieces of writing, such as headings and titles. Serif typefaces work well as body copy.

Of all the typefaces, whether serif or sans serif, which is best? In many cases, the answer depends on your project. Each font has a personality of its own and makes a different impression on the reader. For example:

> *This is French Script MT and might be fun to use in an invitation to a special birthday party.*
>
> **This is Playbill and would look great on a poster advertising a melodrama by the Theater Club.**
>
> **This is Stencil and would be an effective way to say "Top Secret" on a letter to a friend.**

As much fun as they are, these three typefaces are probably inappropriate for a school report or term paper. Specialized fonts are great for unique projects (posters, invitations, and personal correspondence) but less appropriate for writing assignments for school or business.

Since most school writing is considered formal, good font choices include Times New Roman, Arial, Helvetica, or Bookman Antiqua. These type styles are fairly plain and straightforward. They allow the reader to focus on the meaning of your words instead of being distracted by the way they appear on the page.

One last word about fonts: With so many to choose from, you may be tempted to include a dozen or so in your document. Be careful! Text **printed** *in* **multiple** fonts *can* be extremely *confusing* **to read.** The whole idea of different typefaces is to enhance and clarify your message, not the other way around!

A Sizable Choice

Another way to add emphasis to your writing is to adjust the size of the type. Type size is measured in points. One inch is equal to 72 points. Therefore, 72-point type would have letters that measure approximately one inch high. To change the point size of your type, open the Format menu and click Font.

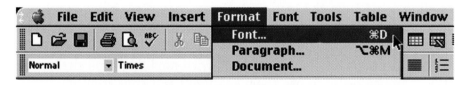

Or use the small number box on the toolbar that usually appears at the top left side of your screen.

For most school and business writing projects, 10 or 12 points is the best size type for the main body copy of your text. However, it's very effective to change the type size for titles, headings, and subheadings to give the reader a clear understanding of how your information is organized. For example, notice how the type in the subheading "A Sizable Choice" is different from the rest of the type on this page, indicating the beginning of a new section.

Another way to add emphasis is to apply a style to the type, such as **bold,** *italics,* or <u>underline</u>. Styles are also found in the Format menu under Font.

Or look for them in the top center section of the toolbar on your screen abbreviated as **B** for bold, *I* for italics, and <u>U</u> for underline.

Here's one more suggestion—color. If you have access to a color printer, you may want to consider using colored type to set your heading apart from the rest of the body copy. Red, blue, or other dark colors work best. Avoid yellow or other light shades that might fade out and be difficult to read.

As with choosing fonts, the trick with applying type sizes, styles, and colors is to use them sparingly and consistently throughout your work. In other words, all the body copy should be in one style of type, all the headings should be in another, and so on. If you pepper your copy with too many fonts, type sizes, styles, and colors, your final product could end up looking more like a patchwork quilt than a polished report.

Layout Help from Your Computer

One way to organize the information in your document is to use one of the preset page layouts provided by your word-processing program. All you have to do is write your document using capital letters for main headings, and uppercase and lowercase letters for subheadings. Set the headings apart from the body copy with returns. Then open the Format menu and click the Autoformat heading.

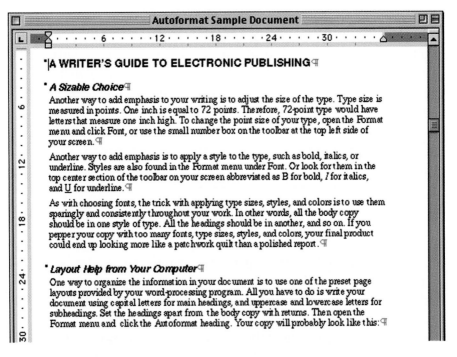

This automatic, preset format is probably fine for most of the writing you do in school. You'll also find other options available in the File menu under Page Setup.

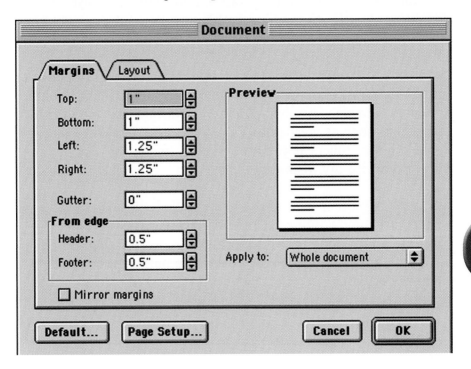

Here you can change the margins and add headers, footers, and page numbers. **Headers** and **footers** are descriptive titles that automatically appear at the top or bottom of each page without having to be retyped each time. For example, you may wish to add the title of your project and the date as a header or footer to each page.

```
 Header
|Project Title Here ¶
|Date Here ¶
```

Let's Get Graphic

The old saying "A picture is worth a thousand words" is particularly true when it comes to spicing up papers and reports. Desktop publishing programs (such as Adobe PhotoDeluxe Home Edition, Macromedia FreeHand, Microsoft PhotoDraw, and Microsoft PowerPoint) give you the ability to include photographs, illustrations, and charts in your work that can express your ideas more clearly and succinctly than words alone.

The key to using graphics effectively is to make sure each one conveys a message of importance. Don't use them just for decoration. Be sure they add something meaningful, or you'll actually detract from your written message.

Drawings   Many paint and draw programs allow you to create or **import** (bring in from another program) an illustration for your document. Drawings can help illustrate concepts that are difficult to describe, such as mechanical parts or procedures. Cartoons can also add a nice touch. If you use them sparingly, they can lighten up an otherwise dry, technical report.

Clip Art   Another kind of drawing is called **clip art.** These simple, black-and-white or color line drawings are often included in desktop publishing or word-processing programs. Predrawn clip art usually is not very good for illustrative purposes, but it does work well as graphic icons that can help guide your reader through various parts of a long report.

For example, suppose you are writing a report on the top arts programs in the United States. You might choose the following clip art for each of the sections:

When you introduce the section of your report that deals with music, you might use the music icon at the large size pictured above. Then, in the headers of all the following sections that deal with music, you might use a smaller version of the icon that looks like this:

 **Music Trends**

Using clip art as icons in this manner lets your readers know at a glance which part of the report they are reading.

Charts and Graphs   If your project, or part of your project, deals with comparing numbers and statistics, one of the best ways to communicate this information is by using charts and graphs. Programs such as Microsoft PowerPoint allow you to create bar graphs, pie charts, and line graphs that can communicate fractions, figures, and comparative measurements much more powerfully than written descriptions.

Photographs   When you flip quickly through a book or a magazine, what catches your eye? Probably photographs. Most of us are naturally curious and want to see what we are reading about. Photos are the perfect companions to written work. With the widespread availability of digital cameras and scanners, adding photos to your project is an easy and effective way to enhance your content.

Using a digital camera or a scanner, you can load photos directly into your computer. Another option is to shoot photographs with a regular camera, but when you have them developed, specify that they be returned to you as "pictures on disc," which you can open on your computer screen.

Photographic images are stored as bits of data in an electronic file. Once you have the photos in your computer, you can use a graphics program such as Adobe PhotoDeluxe Home Edition to manipulate the images in a variety of ways and create amazing visual effects. You can crop elements out of the photo, add special filters and colors, combine elements of two different pictures into one—the possibilities are endless.

After you have inserted the edited photo into your document, be careful when you print out your final draft. Standard printers often don't reproduce photographs well. You may want to take your document on disk to a professional printing company and have it printed out on a high-resolution printer to make sure you get the best quality.

Captions and Titles   While it's true that a single photo can say a great deal, some pictures still need a little explanation in order to have the strongest impact on your reader. Whenever you include an illustration or photograph in a document, also include a simple caption or title for each image.

Add captions in a slightly smaller type size than the body copy and preferably in a sans serif typeface. Use the caption to add information that isn't immediately apparent in the photo. If there are people in the picture, tell us who they are. If the photo features an odd-looking structure, tell us what it is. Be smart with your captions. Don't tell the reader the obvious. Give him or her a reason to read your caption.

For example, suppose you are doing a report about Mt. Everest and you include a dramatic photo of its snowy peak.

| WEAK CAPTION | The summit of Mt. Everest is very high and treacherous. |
| STRONG CAPTION | At its summit, Mt. Everest soars to 29,028 feet, making it the tallest mountain in the world. |

Stand-Alone Graphics   Occasionally you may include well-known graphics or logos in a story or report. These graphics convey powerful messages on their own and don't require captions. Examples of these logos or symbols include:

Nonprint Media—Audio and Video

The world we live in is becoming increasingly more multimedia-savvy. The power of the spoken word and the visual image is widely recognized for the impact it carries. Many businesses rely extensively on multimedia presentations to market their products or convey messages to consumers and employees. Exciting opportunities exist for people who can produce clear, concise messages in audio and visual formats.

Preproduction—Put It on Paper First

Although the final presentation of your subject material may be an audiotape or a video, your project needs to begin on paper first. When you write down your ideas, you do four things:

- Organize your thoughts.
- Narrow your focus.
- Isolate the main messages.
- Identify possible production problems.

Grabbing a tape recorder or camcorder and then running off to record your project is a sure-fire way to create an unorganized mess. This helter-skelter collection of shots and sound bites probably takes hours longer to unravel and fix than if you had taken the time to plan your production in the first place. Resist the urge to jump right in! You'll be glad you did.

Concept Outline   The first task in the writing process is a short, one-page document that describes the basic idea of the project. Ideally this should be three paragraphs—one paragraph each describing the beginning, the middle, and the end. Do not go forward until you have clearly identified these three important parts of your project.

Brief   Next ask yourself, What is the purpose of this video or audiotape? Who is the audience? What is the result you hope to achieve when this group of people sees or hears your presentation? Do you want them to be informed about something? motivated to do something? emotionally moved in some way? or excited about something? Write one to two pages that describe in detail the point of your project: how it will be used, who the intended audience is, and what you hope to achieve with the presentation.

Treatment   The next phase of the writing process fleshes out the ideas you expressed in your outline and brief. The treatment is several pages long. It contains descriptions of the characters, dialogue, and settings, and describes the presentation scene by scene in order of how it will appear. Include in your treatment descriptions of the mood and the tone of your piece. Is it upbeat and whimsical, or dark and ominous? If your project is a video, set the stage by describing the overall look and feel of the production.

Script   Once you've completed the first three steps, you are ready to go to script. The script is the blueprint for your production, similar to a blueprint for a house. Everything that is mentioned in the script is what will wind up in the audio recording or on the screen. Conversely anything that is left out of the script will likely be overlooked and omitted from the final production. So write this document carefully.

For an audio recording, the script contains all narration, dialogue, music, and sound effects. For a videotape, it contains all of these elements plus descriptions of the characters, any sets, props, or costumes, plus all camera shots and movements, special visual effects, and onscreen titles or graphic elements. In short the audio script encompasses everything that is heard, and the video script covers everything that is seen and heard.

Storyboard   Last, for video productions, it's also helpful to create storyboards—simple frame-by-frame sketches with explanatory notes jotted underneath—that paint a visual picture of what the video will look like from start to finish.

The final stages of preproduction include assembling all of the elements you will need before you begin recording your audiotape or shooting your video. Here's a general checklist.

> ## Preproduction Checklist

Audiotape Tasks

- ✓ Arrange for audio recording equipment
- ✓ Cast narrator/actors
- ✓ Find music (secure permission)
- ✓ Arrange for sound effects
- ✓ Set up recording schedule
- ✓ Coordinate all cast and crew
- ✓ Arrange for transportation if needed
- ✓ Rehearse all voice talent

Videotape Tasks

- ✓ Arrange for video equipment (including lighting and sound recording equipment)
- ✓ Cast narrator/host/actors
- ✓ Find music (secure permission)
- ✓ Arrange for sound/visual effects
- ✓ Set up shooting schedule
- ✓ Coordinate all cast and crew
- ✓ Arrange for transportation if needed
- ✓ Set up shooting locations (secure permission)
- ✓ Arrange for costumes, props, sets
- ✓ Arrange for makeup if needed
- ✓ Rehearse all on-camera talent

Video Production Schedule   Tucked into the list of pre-production tasks is "Set up recording/shooting schedule." For videotaping, this means much more than just deciding what day and time you will begin shooting.

During the video production phase of your project, the idea is to shoot everything that your script calls for in the final production. Often the most efficient way to do this is what is called "out-of-sequence" filming. This means that, rather than shoot scenes sequentially (that is, in the order that they appear in the script), you shoot them in the order that is most convenient. Later you will edit them together in the correct order in post-production.

For example, your video might begin and end in the main character's office. Rather than shoot the first office scene, then move the cast and crew to the next location, then later at the end of the day return to the office, it might be easier to shoot both office scenes back-to-back. This will save a great deal of time and effort of moving people, lights, and props back and forth.

Lighting may be a factor in the order in which you shoot your scenes. For example, scenes 3, 4, and 7 may take place in the daytime, and scenes 1, 2, 5, and 6 may take place at night.

To accommodate all of these factors, you will need to plan your shooting schedule carefully. The difference between a smooth shoot day and chaos is a well thought-out shooting schedule.

Last, for video or audio recording, it's also a good idea to assemble your team for a preproduction meeting before you begin. This is your chance to read through the script together, go over time schedules, review responsibilities of each person involved, plus answer any questions or discuss potential problems *before* you begin rolling tape. Preproduction meetings are worth their weight in gold for reducing stress levels and headaches during production!

Production—We're Rolling!

At last, you've completed all your preparation. Now it's time to roll tape!

Audio Production   The better the recording equipment, the higher-quality sound recording you will be able to achieve. The most convenient format for student audio recording is the audiocassette—a high-quality tape in a plastic case that you simply drop inside your cassette recorder.

The forerunner of the audiocassette was reel-to-reel tape in which audiotape was threaded through a recording machine from one reel to another. This format is still used in some recording studios, although recording on CDs—compact discs—has become increasingly more common.

Most professional recording facilities record on DAT—digital audiotape. DAT provides the cleanest, highest-quality sound of all, but the equipment is still quite expensive and limited usually to professional recording situations.

If you are using an audiocassette recorder, use an external microphone rather than the built-in microphone on the tape recorder for best results. Ways to improve the quality of your production include the following:

- Select a high-quality, low-noise tape stock.

- Choose a quiet place to do your recording. Look for a quiet room with carpeting, soft furniture, and a door you can close firmly. Hang a sign outside the door that says, "Quiet Please—Recording in Progress" so you will not be disturbed in the middle of your session.

- Do a voice check before you begin recording so you know whether the sound level on the recorder is set correctly.

- Lay the script pages out side-by-side to eliminate the rustling sound of turning pages.

- If music is part of your production, cue up the correct cut and practice turning it on and fading the volume up and down at the appropriate parts. Do a sound check on the music volume before you start. Do the same with any sound effects.

Video Production　As with audio recording, there are a number of different formats to choose from for video recording. Some of the more common ones include those listed on the following page.

VHS	A full-sized tape machine that produces moderate quality video. The camera is large, heavy, and requires some skill to operate effectively.
VHSC	A compact version of the VHS model. The camera is easier to hold and use. You will need a special adapter to play the tape back on a standard VCR tape player.
Super VHS	A format that produces excellent picture and sound quality, but is very expensive to buy or rent. Super VHS cannot be played on a standard VCR tape machine.
Super VHSC	A compact version of Super VHS.
Video 8	A format sometimes referred to as a camcorder. The Video 8 shoots 8-millimeter videotape. It produces a good quality picture and hi-fi sound. With special cable attachments, you can play the tape back through your VCR or television.
High 8	A compact and lightweight format. High 8 is substantially more expensive than Video 8, but the quality of sound and picture is excellent. High 8 video can be played back on a TV or VCR using special cable attachments.
Betacam	A professional-standard video that delivers top-quality sound and picture. Most news crews shoot Betacam video. Betacam tape can only be played back on a Betacam tape deck.

Ideally you will have ironed out issues regarding shooting sequence when you wrote your production schedule back in the preproduction phase. This will leave you free during production to focus on your production values, your camera shots, and your actors' performances.

Production value is another way of describing how polished and professional your project turns out. There are many ways to increase the production value of your presentation. Some of the easiest include the following:

- Use a tripod to keep the camera steady. Nothing screams "Amateur!" louder than shaky, hand held camera shots. If you can't get your hands on a tripod, lean against something sturdy, such as a tree or the side of a car, to keep your subjects from bouncing around in the frame.

- Use sufficient light. If your audience can't see what's happening, they will quickly lose interest in your show. The best way to light a subject is from one side at a 45-degree angle with the light shining in a downward direction. Supplement this with a slightly less powerful light from the other side and even from behind your subject to avoid unsightly shadows.

- Check your focus frequently. Don't wait until your entire production is nearly finished to check whether the shots are clear. Sometimes the manual focus on some cameras is more reliable than the auto-focus feature. Experiment with your camera using both methods *before* your shoot day to see which gives you the better result.

- Use an external microphone. The built-in microphone on the camera will only pick up sounds that are very close by. If you want to record sounds that are farther off, try using an external microphone that can plug into the video recorder. Poor sound quality can greatly diminish the production values of your video.

Next think about *how* you shoot your video. One way to keep your production lively and interesting is to vary your camera shots. The next time you watch a television show or movie, keep a little notepad handy. Every time you notice a different camera move or cut, make a hash mark on your notepad. At the end of 15 minutes, count the hash marks. You may be amazed to find out how many shots were used!

To hold the interest of your audience, use a variety of camera shots, angles, and moves. Check your local library or media center for good books on camera techniques that describe when and how to use various shots—from long shots to close-ups, from low angles to overhead shots. As a rule, every time you change camera shots, change your angle slightly as well. This way, when the shots are edited together, you can avoid accidentally putting two nearly identical shots side-by-side, which creates an unnerving jarring motion called a "jump cut."

Do some research on framing techniques as well to make sure you frame your subjects properly and avoid cutting people's heads off on the screen. Also, try to learn about ways to move the camera in order to keep your audience interested. For example, three common, but effective camera moves include panning, tracking, and zooming.

Panning means moving the camera smoothly from one side of the scene to another. Panning works well in an establishing shot to help orient your audience to the setting where the action takes place.

Tracking means moving the camera from one place to another in a smooth action as well, but in tracking, the camera parallels the action, such as moving alongside a character as he or she walks down the street. It's called *tracking* because in professional film-making, the camera and the operator are rolled forward or backward on a small set of train tracks alongside the actor or actress.

Zooming means moving the camera forward or back, but zooming actually involves moving the lens rather than the camera. By touching the zoom button, you can push in on a small detail that you would like to emphasize, or you can pull out to reveal a wider perspective.

The important factor in any kind of camera move is to keep the action fluid and, in most cases, slow and steady. Also, use camera movement sparingly. You want to keep your audience eager and interested, not dizzy and sick!

Another good way to keep your presentation moving is to use frequent cuts. While the actual cuts will be done during post-production, you need to plan for them in production. Professional filmmakers use the word *coverage* for making sure they have ample choices for shots. You can create "coverage" for your production by planning shots such as the following:

Kinds of Video Shots

establishing shot	This shot sets up where the action of the story will take place. For example, if your story takes place inside an operating room, you might begin with an establishing shot of the outside of the hospital.

reaction shot	It's a good idea to get shots of all on-camera talent even if that person does not have any dialogue but is listening to, or reacting to, another character. This gives you the chance to break away from the character who is speaking to show how his or her words are affecting other people in the scene.
cutaway shot	The cutaway shot is a shot of something that is not included in the original scene but is somehow related to it. Cutaways are used to connect two subjects. For example, the first shot may be of a person falling off a boat. The second shot could be a cutaway of a shark swimming deep below the water.

If you are adventurous, you might also want to try some simple special effects. Dry ice can create smoke effects. You can also make objects seem to disappear as if by magic. To do this, have your actors freeze; then stop the camera, remove an object from the set, and restart the camera. Other effects can be achieved using false backdrops, colored lights, and filters. Just use your imagination!

Postproduction—The Magic of Editing

Without access to a sound mixing board, it's difficult to do postproduction on audio recordings. However, there's a vast amount of creative control you can have over your video project in post-production using your camera and your VCR.

Once all of your videotaping is complete, it's time to create the **final cut**—that is, your choice of the shots you wish to keep and the shots you wish to discard. The idea, of course, is to keep only your very best shots in the final production. Be choosy and select the footage with only the best composition, lighting, focus, and performance to tell your story.

There are three basic editing techniques:

Video Editing Techniques

in-camera editing

In this process you edit as you shoot. In other words, you need to shoot all your scenes in the correct sequence in the proper length that you want them to appear. This is the most difficult editing process because it leaves no margin for error.

insert editing

In insert editing you transfer all your footage to a new video. Then on your VCR you record over any scenes that you don't want with scenes that you do want in the final version.

assemble editing

This process involves electronically copying your shots from the original source tape in your camera onto a new blank tape, called the edited master, in the order that you want the shots to appear. This method provides the most creative control.

In the best scenario, it's ideal to have three machines at your disposal—the camera, a recording VCR for transferring images, and a post production machine or computer program for adding effects. These effects might include a dissolve from one shot to another instead of an abrupt cut. A **dissolve** is the soft fading of one shot into another. Dissolves are useful when you wish to give the impression that time has passed between two scenes. A long, slow dissolve that comes up from black into a shot, or from a shot down to black, is called a **fade** and is used to open or close a show.

In addition to assembling the program, post production is the time to add titles to the opening of your program and credits to the end of the show. Computer programs such as Adobe Premiere can help you do this. Some cameras are equipped to generate titles too. If you don't have any electronic means to produce titles, you can always mount your camera on a high tripod and focus it downward on well-lit pages of text and graphics placed on the floor. Then edit the text frames into the program.

Post production is also the time to add voice-over narration and music. Voice-overs and background music should be recorded separately and then edited into the program on a separate sound track once the entire show is edited together. Video editing programs for your computer, such as Adobe Premiere, allow you to mix music and voices with your edited video. Some VCRs will allow you to add additional sound tracks as well.

Publishing on the World Wide Web

The World Wide Web is an exciting part of the Internet where you can visit thousands of Websites, take part in online discussion groups, and communicate with other people all over the world via E-mail. You can also become a part of the exciting Web community by building and publishing a Website of your own.

Scoping Out Your Site

There are no hard and fast rules on how to build a Website. However, the Web is a unique medium with distinctive features that make it different from any other form of communication. The Web offers:

- universal access to everyone;
- interactive communication;
- the ability to use photos, illustrations, animation, sound, and video;
- unlimited space;
- unlimited branching capabilities;
- the ability to link your site with other Websites.

If you are going to publish on the Web, it makes sense to take advantage of all of these features. In other words, it's possible to take any written composition, save it in a format that can be displayed in a Web browser, upload it to a server, and leave it at that. But how interesting is it to look at a solid page of text on your computer screen?

Just as you plan a video, you need to plan your Website. Don't just throw text and graphics together up on a screen. The idea is to make your site interesting enough that visitors will want to stay, explore, and come back to your site again—and that takes thought and planning.

Back to the Drawing Board

Again, you need to capture your thoughts and ideas on paper before you publish anything. Start with a one-page summary that states the purpose of your Website and the audience you hope to attract. Describe in a paragraph the look and feel you think your site will need in order to accomplish this purpose and hold your audience's attention.

Make a list of the content you plan to include in your Website. Don't forget to consider any graphics, animations, video, or sound you may want to include. Next go on a World Wide Web field trip.

Ask your friends and teachers for the URLs of their favorite Websites. Visit these sites and bookmark the ones you like. Then click around these sites and ask yourself, Do I like this site? Why or why not? Determine which sites are visually appealing to you and why. Which sites are easy to navigate and why? Print out the pages you like best, and write notes on your reactions.

On the other hand, which sites are boring and why? Print out a few of these pages too, and keep notes on how you feel about them. Chances are the sites you like best will have clean, easy-to-read layouts, be well written, contain visually stimulating graphic elements, and have intuitive **interfaces** that make it simple to find your way around.

One sure kiss of death in any Website is long, uninterrupted blocks of text. Scrolling through page after page of text is extremely boring. Plan to break up long passages of information into manageable sections. What will be the various sections of your site? Will there be separate sections for editorial content? news? humor? feedback? What sections will be updated periodically and how often?

Pick up your drawing pencil and make a few rough sketches. How do you envision the "home" page of your site? What will the icons and buttons look like? Then give careful thought to how the pages will connect to each other starting with the home page. Your plan for connecting the pages is called a **site map**.

Because the Web is an interactive medium, navigation is critical. Decide how users will get from one page to another. Will you put in a navigation bar across the top of the page or down the side? Will there be a top or home page at the beginning of each section?

Once you have planned the content, organized your material into sections, and designed your navigation system, you are ready to begin creating Web pages.

Planning Your Pages

In order to turn text into Web pages, you need to translate the text into a special language that Web browsers can read. This language code is called HTML—HyperText Markup Language. There are three methods available:

- You can use the Save as HTML feature in the File menu of most word-processing programs.

- You can import your text into a Web-building software program and add the code yourself if you know how.

- You can use a software program such as Adobe PageMill that does the work for you. Web-building software programs are referred to as WYSIWYG (pronounced "Wiz-E-Wig"), which stands for **W**hat **Y**ou **S**ee **I**s **W**hat **Y**ou **G**et.

Web-building software also allows you to create links to other Web pages using a simple process called **drag-and-drop.** Be sure to read the directions that come with your software package for complete instructions.

Putting It All Together

Writing for the Web is different from writing for print. The Web is a fast medium. It's about experiences, not study time, so write accordingly. Keep your messages succinct and to the point. Use short, punchy sentences. Break up your copy with clever subheads. Try not to exceed 500 to 600 words in any single article on any one page.

Compose your Web copy on a standard word-processing program. This will give you access to your formatting tools and spell-check features. You can then save the file as HTML or import the completed text into a web-building software program for placement on your Web page.

Next you will want to lay out your Web page and flow the text around some interesting graphics. Be sure to include blank space on the page as well. Blank space lets your page "breathe" and makes for a much more inviting experience.

You can use a variety of images on your Website including charts, graphs, photographs, clip art, and original illustrations. Collect graphics for the Web in exactly the same way you would get graphics for any desktop publishing project—scan in images, use a digital camera, or create your own graphics using a graphics software program.

It's also possible to add audio files and video files (referred to as QuickTime Video) to your Website. These are fun and interesting additions. However, there are two drawbacks—audio and video files are very time-consuming to prepare and they take a long time for the user to load. Also, audio quality can be quite good on the Net, but full-motion video is still not at the broadcast-quality level most people have come to expect.

As an alternative to video, consider animated graphics. Animated graphics are much easier to create using graphics software programs. These programs also allow you to compress the animations so that they load much faster than video files and still run smoothly on screen.

If you would like to learn more about adding audio and video features, as well as graphics, to your Web pages, visit http://msc. pangea.org/tutorials/www/cap 5-eng.htm. For more information about adding other multimedia features, check out Plug-ins for Browsers at http://www.seidata.com/~city/reference/plugins/.

Going Live

Once all your pages are put together you are ready to go live on the World Wide Web, right? Not quite.

Before you upload your new Website, it's a good idea to test all your pages first, using common Web browsers such as Netscape's Navigator or Microsoft's Internet Explorer—browsers your visitors are likely to use. Open your pages on these browsers and look at them closely. Do the text and graphics appear the way you had designed them? Are all the page elements fitting neatly into the screen space, or do you need to tweak the copy or graphics a little to make them fit better?

Test all links on your page. Click on every page and be sure that it takes you to the site you originally intended. Click on all your navigation elements and buttons. Is everything working the way it's supposed to work? Make any corrections on your home or classroom computer before uploading your Website to a host server and going live to the world.

Your Web-building software program has built-in features that make uploading and adding files to your Website a snap. In fact, some of this software is even available free on the Internet and is easy to download right onto your home or classroom computer.

For more information on how to build and launch your own Website, check the Web. You'll find some great tips at http://www. hotwired.com/webmonkey/kids.

This site even features a guided lesson plan called "Webmonkey for Kids" with step-by-step directions on how to create your own site. It also has information about useful software programs that schools and other educational institutions can download free.

Here's one more shortcut to building a Website. If you or your school already has an Internet Service Provider (ISP), you may be entitled to a free Website as part of your service package. In fact, if you already have an E-mail address for correspondence, this address can be modified slightly to serve as the URL address of your Website. Call your ISP and ask about Website services included in your account.

Last, beware of small errors that can occur during the transmission of your Website material to the Web. As soon as you have finished uploading your Website, open your browser, enter the URL address, and take your new site out for a test drive. Click on all your navigational buttons, links, animations, or any other multimedia features. Check to make sure all the pages are there and that everything looks the way you planned it.

Does everything check out? Great. Now all you have to do is send an E-mail to everyone you know and invite each person to visit your brand new Website!

A Writer's Guide to Using the Internet

The Internet is a global network of computers that are connected to one another with high-speed data lines and regular telephone lines. Anyone with a computer, a modem, and a telephone or cable line can be connected to it—just like you!

The idea of the Internet began in 1969 when a government agency called ARPA (**A**dvanced **R**esearch **P**rojects **A**gency) connected the computers of four universities together. They called this connection the ARPANET, and it was used primarily to exchange research and educational information between scientists and engineers.

Gradually people outside the scientific community began to realize the potential of this tool. By 1980, the U.S. Department of Defense created an early version of the Internet, and soon most universities and government agencies were using it too.

Up to this point, the information was not organized in any way. Imagine a library with thousands of books and no catalog! The next challenge was to find a way to locate and access information quickly and efficiently. Over the next few years, several different search tools were proposed. The names of these systems included Archie, Jughead, and Veronica. If you haven't already guessed, these program names were inspired by the *Archie* comics.

One of the best search systems developed, and today the most widely used, is the World Wide Web. The Web is a network of computers *within* the Internet. This network is capable of delivering multimedia content—images, audio, video, and animation—as well as text. Like the Internet, it comes over the same communication lines into personal computers worldwide, including yours.

How Does the Internet Work?

The Internet is made up of literally thousands of networks all linked together around the globe. Each network consists of a group of computers that are connected to one another to exchange information. If one of these computers or networks fails, the information simply bypasses the disabled system and takes another route through a different network. This rerouting is why the Internet is so valuable to agencies such as the U.S. Department of Defense.

No one "owns" the Internet, nor is it managed in a central place. No agency regulates or censors the information on the Internet. Anyone can publish information on the Internet as he or she wishes.

In fact, the Internet offers such a vast wealth of information and experiences that sometimes it's described as the "Information Superhighway." So how do you "get on" this highway? It's easy. Once you have a computer, a modem, and a telephone or cable line, all you need is a connection to the Internet.

The Cyberspace Connection

A company called an **I**nternet **S**ervice **P**rovider (ISP) connects your computer to the Internet. Examples of ISPs that provide direct access are AT&T, Microsoft Network, Earthlink, MediaOne, and Netcom. You can also get on the Internet indirectly through companies such as America Online (AOL), Prodigy, and CompuServe.

ISPs charge a flat monthly fee for their service. Unlike the telephone company, once you pay the monthly ISP fee, there are no long-distance charges for sending or receiving information on the Internet—no matter where your information is coming from, or going to, around the world! Once you are connected to the Information Superhighway, all you have to do is learn how to navigate it.

Alphabet Soup—Making Sense of All Those Letters!

Like physical highways, the Information Superhighway has road signs that help you find your way around. These road signs are expressed in a series of letters that can seem confusing at first. You've already seen several different abbreviations so far—ARPA, ISP, AOL. How do you make sense out of all these letters? Relax. It's not as complicated as it looks.

Each specific group of information on the World Wide Web is called a **Website** and has its own unique address. Think of it as a separate street address of a house in your neighborhood. This address is called the URL, which stands for **U**niform **R**esearch **L**ocator. It's a kind of shorthand for where the information is located on the Web.

Here's a typical URL: **http://www.bkschoolhouse.com.**

All addresses, or URLs, for the World Wide Web begin with **http://**. This stands for **H**yper**T**ext **T**ransfer **P**rotocol and is a programming description of how the information is exchanged.

The next three letters are easy—**www**—and they let you know you are on the World Wide Web. The next part of the URL—**bkschoolhouse**—is the name of the site you want to visit. And the last three letters, in this case **com**, indicate that this Website is sponsored by a **com**mercial company. Here are other common endings of URLs you will find:

- "org" is short for organization, such as in http:// www.ipl.org, which is the URL of the Website for the Internet Public Library.

- "edu" stands for education, as in the Web address for the Virtual Reference Desk, http://thorplus.lib.purdue. edu/reference/index.html, featuring online telephone books, dictionaries, and other reference guides.

- "gov" represents government-sponsored Websites, such as http://www.whitehouse.gov, the Website for the White House in Washington, D.C.

To get to a Website, you use an interface called a **browser.** Two popular browsers are Netscape Navigator and Microsoft Internet Explorer. A browser is like a blank form where you fill in the information you are looking for. If you know the URL of the Website you want to explore, all you have to do is type it in the field marked Location, click Enter on your keyboard, and wait for the information to be delivered to your computer screen.

There are many other ways to find information on the Web. They will be discussed later in this guide.

▢ Basic Internet Terminology

Here are some of the most frequently used words you will hear associated with the Internet.

address
The unique code given to information on the Internet. This may also refer to an E-mail address.

bookmark
A tool that lets you store your favorite URL addresses, allowing you one-click access to your favorite Web pages without retyping the URL each time.

browser
Application software that supplies a graphical interactive interface for searching, finding, viewing, and managing information on the Internet.

chat
Real-time conferencing over the Internet.

cookies
A general mechanism that some Websites use both to store and to retrieve information on the visitor's hard drive. Users have the option to refuse or accept cookies.

cyberspace
The collective realm of computer-aided communication.

download
The transfer of programs or data stored on a remote computer, usually from a server, to a storage device on your personal computer.

E-mail
Electronic mail that can be sent all over the world from one computer to another. May also be short for Earth-mail because no paper (and no rainforest acreage) is involved.

FAQs
The abbreviation for Frequently Asked Questions. This is usually a great resource to get information when visiting a new Website.

flaming	Using mean or abusive language in cyberspace. Flaming is considered to be in extremely poor taste and may be reported to your ISP.
FTP	The abbreviation for **F**ile **T**ransfer **P**rotocol, a method of transferring files to and from a computer connected to the Internet.
home page	The start-up page of a Website.
HTML	The abbreviation for **H**yper**T**ext **M**arkup **L**anguage—a "tag" language used to create most Web pages, which your browser interprets to display those pages. Often the last set of letters found at the end of a Web address.
http	The abbreviation for **H**yper**T**ext **T**ransport **P**rotocol. This is how documents are transferred from the Web site or server to the browsers of individual personal computers.
ISP	The abbreviation for **I**nternet **S**ervice **P**rovider— a company that, for a fee, connects a user's computer to the Internet.
keyword	A simplified term that serves as subject reference when doing a search.
link	Short for Hyperlink. A link is a connection between one piece of information and another.
Net	Short for Internet.
netiquette	The responsible and considerate way for a user to conduct himself or herself on the Internet.
network	A system of interconnected computers.
online	To "be online" means to be connected to the Internet via a live modem connection.
plug-in	Free applications that can be downloaded off the Internet to enhance your browser's capabilities.
real time	Information received and processed (or displayed) as it happens.
search engine	A computer program that locates documents based on keywords that the user enters.

server	A provider of resources, such as a file server.
site	A specific place on the Internet, usually a set of pages on the World Wide Web.
Spam	Electronic junk mail.
surf	A casual reference to browsing on the Internet. To "surf the Web" means to spend time discovering and exploring new Websites.
upload	The transfer of programs or data from a storage device on your personal computer to another, remote computer.
URL	The abbreviation for **U**niform **R**esource **L**ocator. This is the address for an Internet resource, such as a World Wide Web page. Each Web page has its own unique URL.
Website	A page of information or a collection of pages that is being electronically published from one of the computers in the World Wide Web.
WWW	The abbreviation for the **W**orld **W**ide **W**eb. A network of computers within the Internet capable of delivering multimedia content (images, audio, video, and animation) as well as text over communication lines into personal computers all over the globe.

Why Use the Internet?

By the end of the 1990s, the Internet had experienced incredible growth. An estimated 196 million people were using the Internet worldwide, spending an average of 8.8 hours a week online. By 2003, this number is estimated to increase to more than 500 million people who will be surfing the Web. Why? What does the Internet offer that makes so many people want to go online? And what are the advantages of using the Internet for writers in particular?

The World at Your Fingertips

The answer is, the Internet offers an amazing amount of knowledge and experiences at the touch of your computer keyboard. For writers, it's a great way to get ideas and do in-depth research. You'll find thousands upon thousands of Websites offering a mind-boggling array of subjects. You can explore the Web as a way to jump start your creativity or tap into unlimited information.

The Internet also lets you communicate with experts that you might not otherwise have access to. Plus, you can connect with other people all over the world who have the same interests you do—maybe even find a new writing partner!

In short, the Internet is an invaluable tool for creating great writing. The next section will explore just some of the exciting advantages.

Just an E Away

One of the most popular features of the Internet is electronic mail, or E-mail for short. Unlike traditional mail (nicknamed "snail mail" by tech-savvy people), E-mail messages are practically instantaneous. E-mail is so convenient that, by 1999, 46 percent of Americans were sending or receiving E-mail messages every day.

E-mail is a fun and easy way to keep in touch with friends and relatives. You can send anything from a lengthy family newsletter to a quick question or "news flash." E-mail is also appropriate for formal correspondence, such as responding to a job opening and sending a résumé. In this case, it's a good idea to follow up with hard copies in the traditional mail.

Have you ever teamed up with another student or a maybe a group of students in your class to work on a project together? With E-mail, you can collaborate with other students in other states or even other countries! Many schools are taking advantage of E-mail to pair a class in say, San Jose, California, to work on a cooperative project with a class in New York City, or maybe as far away as Sydney, Australia.

For writers, E-mail is an especially valuable tool. It's a great way to communicate with people who are experts in their fields. Many times well-known authorities, who are difficult to reach by phone or in person, will respond to questions and requests for information via E-mail. E-mail is particularly useful when the person you would like to communicate with lives in another part of the world. It eliminates the expense of long-distance phone calls plus awkward problems due to different time zones.

An easy way to locate experts in a particular area is to visit Websites about that subject. Many times these Websites will list an E-mail address where you can send questions.

Another way writers can use E-mail is to gather information and make contacts. E-mail queries can be sent out to many people in a single click by simply adding multiple addresses to the same message.

For example, suppose you are writing a paper about raising exotic birds. With one click, you can send out an E-mail to 30 friends and associates that asks, "Do you know anyone who has an exotic bird?" Chances are at least a few of the people you ask will have one or two contacts they can provide—and think how much faster corresponding by E-mail is than making 30 phone calls!

You can learn more about sending E-mail on pages C736–C739.

Widening Your World

Your E-mail account also gives you access to **mailing lists**—discussion groups that use E-mail to exchange ideas. Subscribing to a mailing list is free and opens a floodgate of information about specific subjects that is sent directly to your E-mail box.

There are hundreds of lists to choose from, with topics ranging from animal rights to Olympic volleyball. Join a mailing list about the subject you are currently writing about, and it will net you dozens of messages about your topic every day. (Don't worry— you can always *un*subscribe at any time from these lists!)

A similar way to get information and contacts about a particular topic is through the Users Network, called Usenet for short. Usenet is the world's largest discussion forum, providing people with common interests the opportunity to talk to one another in smaller groups called **newsgroups.**

Like mailing lists, there are thousands of newsgroups you can join. Instead of receiving information via E-mail, newsgroups post articles and information on their sites. Subscribing to a newsgroup is more like subscribing to a magazine. By visiting the newsgroup site, you can select which articles you wish to read. You can also reply to articles and discuss them with other people in the newsgroup to gather more ideas.

You can find out more about mailing lists and newsgroups on pages C740–C741.

 One **cautionary note** when surfing the Web:

- No matter how tempting, do not give out your name, address, telephone number, or school name to any site that may ask for this information.
- If you are interested in getting on a mailing list or joining a newsgroup, check with your teacher and/or your parents first.

Picture This

Whatever you write will probably have more impact if it's accompanied with some sort of visual. Many sites on the World Wide Web offer photos, illustrations, and clip art that can be downloaded and integrated into your work. Sometimes there are fees associated with this artwork, but many times it's free.

Another way to illustrate your writing is to take your own photos, turn them into electronic images, and integrate them into your work. One way to do this is to use a digital camera and download the images directly into your computer. If you don't have a digital camera, you can also take pictures using a regular camera. When you have the photos developed, ask the developer if you can have them returned to you either on disk or via E-mail.

Another option is to use a scanner, a device that looks some-what like a copy machine. You place the photo on the glass, and the image is scanned into your computer.

Once you have an image in your computer, you can add it to a report or article in a number of ways—for example, on the cover page as a graphic or border design. There are even a number of photo-editing programs available that give you the ability to manipulate images in all sorts of creative ways.

Sometimes a graph or chart can help you illustrate your point more clearly than text alone. Using a program such as Microsoft PowerPoint, you can create a myriad of graphs and tables that you can incorporate into your writing project for extra emphasis.

One advantage of photos, graphs, and artwork that are stored as electronic images is that you can also send them as E-mail attachments. Imagine—with a click of a button, you can:

- share photos of your last soccer game instantly with friends and relatives anywhere in the world;

- take your pen pals on a "virtual" tour of your home, school, or neighborhood;

- swap pictures and graphs with writing partners in other classrooms across the globe and double your resources.

Online Help

You're working on a paper for your Shakespeare class. You come across the phrase, "Thou craven rough-hewn maggot-pie" in the text. Huh? Find out all about how to make sport of someone using Shakespearean language at The Shakespearean Insult Server at http://www.alabanza.com/kabacoff/Inter-Links/sgi/bard.cgi.

This is only one of hundreds of Websites that can help you with specific subjects you are probably studying right now. These sites cover a variety of topics in English, history, math, science, foreign languages, and more. Here's just a sample of some of the sites waiting to help you.

- How to Be a Web Hound! (http://www.mcli.dist.maricopa.edu/webhound/index.html)

- The Guide to Grammar and Writing (http://webster.commnet.edu/HP/pages/darling/grammar.htm)

- The Math Forum—featuring interesting math challenges and the whimsical "Ask Dr. Math" (http://forum.swarthmore.edu/students)

- MapQuest—type in your starting point and destination and get exact mileage and directions (http://www.mapquest.com)

- The Guide to Experimental Science Projects (http://www.isd77.k12.mn.us/resources/cf/SciProj Inter.html)

- The Human Languages Page—gateways to foreign-language resources on the Web (http://www.june29.com/HLP/)

- The Smithsonian Institution—featuring links to sites ranging from Aeronautics to Zoology (http://www.si.edu)

- The Perseus Project—*the* online resource for studying the ancient world (http://www.perseus.tufts.edu/)

- Education Index—a guide to useful educational Websites (http://www.educationindex.com/)

- Up Your Score—the underground guide to scoring well on the SAT (http://www.workmanweb.com/upyourscore/)

- My Homework Helpers/My Virtual Reference Desk (http://www.refdesk.com/homework.html)

- The Writing Center (http://researchpaper.com/writing.html)

The Internet also offers free programs and services that can be of use to writers. For example, sometimes valuable articles are available in a format called PDF, which stands for **P**ortable **D**ocument **F**ormat. In order to view this kind of document, you must have software called Adobe Acrobat Reader. You can download this software free of charge by visiting the Adobe Website at http://www.adobe.com.

Fun and Games

Many people enjoy the fun side of the Internet's personality. A vast number of Websites offer news, entertainment, online games, and adventures in shopping (often referred to as **E-commerce)**.

While these areas may not seem to be related to writing, if the topic you are working on crosses into the realm of news or the entertainment industry, a gold mine of material awaits you. Then again, maybe a quick game is just what you need to shake off a touch of writer's block!

Don't Believe Everything You Read

Wow, all this terrific information—just a click away. There's only one problem: Not all of it is credible or accurate.

When you check out a book from the library, a librarian or a committee of educators has already evaluated the book to make sure it's a reliable source of information, but remember, no one owns or regulates the Internet. Just because you read something online doesn't mean it's true. How can you tell the difference? Here are a few guidelines on how to evaluate an online source.

- **Play the name game.**
  First, find out who publishes the site. Does the URL end in ".com" (which means it's a commercial company)? If so, is it a large, reputable company, or one you've never heard of that might just be trying to sell you something? An educational site in which the URL ends in ".edu," such as a college or university, might be a more reliable choice. Or a site sponsored by a well-known organization (with a URL that ends in ".org"), such as the American Red Cross (http://www.crossnet.org), would also probably be a credible source.

- **Scope it out.**
  Click around the site and get a feel for what it's like. Is the design clean and appealing? Is it easy to navigate the site and find information? Are the sections clearly labeled? Does the site accept advertising? If you think the site seems disjointed or disorganized, or you just have a negative opinion of it, listen to your instincts and move on to another one.

- **Says who?**
  Suppose you find an article on the Web that seems full of great information. The next question you need to ask yourself is, Who is the author? Is the person an acknowledged expert on the subject? If you don't recognize the author's name, you can send a question to a newsgroup asking if anyone knows about the person. You can also do a search on the Web, using the author's name as the keyword, to get more information about him or her.

In some cases, an article won't list any author at all. If you don't find an author's name, be skeptical. A credible site clearly identifies its authors and usually lists the person's professional background and his or her credentials.

- **Is this old news.**
  If you are doing research on the Roman Empire, it's probably all right if the information wasn't posted yesterday. But if you're looking for information in quickly changing fields, such as science and politics, be sure to check the publication date before you accept the data as true.

- **Ask around.**
  Reliable Web sites frequently provide E-mail addresses or links to authors and organizations connected to the content on the site. Send off a quick E-mail to one of these sources, tell them what you are writing, and ask them: Is this material accurate?

Perhaps the best way to find out if the information on any Website or the information in any article (signed or unsigned) is accurate is to check it against another source—and the best source is your local library or media center.

Internet + Media Center = Information Powerhouse!

Although the Internet is a limitless treasure chest of information, remember that it's not catalogued, so it can be tricky to locate the information you need, and sometimes the information you find is not reliable. The library is a well-organized storehouse of knowledge, but it has finite resources. If you use the Internet in *conjunction* with your local media center, you have everything you need to create well-researched articles, reports, and papers.

> **Use the Internet to**

- get great ideas for topics to write about;
- gather information about your topic from companies, colleges and universities, and professional organizations;
- connect with people who are recognized experts in your field of interest;
- connect with other people who are interested in the same subject and who can provide you with information or put you in touch with other sources.

> **Use the Media Center to**

- find additional sources of information either in print or online;
- get background information on your topic;
- cross-check the accuracy and credibility of online information and authors.

I Don't Own a Computer

You can still access the Internet even if you don't have your own computer. Many schools have computer labs that are open after school and on weekends. Some schools will even allow students to use these labs even though they are not enrolled at that particular school. Many libraries are also equipped with computers and Internet connections.

Consider taking a computer course after school or even attending a computer camp. You'll find information about these programs listed at the library, the YMCA, and in parenting magazines.

Last, maybe you have a friend or neighbor with a computer that you can use in exchange for a service you might provide, such as babysitting or yard work.

How to Communicate on the Internet

E-mail, mailing lists, and news groups are all great ways of exchanging information with other people on the Internet. Here's how to use these useful forms of communication, step-by-step.

Keep in Touch with E-mail

Any writer who has ever used E-mail in his or her work will agree that sending and receiving electronic messages is one of the most useful ways of gathering information and contacts for writing projects. It's fast, inexpensive, and fun!

Once you open your E-mail program, click on the command that says Compose Mail. This will open a new blank E-mail similar to the one pictured below. Next, fill in the blanks.

Type the person's E-mail address here. There is no central listing of E-mail addresses. If you don't have the person's address, the easiest way to get it is to call and ask the person for it. You can address an E-mail to one or several people, depending on the number of addresses you type in this space.

CC stands for **c**ourtesy **c**opy. If you type additional E-mail addresses in this area, you can send a copy of the message to other people.

BCC stands for **b**lind **c**ourtesy **c**opy. By typing one or more E-mail addresses here, you can send a copy of the message to others without the original recipient knowing that other people have received the same message. Not all E-mail programs have this feature.

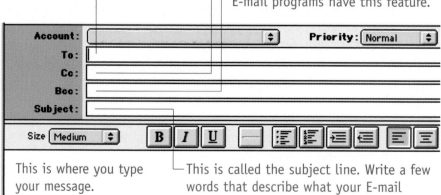

This is where you type your message.

This is called the subject line. Write a few words that describe what your E-mail message is about.

Say It with Style

Like regular letters, E-mail can assume a different tone and style depending on to whom you are writing. Usually informal E-mails, such as **Instant Messages (IMs)** to close friends, are light, brief, and to the point. In the case of more formal E-mails, such as a request for information from an expert or a museum, it's important to keep the following guidelines in mind.

- Make sure your message is clear and concise.
- Use proper grammar and punctuation.
- Check your spelling. (Some E-mail programs have their own spell-check function—use it!)
- Double-check the person's E-mail address to be sure you've typed it correctly.

Because E-mail is a fast medium designed for quick communication, E-mail users have developed a kind of shorthand that helps them write their messages even faster. Here are a few commonly used abbreviations that you may find in informal E-mail.

COMMON E-MAIL ABBREVIATIONS

BRB	be right back	BTW	by the way
FYI	for your information	F2F	face-to-face
HAND	Have a nice day	J/K	just kidding
IMHO	in my humble opinion	IOW	in other words
LOL	laughing out loud	L8R	later
OIC	Oh, I see	ROFL	rolling on the floor laughing
WU	What's up?		

IMHO, TBC RTTR ETU, FWIW!
(*Translation:* In my humble opinion, the best conversations are those that are easiest to understand, for what it's worth!)

Are you sending the E-mail to a friend or relative? If so, would you like to add a touch of fun? Then you may want to explore **emoticons** (also know as "smileys")—little faces made out of keyboard symbols that you add to your messages to express how you feel about something.

EMOTICONS				
:)	happy	:(	sad	
:-D	laughing	:`-(	crying	
;-)	winking	:-}	smirking	
:-0	shocked	:-/	skeptical	
:-#	my lips are sealed	*<|:-)	Santa Claus	
:s	confused	:<>	bored	
8)	I'm wearing glasses	B)	I'm wearing sunglasses/shades	

Attach a Little Something Extra

When you send E-mail, you can also send other information along with your message. These are called **attachments**. Depending on your E-mail program's capabilities, you can attach documents, photos, illustrations—even sound and video files. Click Attach, and then double-click on the document or file on your computer that you wish to send.

After you have composed your message and added any attachments you want to include, click the Send button. Presto! Your message arrives in the other person's mailbox seconds later, whether that person lives right next door or on the other side of the world. Because there is usually no charge to send E-mail, it's a great way to save money on postage and long-distance telephone calls.

Follow Up

It's important to note, however, that just because you have sent a message, you shouldn't automatically assume that the other person has received it. Internet Service Providers (ISPs) keep all messages that are sent until the recipient requests them. The person you sent your E-mail to might be away from his or her computer or may not check messages regularly.

Also, the Internet is still an imperfect technology. From time to time, servers go down or other "hiccups" in electronic transmissions can occur, leaving your message stranded somewhere in cyberspace. If you don't get a reply in a reasonable amount of time, either resend your original E-mail message or call the person and let him or her know that your message is waiting.

You've Got Mail

When someone sends YOU an E-mail message, you have several options:

Reply: Click Reply, and you can automatically send back a new message without having to retype the person's E-mail address. (Be sure you keep a copy of the sender's E-mail address in your Address Book for future use.)

Forward: Suppose you receive a message that you would like to share with someone else. Click Forward, and you can send a copy of the message, plus include a few of your own comments, to another person.

Print: In some instances, you may need to have a paper copy of the E-mail message. For example, if someone E-mails you directions to a party, click Print to take a hard copy of the instructions with you.

Store: Do you want to keep a message to refer to later? Some E-mail programs allow you to create folders to organize stored messages.

Delete: You can discard a message you no longer need just by clicking Delete. It's a good idea to throw messages away regularly to keep them from accumulating in your mailbox.

Care to Chat?

Another way to communicate online is **I**nternet **R**elay **C**hat (IRC), or "chat rooms" for short. Chat rooms focus on a large variety of topics, so you may be able to find a chat room where people are discussing the subject you are writing about.

"Chat" is similar to talking on the telephone except that, instead of speaking, the people in the chat room type their responses back and forth to each other. As soon as you type your comment, it immediately appears on the computer screen of every person involved in the "conversation." There are also more advanced forms of chat available on the Net, such as 3-D chat and voice chat.

To participate in a chat room, you'll need to invent a nickname for yourself. This name helps to identify who is speaking, yet allows you to remain anonymous. Everyone uses a made-up name in chat rooms (like Zorro, Twinkle, Madonna, or Elvis), so don't make the mistake of believing that people really are who their name says they are!

To get started, you will need a special program for your computer. Two sites that offer this program free of charge include mIRC program (http://huizen.dds.nl/~mirc/index.htm) and Global Chat (http://www.prospero.com/globalchat).

 One last word about chat rooms: While they are a great way to meet and communicate with other people, the anonymous nature of a chat room can make people less inhibited than they might otherwise be in person. If you sense that one of the participants in your chat room is responding inappropriately, ask your parents or teacher to step in, or simply sign off.

Join the Group

Mailing lists and newsgroups are larger discussion forums that can help you get even more information about a specific subject.

Mailing Lists   To find a directory of available mailing lists, check out http://www.neosoft.com/internet/paml. If you find a mailing list that interests you and wish to subscribe to it, just send a message to the administrative address. You will start to receive messages from the mailing list within a few days.

Remember, mailing lists use E-mail to communicate, so be sure to check your E-mail often because once you subscribe to a list, it's possible to receive dozens of messages in a matter of days. In fact, you might want to unsubscribe from mailing lists whenever you go on vacation. Otherwise, you might come home to a mailbox stuffed to overflowing with messages!

Another good idea is to read the messages in your new mailing list for a week or so before submitting a message of your own. This will give you a good idea of what has already been discussed so you can be considerate about resubmitting old information.

You can reply to a message any time you wish. However, it doesn't do anyone any good to respond by saying, "Yes, I agree." Get in the habit of replying to messages only when you have something important to add. Also, be sure to repeat the original question in your reply so that people understand which message you are responding to.

Be sure that you really want to belong to a mailing list before you subscribe. Unwanted E-mail can be a nuisance. Fortunately, if you change your mind, you can always unsubscribe to mailing lists at any time.

Newsgroups To join a newsgroup, check with your ISP. Service providers frequently list available topics under the heading "Newsgroups." Another way to find a newsgroup about a topic you want to research is to visit Deja News at http://www.dejanews.com on the World Wide Web.

Newsgroups are named with two or more words separated by a period. For example, there is a newsgroup named rec.sport.baseball. college. The first three letters—"rec"—defines the main subject, in this case *recreation*. Each word that follows—*sport, baseball,* and *college*—narrows the scope of the subject to an increasingly more specific area of interest.

As with mailing lists, you can always unsubscribe to newsgroups at any time.

Mind Your Manners!

As in any social setting, there are a few guidelines to follow when you are talking to people online—via E-mail, in a chat room, or in a newsgroup. These suggestions will help you be considerate of others in cyberspace. This conduct is called **netiquette.**

E-mail and Chat

- Never use harsh or insulting language. This is called **flaming** and is considered rude. A continuing argument in which derogatory terms are swapped back and forth is called a **flamewar**. Avoid this situation.

- Type your messages using uppercase and lowercase letters. WRITING IN ALL CAPITAL LETTERS IS DIFFICULT TO READ AND IS REFERRED TO AS "SHOUTING."

- Respect other people's ideas and work. Don't forward a message or attach documents written by someone else without first asking the author's permission.

- Don't send Spam. **Spamming** refers to sending messages to entire lists of people in your E-mail addresses, on mailing lists, or in newsgroups for the purpose of selling something. Don't use the Internet to spread rumors or gossip.

- Respect other people's privacy. The Internet is an enormous public forum, so be careful what you write and post on the Internet that hundreds or thousands of people might see.

Newsgroups

- Read the articles in a newsgroup for 7 to 10 days before posting articles yourself. No one in a newsgroup wants to read the same article twice.

- Make sure the article you are proposing is appropriate to the subject of the newsgroup.

- If you are going to post an article, be sure you express the title clearly in the subject heading so readers will know what the article is about.

- Read the FAQ (Frequently Asked Questions) so you can avoid repeating a question that has already been discussed.

How to Do Research on the Internet

The Information Superhighway could be the best research partner you've ever had. It's fast, vast, and always available. But like any other highway, if you don't know your way around, it can also be confusing and frustrating. This is particularly true of the Internet because the sheer volume of information often can be intimidating.

This section will explore ways to help you search the Web effectively. Be patient. It takes time to learn how to navigate the Net and zero in on the information you need. The best thing to do is practice early and often. Don't wait until the night before your term paper is due to learn how to do research on the Internet!

Getting Started

Just as there are several different ways to get to your home or school, there are many different ways to arrive at the information you're looking for on the Internet.

CD-ROM Encyclopedia   One way to begin is not on the Web at all. You might want to start your search by using a CD-ROM encyclopedia. These CD-ROMs start with an Internet directory. Click the topic that is closest to your subject. This will link you to a site that's likely to be a good starting point. From there, you can link to other resources suggested in the site.

Search Page   Another good first step is your browser's search page.

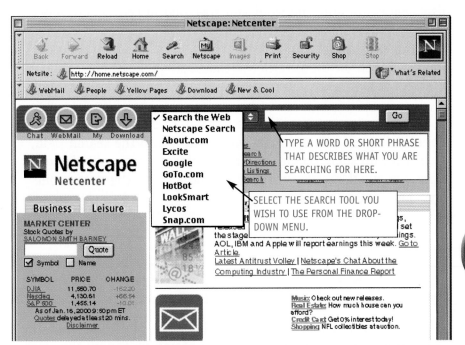

Netscape Center screenshot ©2000 Netscape Communications Corporation. Used with permission.

Search Tools   There are several different free search services available that will help you find topics of interest by entering words and phrases that describe what you are searching for. Just some of these tools, sometimes referred to as **search engines,** include:

- AltaVista—http://www.altavista.com
- Excite—http://www.excite.com
- HotBot—http://www.hotbot.com
- InfoSeek—http://www.infoseek.com
- Lycos—http://www.lycos.com
- WebCrawler—http://www.webcrawler.com
- Yahoo!—http://www.yahoo.com

Search services usually list broad categories of subjects, plus they may offer other features, such as "Random Links" or "Top 25 Sites," and customization options. Each one also has a search field. Type in a word or short phrase, called a **keyword**, which describes your area of interest. Then click Search or the Enter key on your keyboard. Seconds later a list of Websites known as "hits" will be displayed containing the word you specified in the search field. Scroll through the list and click the page you wish to view.

So far this sounds simple, doesn't it? The tricky part about doing a search on the Internet is that a single keyword may yield a hundred or more sites. Plus, you may find many topics you don't need.

For example, suppose you are writing a science paper about the planet Saturn. If you type the word *Saturn* into the search field, you'll turn up some articles about the planet, but you'll also get articles about NASA's Saturn rockets and Saturn, the automobile company.

Search Smart!

Listed below are a few pointers on how to narrow your search, save time, and search *smart* on the Net.

1. The keyword or words that you enter have a lot to do with the accuracy of your search. Focus your search by adding the word *and* or the + sign followed by another descriptive word. For example, try *Saturn* again, but this time, add "+ space." Adding a third word, "Saturn + space + rings," will narrow the field even more.

2. On the other hand, you can limit unwanted results by specifying information that you do *not* want the search engine to find. If you type "dolphins not football," you will get Web sites about the animal that lives in the ocean rather than the football team that lives in Miami.

3. Specify geographical areas using the word *near* between keywords as in "islands near Florida." This lets you focus on specific regions.

4. To broaden your search, add the word *or* between keywords. For example, "sailboats or catamarans."

5. Help the search engine recognize familiar phrases by putting words that go together in quotes; for example, "Tom and Jerry" or "bacon and eggs."

6. Sometimes the site you come up with is close to what you are searching for, but it is not exactly what you need. Skim the text quickly anyway. It may give you ideas for more accurate keywords. There might also be links listed to other sites that are just the right resource you need.

7. Try out different search engines. Each service uses slightly different methods of searching, so you may get different results using the same keywords.

Last, check the spelling of the keywords you are using. A misspelled word can send a search engine in completely the wrong direction. Also, be careful how you use capital letters. If you type the word *Gold*, some search services will only bring up articles that include the word with a capital *G*.

Pick a Category

Another way to search for information is by using subject directories. Many of the search engines on the Web provide well-organized subject guides to a variety of handpicked Websites. On the next page, you can see what a sample subject-tree directory looks like on Yahoo! under the topic "Food Safety."

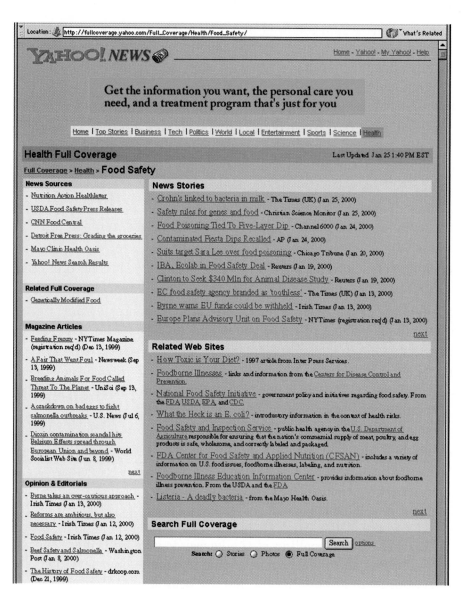

Saving a Site for Later

You may want to keep a list handy of favorite Websites, or sites you are currently using in a project. This will save you time because you can just click on the name of the site in your list and return to that page without having to retype the URL.

Different browsers have different names for this feature. For example, Netscape Navigator calls it a **bookmark**, while Microsoft Internet Explorer calls it **Favorites**.

Searching Out a Subject

Suppose you are writing a paper about the unique role computer-generated special effects play in today's blockbuster motion pictures. Here's an idea of one way to research this topic.

- First, we'll select a search engine. We'll start with WebCrawler—at http://www.webcrawler.com. The first keywords we enter are "computer generated graphics." The search engine found these sites:

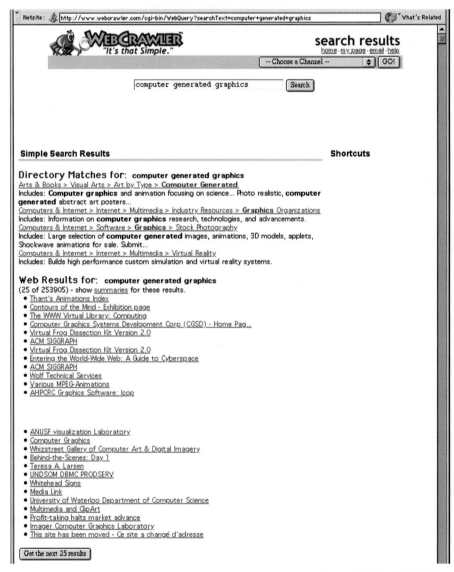

No good. Few sites on this list seem to mention special effects or computer graphics. Let's narrow the search. We'll try again, but this time we'll enter the keywords "computer generated effects + films." Now look at the list of topics:

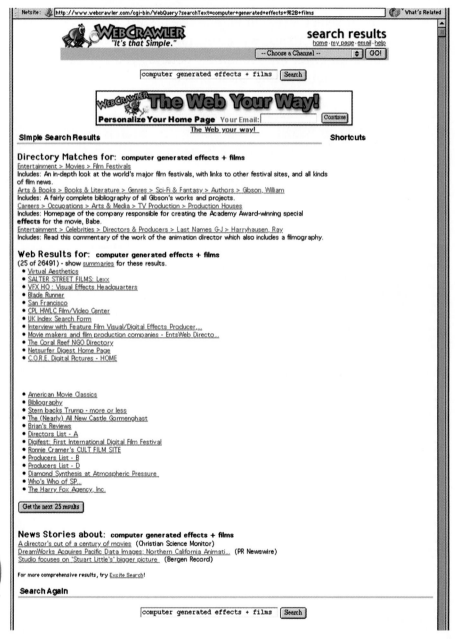

Copyright ©1995–2000 Excite Inc.

As you can see, there are many more choices to pick from. We'll click Visual Effects Headquarters Archive.

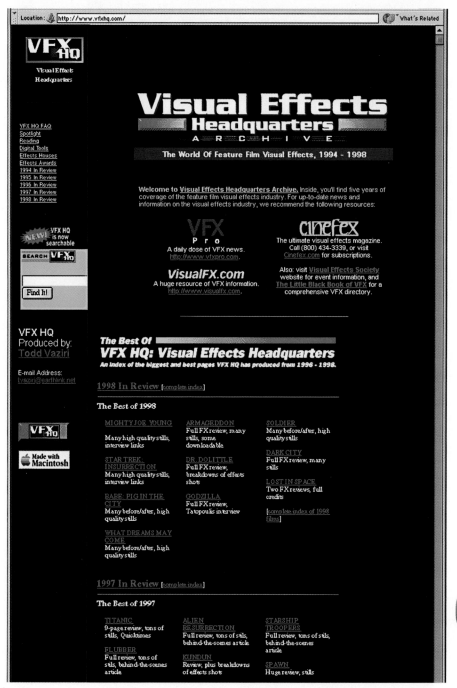

VFX HQ produced by Todd Vaziri ... http://www.vfxhq.com ... email tvaziri@earthlink.net.
All text Copyright ©Todd Vaziri, unless otherwise noted.

stils, behind-the-scenes
article

Review, plus breakdowns
of effects shots

SPAWN
Huge review, stills

CONTACT
Huge review, stills,
Quicktime movie

MEN IN BLACK
Full review, tons of stills

THE FIFTH
ELEMENT
Huge review, tons of
stills, Stetson interview

THE LOST WORLD
Full review, stills

VOLCANO
Full review, tons of stills,
behind-the-scenes article

SPEED 2
Huge review, tons of
stills

STAR WARS:
SPECIAL EDITION
Reviews of all three
movies

[complete index of 1997
films]

1996 In Review [complete index]

The Best of 1996

INDEPENDENCE DAY
Full review, stills, Quicktime movie

STAR TREK: FIRST CONTACT
Huge review, stills

MARS ATTACKS
Huge review, tons of stills

[complete index of 1996 films]

Visual Effects Headquarters Awards [complete index]

The Best of Awards

The 1997 VFX HQ
Awards
Winners included
TITANIC, THE LOST
WORLD and
STARSHIP
TROOPERS

The 1996 VFX HQ
Awards
Winners included
TWISTER,
INDEPENDENCE DAY
and THE FRIGHTENERS

Academy Award
Winners
A full list of winners
from 1939-1997

Spotlight Articles [complete index]

The Best of>

Transfer interrupted!

0" width="100%">

Patrick Tatopoulis: The Man Behind The Monster
2-part interview with the GODZILLA designer (6/98), Part One, Part Two

Time, Money and Effects
Carl Rosendahl's wisdom (6/98)

Bedtime for Deadtime
Frozen in time (6/98)

30th Anniversary Tribute to 2001
2-part interview with Con Pederson (4/98), Part One, Part Two

Boldly Trekking Into The Digital World
CG versus miniatures (5/98)

Letter to the Editor
The only one ever posted (2/98)

The Modern, Digital Illusion
The dehumanization of visual effects (1/98)

Looking
Back at
1997
The year in
effects (12/97)

The Secret's
Out...
SPEED 2's
bovine secret
(11/97)

The Touchy
Issue of
Credits
Crediting
artists (11/97)

Boss Shuts
Down
Three articles:
The Industry
Reacts, The
Best of Boss
and The
Closeout (9/97)

Super35
and "The
Fifth
Element"
VFX Sup.
Mark Stetson
talks about the
format (7/97)

The
Morphing
Artist
From
stop-motion to
CGI (5/97)

Mat Beck
Goes With
The Flow
An interview
with
VOLCANO's
supervisor (7/97)

"Star Wars"
Strikes Back
The pro's and
con's of the
Special
Editions (4/97)

The Magic of
ILM
A look at the
effects house
(12/96)

A Look at
the '80's and
'90's
A commentary
on the state of
effects films
(5/96)

VFX HQ produced by Todd Vaziri ... http://www.vfxhq.com ... email tvaziri@earthlink.net.
All text Copyright ©Todd Vaziri, unless otherwise noted.

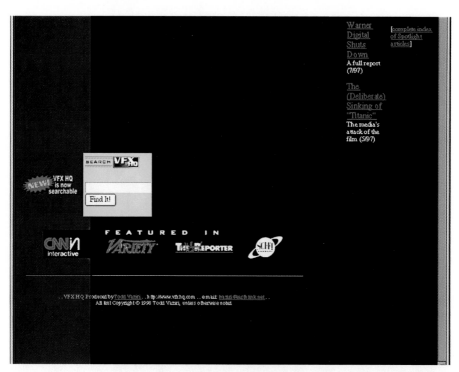

VFX HQ produced by Todd Vaziri ... http://www.vfxhq.com ... email tvaziri@earthlink.net.
All text Copyright ©Todd Vaziri, unless otherwise noted.

Wow—look at all these articles about computer-generated effects in well-known movies! Let's click "Babe, Pig in the City."

VFX HQ produced by Todd Vaziri ... http://www.vfxhq.com ... email tvaziri@earthlink.net.
All text Copyright ©Todd Vaziri, unless otherwise noted.

Even more talking animals are featured in BABE: PIG IN THE CITY, sequel to 1995's highly successful BABE. The original won an Academy Award for Best Visual Effects in 1995, and Mill Film, Rhythm & Hues, and Animal Logic contributed to the visual effects to the sequel.

These shots, accomplished by Rhythm & Hues Studios, feature real-life animals 'fitted' with digital prosthetics. The snouts of the animals were meticulously matchmoved in 3D, where a photorealistic mouth was animated and composited over the real mouth. In many cases, parts of the animals' real mouth (if not the entire mouth, snout, chin, etc.) had to be digitally erased.

Official Web Site: http://www.babeinthecity.com

Back to the 1998 Menu

 **Visual Effects** Headquarters ARCHIVE

Home   Spotlight   FAQ   Digital Tools
Effects Houses   Awards   Reading
Movies: 1994   1995   1996   1997   1998

There's some interesting information here about how they made the animals appear to speak using computer effects. We might also want to incorporate some of these fun pictures of the talking pig into our finished project. Again, more interesting information about how computer-generated effects contributed to the making of the film. For now, let's click the Back button and return to the Visual Effects Headquarters Archive to check out another film—"Godzilla."

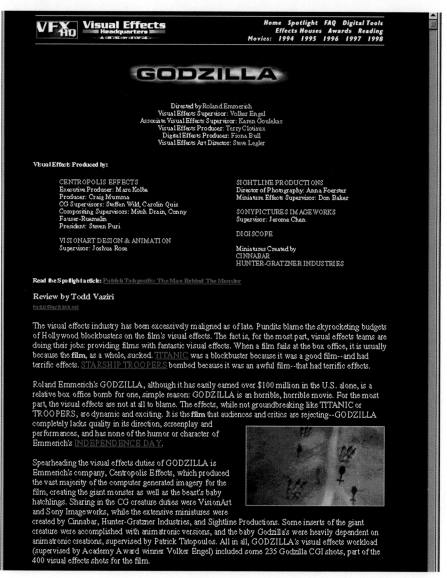

VFX HQ produced by Todd Vaziri ... http://www.vfxhq.com ... email tvaziri@earthlink.net.
All text Copyright ©Todd Vaziri, unless otherwise noted.

Much has been said and written about the incessant rain that obscures the giant creature in its New York setting. While the addition of rain to these night shots obscures some artifacts and allows artists to 'get away' with more, it also complicates the CG process, since the creature must appear to be rain-soaked in nearly every scene. Looking at the entire film, the most satisfying Godzilla shots are those where he is completely visible, in daylight, with the camera not moving. Godzilla's first appearance in a New York's harbor featured plenty of daylight (albiet overcast) shots of the giant monster--beginning with tight shots of his massive foot smashing cars, and ending with his dazzling confrontation with cameraman Hank Azaria, where Godzilla is fully revealed. Early shots of the sequence contained terrific matchmoving--the real camera and the CG camera were perfectly in synch--and the interaction between the CG creature and the real-life elements, like cars and people, was very convincing. Careful attention to shadows and extensive rotoscoping of foreground elements allowed these sequences to be successful, although the lack of motion blur on the creature frequently hurt CG shots.

The mutated lizard wanders its way through New York City. The CGI Godzilla was created by newly formed Centropolis Effects. Only a handful of shots of the title creature were completed with animatronic versions of the beast.

©1998 Tri-Star Pictures

The subsequent full-body shots of Godzilla confronting Azaria are brilliant, especially because of the kinetic camera movement. The director was able to use as many dollys and cranes as he wanted, and the CG and compositing teams were able to place the creature realistically within the scene. The best shot of the sequence is a terrific rotational camera move around Azaria as Godzilla approaches his position. Once again, lighting and rotoscoping of these shots make them successful.

Less successful is the design and texture of Godzilla. A monster movie's main creature needs to have character--something inherent to the design of the beast that lends an idea as to its character, its emotions, its desires. TROOPERS' bugs, JURASSIC PARK's dinosaurs, even T2's T-1000 all have some visual characteristics that give us a glimpse of what drives them. Godzilla looks like a man in a lizard suit, plainly and simply. This is not only due to the design, but the choreography and direction of the Godzilla sequences. There seems to be no rhyme or reason to his movements; the audience subsequently cares very little about this creature.

Not to be forgotten are some of the film's non-lizard effects shots. The very best of which is the fantastic helicopter shot of the beached tanker found on the Panamanian coast. From the POV of a hovering helicopter, the camera rotates around the massive liner, perched on the sandy shores of the beach. The shot is incredible--the CG boat is perfectly lit and matchmoved into the scene, even with the bouncy nature of the helicopter-shot background plate. The subsequent bluescreen shot of Matthew Broderick staring at the clawprint on the hull of the ship is less successful, due to the widly varying contrast levels of that shot, relative to the rest of the sequence.

"...the compositing of the creature into the backgrounds make these effects shots look like... well... effects shots."

Speaking of helicopters, they're all over GODZILLA. Flying overhead, helicopter POVs, even in the distant background, there are dozens upon dozens of shots involving the compositing of CG and model helicopters

VFX HQ produced by Todd Vaziri . . . http://www.vfxhq.com . . . email tvaziri@earthlink.net.
All text Copyright ©Todd Vaziri, unless otherwise noted.

into background plates. The most convincing shots are those where the camera is on the ground, slightly drifting to follow the path of the choppers. The most obvious are those where the helicopters fly only a few feet away from the camera, in situations where no real camera could possibly photograph the action. Overall, textures and lighting of the helicopters are quite realistic.

As these choppers pursue Godzilla through the streets of New York, the camera weaves down city streets. The CG creature and (mainly) CG helicopters were composited into background plates of miniature cityscapes, and although these shots are exciting, they do not look photorealistic. The lights from buildings' windows are far too bright and have an unnatural glow, and the compositing of the creature into the backgrounds make these effects shots look like... well... effects shots. The miniatures for the film, overall, are quite fantastic--the best of which appear in daylight shots, where miniature buildings are destroyed right and left with the accurate appearance of scale.

As revealed by a massive panning shot of the Madison Square Garden interior, Godzilla has laid hundreds of eggs. The reveal shot, realized with extensive miniatures, looks muddy and blurry, while subsequent shots of the Garden interior are much more successful. (An earlier version of this review incorrectly stated that a matte painting was used for the reveal shot. VFX HQ regrets the error.) The hatchlings were executed with a combination of animatronic and CG techniques, and the visual differences between them is obvious. Many of the CG baby shots seemed rushed--lighting, animation and compositing are sometimes brilliant, integrating the raptors--ahem, lizards into their background plates, and at other times awful, as if the CG elements were cut and pasted into plates without concern to shadows, reflections, or color levels. There are a ton of baby Godzilla shots, and only half of them achieve the realistic integration of CG element and background plate as such films as JURASSIC PARK and STARSHIP TROOPERS.

"It's too bad that director Emmerich and producer Dean Devlin couldn't have done a better job creating the non-effects shots."

The single best Godzilla sequence occurs after his 'resurrection'--his chase of our heroes, fleeing in a NYC cab, as Godzilla pursues them. Although one must suspend disbelief heavily for the sequence to work (as if big 'G' couldn't smash the cab with one swoop of his foot), the scene displays the best animation, lighting, and compositing of any other of the film. The Brooklyn Bridge sequence is perhaps more complicated than it has to be, with the bridge disintegrating around Godzilla, poles and supports flying all over the place. The eventual destruction of the beast isn't particularly interesting, with explosions obviously composited over and behind big 'G'.

The few effects' shortcomings aside, the effects teams did a terrific job on GODZILLA. It's just too bad that director Emmerich and producer Dean Devlin couldn't have done a better job creating the non-effects shots.

Check out **Cinefex 74.**
Official Web Site: http://www.godzilla.com
GODZILLA ©1998 Tri-Star Pictures

One more time, let's go back to Visual Effects Headquarters Archive, but this time, we're going to scroll down to the bottom of the page. Here, they have links to more than a dozen articles about effects and the movie industry. Let's try "The Magic of ILM."

The Magic of ILM
By Todd Vaziri

If you've visited the Effects Houses section of the VFX HQ, you have seen over a dozen of the biggest names in visual effects. Every house listed creates great images for today's feature films. Although parity of the industry exists, there is a definitive leader of the pack: Lucas Digital's Industrial Light & Magic (ILM).

Effects technology has become much cheaper over the years, and the capital it takes to start a new company has slowly been shrinking. Software like Softimage is now available to the consumer market, and SGIs are becoming a bit more affordable. Also, the talent pool seems to be getting larger as universities train students on valuable animation software.

Amidst all of the competition, ILM remains on top. They have the experience, the creativity, the tools, the history and the power to work on high profile shows and consistently perform well. The folks who built ILM pioneered the use of many techniques that are commonplace today. Think of how important CG imagery is in today's films. Where did feature film's use of CG begin? The most significant step in CG, in my opinion, was 1982's STAR TREK II: THE WRATH OF KHAN, whose dramatic Genesis simulation was an entirely computer generated sequence, the first of its kind. The group that worked on the sequence at ILM later separated from LucasArts and became a company called Pixar, whose TOY STORY represented yet another huge step in CG animation.

The Pixar example is just one of many arms of ILM's far-extending reach. Nearly every respected effects veteran is or was connected to ILM. The president of Sony Pictures Imageworks, Ken Ralston, spent almost two decades at ILM. Richard Edlund, who was integral to the effects of STAR WARS founded his own company, Boss Film Studios, Phil Tippett, the go-motion innovator, did the same and is currently running Tippett Studios. Digital Domain was founded by three men, all of which had serious relationships with ILM; James Cameron worked with ILM on THE ABYSS and T2, Stan Winston collaborated with them on JURASSIC PARK and T2, and Scott Ross was ILM's general manager.

The past ten years have been extraordinary for ILM in terms of the shows on which they've worked. (Never mind the fact that ILM provided effects for such blockbusters as E.T., RAIDERS OF THE LOST ARK, the STAR WARS trilogy, etc.) Since 1987, ILM has earned seven out of nine Academy Awards for visual effects. Just like other effects houses, ILM must prove its worth during the negotiations period--productions do not simply hand off their project to ILM blindly. Take TWISTER, for example. Director Jan DeBont and producer Steven Spielberg needed to be convinced that a CG tornado would work on film, or else the picture wouldn't have been made at all. The ILM test team was led by effects veteran Dennis Muren, and consisted of fx producer Kim Bromley, animator Dan Taylor, and CG artists Scott Frankel, Carol Hayden, Stewart Lew and Scott Frankel. The test was overwhelmingly successful--you may have even seen it. It was so fantastic, Warner Bros. attached it to the end of the teaser and trailer for the film.

The continuing power of ILM is also due to the snowball effect. ILM revolutionized effects in 1977, they get more high-profile, big-budget projects, ILM grows, the tools and resources expand, ILM gets more big-budget projects, ILM expands its talent, ILM gets another $80 million movie, etc.

ILM has brought about effects revolutions; techniques such as the morph and CG creation and animation were used effectively in their shows. They successfully graduated from the optical world to the digital world. Just look at the compositing in MISSION: IMPOSSIBLE and TWISTER. It is impeccable.

High profile, risky projects are nothing new to ILM. No matter what imagery is presented before them in a screenplay--not even if the technology isn't available yet--the effects house comes through with stunning results. A mysterious water tentacle? "We can do that (THE ABYSS)." Fully computer generated dinosaurs? "We can do that (JURASSIC PARK)." A chase scene with a virtual helicopter, a virtual train and a virtual tunnel? "We can do that (MISSION: IMPOSSIBLE)." They are constantly given the impossible and achieve it.

Owner George Lucas has crafted the company into an image factory. Easily the largest of all the effects houses, ILM is sometimes criticized for its 'assembly line' attitude in creating visual effects. No matter how ILM runs its business, they are at the top of their game.

The effects industry should be very proud of itself right now. Fantastic images are being created by the big companies, like ILM and Digital Domain, as well as other companies like Boss Film and Rhythm & Hues. But ILM is the heart of the industry--they are the most consistent effects house in terms of quality and quantity of images. The company is synonymous with special effects because of its rich history and continually expanding resources and talent.

Back to the Spotlight Main Menu

This article is more about the history of the company, ILM, than it is about how computer-generated effects are used in movies. Let's scroll down a little farther. Inside this article is some hot type on "Star Wars." The "Star Wars" movies introduced some amazing advances in computer-generated effects. This might be a good place to investigate.

Again, still no specific information. Let's keep looking. We'll click "Star Wars Special Edition."

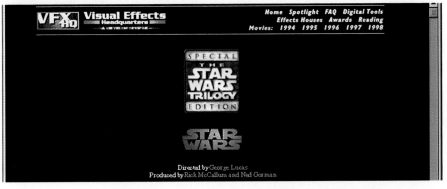

INDUSTRIAL LIGHT & MAGIC
Visual Effects Supervisors: Dave Carson, John Knoll, Steven Williams, Bruce Nicholson and Alex Seiden
Visual Effects Producer: Tom Kennedy
Visual Effects Consultant: Dennis Muren
CG Supervisors: Joe Letteri and John Berton

The impetus of the STAR WARS project was the desire to restore of the classic film for its 20th Anniversary. Lucas and Fox jumped at the chance to re-release all three films in grand fashion, adding and enhancing certain visual effects shots.

Certain effects shots from the film have been completely replaced using digital technology, while others use original photography as plates for brand new background and foreground elements. With a few exceptions, the new and enhanced shots fit seamlessly into the classic sci-fi flick.

The first of the brand new shots is a gorgeous establishing shot of R2D2 on Tatooine, just before the Jawas capture him. The shot begins on a stunning Tatooine sky at dusk, and tilts down to the lonely droid navigating the Tatooine surface.

In addition to the new R2 establishing shot, two more new 'replacement' establishing shots were made for Obi-Wan's home and Luke's moisture farm. The 1977 Obi-Wan establishing shot was an odd, nondescript, low angle of Luke's speeder parked outside a hut. This new shot is very wide and beautiful, featuring a lot of great colors and textures of the Tatooine surface. A slight zoom was added to the shot--if the artists had created a dolly-in instead of a zoom, the shot wouldn't have fit into the film. If you look carefully at the original film, there are very few dynamic camera movements, like cranes and dollys. The other establishing shot is an extended wide shot of Luke's farm. Using the original 1977 shot, the artists shrunk the footage, and added more sky, more of the Jawa's cruiser and more of Luke's farm in this breathtaking shot.

An isolated shot of the new CG Dewback and CG Stormtrooper. The background plate is a new shot, photographed in Yuma, AZ. Notice the slight highlight added to the trooper's helmet, consistent with the filters used back in 1977 for Tatooine scenes.

A CG Stormtrooper dismounts from a CG Dewback in this enhanced shot. The animation of the Trooper getting off the beast is phenomenal.

The first shot of the search sequence features real Stormtroopers and the synthetic Dewback and trooper in the background, along with an Imperial craft zooming across the sky.

Searching for the C3PO and R2D2, Imperial Stormtroopers use Dewbacks to help in the search. Originally, the scene consisted of a single shot of a Stormtrooper on an unmoving Dewback far in the distance--then the camera pans left to two troopers in the foreground. The sequence is now three shots long, with two brand new shots using newly shot Stormtrooper footage in Yuma, Arizona (the original photography took place in Tunisia). The two brand new shots feature fully computer generated Dewbacks with CG Stormtroopers riding them. The CG models look great, and the compositing of these two shots have the same 'look' as the original 1977 photography. The last shot is the 1977 pan, but instead of the immobile Dewback in the distance, we now see fully mobile CG Dewbacks and Stormtroopers. The CG elements and plate photography are perfectly married together.

A great new tigher shot of the Jawa's land cruiser is included in the Special Edition, replacing a very long, wide shot of the same cruiser.

Many of Luke's landspeeder shots (around 6 in all) have been 'fixed'--the orange optical blur underneath the floating speeder from the 1977 version has been erased and a new shadow was created.

VFX HQ produced by Todd Vaziri . . . http://www.vfxhq.com . . . email tvaziri@earthlink.net.
All text Copyright ©Todd Vaziri, unless otherwise noted.

The enhanced landspeeder shots (4 in all) add the illusion of the floating craft.

This enhanced shot features a man walking a Ronto (frame left) and the elimination of the orange distortion pattern underneath the floating landspeeder.

A speeder-bike nearly hits a Ronto as its Jawa riders get flung off the beast in this all-new shot from the Mos Eisley sequence.

Luke, Obi-Wan Kenobi and the two droids then venture off to Mos Eisley, Tatooine's bustling spaceport. The new Mos Eisley sequences feature both completely brand new shots as well as many brilliant enhanced shots.

The first is a brand new wide shot of the spaceport--the view that Obi-Wan and the gang sees as Kenobi calls it "a wretched hive of scum and villany." Spacecraft can be seen zooming in and out of the port, and the buildings look a lot more dense in this great establishing shot.

The landspeeder zooms over the camera into the city in another replacement shot. Instead of a blank sandy surface, many tiny creatures are seen hanging around the city--the Mos Eisley equivalent of pigeons. The design is very cute and the animation is really nice as the landspeeder zooms overhead, although it was quite apparent that the effect was accomplished in post-production. The contrast levels seemed a bit too high--the animals didn't seem as if they were actually in front of the camera.

The hero shot of the sequence appears next, as a completely new shot begins on two fighting droids, follows the landspeeder with a pan right, and cranes up, dozens of feet above the ground, allowing the audience to see the large, bustling city for the first time. The animation of the two droids (one a human-like droid and the other a floating probe droid) is fanatstic and quite funny. Numerous CG elements made up the shots, along with many digital matte paintings and miniatures. Although the shot technically and aesthetically brilliant, it simply does not fit into STAR WARS. The establishing crane shot is a standard in many films, but the 1977 version of STAR WARS had very little camera movement.

The hero shot of the sequence appears next, as a completely new shot begins on two fighting droids, follows the landspeeder with a pan right, and cranes up, dozens of feet above the ground, allowing the audience to see the large, bustling city for the first time. The animation of the two droids (one a human-like droid and the other a floating probe droid) is fanatstic and quite funny. Numerous CG elements made up the shots, along with many digital matte paintings and miniatures. Although the shot technically and aesthetically brilliant, it simply does not fit into STAR WARS. The establishing crane shot is a standard in many films, but the 1977 version of STAR WARS had very little camera movement.

Another five shots follow (some brand new, some enhanced), and many include new, thirty foot tall creatures, called Rontos. The animation and models of these CG models look fantastic, and compositing of these shots integrated them into the plate photography. If the Ronto's shape looks familiar, it should--it's actually a altered version of the CG model created for JURASSIC PARK's Brontosaurus, hence the name Ronto. In a few other shots outside the cantina, CG Rontos and Dewbacks, along with the floating Imperial droids are featured in the backgrounds of original 1977 photography. The match-moving and rotoscoping of these shots are **fantastic**--the shadows created for the floating droid are right on the money and are completely integrated into the 1977 shot.

The CG Stormtrooper makes another appearance in an enhanced shot--the Stormtrooper dismounts from the Dewback in some of the best humanoid CG animation I've ever seen.

VFX HQ produced by Todd Vaziri . . . http://www.vfxhq.com . . . email tvaziri@earthlink.net.
All text Copyright ©Todd Vaziri, unless otherwise noted.

Jabba the Hutt makes a cameo in STAR WARS in this newly restored sequence.

One of the biggest new scenes is the restored conversation between Han Solo and Jabba the Hutt. Originally shot with a human actor as Jabba, CG Supervisor Joe Letteri and animator Steve "Spaz" Williams replaced him with a fully CG Jabba slug, as he appeared in RETURN OF THE JEDI. This Jabba can slithers and squirms his way to Han, and has a discussion with Solo in the 5 shot sequence. Small alterations to Harrison Ford's movements were made to accomplish a seamless (and sometimes very funny) encounter between the human and the CG creature. A new feature to the sequence is Boba Fett--an actor in costume performed in front of a bluescreen in order to integrate the bounty hunter into the sequence. One problem I have with the new Jabba sequence is Jabba's eyes. The bright orange eyes of the puppet Jabba in JEDI are realized in the new shots as glossy, desaturated bulbs. Also, Jabba is far too expressive in this chapter of the STAR WARS saga, which betrays the way Jabba appears in RETURN OF THE JEDI.

An exclusive side-by-side comparison of the 1977 production footage and the newly enhanced shot including a computer generated Jabba. Careful erasure of the original actor as well as extensive rotoscoping and animation of Solo add to the realism of the sequence.

As the Falcon takes off from Mos Eisley, one brand new shot shows a CG Falcon rising from Bay 94, and an enhanced wide shot of the Falcon zooming into the air features a new, dynamic aerial move. As the Falcon tries to escape the Death Star's tractor beam, new, accurate camera shake animation was added to the interior shots.

A new explosion was shot for Alderaan's destruction, and features a colorful shockwave, very similar to ILM's shockwave created for STAR TREK VI. The Death Star's explosion was enhanced with this shockwave, as well.

A terrific enhanced shot was created for Han Solo's furious attack on a group of Stormtroopers. In the original shot, eight Stormtroopers turn around and fire on Solo. In the hilarious enhanced shot, an entire legion of Stormtroopers appear in the background.

In this incredible composite, the Rebel base exterior has been enhanced, giving the huge structure a new, rougher exterior.

No new model photography was used for space sequences for the Special Edition of STAR WARS--all spacecraft were created as CG models. Textures were scanned directly off of the original miniature models created in the late 70's, however. CG representations of the Millennium Falcon, the X- and Y-Wing fighters, as well as TIE Fighters will appear onscreen.

Intending to keep the pacing of the original film intact, the effects artists crafted each new space shot (around 30) to be the same frame length as the original shot. The choreography of the shots in question was enhanced--the new CG craft afford the animators a greater range of movement than the motion-control shot models. Instead of a limited three dimensional space for which the camera and the model to interact (due to stage size, model and camera rigging, etc.), the virtual camera and virtual model have infinite possibilities in terms of distance and perspective. New, exciting dynamics have been created to **enhance** the sequences' drama, not alter them.

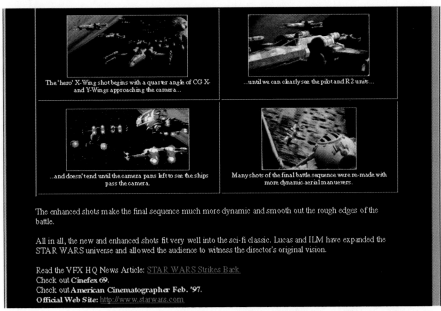

The 'hero' X-Wing shot begins with a quarter angle of CG X- and Y-Wings approaching the camera...

...until we can clearly see the pilot and R2 units...

...and doesn't tend until the camera pans left to see the ships pass the camera.

Many shots of the final battle sequence were re-made with more dynamic aerial manuevers.

The enhanced shots make the final sequence much more dynamic and smooth out the rough edges of the battle.

All in all, the new and enhanced shots fit very well into the sci-fi classic. Lucas and ILM have expanded the STAR WARS universe and allowed the audience to witness the director's original vision.

Read the VFX HQ News Article: STAR WARS Strikes Back
Check out **Cinefex 69**.
Check out **American Cinematographer Feb. '97**.
Official Web Site: http://www.starwars.com

VFX HQ produced by Todd Vaziri ... http://www.vfxhq.com ... email tvaziri@earthlink.net.

Here's the payoff! This article talks about how several years after the original "Star Wars" film was completed, advanced computer-graphic effects enhanced the Special Edition version of the film.

The Visual Effects Headquarters Archive produced a wealth of articles for our project. We could spend much longer on this one site alone. For now, let's set a bookmark here and go back to the Webcrawler site listing one more time.

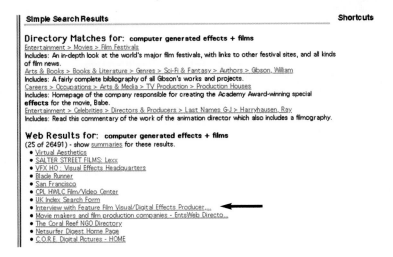

Simple Search Results   **Shortcuts**

Directory Matches for: computer generated effects + films
Entertainment > Movies > Film Festivals
Includes: An in-depth look at the world's major film festivals, with links to other festival sites, and all kinds of film news.
Arts & Books > Books & Literature > Genres > Sci-Fi & Fantasy > Authors > Gibson, William
Includes: A fairly complete bibliography of all Gibson's works and projects.
Careers > Occupations > Arts & Media > TV Production > Production Houses
Includes: Homepage of the company responsible for creating the Academy Award-winning special **effects** for the movie, Babe.
Entertainment > Celebrities > Directors & Producers > Last Names G-J > Harryhausen, Ray
Includes: Read this commentary of the work of the animation director which also includes a filmography.

Web Results for: computer generated effects + films
(25 of 26491) - show summaries for these results.
- Virtual Aesthetics
- SALTER STREET FILMS: Lexx
- VFX HQ : Visual Effects Headquarters
- Blade Runner
- San Francisco
- CPL HWLC Film/Video Center
- UK Index Search Form
- Interview with Feature Film Visual/Digital Effects Producer,... ◄━━━
- Movie makers and film production companies - EntsWeb Directo...
- The Coral Reef NGO Directory
- Netsurfer Digest Home Page
- C.O.R.E. Digital Pictures - HOME

- American Movie Classics
- Bibliography
- Stern backs Trump - more or less
- The (Nearly) All New Castle Gormenghast
- Brian's Reviews
- Directors List - A
- Digifest: First International Digital Film Festival
- Ronnie Cramer's CULT FILM SITE
- Producers List - B
- Producers List - D
- Diamond Synthesis at Atmospheric Pressure
- Who's Who of SP...
- The Harry Fox Agency, Inc.

Get the next 25 results

News Stories about: computer generated effects + films
A director's cut of a century of movies (Christian Science Monitor)
DreamWorks Acquires Pacific Data Images; Northern California Animati... (PR Newswire)
Studio focuses on 'Stuart Little's' bigger picture (Bergen Record)

For more comprehensive results, try Excite Search!

Search Again

Here we find another article about computerized visual effects, but from a producer's perspective.

An Interview with Robert O'Haver

The Reel Site

Interview conducted in October 1998. Bio updated as needed.

It's my pleasure to be able to present you this interview with Robert O'Haver, a **Feature Film Visual/Digital Effects Producer**.

I would like to give a big thanks to Mr. O'Haver for allowing me to interview him. He's a very busy man and I appreciate his time greatly.

I hope you find this an entertaining piece of writing. Please send any comments my way.

Michael T. Grace

Make sure to check out VisualFX.com, which Robert is the co-webmaster of.

Filmography:

Production Supervisor - *Dinosaurs*
Spikes Up Productions / Disney Feature Animation
Visual Effects Supervisor: Neil Krepla

Visual Effects Producer - *CutThroat*

> **What got you interested in the Visual FX field?**

I got the chance to work as a PA at Apogee. I was lucky to work with a lot of great people and saw that it was a fun way to make a living.

> **What did you study in school?**

Mostly business and some theater.

> **How did you go from business school to jobs that are FX-related? I mean, how are your interests related? You run a web site that's involved in Visual FX, yet you say you're mostly into the money aspects, etc. How's all this connected?**

A producer or production manager has to understand what everyone on a visual effects crew does, how much it costs, and how long it will take, so it's basically business. I've been around computers all my life so starting a website seemed natural. Terrence Masson and I opened VisualFx.com in 1994 to provide an on-line center for Visual FX professionals and enthusiasts alike. (VisualFx.com)

> **You studied business... but I imagine if you want to stay away from the producing and want to get specifically into the creative aspects, other classes would be better to take. What do you recommend people study if they're interested in the visual FX field?**

If you want to get into VFX take film classes, life drawing, computer classes, etc. You need to learn about the art of Visual Effects for motion pictures. This will give you more to draw from later.

Starting in December, VisualFx.com will have a complete section devoted to "Getting Started In The Visual Effects Industry." We will have interviews with award winning Visual Effects Supervisors with their answers to this question. Check it out.

> **Are more schools offering special-effects specific curriculum these days?**

Check out the Schools and Training Center Page on our site. The list is growing, with places from all over the world.

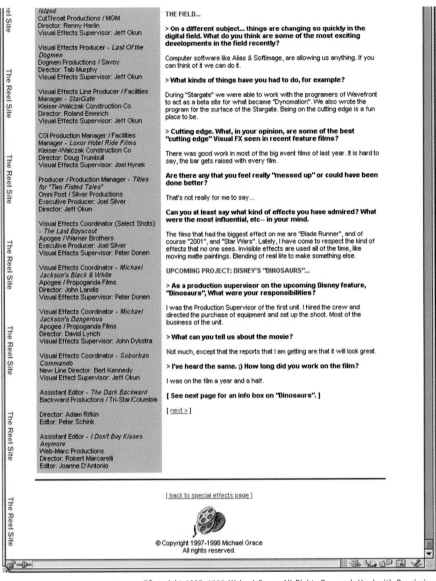

el Site

The Reel Site

The Reel Site

The Reel Site

The Reel Site

The Reel Site

The Reel Site

Island
CutThroat Productions / MGM
Director: Renny Harlin
Visual Effects Supervisor: Jeff Okun

Visual Effects Producer - *Last Of the Dogmen*
Dogmen Productions / Savoy
Director: Tab Murphy
Visual Effects Supervisor: Jeff Okun

Visual Effects Line Producer / Facilities Manager - *StarGate*
Kleiser-Walczak Construction Co
Director: Roland Emmrich
Visual Effects Supervisor: Jeff Okun

CGI Production Manager / Facilities Manager - *Luxor Hotel Ride Films*
Kleiser-Walczak Construction Co
Director: Doug Trumbull
Visual Effects Supervisor: Joel Hynek

Producer / Production Manager - *Titles for "Two Fisted Tales"*
Omni Post / Silver Productions
Executive Producer: Joel Silver
Director: Jeff Okun

Visual Effects Coordinator (Select Shots) - *The Last Boyscout*
Apogee / Warner Brothers
Executive Producer: Joel Silver
Visual Effects Supervisor: Peter Donen

Visual Effects Coordinator - *Michael Jackson's Black & White*
Apogee / Propoganda Films
Director: John Landis
Visual Effects Supervisor: Peter Donen

Visual Effects Coordinator - *Michael Jackson's Dangerous*
Apogee / Propoganda Films
Director: David Lynch
Visual Effects Supervisor: John Dykstra

Visual Effects Coordinator - *Suburban Commando*
New Line Director: Bert Kennedy
Visual Effect Supervisor: Jeff Okun

Assistant Editor - *The Dark Backward*
Backward Productions / Tri-Star/Columbia

Director: Adam Rifkin
Editor: Peter Schink

Assistant Editor - *I Don't Buy Kisses Anymore*
Web-Marc Productions
Director: Robert Marcarelli
Editor: Joanne D'Antonio

THE FIELD...

> On a different subject... things are changing so quickly in the digital field. What do you think are some of the most exciting developments in the field recently?

Computer software like Alias & Softimage, are allowing us anything. If you can think of it we can do it.

> What kinds of things have you had to do, for example?

During "Stargate" we were able to work with the programers of Wavefront to act as a beta site for what became "Dynomation". We also wrote the program for the surface of the Stargate. Being on the cutting edge is a fun place to be.

> Cutting edge. What, in your opinion, are some of the best "cutting edge" Visual FX seen in recent feature films?

There was good work in most of the big event films of last year. It is hard to say, the bar gets raised with every film.

Are there any that you feel really "messed up" or could have been done better?

That's not really for me to say...

Can you at least say what kind of effects you have admired? What were the most influential, etc-- in your mind.

The films that had the biggest effect on me are "Blade Runner", and of course "2001", and "Star Wars". Lately, I have come to respect the kind of effects that no one sees. Invisible effects are used all of the time, like moving matte paintings. Blending of real life to make something else.

UPCOMING PROJECT: DISNEY'S "DINOSAURS"...

> As a production supervisor on the upcoming Disney feature, "Dinosaurs", What were your responsibilities?

I was the Production Supervisor of the first unit. I hired the crew and directed the purchase of equipment and set up the shoot. Most of the business of the unit.

> What can you tell us about the movie?

Not much, except that the reports that I am getting are that it will look great.

> I've heard the same. ;) How long did you work on the film?

I was on the film a year and a half.

[See next page for an info box on "Dinosaurs".]

[next >]

[back to special effects page]

The keywords "computer generated effects + films" seemed to work well. Let's try our search again using the Lycos search engine this time. We'll also narrow our search even further by adding the word *visual,* so our keywords will be "computer generated visual effects + films." Here's the list the service retrieved.

The LYC🔵S, Network   Find it · Talk about it · Shop for it

SEARCH FOR computer generated visual effe   [Go Get It!]®   Save this Search

Advanced Search | Parental Controls | Multimedia Search

🖐 Buy the top programming books   🖐 Movie magazines

POPULAR   [POPULAR· WEB SITES· NEWS ARTICLES]

1 of the Web sites reviewed by Lycos Editors match your search

START HERE: Effects News, Click Here!

1. Digital Hollywood - Hollywood's latest creative and entertaining applications for digital film and video, computer-generated animation, and webcasting.
    http://www.wired.com/news/news/digiwood/

WEB SITES   [POPULAR· WEB SITES· NEWS ARTICLES]

424 Web sites were found in a search of the complete Lycos Web catalog

1. CyberTech Productions : The Visual Effects & Animation Co. - **Visual Effects** & Animation for TV & Film makers .
    CyberTech Productions is a **visual effects** & animation facility established in 1994 to bring **computer-generated** imagery
    (CGI) closer to the
    http://www.singnet.com.sg/~cybertch/

2. Cinema Sites: Animation & Visual Effects - [Previous Section] [Table of Contents] [Next Section] Animation & Visual
    Effects: _____ Conventional: _____ AnimeExpo97: The International Comics & Animation Exposition, was
    held Ju
    http://www.cinema-sites.com/Cinema_Sites_ANI.html

3. Compufield-2d cell animation, computer-generated cartooning, animator pro press - Home Page Desktop Publishing
    Digital Graphics Commercial Arts Multimedia Jewellery Designing Fashion Designing Textile Designing Interior
    Designing Mechanical Engineering Coreldraw Adobe Photoshop Ani
    http://www.compufield.com/3d_studio_max.html

4. Computer Effects: Extras - Extras Animation Humans Vehicles Creatures Extras Cg vs Models Home Glossary Comments   PC, MAC, and CPUs at eBay
    Media About Our Team Computers are not always used for large scale projects, where the companies love to promote t
    http://tqdadvanced.org/8496extras.html

5. Computer Effects: Extras - Extras Animation Humans Vehicles Creatures Extras Cg vs Models Home Glossary Comments Media About Our Team
    Computers are not always used for large scale projects, where the companies love to promote t
    http://tqdadvanced.org/8496extras.html

6. Starship Troopers and Fall Blockbuster Films Powered by Adobe After Effects - FOR THE LATEST IN TECHNOLOGY Join TechMall's Custom News
    And Information Resource Service! Complete listing of past top stories and new product releases. Search Top Tech Stories Get stock quotes, news
    http://www.techmall.com/techdocs/TS971112-4.html

7. Star Trek: The Experience - news virtual tour comm center background the team Rhythm & Hues Studios -- Producer (Film) Rhythm & Hues Studios
    produces live-action commercials as well as **computer-generated** images and **visual effect**
    http://www.startrekexp.com/6kg4t/rhythm.html

8. Visual FX - Picture this: 100100101 **Visual Effects** by the Numbers by Frank Garcia Clue: Godzilla toys, BC Tel, X-Files and Knowledge Network If you were
    playing Jeopardy! responding to the category of Special FX
    http://204.191.245.9/Dev94/VisualEffect.html

9. Computer Graphics vs. Models - CG vs. Models Nobody that has seen Star Wars can ever forget the exhilarating feeling of watching the spaceships fly
    through space in what was the pinacle of special effects in 1977. However, now Geor
    http://tqdadvanced.org/8496cgvsmodels.html

10. Topic 1: Introduction to Computer Graphics - SCC308 banner Topic 1 banner Development of **Computer** Graphics Given how accustomed the general public
    has become to seeing various forms of **computer-generated** imagery (CGI) in **films** and on television
    http://www.deakin.edu.au/A-agoodman/scc308/topic1.html

[414 More Web Sites about **computer generated visual effects** + **films**]

NEWS ARTICLES   [POPULAR· WEB SITES· NEWS ARTICLES]

9 articles were found from a search of the Web's leading news sites

1. NOVA Online | Special Effects: Titanic and Beyond | Resources - NOVA Online (click here for NOVA home) Special **Effects** Titanic and Beyond Site Map
    Resources Links | Books | Magazines | Schools | Job Opportunities/Internships | Credits | Special Thanks Links SIGGRA
    More Articles about **computer generated visual effects** + **films** from pbs.org

2. NOVA Online | Special Effects: Titanic and Beyond | Virtual Humans - NOVA Online (click here for NOVA home) Special **Effects** Titanic and Beyond Site
    Map Virtual Humans By Kelly Tyler After millions of years of natural selection, humans beings have some serious competiti
    More Articles about **computer generated visual effects** + **films** from pbs.org

3. U.S. News: A step closer to creating a wholly digital cinematic human (5/24/99) - U.S. News Online This Week's Highlights News & Views U.S. News U.S. News Ads
    Urban campuses finally join their neighbors Rubin's sense of timing is exquisite to the end U.S. News Ads U.S. News Ads Search the sit
    More Articles about **computer generated visual effects** + **films** from usnews.com

[6 More News Articles about **computer generated visual effects** + **films**]

🛒 PC, MAC, and CPUs at eBay   💻 Download Free Lycos Browser Now!

SEARCH FOR computer generated visual effe [Go Get It!]®

Advanced Search | Parental Controls | Multimedia Search

Again, we've found a great assortment of articles. Here are two that look interesting.

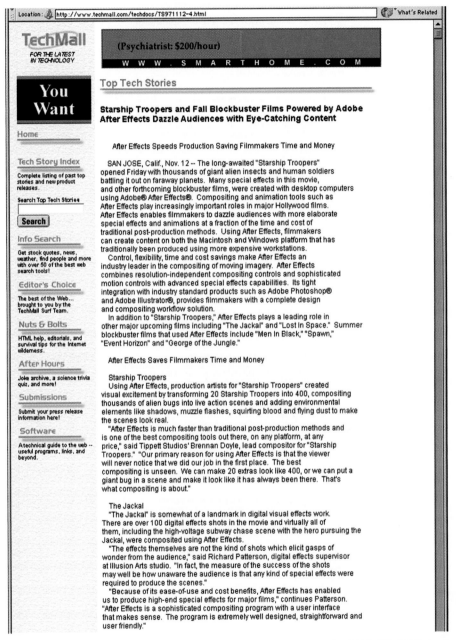

Spawn

Los Angeles-based Banned From the Ranch Entertainment (BFTR) used After Effects for the majority of their supernatural visual effects and graphics work on the movie "Spawn." After Effects was used in combination with MetaCreations' particle system plug-ins to generate elements -- from rolling storm clouds to animated fire -- and composite the final film-resolution shots.

"After Effects allowed us to dial up a wide variety of special effects, from light rays to particle systems, that would typically require a 3D package," said BFTR lead digital artist, Erich Ippen. "After Effects gave us the ability to do everything we wanted and more, with respect to compositing, at a fraction of the cost of other film compositing systems."

After Effects Improves Productivity

Lost In Space

The challenge of making spaceship data screens appear both real and futuristic for the forthcoming film "Lost In Space" was met with the help of After Effects. Using After Effects, a team of six generated graphics for on-set screens that were made to look like spaceship 'communicators' used to present navigational, engineering, weapons systems and life support information to the crew throughout the film.

"We found After Effects to be a vital piece of software for our production methods. Indeed, I cannot think of any other animation programs that could provide such intuitive yet powerful flexibility," said Richard Briscoe, freelancer for Bionics Productions, Ltd. "Both the timeline and motion path controls, as well as the filters, allow for an enormous range of possibilities. After Effects allows for the production of the highest quality material, with all the control one could wish for."

George of the Jungle

In "George of the Jungle," After Effects and Photoshop were used in combination exclusively for the film's matte painting work, bringing the mysterious Ape Mountain to life. Sophisticated composites of George's pet, Shep the elephant, were accomplished quickly utilizing After Effects.

"We knew from the outset that After Effects would be an integral part of 'George of the Jungle's visual effects," said Tim Landry. "Features such as the integration of Photoshop layers, offer effects options that are simply not available in any other compositing package."

Event Horizon

AMXdigital used After Effects in conjunction with Photoshop and Illustrator to design and produce computer screen graphics for the two spaceships in "Event Horizon." AMX developed a series of animated sequences displaying internal computer systems, ship's log, video consoles and communications devices for each of the space vessels. In total, 11,520 frames were generated for eight minutes of special effects.

According to Zoe Black, the producer on the project, "Going from basic animation to sophisticated project structure was easy and straightforward with After Effects. The software was also extremely stable and coped well with multiple animated layers."

About Adobe After Effects

With After Effects, users can combine unlimited layers of moving and still images, add any number of keyframes, animate and apply special effects to each layer and adjust layers until the composite looks and moves exactly as intended. After Effects gives users precise control over every aspect of the composite -- from sub-pixel positioning to controlling the shape and velocity of each animation path. After Effects is available on both the Macintosh and PC platforms, and offers sophisticated support for multiprocessing to take advantage of today's high-performance desktop systems.

About Adobe Systems Inc.

Based in San Jose, California, Adobe Systems Incorporated develops and supports products to help people express and use information in more imaginative and meaningful ways across print and electronic media. Founded in 1982, Adobe helped launch the desktop publishing revolution. Today, the company offers a market-leading line of application software and type products for creating and distributing visually rich communication materials; licenses its industry-standard technologies to major hardware manufacturers, software developers, and service providers; and offers integrated software solutions to businesses of all sizes. For more information, see Adobe's home page at http://www.adobe.com on the World Wide Web.

SOURCE Adobe Systems Inc.

CONTACT: Press/Analyst Contact: Heidi White of Cunningham Communication, Inc., 650-858-3759, or hwhite@ccipr.com

COMPUTER GRAPHICS vs. MODELS

Nobody that has seen Star Wars can ever forget the exhilerating feeling of watching the spaceships fly through space in what was the pinacle of special effects in 1977. However, now George Lucas and Industrial Light and Magic are investing $10 million to recreate the Star Wars trilogy in special editions to be released in 1997. Almost all of the ships from the previous films will be replaced with computer generated vehicles. Which raises an interesting question: which works better? Hand-built models or computer graphics?

As in just about any effects shot, with models it's the details that count. Model builders, computer or otherwise, will spend hours working on the smallest items to bring the level of realism to the highest possible. After all, an audience will quickly get bored with an object if there isn't anything interesting to see after the first look. Details are a big part, and it's relatively easy to modify a hand-built model with a small piece from a battleship model, or other off-the-shelf set. However, computer graphics people can't do that. A little spray of paint for the model builder is several days of drawing textures and then applying them for the computer people. A quick dent in the plastic will translate into a couple hours of reworking the wireframe, and then rerendering the entire object. If it's one large, static model you're trying to build, a hand-built model will probably be the fastest, easiest and cheapest. But once you begin to grow beyond just the one model, the pros begin to move toward the computer's side.

When creating the large number of spaceships for his Star Wars films, Lucas had a couple of options to make the large space battles come to life. The first was much more time consuming: he could have the effects people build a different model for each craft. Or he could take a quicker and cheaper way, and take numerous shots of the same model, or a small number of models, and composite them together to make it appear as if there were a number of ships flying about. But there are problems with both of these approaches. To build a large number of models is expensive and takes time. But to shoot just a few models limits what the audience is seeing, and to pull off such an effect, the camera couldn't stay on one ship too long, or the viewers will realize it's the same ship over and over.

The problem is further complicated by lighting. To get a certain level of lighting on one ship is not a problem; just position a light and let the camera roll. But to get the lighting to fit the same on hundreds of ships is almost impossible. Small flaws quickly become amplified, and the shot becomes transparent. Computers can solve the lighting problem and the difficulty of creating numerous ships.

By taking the original model on the computer and replicating it several times, a graphics artist can make small changes on each of the wireframes to keep the ship from looking the same, and then combine the models into the same shot with a static light source. This ensures that all the models will have the same amount of shading, as if they were all being filmed at the same time.

Computer models also allow for a much greater degree of maneuverability. Rather than needing to reposition the wires and bars that keep a hand-built model in place, and then moving the camera to keep the shot right. With a computer model, moving the wireframe to fit the request is faster and easier. And rather than needing to set the camera on a robotic arm and move it past the model, often resulting in a blocky effect, a computer can simulate a path of motion for a ship and execute it numerous times without error or need for adjustment. Computer generated ships can also be manipulated to fit the constraints of gravity and centripital force. Mathematical models guarantee that a tight turn by a fighter plane will look as if the ship were turning in real life.

Independence Day
[Image courtesy of the VFXHQ]

Basically, models have one big plus working for them. There's nothing more impressive than a large pyrotechnic display to amaze the audience. As Independence Day demostrated, models still have a good grip on the explosion area. Small charges can be set and sequenced to obliterate a scale model of a structure. Explosions are one thing that computer artists haven't been able to emulate correctly. The small particles that explosions create have to be individually built and rendered. Mathematical models can create realistic flight paths for the debris, but a computer can't really work out the structural weaknesses of a building and pinpoint where the blast will break out the walls. And if any fire is required (it usually is), programmers have yet to render a realistic looking flame. Models are quite simply more realistic, faster and more cost effective when dealing with explosions.

For the most part, models and computer graphics each have their pros and cons. They work best when put together. A prime example is a certain shot from Twister. A oiltanker was scripted to fly down from the sky and then explode ahead of the character's truck. A CG rendered tanker was created to fly from the sky, and a large full scale model was built to drop in front of the truck and explode. A perfect combination of two technologies, the scene comes off flawlessly.

To conclude, each technique has it's own uses. Computers are quickly replacing what models used to do, but the models still have a position to fill. Until the next generation of computer artists works out the kinks in 3d rendering, we'll continue to see a small version of the White House exploding on screen, and we'll still be content.

RELATED LINKS

Obviously we could go on and on. The important thing to remember is to use your imagination plus a little deductive reasoning. Just imagine you are a cyberspace detective sniffing out clues on a case!

 When doing research on the Internet, never give out your name, address, telephone number, or school name without checking with your teacher and/or your parents. Although most sites are safe, a few sites may not use the information in the way they say they are going to use it.

LANGUAGE

CHAPTER 1

The Parts of Speech

 **Pretest**

Directions

Write the letter of the term that correctly identifies the underlined word in each sentence.

EXAMPLE

1. Oregon is known for <u>its</u> apples and lumber.

1 A noun

B pronoun

C verb

D adverb

ANSWER **1 B**

1. Oregon is one of the <u>northwestern</u> states.
2. On the east <u>it</u> is bordered by Idaho.
3. The Cascade Mountains <u>run</u> from north to south in the eastern part of the state.
4. The mountains end <u>gradually</u> in the river valleys further west.
5. The major cities include Portland, <u>Salem</u>, and Eugene.
6. Lumber is the state's <u>foremost</u> product.
7. With the lumber industry come related industries: paper, furniture-making, <u>and</u> many others.
8. Fishing is also a major source of <u>income</u>.
9. Tourism <u>is</u> very important in Oregon as well.
10. Crater Lake National Park is a major attraction for tourists <u>from</u> all parts of the world.

1   **A**   adjective
    B   adverb
    C   preposition
    D   noun

2   **A**   noun
    B   pronoun
    C   verb
    D   adverb

3   **A**   noun
    B   pronoun
    C   verb
    D   adverb

4   **A**   adjective
    B   adverb
    C   preposition
    D   noun

5   **A**   adjective
    B   adverb
    C   preposition
    D   noun

6   **A**   adjective
    B   adverb
    C   preposition
    D   noun

7   **A**   conjunction
    B   interjection
    C   preposition
    D   adjective

8   **A**   adjective
    B   adverb
    C   preposition
    D   noun

9   **A**   noun
    B   pronoun
    C   verb
    D   adverb

10 **A**   conjunction
    B   interjection
    C   preposition
    D   adjective

Frida Kahlo. *Long Live Life,* 1954.
Oil on masonite, 20¼ by 28⅛ inches. Reproduction authorized by the National Institute of Fine Arts and Literature, Mexico City, Mexico.

Describe   What do you see in the painting? What shapes do you see?

Analyze   Based on the title of the painting, what do you think the author meant to convey through her work?

Interpret   How could a writer use description and vivid words to communicate the same ideas?

Judge   What could a written description include that a painting could not? What could a painting include that a written description could not?

At the end of this chapter, you will use the artwork as a visual aid for writing.

Nouns

As you write, you use words in different ways. You might, for example, use the word *plant* as a thing—a *plant* for your mother. You also might use it to describe a piece of furniture—a *plant* stand. You could even use it to explain an action—*plant* a tree. How a word is used in a sentence determines that word's **part of speech.** A noun is one part of speech. In the English language, there are eight parts of speech.

THE EIGHT PARTS OF SPEECH	
noun (names)	**adverb** (describes, limits)
pronoun (replaces)	**preposition** (relates)
verb (states action or being)	**conjunction** (connects)
adjective (describes, limits)	**interjection** (expresses strong feeling)

When you use the word *plant* as a thing—a plant for your mother—you are using the word *plant* as a noun.

A **noun** is the name of a person, place, thing, or idea.

> **Edward** has achieved **fame** at our **school** for his academic **achievement.**
>
> Another **student** on the swim **team** won a **competition** in **Dallas, Texas.**
>
> **Sarah** excels in **drama** and wants to act on **Broadway** after **graduation.**

Nouns may be classified in several ways.

Concrete and Abstract Nouns

Nouns are often categorized in two main groups: concrete nouns and abstract nouns. Because **concrete nouns** name people, places, and things, they are easy to identify. **Abstract nouns** are often harder to recognize because they name ideas and qualities.

CONCRETE NOUNS	
PEOPLE	boy, teacher, parent, aunt, Mr. Jones, Dr. Holly
PLACES	school, Earth, Chicago, America, Madison Avenue
THINGS	ocean, cat, car, credit, cash

ABSTRACT NOUNS	
IDEAS AND QUALITIES	love, hope, grief, sorrow, dream, belief, beauty, happiness

You can learn about plural nouns on pages L537–L544 and possessive nouns on pages L485–L486.

PRACTICE YOUR SKILLS

 Check Your Understanding

Finding Nouns

 Science Topic **Write the nouns in each sentence.**

1. Coral comes from an animal in the ocean that is known as a coral polyp.

2. The polyp can be smaller than a fingernail.

3. The polyp secretes a chemical to form a skeletal "house."

4. When a polyp dies, a new generation grows on the skeleton.

5. Millions of these skeletons form reefs of coral.

6. The reefs grow in the shallow oceans near the equator.

7. Reefs provide homes to billions of creatures.

8. Living reefs host one of every four species that live in the ocean.

9. At half an inch a year, colonies of coral grow slowly.

10. Commercial fishers, chemical runoff, and the aquarium industry are destroying the beauty of the reefs.

Common and Proper Nouns

Nouns may also be classified as common and proper nouns.

A **common noun** names any person, place, or thing.

A **proper noun** names a particular person, place, or thing.

COMMON AND PROPER NOUNS	
COMMON NOUNS	friend, city, spacecraft, holiday
PROPER NOUNS	Maria Rodriguez, Houston, *Voyager*, Memorial Day, August, Carson's

Some proper nouns include more than one word. They are still considered one noun. *Maria Rodriguez* is the name of one person, and *Memorial Day* is the name of one holiday.

You can learn about capitalizing proper nouns on pages L382–L384.

PRACTICE YOUR SKILLS

 Check Your Understanding
Finding Common and Proper Nouns

> Music Topic
>
> **Write the nouns in each sentence. Label each one C for common noun or P for proper noun.** (A date is considered a proper noun.)

1. Franz Joseph Haydn was born in Rohrau, Austria.

2. "Papa" Haydn was one of the greatest composers of the classical period.

3. Mozart and Beethoven were influenced by Haydn's development of the sonata form.

4. Young Haydn studied in Vienna, a city in Austria.

5. In 1762, Haydn entered the service of Prince Nicolaus, who helped Haydn develop as a composer.

6. The prince gave Haydn a huge musical staff.

7. Haydn's schedule included daily performances of chamber music and four weekly performances.

8. For these occasions Haydn composed new works.

9. Haydn's fame spread, first to Vienna and then throughout Europe.

10. His most famous choral work is entitled *The Creation*.

● Connect to the Writing Process: Editing
Capitalizing Proper Nouns

Write each sentence and capitalize the proper nouns.

11. mozart and haydn were friends in vienna.

12. haydn also taught beethoven.

13. On new year's day in 1791, haydn arrived in england.

14. haydn wrote twelve symphonies for london, which are called the *london symphonies*.

15. One of haydn's compositions is entitled *the seasons*.

Communicate Your Ideas

APPLY TO WRITING

Movie Review: *Common and Proper Nouns*

The editor of your school paper has asked you to write a review of a recent movie. Write a brief description of the movie and explain why you would or would not recommend it to high school students. In your introduction include details such as the movie title, names of the main actors, and the director. These details will help make your review specific and interesting to read.

Compound Nouns

Some nouns include more than one word. Such words are **compound nouns.** Compound nouns can take three different forms. Always check a dictionary to find out which form to use.

COMPOUND NOUNS	
Two Words	first aid, coffee roll, sleeping bag
Hyphenated Words	ambassador-at-large, baby-sitter
Single Words	turtleneck, officeholder, onlooker

You can learn how to form the plural of compound nouns on page L542.

Collective Nouns

Other nouns, such as *team* and *orchestra,* name groups of people or things. These nouns are **collective nouns.**

COMMON COLLECTIVE NOUNS			
band	congregation	flock	orchestra
class	crew	gang	swarm
colony	crowd	herd	team
committee	family	league	tribe

CONNECT TO WRITER'S CRAFT

When a writer uses a collective noun for a subject, the verb must agree. Even though collective nouns represent a group of people or things, most are singular unless an *s* is added.

SINGULAR   Our French **class** sponsors five exchange students.

PLURAL   The language **classes** sponsor twenty exchange students in all.

PRACTICE YOUR SKILLS

● Check Your Understanding
Finding Compound and Collective Nouns

General Interest **Make two columns on your paper. Label the first column *compound nouns.* Label the second column *collective nouns.* Then, in the proper column, write each noun.**

1. The students look forward to the annual awards assembly.
2. This year's assembly will take place during study hall.
3. The football team will be honored for winning the state championship.
4. The band will play a special song.
5. Shelia Smith will receive an award for saving a man who had a heart attack.
6. The audience will be on its best behavior.
7. The officeholders of the senior class will say a final good-bye to their classmates.
8. Onlookers will include parents, family, and friends.
9. The staff will honor the seniors with a reception in the cafeteria.
10. A group of parents will provide ice cream for the crowd.

● Connect to the Writing Process: Editing
Spelling Compound Nouns

Write each sentence, checking to see that each compound noun is in the proper form. Use a dictionary if necessary.

11. My brother in law went to see a movie.
12. He had to get a baby sitter for my niece, who is only four.
13. A four year old can get into trouble easily.
14. The last time that she had a sitter, my niece cut up all my brother in law's turtlenecks.
15. At least she did not need first aid.

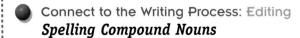

General Interest **Write the nouns in each sentence below.**

1. Huge snowdrifts caused Jim Maxwell to arrive late at the auction on a cold day in December.

2. He arrived as a group of horses were being loaded into a truck headed for a slaughterhouse.

3. As Jim watched, he noticed Cassidy, a horse that had worked nine years on a farm.

4. The horse was in bad shape; his ribs stuck out, and mud covered his coat.

5. Jim paid the dealer a few dollars and returned to his family.

6. Because the children showed Cassidy so much affection, he soon fattened up and looked like a new animal.

7. With great sadness Jim had to sell him ten months later to a neighbor, Dr. Mason Adams.

8. Cassidy, however, did not like the idea of new quarters at all.

9. That night, he jumped a fence, ran across a field, wandered through gardens and yards, and returned to Jim.

10. After higher fences did not stop Cassidy, Jim bought him back.

11. Impressed by his jumps, Jim started to train him.

12. By the following spring, Cassidy was ready to participate in competitions.

13. After defeating thoroughbreds at exhibitions in nearby arenas, Cassidy entered a national competition.

14. He became the winner, the best jumper in the United States.

15. Jim accepted the trophy before a crowd of cheering fans in Madison Square Garden.

Pronouns

A **pronoun** is a word that takes the place of one or more nouns.

Pronouns make it possible to eliminate awkward repetition in writing. The second sentence in the following example flows more smoothly and is easier to understand because pronouns were used.

> Mary told Paul that Mary received an *A* on Mary's math test.
> Mary told Paul that **she** received an *A* on **her** math test.

Personal Pronouns

Personal pronouns are the most common kind of pronoun. They are divided into three groups, depending on whether they are first-person, second-person, or third-person pronouns.

PERSONAL PRONOUNS	
FIRST PERSON	(the person speaking)
SINGULAR	I, me, my, mine
PLURAL	we, us, our, ours
SECOND PERSON	(the person spoken to)
SINGULAR	you, your, yours
PLURAL	you, your, yours
THIRD PERSON	(the person or thing being spoken about)
SINGULAR	he, him, his, she, her, hers, it, its
PLURAL	they, them, their, theirs

> **You** can meet **them** at **my** house.
> **We** should take **your** umbrella with **us.**

CONNECT TO WRITER'S CRAFT

Good writers make certain that each personal pronoun has an antecedent. An **antecedent** is the noun that the pronoun refers to or replaces. Using pronouns and antecedents correctly helps to clarify meaning.

Andrea and **Lynn** said **they** enjoyed the fair.

The **fair** made more money than **it** has in recent years.

You can learn about pronouns and their antecedents on pages L274–L278.

Reflexive and Intensive Pronouns

Reflexive and intensive pronouns are formed by adding *–self* or *–selves* to certain personal pronouns. They are used to refer to or to emphasize nouns or other pronouns.

Jason makes **himself** a snack before the game. (reflexive)
I **myself** do not like to cook. (intensive)
Some fans could see **themselves** on the monitor. (reflexive)
We **ourselves** did not have a good view. (intensive)

REFLEXIVE AND INTENSIVE PRONOUNS	
SINGULAR	myself, yourself, himself, herself, itself
PLURAL	ourselves, yourselves, themselves

PRACTICE YOUR SKILLS

● Check Your Understanding
Finding Pronouns

Contemporary Life | **Write the pronouns and label them *P* for personal, *R* for reflexive, and *I* for intensive.**

1. The school is holding its football tryouts at three-thirty.

2. "Ari said he would try out for the team," Rob stated.

3. Ari's friends decided they themselves would go to the tryouts.

4. Janice told Bonnie, "We should have brought our raincoats with us."

5. "Lani said she couldn't meet us," Lily told Rob.

6. Ari found himself with his own private cheering section at the tryouts.

7. Coach Mayer said he was looking forward to a good season if the players would do their part.

8. "Your passing is fine, but I think you should work on your running game," Coach told his players.

9. Janice and Bonnie worked themselves hard.

10. Ari himself decided to work harder, too.

● Connect to the Writing Process: Editing
Correcting Pronoun and Antecedent Agreement

Decide whether the underlined pronoun in the second sentence agrees with the antecedent in the first sentence. If the pronoun and antecedent agree, write C for correct. If the pronoun is incorrect, rewrite the second sentence using the correct pronoun.

11. Bob climbed the stairs into the bleachers. They sat in the top row.

12. The two teams were on the field. It was groomed and ready for the big game.

13. The referees began the trek out onto the field. He were ready for the game.

14. The usher spoke to the fans. He asked her to stand.

15. Polly held her purse. I did not want to lose it.

16. Polly found a dollar in her purse. He gave it to Kent.

17. Kent and Edie went for refreshments. We were hungry.

18. Our friends wandered around the stadium. We were lost.

19. The referee blew the whistle. We was loud.

20. The quarterback threw the ball. They completed the pass.

Other Kinds of Pronouns

In addition to personal pronouns, there are other kinds of pronouns. Three of the most common are indefinite pronouns, demonstrative pronouns, and interrogative pronouns.

Indefinite pronouns quite often refer to unnamed people or things. Therefore, they usually do not have definite antecedents as personal pronouns do.

> **Everyone** likes a good book.
> At the library meeting, **nothing** important happened.
> After class **no one** was ready for homework.

COMMON INDEFINITE PRONOUNS			
all	both	few	no one
another	each	many	nothing
any	either	most	others
anybody	everybody	neither	several
anyone	everyone	nobody	some
anything	· everything	none	someone

Demonstrative pronouns are used to point out specific people, places, or things.

> **This** is my favorite book.
> Can you also carry **these?**
> We bought **those** at the discount store.

DEMONSTRATIVE PRONOUNS			
this	that	these	those

The pronouns *this* and *these* refer to something nearby. *That* and *those* refer to something in the distance.

Interrogative pronouns are used to ask questions.

What did you find out about the author?
Who is waiting for your response?
Whose are these?

INTERROGATIVE PRONOUNS				
what	which	who	whom	whose

You can learn about another kind of pronoun, the relative pronoun, on pages L164–L167.

PRACTICE YOUR SKILLS

Check Your Understanding
Finding Indefinite, Demonstrative, and Interrogative Pronouns

Literature Topic | **Write each pronoun. Then use the label *ind.* for indefinite, *dem.* for demonstrative, and *int.* for interrogative.**

1. Few can put down a good mystery.

2. That is my favorite story about Sherlock Holmes.

3. I loaned my copy to someone.

4. Who could put it down?

5. Some would call it a detective story.

6. What does Ashton think?

7. Everybody has a different opinion.

8. Several agreed it is a detective story.

9. One police captain said several of his officers use stories about Holmes as a detective manual.

10. Most would agree the stories are fiction.

11. Whom do you believe?

12. After careful consideration, these are only opinions.

Using Pronouns

History Topic **Write each sentence adding the kind of pronoun indicated in parentheses.**

13. ■ was Mariah Vance? (interrogative)

14. ■ was the family that employed her? (interrogative)

15. ■ knew that she was once Lincoln's housekeeper. (indefinite)

16. ■ was revealed to Adah Sutton. (demonstrative)

17. Ms. Vance shared stories that ■ had heard. (indefinite)

18. Ms. Sutton wrote down ■ in shorthand in the early 1900s. (demonstrative)

19. She thought that ■ would be interested. (indefinite)

20. ■, however, was interested in publishing the manuscript until recently. (indefinite)

● Connect to the Writing Process: Revising
Changing Indefinite Pronouns to Change Meaning

21.–25. Some indefinite pronouns are exact opposites and can change the meaning of a sentence. Choose five of the preceding sentences that have indefinite pronouns, and rewrite them with different indefinite pronouns to change the meaning of each sentence.

Communicate Your Ideas

APPLY TO WRITING

Journal Entry: *Pronouns*

Last week you had a most amazing experience. You want to be able to remember every detail clearly, so you will be able to share this story with your grandchildren someday. In a journal, write an entry that captures this experience. Make use of personal pronouns to avoid overusing nouns. You may choose to write using all first-person pronouns or all third-person pronouns.

General Interest **Write the nouns and pronouns in each sentence.**

1. During the Great Depression, Charles Darrow lost his job.

2. With time on his hands, he began to invent things like puzzles.

3. One day he got an idea for a game about Atlantic City, the place where he and his wife had spent their vacations.

4. First he drew the outline of the board on the tablecloth.

5. Then he built little houses and hotels from scraps of wood.

6. Colored buttons became tokens, and pieces of cardboard became the deeds to properties.

7. Next Charles bought play money and a pair of dice.

8. Everyone loved the game and wanted one.

9. When he could not keep up with the orders, Darrow tried to sell his game to a large company.

10. What do you think happened?

11. They came up with fifty-two reasons why no one would play it.

12. Darrow himself then arranged for the printer to make five thousand copies of the game.

13. This is now the most popular game in the world.

14. The rules are printed in eighteen different languages.

15. Do you know what game this is?

A **verb** expresses action or being and is the main part of the predicate of a sentence.

ACTION | The shadow of the clouds **moves** across the snow.

The snow **sparkles** beneath the sun's rays.

BEING | The snow **is** pearly white.

Footprints **are** visible in the snow.

Verbs are an important part of speech because you cannot write a complete sentence without a verb. This section will explain the different kinds of verbs and will show you how to use them effectively in your writing. Most of the verbs that you will use when you speak or write are called action verbs.

 Action Verbs

An **action verb** tells what action the subject of a sentence is performing.

The action verbs in the following sentences each show a physical action.

Martha **marched** with her dogs across the snowy road.
Charlie **mailed** the package to Alaska yesterday.
Toby **loaded** supplies on the sled.

Action verbs can also show mental action or ownership.

I **remembered** the day of the race well.
Jerry **had** his winter gear with him.
Chen **forgot** the package.

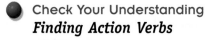

CONNECT TO SPEAKING AND WRITING

The verb is the most powerful word in a sentence. If you choose your verbs carefully, you can make your sentences come alive and give your listeners or readers an exact mental image. Notice the difference in the following sentences.

The young boy **came** into the room.
The young boy **ambled** into the room.
The young boy **bolted** into the room.

PRACTICE YOUR SKILLS

Check Your Understanding
Finding Action Verbs

General Interest **Write the action verb in each sentence.**

1. Hardy dogs run in the Iditarod.

2. Mushers and dogs endure razor-sharp ice fields, waist-deep snow, and knee-deep creeks.

3. The race takes about nine days.

4. It lasts as long as two weeks for the slowest mushers.

5. The race commemorates the 1925 run from Nome to Nenana, Alaska.

6. Mushers and dog teams delivered serum for a diphtheria epidemic.

7. Twenty dog teams relayed the medicine 6,874 miles in 5 days.

8. Today's race starts early in the day on Fourth Avenue in Anchorage, Alaska.

9. Onlookers line the trail.

10. Mushers from all around the world enter the race.

11. The teams travel through tiny villages and major cities.

12. Race announcers compete with each other for an interview with the winner.

Using Specific Verbs

The verb *said* is often overused. Substitute four more specific verbs for the verb *said* in the sentence below to change the sentence's meaning. Use a dictionary or thesaurus to help you. Write each sentence.

13.–16. "It's time to begin the celebration," **said** the winner of the race.

Communicate Your Ideas

APPLY TO WRITING

News Article: *Action Verbs*

You have been given the assignment of describing the championship football game for your yearbook. Write a news story about the game, being sure to include specific action verbs so that your fellow students will be able to remember the game for years to come.

Before writing, brainstorm answers to the following questions.

- What are the names of the two teams?
- What is the date and the final score?
- What does the quarterback do?
- What was the best play?

Transitive and Intransitive Verbs

An action verb that takes an object is a **transitive verb.**

To find an object, say the subject and the verb and then ask the question *What?* or *Whom?* A word that answers either question is the object.

TRANSITIVE   I **saw** the ducks in the middle of the road.
(I saw *What?* or *Whom? Ducks* is the object; therefore, *saw* is a transitive verb.)

An action verb that does not have an object is an
intransitive verb.

> INTRANSITIVE The ducks **waddled** safely across the road.
> (The ducks waddled *What?* or *Whom?* There
> is no object; *waddled* is an intransitive verb.)

Some verbs may be transitive in one sentence and intransitive in
another sentence.

> TRANSITIVE The rabbit **nibbled** the carrot.
> (*Carrot* is the object.)

> INTRANSITIVE The rabbit **nibbled** around the lettuce leaves.
> (There is no object.)

PRACTICE YOUR SKILLS

● Check Your Understanding
Finding Transitive and Intransitive Verbs

General
Interest **Write the action verb in each sentence. Then label
each one *T* for transitive or *I* for intransitive.**

1. Coyotes howl along with the music at outdoor concerts in Los Angeles.
2. Beavers build dams in the Potomac River near Washington, D.C.
3. For a while, a fox lived in New York's Yankee Stadium.
4. Most raccoons tip garbage cans over.
5. The cans' contents provide food for the raccoons.
6. Some types of falcons live on the tops of skyscrapers.
7. Many animals make their homes on the center strips of highways.
8. In some cities police on horses patrol streets.
9. Pigeons existed everywhere for centuries.
10. They often live in cities.

Verb Phrases

A **verb phrase** is a main verb plus one or more helping verbs.

Following is a list of common helping verbs.

COMMON HELPING VERBS	
be	am, is, are, was, were, be, being, been
have	has, have, had
do	do, does, did
OTHERS	may, might, must, can, could, shall, should, will, would

> The small black dog **has disappeared.**
> It **was wearing** a blue collar.
> It **might respond** to a whistle.

Notice in the following examples that a verb phrase may be interrupted by other words.

> The little dog **should** never **have gone** near the lake.
> It **was** always **looking** for new adventures.
> It **wasn't looking** for an alligator, though.

You can learn more about contractions on page L495.

CONNECT TO SPEAKING AND WRITING

The word *not* and its contraction *n't* often interrupt verb phrases. Neither is part of the verb.

Cats **do** not **fetch** very well.
They **don't like** loud noises.

When you are doing a piece of formal writing, such as a research paper, you should spell out the word *not.* Use the contraction *n't* only in speaking and in informal writing situations.

Practice Your Skills

● Check Your Understanding
Finding Verb Phrases

General Interest **Write the verb phrase in each sentence.**

1. Today, many people are viewing their pets as members of their family.

2. Veterinary schools are teaching their students about pet owners' problems, too.

3. In the past pets were kept for protection from pests and strangers.

4. Now, a cat or a dog is often treated like a child by its owners.

5. Almost 79 percent of pet owners may give their pets holiday presents.

6. Some companies do allow dogs in the workplace.

7. Day-care enterprises for dogs and cats are springing up.

8. People can turn to animals for companionship.

9. Dogs do help people in many ways.

10. Seeing-eye dogs can enter many places not accessible to other dogs.

11. Usually dogs are not allowed in the cabin of an airplane.

12. American pet owners might spend as much as twenty billion dollars a year on their pets.

● Connect to the Writing Process: Revising
Using Verb Phrases

13.–15. Match each helping verb on the left to the correct main verb on the right to create verb phrases. Then write a sentence about a cat for each verb phrase.

might have	protect
are	protected
did	protecting

APPLY TO WRITING

Summary: *Verb Phrases*

You have just seen an action movie that you want to encourage your friends to see. Write a summary of that movie for your friends and be sure to use some of the verb phrases listed below.

- was running
- should go
- have been seeing
- could lift
- will recommend
- would act
- did not like

Linking Verbs

A **linking verb** links the subject with another word in the sentence. The other word either names or describes the subject.

Chico **was** the winner of the election.

(*Was* links *winner* and the subject, *Chico*. *Winner* renames the subject.)

You **will be** happy with the results.

(*Will be* links *happy* with the subject, *you*. *Happy* describes the subject.)

Forms of the verb *be* are the most common linking verbs. In fact, any verb phrase ending in *be* or *been* can be a linking verb.

COMMON FORMS OF *BE*		
be	will be	has been
being	can be	had been
is	could be	could have been
am	should be	should have been
are	would be	would have been
was	may be	may have been
were	might be	might have been
been	must be	must have been
shall be	have been	

Meg Hedren **could be** next year's class president.
(*President* renames the subject, *Meg Hedren*.)

The campaign **has been** long and difficult.
(*Long* and *difficult* describe the subject, *campaign*.)

The forms of the verb *be* are not always linking verbs. To be a linking verb, a verb must link the subject with another word that renames or describes the subject. In the following examples, the verbs simply make statements.

She **was** there.
Her candidate **is** on the stage.

Additional Linking Verbs

The verbs in the following list may also be used as linking verbs. All these verbs can be used with helping verbs as well.

ADDITIONAL LINKING VERBS					
appear	feel	look	seem	sound	taste
become	grow	remain	smell	stay	turn

Carmen **will become** the treasurer.
(*Treasurer* renames the subject, *Carmen.*)

The speaker on the stage **appeared** nervous.
(*Nervous* describes the subject, *speaker.*)

You can learn about subject complements on pages L90–L91.

PRACTICE YOUR SKILLS

● Check Your Understanding
Finding Linking Verbs

History Topic **Write the verb or verb phrase in each sentence. Then write the two words that the verb links.**

1. Thomas Jefferson may have been one of the most influential people of his time.

2. He was president from 1801 until 1809.

3. Jefferson had been a representative in the Virginia House of Burgesses.

4. He is famous for the Declaration of Independence.

5. Some of Jefferson's ideas were radical for his time.

6. He was a successful statesman.

7. He remained minister to France from 1784 until 1789.

8. His life could have been peaceful and ordinary.

9. Instead, Jefferson became the third president of the United States.

10. He must have been very intelligent.

● Connect to the Writing Process: Drafting
Using Linking Verbs

Draft four sentences of your own about a famous person, using the following linking verbs.

11. will be   **12.** looks   **13.** may be   **14.** has been

Linking Verb or Action Verb?

Most of the additional linking verbs can also be action verbs if they show action. They are linking verbs if they link the subject with another word that renames or describes the subject.

LINKING	The scientist **looked** skeptical.
ACTION	She **looked** all over the lab for her pen.
LINKING	The lab **grew** quiet in the afternoon.
ACTION	Steve **grew** bean plants for his experiment.

PRACTICE YOUR SKILLS

● Check Your Understanding
Distinguishing between Linking Verbs and Action Verbs

Science Topic **Write the verb or verb phrase in each sentence. Then label each one L for linking or A for action.**

1. Many tiny insects appear sinister under a microscope.

2. Huge hairy monsters appear under the magnifying lens.

3. Some bugs grow no larger than the size of a period.

4. At times bugs do not seem very helpful.

5. Leeches became useful in the field of medicine during the Middle Ages.

6. Even today, leeches remain useful in certain types of medicine.

7. Some people grow squeamish at the sight of a spider.

8. Mosquitoes remain a pesky problem.

9. Moths look for light.

10. Butterflies seem more colorful than moths.

● Connect to the Writing Process: Drafting
Using Linking Verbs and Action Verbs

Use the following verbs first as a linking verb and then as an action verb in your own original sentences about insects.

11. feel   **12.** turn   **13.** sound   **14.** stay   **15.** grow

Communicate Your Ideas

APPLY TO WRITING

E-mail Message: *Verbs*

Your best friend is anxious to go out with your cousin. Your cousin, however, is reluctant to accept a date until she knows more about your best friend. Write an E-mail message to your cousin in which you describe what kind of a person your best friend is. Include a description of the types of things your friend likes to do. Then identify the action verbs and the linking verbs.

 QuickCheck Mixed Practice

General Interest **Write the verb or verb phrase in each sentence. Label each verb *L* for linking or *A* for action.**

1. For many people Clyde Beatty has remained the greatest animal trainer of all time.

2. Without protection he would enter a cage of twelve to twenty-four animals.

3. His only weapon was a pistol with blanks in it.

4. During his long career, Beatty faced thousands of lions and tigers.

5. Once in a while, these animals would become uncontrollable.

6. Several times, five-hundred-pound beasts clawed him.

7. In one act he handled forty big cats at once.

8. This feat was unusually dangerous.

9. Beatty could not keep all the animals in his range of vision.

10. He performed this act only one time.

Adjectives

An **adjective** is a word that modifies a noun or pronoun.

Adjectives can be compared to the colors an artist uses to make a drawing come alive. Because they can totally transform ordinary, dull nouns or pronouns, adjectives can add a vividness and richness to your writing. For instance, notice how the adjectives in **bold** type below make the car easy to visualize in your mind.

The **old green** sedan has a **rusty** bumper and **bald** tires.

To find an adjective, first find each noun and pronoun in a sentence. Then ask yourself, *What kind? Which one(s)? How many?* or *How much?* about each one. The answers will be adjectives.

ADJECTIVES		
WHAT KIND?	**fresh** smell **tall** grass	**loud** horn **strong** wind
WHICH ONE(S)?	**these** windows **that** woman	**red** carpets **sleek** dress
HOW MANY?	**twenty** seats **six** men	**one** car **fifty** cents
HOW MUCH?	**great** amount **small** dose	**much** help **little** aid

Most adjectives come before the nouns or the pronouns they modify. A few adjectives come after the nouns or pronouns they modify, and some adjectives follow linking verbs. Notice that more than one adjective can modify the same noun or pronoun.

BEFORE A NOUN	The **frisky, playful** kitten woke us.
AFTER A NOUN	The kitten, **frisky** and **playful,** woke us.
AFTER A LINKING VERB	The kitten is **frisky** and **playful.**

PUNCTUATION WITH TWO ADJECTIVES

Sometimes you will write two adjectives before or after the noun or pronoun they describe. If those adjectives are not connected by a conjunction—such as *and* or *or*—you might need to put a comma between them.

To decide whether a comma belongs, read the adjectives and add the word *and* between them.

- If the adjectives make sense, put a comma in to replace *and*.
- If the adjectives do not make sense with the word *and* between them, do not add a comma.

COMMA NEEDED	The soft, fluffy kitten turned somersaults in every room. *(The soft and fluffy kitten reads well.)*
NO COMMA NEEDED	It was a cute brown kitten. *(A cute and brown kitten does not read well.)*

You can learn more about linking verbs and find a complete list of them on pages L25–L28.
You can learn more about predicate adjectives on page L92.
You can learn more about commas with adjectives on pages L419–L420.

Proper Adjectives and Compound Adjectives

Two special kinds of adjectives also answer the adjective questions. A **proper adjective** is formed from a proper noun and begins with a capital letter. A **compound adjective,** like a compound noun, takes different forms. The words in a compound adjective may be combined into one word or may be joined by a hyphen.

PROPER AND COMPOUND ADJECTIVES		
PROPER ADJECTIVES	**Swiss** watches	**Italian** bread
COMPOUND ADJECTIVES	**high-school** student	**third-class** mail

You can learn more about proper adjectives on page L395.

Writers create better descriptions for readers by using a variety of adjectives.

ADJECTIVE	Eva's costume is **pretty.**
PROPER ADJECTIVE	Eva's costume is **South American.**
ADJECTIVE	The **silent** crowd watched Eva dance.
COMPOUND ADJECTIVE	The **spellbound** crowd watched Eva dance.

▶ Articles

A, an, and *the* form a special group of adjectives called **articles.** *A* comes before words that begin with a consonant sound, and *an* comes before words that begin with a vowel sound.

> **A** doughnut was on **a** dish in the middle of the table.
> **An** orange was left on **an** ivory plate.

You will not be asked to list articles in the exercises in this book.

PRACTICE YOUR SKILLS

● Check Your Understanding
Finding Adjectives

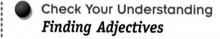

Social Studies Topic **Write the adjective or adjectives in each sentence. Beside each adjective, write the noun or pronoun each adjective modifies.**

1. The doughnut has been called a delicious accident.

2. Soldiers during World War I have been credited with the discovery of the popular doughnut.

3. Rain, cold and heavy, had fallen for many days in a village in France.

4. The morale of the men was low.

5. Two top-notch representatives of the Salvation Army looked for a quick remedy.

6. According to the story, they mixed a pot of dough and rolled the lumpy mixture with a large bottle.

7. Then they cut round pieces of dough with a can.

8. The small pieces of dough were then fried on a crude, homemade stove.

9. The unusual results, warm and tasty, did the trick for the soldiers.

10. Temporarily, the men did not feel homesick.

Connect to the Writing Process: Editing
Writing Adjectives and Articles Correctly

Edit the sentences below. Watch for mistakes in capitalizing proper adjectives and in using articles. Write the sentences correctly.

11. Doughnuts were probably first made in an french hamlet in 1917.

12. Nearly a thousand american soldiers were stationed in a tiny village.

13. The modern doughnut was born when the tasty discovery eventually made a atlantic crossing to the United States.

14. Today, doughnuts come in a assortment of flavors, sizes, and shapes.

15. A boston cream doughnut is an particular favorite of many people.

16. A cream-filled doughnut does not have an hole cut in the round pastry.

17. The round pastry can also be filled with an fruit-flavored jelly.

18. Some bakers make an hawaiian doughnut.

19. The icing tastes like an pineapple.

20. Near an holiday some bakeries add bright decorations and colorful frostings.

APPLY TO WRITING
Description: *Adjectives*

Doris Lee. *Thanksgiving,* 1935.
Oil on canvas, 28⅒ by 40 inches. The Art Institute of Chicago.

You have been to an art exhibit at a local museum. For you, one of the most interesting pictures was Doris Lee's painting called *Thanksgiving.* Your younger sister is also interested in art and has asked you to describe to her the most interesting painting at the exhibit. Write a note to your sister that describes this painting. Be sure to use a good variety of adjectives to bring this painting to life.

Other Parts of Speech Used as Adjectives

The same word may be used as an adjective in one sentence and a noun in another sentence.

ADJECTIVE	**Porch** furniture is on sale now.
	(*Porch* tells what kind of furniture.)
NOUN	We built a **porch** on our house.
	(*Porch* is the name of a thing.)
ADJECTIVE	**Name** tags were given to the people at the convention.
	(*Name* tells what kind of tags.)
NOUN	Patios and Porches was the **name** of the sponsor.
	(*Name* is a thing.)

Name can also be used as a verb.

| VERB | They will **name** the winner at the banquet. |

Some words can also be used as pronouns or adjectives. The following words are adjectives when they come before a noun and modify a noun. They are pronouns when they stand alone.

WORDS USED AS ADJECTIVES OR PRONOUNS		
Demonstrative	**Interrogative**	**Indefinite**
that	what	all · · · · · · · many
these	which	another · · · more
this	whose	any · · · · · · · · most
those		both · · · · · · · neither
		each · · · · · · · other
		either · · · · · several
		few · · · · · · · · some

ADJECTIVE	**These** boots are too large for me.
PRONOUN	**These** are too large for me.
ADJECTIVE	**What** answer did he give you?
PRONOUN	**What** did he give you?

The possessive pronouns *my, your, his, her, its, our,* and *their* are sometimes called pronominal adjectives because they answer the adjective question *Which one(s)?* Throughout this book, however, these words will be considered pronouns.

PRACTICE YOUR SKILLS

● Check Your Understanding
Determining Word Use

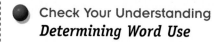 Art Topic **Write the underlined word in each sentence. Then label each word *A* for adjective, *N* for noun, or *P* for pronoun.**

1. <u>Most</u> people agree that Winslow Homer was an interesting American artist.

2. He changed the way Americans saw <u>watercolors</u> by developing Impressionist techniques.

3. <u>Many</u> of his paintings feature the New England seashore.

4. <u>Those</u> who knew him well thought him to be an eccentric person.

5. His <u>watercolor</u> paintings are vivid and lyrical.

6. <u>Most</u> of his work can be interpreted on many levels.

7. It is <u>this</u> complexity that makes his work so interesting and attractive.

8. His <u>many</u> nature paintings seem as if they are about to come to life.

9. He was one of <u>those</u> reclusive painters, and he was shy.

10. <u>This</u> first painting of his was purchased secretly by his brother when no one else would buy it.

11. <u>One</u> of Homer's famous paintings was featured on a postage stamp.

12. A <u>retrospective</u> of his work has been in museums in Boston, New York, and Washington, D.C.

13. A <u>retrospective</u> book has been written about Homer's depictions of African Americans.

14. The Civil War provided <u>another</u> subject for his artistry.

15. <u>Several</u> of the best art museums in the United States now house Homer's paintings.

● Connect to the Writing Process: Drafting
Using Adjectives as Different Parts of Speech

Write two sentences for each word listed below, using the word as an adjective the first time and as a noun or pronoun the second time.

16. plant   **17.** which   **18.** all   **19.** these   **20.** wool

Communicate Your Ideas

APPLY TO WRITING

Instructions: *Adjectives*

You have been invited to a Mardi Gras party that requires costumes. You need help putting together your costume. Think about the kinds of things you might need. Choose an idea for your costume, and write instructions so that your parents will be able to help you assemble this costume. Brainstorm answers to the following questions before writing your instructions.

- What kind of costume would you like to wear?
- What color of fabric would you like to use?
- What should the mask look like?
- Will you be able to easily assemble, glue, or sew the parts together?
- How will you decorate the costume?
- Do you need any props?

Be sure to use colorful adjectives in your instructions.

Adverbs

An **adverb** is a word that modifies a verb, an adjective, or another adverb.

To find an adverb, ask yourself, *Where? When? How?* or *To what extent?* Words answering these questions will be adverbs. Another way to find adverbs is to look for words ending in *–ly*. Some adverbs, however, do not end in *–ly*.

COMMON ADVERBS			
afterward	fast	now	soon
again	hard	nowhere	still
almost	here	often	straight
alone	just	outside	then
already	later	perhaps	there
also	long	quite	today
always	low	rather	tomorrow
away	more	seldom	too
down	near	so	very
even	never	sometimes	well
ever	next	somewhat	yesterday
far	not (n't)	somewhere	yet

● Adverbs That Modify Verbs

Most adverbs modify verbs. An adverb that modifies a verb modifies the whole verb phrase.

WHERE   We looked **everywhere** for Paul.

WHEN   He is **always** speaking before groups.

HOW   This one was **carefully** listening to him.

PRACTICE YOUR SKILLS

● Check Your Understanding
Finding Adverbs

Contemporary Life **Write the adverb in each sentence. Then, next to each adverb, write the word or words it modifies.**

1. That candidate unexpectedly won.

2. The campaign manager carefully planned the New Hampshire primary.

3. Many people strongly disagreed with the candidate's views on tax reform.

4. Both candidates debated well.

5. The voters waited eagerly for the election results.

6. The incumbent conceded graciously.

7. The candidates did not resort to mudslinging during the campaign.

8. The president's arrival at the inaugural ball was perfectly timed.

9. The guests happily cheered when the president and first lady danced.

10. The new president should always put our nation's well-being at the top of his agenda.

● Connect to the Writing Process: Revising
Using Adverbs to Modify Verbs

Add adverbs to modify the verbs that are underlined in the following sentences. Write the new sentence.

11. Walk over the ice on the sidewalk.

12. The snow fell during the night.

13. You should prepare for sudden snowfalls this winter.

14. Many people were shoveling their sidewalks.

15. The children listened to the radio for school cancellation announcements.

Adverbs That Modify Adjectives and Other Adverbs

A few adverbs modify adjectives or other adverbs. The adverbs in the following examples answer the question *To what extent?*

| MODIFYING AN ADJECTIVE | The weather this winter has been **extremely** cold. |
| MODIFYING AN ADVERB | My grandparents visit **quite** often. |

Finding adverbs that modify adjectives and other adverbs is easy if you first identify all the adjectives and adverbs in the sentence. Then ask yourself, *To what extent?* about each one. Notice in the preceding examples that the adverbs that modify adjectives and other adverbs usually come before the word they modify.

PRACTICE YOUR SKILLS

 Check Your Understanding
Finding Adverbs

General Interest **Write the adverb or adverbs in each sentence. Then, beside each one, write the word or words that it modifies.**

1. Joe Campana's poorly maintained house was rapidly decaying.

2. City officials almost condemned the building and ordered it demolished.

3. Unfortunately Joe did not have the money for a new house.

4. Then something happened that Joe thought was absolutely incredible.

5. Volunteers offered help and quickly built Joe a new home.

6. Joe was very thankful.

7. "Nothing like this has ever happened to me," the old man said.

8. It was a rather impressive effort on the part of the volunteers.

9. Large corporations generously donated appliances and furniture to the project.

10. Joe told the volunteers he would never forget the wonderful gift.

● Connect to the Writing Process: Drafting
Using Adverbs

Write a sentence about volunteer work for each of the following adverbs. Underline the word that the adverb modifies.

11. rather

12. very

13. somewhat

14. seldom

15. often

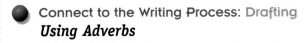

Communicate Your Ideas

APPLY TO WRITING

Feature Article: *Adverbs*

The local newspaper has asked you to write a feature about student athletes. You are to evaluate one athlete's performance for an upcoming special edition of your hometown paper. Choose an athlete whom you admire. He or she may excel in the areas of academics and community service as well as in sports. Write the article, focusing on the student's achievements on and off the field. Use adverbs to answer the questions *How? When? Where?* and *To what extent?*

Sports Topic **Write and label all the adjectives and adverbs in the following paragraph.**

Rice University and Alabama were extremely well matched in the Cotton Bowl in 1954. In the fourth quarter, Rice's Dicky Moegle was clear. With great speed he raced for a ninety-five-yard touchdown. As Moegle passed the Alabama bench, Tommy Lewis suddenly jumped up. The fullback, anxious and eager, flung himself forcefully at Moegle. Moegle crashed to the ground. Lewis instantly realized what he had done. His face turned very red with embarrassment. Timidly he crawled back to the bench. The 75,000 fans in the stands were silent with disbelief. The referee, believing Moegle would have ultimately reached his goal without interference, declared a touchdown for Rice. Rice later won 28–6, and Moegle eventually set a new record for the Cotton Bowl. He rushed 265 yards.

Other Parts of Speech

The other three parts of speech are prepositions, conjunctions, and interjections. A preposition shows relationships between words. A conjunction connects words, and an interjection shows strong feeling.

 Prepositions

A **preposition** is a word that shows the relationship between a noun or pronoun and another word in the sentence.

If your brother asked you to get a book for him from the living room, you would save time if he told you whether he wanted the book on the couch, the one under the couch, or the one beside the couch. *On, under,* and *beside* are prepositions. Each of them shows a different relationship between the book and the couch.

Following is a list of common prepositions.

COMMON PREPOSITIONS				
aboard	before	down	off	till
about	behind	during	on	to
above	below	except	onto	toward
across	beneath	for	opposite	under
after	beside	from	out	underneath
against	besides	in	outside	until
along	between	inside	over	up
among	beyond	into	past	upon
around	but ("except")	like	since	with
as	by	near	through	within
at	concerning	of	throughout	without

Following is a list of common compound prepositions.

COMMON COMPOUND PREPOSITIONS		
according to	by means of	instead of
ahead of	in addition to	in view of
apart from	in back of	next to
aside from	in front of	on account of
as of	in place of	out of
because of	in spite of	prior to

Prepositional Phrases

A preposition is always part of a group of words called a prepositional phrase. A **prepositional phrase** begins with a preposition. It ends with a noun or pronoun called the **object of the preposition.** A prepositional phrase may also contain modifiers.

In the early evening, we hiked **to the park.**

He would not go **near the lake or the ruins.**
(The words *lake* and *ruins* form a compound object of the preposition *near*.)

CONNECT TO WRITER'S CRAFT

One way that writers create sentence variety is to vary how the sentences begin. If every sentence begins with the subject, the writing becomes monotonous. Writers sometimes vary the beginning of sentences by starting with a prepositional phrase.

A pot with a lone flower stood by the gate to the zoo.
By the gate to the zoo stood a pot with a lone flower.

She picked the trail to the right for their walk.
For their walk she picked the trail to the right.

You can learn more about prepositional phrases on pages L111–L117.

Preposition or Adverb?

Some prepositions can also be adverbs. They are prepositions when they are part of a prepositional phrase. They are adverbs when they stand alone.

| PREPOSITION | Put the thermos *inside* **the backpack.** |
| ADVERB | Put the thermos **inside.** |

PRACTICE YOUR SKILLS

● Check Your Understanding
Finding Prepositional Phrases

 Geography Topic **Write each prepositional phrase in the following paragraph.**

The greatest mountain range, called the Dolphin Rise, lies under the sea! It extends from the Arctic to the Antarctic. At certain points the tops of the mountains rise out of the water. Some of these points are the Azores and Canary Islands. In some places the deepest valleys between these mountains descend five miles below the surface of the ocean. Mount McKinley is the highest mountain in North America. If it were dropped into such a spot, it would be completely covered with water.

● Connect to the Writing Process: Drafting
Using Prepositions and Adverbs

Write two sentences about the outdoors for each of the following words. In the first sentence, use the word as a preposition. In the second sentence, use it as an adverb. Label the use of each one.

1. by

2. outside

3. below

4. around

5. near

6. above

7. through

8. within

9. across

10. toward

11. beside

12. between

Communicate Your Ideas

APPLY TO WRITING

Tall Tale: *Prepositional Phrases*

Your class has "adopted" a group of first graders to mentor. In order to break the ice at your first meeting, you have been asked to write a tall tale, using one of the children as the main character and the mountains as a setting. Brainstorm a list of character traits that would be good hero traits, and write a short tall tale for your first grader. Remember that a tall tale is humorous. As you revise your tale, vary your sentence beginnings by using prepositional phrases.

Conjunctions

A **conjunction** connects words or groups of words.

In English there are three kinds of conjunctions. **Coordinating conjunctions** are single connecting words. **Correlative conjunctions** are pairs of connecting words. The third type, subordinating conjunctions, is covered on pages L159–L160.

CONJUNCTIONS				
Coordinating			**Correlative**	
and	nor	yet	both/and	not only/but also
but	or		either/or	whether/or
for	so		neither/nor	

A bike **or** skates will do.

(connects nouns)

Let's sit **and** rest for a short while.

(connects verbs)

That road is **not only** dusty **but also** bumpy.

(connects adjectives)

I remembered my helmet, **but** I forgot my snack.

(connects sentences)

Notice that a comma comes before a coordinating conjunction that connects two sentences.

You can learn about subordinating conjunctions on pages L159–L160.

CONNECT TO WRITER'S CRAFT

Writers often vary the length of their sentences. Sometimes this variety is achieved by using conjunctions to link sentences that contain similar ideas. Varying the lengths of sentences helps to keep the reader's attention.

SHORT SENTENCES	I fell from my bike. I landed in the dusty road. I skinned my knee.
VARYING LENGTHS	I fell from my bike. I landed in the dusty road **and** skinned my knee.

PRACTICE YOUR SKILLS

● Check Your Understanding
Finding Conjunctions

Contemporary Life **Write the coordinating or correlative conjunctions in each sentence.**

1. Both exercise and a healthy diet help people live longer.
2. Each day I jog two miles or do exercises.
3. I do not like sweets, nor do I like fatty foods.
4. Some people exercise regularly, but they eat poorly.
5. Walking and swimming are good forms of exercise.
6. Neither potato chips nor chocolate is good for you.
7. Some people exercise, yet they complain about it.
8. Jamie likes either to dance or to run as a way to exercise.
9. The five-kilometer race was not only good exercise but also a good way to raise money for charity.
10. I wanted extra exercise today, so I rode my bike to school.

● Connect to the Writing Process: Revising
Using Conjunctions to Combine Sentences

Combine each pair of sentences into one sentence, using coordinating or correlative conjunctions.

11. Dinner was delicious and filling. Dessert was delicious and filling.
12. The fire warmed us. The fire dried our wet clothes.
13. Our run was fun. The rain cut our run short.
14. The roads became slippery. The roads became extremely dangerous.
15. Melvin did not like the sound of the wind. Roger did not like the sound of the wind.

APPLY TO WRITING

Postcard Message: *Conjunctions*

Grandma Moses. *Joy Ride,* 1953.
Oil on pressed wood, 18 by 24 inches. ©1992, Grandma Moses Properties Co., New York.

During the winter break, you had a chance to visit the countryside pictured here. You decide to write on the back of this postcard to your best friend. Since you do not have much room on the back of the postcard, be sure to combine sentences by using conjunctions whenever possible.

▶ Interjections

An **interjection** is a word that expresses strong feeling or emotion.

Surprise, disbelief, joy, disappointment—these and other emotions or feelings are often expressed by interjections. An interjection is separated from the rest of the sentence by an exclamation point or a comma.

Ouch! That hurts.
Well! That's finally over.
Oh, I can't believe it!
Great! I like that idea.

CONNECT TO SPEAKING AND WRITING

When you use interjections, oftentimes the punctuation that comes after them will determine the volume of your voice, as well as the intensity of emotion involved. Generally speaking, an exclamation point indicates stronger emotions and a louder volume on the part of the speaker.

PRACTICE YOUR SKILLS

● Check Your Understanding
Finding Interjections

Contemporary Life **Write the interjections from the following sentences.**

1. "Wow!" said Susie. "I can't believe we got tickets to the concert."

2. "Oh, it was fun to wait in line," said a grinning Steve.

3. "Well, I know I am going to have a great time at the show," added Rhonda.

4. "Hey, did you tell Mark about the show?" asked Susie.

5. "Oops! I guess I forgot," said Steve sheepishly.

6. "No! Please tell me that he won't have to work," begged Rhonda.

7. "Yeah, that would be terrible," Susie agreed.

8. "Quick! Here he comes," said Rhonda. "Ask him, Steve."

9. "Um, Mark," asked Steve, "do you have to work tonight?"

10. "No, I'm off," said Mark. "I hope you have some good ideas."

Connect to the Writing Process: Drafting
Using Interjections

Write a sentence about a concert for each interjection.

11. Uh-oh!

12. Wow!

13. Yikes!

14. Aha!

15. Ugh!

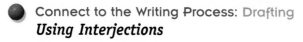

Art Topic **Write the prepositional phrases, conjunctions, and interjections found in the paragraph below. Label each one.**

Quick! Make a choice. Which one would you prefer to be: a painter, sculptor, musician, poet, or philosopher? Leonardo da Vinci was not only all of these but also an inventor, a biologist, an astronomer, a geologist, and a mathematician. Da Vinci was born near Florence, Italy, in 1452. In his early forties, he painted the *Last Supper.* Within a short period of time, he also painted the *Mona Lisa,* the most famous painting in the world. During his lifetime he was a recognized artist, yet his notebooks also contain sketches of fantastic inventions. There are drawings of an airplane, a helicopter, and a submarine. Yes! Leonardo da Vinci was centuries ahead of his time.

You know that a word can be used as more than one part of speech. The way a word is used in a sentence determines its part of speech. For example, the word *well* can be used as five different parts of speech.

NOUN	There's a **well** in my uncle's backyard.
VERB	Tears **well** up in his eyes when he talks about the accident.
ADJECTIVE	Don't you feel **well** today?
ADVERB	Stir the pudding **well,** or it will scorch.
INTERJECTION	**Well!** You should have told me that before.

Before deciding what part of speech a particular word is, ask yourself, *What is this word doing in this sentence?* The following summary with questions should help you.

NOUN	Is the word naming a person, a place, a thing, or an idea? His **bicycle** was a **means** of **transportation.**
PRONOUN	Is the word taking the place of a noun? **They** presented licenses to **her** and **me.**
VERB	Is the word showing action? Timothy **is driving** that truck. Does the word link the subject with another word in the sentence? In many areas today, cars **are** a necessity.
ADJECTIVE	Is the word modifying a noun or pronoun? Does it answer the question *What kind? Which one(s)? How many?* or *How much?* The **two brand-new** vans were **American.** **These** few were donated.

ADVERB	Is the word modifying a verb, an adjective, or another adverb? Does it answer the question *How? When? Where?* or *To what extent?*
	The **somewhat** shy child rides **quite well**.
PREPOSITION	Is the word showing a relationship between a noun or a pronoun and another word in the sentence? Is it part of a phrase? **According to** the report, everyone **in** our area pays too much money **for** insurance.
CONJUNCTION	Is the word connecting words or groups of words? Take **either** the bus **or** the train, **for** you have plenty of time.
INTERJECTION	Is the word expressing strong feeling? **Oh!** I forgot my registration form. **Whew!** We worked on the engine until midnight.

Practice Your Skills

● Check Your Understanding
Determining Parts of Speech

General Interest **Write the underlined words. Then beside each word, write its part of speech: *noun, pronoun, verb, adjective, adverb, preposition, conjunction,* or *interjection.***

1. The <u>stop</u> sign was missing.

2. <u>This</u> accident could have been prevented.

3. <u>Most</u> injuries were minor.

4. Why did you <u>stop</u> at the scene?

5. The driver's <u>stamp</u> collection was damaged.

6. How did the <u>ink</u> spill on it?

7. Stamp the time of the accident on the witness report.

8. No! Don't move the cars yet.

9. Ink the stamp pad before you date the report.

10. Empty the trash from that car, for it is spilling over.

11. What is that?

12. I found several at the scene.

13. Give her the cell phone.

14. It is in the top compartment of my van.

15. The top is damaged, and the side is scratched.

16. Does that stamp belong to the driver's collection?

17. Most are scattered in the car.

18. Please be a witness for us.

19. The wind will blow the stamps about.

20. This is for you.

21. The insurance company might not top that offer.

22. They were driving about the town.

23. They did stop and ask for directions.

24. Turn left at the stop sign.

25. He looked carefully for the sign.

26. Oh! The sign must be missing again.

27. Several are coming to help.

28. Those stamps are priceless.

29. I took photos of the collection before the accident.

30. All will wait for the officer.

● Connect to the Writing Process: Drafting
Using the Eight Parts of Speech

31. Is it possible to write a sentence that includes the eight parts of speech? Try it and see. When you have finished your sentence, identify each part of speech: *noun, pronoun, verb, adjective, adverb, preposition, conjunction,* and *interjection.*

APPLY TO WRITING

Persuasive E-mail: *Parts of Speech*

Carmen Lomas Garza. *Birthday Party,* 1989.
Oil on canvas, 36 by 48 inches. Collection of the artist.

Your family is planning a large party like the one in the picture above. Mostly family will attend, but your mother has told you that you may invite one of your best friends. Write an E-mail message to your best friend describing the party and persuade your friend to spend the afternoon with your family. Be sure to use a variety of specific nouns, precise verbs, and vivid adjectives and adverbs. Vary the length of your sentences by using conjunctions to combine ideas. Vary the beginnings of your sentences by using prepositional phrases.

Determining Parts of Speech

Write each underlined word. Then, beside each word, write its part of speech using the following abbreviations.

noun = *n.*	pronoun = *pron.*	verb = *v.*
adjective = *adj.*	adverb = *adv.*	preposition = *prep.*
conjunction = *conj.*		

1. Dolley Madison, the wife of the fourth United States president, is <u>one</u> of history's <u>many</u> interesting women.

2. The <u>first</u> name of this unusual woman is <u>often</u> misspelled.

3. The official name on her <u>birth certificate</u> is spelled <u>with</u> an *e.*

4. <u>Throughout</u> her life, <u>many</u> incorrectly wrote her name.

5. Dolley Madison <u>was</u> the foremost woman in the nation's <u>capital</u> in the opening years of the 1800s.

6. Thomas Jefferson <u>chose</u> James Madison as <u>his</u> secretary of state.

7. The dynamic wife of <u>James Madison</u> became the unofficial First Lady <u>during</u> Jefferson's eight years as president.

8. <u>Later</u> this charming and talented woman became the official First Lady during her husband's <u>eight</u> years in office.

9. Most historians give Dolley Madison credit for the <u>style</u> <u>and</u> tone of the nation's capital in those years.

10. Dolley Madison's attractive face later <u>appeared</u> on a <u>United States</u> stamp.

Determining Parts of Speech

Write each underlined word. Then, beside each word, write its part of speech using the following abbreviations.

noun = *n.*   pronoun = *pron.*   verb = *v.*
adjective = *adj.*   adverb = *adv.*   preposition = *prep.*
conjunction = *conj.* interjection = *interj.*

> <u>In</u> 1823, Captain John Cleves Symmes appeared <u>before</u> <u>Congress</u>. He wanted money for a ship and a few <u>extremely</u> brave scientists to make a trip to the North Pole. <u>You</u> see, Symmes believed the earth was <u>hollow</u>. There's more. Not only <u>his</u> research but also his documents seemed to prove that the <u>earth</u> was open at the poles. <u>He</u> was convinced that the <u>inside</u> of the earth <u>was</u> "a warm, <u>rich</u> land, stocked <u>generously</u> with <u>thrifty</u> vegetables and animals—if not men."

Understanding Parts of Speech

Write sentences that use the following words as the different parts of speech. Underline each word and label its use in the sentence using the following abbreviations.

noun = *n.*   pronoun = *pron.*   verb = *v.*
adjective = *adj.*   adverb = *adv.*   preposition = *prep.*
conjunction = *conj.* interjection = *interj.*

1. flower—noun, verb, adjective
2. beyond—adverb, preposition
3. neither—pronoun, adjective, conjunction
4. those—pronoun, adjective
5. light—noun, verb, adjective

Language and *Self-Expression*

Frida Kahlo was a Mexican artist whose worth was not widely recognized until after her death. She produced more than two hundred paintings, primarily still lifes and self-portraits.

A descriptive paragraph uses words to paint a picture of a real or imagined person, place, or thing. The writer includes vivid words to make the subject come alive in the mind of the reader. The key to good description is precision, using words that are specific to the subject being described.

Look closely at the painting *Long Live Life.* Think about what the title means to you. Then use the painting as a focal point for a paragraph of description. Use concrete nouns to tell what you see and precise verbs to tell what is happening. Use colorful adjectives and adverbs to describe what you see. Always keep the painting's title in mind as you write.

Prewriting Brainstorm a list of words that come to your mind when you look at the painting. Divide these words into lists of nouns, verbs, adjectives, and adverbs. Add more words if you wish.

Drafting Begin with a sentence that states the main idea of your paragraph. Add details in an order that makes sense. Conclude with a summary sentence that incorporates the theme of the painting.

Revising Reread your paragraph and check it for precision. Replace dull, ordinary nouns and verbs with vivid, precise nouns and verbs. Add adjectives and adverbs that will help the reader "see" the painting.

Editing Review your paragraph, looking for errors in grammar, capitalization, punctuation, and spelling. Make any corrections that are necessary.

Publishing Prepare a final copy of your paragraph. Share your paragraph by reading it aloud to a group. Talk about how group descriptions vary and how they are similar.

Another Look

A **noun** is the name of a person, place, thing, or idea.

Kinds of Nouns
A **common noun** names any person, place, or thing. *(page L7)*
A **proper noun** names a particular person, place, or thing. *(page L7)*

A **pronoun** is a word that takes the place of one or more nouns.

Kinds of Pronouns
A **reflexive pronoun** is formed by adding *-self* or *-selves* to certain personal pronouns. *(page L13)*
An **indefinite pronoun** usually refers to unnamed people or things. *(page L15)*
A **demonstrative pronoun** points out a specific person, place, or thing. *(page L15)*
An **interrogative pronoun** is used to ask a question. *(page L16)*

An **action verb** tells what action a subject is performing. A **verb phrase** is an action verb plus one or more helping verbs.

A **linking verb** links the subject with another word in the sentence. The other word either renames or describes the subject.

An **adjective** is a word that modifies a noun or pronoun.

An **adverb** is a word that modifies a verb, an adjective, or another adverb.

Other Parts of Speech
A **preposition** is a word that shows the relationship between a noun or a pronoun and another word in the sentence. *(pages L43–L45)*
A preposition is always part of a group of words called a **prepositional phrase.** *(page L44)*
A **conjunction** connects words or groups of words. *(pages L46–L47)*
An **interjection** is a word that expresses strong feeling or emotion. *(pages L49–L50)*

Posttest

Directions

Write the letter of the term that correctly identifies the underlined word in each sentence.

EXAMPLE   **1.** Ragtime is a <u>form</u> of popular American music.

             1   **A**   noun

                  B   pronoun

                  C   verb

                  D   adverb

ANSWER   **1**   **A**

1. <u>Ragtime</u> is one of the ancestors of jazz.

2. It was popular from the 1890s <u>until</u> the end of the first World War.

3. In <u>ragtime</u> music, melodies are syncopated.

4. The style derived from street bands in New Orleans, St. Louis, <u>and</u> Memphis.

5. It was related to a popular dance at the turn of the century called the "<u>cakewalk</u>."

6. Scott Joplin is <u>probably</u> the best known of the ragtime composers.

7. *Maple Leaf Rag* is still played regularly <u>today</u>.

8. <u>Hey</u>, wasn't that one of our school band's songs?

9. Scott Joplin actually <u>wrote</u> a ragtime opera called *A Guest of Honor*.

10. Have <u>you</u> heard of Jelly Roll Morton?

1	**A**	adjective	**6**	**A**	conjunction
	B	adverb		**B**	interjection
	C	preposition		**C**	preposition
	D	noun		**D**	adverb
2	**A**	adjective	**7**	**A**	adjective
	B	adverb		**B**	adverb
	C	preposition		**C**	preposition
	D	noun		**D**	noun
3	**A**	adjective	**8**	**A**	conjunction
	B	adverb		**B**	interjection
	C	preposition		**C**	preposition
	D	noun		**D**	adjective
4	**A**	noun	**9**	**A**	noun
	B	pronoun		**B**	pronoun
	C	conjunction		**C**	verb
	D	adverb		**D**	adverb
5	**A**	noun	**10**	**A**	conjunction
	B	pronoun		**B**	interjection
	C	verb		**C**	pronoun
	D	adverb		**D**	adjective

CHAPTER 2

The Sentence Base

• •

 **Pretest**

Directions
Write the letter of the term that correctly identifies the underlined word or words in each sentence.

EXAMPLE	**1.** A <u>warm-up</u> prepares the body for vigorous exercise.

> **1 A** simple subject
>   **B** simple verb
>   **C** complete subject
>   **D** complete predicate

ANSWER   **1 A**

1. Here is <u>a good fitness program.</u>

2. Always <u>stretch</u> at the beginning of a workout.

3. You <u>should warm up for the first ten or fifteen minutes.</u>

4. This <u>increases</u> the temperature of your muscles.

5. In winter you <u>will need</u> more of a warm-up.

6. A steady jog is a good <u>warm-up</u> or <u>cool-down.</u>

7. <u>Respiration</u> and <u>heart efficiency</u> are the goals of a good exercise program.

8. You <u>should reach</u> and <u>maintain</u> a target heart rate for at least twenty minutes.

9. Some good activities for this include a <u>jog</u> or a <u>swim.</u>

10. You might also try <u>dance.</u>

1	**A**	simple subject	**6**	**A**	compound subject
	B	simple predicate		**B**	compound predicate
	C	complete subject		**C**	compound direct object
	D	complete predicate		**D**	compound predicate nominative

2	**A**	simple subject			
	B	simple predicate	**7**	**A**	compound subject
	C	complete subject		**B**	compound predicate
	D	complete predicate		**C**	compound direct object
				D	complete subject

3	**A**	simple subject			
	B	simple predicate	**8**	**A**	compound subject
	C	complete subject		**B**	compound predicate
	D	complete predicate		**C**	compound direct object
				D	complete predicate

4	**A**	simple subject			
	B	simple predicate	**9**	**A**	compound subject
	C	complete subject		**B**	compound predicate
	D	complete predicate		**C**	compound direct object
				D	complete predicate

5	**A**	simple subject			
	B	simple predicate	**10**	**A**	complete subject
	C	complete subject		**B**	complete predicate
	D	complete predicate		**C**	direct object
				D	predicate nominative

"He knows all about art,
but he doesn't know
what he likes."

James Thurber. "He
knows all about art,
but he doesn't know
what he likes," 1943.
© 1943 James Thurber.
Copyright © 1971 Rosemary
A. Thurber. From *Men,
Women & Dogs,* published
by Harcourt Brace.

Describe   Without rereading the caption, describe what is happening in this cartoon.

Analyze   This caption reverses a well-known saying: "I don't know much about art, but I know what I like." Whom is the cartoonist mocking? What do you think he is saying about so-called experts?

Interpret   A good cartoonist can make a political or social statement using only a simple drawing and caption. What form might a writer use to involve the audience in a similar way?

Judge   James Thurber wrote essays and short stories as well as drawing cartoons. When do you suppose an essay might be more appropriate than a cartoon? When might a short story be a better way of making a point?

At the end of this chapter, you will use the artwork to stimulate ideas for writing.

A Sentence

A **sentence** is a group of words that expresses a complete thought.

Recognizing complete thoughts as sentences is the first step in communicating your ideas clearly.

CONNECT TO SPEAKING AND WRITING

When you speak, you convey your ideas not only with your words but also with your facial expressions, body language, and tone of voice. When you write, you cannot depend on your body language, and so you must express your ideas clearly.

The groups of words below do not express complete thoughts. They are called **sentence fragments.**

> The tea in the cup.
> Brewed some tea last night.
> Drinking my tea.
> After the tea was ready.
> Best I ever had.
> Tonight I will.

Fragments become sentences when each idea is expressed completely.

> The tea in the cup **is very bitter.**
> **Jamie** brewed some tea last night.
> Drinking my tea **made me feel better.**
> After the tea was finished, **everyone went home.**
> **It was the** best **tea** I ever had.
> Tonight I will **buy a box of it.**

You can learn more about sentence fragments on pages L82–L83 and L180–L181.

PRACTICE YOUR SKILLS

● Check Your Understanding
Recognizing Sentences and Fragments

General Interest **Label each group of words *S* if it is a sentence or *F* if it is a fragment.**

1. Since many people drink tea.
2. Tea has a soothing effect.
3. Comforting though it is.
4. It feels good to inhale the steam.
5. Teas made from tea leaves, *Camellia sinensis*.
6. After a long day.
7. Tea is also rich in fluoride.
8. Just as coffee contains caffeine.
9. The tea leaves during the brewing process.
10. After people eat dinner.
11. More popular in England.
12. Even in hot places like India.
13. Iced tea is also delicious.
14. Freshly brewed or made from a mix.
15. Now there are many varieties of iced-tea mixes.
16. Just like different types of tea leaves.
17. Herbal teas, flavored teas.
18. Some teas may even help to prevent cancer.
19. Many studies conducted.
20. The evidence is considered strong but not yet conclusive.

● Connect to the Writing Process: Revising
Writing Complete Sentences

21.–33. Add information to expand each fragment above into a sentence. When you write your sentences, remember to begin each sentence with a capital letter and end it with a punctuation mark.

APPLY TO WRITING
Summary: *Complete Sentences*

Henri Rousseau. *Tropical Storm with a Tiger (Surprise)*, 1891.
Oil on canvas, 51⅛ by 31³⁄₁₆ inches. Trustees, National Gallery, London.

You are working as a field biologist in India for the National Geographic Society. You find yourself caught in a tropical storm, and then a tiger crosses a few yards from where you are hidden. Write a summary of the experience for the lead biologist on your team.

Before writing your summary, brainstorm for the following details:

- What was your first response when you saw the tiger?
- If the tiger saw you, did it respond?
- Did either you or the tiger make any sounds?

Be sure to use complete sentences to capture the experience fully.

Subjects and Predicates

A **subject** names the person, place, thing, or idea the sentence is about.

A **predicate** tells something about the subject.

To express a complete thought, a sentence must have a subject and a predicate.

	SUBJECT	PREDICATE
PERSON	My sister Rhoda	works at the downtown art gallery.
PLACE	The art gallery	will be open every other Sunday.
THING	The Impressionist seascape painting	belongs to Carlos.
IDEA	His interpretation of the painting	is unique.

▶ Complete and Simple Subjects

The **complete subject** is the group of words that names the person, place, thing, or idea the sentence is about.

Every sentence has a subject. To find a subject, ask yourself *Whom?* or *What?* the sentence is about.

Many famous paintings from the past are displayed in the gallery.

(*Many famous paintings from the past* tells what the sentence is about.)

> **Mrs. Mason of the art department** has become the gallery's new owner.
>
> *(Mrs. Mason of the art department* tells whom this sentence is about.)

In both of the preceding examples, one word—more than the others—answers the question *Whom?* or *What?* This main word in the complete subject is called the simple subject. When finding a simple subject, keep in mind that a subject is never part of a prepositional phrase.

You can learn more about prepositional phrases on pages L111–L117.

A **simple subject** is the main word in the complete subject.

In the following examples, the simple subjects are underlined.

> Many famous **paintings** from the past are displayed in the gallery.
>
> *(Paintings* is the main word that tells what the sentence is about.)
>
> **Mrs. Mason** of the art department has become the gallery's new owner.
>
> *(Mrs. Mason* is the main word that tells whom the sentence is about.)

Even though *Mrs. Mason* is two words, it is considered the simple subject because it is the name of one person.

Sometimes the complete subject and the simple subject are the same word or group of words.

> **She** adjusted the painting correctly.
> **Vincent van Gogh** led an unusual life.

Throughout the rest of this book, the simple subject will be called the *subject*.

PRACTICE YOUR SKILLS

● Check Your Understanding
Finding Complete and Simple Subjects

Art Topic **Write the complete subject in each sentence. Then underline the simple subject.**

1. Vincent van Gogh was a very prolific artist.
2. Young Vincent worked in an art gallery.
3. He chose art as his vocation around 1880.
4. *The Potato Eaters* was painted in 1885.
5. This painting underscores his interest in peasant life.
6. The Paris period was important to van Gogh's artistic development.
7. The artist completed many self-portraits, still lifes, and cityscapes in Paris.
8. Postimpressionist painting is the name given to van Gogh's style toward the end of his career.
9. *The Starry Night* reflects his bold style with swirling brushstrokes in greens, yellows, and blues.
10. None of his works became famous until after his death.

Different Positions of Subjects

A sentence is said to be in **inverted order** when the subject-verb order is changed.

Normally the subject comes before the verb in a sentence. To create sentence variety, you can sometimes change the subject-verb order. In inverted sentences the subject is harder to find or may even seem to be missing. To find a subject in an inverted sentence, first find the verb. Then ask yourself, *Who or what is doing the action?* or *About whom or what is a statement being made?*

> Across the stage **paced** the **actor.**
>
> (*Paced* is the verb. Who paced? *Actor* is the subject—even though it follows the verb.)

Finding the subject and the verb in an inverted sentence is easy if you turn the sentence around to its natural order. Each subject is underlined once and each verb is underlined twice in the following examples.

> INVERTED ORDER   At the back of the stage is a trapdoor.
>
> NATURAL ORDER   A trapdoor is at the back of the stage.

Questions are usually in inverted order. The subject often comes between parts of a verb phrase. To find the subject in a question, turn it around so that it makes a statement.

> QUESTION   Has Lani auditioned for the play?
>
> STATEMENT   Lani has auditioned for the play.

CONNECT TO SPEAKING AND WRITING

When you ask a question, your voice usually rises at the end of the sentence. This emphasizes that you are asking a question and not making a statement. The rising tone of voice signals a question in speech just as a question mark signals a question in writing.

Sentences beginning with *there* or *here* are also in inverted order. When a sentence begins with *there* or *here,* the subject will come after the verb. To find the subject, drop the word *there* or *here* and put the other words in the sentence in natural order.

> INVERTED ORDER   There are two leads in this play.
>
> NATURAL ORDER   Two leads are in this play.

You can learn about subject-verb agreement in sentences that are in inverted order on page L306.

Understood subjects occur in sentences that give a command or make a request. Most often the subject *you* is not stated. It is, however, understood to be there.

> <u>Lend</u> me your script.
>
> (If you ask who should lend, the answer is an understood *you*—the person requested or commanded to do something.)

Notice that *you* is the understood subject of each of the following sentences.

> **(you)** Answer the stage manager.
> **(you)** Strike the set after rehearsal.
> Dana, **(you)** please return my script to the director.

Although the person receiving the request in the last example is called directly by name, *you* is still the understood subject.

PRACTICE YOUR SKILLS

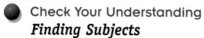 Check Your Understanding
Finding Subjects

Contemporary Life **Write the subjects in the following sentences. If the subject is an understood *you*, write (you).**

1. Find your seats quickly.

2. During open auditions there are very few empty seats in the auditorium.

3. Have you heard the director's name?

4. Down the aisle runs the eager actress.

5. Here comes the new director.

6. Did you sign the audition slip?

7. Rick, please turn on the stage lights.

8. Where did you find your monologue?

9. There are more than one hundred students at this audition.

10. Answer the director now!

11. The role of Amelia is the most challenging.

12. Read the narrative, please.

13. On the table is an extra script.

14. Speak clearly and loudly to the audience.

15. Will you read another part for me, please?

● Connect to the Writing Process: Revising
Changing Inverted Sentences to Natural Order

16.–20. Choose any five of the preceding sentences that are in inverted order, and rewrite them in natural order.

Communicate Your Ideas

APPLY TO WRITING

Press Release: *Position of Subjects*

The director of the school play has asked you to write a short press release for the play. The press release will be read during the morning announcements. Write a short summary of the play, tell about the cast, and include information about when the play will take place. Use a variety of subject-verb orders to grab the attention of your classmates. Think about answers to the following questions before writing.

- Who are the main characters?
- What is the setting and the conflict?
- Why would someone want to see this play?

● Complete and Simple Predicates

The **complete predicate** is a group of words that tells something about the subject.

In addition to a subject, every sentence needs a predicate. To find a predicate, first find the subject. Then ask yourself, *What is the subject doing?* or *What is being said about the subject?* In the following sentences, the complete predicates are in **bold** type.

Mozart **composed many different types of music.**

(The subject is *Mozart. Composed many different types of music* tells what Mozart did.)

The music **is nearly perfect.**

(The subject is *music. Is nearly perfect* tells something about the subject.)

Complete predicates usually have one main word or phrase that tells what the subject is doing or tells something about the subject. This main word or phrase is called the simple predicate, or verb.

A **simple predicate,** or **verb,** is the main word or phrase in the complete predicate.

In the following examples, the verbs are underlined twice.

Mozart **composed many different types of music.**
People **perform his music even today.**

Verb Phrases

Action verbs can be used with helping verbs. The verb and any helping verbs form a **verb phrase.** In the following examples, the verb phrases are underlined twice and the helping verbs are in **bold** type.

We **will be** spending this evening at the opera.
The performers' names **must have been** announced already.

Following is a list of common helping verbs.

COMMON HELPING VERBS	
be	am, is, are, was, were, be, being, been
have	has, have, had
do	do, does, did
OTHERS	may, might, must, can, could, shall, should, will, would

Notice in the following examples that a verb phrase may be interrupted by other words.

Sheila **has** never **performed** a solo before an audience in her life.

Will Tom **meet** us backstage?

I **did** not **need** a new oboe reed.

You can learn more about helping verbs on page L23.

Linking Verbs

Verbs that tell what a subject is doing are usually easy to find because they show action. However, **linking verbs** that tell something about the subject may be harder to find. Just remember that a linking verb links a subject with another word in the sentence that either renames or describes the subject. Following is a list of common linking verbs.

COMMON LINKING VERBS			
is	am	are	was
were	be	being	been

In the following examples, the linking verbs are underlined twice.

> George **will be** the new **conductor.**
> The musicians **have been** anxious.

You can learn more about linking verbs and find a complete list on pages L25–L28.

CONNECT TO SPEAKING AND WRITING

Using vivid verbs when you speak or write can make your ideas more interesting. Because the predicate conveys action in a sentence, choosing strong verbs can help your audience visualize what is happening.

LESS VIVID	The tempo of the music **affected** the audience.
MORE VIVID	The tempo of the music **soothed** the audience. 

PRACTICE YOUR SKILLS

● Check Your Understanding
Finding Complete Predicates and Verbs

Music Topic **Write the complete predicate in each sentence. Then underline each verb.**

1. Wolfgang Amadeus Mozart was born in Salzburg, Austria.

2. *The Marriage of Figaro* gave him his greatest operatic success.

3. The 1786 opera was composed for the Vienna Opera.

4. Mozart wrote many sacred and secular works.

5. He excelled in every form of music composition.

6. Many of his contemporaries misunderstood Mozart.

7. Mozart's music influenced Haydn and Beethoven.

8. Mozart died of kidney failure on December 5, 1791.

9. Much of his work is brilliant.

10. Classical musicians play his works even today.

● **Check Your Understanding**
Finding Verbs

 Contemporary Life **Write the verb in each sentence. Remember that words that interrupt a verb phrase are not part of the verb.**

11. We have practiced the piano for two hours every night this week.

12. Can you do the arpeggio?

13. Ken should have joined the orchestra with us.

14. Someone must have taken your clarinet case by mistake.

15. Have you ever tried warm-ups?

16. You could be practicing every day in the soundproof practice room.

17. No one has ever attempted two solos in one performance.

18. Where did you put your reeds?

19. The new conductor did not appear until right before curtain time.

20. The auditorium can hold five hundred people at a time.

● **Connect to the Writing Process:** Revising
Using Vivid Verbs

Write each sentence, replacing each verb with a more vivid verb.

21. The music went into the auditorium.

22. The conductor went to the center of the stage.

23. The drums sounded loudly.

24. The soloist appeared at the corner of the stage.

25. The loud trumpet music filled the air.

APPLY TO WRITING

Description: *Predicates*

Your grandmother was unable to attend the music concert at your school and missed your solo. Write a description for her, telling her about the concert and your solo. Include details about how you felt and the sights and sounds of the concert from your viewpoint on the stage. Use vivid verbs to make your writing come alive.

Compound Subjects and Verbs

A **compound subject** is two or more subjects in one sentence that have the same verb and are joined by a conjunction.

In the following examples, each subject is underlined once, and each verb is underlined twice.

Bill **or** Mike will buy a ring today.

Many rings, bracelets, **and** necklaces are made of gold.

A sentence may also have more than one verb, called a compound verb.

A **compound verb** is two or more verbs in one sentence that have the same subject and are joined by a conjunction.

Marty has purchased the ring **but** will take it home tomorrow.

Susan stopped at the jeweler's window, looked inside, **and** then opened the door.

A sentence may include a compound subject and a compound verb.

> My sister **and** I collected old jewelry **and** sold it at flea markets.

The conjunctions *and* and *or* can connect compound subjects. *And, or,* and *but* can connect compound verbs. *Either/or, neither/nor, not only/but also, both/and,* and *whether/or* may also be used with either compound subjects or compound verbs.

You can learn more about conjunctions on pages L46–L47.

PRACTICE YOUR SKILLS

● Check Your Understanding
Finding Compound Subjects and Verbs

General Interest **Write the subjects and verbs in each sentence.**

1. Wedding bands and engagement rings encompass a lifetime of memories.
2. Most are either silver or gold.
3. Stephen and Judy used a plastic ring but replaced it with a gold one.
4. Would you prefer a traditional ring or something unusual?
5. John and Mary found a meteor and made their rings from it.
6. Keith and Lindsay put their rings on chains and wore them around their necks.
7. Old family heirlooms and loose gemstones have been used in rings.
8. Some people attend auctions and buy antique rings.
9. Sue and her husband accidentally threw their rings away but found them at the dump.

10. Ken not only designed his ring but also supplied the stones for it.

11. Luke's ring was purchased in Amsterdam and shipped to Houston, Texas.

12. Luke, Jeanette, and Tess analyzed the stones and selected their favorites.

13. The stonecutters cut and polish diamonds before a crowd of onlookers.

14. Kayla searches for beautiful turquoise stones and designs settings for them.

● Connect to the Writing Process: Revising
Combining Subjects and Verbs

Combine the following pairs of sentences to create compound subjects or compound verbs.

15. Ashley went to the store. Ashley bought a necklace.

16. Bill washed the floor in the music store. Bob waxed it.

17. Sarah ate at the food court. Dave ate at the food court.

18. Christopher went to the bookstore. Christopher bought a mystery novel and a calendar.

19. Gabrielle looked at the computer games. Michael looked at the computer games.

20. Riley chose a microscope. Riley purchased lunch.

Communicate Your Ideas

APPLY TO WRITING

Thank-You Note: *Compound Subjects and Verbs*

Your grandmother has sent you a gift certificate that you can use at any store at the mall. Write a thank-you note to her, explaining what you are going to do with the gift certificate. At least one sentence of your explanation should have a compound subject, and one other sentence should have a compound verb.

 **Mixed Practice**

Health Topic **Write the subject and verb in each sentence. If the subject is an understood *you*, write (you).**

1. You and a friend are dining in a restaurant.

2. A man at the next table chokes on a piece of food.

3. Without prompt help that person could die in four minutes.

4. What should you do?

5. Get behind the man and place your arms around him above his waist.

6. The man's head and torso will automatically lean forward.

7. Tightly grasp your own wrist and press your fist into his abdomen forcefully.

8. You should not worry about damage to his ribs.

9. These actions should be repeated several times and should finally force the piece of food out.

10. This maneuver was successfully developed by Dr. H. J. Heimlich.

Sentence Fragments

A **sentence fragment** is a group of words that does not express a complete thought.

At the beginning of this chapter, you learned that a sentence is a group of words that expresses a complete thought. Then you learned that no sentence can express a complete thought unless it has a subject and a verb. A group of words that lacks either a subject or a verb is called a sentence fragment. An important step in the writing process is to check for these kinds of sentence fragments.

Fragments due to incomplete thoughts are a common kind of fragment.

NO SUBJECT	Howling at the moon.
	Are intelligent.
	Have resources for survival.
NO VERB	Wolves in Alaska.
	Tracks in the snow.
	The fur of a wolf.

Fragments due to incorrect punctuation are another kind of fragment.

PARTS OF A COMPOUND VERB	Have you heard the howls of the wolves? **And seen the tracks they left in the snow?**
ITEMS IN A SERIES	Wolves have everything they need for survival. **Warm fur, intelligence, large territories, and powerful jaws.**

You can learn about additional kinds of fragments on pages L140–L142 and L180–L181.

Ways to Correct Sentence Fragments

A fragment can be corrected in either of two ways. One way to correct a fragment is to add words to make the fragment a separate sentence. Sometimes you might need to add a subject or a verb to a sentence. Occasionally, you might need to add both a subject and a verb. A second way to correct a fragment is to attach it to the sentence next to it.

SENTENCE AND FRAGMENT	Have you heard the howls of the wolves? **And seen the tracks they left in the snow?**
SEPARATE SENTENCES	Have you heard the howls of the wolves? **Have you seen the tracks they left in the snow?**
ATTACHED	Have you heard the howls of the wolves **and seen the tracks they left in the snow?**
SENTENCE AND FRAGMENT	Wolves have everything they need for survival. **Warm fur, intelligence, large territories, and powerful jaws.**
SEPARATE SENTENCES	Wolves have everything they need for survival. **They have warm fur, intelligence, large territories, and powerful jaws.**
ATTACHED	Wolves have everything they need for survival: **warm fur, intelligence, large territories, and powerful jaws.**

CONNECT TO SPEAKING AND WRITING

In conversation, people often speak in fragments to one another. Likewise, when a writer uses dialogue, he or she might use fragments to make the conversation between characters sound more natural.

PRACTICE YOUR SKILLS

● Check Your Understanding
Recognizing Sentences and Fragments

Science Topic **Label each group of words S if it is a sentence or F if it is a fragment.**

1. But are facing extinction.
2. A wolf in a pack.
3. The wolves will be extinct in a few years.
4. A keen sense of smell, excellent hearing, and the will to survive.
5. Are running quickly through the mountain ranges of Denali National Park.
6. And dragged the moose down on its knees.
7. Ground squirrels, deer, or moose.
8. Have survived for centuries.
9. A threat to domestic animals.
10. Change your thinking about wolves.

● Connect to the Writing Process: Revising
Changing Sentence Fragments to Complete Sentences

11.–18. **Rewrite the fragments from the exercise above as sentences. Add words, capital letters, and punctuation where needed.**

Communicate Your Ideas

APPLY TO WRITING

Writer's Craft: *Analyzing the Use of Fragments*

Writers often use sentence fragments in dialogue. Read the following passage from D. H. Lawrence's short story "The Rocking-Horse Winner." Then answer the questions that follow it.

(*Note: Honor bright* is an expression that means "on your honor," and *Daffodil* and *Mirza* are the names of racehorses in the story.)

> The car sped into the country, going down to Uncle Oscar's place in Hampshire.
> "Honor bright?" said the nephew.
> "Honor bright, son!" said the uncle.
> "Well, then, Daffodil."
> "Daffodil! I doubt it, sonny. What about Mirza?"
> "I only know the winner," said the boy. "That's Daffodil."
> "Daffodil, eh?"
> There was a pause. Daffodil was an obscure horse comparatively.
> "Uncle!"
> "Yes, son?"
> "You won't let it go any further, will you? I promised Bassett."
>
> —*D. H. Lawrence*, "The Rocking-Horse Winner"

- Identify all the fragments in the excerpt. (You should find eight.)
- Rewrite the fragments so they are complete sentences.
- Read the new sentences and compare the passage with the original. Why do you think the writer chose to use fragments?

Complements

Subjects and verbs often need another word to complete the meaning of a sentence. This word is called a completer, or **complement.**

> Spiders spin **webs.**
> The horse's eyes were **blue.**
> The prize thrilled **him.**
> The soccer team felt **tired.**

There are four major kinds of complements. Direct objects and indirect objects follow action verbs. Predicate nominatives and predicate adjectives follow linking verbs. Together, a subject, a verb, and a complement are called the **sentence base.**

Direct Objects

A **direct object** is a noun or pronoun that receives the action of the verb.

Direct objects complete the meaning of action verbs. To find a direct object, first find the subject and the action verb. Then ask the question *What?* or *Whom?* The answer to either of these questions will be a direct object.

>   ┌d.o.┐
> I will take **Dan** to the lake.
>
> (I will take whom? *Dan* is the direct object.)
>
>   ┌d.o.┐   ┌d.o.┐
> The bear caught a **fish** and ate **it.**
>
> (The bear caught what? *Fish* is the direct object of *caught.*
> The bear ate what? *It* is the direct object of *ate.*)

Two or more direct objects following the same verb are called a **compound direct object.**

          ┌**d.o.**┐   ┌**d.o.**┐
Dan watched the **fish** and the **birds.**

(Dan watched what? *Fish* and *birds* are both direct objects.)

A complement is never part of a prepositional phrase.

            ┌**d.o.**┐
Did the birds eat **any** of those crumbs?

(The birds did eat what? *Any* is the direct object. *Crumbs* cannot be the direct object since it is part of the prepositional phrase *of those crumbs.*)

You can learn more about action verbs and transitive verbs on pages L19–L22.

PRACTICE YOUR SKILLS

● Check Your Understanding
Finding Direct Objects

 **Write the direct objects from the sentences below.**

1. Sea otters love all kinds of shellfish.

2. Lying on their backs, they hold unopened shells on their chests and smash them with a rock.

3. Termites do not like the sun.

4. They often make paper umbrellas and shade their heads outside the mound.

5. Chimpanzees chew the ends of sticks and make brushes.

6. With the brushes they dig termites and other insects out of the ground.

7. An elephant holds a stick in its trunk and scratches its back.

8. The Egyptian vulture takes a rock in its beak and opens an ostrich egg with it.

9. Bowerbirds often build fancy nests for themselves.

10. They will use shells, leaves, and even clothespins.

Indirect Objects

An **indirect object** answers the questions *To or for whom?* or *To or for what?* after an action verb.

An indirect object can be included in a sentence that already contains a direct object. To find an indirect object, first find the direct object. Then ask, *To or for whom?* or *To or for what?* about each direct object. The answer to either of these questions will be an indirect object. Notice in the following examples that an indirect object comes before a direct object.

          — i.o. —   ┌ d.o. ┐
Jennifer wrote **Mr. Leary** a **report.**

(*Report* is the direct object. Jennifer wrote a report for whom? *Mr. Leary* is the indirect object.)

          ┌ i.o. ┐ ┌d.o.┐
Jerry gave his **report** a **title.**

(*Title* is the direct object. Jerry gave a title to what? *Report* is the indirect object.)

          ┌i.o.┐   ┌i.o.┐   ┌ d.o. ┐
Mrs. Reynolds assigned **Jeff** and **me** a special **project.**

(*Project* is the direct object. Mrs. Reynolds assigned a project to whom? The compound indirect object is *Jeff* and *me.*)

An indirect object cannot be part of a prepositional phrase.

    ┌ i.o.┐
Give **Dad** the report on the computer.

(*Dad* is the indirect object. It comes before the direct object *report* and is not part of the prepositional phrase.

Give the report on the computer to Dad.

(*Dad* is not the indirect object because it follows the direct object and is part of the prepositional phrase *to Dad*.)

You can learn about objective case pronouns on pages L250–L251.

PRACTICE YOUR SKILLS

● Check Your Understanding
Finding Direct and Indirect Objects

 Write each direct object and each indirect object. Then label each one *D* for direct object or *I* for indirect object.

1. Mr. Leary assigned Mary a report on George Washington.
2. Mary promised Mr. Leary the report on Tuesday.
3. George Washington dedicated his life to our country.
4. In return, our country offered him the presidency.
5. Almost one million people visit Mount Vernon each year.
6. George Washington left his nephew Mount Vernon.
7. Washington kept seven rifles, several pistols, swords, and a small cannon in his library.
8. He fired salutes at passing boats on the Potomac.
9. Washington and his wife entertained visitors often.
10. Many people mourned his death in 1799.

● Connect to the Writing Process: Drafting
Composing Sentences with Direct Objects

Write a sentence that answers each of the following questions. Then underline each direct object.

11. What do you see to your right?
12. Whom did you recently visit?
13. What did you eat for breakfast this morning?

14. What courses are you taking this year?

15. What are you holding in your hand right now?

Communicate Your Ideas

APPLY TO WRITING

Writing Diary Entries: *Direct and Indirect Objects*

You have fallen asleep for twenty years, just as Rip Van Winkle did in Washington Irving's story. When you awake, you cannot believe how things have changed. Write a diary entry that explains the changes that have taken place in the past twenty years. Use at least three direct objects and three indirect objects in your writing.

Predicate Nominatives

The types of complements that follow linking verbs are called **subject complements.** One of these subject complements is the predicate nominative.

A **predicate nominative** is a noun or pronoun that follows a linking verb and identifies, renames, or explains the subject.

To find a predicate nominative, first find the subject and the linking verb. Then find the noun or pronoun that follows the verb and that identifies, renames, or explains the subject. This word will be the predicate nominative.

Retrievers are the most popular **dogs.**

(*Dogs* = *retrievers.* The predicate nominative is *dogs.*)

Sometimes more than one predicate nominative follows a linking verb. Two or more predicate nominatives following the same verb are a **compound predicate nominative.**

The winners of the dog show were a **poodle** and a **beagle.**

(*Poodle* and *beagle* = *winners*. The compound predicate nominative is *poodle* and *beagle*.)

A predicate nominative, like other complements, cannot be part of a prepositional phrase.

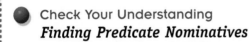

Charlie is **one** of the best dogs.

(*One* = *Charlie. Dogs* is part of the prepositional phrase *of the best dogs*.)

You can learn more about linking verbs on pages L25–L28 and about nominative case pronouns on pages L244–L247.

PRACTICE YOUR SKILLS

● Check Your Understanding
Finding Predicate Nominatives

General Interest **Write the predicate nominatives from the sentences below.**

1. Labrador retrievers are intelligent dogs and excellent hunters.

2. However, they are also champion eaters.

3. Of course, any kind of food can be a meal for them.

4. Anything from shoes to fishing reels might be a snack.

5. This is a problem for their owners.

6. Their owners must be patient people.

7. The solution to the problem remains a mystery to vets.

8. Many labradors have been steady customers at the veterinarian's office.

9. Labrador retrievers, though, can be wonderful companions.

10. They remain good pets for families with children.

● Predicate Adjectives

A **predicate adjective** is an adjective that follows a linking verb and modifies the subject.

A predicate adjective is another kind of subject complement. To find a predicate adjective, first find the subject and the linking verb. Then find the adjective that follows the verb and describes the subject. This word will be a predicate adjective.

> The surfer was very **confident.**
>
> (*Confident* describes the surfer—*the confident surfer.* *Confident* is the predicate adjective.)

> The waves were **tall** and **powerful.**
>
> (*Tall* and *powerful* describe the waves—*the tall, powerful waves.* *Tall* and *powerful* are the two parts of a compound predicate adjective.)

Do not confuse a regular adjective with a predicate adjective. A predicate adjective follows the linking verb and describes the subject.

> REGULAR ADJECTIVE   Maui is a **beautiful** island.
>
> PREDICATE ADJECTIVE   Maui is always **beautiful.**

PRACTICE YOUR SKILLS

● Check Your Understanding
Finding Predicate Adjectives

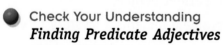 Contemporary Life **Write each predicate adjective in the following sentences.**

1. The waves at Maui are large.

2. Normal waves seem small.

3. Surfing can be fun and dangerous.

4. Surfers always appear enthusiastic.

5. For an inexperienced surfer, a mistake could be disastrous.

6. No two waves are exactly alike.

7. The clear blue waters of Maui are irresistible.

8. The weather has been unusually stormy.

9. Waves grow higher and stronger around the reef.

10. Surfers feel wary around sharks.

● Check Your Understanding
Finding Subject Complements

Geography Topic **Write each complement. Label each one *predicate nominative* or *predicate adjective*.**

11. Many people are unaware of basic geography facts.

12. The Hawaiian pineapple was first a native of South America.

13. The South Pole is colder than the North Pole.

14. The rainiest spot on Earth is Mount Waialeale in Hawaii.

15. Tahiti is fragrant with tropical flowers.

16. Texas was once an independent republic.

17. England can be cold and damp.

18. South America is home to penguins.

19. Rain forests appear significant to the world's climate and ecology.

20. Deserts may be more diverse than you think.

● Connect to the Writing Process: Prewriting
Clustering Sentences for a Rough Draft

Make a cluster of possible sentences for a paragraph that describes the geography of the area where you live. Make sure that your sentences include predicate nominatives and predicate adjectives.

Communicate Your Ideas

APPLY TO WRITING
Friendly Letter: *Complements*

You are writing a friendly letter to your pen pal who lives in a foreign country. Using some of the sentences from your cluster, write your pen pal a description of the area where you live. Be sure to include in your description things that someone in a foreign country might find unusual or interesting. Be prepared to identify all the complements in your letter. Brainstorm answers to the following questions before you begin to write.

- What would you see if you were to drive outside your city or town?
- Is land in your area flat, hilly, or mountainous?
- What color is the soil where you live?
- What kinds of plants grow naturally in your area?
- Are there any extreme features: high or low, wet or dry, hot or cold?

 QuickCheck Mixed Practice

> History Topic **Write the complement or complements in each sentence. Then label each one, using the following abbreviations.**
>
> direct object = *d.o.*   indirect object = *i.o.*
> predicate nominative = *p.n.*   predicate adjective = *p.a.*

1. Thomas Edison was not popular at his high school in Port Huron, Michigan, in 1854.

2. He was sick much of the time.

3. Sometimes his fellow students were cruel to him.

4. After a time his mother ended his formal education.

5. From then on she taught him lessons at home.

6. At age ten Tom read a complete science book.

7. Immediately afterward he built himself a chemical laboratory in the basement of his home.

8. At twelve Edison started his own business.

9. On a train route between Port Huron and Detroit, he sold passengers newspapers.

10. The work was hard and tiresome.

11. Surprisingly, Tom still found time for other ventures.

12. He published his own one-page newspaper and sold each copy for three cents.

13. He learned Morse code and took a job in a telegraph office.

14. The pay was twenty-five dollars per month.

15. Often he was idle at work.

16. At these times he did chemical experiments.

17. One day an experiment exploded and destroyed the office!

18. Tom became an inventor at the age of sixteen.

19. His best-known inventions are the electric light and the phonograph.

20. Later in life Thomas Edison became a millionaire.

Sentence Patterns

Using Sentence Patterns

Surprisingly, all written sentences follow a few basic sentence patterns. Sentences can vary greatly because each element in a given pattern can be expanded differently. Following are the most common sentence patterns. Knowing them will help you plan your writing effectively.

Pattern 1: S-V (subject-verb)

     S   V
Icebergs drifted.

              S   V
The large icebergs with their huge crags drifted into the shipping lanes.

Pattern 2: S-V-O (subject-verb-object)

     S   V   O
Grubs destroy grass.

        S   V   O
Fat grubs often destroy the grass in our lawn.

Pattern 3: S-V-I-O (subject-verb-indirect object-direct object)

         S   V   I   O
Grandmother sent me jewelry.

          S   V   I   O
My grandmother in Colorado recently sent me silver jewelry with turquoise stones.

Pattern 4: S-V-N (subject-verb-predicate nominative)

     S   V   N
Porpoises are performers.

             S   V   N
The friendly porpoises in Marineland are popular performers.

Pattern 5: S-V-A (subject-verb-predicate adjective)

      S   V   A
Dragonflies are harmless.

               S   V   A
The fierce-looking dragonflies are actually harmless to people.

PRACTICE YOUR SKILLS

Check Your Understanding

Write the sentence pattern that each sentence follows, using the abbreviations on the preceding page.

1. The quarterback's abilities were obvious to everyone.
2. The animal with the longest life span is the giant tortoise.
3. Roger Tory Peterson wrote many books about nature.
4. The baseball team practices daily in the early afternoon.
5. The teacher promised Jerry some extra help after school.
6. Mr. Murphy assigned us a new chapter.
7. The capital of Puerto Rico is San Juan.
8. Mauna Loa in Hawaii is the world's most active volcano.
9. Mary L. Petermann is an outstanding American scientist.
10. A griffin resembles a cross between an eagle and a lion.
11. Dolphins are really whales.
12. The guests wished the couple a long and prosperous life.
13. Southern colonial homes are famous for their stately columns.
14. Jim gladly accepted the prize of one hundred dollars.
15. The Adams family gave their country two presidents.
16. Australia is the home of many unusual creatures.
17. You can have the last slice of the roast.
18. The brain is the most complex group of cells on Earth.
19. David loaned his brother his new catcher's mitt.
20. The ears of the African elephant are the largest in the world.

Writing a Personal Essay

Suppose you awoke one morning speaking a language that no one around you understood. Write a short narrative relating one incident that might occur. Use your imagination to include specific details of your experience. As you revise, make sure you have included different kinds of sentence patterns. Then edit your work, looking for misspelled words and incorrect punctuation before you write a final copy.

Diagraming the Sentence Base

A **sentence diagram** shows at a quick glance how a sentence is put together because it depicts the relationship among all parts of the sentence. Sentence diagrams, therefore, help you easily see how you can change sentences to add more variety to your writing.

Subjects and Verbs The subject and the verb of a sentence are written on a straight baseline and are separated by a short vertical line. Although capital letters are included, punctuation is omitted. In the second and third examples, compound subjects and verbs are written on parallel lines. The conjunction or conjunctions connecting them are written on a broken line between them.

Traffic had stopped.   Joyce smiled and bowed.

Turtles, parakeets, and rabbits are being sold.

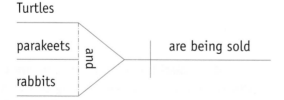

Inverted Order and Understood Subjects A sentence in inverted order is diagramed as if it were in its natural order. When a sentence has an understood subject, the *you* is diagramed in the subject position—in parentheses.

Did you sing?   Listen!

| you | Did sing | | (you) | Listen |

Adjectives and Adverbs   In a sentence diagram, adjectives and adverbs are connected to the words they modify by a slanted line. Two adjectives or adverbs are connected by a conjunction on a broken line.

The boisterous audience cheered wildly and happily.

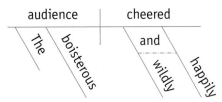

Adverbs That Modify Adjectives or Other Adverbs   These adverbs are also connected to the words they modify, but they are written on a line parallel to that word.

The extremely hard worker was promoted.

My sister writes quite often.

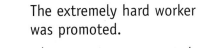

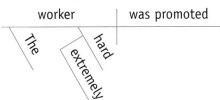

Complements

All complements except the indirect object are diagramed on the baseline—along with the subject and verb—because they are part of the sentence base.

Direct Objects   A direct object is separated from the verb by a short vertical line. Notice in the second example on page L100 that the conjunction connecting the parts of a compound direct object is written on a broken line between them.

Our car gets good mileage.

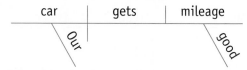

Tony served milk and sandwiches.

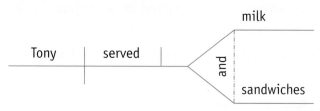

Indirect Objects An indirect object is diagramed on a horizontal line that is connected to the verb. In the second example, the conjunction connecting the parts of the compound indirect object is written on a broken line between them.

Dad cooked me a hamburger.

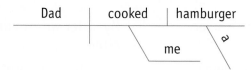

Teach Rob and me a few basic rules.

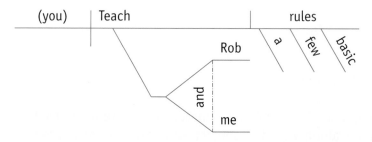

Subject Complements A predicate nominative and a predicate adjective are both diagramed on the baseline after the verb. They are separated from the verb by a slanted line pointing back to the subject. The conjunction that joins a compound subject complement is placed on a broken line between the compound parts.

The first speaker was she.   Her speech was very long.

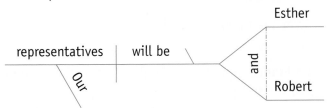

Our representatives will be Esther and Robert.

PRACTICE YOUR SKILLS

Diagraming Sentences

Diagram the following sentences or copy them. If you copy them, draw one line under each subject and two lines under each verb. Then label each complement, using the following abbreviations.

direct object = *d.o.*   predicate nominative = *p.n.*
indirect object = *i.o.*   predicate adjective = *p.a.*

1. Do you have a pet?

2. Some pets are strange and unusual.

3. Look here!

4. Some people keep cockroaches or tarantulas.

5. Snakes and ferrets have also become pets.

6. White House visitors quite often give presidents gifts.

7. Occasionally these gifts are small puppies or other animals.

8. President Theodore Roosevelt must have had the most pets.

9. Two unusual pets were a one-legged chicken and a six-toed cat.

10. The Humane Society recently gave me a very ordinary rabbit.

Identifying Subjects and Verbs

Write each subject and verb. If the subject is an understood *you*, write *you* in parentheses.

1. Have you ever read about the history of Mississippi?
2. Listen to this.
3. At one time France, Spain, and England have flown their flags over areas of Mississippi.
4. Originally this land was the home of almost thirty thousand Natchez, Choctaw, and Chickasaw.
5. Eventually this area became an American territory in 1798.
6. Farmers liked Mississippi's rich soil and soon settled there.
7. There were huge cotton plantations even in Mississippi's early history.
8. Peanuts, soybeans, and sugar were other crops grown in Mississippi.
9. Today people in Mississippi still farm but are also involved in such industries as timber, furniture, and natural gas.
10. Who are some famous people from Mississippi?
11. Perhaps the most famous person is Elvis Presley.
12. There were also three great writers, Eudora Welty, Tennessee Williams, and William Faulkner.
13. Of course, the most famous attraction must be the Mississippi River itself.
14. This river has been called a liquid highway.
15. It borders ten states and carries tons of goods to market every year.

Identifying Complements

Write each complement. Then label each one, using the following abbreviations:

> direct object = *d.o.* predicate nominative = *p.n.*
> indirect object = *i.o.* predicate adjective = *p.a.*

1. The year 1975 was very important.
2. In 1975, Margaret Thatcher became famous as the first woman leader of the British Conservative Party.
3. The Library of Congress celebrated its 175th birthday.
4. The New York Drama Critics gave *A Chorus Line* an award.
5. This play became the best musical play of 1975.
6. Andrei Sakharov was the winner of the Nobel Peace Prize.
7. Steven Spielberg scared the public with a new film, *Jaws*.
8. The postage for a first-class letter became more expensive.
9. The increase in price was 30 percent.
10. The United States began its bicentennial celebrations and ceremonies at the Old North Church in Boston.

Using the Sentence Base

Write five sentences that follow the directions below. (The sentences may come in any order.) Write about one of the following topics or a topic of your choice: the best things that have happened to you so far this year, the best year of your life, or things that you predict will happen later in your life.

Write a sentence that . . .

1. includes a direct object.
2. includes an indirect object.
3. includes a predicate nominative.
4. includes a predicate adjective.
5. includes a compound complement.

Underline each subject once, each verb twice, and label each complement.

Language and *Self-Expression*

"He knows all about art, but he doesn't know what he likes."

James Thurber was an author and cartoonist. He began his writing career as a reporter and later joined the staff of the *New Yorker*. He is known for his humor about the extremes of twentieth-century life. "The Secret Life of Walter Mitty" is an excellent example.

Thurber's cartoon makes fun of people who think they know everything about a subject but are unable to express an opinion about it. Think of a subject in which you consider yourself an expert—such as state history, basketball, or cooking. Sift through all the facts you know, then write an opinion statement about some aspect of the subject. Use this statement as the focus of an essay and support it with reasons. Use a variety of sentence patterns.

Prewriting Choose your area of expertise. Use an inverted pyramid like the one below to narrow your topic. Then write a statement of opinion.

New York state history

the history of the Finger Lakes

recent occurrences in the Finger Lakes

the Lake Source Cooling Project

Drafting Add details that support your opinion. Conclude with a paragraph that sums up your ideas.

Revising Read your essay critically for material unrelated to your main idea. Cut and add details as needed.

Editing Review your essay, correcting errors in grammar, capitalization, punctuation, and spelling.

Publishing Prepare a final copy of your essay. Consider publication in your school newspaper or magazine.

Another Look

A **sentence** is a group of words that expresses a complete thought.

Subjects and Predicates

A sentence has two main parts: a **subject** and a **predicate.** *(page L68)*

The **complete subject** is the group of words that names the person, place, thing, or idea the sentence is about. *(pages L68–L69)*

The **simple subject** is the main word in the complete subject. *(page L69)*

A **compound subject** is two or more subjects in one sentence that have the same verb and are joined by a conjunction. *(page L78)*

The **complete predicate** is the group of words that tells something about the subject. *(pages L73–L74)*

The **simple predicate,** or **verb,** is the main word or phrase in the complete predicate. *(page L74)*

A **compound verb** is two or more verbs in one sentence that have the same subject and are joined by a conjunction. *(pages L78–L79)*

Other Information About Subjects and Predicates

Recognizing inverted order in questions *(page L71)*

Recognizing inverted order in sentences beginning with *here* or *there* *(page L71)*

Recognizing understood subjects *(page L72)*

Combining sentences *(page L83)*

Sentence Errors

A **sentence fragment** is a group of words that does not express a complete thought. *(page L82)*

Complements

A **direct object** is a noun or pronoun that receives the action of the verb. *(pages L86–L87)*

An **indirect object** answers the questions *To or for whom?* or *To or for what?* after an action verb. *(pages L88–L89)*

A **predicate nominative** is a noun or pronoun that follows a linking verb and identifies, renames, or explains the subject. *(pages L90–L91)*

A **predicate adjective** is an adjective that follows a linking verb and modifies the subject. *(page L92)*

Posttest

Directions
Write the letter of the term that correctly identifies the underlined word or words in each sentence.

EXAMPLE

1. The nation of Canada <u>covers</u> an enormous tract of land.

    1   **A**   simple subject
        B   simple predicate
        C   complete subject
        D   complete predicate

ANSWER   1   **B**

1. Nearly 40 percent of Canada <u>is forest land.</u>
2. Logging <u>was</u> uncontrolled in Canada for centuries.
3. <u>The Canadian Pacific Railway</u> linked the country's coasts.
4. The Trans-Canada Highway <u>has opened</u> up the country to travelers.
5. Wooden <u>snowshoes</u> were once the best mode of travel.
6. Today people take <u>trains</u>, <u>cars</u>, or <u>airplanes</u>.
7. The <u>vastness</u> and <u>isolation</u> of Canada no longer impede its progress.
8. Railroads <u>allowed</u> for the development of farming and <u>led</u> to the settlement of remote communities.
9. Important areas of wheat production are <u>Saskatchewan</u> and <u>Alberta</u>.
10. Vancouver <u>became</u> a major port.

1	**A** simple subject	**6**	**A** compound subject
	B simple predicate		**B** compound predicate
	C complete subject		**C** compound direct object
	D complete predicate		**D** complete predicate

1
A simple subject
B simple predicate
C complete subject
D complete predicate

2
A simple subject
B simple predicate
C complete subject
D complete predicate

3
A simple subject
B simple predicate
C complete subject
D complete predicate

4
A simple subject
B simple predicate
C complete subject
D complete predicate

5
A simple subject
B simple predicate
C complete subject
D complete predicate

6
A compound subject
B compound predicate
C compound direct object
D complete predicate

7
A compound subject
B compound predicate
C complete subject
D complete predicate

8
A compound subject
B compound predicate
C compound direct object
D complete predicate

9
A compound subject
B compound predicate
C compound direct object
D compound predicate nominative

10
A simple subject
B simple predicate
C direct object
D predicate nominative

Phrases

• •

Directions
Write the letter of the term that correctly identifies the underlined phrase in each sentence.

EXAMPLE **1.** Our literature class looked at motifs <u>in folktales</u>.

      1 A prepositional
         B participial
         C gerund
         D infinitive

ANSWER **1 A**

1. Wicked ogres with magical powers are common <u>to many folktales</u>.
2. "Come <u>into my parlor</u>," croak the evil creatures.
3. The stories' climaxes often feature the beast ready <u>to eat some hapless person</u>.
4. <u>Having a good heart</u> saves many a character from an unfortunate demise.
5. <u>Using their wits</u>, the good people usually escape from the wicked beast.
6. Another motif involves <u>transforming oneself</u>.
7. "The Frog Prince" features examples <u>of magical transformations</u>.
8. The handsome prince, <u>now a lowly frog</u>, is under a spell.
9. <u>To save him</u>, some gentle soul must kiss the frog.
10. "Beauty and the Beast," <u>another example of this genre</u>, is well known around the world.

1	A	prepositional	6	A	participial
	B	participial		B	infinitive
	C	gerund		C	appositive
	D	infinitive		D	gerund

2	A	prepositional	7	A	prepositional
	B	participial		B	participial
	C	appositive		C	gerund
	D	gerund		D	infinitive

3	A	prepositional	8	A	prepositional
	B	participial		B	participial
	C	gerund		C	appositive
	D	infinitive		D	gerund

4	A	infinitive	9	A	prepositional
	B	participial		B	participial
	C	appositive		C	gerund
	D	gerund		D	infinitive

5	A	prepositional	10	A	prepositional
	B	participial		B	infinitive
	C	gerund		C	appositive
	D	infinitive		D	gerund

Elizabeth Layton. *Self-Portrait Holding Rose with Thorns,* 1985.
Pastel with pencil on paper, 18 by 7 inches. The National Museum of Women in the Arts. Gift of Wallace and Wilhelmina Holladay.

Describe Tell what you notice first, second, and third as you look at this artwork.

Analyze A rose has specific qualities that make it highly symbolic. Why do you suppose the artist used a rose in her self-portrait?

Interpret To present themselves to the world, artists often draw self-portraits, and authors write memoirs or autobiographies. How are these two processes similar? How do they differ?

Judge Would you rather have an artist paint your picture or a writer compose your biography? Why?

At the end of this chapter, you will use the artwork to stimulate ideas for writing.

Prepositional Phrases

A **phrase** is a group of related words that functions as a single part of speech. A phrase does not have a subject and a verb.

There are several kinds of phrases. In addition to prepositional phrases and appositive phrases, there is a group of phrases called verbal phrases. They include participial phrases, gerund phrases, and infinitive phrases.

Although all phrases have unique characteristics, they do share three things in common. First, all the words in a phrase work together as a single part of speech. Second, a phrase does not have a subject and a verb. Finally, all phrases can add variety and conciseness to your writing.

Prepositional phrases, as you know, begin with a preposition. You also know that a prepositional phrase ends with a noun or pronoun called the object of the preposition. The prepositional phrases in the following examples are in **bold** type.

The Michael Jordan Award **from the athletic club** will be presented **to Richard and Thomas.**

According to the announcement, the ceremony will begin **by seven o'clock.**

Look **for our basketball coach** either **on the stage** or **in the front row.**

One **of the journalism teachers** is making a videotape **about our coach.**

Of all the coaches we've had, Mr. Connolly is the best.

Because of his outstanding leadership, Mr. Connolly will receive the Coach of the Year Award.

You can find lists of prepositions on pages L43–L44.

PRACTICE YOUR SKILLS

● Check Your Understanding
Finding Prepositions

Sports Topic **Write the prepositional phrases in the following paragraph.**

The only major sport with a totally American origin is basketball. It was invented in December 1891 by James Naismith. He was an instructor at the YMCA training school in Springfield, Massachusetts. Because his students continually complained about boring gym classes, he created a game with peach baskets and a soccer ball. In a few years, basketball was being played throughout the country. After World War I, it became a major international sport.

▶ Adjective Phrases

An **adjective phrase** is a prepositional phrase used to modify a noun or pronoun.

Like a single adjective, a prepositional phrase can modify a noun or a pronoun. When it does, the prepositional phrase is called an adjective phrase.

| SINGLE ADJECTIVES | Did you see the **shuttle** launch? |
| ADJECTIVE PHRASES | Did you see the launch **of the shuttle?** |

A single adjective and an adjective phrase answer the same questions: *Which ones?* and *What kind?*

WHICH ONE(S)?	Did you read the article **about the space shuttle?**
WHAT KIND?	The launch was one chance **in a million.**

An adjective phrase usually modifies the noun or the pronoun directly in front of it. Occasionally, that word will be the object of the preposition of another phrase.

The new part *for the shuttle* has been painted a strange shade *of green.*

Some *of the tickets to the launch* have been lost.

Two adjective phrases can modify the same noun or pronoun.

The parts *of the rocket beside the booster* are new.

PRACTICE YOUR SKILLS

● Check Your Understanding
Recognizing Adjective Phrases as Modifiers

Science Topic **Write each adjective phrase. Then, beside each phrase, write the word it modifies.**

1. The article in the newspaper about the NASA space shuttle was interesting.

2. The scientists at NASA needed new parts for the space shuttle.

3. A lack of funds prevented the manufacture of new parts.

4. A space museum in Alabama had an exhibit of the space shuttle with actual parts.

5. The cost of new parts for the shuttle would have been between five million and ten million dollars.

6. The estimated cost of the museum's shuttle parts was $300,000.

7. NASA wanted the forward assemblies from the solid rocket boosters on the museum's exhibit.

8. The rocket boosters at 149 feet in length are the largest solid propellant motors ever flown.

9. The savings to the project manager at NASA were substantial.

10. The people from the museum helped gladly.

11. Information from the space shuttle's missions further advances our knowledge of science and technology.

12. One area of advancement has been an increase in knowledge about the planet Mars.

13. The extreme forces of nature are constantly reshaping the surface of Mars.

14. A few of these forces include pink dust clouds, wind storms, and frost and polar ice caps.

15. The polar ice caps cover an area of both the north and south poles.

Connect to the Writing Process: Revising
Adding Adjective Phrases

Revise the following sentences to make them more descriptive by adding adjective phrases.

16. The documentary was interesting.

17. A single launch can use much fuel.

18. A special compartment contains food.

19. The astronauts eat each day.

20. The woman is an astronaut.

21. Astronauts train.

22. The Cassini spacecraft was launched.

23. Meteor showers are monitored.

24. We use telescopes.

25. The students learn about space.

APPLY TO WRITING
News Article: *Adjective Phrases*

It is the early 1980s, and you are a newspaper reporter. You are in Florida to cover one of the first launches of the space shuttle. This photograph is the scene before you. Write an article for your readers back home that will give them an idea of what a space shuttle launch is like. Ask yourself the following questions before writing your first draft.

- What would the shuttle launch sound like?
- How would the shuttle look before the launch?
- What adjective phrases would paint a clear picture of a shuttle launch?
- What might you feel during a launch?

In your article be sure to use adjective phrases to help your readers clearly "see" what is happening.

Adverb Phrases

An **adverb phrase** is a prepositional phrase used to modify a verb, an adjective, or an adverb.

SINGLE ADVERBS   The shuttle soared **upward.**

ADVERB PHRASES   The shuttle soared **into the sky.**

A single adverb and an adverb phrase answer the same questions: *Where? When? How? To what extent?* and *To what degree?* Adverb phrases also answer the question *Why?*

WHERE?   Please take me **to China.**

WHEN?   **During the last century,** China changed.

HOW?   I drank the hot tea **with great pleasure.**

WHY?   **Because of the floods,** the villagers built a dam.

Notice in the preceding examples that an adverb phrase does not always come next to the word it modifies.

When an adverb phrase modifies a verb, it modifies the whole verb phrase. Notice in the following example that more than one adverb phrase can modify the same verb.

At noon the villagers will arrive **for the celebration.**

Although most adverb phrases modify verbs, some modify adjectives and adverbs.

MODIFYING AN
ADJECTIVE   The people were happy **with the leaders.**

MODIFYING AN
ADVERB   The Great Wall extends far **across China.**

PUNCTUATION WITH ADVERB PHRASES

If a short adverb phrase comes at the beginning of a sentence, usually no comma is needed. You should, however, place a comma after an adverb phrase of four or more words, after several introductory phrases, or after a phrase that ends with a date.

No COMMA	**With their help** we finished early.
COMMA	**According to the latest news release,** China has many modern cities.

PRACTICE YOUR SKILLS

● Check Your Understanding
Recognizing Adverb Phrases as Modifiers

Social Studies **Write each adverb phrase. Then, beside each phrase, write the word or words the adverb phrase modifies.**

1. China has existed for many centuries.

2. Spaghetti was invented by the Chinese.

3. During our history class, we learned about Marco Polo and China.

4. For many years most Chinese have been farmers.

5. Throughout the centuries the Chinese have supported their population by farming.

6. In spite of population predictions, the farmers will be feeding more people with less farmland.

7. China's current building boom is similar to the 1950s and 1960s United States building boom.

8. In September 1998, a law that protects "fundamental farmland" was passed.

9. Farmland no longer can be converted for development.

10. Despite the stiff penalty, the government expects additional problems.

Punctuating Adverb Phrases

Rewrite the following sentences, placing commas after the introductory phrases, if needed. If a comma is not necessary, write C for correct.

11. Within the week your debate notes must be given to Mr. Johnson.

12. During our history class Anthony appeared nervous as the debate monitor.

13. Throughout the research assignment he complained that he didn't like the topic.

14. Before class Tom found his notecards.

15. After history class we put our books away.

16. In a few minutes it will be time for our next class.

17. Through the halls we will walk.

18. In one direction is the chemistry laboratory.

19. On the opposite side Mr. Garcia teaches Spanish.

20. From here it is a long walk to trigonometry class.

Communicate Your Ideas

APPLY TO WRITING

Directions: *Adverb Phrases*

The new student at school has offered to help you study for a test but has to stay late at school for practice. Write directions to your house from school so that this new student can find your house easily. Be as specific as possible with your directions, mentioning landmarks where appropriate. Include adverb phrases to make your directions clear. Be prepared to identify the phrases you used.

Appositives and Appositive Phrases

An **appositive** is a noun or pronoun that identifies or explains another noun or pronoun in the sentence.

An appositive usually follows the word it identifies or explains.

Raymond wrote his history report on the sixteenth president, **Lincoln.**

Lincoln's home state, **Illinois,** is very proud of him.

An appositive usually includes modifiers. When it does, it is called an appositive phrase.

An **appositive phrase** is a group of words that contains an appositive and its modifiers.

Notice in the third example below that an appositive phrase can include a prepositional phrase.

During his presidency the Civil War, **a lengthy U.S. war,** ended.

Lincoln wrote the Gettysburg Address, **a famous speech.**

The war, **the bloodiest in U.S. history,** was divisive.

PUNCTUATION WITH APPOSITIVES AND APPOSITIVE PHRASES

If an appositive contains information essential to the meaning of a sentence, no punctuation is needed. Information is considered essential if it identifies a person, place, or thing.

ESSENTIAL   The stage actor **John Wilkes Booth** shot Lincoln.

(No commas are used because *John Wilkes Booth* is needed to identify the actor.)

If an appositive or an appositive phrase contains nonessential information, a comma or commas should be used to separate it from the rest of the sentence. Information is nonessential if it can be removed without changing the basic meaning of the sentence.

| NONESSENTIAL | John Wilkes Booth, **the stage actor,** shot Lincoln. |
| | (Commas are used because the appositive phrase could be removed without changing the meaning of the sentence.) |

PRACTICE YOUR SKILLS

 Check Your Understanding
Finding Appositives and Appositive Phrases

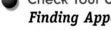 History Topic **Write the appositive or appositive phrase in each sentence. Then, beside each one, write the word or words it identifies or explains.**

1. Abraham Lincoln's birthday, February 12, falls on a Tuesday this year.

2. The sixteenth president of the United States, Abraham Lincoln, belonged to the Republican Party.

3. Thomas Lincoln, his father, was a carpenter.

4. Little is known about his mother, Nancy Hanks Lincoln.

5. Lincoln's first home, a log cabin in Kentucky, was located in Larue County.

6. Abraham Lincoln married Mary Todd, a fellow Kentuckian, on November 4, 1842.

7. As the underdog in the 1858 senatorial campaign, Lincoln debated his opponent Stephen Douglas.

8. Douglas, a Democrat, lost the debates but won the Senate seat.

9. Lincoln, a virtual unknown, was able to win the presidency in 1860.

10. Lincoln was assassinated by John Wilkes Booth, a radical, in April of 1865.

● Connect to the Writing Process: Drafting
Writing Sentences with Appositive Phrases

Match each of the following nouns listed on the left with an appropriate appositive phrase from the list on the right. Then write a sentence that includes both, using commas where needed.

11. Kentucky   a biblical name

12. Abraham   the prettiest state in the United States

13. the Civil War   the capital of the United States

14. Washington, D.C.   a small town in Illinois

15. Springfield   the bloodiest war in U.S. history

Communicate Your Ideas

APPLY TO WRITING

Persuasive Letter: *Appositives and Appositive Phrases*

Your school paper is conducting a poll to select the most influential person in history. You decide to write a letter that will persuade the staff of the paper to choose a historical figure you think is very significant. Write a paragraph explaining who the person is (or was) and why you think that person should be voted most influential.

Brainstorm with the following questions before writing:

- What historical events are the most significant?

- Who were the key people behind these events?

Include at least three appositives or appositive phrases.

Verbals and Verbal Phrases

A **verbal** is a verb form that is used as some other part of speech.

A verbal can be used alone, or it can be combined with modifiers or complements to form a **verbal phrase.** Verbals are part of your daily conversation. They also add interest to your writing. The three kinds of verbals are participles, gerunds, and infinitives.

 **Participles**

A **participle** is a verb form that is used as an adjective.

When weather forecasters talk about *rising* tides or *howling* winds, they are using participles. Used as an adjective, a participle modifies a noun or pronoun. To find a participle, simply ask the adjective questions: *Which one(s)?* and *What kind?* A verb form that answers one of these questions and describes a noun or a pronoun will be a participle. The participles in the following examples are in **bold** type. An arrow points to the word each participle modifies.

The **howling** winds scared the **frightened** children.

The **blazing** sun melted the **frozen** pond.

There are two kinds of participles. Present participles end in *–ing.* Past participles often end in *–ed,* but they can also have irregular endings such as *–n, –t,* or *–en.*

PARTICIPLES	
PRESENT PARTICIPLES	clinging, running, sinking, winding
PAST PARTICIPLES	reserved, buried, worn, bent, broken

Since a participle is a verb form, you must be careful not to confuse it with the verb in a verb phrase. Also, do not confuse a participle with the main verb. Sometimes, the participle form is the same as the past tense verb form.

PARTICIPLE	Tim and his father carefully repaired their **damaged** roof.
VERB IN VERB PHRASE	The wind **had damaged** the roof in several places.
PAST TENSE VERB	The heavy rains **damaged** the plants.

PRACTICE YOUR SKILLS

● Check Your Understanding
Finding Participles

General Interest **Write each participle. Then write the word it modifies.**

1. Dark clouds warn of an approaching storm.
2. Scientists worry about our changing climate.
3. No one could cross the flooded roadway.
4. The torn roof was on the ground after the tornado.
5. Lingering rains damaged the crops.
6. Freezing rain coated tree limbs.
7. Under the extra weight, bent branches touched the ground.
8. Frozen tree limbs fell on houses.
9. The parched land yielded few crops.
10. The rising temperatures caused high electric use.
11. Scorching lava spewed from the volcano.
12. Scared creatures ran for safety.
13. Dancing winds tossed signs and debris.
14. Surging tides announced the hurricane's arrival.

Participial Phrases

A **participial phrase** is a participle with its modifiers and complements all working together as an adjective.

As a verb form, a participle can have modifiers and complements. The following examples show variations of the participial phrase.

PARTICIPLE WITH AN ADVERB	**Reading carefully,** the student followed the instructions.
PARTICIPLE WITH A PREPOSITIONAL PHRASE	The notes, **written in French,** were impossible for me to read.
PARTICIPLE WITH A COMPLEMENT	Every student **passing the test** will receive a good grade.

The participles *being* and *having* may be followed by a past participle.

Having read the article before, I just skimmed it.

PUNCTUATION WITH PARTICIPIAL PHRASES

Always place a comma after an introductory participial phrase. If the information in an internal phrase is essential, no commas are needed. Information is essential if it identifies a person, place, or thing.

ESSENTIAL   The person **talking to the teacher** is my dad.
(No commas are used because the phrase is needed to identify the person.)

If the information in an internal phrase is nonessential, commas are used to separate it from the rest of the sentence. A nonessential phrase contains information that can be removed without changing the basic meaning of the sentence.

NONESSENTIAL   Pete Jons, **talking to the teacher,** is my friend.
(Commas are needed because the phrase could be removed from the sentence.)

Practice Your Skills

● Check Your Understanding
Recognizing Participial Phrases as Modifiers

General Interest **Write each participial phrase. Then write the word it modifies.**

1. Having studied for my geography test, I headed for school.

2. The test, given by Mr. Stephens, will be difficult.

3. Studying for the test, I learned many interesting facts.

4. The country of Tonga issued a stamp shaped like a banana.

5. Dates grown in the Sahara Desert are among the very best in the world.

6. Requiring heavy rainfall, tea does not grow very well in dry regions.

7. Paper money is a Chinese invention dating from the seventeenth century.

8. Clam chowder was invented by a group of hungry sailors shipwrecked off the coast of Maine.

9. I found a textbook packed with information for my test.

10. Brimming with confidence, I will pass Mr. Stephens's geography test.

● Connect to the Writing Process: Editing
Using Commas with Participial Phrases

Write each sentence. Add commas if needed.

11. Studying for the test I fell asleep.

12. My grade point average totaling 3.8 will help me get into college.

13. Information learned for the test will be helpful for the research paper.

14. Having organized my notes I found it easy to study.

15. The first test made by Mr. Stephens was quite difficult.

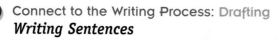*Writing Sentences*

Write two sentences for each word. Use the word in the first sentence as a verb and in the second sentence as a participle in a participial phrase. Be sure to punctuate your sentences correctly.

16. learning

17. listening

18. tested

19. connecting

20. written

21. speaking

22. taped

APPLY TO WRITING

Brochure: *Participial Phrases*

Your guidance counselor has asked you to prepare a brochure that will help the incoming freshmen at school become more successful academically. Write the text for your brochure, being sure to include tips on studying, taking notes, and reading. Use participial phrases and be prepared to identify them.

Gerunds

A **gerund** is a verb form that is used as a noun.

A gerund is another kind of verbal. Like a present participle, a gerund ends in *–ing*. Unlike a participle, a gerund is used as a noun, not as an adjective.

GERUND	**Cheating** is not allowed in sports. (*Cheating* is used as a noun—the subject of the sentence.)
PARTICIPLE	The **cheating** player annoyed everyone. (*Cheating* is used as an adjective to describe *player.*)

A gerund can be used in all the ways in which a noun is used.

SUBJECT	**Surfing** is fun.
DIRECT OBJECT	Pamela likes **skating.**
INDIRECT OBJECT	She gives her **running** one hour each day.
OBJECT OF A PREPOSITION	My friend went a whole day without **walking.**
PREDICATE NOMINATIVE	This year my favorite winter sport was **skiing** at Loon Mountain.
APPOSITIVE	Tim has a new hobby, **windsurfing.**

PRACTICE YOUR SKILLS

● Check Your Understanding
Recognizing Gerunds

 **Write the gerund in each sentence. Then use the following abbreviations to tell how each one is used.**

direct object = *d.o.*   indirect object = *i.o.*
predicate nominative = *p.n.*   subject = *s.*
object of a preposition = *o.p.* appositive = *a.*

1. Do you enjoy exercising?

2. Snowboarding is a very popular sport.

3. Lessons in diving will be given on Tuesdays after school.

4. His favorite pastime is bicycling.

5. Sarah signed up for swimming.

6. Running is a very important part of conditioning.

7. They give their skating all their free time.

8. Clear your mind of all possible distractions before starting.

9. Since her early childhood, Vanessa has developed a great talent, riding.

10. Sailing is my favorite sport.

 Gerund Phrases

A **gerund phrase** is a gerund with its modifiers and complements all working together as a noun.

Gerunds, like participles, can be combined with modifiers and complements. The following examples show some variations of the gerund phrase.

GERUND WITH AN ADVERB	**Traveling inexpensively** is a necessity for naturalists.
GERUND WITH PREPOSITIONAL PHRASES	Brian surprised us by **going to the insect exhibit at the museum.**
GERUND WITH A COMPLEMENT	**Photographing insects** is Rebecca's specialty.

The possessive form of a noun or pronoun is used before a gerund and is considered part of the phrase.

Paul's **photographing the caterpillar** was a surprise.

His parents encouraged *his* **studying botany.**

His **reading books about insects** as a child led Paul to a career in botany.

Our **walking in the woods and around rivers** is still a favorite vacation activity.

PRACTICE YOUR SKILLS

● Check Your Understanding
Recognizing Gerund Phrases

Science Topic · **Write the gerund phrase in each sentence. Then underline each gerund.**

1. Venturing into the rain forest is not everyone's idea of a great vacation.

2. Credit for saving the rain forest can be given to amateur naturalists.

3. Rain forests should be preserved for containing diverse life forms.

4. Scientists appreciate amateurs' collecting specimens.

5. Until recently most people encouraged farming in rain forest areas.

6. Scientists have a new goal, cataloging the diverse species within the rain forests.

7. Identifying thousands of different insects and plants is not an easy task.

8. Holly's summer job is identifying different types of caterpillars.

9. She enjoys explaining her work.

10. Some rain forest insects are capable of jumping a distance of more than two feet.

● Check Your Understanding
Understanding the Uses of Gerund Phrases

General Interest · **Write the gerund phrase in each sentence. Then use the following abbreviations to tell how each one is used.**

direct object = *d.o.*   indirect object = *i.o.*
predicate nominative = *p.n.*   subject = *s.*
object of a preposition = *o.p.* appositive = *a.*

11. My uncle enjoys a different hobby, hunting animals with a camera.

12. He has learned many things by photographing animals.

13. I enjoy accompanying him on his assignments.

14. My job is scouting appropriate locations.

15. We both like learning unusual facts about animals.

16. A flea is capable of jumping thirteen inches in a single leap.

17. Most snakes can go a year without eating anything.

18. Photographing insects takes a great deal of patience.

19. My uncle accomplished his goal, taking pictures of the rain forest insects.

20. His reward was the accepting of his photographs for publication.

● Connect to the Writing Process: Drafting
Using Verbs as Gerunds and Participles

Write two sentences for each of the following words. The first sentence should use the word as a gerund. The second sentence should use the same word as a participle. Use punctuation where needed.

21. flying

22. observing

23. jumping

24. watching

25. recording

Communicate Your Ideas

APPLY TO WRITING

Persuasive Letter: *Gerunds and Gerund Phrases*

Your biology teacher has told your class about a proposal in your city to cut down a forest to make way for a shopping mall. Write to the city planning commission and explain to them why they must preserve the diversity of this forest area. Persuade them to build the mall in another area of town that needs renovating instead of destroying this forest, which is home to many unusual animals. Be sure to use gerunds and gerund phrases in your letter to the city planning commission.

 **Infinitives**

An **infinitive** is a verb form that usually begins with *to*. It is used as a noun, an adjective, or an adverb.

The infinitive is the third kind of verbal. It is different in form from the other verbals because it usually begins with the word *to*. Unlike other verbals, though, it can be used as more than one part of speech. The following sentences show some of the ways in which an infinitive can be used.

NOUN	**To err** is human.
	(subject)
	Everyone should learn **to act.**
	(direct object)
ADJECTIVE	This year Danvers is the debate team **to beat.**
	(*To beat* modifies the noun *team.*)
ADVERB	Good actors are quick **to learn.**
	(*To learn* modifies the adjective *quick.*)

Because an infinitive begins with the word *to,* it is sometimes confused with a prepositional phrase. An infinitive ends with a verb form, but a prepositional phrase ends with a noun or pronoun.

INFINITIVE	This will be difficult **to perform.**
	(ends with a verb form.)
	Comic roles are fun **to play.**
PREPOSITIONAL PHRASE	You should take this **to the performance.**
	(ends with a noun or pronoun)
	Our grandparents went **to the play.**

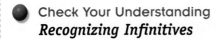

PRACTICE YOUR SKILLS

● Check Your Understanding
Recognizing Infinitives

> Music
> Topic
> **Write the infinitive in each sentence. Then use the following labels to tell how each one is used:** *noun, adjective, adverb.*

1. Carnegie Hall, which is located in New York City, has a reputation to maintain.

2. Pilar's desire to perform is strong.

3. This weekend Kari plans to practice.

4. At an early age, children can learn to sing.

5. That instrument is hard to play.

6. This piano concerto is the one to learn for the competition.

7. The purpose of music class is to instruct.

8. At our school the best place to practice is the recital hall.

9. Do you have to sing?

10. Music is almost impossible to hate.

● Infinitive Phrases

An **infinitive phrase** is an infinitive with its modifiers and complements all working together as a noun, adjective, or an adverb.

Like other verbals infinitives can be combined with modifiers and complements to form an infinitive phrase. The following sentences show some of the variations of the infinitive phrase.

> INFINITIVE
> WITH AN ADVERB
> Everyone on the crew promises **to work hard.**

INFINITIVE WITH A PREPOSITIONAL PHRASE	**To win at drama competitions** requires concentration and patience.
INFINITIVE WITH A COMPLEMENT	It's fun **to try different roles** with new directors.

Usually you can recognize an infinitive because it begins with *to*. Sometimes *to* is omitted when an infinitive follows such verbs as *dare, feel, hear, help, let, make, need, see,* or *watch*.

Will you help **collect** the scripts?
(to collect)

PRACTICE YOUR SKILLS

● Check Your Understanding
Recognizing Infinitive Phrases

Theater Arts Topic
Write the infinitive phrase in each sentence. Then underline each infinitive. Remember that *to* is sometimes omitted.

1. As an actor, Bob had to learn many lines.

2. It took him about three weeks to memorize his part.

3. Actors seem to prefer the company of other actors.

4. We did not dare interrupt him.

5. Directors are known to demand long hours from casts.

6. From the middle of the balcony, we were unable to hear the actors.

7. To project his voice, an actor learns to breathe differently.

8. An actress can learn to whisper loudly.

9. It was very thoughtful of you to send Veronica those flowers on opening night.

10. A good actor is able to learn any part.

● Check Your Understanding
Understanding the Uses of Infinitive Phrases

Write the infinitive phrase in each sentence. Then use the following labels to tell how each one is used: *noun, adjective, adverb*.

11. We had two hours to learn Hamlet's soliloquy.

12. I decided to memorize the entire play.

13. We plan to perform *Hamlet* for the entire school.

14. No one would dare begin without the lead actor.

15. To save time, we skipped the line rehearsal.

16. To perform Shakespeare takes plenty of skill.

17. Which is the best play to perform for our school?

18. Her skill as an actress continues to grow as she studies.

19. His secret ambition is to become an actor.

20. Marty studied to become a director.

● Connect to the Writing Process: Revising
Adding Infinitives to Sentences

Rewrite the following sentences so that they include an infinitive or infinitive phrase.

21. Marsha is choosing acting for a career.

22. Memorizing dialogue is difficult.

23. Acting is her life's ambition.

24. The coach likes working with different dialects.

25. The stage manager tries adjusting the lights.

26. Changing the appearance of the characters is the makeup artist's goal.

27. She works hard making old faces from young ones.

28. Marsha needs extra practice sessions for learning lines.

29. Painters attempt transforming their stage into a castle.

30. Jason's job is creating the costumes.

Communicate Your Ideas

APPLY TO WRITING

Analyzing the Writer's Craft: *Infinitives*

Read the following passage from *Hamlet*. Answer the
questions that follow.

> HAMLET: To be, or not to be: that is the question:
> Whether 'tis nobler in the mind to suffer
> The slings and arrows of outrageous fortune,
> Or to take arms against a sea of troubles,
> And by opposing end them?—To die: to sleep. . . .
>
> *—William Shakespeare,* Hamlet

- Write the infinitives in this passage.
- Rewrite the passage, using gerunds instead of
  infinitives.
- Which version is more effective? Explain your choice.
- What is the total effect of Shakespeare's repetition of
  infinitives in this passage?

✓ QuickCheck   Mixed Practice

Social
Studies   **Write each verbal phrase in the following paragraphs.
Then label each one *P* for participle, *G* for gerund, or
I for infinitive.**

The Great Wall of China, twisting and turning for over

2,500 miles, is the only man-made structure that can be seen

from the moon. Covering more than one-twentieth of Earth's

circumference, the Great Wall stretches over mountains, deserts, and plains. In the third century B.C., the first emperor of China began to build the wall. However, the rulers during the Ming Dynasty (1386–1644) were responsible for constructing the major portion of the wall. Built over a period of 1,700 years, the Great Wall is unquestionably an incredible feat. For example, the stone used to build the wall is equal to the amount needed to construct an eight-foot wall encircling the entire globe at the equator.

Determining the reason for the Great Wall is not easy. To defend China against hostile tribes to the north is one theory. This, however, may not have been the reason for creating the wall. Many times armies were successful in breaching it. To defend the limits of Chinese authority is a second theory. In fact, the wall did serve as a boundary between the Orient and the rest of the world for hundreds of years. To provide employment is still another theory. Of course, the real reason will probably never be known. Nevertheless, the Great Wall stands as one of the greatest—and certainly the largest—feats accomplished by humans.

Misplaced and Dangling Modifiers

A phrase that is used as a modifier should be placed as close as possible to the word it modifies. When a phrase is placed far away from the word it modifies, it often becomes a **misplaced modifier.**

MISPLACED	Rick saw two owls camping on Mount Greylock.
CORRECT	**Camping on Mount Greylock,** Rick saw two owls.
MISPLACED	I saw a pheasant riding my bike through the camp.
CORRECT	**Riding my bike through the camp,** I saw a pheasant.

Another problem arises when a phrase that is being used as a modifier lacks a word to modify. This kind of phrase is called a **dangling modifier.**

DANGLING	To build a good campfire, twigs are helpful.
CORRECTED	**To build a good campfire,** you will need twigs.
DANGLING	Crying with pain, a splinter was removed from his hand.
CORRECTED	**Crying with pain,** he had a splinter removed from his hand.
DANGLING	Hurrying from store to store, it was easy to lose track of time.
CORRECTED	**Hurrying from store to store,** we easily lost track of time

PRACTICE YOUR SKILLS

● Check Your Understanding
Recognizing Misplaced and Dangling Modifiers

General
Interest
If a sentence contains a misplaced modifier, label it MM. If it contains a dangling modifier, label it DM. If a sentence is correct, label it C.

1. We saw a graceful willow tree strolling around the lake.

2. Sailing into the harbor, we had our first glimpse of the campground.

3. That's my mother's camper parked at the dock with the red upholstery.

4. Paddling across the lake, I saw a swimmer fall off the dock.

5. Skiing at the end of a towrope, we saw a water skier.

6. Balancing in the front of the canoe, Todd kept his eye on the dock.

7. From rowing the canoe, we had some sore muscles.

8. To tie up at the dock properly, you should take extreme care.

9. We saw a flock of geese camping at the lake.

10. Sleeping under the stars, we could see the Big Dipper.

11. We spent a lot of time swimming in the lake.

12. Resting in the shade, we saw our parents.

13. To keep from getting sunburned, sunscreen is necessary.

14. Our dad found a scenic spot driving through the park.

15. Surrounding the park, we were all impressed by the beautiful mountains.

● Connect to the Writing Process: Editing
Editing for Misplaced and Dangling Modifiers

16.–23. Rewrite the sentences that have misplaced or dangling modifiers so that the modifiers are used correctly.

APPLY TO WRITING

Directions: *Verbals as Modifiers*

Your friends are going camping this weekend and have never cooked out before. Write them directions for making a meal over the campfire. Consider the photograph above. What food and utensils would you recommend that your friends take? You might want to include safety guidelines for cooking over an open fire, as well as information on how to properly extinguish a campfire. Be sure to use participial phrases, gerund phrases, and infinitive phrases properly in your instructions. Be prepared to identify the verbals and verbal phrases you used.

Phrase Fragments

Because some phrases are long, they may look like a sentence. Phrases can never be a sentence, however, because they do not have a subject or a verb. When phrases are written as if they were sentences, they result in **phrase fragments.**

Following are examples in **bold** type of different phrase fragments. Notice that they are capitalized and punctuated as if they were sentences.

PREPOSITIONAL PHRASE FRAGMENTS	I have a meeting with Mr. Hayes. **During my study period on Thursday afternoon.**
	After the game against Kenmore High. Everyone went to a celebration dance.
APPOSITIVE PHRASE FRAGMENTS	Our school mascot is a Viking. **A fierce warrior.**
	A tiebreaker. The extra point meant a ticket to the state championship.
PARTICIPIAL PHRASE FRAGMENTS	The school picnic will be held at Grange Park. **Located off Route 24 in Brighton.**
	Washing cars on weekends. The club members raised money for Children's Hospital.
INFINITIVE PHRASE FRAGMENTS	I am going to Otis's house. **To study for the semester exam in history.**
	To find the answer to the question. Gregory looked in five different reference books.

Ways to Correct Phrase Fragments

When you edit your written work, always look for phrase fragments. If you find any, you can correct them in one of two ways: (1) Add words to make them into separate sentences, or (2) attach them to a related group of words that has a subject and a verb.

PREPOSITIONAL PHRASE FRAGMENT	I have a meeting with Mr. Hayes. **During my study period on Thursday afternoon.**
SEPARATE SENTENCES	I have a meeting with Mr. Hayes. **It is during my study period on Thursday afternoon.**
ATTACHED	I have a meeting with Mr. Hayes **during my study period on Thursday afternoon.**
APPOSITIVE PHRASE FRAGMENT	Our school mascot is a Viking. **A fierce warrior.**
SEPARATE SENTENCES	Our school mascot is a Viking. **A Viking is a fierce warrior.**
ATTACHED	Our school mascot is a Viking, **a fierce warrior.**
PARTICIPIAL PHRASE FRAGMENT	The school picnic will be held at Grange Park. **Located off Route 24 in Brighton.**
SEPARATE SENTENCES	The school picnic will be held at Grange Park. **The park is located off Route 24 in Brighton.**
ATTACHED	The school picnic will be held at Grange Park, **located off Route 24 in Brighton.**

INFINITIVE PHRASE	I am going to Otis's house. **To study for the semester exam in history.**
SEPARATE SENTENCES	I am going to Otis's house. **We plan to study for the semester exam in history.**
ATTACHED	I am going to Otis's house **to study for the semester exam in history.**

You can learn more about other types of fragments on pages L82–L83 and L180–L181.

PRACTICE YOUR SKILLS

● Check Your Understanding
Recognizing Phrase Fragments

Contemporary Life **Label each group of words *S* for sentence or *PF* for phrase fragment.**

1. As a result of the survey of students at Kent High School.

2. My appointment with the yearbook editor is at three-thirty this afternoon.

3. The newly appointed principal.

4. To finish my work faster.

5. By far the most difficult subject on her schedule.

6. Answer the teacher.

7. The one assigned to us in history.

8. Copying from the chalkboard.

9. That was my assignment.

10. The one about the young soldier wounded in the Revolutionary War.

● Connect to the Writing Process: Revising
Correcting Sentence Fragments

11.–17. Rewrite each fragment from the previous exercise as a complete sentence.

APPLY TO WRITING

Writer's Craft: *Analyzing the Use of Phrase Fragments*

Rather than use complete sentences, writers often intentionally use phrase fragments to express themselves. Read the following stanza from a poem by Robert Frost, and then follow the directions.

My little horse must think it queer
To stop without a farmhouse near
Between the woods and frozen lake
The darkest evening of the year.

—*Robert Frost,* "Stopping by Woods on a Snowy Evening"

- Write the lines that are phrase fragments when read alone.

- Why do you think Frost chose to break the lines this way?

- Try correcting the phrase fragments by making them into separate sentences. What happens to the sound of the poem?

Diagraming Phrases

How a phrase is used in a sentence determines how it is diagramed.

Prepositional Phrases An adjective phrase or an adverb phrase is always connected to the word it modifies. The preposition is placed on a connecting slanted line. The object of a preposition is put on a horizontal line attached to the slanted line.

A loud round of applause came from the stands on the left.

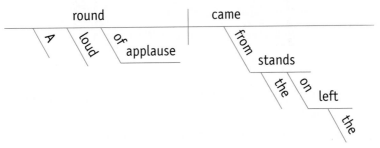

Appositive Phrases An appositive is diagramed in parentheses next to the word it identifies or explains.

I met Mr. Monroe, the director of personnel.

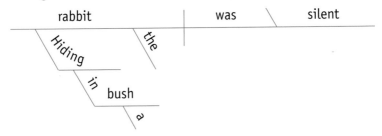

Participial Phrases A participial phrase is diagramed under the word it modifies. Participles are written in a curve.

Hiding in a bush, the rabbit was silent.

Gerund Phrases As a noun a gerund phrase can be diagramed in many places. In the following diagram the gerund phrase is used as a direct object and diagramed on a pedestal.

Talbot enjoys discussing politics with everyone.

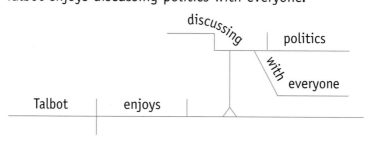

Infinitive Phrases An infinitive phrase that is used as an adjective or an adverb is diagramed just like a prepositional phrase. An infinitive phrase that is used as a noun is diagramed in any noun position. In the following example, an infinitive phrase is used as the subject of the sentence.

To write clearly is important.

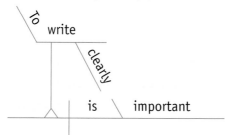

PRACTICE YOUR SKILLS

Diagraming Phrases

Diagram the following sentences or copy them. If you copy them, draw one line under each subject and two lines under each verb. Put parentheses around each phrase. Then label each phrase prepositional, appositive, participial, gerund, or infinitive.

1. My grandparents moved to California.
2. I like reading their letters.
3. Sacramento is the capital of California, the third-largest state.
4. Surfing the Pacific Ocean would become my hobby.
5. I would also like to visit the Redwood National Park.

Identifying Phrases

**Write the phrases in the following sentences. Then label each one
prepositional, appositive, participial, gerund, or *infinitive*.**

1. Porpoises have been trained to play basketball.
2. I will be going to the library soon.
3. Built of mud, the oldest house in the United States stands in New Mexico.
4. Saccharin, one kind of artificial sweetener, is a coal-tar product.
5. Their moving away made my little cousins sad.
6. Camping out is my idea of a really great vacation.
7. Twenty-four percent of California is desert.
8. Tigers, the present-day Asian mammals' prehistoric relations, once roamed the North American plains.
9. No one over six feet can qualify to become an astronaut.
10. Having read the chapter, Bernie answered the questions at the end.
11. Being elected a Hall of Famer establishes a player as a baseball immortal.
12. The fruit with the greatest number of calories is the delicious, rich avocado.
13. Almost everyone I know likes leaving school early.
14. Are you going to refinish the table's surface?
15. Jupiter, the largest planet, has the shortest day of all the planets.

Identifying Phrases

Write the phrases in the following sentences. Then label each one *prepositional, appositive, participial, gerund,* **or** *infinitive.*

Dinosaurs have not been seen for approximately 65 million years. To understand the animals' disappearance, scientists have turned to geology. One theory belongs to Luis and Walter Alvarez, a father-and-son team. Digging down, the Alvarezes discovered a thin layer of clay containing iridium. Iridium, a rare chemical here, is common in outer space.

Connecting iridium and dinosaurs was the hard part of their job. The Alvarezes proposed that a meteorite, a huge space rock, landed on Earth and created tons of dust. Spreading widely, the dust blocked the sunlight from Earth. The planet fell into darkness, and temperatures dropped severely. As a result, plant life died. Without plants to eat, the dinosaurs died, too.

Using Phrases

Write five sentences that follow the directions below. (The sentences may come in any order.) Write about one of the following topics or a topic of your choice: a farm animal, a wild animal, or a pet.

Write a sentence that . . .

1. includes at least two prepositional phrases.
2. includes an appositive phrase.
3. includes an introductory participial phrase.
4. includes a gerund phrase.
5. includes an infinitive phrase.

Underline and label each phrase.

Language and *Self-Expression*

Elizabeth Layton came late to art, making her first drawings at the age of sixty-eight as part of her recovery following a stroke. Her deeply personal self-portraits, portraits of family members, and drawings of the world around her made her famous.

A self-portrait expresses how you see yourself and your world. Elizabeth Layton's self-portrait shows her underlying joy in life. What feelings and characteristics would you express in a self-portrait? Think of yourself as you would wish the world to see you, then write a one-page self-portrait. In the portrait, you might explore your positive and negative traits, your special talents, and/or your beliefs. Vary your sentences by including phrases of different kinds.

Prewriting Focus your self-portrait by imagining yourself posing in a place that has some meaning to you. Sketch yourself in that place and use the sketch to brainstorm words and phrases to use in your self-portrait.

Drafting Use your sketch and list of words and phrases to draft a self-portrait. Begin with a sentence that introduces you to your audience. Add details that tell about your feelings, traits, and beliefs. Conclude your self-portrait with a summary.

Revising Ask a partner to read your self-portrait and give you feedback on its flow and sentence variety. Find places where you might add phrases to clarify details or move phrases to vary sentence construction.

Editing Check your self-portrait for errors in grammar, capitalization, punctuation, and spelling. Make any needed corrections.

Publishing Prepare a final copy of your self-portrait. You might publish it by putting it in a folder with a photograph or sketch and share it with your classmates.

Another Look

A **phrase** is a group of related words that functions as a single part of speech. A phrase does not have a subject or a verb.

Prepositional Phrases

An **adjective phrase** is a prepositional phrase that is used to modify a noun or pronoun. *(pages L112–L113)*

An **adverb phrase** is a prepositional phrase that is used to modify a verb, an adjective, or an adverb. *(pages L116–L117)*

Appositives and Appositive Phrases

An **appositive** is a noun or pronoun that identifies or explains another noun or pronoun in the sentence. *(page L119)*

An **appositive phrase** is a group of words that contains an appositive and its modifiers. *(pages L119–L120)*

Verbals and Verbal Phrases

A **participle** is a verb form used as an adjective. *(pages L122–L123)*

A **participial phrase** is a participle with its modifiers and complements all working together as an adjective. *(page L124)*

A **gerund** is a verb form used as a noun. *(pages L126–L127)*

A **gerund phrase** is a gerund with its modifiers and complements all working together as a noun. *(page L128)*

An **infinitive** is a verb form that usually begins with *to*. It is used as a noun, an adjective, or an adverb. *(page L131)*

An **infinitive phrase** is an infinitive with its modifiers and complements all working together as a noun, an adjective, or an adverb. *(pages L132–L133)*

Other Information About Phrases

Punctuating adverb phrases *(page L117)*
Punctuating appositives and appositive phrases *(pages L119–L120)*
Punctuating participial phrases *(page L124)*
Avoiding misplaced modifiers *(page L137)*
Avoiding dangling modifiers *(page L137)*
Correcting phrase fragments *(pages L141–L142)*

Posttest

Directions

Write the letter of the term that correctly identifies the underlined phrase in each sentence.

EXAMPLE   **1.** The structure <u>of the brain</u> is amazing.

     1   **A**   prepositional
         B   participial
         C   gerund
         D   infinitive

ANSWER   **1 A**

1. The brain enables us <u>to reason and react</u>.

2. The *cerebrum,* <u>the two cerebral hemispheres</u>, forms the largest part of the brain.

3. <u>Controlling the voluntary movements of a person</u> is the job of the cortex.

4. Many grooves mark the surface <u>of the cortex</u>.

5. <u>Subdividing the cortex</u>, the grooves raise ridges that appear only in the brains of mammals.

6. <u>In some unknown way</u>, these grooves may actually affect intelligence.

7. This fascinating idea, <u>proposed decades ago</u>, has not yet been proved.

8. Two olfactory lobes extend <u>from the forebrain</u>.

9. These are designed <u>to help us smell</u>.

10. <u>In humans</u>, these lobes are rather small.

1 **A** prepositional
   B participial
   C gerund
   D infinitive

2 **A** prepositional
   B gerund
   C appositive
   D infinitive

3 **A** prepositional
   B participial
   C gerund
   D infinitive

4 **A** infinitive
   B prepositional
   C appositive
   D gerund

5 **A** prepositional
   B participial
   C gerund
   D infinitive

6 **A** prepositional
   B participial
   C appositive
   D gerund

7 **A** prepositional
   B participial
   C gerund
   D infinitive

8 **A** infinitive
   B prepositional
   C appositive
   D gerund

9 **A** prepositional
   B participial
   C gerund
   D infinitive

10 **A** prepositional
    B participial
    C appositive
    D gerund

CHAPTER 4

Clausas

Pretest

Directions
Write the letter of the term that correctly identifies each sentence or the underlined word or words in the sentence.

EXAMPLE **1.** A story that I like very much is "The Legend of Sleepy Hollow."

   1 A simple sentence

     B compound sentence

     C complex sentence

     D compound-complex sentence

ANSWER   **1 C**

1. This famous tale was first published in 1820.

2. Washington Irving wrote this tale, and it quickly established itself as a classic.

3. It features Ichabod Crane, who is a naive schoolmaster.

4. Ichabod loves Katrina, but he has a rival who loves her too.

5. As soon as Ichabod appears on the scene, Brom begins a series of practical jokes.

6. <u>After the jokes have gone on for some time</u>, Katrina invites guests to a quilting party.

7. <u>The guests tell ghost stories</u>, and everyone becomes nervous.

8. Brom tells of a headless horseman <u>who haunts the area</u>.

9. Ichabod doubts <u>that the story is true</u>.

10. <u>His love for Katrina seems unrequited</u>, and he rides away sadly.

1	A	simple sentence	6	A	independent clause
	B	compound sentence		B	adverb clause
	C	complex sentence		C	adjective clause
	D	sentence fragment		D	noun clause

2	A	simple sentence	7	A	independent clause
	B	compound sentence		B	adverb clause
	C	complex sentence		C	adjective clause
	D	run-on		D	noun clause

3	A	simple sentence	8	A	independent clause
	B	compound sentence		B	adverb clause
	C	complex sentence		C	adjective clause
	D	run-on		D	noun clause

4	A	simple sentence	9	A	independent clause
	B	compound sentence		B	adverb clause
	C	complex sentence		C	adjective clause
	D	compound-complex sentence		D	noun clause

10	A	independent clause
	B	adverb clause

5	A	simple sentence	10	C	adjective clause
	B	compound sentence		D	noun clause
	C	complex sentence			
	D	compound-complex sentence			

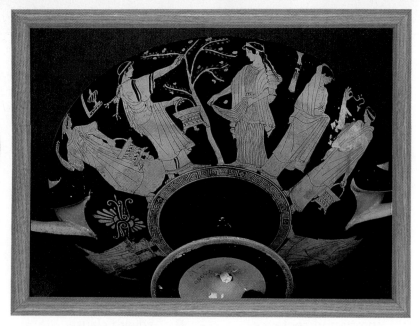

Artist unknown, Greek. *Women Gathering Fruit,* ca. 5th century B.C.
Red-figured cup. Musée Vivenel, Compiègne, France.

Describe   What are the women in the design doing? How
            are they dressed? How does the artist use
            symmetry?

Analyze   What can you learn about ancient Athens from
            studying this cup?

Interpret   How might ancient writings also serve to teach
            people today about past cultures?

Judge   Which is more important to your understanding
            of ancient cultures, written works or practical
            art? If both are important, why do you think so?

At the end of this chapter, you will use the artwork as a visual aid
for writing.

Independent and Subordinate Clauses

A clause is a group of words that has a subject and a verb.

A phrase, as you learned in the last chapter, can be used as a noun, an adjective, or an adverb. A clause can also be used as these parts of speech. A clause, however, has a subject and verb; a phrase does not. In the following examples, both the phrase and the clause are used as an adverb to modify the word *empty*.

PHRASE	Empty the trash **before dinner.**
CLAUSE	Empty the trash **before you eat dinner.** (*You* is the subject of the clause; *eat* is the verb.)

Understanding clauses and being able to include them in your own writing is valuable because clauses show important relationships between ideas. Clauses also combine ideas and in that way create clearer sentences.

There are two kinds of clauses: the independent clause and the subordinate clause.

An **independent,** or **main, clause** can stand alone as a sentence because it expresses a complete thought.

When an independent clause stands by itself, it is called a sentence. When it appears in a sentence with another clause, it is called a clause. In the following examples, each subject is underlined once, and each verb is underlined twice. Notice that each independent clause can stand alone as a separate sentence.

┌──── independent clause ────┐   ┌── independent clause ──┐
Lynn washed the bottles, and Bill emptied the trash.

┌──────── sentence ────────┐ ┌──────── sentence ────────┐
Lynn washed the bottles. Bill emptied the trash.

A **subordinate,** or **dependent, clause** cannot stand alone as a sentence because it does not express a complete thought.

In the examples below, the subordinate clauses do not express complete thoughts—even though they have a subject and a verb.

```
        ┌──────subordinate clause──────┐  ┌──independent clause──┐
```
After the <u>trash</u> <u>had been emptied,</u> <u>Nathan</u> <u>rinsed</u> the cans.

```
        ┌──────────independent clause──────────┐ ┌──subordinate clause──┐
```
<u>Are</u> <u>you</u> <u>going</u> to gather the newspapers <u>that</u> <u>are</u> on the table?

CONNECT TO WRITER'S CRAFT

When you are writing to persuade an audience to adopt your viewpoint on a particular topic, you can acknowledge the opposing point of view by presenting it in a subordinate clause rather than in an independent clause.

> **Although some argue that the amount of money high schools spend on athletic programs is fair,** recent findings indicate that some schools spend forty percent more on athletics than on other extracurricular activities.

By beginning the statement with a subordinate clause, you let the audience know that you understand the arguments against spending less money on athletics. However, you believe other extracurricular activities would benefit if high schools spent more money on them.

PRACTICE YOUR SKILLS

● Check Your Understanding
Identifying Subordinate Clauses

Contemporary Life **Write the subordinate clause in each sentence.**

1. Because we recycle, we save space in the city landfill.

2. Take the cans that are in the dish drainer.

3. Did you know that trash day is Monday?

4. You should talk to the sanitary engineer who drives the route on our street.

5. We recycle newspapers whenever we get the chance.

6. While you are at school, tons of garbage are dumped in the landfill.

7. The mayor promised that he would expand the city's recycling program.

8. Because there are so many kinds of plastics, some recycling programs do not accept any plastic products.

9. The phone book is another common item that many communities have difficulty recycling.

10. The city manager wants a dump site that he believes is environmentally safe.

11. We should recycle our trash because we may not have enough landfills in a few years.

12. Before you recycle bottles, you should wash them out.

13. Some cities have special recycling containers that you can use for your recyclable trash.

14. Before we had recycling bins, all of our trash was carried to the dump.

15. We put our recycling containers on the curb on trash pickup days so that the collectors can empty them.

16. After recycling trucks empty these containers, they take the recyclable trash to a special facility.

17. This kind of service makes it easy and convenient for people who want to recycle.

18. See what you can do to get your city to adopt a recycling program.

● Connect to the Writing Process: Drafting
Writing Sentences Using Subordinate Clauses

19.–23. Write five sentences about recycling, including a subordinate clause in each. Then underline each subordinate clause.

Uses of Subordinate Clauses

A subordinate clause in a sentence can be used in several ways. It can be used as an adverb, an adjective, or a noun.

● Adverb Clauses

An **adverb clause** is a subordinate clause that is used like an adverb to modify a verb, an adjective, or an adverb.

Like a phrase, a subordinate clause can be used as if it were a single adverb. The single adverb, the adverb phrase, and the adverb clause in the following examples all modify the verb *had practiced*.

SINGLE ADVERB	He had practiced **continuously.**
ADVERB PHRASE	He had practiced **without rest.**
ADVERB CLAUSE	He had practiced **even though he was tired.**

An adverb clause answers the same questions a single adverb answers: *How? When? Where? How much?* and *To what extent?* An adverb clause also answers the questions *Under what condition?* and *Why?* Notice that in the first three examples below, the adverb clauses modify the whole verb phrase.

WHEN?	We will go **whenever you are ready.**
WHERE?	We will park **wherever we can find an empty spot in the garage.**
UNDER WHAT CONDITION?	We will attend the concert **if we can get tickets.**
WHY?	We left early **so that we would not be late.**

Although most adverb clauses modify verbs, some modify adverbs or adjectives.

MODIFYING AN ADJECTIVE	Mike is more precise **than I am.**
MODIFYING AN ADVERB	Jan arrived sooner **than I did.**

Subordinating Conjunctions

A **subordinating conjunction** begins an adverb clause. Following is a list of common subordinating conjunctions. Remember that words such as *after, before,* and *until* can also be used as prepositions.

COMMON SUBORDINATING CONJUNCTIONS		
after	because	though
although	before	unless
as	even though	until
as far as	if	when
as if	in order that	whenever
as long as	since	where
as soon as	so that	wherever
as though	than	while

If you like jazz, you will enjoy this new CD.

We arrived **after the performance started.**

She was singing **as if she had a cold.**

Unless we hurry, we will miss the concert.

PUNCTUATION WITH ADVERB CLAUSES

Place a comma after an introductory adverb clause.

If you win the music competition, what will you do with the prize money?

If an adverb clause interrupts an independent clause, place a comma before and after it.

The audience, **after the band finished the medley,** gave a standing ovation.

When an adverb clause follows an independent clause, no comma is needed.

Call me **as soon as you have the tickets.**

PRACTICE YOUR SKILLS

● Check Your Understanding
Identifying Subordinating Conjunctions

Music Topic **Write each adverb clause. Then underline each subordinating conjunction.**

1. You cannot play jazz unless you practice regularly.
2. Jazz is unique because it is characterized by syncopation.
3. Although jazz is American, it has also influenced other Western music.
4. Playing jazz is harder than most people realize.
5. Good musicians play jazz as though it were effortless.
6. Although some listeners prefer Miles Davis's music, others like Herbie Hancock's style.
7. Bebop, because it was unusual, resulted in the first breakaway of jazz from mainstream music.
8. Bebop is unusual because it is very difficult.

9. Good jazz musicians improvise whenever they get together to play.

10. When a band plays swing jazz, many people feel like dancing.

Recognizing Adverb Clauses as Modifiers

> Music
> Topic
>
> **Write each adverb clause. Then, beside each one, write the word or words it modifies.**

11. After I studied the history of jazz, I found a new love.

12. When I heard Scott Joplin's music, it spoke to me.

13. Although his family was poor, young Joplin studied classical piano as a child.

14. He became a traveling pianist as soon as he reached his twenties.

15. Wherever he went, people flocked to hear him play.

16. Because he wrote "The Maple Leaf Rag," he earned the title of "King of Ragtime."

17. Before he died in 1917, he had published about sixty compositions.

18. He was never acknowledged as a serious composer because he wrote ragtime music.

19. As soon as his music was republished in the early 1970s, it found an appreciative audience.

20. The Advisory Board on the Pulitzer Prizes, when it met in 1976, gave Joplin a special citation for his contribution to American music.

● Connect to the Writing Process: Editing
Punctuating Adverb Clauses

Write the following sentences, adding commas where needed. If a sentence is correct, write C.

21. Since I have been practicing I have been improving.

22. Do not applaud until the bandleader drops her hands.

23. While you are practicing I will review the next song.

24. We will perform outside unless it rains.

25. The sponsors when they heard the thunder moved the concert inside.

APPLY TO WRITING

Press Release: *Adverb Clauses*

Your band director has given you this picture of a recent activity of the band and asked you to write a short press release for the lifestyle section of the local newspaper. While organizing information for your press release, determine the answers to the questions that news articles should answer: *Who? What? When? Where?* and *Why?* Remember to arrange the events in chronological order and use adverb clauses wherever possible to give readers a better description of the action.

Adjective Clauses

An **adjective clause** is a subordinate clause that is used like an adjective to modify a noun or pronoun.

When a subordinate clause is used like a single adjective, it is called an adjective clause. In the following examples, the single adjective, the adjective phrase, and the adjective clause all modify the word *business* or *designer*.

SINGLE ADJECTIVE	The fashion industry is a **risky** business.
	Jean became a **fashion** designer.
ADJECTIVE PHRASE	The fashion industry is a business **with many risks.**
	Jean became a designer **with her own fashion style.**
ADJECTIVE CLAUSE	The fashion industry is a business **that has many risks.**
	Jean became a designer **who makes her own fashions.**

An adjective clause answers the same questions a single adjective answers: *Which one(s)?* and *What kind?*

WHICH ONE(S)?	The person **who just rang the bell** left a package.
	John found the shoes **that he had been wanting** at the new store.
WHAT KIND?	The package, **which was heavy**, came from our grandmother.
	John is wearing shoes **that have platform soles.**

Professional writers often use adverb and adjective clauses to create a pattern of speech that flows smoothly and naturally. Notice the use of adverb clauses in this passage. They are in **bold** type.

> **When Sir Launcelot awoke** he remounted and rode down the valley **until he came to a small chapel.** Through the window he could see a recluse kneeling before the altar. She called him into the chapel and asked him **whence he had come.**
>
> —*Sir Thomas Malory*, Le Morte D'Arthur

Relative Pronouns

An adjective clause usually begins with a relative pronoun. A **relative pronoun** relates an adjective clause to its antecedent— the noun or pronoun the clause modifies.

RELATIVE PRONOUNS				
who	whom	whose	which	that

The clerk **who sold me these pants** no longer works there.

Samantha found the receipt **that you lost.**

Sometimes the word *when* or *where* will also begin an adjective clause.

Autumn is the time **when the new spring fashions are shown.**

The city **where many fashion shows in Europe are held** is Paris.

Occasionally the relative pronoun *that* is dropped from an adjective clause. However, it is still understood to be there.

I have some shopping **I must do tonight.**
(The entire adjective clause is *[that] I must do tonight.*)

Practice Your Skills

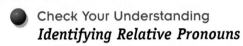

Check Your Understanding

Identifying Relative Pronouns

General Interest **Write each adjective clause. Then underline the relative pronoun or the word introducing each adjective clause.**

1. I have not seen a jacket that I have liked.

2. Ms. Henderson, whom I know from the mall, will be teaching a sewing class this year.

3. Saturday is the day when we like to go shopping.

4. Mr. Alonzo, whose store is at the center of the mall, can hem your pants.

5. Minnesota is home to a mall that has a roller coaster in it.

6. Are these the jeans that you saw in the window?

7. The man who made the first blue jeans was Levi Strauss.

8. The mall where my friends shop is on the other side of town.

9. Carmen's mother, who works at the information center, tells us about the new stores in the mall.

10. My grandparents joined a walking club whose members meet every morning in the mall.

11. The Southport Mall, which has many shops for teenagers, also has a large food court.

12. Many students who like to shop spend hours at the mall.

History Topic **Write each adjective clause. Then, beside each one, write the word it modifies.**

13. An item of clothing that is popular among people of all ages is blue jeans.

14. The first jeans, which were made in 1850, cost $13.50 a dozen!

15. They were made by a German immigrant whose name was Levi Strauss.

16. Strauss, who had a dream of success, went to San Francisco during the Gold Rush.

17. He took with him several bales of cloth, which he planned to use to make tents.

18. Other people who had arrived before him were already making tents.

19. San Francisco was still a place where ingenuity paid off.

20. He got an idea from a miner who complained about his trousers.

21. The heavy-duty material, which Strauss had intended for tents, soon became jeans.

22. The jeans that Strauss made are still copied today.

23. These jeans, which are made with cotton, are very comfortable.

24. My brother is one of those people who wear nothing but blue jeans and T-shirts.

Additional Functions of a Relative Pronoun

Besides introducing an adjective clause, a relative pronoun has another function. Within the adjective clause, it can serve as a subject, a direct object, or an object of a preposition. A relative pronoun can also show possession.

SUBJECT	Mrs. Brown, **who teaches British history,** is my next-door neighbor. *(Who is the subject of teaches.)*
DIRECT OBJECT	The school **she attends** is in Portland, Maine. *(The understood that is the direct object of she attends.)*
OBJECT OF A PREPOSITION	The book **from which I got most of my information** is in the library. *(Which is the object of the preposition from. Notice that from is part of the clause.)*
POSSESSION	Mrs. Brown is the person **whose classes I enjoy the most**. *(Whose shows possession of classes.)*

PUNCTUATION WITH ADJECTIVE CLAUSES

No punctuation is used with an adjective clause containing information that is essential to identify a person, place, or thing in a sentence.

ESSENTIAL	The person **who captured the imagination of England** was Lawrence of Arabia. (No commas are used because the clause is needed to identify which person.)

A comma or commas, however, should set off an adjective clause that is nonessential. A clause is nonessential if it can be removed from the sentence without changing the basic meaning.

NONESSENTIAL	Lawrence of Arabia, **who loathed human contact,** was a respected military leader. (Commas are used because the clause can be removed from the sentence.)

The relative pronoun *that* is usually used in an essential clause, whereas *which* is often used in a nonessential clause.

PRACTICE YOUR SKILLS

● Check Your Understanding

Determining the Function of a Relative Pronoun

History Topic **Write each adjective clause and underline the relative pronoun. If an adjective clause begins with an understood *that*, write *T* after the number. Label the usage of each relative pronoun, including understood *that*, in the adjective clauses, using the following abbreviations.**

direct object = *d.o.*   object of the preposition = *o.p.*
subject = *s.*   possession = *p.*

1. Thomas Edward Lawrence, whose adventures in Arabia made him famous, was a most unusual man.

2. Lawrence, who loathed physical contact, bowed to people instead of shaking hands.

3. He was a child who enjoyed history.

4. In 1907, he entered Oxford University, which is located in England.

5. In his senior year, he decided to study the influences the Crusades had had on European architecture in Arabia.

6. Arab officials, who were worried about his safety, warned him about the danger of traveling alone.

7. The Arab people, whom Lawrence greatly respected, became his best friends.

8. The happiest period of his life was one in which he worked at an archaeological dig site in Turkey.

9. Lawrence, who had many talents, also served in the British military in Arabia.

10. During his retirement Lawrence enjoyed riding motorcycles that were known for high speeds.

11. He also wrote the book *The Seven Pillars of Wisdom* for which he received great recognition.

12. Because of this book, people remember Lawrence as a man who was a romantic adventurer.

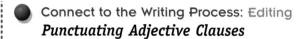
Punctuating Adjective Clauses

Write the following sentences, adding commas where needed. If a sentence is correct, write C.

13. History is a subject in which you can meet interesting people from the past.

14. Linda White whom you just met always earns high grades in history.

15. Mr. Lewallen whose essay tests are very difficult always makes history an interesting class.

16. This book which had fifteen chapters gave the class a great deal of background on Arabia.

17. I was the only person who had read the book before.

18. Arabia, which is situated between the Red Sea and the Persian Gulf, forms the southwest corner of Asia.

19. Much of Arabia is a barren desert in which few people live.

20. In the past, Arabia was a place to which people came to trade and learn.

21. In the 1100s, Western traders brought the Arabic system of numbers on which math is based today to Europe.

22. Today, Arabia is known for its oil industry, which is a rich economic resource.

Communicate Your Ideas

APPLY TO WRITING

Autobiography: *Adjective Clauses*

For geography class you are exchanging letters with a student in a foreign country. To get to know your pen pal, you decide to tell her what your life has been like so far. Write a short autobiography and be sure to use adjective clauses to describe yourself, your family, and your friends.

Misplaced Modifiers

An adjective clause should be placed as near as possible to the word it modifies. A clause placed too far away from the word it modifies is called a **misplaced modifier**.

MISPLACED   The enormous dinosaur display crashed to the ground, which had just been acquired by the museum.

CORRECT   The enormous dinosaur display, **which had just been acquired by the museum,** crashed to the ground.

PRACTICE YOUR SKILLS

● Check Your Understanding
Identifying Misplaced Modifiers

Contemporary Life   **If the underlined modifier is placed correctly in the sentence, write C for correct. If the underlined modifier is misplaced, write MM for misplaced modifier.**

1. I spent Monday, <u>which was a holiday</u>, at the museum.

2. We saw a reconstructed dinosaur at the museum, <u>which existed millions of years ago</u>.

3. Mr. Hale, <u>who collects rare Indian relics</u>, often contributes to the museum.

4. Mr. Hale donated his arrowhead collection to the museum, <u>which is very rare</u>.

5. I used the computer <u>that is located in the gemstone exhibit</u>.

6. I bought a beautiful book from the gift shop <u>that is about archaeology</u>.

7. My five-year-old sister enjoyed watching the artist <u>who taught pottery</u>.

8. Our museum contains many unusual pieces of sculpture, which sits at the corner of Second Street and Grand Avenue.

9. We read the books from the museum that we had bought.

10. Did Alexandra find all of the information that she will need for her report on dinosaur extinction?

11. The exhibit that the museum showed last week included Roman art.

12. One item of the exhibit, which is in Rome, Italy, was a miniature of the Colosseum.

13. The Colosseum could seat almost 50,000 people, which was built nearly two thousand years ago.

14. The marble, stucco, and metal decorations exist no longer on the remaining Colosseum walls which were destroyed by neglect, earthquakes, and builders.

Connect to the Writing Process: Revising
Correcting Misplaced Modifiers

15.–22. Correctly rewrite the sentences above that contain misplaced modifiers. Remember to use commas where they are needed.

Noun Clauses

A **noun clause** is a subordinate clause that is used like a noun.

Both the single noun *news* and the noun clause in the following examples are used as objects of a preposition.

SINGLE NOUN	The scientists were elated by the **news.**
NOUN CLAUSE	The scientists were elated by **what they had heard.**

Within a sentence, a noun clause can be used in the same ways that a single noun can be used.

SUBJECT	**Whatever you choose** is fine with me.
DIRECT OBJECT	Did you know **that the volcano erupted?**
INDIRECT OBJECT	Give **whoever comes to the site** a flier.
OBJECT OF A PREPOSITION	Award the prize to **whoever has the best project.**
PREDICATE NOMINATIVE	Helen's reason for visiting Mexico was **that she had planned to study the volcano.**

The words in the following list often introduce a noun clause. You may recall that *who, whom, whose, which,* and *that* also introduce adjective clauses. For this reason, do not rely on an introductory word alone to identify a clause. Instead, determine how a clause is used in a sentence.

COMMON INTRODUCTORY WORDS FOR NOUN CLAUSES			
how	whatever	which	whomever
if	when	who	whose
that	where	whoever	why
what	whether	whom	

PRACTICE YOUR SKILLS

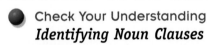

Check Your Understanding
Identifying Noun Clauses

 Science Topic **Write the noun clause from each sentence.**

1. Most people know that the Popocatépetl volcano is dangerous.

2. Scientists give whoever lives near the volcano information about it.

3. I read that the volcano is due to erupt soon.

4. National Geographic Society research grants help scientists learn more about why volcanos errupt.

5. They have learned that El Popo can be very unpredictable.

6. Information about the volcano will be given to whoever asks for it.

7. The Mexican government's wish is that the volcano will not erupt.

8. That the soil around a volcano is rich farmland surprises most people.

9. Do you know what the scientists have learned about the volcano?

10. What they have discovered over the past few years must not be kept a secret.

● Check Your Understanding
Determining the Uses of Noun Clauses

Science Topic **Write each noun clause. Then label how it is used in the sentence with one of the following abbreviations.**

direct object = *d.o.*   predicate nominative = *p.n.*
subject = *s.*   object of the preposition = *o.p.*
indirect object = *i.o.*

11. Many people once believed that angry gods lived inside volcanoes.

12. What scientists hypothesize often occurs.

13. The government will make evacuation plans for whoever lives near El Popo.

14. The only trouble with the evacuation plan is that it may not work.

15. Give whoever lives near the volcano the evacuation plan.

16. Tell me what you will attempt to do to help the scientists.

17. How volcanoes erupt was thoroughly explained in science class today.

18. The scientists' opinion is that the volcano will erupt soon.

19. Did you know that even dormant volcanoes can become dangerous?

20. How the government responds depends on the scientists' plans.

● Connect to the Writing Process: Drafting
Writing Sentences with Noun Clauses

Complete the following sentences by adding noun clauses.

21. The scientists hope ▉.

22. Did you know ▉?

23. I wonder ▉.

24. The difficulty is ▉.

25. ▉ is no surprise.

26. They will bring back ▉.

27. Have they decided ▉?

28. ▉ depends on the day's weather.

29. The evacuation will use ▉.

30. ▉ will lead the expedition.

Communicate Your Ideas

APPLY TO WRITING

News Story: *Noun Clauses*

The editor of your school paper has asked you to write a news story about a natural disaster. Select a natural event that might occur in your geographical area. List facts and interesting details about the disaster. Incorporate them into your news article. Write a final copy, and be sure to include noun clauses wherever possible. Then, write an eye-catching title for your news article.

 **QuickCheck** Mixed Practice

General Interest **Write each subordinate clause in the paragraphs and label each one *adv.* for adverb, *adj.* for adjective, or *n.* for noun.**

Brazilian scientists knew that killer bees were fierce. They also knew that killer bees made more honey than European bees did. It seemed worth the chance to fly in some killer bees from Africa. If they could be crossed with the European bees, the results might be gentle bees that would make a great deal of honey. Special hives from which the larger queen bees and drones could not escape were constructed. As long as the queen bees were locked up in the hives, the workers would come home to them.

Accidents, however, do happen. A beekeeper who did not know about the killer bees removed the grids from the hives. Twenty-six queen bees escaped—along with all their workers and drones. The killer bees, which traveled about two hundred miles farther north every year, reached the United States during the 1990s. Most experts say that people in northern states should not worry. Killer bees cannot live through cold winters.

Kinds of Sentence Structure

Sentences are classified according to the number and kinds of clauses within them. The four basic kinds of sentences are simple, compound, complex, and compound-complex.

A simple sentence consists of one independent clause.

This sponge is dirty.

A simple sentence can have a compound subject, a compound verb, or both. In the following sentence, the compound subject is underlined once, and the compound verb is underlined twice.

Jason and Luis finished their dive and have gone home.

A compound sentence consists of two or more independent clauses.

┌── independent clause ──┐   ┌── independent clause ──┐
Sponges are not plants, but they are ocean animals.

┌── independent clause ──┐ ┌ independent clause ┐
Diving can be difficult; snorkeling is easy.

CONNECT TO WRITER'S CRAFT

Before you write a compound sentence, ask yourself if the clauses belong together. Independent clauses should not be combined to make a compound sentence unless the ideas are closely related. Notice that the clauses in the following sentences are not closely related, so a compound sentence is not a good choice.

Diving is my favorite sport, but it is getting late.

Diving is my favorite **sport. It** is getting late.

You can learn about punctuating a compound sentence on pages L423–L424.

PUNCTUATION WITH COMPOUND SENTENCES

You can join independent clauses in a compound sentence with a comma and a conjunction.

The sun will set soon, **but** it will still be hot.

You can also join independent clauses with a semicolon and no conjunction.

The sun will set soon; we will need our lanterns.

A **complex sentence** consists of one independent clause and one or more subordinate clauses.

┌─── independent clause ───┐ ┌── subordinate clause ──┐
I enjoy scuba diving more than I enjoy snorkeling.

┌──── subordinate clause ────┐ ┌── independent clause ──┐
Although I have tried many times, snorkeling is one sport

┌─ subordinate clause ─┐
that I cannot master.

You can learn about punctuating a complex sentence on page L427.

A **compound-complex sentence** consists of two or more independent clauses and one or more subordinate clauses.

┌───── subordinate clause ─────┐ ┌─independent clause─┐
If you ascend too quickly after a dive, gas bubbles form in

┌──────── independent clause ────────┐
your blood, and you will suffer from the bends.

┌──── independent clause ────┐ ┌─independent clause─┐
This complication can be avoided, and you will feel much

┌───── subordinate clause ─────┐
better if you rise slowly after a dive.

When you punctuate compound-complex sentences, follow the rules for both compound and complex sentences.

● Check Your Understanding
Classifying Sentences

Science Topic **Label each sentence *simple, compound, complex,* or *compound-complex.***

1. When you wash the dishes with a natural sponge, you are actually using the skeleton of an ocean animal.

2. The sponge is not a plant; it is an animal that is covered with flesh.

3. The skeleton is gradually formed as hard materials become imbedded in the body.

4. The sponge is alive, yet it has no legs or fins.

5. As a result, the sponge must attach itself to some firm object.

6. Nature's plan for the sponge was ingenious, for tiny holes exist in the sponge.

7. As water flows into these holes, food and oxygen are carried in.

8. Through the holes, waste materials are carried out.

9. Some sponges can regenerate themselves; they can grow whole new sponges from small fragments.

10. People plant sponge fragments in the sea, and the sponges are harvested two or three years later when they have grown large.

11. Some of the oldest animal fossils that have been found are sponges.

12. Although there are about 5,000 species of sponges, only about 150 species live in fresh water, and the rest are found in the oceans.

13. Many sponges secrete toxic fluids and are used as protection by some marine creatures.

14. Some sponges bore into coral and anchor themselves to an area where protection is available.

Creating a Variety of Sentence Structures

15.–20. Choose any six of the sentences on the preceding page and rewrite them so that they form another sentence structure.

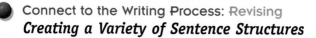

APPLY TO WRITING

Writer's Craft: *Analyzing Sentence Structure*

Read the following passage from *The Pearl* and answer the questions that follow.

> Kino and Juana came slowly down to the beach and to Kino's canoe, which was the one thing of value he owned in the world. It was very old. Kino's grandfather had brought it from Nayarit, and he had given it to Kino's father, and so it had come to Kino. It was at once property and source of food, for a man with a boat can guarantee a woman that she will eat something.
>
> —*John Steinbeck,* The Pearl

- Identify the different sentence structures Steinbeck uses. Why do you think he uses them?
- What value or impact does the author add to the excerpt by including a simple sentence?
- What qualities do the other sentences add to the excerpt?
- One of the sentences written by Steinbeck has three independent clauses. How does this relate to the content of the sentence?
- Try to rewrite the passage using all simple sentences. What is the effect of using only one type of sentence?

Clause Fragments

Although all clauses have a subject and a verb, only an independent clause can stand alone as a sentence. When subordinate clauses stand alone, they do not express a complete thought. A **clause fragment**, therefore, results when a subordinate clause stands alone. Following are examples of clause fragments in **bold** type. Notice that they are punctuated and capitalized as if they were complete sentences.

ADVERB CLAUSE FRAGMENTS	The birthday party was canceled. **Because it rained.**
	Before you choose a gift. Think carefully.
ADJECTIVE CLAUSE FRAGMENTS	Here is the invitation. **That you wanted me to copy for you.**
	Jennifer ordered a chocolate cake. **Which everyone seems to like.**

Correcting Clause Fragments

When you edit your written work, always look for clause fragments. If you find any, you can correct them in one of two ways. First, you can add words to make them into separate sentences. Second, you can attach them to a related sentence next to them.

SENTENCE AND CLAUSE FRAGMENT	We had planned a big party. **That was supposed to be a surprise.**
SEPARATE SENTENCES	We had planned a big party. **It was supposed to be a surprise.**
ATTACHED	We had planned a big party **that was supposed to be a surprise.**

SENTENCE AND CLAUSE FRAGMENT	Have you seen Julie? **Who was supposed to order the balloons.**
SEPARATE SENTENCES	Have you seen Julie? **She was supposed to order the balloons.**
ATTACHED	Have you seen Julie, **who was supposed to order the balloons?**

You can learn about other kinds of fragments on pages L82–L83 and L140–L142.

PRACTICE YOUR SKILLS

● Check Your Understanding
Recognizing Clause Fragments

Contemporary Life **Label each group of words *S* for sentence or *CF* for clause fragment.**

1. After dinner and dessert, she will open all her birthday presents.

2. Who is making the decorations for the party?

3. While you hang the balloons.

4. Who never likes surprises.

5. Because the party is so early.

6. Which balloon do you want?

7. Which was impossible to plan.

8. Since the party will be tonight.

9. If the weather forecaster on Channel 6 was right.

10. Now is the time to decide.

11. Even though the party is at the park?

12. The weather should be perfect!

● Connect to the Writing Process: Revising
Correcting Sentence Fragments

13.–19. Rewrite the clause fragments from the previous exercise as complete sentences.

APPLY TO WRITING

Thank-You Note: *Complete Sentences*

Your best friend gave you a surprise party, which you enjoyed so much that you posted the pictures on your Website. Write a thank-you note to your friend. Explain how much you enjoyed the party. Be sure to avoid using clause fragments in your note. Before writing your first draft, brainstorm answers to the following questions.

- What role did your friend play in putting the party together?

- Which specific details were particularly thoughtful and difficult to coordinate?

- What did this party mean to you?

Run-on Sentences

Writing too fast often results in run-on sentences because one sentence flows right into another one. Readers often get confused when they read run-on sentences because too much information comes all at once.

A **run-on sentence** is two or more sentences that are written as one sentence and are separated by a comma or no mark of punctuation at all.

Run-on sentences usually are written in one of two ways.

WITH A COMMA	Laurie arrived on time, **everyone else came fifteen minutes late.**
WITH NO PUNCTUATION	The skis were too large for my feet **they had to be returned.**

▶ Ways to Correct Run-on Sentences

There are three ways to correct a run-on sentence. You can turn it into (1) separate sentences, (2) a compound sentence, or (3) a complex sentence.

RUN-ON SENTENCE	Art hurt his leg Hank skied the run for him. (two independent clauses with no punctuation)
SEPARATE SENTENCES	Art hurt his leg. **H**ank skied the run for him. (separated, using a period and a capital letter)
COMPOUND SENTENCE	Art hurt his leg, **and** Hank skied the run for him. (combined, using a comma and a conjunction)
	Art hurt his leg; Hank skied the run for him. (combined, using a semicolon)

COMPLEX SENTENCE	**When** Art hurt his leg, Hank skied the run for him.
	(combined by changing one independent clause into a subordinate clause)

PRACTICE YOUR SKILLS

● Check Your Understanding
Recognizing Run-on Sentences

Contemporary Life **Label each group of words *S* for sentence or *R* for run-on.**

1. Winter is the season of the year that I like the best.

2. Although the snow was not very deep, skiing was surprisingly good.

3. May I borrow your camera I want to take pictures during my ski vacation in Colorado.

4. For my first experience skiing, I chose the beginner's slope.

5. The skiers do best in clear weather, it is easier to see the trails.

6. On the expert trail, I am not very good I am a beginner.

7. Skiers can use a variety of skis, it depends on what type of skiing they are going to do.

8. I followed the instructor, traveling as fast as my legs could carry me.

9. I brought several jackets with me the first time I went skiing, for I wasn't sure of the weather.

10. The longest trail at the resort is the cross-country trail it is 38 miles long.

11. Only the most adventurous and physically fit skiers can finish the entire trail.

12. I was able to finish only three miles it was a long trek, but I had a good time.

13. Extreme skiing is exciting to watch the skiers take incredible risks.

14. Don't let these daredevils fool you they are very well trained and have a lot of experience.

15. After my vacation, I kept thinking about how enjoyable it was I want to go skiing again next year.

● Connect to the Writing Process: Revising
Correcting Run-on Sentences

16.–24. **Rewrite the run-on sentences from the previous exercise as complete sentences.**

Communicate Your Ideas

APPLY TO WRITING

Proposal: *Complete Sentences*

Your sports club has decided to enter the school science fair. You have designed an invention that will improve a piece of sports equipment. However, in order to enter the science competition, you must first submit a proposal for your project to the judges of the competition. Write a description of your invention and your project and be certain to avoid run-on sentences. While writing the first draft of your proposal, be sure to incorporate the following ideas.

- Name your invention.
- Explain how it is to be used.
- State why it is an improvement over the original invention.
- Determine your market.
- Request action.

Diagraming Sentences

A simple sentence is diagramed on a single baseline. In compound, complex, and compound-complex sentences, however, each clause is diagramed on a separate baseline.

Compound Sentences   Each independent clause in a compound sentence is diagramed like a simple sentence. The clauses are joined with a broken line that connects the verbs. The conjunction is then placed on the broken line.

You make the salad, and I will make dessert.

You	make	salad

and

the

I	will make	dessert

Complex Sentences   In a complex sentence, an adverb clause is diagramed beneath the independent clause it modifies. The subordinating conjunction goes on a broken line that connects the verb in the adverb clause to the verb, the adjective, or the adverb that the clause modifies. In the following diagram, the adverb clause modifies the verb in the independent clause.

Take the dog out before you leave.

(you)	Take	dog

out   before   the

you	leave

In a complex sentence, an adjective clause is also diagramed beneath the independent clause it modifies. The relative pronoun in the clause is connected by a broken line to the noun or pronoun the clause modifies. In the following diagram, the adjective clause modifies the noun *book* in the independent clause.

This is the book that you should read.

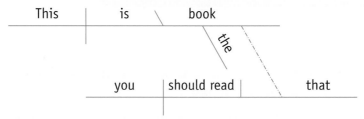

A noun clause is diagramed on a pedestal in the same place that a single noun would be if it had the same function. In the following diagram, the noun clause is used as the subject.

Whatever will be will be.

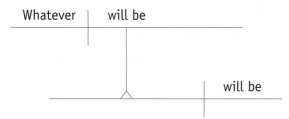

Compound-Complex Sentences Apply what you just learned about diagraming compound and complex sentences.

PRACTICE YOUR SKILLS

● Check Your Understanding
Diagraming Sentences

Diagram the following sentences or copy them. If you copy them, draw one line under each subject and two lines under each verb. Then put parentheses around each subordinate clause and label each one *adverb, adjective,* or *noun*.

1. If you look at the clouds, you can usually predict the weather.
2. Tell me what you see now.
3. Cumulus clouds are fluffy, and they signal fine weather
4. Cirrus clouds, which are wisps with tails, may signal rain.
5. Did you know that clouds predict weather?

Identifying Subordinate Clauses

Write the subordinate clause in each sentence. Then label the use of each one *adverb, adjective,* or *noun*.

1. A little-known invention by Thomas Edison was a doll that talked.
2. Although people eat the harmless eggplant, its vines are poisonous.
3. It is estimated that Niagara Falls will disappear into Lake Erie in about 23,000 years.
4. If diamonds are heated sufficiently, they will burn.
5. Venus, which is the third brightest object in the sky, can sometimes be seen clearly at noon.
6. Sailing is what I like best.
7. They agreed on a place where they would meet.
8. Whoever just called didn't leave a message.
9. When it is provoked, a rhinoceros can charge at a speed of thirty miles per hour.
10. Of the millions of bison that once roamed North America, only about 200,000 now exist.
11. I don't know where I put my sunglasses.
12. A French astronomer found helium on the sun before anyone found it on the earth.
13. Napoleon had conquered Italy by the time that he was twenty-six years old.
14. Stanley Lopez, whom you have not met, will be the new soccer captain.
15. Sir Arthur Conan Doyle, who created Sherlock Holmes, was a doctor.

Classifying Sentences

Label each of the following sentences _simple, compound, complex,_ or _compound-complex._

1. Records and tapes are out, and compact disks are in.
2. Compact disks are often called CDs.
3. Although a CD may look like a little record, it doesn't work like one.
4. Records have a thin groove, and different sounds are recorded as bumps and dents in the groove's sides and floor.
5. The sound is produced when a needle moves up and down and from side to side along the groove.
6. A CD, however, is covered with microscopic pits that make up a digital code.
7. When you play a CD, a laser bounces off the CD and reads the little pits, and the code is translated into sound.
8. In spite of the cost of CDs, they have many advantages.
9. They produce extraordinary sound, and because a needle never touches them, they last and last.
10. Some music lovers would rather not listen to anything but CDs.

Using Sentence Structure

Write five sentences that follow the directions below. (The sentences may come in any order.) Write about one of the following topics or a topic of your choice: your favorite kind of music, your favorite singer or group, or your own musical talents.

1. Write a simple sentence.
2. Write a complex sentence with an introductory adverb clause.
3. Write a complex sentence with an adjective clause.
4. Write a compound sentence.
5. Write a complex sentence with a noun clause.

Label each sentence and check its punctuation.

Language and *Self-Expression*

This cup from the fifth century B.C. is an example of red-figured technique. The artist left the figures in the red color of the clay and used black paint to fill in the background. This technique allowed artists to show precise details and to experiment with perspective. The mood of the cup is peaceful, and the figures seem relaxed in their task. From painted works of this kind, people can infer many things about Athenians in these ancient times.

Make up a story about the figures you see on the cup. Assign each woman a personality and use the details you see to suggest a plot. Have this scene at the orchard play a pivotal role. Be sure your story has a beginning, middle, and end. Plan to share your story with your classmates.

Prewriting Give each woman a name and make a chart like this one. Fill in details about each woman.

Name	Family Home	Personality Traits

Choose a main character and decide on a problem she will face. Use a chart with these headings.

Problem	Steps to Solve It	Solution

Drafting Begin by introducing characters, setting, and problem. Continue with plot points that lead to the solution. End with a satisfying conclusion that ties up any loose ends.

Revising Look for ideas that do not flow or that seem unrelated. Cut and add material as needed. Include simple, compound, complex, and compound-complex sentences.

Editing As you review your story, correct errors in grammar, capitalization, punctuation, and spelling.

Publishing Prepare a final copy of your story and present it to your classmates.

 **Another Look**

A **clause** is a group of words that has a subject and a verb.

Kinds of Clauses

An **independent (or main) clause** can stand alone as a sentence because it expresses a complete thought. *(page L155)*

A **subordinate (or dependent) clause** cannot stand alone as a sentence because it does not express a complete thought. *(page L156)*

Uses of Subordinate Clauses

An **adverb clause** is a subordinate clause that is used like an adverb to modify a verb, an adjective, or an adverb. *(pages L158–L159)*

All adverb clauses begin with a **subordinating conjunction.** *(page L159)*

An **adjective clause** is a subordinate clause that is used like an adjective to modify a noun or pronoun. *(pages L163–L164)*

Most adjective clauses begin with a **relative pronoun.** *(pages L164–L165)*

A **noun clause** is a subordinate clause that is used like a noun. *(pages L171–L172)*

Kinds of Sentence Structure

A **simple sentence** consists of one independent clause. *(page L176)*

A **compound sentence** consists of two or more independent clauses. *(pages L176–L177)*

A **complex sentence** consists of one independent clause and one or more subordinate clauses. *(page L177)*

A **compound-complex sentence** consists of two or more independent clauses and one or more subordinate clauses. *(page L177)*

Other Information About Clauses

Punctuating adverb clauses *(page L160)*

Punctuating adjective clauses *(page L167)*

Avoiding misplaced modifiers *(page L170)*

Correcting clause fragments *(pages L180–L181)*

Correcting run-on sentences *(pages L183–L184)*

Posttest

Directions

Write the letter of the term that correctly identifies each sentence or the underlined word or words in a sentence.

EXAMPLE **1.** The meanings of names is a subject that fascinates me.

    1 A simple sentence

       B compound sentence

       C complex sentence

       D compound-complex sentence

ANSWER   **1 C**

1. My name, *Cynthia,* is from a Greek word for *moon.*

2. I was not surprised when I learned that.

3. After all, I have always been a night owl, and I prefer moonlight to sunlight.

4. I have a friend named *Jalila,* and I just learned that her name means "great" in Arabic.

5. I know that Jalila has always seemed great to me!

6. The most popular girl's name <u>when I was born</u> was *Ashley.*

7. <u>Although I go to school with hundreds of kids</u>, I don't know any Ashleys at all.

8. I guess <u>that *Ashley* wasn't popular in our town</u>.

9. <u>I do know three Caitlyns</u>, and my brother knows at least three Kaylas.

10. My middle name, *Abigail,* is the name <u>that I like best</u>.

1	**A**	simple sentence	**6**	**A**	independent clause
	B	compound sentence		**B**	adverb clause
	C	complex sentence		**C**	adjective clause
	D	compound-complex sentence		**D**	noun clause

1
- **A** simple sentence
- **B** compound sentence
- **C** complex sentence
- **D** compound-complex sentence

2
- **A** simple sentence
- **B** compound sentence
- **C** complex sentence
- **D** compound-complex sentence

3
- **A** simple sentence
- **B** compound sentence
- **C** complex sentence
- **D** compound-complex sentence

4
- **A** simple sentence
- **B** compound sentence
- **C** complex sentence
- **D** compound-complex sentence

5
- **A** simple sentence
- **B** compound sentence
- **C** complex sentence
- **D** compound-complex sentence

6
- **A** independent clause
- **B** adverb clause
- **C** adjective clause
- **D** noun clause

7
- **A** independent clause
- **B** adverb clause
- **C** adjective clause
- **D** noun clause

8
- **A** independent clause
- **B** adverb clause
- **C** adjective clause
- **D** noun clause

9
- **A** independent clause
- **B** adverb clause
- **C** adjective clause
- **D** noun clause

10
- **A** independent clause
- **B** adverb clause
- **C** adjective clause
- **D** noun clause

CHAPTER 5

Using Verbs

Pretest

Directions
Write the letter of the term that correctly identifies the underlined word or words in each sentence.

EXAMPLE   **1.** We have <u>gone</u> to the pool every summer for years.

    1 A   present tense
       B   present participle
       C   past tense
       D   past participle

ANSWER   **1 D**

1. Almost everyone I know at school <u>likes</u> the swim classes at the pool.

2. My friends <u>arrive</u> there early in the morning.

3. Last week my friends and I <u>stayed</u> there all day every day.

4. We are <u>practicing</u> as many different strokes as possible.

5. I have <u>mastered</u> the crawl and the backstroke.

6. The instructor is <u>teaching</u> us the butterfly stroke.

7. I <u>do find</u> it very difficult.

8. It <u>will take</u> me a long time to master it.

9. I <u>have been practicing</u> for the swim team tryouts this fall.

10. My father also <u>had swum</u> on his school team when he was my age.

1 **A** present tense
   B present participle
   C past tense
   D past participle

2 **A** present tense
   B present participle
   C past tense
   D past participle

3 **A** present tense
   B present participle
   C past tense
   D past participle

4 **A** present tense
   B present participle
   C past tense
   D past participle

5 **A** present tense
   B present participle
   C past tense
   D past participle

6 **A** present tense
   B present participle
   C past tense
   D past participle

7 **A** present participle
   B past tense
   C emphatic form
   D past perfect tense

8 **A** present tense
   B past tense
   C future tense
   D emphatic form

9 **A** present progressive
   B past tense
   C present perfect progressive form
   D past perfect tense

10 **A** future perfect tense
   B past tense
   C future tense
   D past perfect tense

Sandy Skoglund. *The Green House,* 1990.
Photo cibachrome, 52¼ by 64 inches.

Describe   What does this image show? What are the
human figures in the background doing?

Analyze   What colors does the artist use in this image?
Are they warm colors or cool colors?

Interpret   What mood do you think the artist wishes to
convey in this image? How does the use of
color affect the mood? How might a writer
portray the same mood?

Judge   How does the image make you feel?
Thoughtful? Sleepy? Serene? Some other way?
Explain.

At the end of this chapter, you will use the artwork to stimulate
ideas for writing.

The Principal Parts of Verbs

In the preceding section of this book, you learned the various elements of grammar. In this section on usage, you will see how to use those elements properly in your writing and speaking. This chapter will review the many forms of verbs and the uses of those forms.

The four basic forms of a verb are called its principal parts. Knowing the principal parts of a verb is important because all the tenses of a verb are formed from them.

> The **principal parts** of a verb are the present, the present participle, the past, and the past participle.

Notice in the following examples that the present participle and the past participle have helping verbs when used as the main verb of a sentence.

PRESENT	I **study** each night.
PRESENT PARTICIPLE	I *am* **studying** now.
PAST	I **studied** last night.
PAST PARTICIPLE	I *have* **studied** every night this week.

● Regular Verbs

> A **regular verb** forms its past and past participle by adding *–ed* or *–d* to the present.

Most verbs are regular verbs. They form their past and past participle the same way. *Sail, ask, smile,* and *drip* are just four of the many regular verbs. As you look at their four principal parts, notice that the present participle is formed by adding *–ing* to the present form, and that, as the rule says, the past participle is formed by adding *–ed* or *–d* to the present form.

PRESENT	PRESENT PARTICIPLE	PAST	PAST PARTICIPLE
sail	(is) sailing	sailed	(have) sailed
ask	(is) asking	asked	(have) asked
smile	(is) smiling	smiled	(have) smiled
drip	(is) dripping	dripped	(have) dripped

When endings such as *–ing* and *–ed* are added to some verbs like *smile* and *drip,* the spelling changes. If you are unsure of the spelling of a verb form, look it up in a dictionary.

CONNECT TO SPEAKING AND WRITING

When you speak, pay particular attention to verb endings. Dropping the *–ed* or *–d* from the past participle of a verb is a common error. Watch especially when you use the verbs *asked, hoped, supposed,* and *used.*

> INCORRECT   We **use** to have picnics here in the summer.
> CORRECT   We **used** to have picnics here in the summer.

PRACTICE YOUR SKILLS

● Check Your Understanding
Determining the Principal Parts of Verbs

Write the four principal parts of the following regular verbs. Remember that the principal parts are present, present participle, past, and past participle.

1. wait	**3.** stop	**5.** paint	**7.** open	**9.** plan
2. cook	**4.** bake	**6.** dream	**8.** climb	**10.** play

Irregular Verbs

An irregular verb does not form its past and past participle by adding *-ed* or *-d* to the present.

The irregular verbs form their past and past participle in different ways. The following irregular verbs have been divided into groups according to the way they form their past and past participle. Remember, though, that the word *is* is not part of the present participle and the word *have* is not part of the past participle. They have been added to the following lists of irregular verbs, however, to remind you that all present and past participles must have a form of one of these verbs when they are used as a verb in a sentence.

Group 1 The following irregular verbs have the same form for the present, the past, and the past participle.

PRESENT	PRESENT PARTICIPLE	PAST	PAST PARTICIPLE
burst	(is) bursting	burst	(have) burst
cost	(is) costing	cost	(have) cost
hit	(is) hitting	hit	(have) hit
hurt	(is) hurting	hurt	(have) hurt
let	(is) letting	let	(have) let
put	(is) putting	put	(have) put
set	(is) setting	set	(have) set
spread	(is) spreading	spread	(have) spread

Group 2 The irregular verbs on the following page have the same form for the past and the past participle.

PRESENT	PRESENT PARTICIPLE	PAST	PAST PARTICIPLE
bring	(is) bringing	brought	(have) brought
buy	(is) buying	bought	(have) bought
catch	(is) catching	caught	(have) caught
feel	(is) feeling	felt	(have) felt
fight	(is) fighting	fought	(have) fought
find	(is) finding	found	(have) found
get	(is) getting	got	(have) got or gotten
hold	(is) holding	held	(have) held
keep	(is) keeping	kept	(have) kept
lead	(is) leading	led	(have) led
leave	(is) leaving	left	(have) left
lose	(is) losing	lost	(have) lost
make	(is) making	made	(have) made
say	(is) saying	said	(have) said
seek	(is) seeking	sought	(have) sought
sell	(is) selling	sold	(have) sold
send	(is) sending	sent	(have) sent
sit	(is) sitting	sat	(have) sat
teach	(is) teaching	taught	(have) taught
think	(is) thinking	thought	(have) thought
tell	(is) telling	told	(have) told
win	(is) winning	won	(have) won

PRACTICE YOUR SKILLS

● Check Your Understanding
Using the Correct Verb Form

Contemporary Life **Write the past or past participle of each verb in parentheses. Then read each sentence aloud to check your answers.**

1. Have you (make) the decorations for the high school dance yet?
2. Hank (put) the scissors in the toolbox.
3. I (hold) the ribbon as your mother tied the bows.
4. A teacher from the art department (lead) the union meeting.
5. Someone at the meeting (win) a door prize.
6. Tad has (hit) his thumb with the hammer again.
7. Another balloon has just (burst).
8. They (leave) the gym shortly after it was completely decorated.
9. Have you (sell) any tickets yet?
10. I have looked everywhere, but I have not (find) the ladder.
11. Teresa (feel) extremely happy after helping us put up the decorations.
12. Who (say) you should not go to the dance?
13. Jesse (lose) his end of the streamers.
14. I have (keep) many pictures of our decorations.
15. Have you (let) the air out of the balloons?
16. Yesterday Mrs. Jones (send) me to the store for more paint.
17. Last weekend Lisa (teach) us how to make tissue paper flowers.
18. Who (bring) an extra pencil?
19. She (get) an invitation to the dance.
20. Raymond (catch) some of the balloons that fell from the ceiling.

Correcting Verb Forms

Read aloud the following announcement, correcting any improper verb forms.

Attention all students on the dance committee! By the end of the week, be sure you have brung your artwork to Mrs. Davis, the art teacher. She will put it up in the gym for you in its proper place. Make sure that you have holded onto your sketches for the centerpiece and finded the proper paint for your project. Mrs. Davis would also like to remind you that there will be a prize for whoever selled the most dance tickets last week.

Group 3 The following irregular verbs form the past participle by adding −*n* to the past.

PRESENT	PRESENT PARTICIPLE	PAST	PAST PARTICIPLE
break	(is) breaking	broke	(have) broken
choose	(is) choosing	chose	(have) chosen
freeze	(is) freezing	froze	(have) frozen
speak	(is) speaking	spoke	(have) spoken
steal	(is) stealing	stole	(have) stolen
weave	(is) weaving	wove	(have) woven

Group 4 The following irregular verbs form the past participle by adding −*n* to the present.

PRESENT	PRESENT PARTICIPLE	PAST	PAST PARTICIPLE
blow	(is) blowing	blew	(have) blown
draw	(is) drawing	drew	(have) drawn
drive	(is) driving	drove	(have) driven
give	(is) giving	gave	(have) given
grow	(is) growing	grew	(have) grown
know	(is) knowing	knew	(have) known
see	(is) seeing	saw	(have) seen
take	(is) taking	took	(have) taken
throw	(is) throwing	threw	(have) thrown

PRACTICE YOUR SKILLS

● Check Your Understanding
Determining the Correct Verb Form

 Contemporary Life **Write the correct verb form for each sentence.**

1. Have you ever (drove, driven) across the country?

2. Last summer we (chose, chosen) to drive across the country for our vacation.

3. We (saw, seen) many unusual sights on our trip.

4. The Rocky Mountains (stole, stolen) my heart.

5. Linda (drew, drawn) some sketches of the mountains.

6. We had (took, taken) enough supplies for the whole summer.

7. In the middle of the trip, our radiator (broke, broken).

8. I should have (knew, known) that we would have car trouble.

9. We nearly (froze, frozen) in the mountains at night.

10. I have not (spoke, spoken) to Linda since the trip.

Using the Correct Verb Form

General Interest **Write the past or the past participle of each verb in parentheses.**

11. The gorilla caught the ball and (throw) it to the zookeeper.

12. The baby elephant must have (grow) five inches since my last visit.

13. The polar bears enjoyed the weather when it (freeze) last winter.

14. I have not (see) the new tiger exhibit.

15. Dr. Rosen, the zoo's veterinarian, (speak) at the opening day ceremonies.

16. My friends and I (steal) a peek at the new baby panda.

17. Have you ever (draw) portraits of the animals at the zoo?

18. Seth (give) a talk about endangered species.

19. No one (know) how to use the new camcorder for our trip to the zoo.

20. I should have (take) the bus to the zoo.

21. Who (break) the computer that was part of the exhibit?

22. Maria (choose) to spend all her time looking at the lions.

23. That is the third time a monkey has (steal) a visitor's hat.

24. Who (drive) you to the zoo?

25. Someone has (throw) popcorn to the bears.

26. We have (freeze) some fish for the seals.

27. The wind has (blow) away the balloons.

28. Cindy (draw) us a map to her house from the zoo.

29. I (grow) tired of waiting for the lions to wake up, so I went to see the bears.

30. I think I have (saw) just about every animal at the zoo.

Editing for Correct Verb Forms

Read aloud the following speech by the head zookeeper, correcting any verbs that are used incorrectly.

> I would like to thank those of you who have gave so generously to our most recent fund drive. The city zoo has growed quite a bit in the past few years, and this money will help us tremendously. I knowed I could count on your generosity, and the animals will benefit from your efforts. I speaking for the entire staff and all the animals when I thank you for your help.

Group 5 The following irregular verbs form the past and past participle by changing a vowel.

PRESENT	PRESENT PARTICIPLE	PAST	PAST PARTICIPLE
begin	(is) beginning	began	(have) begun
drink	(is) drinking	drank	(have) drunk
ring	(is) ringing	rang	(have) rung
shrink	(is) shrinking	shrank	(have) shrunk
sing	(is) singing	sang	(have) sung
sink	(is) sinking	sank	(have) sunk
swim	(is) swimming	swam	(have) swum

Group 6 The following irregular verbs form the past and past participle in other ways.

PRESENT	PRESENT PARTICIPLE	PAST	PAST PARTICIPLE
come	(is) coming	came	(have) come
do	(is) doing	did	(have) done
eat	(is) eating	ate	(have) eaten
fall	(is) falling	fell	(have) fallen
go	(is) going	went	(have) gone
ride	(is) riding	rode	(have) ridden
run	(is) running	ran	(have) run
tear	(is) tearing	tore	(have) torn
wear	(is) wearing	wore	(have) worn
write	(is) writing	wrote	(have) written

PRACTICE YOUR SKILLS

 Check Your Understanding
Using the Correct Verb Form

 Write the past or past participle of each verb in parentheses.

1. I have not (write) my science report yet.
2. Roy (run) around all day yesterday looking for supplies for his project.
3. Kenneth (do) his report on the computer.
4. Your pen must have (fall) out of your notebook.
5. Willis (come) to school an hour late.
6. Have you (begin) to write your report yet?
7. The school bell had already (ring).

8. I have never (ride) in a school bus.

9. We (eat) in the school cafeteria earlier today.

10. Mrs. Arthur (go) to the library yesterday.

11. My eraser (tear) a hole in my paper.

12. The football players (wear) their jerseys to class last week.

13. My football jersey (shrink) in the wash.

14. Luella (swim) for the school team last year.

15. Who (sing) the solo during the choir concert last night?

● Check Your Understanding
Supplying the Correct Verb Form

Contemporary
Life
Complete each pair of sentences by supplying the correct form of the verb in parentheses. This exercise includes verbs from all six groups.

16. (write) I ■ for a college application. Have you ■ for one yet?

17. (burst) The pipes ■ in the restroom last week. Have they ■ again?

18. (give) Have you ■ your history speech yet? I ■ mine yesterday.

19. (throw) Today in class I ■ away my old notebook. Have you ■ yours away yet?

20. (swim) Last week I ■ at the city championship. I have never ■ there before.

21. (come) Have your SAT scores ■ yet? Mine ■ last week.

22. (see) Have you ■ Andrew? I just ■ him at the school library.

23. (make) Have you ■ your speech yet? I ■ mine this morning.

24. (choose) Have you ■ your classes for next year? I ■ them a week ago.

25. (begin) Has school ■? It ■ an hour ago!

Correcting Verb Forms

Read aloud the following announcement from a guidance counselor, correcting any incorrect verb forms.

If you have not chose your classes for next year, please do so by next Thursday. You should brung your report card to the counselor's office. Your SAT scores come to our office, and we will share those with you when you have wrote your schedule request. Make sure you have taked all the necessary classes for this year before you gave us your new choices.

Communicate Your Ideas

APPLY TO WRITING

Writer's Craft: *Analyzing the Use of Verb Forms*

Read the passage below from *The Good Earth*. Then answer the questions that follow.

All down the street in a long line the barbers stood behind their small stalls, and Wang Lung went to the furthest one and sat down upon the stool and motioned to the barber who stood chattering to his neighbor. The barber came at once and began quickly to pour hot water, from a kettle on his pot of charcoal, into his brass basin.

—*Pearl S. Buck,* The Good Earth

- List the underlined verbs in this passage and identify which principal part is used in each case.

- Then rewrite the passage, using the past participle with *had* to replace each underlined verb form. What happened to each verb form?
- Which verb forms are regular and which are irregular?
- When writers write, do you think they are aware of whether they are using regular or irregular verb forms? Explain your answer.

Six Problem Verbs

In addition to learning the principal parts of irregular verbs, you should also check to make sure you have chosen the correct verb. The meanings of some verbs are easily confused.

lie and *lay*

Lie means "to rest or recline." *Lie* is never followed by a direct object. *Lay* means "to put or set (something) down." *Lay* is usually followed by a direct object.

You can review direct objects on pages L86–L87.

PRESENT	PRESENT PARTICIPLE	PAST	PAST PARTICIPLE
lie	(is) lying	lay	(have) lain
lay	(is) laying	laid	(have) laid

LIE   My pencils always **lie** on my desk.
They **are lying** there now.
They **lay** there all last evening.
They **have lain** there for an hour now.

LAY **Lay** your pencil on the table.

(You lay what? *Pencil* is the direct object.)

Sam **is laying** his pencil on the table.
His brother **laid** the pencil on the table
yesterday afternoon.
Usually I **have laid** my pencil on the book
on my desk.

rise and *raise*

Rise means "to move upward" or "to get up." *Rise* is never
followed by a direct object. *Raise* means "to lift (something) up,"
"to increase," or "to grow (something)." *Raise* is usually followed
by a direct object.

PRESENT	PRESENT PARTICIPLE	PAST	PAST PARTICIPLE
rise	(is) rising	rose	(have) risen
raise	(is) raising	raised	(have) raised

RISE Some students **rise** very early to catch the bus
each morning.
Cherri **is rising** early to study for her social
studies test.
She **rose** at 5:30 this morning.
She **has risen** early all this week.

RAISE **Raise** your hand.

(You raise what? *Hand* is the direct object.)

Tom **is raising** his hand.
Lee **raised** her hand first.
Jessica **has raised** her hand for fifteen
minutes now.

sit and *set*

Sit means "to rest in an upright position." *Sit* is never followed by a direct object. *Set* means "to put or place (something)." *Set* is usually followed by a direct object.

PRESENT	PRESENT PARTICIPLE	PAST	PAST PARTICIPLE
sit	(is) sitting	sat	(have) sat
set	(is) setting	set	(have) set

SIT   **Sit** down at your desk and start the test.
She is **sitting** at her desk.
She **sat** there for an hour.
She has never **sat** there before today.

SET   **Set** your books on the floor.
(You set what? *Books* is the direct object.)

He **is setting** his books on the floor.
He **set** his books on the floor yesterday.
He **has set** his books on the floor many times before.

You can learn about other problem verbs in "A Writer's Glossary of Usage" on pages L350–L373.

PRACTICE YOUR SKILLS

● Check Your Understanding
Using Problem Verbs Correctly

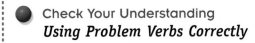

Oral Expression   **Practice using the problem verbs correctly by reading these sentences aloud. Be prepared to explain why the verb is correct.**

1. *Lay* your books on the floor during the test.

2. *Set* your pencil on top of your paper.

3. *Sit* up straight in your chair.

4. Do not *lie* down while you are taking a test.

5. *Raise* your hand if you have any questions.

6. She *rose* early to study for the test.

7. We *sat* in the room waiting for the test to begin.

8. The teacher *had set* the answer key on her desk.

9. It *had lain* there during the entire test.

10. Did you *rise* to the difficult challenge?

● Check Your Understanding
Determining the Correct Verb Form

Contemporary
Life   **Write the correct verb form for each sentence.**

11. Casey has (raised, risen) a steer to enter in this year's rodeo.

12. Julie baked some bread for the bake sale, but the dough did not (raise, rise).

13. Samantha (set, sit) the table as part of the 4-H competition.

14. We (set, sat) in the arena for an hour waiting for the roping competition.

15. The rodeo clown (set, sat) the barrels for the barrel racing event.

16. Why did the clown (lie, lay) in front of the bronco?

17. The cowboy (lies, lays) his hat on the ground.

18. The calf (laid, lay) perfectly still after it was roped.

19. Sidney (rises, raises) to accept the challenge from the champion.

20. We (rose, raised) hogs for last year's competition.

● Connect to the Writing Process: Editing
Correcting Verb Forms

Rewrite each sentence, correcting the verb form. If the verb form is correct, write C.

21. Martha set at the food table at this year's baking competition.

22. Her rolls always rise properly.

23. She lie the blue ribbon beside her pie.

24. Her brother rises chickens for the 4-H club.

25. A lovely ornament is laying on top of the cake.

Communicate Your Ideas

APPLY TO WRITING

E-mail Message: *Problem Verbs*

You have just returned home after the first day of the rodeo competition. Imagine that you have seen an event like the one in the picture. Now your cousin is trying to decide whether to come and see the rodeo with you. Write an E-mail message to your cousin, describing what you have seen during the evening. Be sure to use problem verbs correctly throughout your message.

QuickCheck Mixed Practice

Science Topic **Write the past or past participle of each verb in parentheses.**

1. In 1960, American scientists (raise) a serious concern.

2. Spacecraft (weigh) too much.

3. No solution was (find) until a dried, compressed metal was (invent).

4. It could be (use) for cabinets and panels.

5. The exciting aspect of the discovery was that it could also be (eat)!

6. The early version of this material, however, would have (break) the astronauts' teeth if it had been (eat.)

7. Another version was eventually (make) from powdered milk, cornstarch, flour, banana flakes, and grits.

8. The grits were extremely important because they (hold) the mixture together.

9. The mixture was (call) Edible Structural Material.

10. Once it was (bake), it was hard enough to drill holes in.

11. Before it could be (consume), it first had to be soaked.

12. That (bring) back its edible consistency.

13. The material (taste) like banana-flavored cereal.

14. The scientists, however, were (refuse) a patent because an edible structure had already been (patent).

15. That honor had (go) to the ice cream cone.

The four principal parts of a verb are used to form the tenses of a verb.

The time expressed by a verb is called the tense of a verb.

The six tenses of a verb are present, past, future, present perfect, past perfect, and future perfect. In the following examples, the six tenses of the verb *practice* are used to express action at different times.

PRESENT	I **practice** at least one hour each day.
PAST	I **practiced** last night.
FUTURE	I **will practice** again this weekend.
PRESENT PERFECT	I **have practiced** every day this week.
PAST PERFECT	I **had** not **practiced** much before last year.
FUTURE PERFECT	By the end of the year, I **will have practiced** almost four hundred hours.

 **Uses of Tenses**

The six basic tenses—three simple tenses and three perfect tenses—are used to show whether something is happening now, has happened in the past, or will happen in the future. All these tenses can be formed from the four principal parts of a verb and the helping verbs *have, has, had, will,* and *shall.*

Present tense is the first of the simple tenses and is used mainly to express (1) an action that is going on now, (2) an action that happens regularly, or (3) an action that is usually constant or the same. To form the present tense, use the present form (the first principal part of the verb) or add *–s* or *–es* to the present form.

| PRESENT TENSE | **Listen** to the music. |
| | (current action) |

I **sing** the scales every day after school. (regular action)

The bells in the church **ring** very loudly. (constant action)

The present tense has two other, less common, uses. The **historical present tense** is used to relate a past action as if it were happening in the present.

Paul Revere **warns** the colonists of the British attack.

When writing about literature, you can also use the present tense.

In *Le Morte D'Arthur,* Sir Thomas Malory **tells** a beautiful love story.

Past tense is used to express an action that already took place or was completed in the past. To form the past tense of a regular verb, add *–ed* or *–d* to the present form. To form the past tense of an irregular verb, check a dictionary for the past form or look for it on pages L199–L211.

PAST TENSE	I **listened** to the radio last night.
	Arthur **rang** the church bells on Sunday morning.
	He **went** on vacation yesterday.
	Ann **wrote** us a letter.

Future tense is used to express an action that will take place in the future. To form the future tense, use the helping verb *shall* or *will* with the present form.

| FUTURE TENSE | I **shall listen** to the flute solo. |
| | Arthur **will ring** the church bells next Sunday. |

When you are doing a piece of formal writing, remember that *shall* is used with *I* and *we,* and *will* is used with *you, he, she,* or *it.* In informal speech, *shall* and *will* are generally used interchangeably with *I* and *we.* In questions, however, *shall* should still be used with *I* and *we.*

You can learn more about shall *and* will *on page L365.*

Present perfect tense, the first of the perfect tenses, has two uses: (1) to express an action that was completed at some indefinite time in the past and (2) to express an action that started in the past and is still going on. To form the present perfect tense, add *has* or *have* to the past participle.

PRESENT PERFECT TENSE	I **have listened** for the altos. (action completed at an indefinite time)
	Arthur **has rung** the bells for three years. (action that is still going on)

Past perfect tense expresses an action that took place before some other past action. To form the past perfect tense, add *had* to the past participle.

PAST PERFECT TENSE	I **had listened** for my cue before I heard yours.
	Arthur **had rung** the bells before the bride came into the church.

Future perfect tense expresses an action that will take place before another future action or time. To form the future perfect tense, add *shall have* or *will have* to the past participle.

FUTURE PERFECT TENSE	I **will have listened** to the music for three hours by Friday.
	By Saturday, Arthur **will have rung** the bells for more than twenty weddings.

Verb Conjugation

One of the best ways to study the tenses of a verb is to look at the conjugation of that verb. A **conjugation** is a list of all the singular and plural forms of a verb in its various tenses. Following is a conjugation of the verb *swim,* whose four principal parts are *swim, swimming, swam,* and *swum.*

SIMPLE TENSES OF THE VERB *SWIM*

Present

SINGULAR	PLURAL
I swim	we swim
you swim	you swim
he, she, it swims	they swim

Past

SINGULAR	PLURAL
I swam	we swam
you swam	you swam
he, she, it swam	they swam

Future

SINGULAR	PLURAL
I shall/will swim	we shall/will swim
you will swim	you will swim
he, she, it will swim	they will swim

PERFECT TENSES OF THE VERB *SWIM*

Present Perfect Tense

SINGULAR	PLURAL
I have swum	we have swum
you have swum	you have swum
he, she, it has swum	they have swum

Past Perfect Tense

SINGULAR	PLURAL
I had swum	we had swum
you had swum	you had swum
he, she, it had swum	they had swum

Future Perfect Tense

SINGULAR	PLURAL
I shall/will have swum	we shall/will have swum
you will have swum	you will have swum
he, she, it will have swum	they will have swum

The present participle is used to conjugate only the progressive forms of a verb. You can learn more about those verbs on pages L223–L224.

Because the principal parts of the verb *be* are highly irregular, the conjugation of this verb is very different from the other irregular verbs. The following box shows the conjugation of the verb *be*. The four principal parts of *be* are *am, being, was,* and *been.* On the following page, notice that *been* is always used with helping verbs.

SIMPLE TENSES OF THE VERB *BE*

Present

SINGULAR	PLURAL
I am	we are
you are	you are
he, she, it is	they are

Past

SINGULAR	PLURAL
I was	we were
you were	you were
he, she, it was	they were

Future

SINGULAR	PLURAL
I shall/will be	we shall/will be
you will be	you will be
he, she, it will be	they will be

PERFECT TENSES OF THE VERB *BE*

Present Perfect Tense

SINGULAR	PLURAL
I have been	we have been
you have been	you have been
he, she, it has been	they have been

Past Perfect Tense

SINGULAR	PLURAL
I had been	we had been
you had been	you had been
he, she, it had been	they had been

Future Perfect Tense

SINGULAR	PLURAL
I shall/will have been	we shall/will have been
you will have been	you will have been
he, she, it will have been	they will have been

PRACTICE YOUR SKILLS

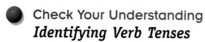

Check Your Understanding
Identifying Verb Tenses

> Music Topic **Write the verb in each sentence. Then label each verb as *present, past, future, present perfect, past perfect,* or *future perfect.***

1. I have practiced the piano for eight hours this week.

2. By this time next week, I will have performed in three recitals.

3. This weekend I will rehearse with the symphony.

4. My favorite composer is Frédéric Chopin.

5. I have worked on Chopin's preludes for almost a year now.

6. Chopin gave his first piano recital at the age of eight.

7. Chopin had been a piano teacher when he met the writer George Sand.

8. The Polish composer's piano sonatas show great structural ingenuity.

9. Chopin influenced Franz Liszt and Richard Wagner.

10. Chopin had suffered from tuberculosis for many years before his death.

● Check Your Understanding
Choosing the Correct Tense

Music Topic **Write the correct verb tense for each sentence.**

11. I (practice, will practice) the new sonatas for the recital next week.

12. Since last summer I (wanted, have wanted) to play some works by Franz Liszt.

13. Liszt (showed, has shown) immense musical gifts at an early age.

14. His innovations in musical form (make, shall make) him one of the most important composers of the nineteenth century.

15. I hope I (play, will play) his compositions well next week.

16. By the end of this semester, I (perform, will have performed) works by three different composers.

17. Learning about these composers (helped, has helped) my performance.

18. Many other nineteenth-century composers apparently (misunderstand, misunderstood) the works of Franz Liszt.

19. His piano writing (incorporates, has incorporated) the styles of Beethoven and Chopin.

20. I always (enjoy, will have enjoyed) his unusual style of music.

● Connect to the Writing Process: Revising
Using the Proper Tense

Revise each of the following sentences, using the verb tense listed in parentheses.

21. Many students at our school participated in the orchestra. (present)

22. Susie played the French horn for three years before she joined the orchestra. (past perfect)

23. Chris practices for hours before most of his recitals. (future)

24. I gave three solos on my piano this year alone. (present perfect)

25. Lucas works very hard during his last year with the orchestra. (past)

26. One of Susie's friends is a member of a French orchestra. (past)

27. Susie travels to France sometimes to visit her friend. (present perfect)

28. Chris enjoys playing solos on his saxophone for the band concerts. (past)

29. Chris and Lucas often perform duets for the school orchestra. (past perfect)

30. By the end of the year, the orchestra will complete more than ten performances. (future perfect)

APPLY TO WRITING

Persuasive Letter: *Verb Tenses*

The school board is considering cutting the budget for the music department from your school as a way to save money. This means that your band will not be able to perform at one of the New Year's bowl parades. Write a letter to the president of the school board, explaining how hard you and the other students have worked. Try to persuade the school board not to cut the budget. Be sure to use at least three different tenses of the verb *work, study,* or *practice.*

 # Progressive and Emphatic Verb Forms

In addition to the six basic tenses, every verb has six progressive forms and an emphatic form for the present and past tenses.

Progressive Forms

The **progressive forms** of verbs are used to express continuing or ongoing action. To write the progressive forms, add a present or perfect tense of the verb *be* to the present participle. Notice in the following examples that all the progressive forms end in *–ing.*

PRESENT PROGRESSIVE	I am swimming.
PAST PROGRESSIVE	I was swimming.
FUTURE PROGRESSIVE	I will (shall) be swimming.
PRESENT PERFECT PROGRESSIVE	I have been swimming.
PAST PERFECT PROGRESSIVE	I had been swimming.
FUTURE PERFECT PROGRESSIVE	I will (shall) have been swimming.

The **present progressive form** shows an ongoing action that is taking place now.

> I **am working** on a big project for art today.

Occasionally the present progressive can also show action in the future when the sentence contains an adverb or a phrase that indicates the future—such as *tomorrow* or *next month*.

> I **am taking** an art history test tomorrow.

The **past progressive form** shows an ongoing action that took place in the past.

> Jill **was working** on the final phase of her painting when I telephoned.

The **future progressive form** shows an ongoing action that will take place in the future.

> Kyle **will be working** on his sculpture during summer vacation.

The **present perfect progressive form** shows an ongoing action that is continuing in the present.

> Stephanie **has been working** on a new painting for three weeks.

The **past perfect progressive form** shows an ongoing action in the past that was interrupted by another past action.

> Valerie **had been working** in the studio when the storm began in earnest.

The **future perfect progressive form** shows a future ongoing action that will have taken place by a stated future time.

> By this time next week, Bill **will have been working** as a museum guide for three months.

Emphatic Forms

The **emphatic forms** of the present and past tenses of verbs are mainly used to show emphasis or force. To write the present emphatic, add *do* or *does* to the present tense of a verb. To write the past emphatic, add *did* to the present tense.

PRESENT	I **swim** every day.
PRESENT EMPHATIC	I **do swim** every day.
PAST	I **swam** yesterday.
PAST EMPHATIC	I **did swim** yesterday.

The emphatic forms are also used in some negative statements and questions.

NEGATIVE STATEMENT	The children **did not swim** during the rain.
QUESTION	**Do** the parents often **swim** with their children?

PRACTICE YOUR SKILLS

● Check your Understanding
Identifying Progressive and Emphatic Forms

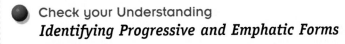 Contemporary Life **Write the verb in each sentence and identify its form.**

1. Everyone in the art room was drawing furiously.

2. Shawn will be entering her painting in the city art contest.

3. She has been painting for two weeks now.

4. David is taking an advanced course in art history.

5. Do you like painting or sculpture better?

6. Before the dance I had been reading a book about Michelangelo.

7. By the end of the summer, I will have been reading about him for three months.

8. George did not like Michelangelo's sculptures.

9. Gina has been working at the art museum for the last five weekends.

10. Sam did paint some wonderful paintings.

● Connect to the Writing Process: Drafting
Writing Sentences

For each verb listed below, write two sentences: one with the verb in progressive form and one with the verb in emphatic form.

11. write

12. act

13. sing

14. direct

15. dance

16. rehearse

17. play

18. go

19. remember

20. enjoy

Communicate Your Ideas

APPLY TO WRITING

Letter of Application: *Progressive and Emphatic Forms*

The counselor at your school has announced that a local museum is going to accept applications from students who would like to spend the summer working in an art gallery. Write a letter to the director of the museum, explaining why you would like to have the job and telling about your past art experience. Be sure to use some progressive and emphatic forms of verbs.

General
Interest **Write the tense of each underlined verb.**

1. Do you <u>know</u> that Michelangelo was a painter and a sculptor?

2. He <u>is</u> the supreme Renaissance artist.

3. He <u>made</u> an imprint on the Western imagination.

4. Everyone at my school <u>is studying</u> his work.

5. I <u>will be studying</u> his painting techniques this summer.

6. Did Laura <u>see</u> his works in Italy last summer?

7. *Bacchus* <u>was</u> Michelangelo's first mature piece of sculpture.

8. Bart <u>told</u> us that he <u>had seen</u> the exhibit three times.

9. I <u>have been sculpting</u> for three weeks now.

10. Michelangelo's techniques <u>have been</u> extremely helpful to me.

11. Tim <u>will have finished</u> his painting by the time we get there.

12. Charlie <u>is taking</u> art lessons from Mr. Joseph.

13. Wendy <u>will be</u> at the museum.

14. Michelangelo's painting style <u>is</u> unique.

15. Before the exhibit I <u>had been finishing</u> the sculpture.

16. Michelangelo's artwork <u>has inspired</u> many people throughout the world.

17. By next December I <u>will have been painting</u> for five years.

18. I <u>did read</u> about Michelangelo's life before class this morning.

19. I <u>have been</u> a student of art for quite some time.

20. There <u>are</u> many reasons that people enjoy art.

Shifts in Tense

Writers use the past tense most often when they write a story. Whatever tense you choose to write in, use it consistently throughout your story or report. A shift in tense can often cause confusion or misunderstanding.

Avoid unnecessary shifts in tense within a sentence or within related sentences.

INCORRECT	┌ past ┐ The outfielder **began** to run and then ┌present┐ suddenly **stops.**
CORRECT	┌ past ┐ The outfielder **began** to run and then ┌ past ┐ suddenly **stopped.**
INCORRECT	┌past perfect┐ After everyone **had seen** the game, three ┌past┐ people **told** their impressions. ┌present┐ The audience **listens** carefully.
CORRECT	┌past perfect┐ After everyone **had seen** the game, ┌past┐ three people **told** their impressions. ┌past┐ The audience **listened** carefully.

Remember, though, that occasionally you will need to mix verb tenses to show a sequence of events. For example, in the second example above, the past perfect verb *had seen* is necessary to show that that action occurred before the people *told* and the audience *listened.*

Often when writers use dialogue, it appears that they are shifting tenses. Shifting tenses in dialogue is necessary to show a sequence of events.

Notice the apparent shifts in tense in this exchange of dialogue. (All the verbs in the passage have been underlined.)

> Siddhartha did not speak; silently he looked into her eyes.
>
> "Have you attained it?" she asked. "Have you found peace?"
>
> He smiled and placed his hand on hers.
>
> "Yes," she said, "I see it. I also will find peace."
>
> "You have found it," whispered Siddhartha.
>
> —Herman Hesse, Siddhartha

PRACTICE YOUR SKILLS

● Check Your Understanding
Identifying Shifts in Tense

Sports Topic **Write the verbs in the following paragraph and identify the tense of each verb.**

William Hoy was an outfielder on six teams between 1888 and 1902. He compiles a .288 lifetime batting average and an impressive record as an outfielder and a base stealer. There is, however, something extra special about Hoy. He is completely deaf as the result of a childhood illness. "I found it no handicap," Hoy says of his deafness. Initially there was one problem. Hoy could not hear the umpire call balls and strikes when he is at bat. Then Hoy has an idea. He asks an umpire to signal a strike with his right arm. Soon all umpires follow suit. This practice has continued ever since.

● Connect to the Writing Process: Revising
Correcting Shifts in Tense

Look over the verb tenses you identified in the above paragraph. Rewrite the paragraph, correcting shifts in tense.

Communicate Your Ideas

APPLY TO WRITING
Summary: *Verb Tenses*

Your best friend is required to work on the night of the championship game. Write your friend an E-mail message that summarizes the game. Before you begin writing, ask yourself the following questions and jot down the answers.

- Which sport will I write about?
- Which team played us in the game?
- How did the game begin?
- What was the most exciting part of the game?
- Which team won?
- Who starred for the opposing team?
- Who starred for our team?

Then write your E-mail message. Be sure to include all the highlights of the game and use verb tenses properly.

Active and Passive Voice

The **active voice** indicates that the subject is performing the action.

The **passive voice** indicates that the action of the verb is being performed on the subject.

In addition to tense, a verb has voice. In the following example, the same verb is used both in the active voice and the passive voice. The verb in the active voice has a direct object. The verb in the passive voice has no direct object.

ACTIVE VOICE   Cal **cleans** the animal cages. ⌐d.o.¬

PASSIVE VOICE   The animal cages **are cleaned** by Cal. ⌐s.¬

Only transitive verbs can be used in the passive voice. When an active verb is changed to passive, the direct object of the active verb becomes the subject of the passive verb. The subject of the active verb is then included in a prepositional phrase.

ACTIVE VOICE   The Siberian tiger **delighted** many visitors. ⌐d.o.¬

PASSIVE VOICE   Many visitors **were delighted** by the Siberian tiger. ⌐s.¬

You can learn more about direct objects on pages L86–L87.

▶ Use of Voice

When you write, use the active voice as much as possible. The active voice adds directness and impact to your writing. Use the passive voice, however, when the doer of the action is unknown or unimportant or when you want to emphasize the receiver of the action.

> Our zoo **has** just **been reopened.**
>
> (doers unknown)
>
> The lion **was given** the meat.
>
> (emphasis on the receiver)

PRACTICE YOUR SKILLS

● Check Your Understanding
Recognizing Active and Passive Voice

General Interest **Write the verb in each sentence and label it *A* for active or *P* for passive.**

1. Many people keep pets.
2. Some people own exotic animals, such as tigers and lions.
3. Crickets are kept as pets in China.
4. City people should not buy large wild animals, such as wolves.
5. Nearly all exotic pets are sold by zoos.
6. Many zoos have "surplus" animals.
7. Some exotic pets are purchased by circuses.
8. A single zoo may earn thousands of dollars from the sale of surplus animals.
9. Exotic animals are enjoyed by many people.
10. In the future some zoos will be monitored by the U.S. Fish and Wildlife Service.

● Connect to the Writing Process: Revising
Using Active Voice

Rewrite each sentence, changing the passive voice to the active voice if appropriate. If a sentence is better in the passive voice, write *C* for correct.

11. All sides of the issue were discussed by the class.

12. Concern for endangered animals is shown by many.

13. Our trip to the zoo was ruined by a gorilla.

14. Water was splashed on us by the gorilla.

15. No warning was posted beside the gorilla's cage.

APPLY TO WRITING

Journal Entry: *Active and Passive Voice*

You have just taken your little sister to the zoo, and you decide to write a journal entry that you will give to her when she is older. Describe how the animals behaved and how she reacted. Be sure to use active and passive voice properly.

 QuickCheck Mixed Practice

Music Topic **Rewrite the following paragraph, correcting all verb errors.**

The world's best violins were made by Antonius Stradivarius. After he play the violin, he become interested in making these instruments. He perform many experiments. He want his violins to sound as lovely as the human voice. Success was achieved by him early in his career. Since his death in 1737, no one had been able to duplicate the sound of his violins. His secret was never shared by him, not even with his sons.

Choosing Verb Forms

Write the correct form of the verb in parentheses.

1. By the time the clouds disappeared, the sun (set, had set).
2. Two months ago I (ordered, have ordered) a bicycle.
3. Pam (beats, beat) me at tennis whenever we play.
4. I (look, will look) for you on the news tonight.
5. Our team (played, has played) very well so far this season.
6. Yesterday Greg (run, ran) the one-hundred-yard dash.
7. By last week Ann (earned, had earned) money for a bike.
8. Before the storm broke, we (closed, had closed) the windows.
9. Lee (ask, asked) for directions to the new stadium.
10. Sharon (began, has begun) playing the drums in May.

Using the Correct Verb Form

Write the past or past participle of each verb in parentheses.

1. The coaches (choose) Otis as most valuable player.
2. You should have (give) him a second chance.
3. Tina (see) the artist sketch an ocean scene.
4. The singer (shrink) back from his admirers.
5. The central water main (burst) yesterday.
6. Where have you (lay) the hammer?
7. My father has (wear) the same tie for years.
8. We (find) some old records in Emily's attic.
9. How long have you (know) about this?
10. The school has (buy) six more computers.

Recognizing Active and Passive Verbs

Write the verb in each sentence. Then label it *active* or *passive*.

1. The first car wash of the year was sponsored by the sophomore class.
2. Surprisingly, the Southern Hemisphere has only one species of bear.
3. Our ripe corn was harvested by a hungry raccoon.
4. All of the flowers in our garden were planted by my dad and mom.
5. Jules Verne wrote *From the Earth to the Moon.*
6. I am taking driver's education this semester.
7. Do you want an apple or a peach?
8. The science awards were announced over the intercom during second period.
9. The SAT tests are taken by many juniors.
10. I need a new pair of warm, fur-lined boots for winter sports.
11. Most of the tourists took the tour to the castle.
12. The audience applause was measured by a sound monitor.
13. The telephone has been ringing all day.
14. Jimmy raised the window without any problem.
15. By mistake your letter was opened by Aunt Louise.

Writing Sentences

Write several paragraphs in which you explain any past working experience. Use at least three different tenses of the verb *work*, including some progressive forms.

Language and *Self-Expression*

Artists use colors to influence the way a viewer feels. For example, warm colors—such as red, yellow, or orange—might be used to create a sunny mood, whereas cool colors—such as green, blue, or violet—might be used to impart fear or loneliness. *The Green House* is a photograph of an installation artwork that includes plastic dogs and surfaces covered in raffia. What mood do you think Sandy Skoglund creates with her use of color, light, and shadow?

Writers also create feelings of warmth or coldness using images, colors, and key words. Certain words or images, for example, might reflect warm, cozy times while others might convey cold, gloomy times. Write a short essay describing scenes of warmth or coldness you have experienced. Be sure to use verbs correctly.

Prewriting Brainstorm images or places that gave you feelings of special warmth or dismal coldness. List them briefly.

Drafting Choose one example of warmth and one of coldness. Then write a thesis statement for your essay. Write a paragraph describing a warm, happy scene in your life. Concentrate on the feeling of warmth or coziness. Do the same in a paragraph describing a cold, dismal scene. Focus on the coldness or gloominess of your experience. End your essay by reflecting on the two experiences.

Revising Reread your draft. Do the sentences flow naturally from one to the next?

Editing Review your work, concentrating on grammar and usage. Be sure your verb tenses are correct.

Publishing Make a clean copy of your essay. Publish your work by joining a classmate and taking turns reading to each other.

Another Look

The **principal parts** of a verb are the *present,* the *present participle,* and the *past participle.*

Regular and Irregular Verbs

A **regular verb** forms its past and past participle by adding *–ed* or *–d* to the present. An **irregular verb** does not form its past and past participle by adding *–ed* or *–d* to the present. *(pages L197–L199)*

Six Problem Verbs

lie and *lay*

Lie means "to rest or recline." *Lay* means "to put or set (something) down." *(pages L209–L210)*

rise and *raise*

Rise means "to move upward" or "to get up." *Raise* means "to lift (something) up." *(page L210)*

sit and *set*

Sit means "to rest in an upright position." *Set* means "to put or place (something)." *(page L211)*

The time expressed by a verb is called the **tense** of a verb. The six tenses of a verb are *present, past, future, present perfect, past perfect,* and *future perfect.* Avoid unnecessary shifts in tense within a sentence or within related sentences.

Progressive and Emphatic Verb Forms

The six **progressive** forms of verbs are *present progressive, past progressive, future progressive, present perfect progressive, past perfect progressive,* and *future perfect progressive. (pages L223–L224)*

The **emphatic** verb form is used to show emphasis or force. Add *do* or *does* to the present tense of a verb, or add *did* to the past tense of a verb. *(page L225)*

Active and Passive Voice

The **active voice** indicates that the subject is performing the action.

The **passive voice** indicates that the action of the verb is being performed on the subject. *(page L231)*

 **Posttest**

Directions

Read the passage and choose the word or group of words that belongs in each underlined space. Write the letter of the correct answer.

EXAMPLE   **1.** We __(1)__ on our summer vacation soon.

             1 **A**   will have gone
                 B   did go
                 C   go
                 D   will go

ANSWER   **1** **D**

My family __(1)__ Sebago Lake in Casco, Maine, every year. We __(2)__ each summer for eight years now. After this summer we __(3)__ for nine years straight. All of us __(4)__ life at the lake. We all __(5)__ to swim and canoe there. This year we __(6)__ our new kayak. My sister always __(7)__ fish for the whole family. Last year she __(8)__ in a three-foot-long eel and was completely horrified. She __(9)__ never _____ one before. Since then, she __(10)__ very careful about what she catches.

1	**A**	will visit	**6**	**A**	will try
	B	visits		**B**	try
	C	will have visited		**C**	tried
	D	had visited		**D**	had tried

1
- **A** will visit
- **B** visits
- **C** will have visited
- **D** had visited

2
- **A** went
- **B** have been going
- **C** will have gone
- **D** go

3
- **A** will have gone
- **B** went
- **C** go
- **D** have gone

4
- **A** will like
- **B** like
- **C** liked
- **D** will have liked

5
- **A** had learned
- **B** will have learned
- **C** learned
- **D** are learning

6
- **A** will try
- **B** try
- **C** tried
- **D** had tried

7
- **A** had caught
- **B** will have caught
- **C** will have been catching
- **D** catches

8
- **A** had reeled
- **B** reeled
- **C** reels
- **D** will reel

9
- **A** had...seen
- **B** have...seen
- **C** will...see
- **D** will...have seen

10
- **A** will be
- **B** is
- **C** was
- **D** has been

CHAPTER 6

Using Pronouns

 **Pretest**

Directions
Read the passage and choose the pronoun that belongs in each underlined space. Write the letter of the correct answer.

EXAMPLE **1.** The best actor at our school is __(1)__ .

1 A him
B he
C he or him
D his

ANSWER **1 B**

My friend Jonas and __(1)__ tried out for a part in a real Broadway play. Jonas practiced __(2)__ part for days before the tryouts. I didn't work that hard on __(3)__ part. The other people at the tryouts all looked like professional actors. Some of __(4)__ even brought __(5)__ agents! I saw a famous actor there, too. At first I wasn't sure it was __(6)__ . After the tryouts, we learned the choice was to be between Jonas and __(7)__ . __(8)__ would they pick? Finally, they chose the famous actor, even though I thought Jonas was better than __(9)__ . Jonas was disappointed and the actor was thrilled, but neither of them showed __(10)__ true feelings.

1	A	me		6	A	them
	B	I			B	his
	C	him			C	he
	D	us			D	him
2	A	him		7	A	he
	B	their			B	him
	C	his			C	his
	D	mine			D	them
3	A	mine		8	A	Whom
	B	my			B	Who
	C	they			C	He
	D	myself			D	They
4	A	them		9	A	them
	B	they			B	he
	C	their			C	him
	D	him			D	his
5	A	they		10	A	him
	B	them			B	their
	C	their			C	its
	D	him			D	his

Philip Evergood. *Her World*, 1948.
Oil on canvas, 48 by 35 ⅝ inches. The Metropolitan Museum of Art, Arthur Hoppock
Hearn Fund, 1950 (50.29). Photograph © 1986 The Metropolitan Museum of Art.

Describe   How would you describe the girl's world—as
the artist shows it?

Analyze   What might the girl in the painting be
thinking?

Interpret   How do you think the girl feels about her
world? What details suggest this to you? How
might a writer show a character's feelings?

Judge   How does this painting make you feel? Why?
Does a painting or a written work usually
evoke a stronger feeling in you? Explain.

At the end of this chapter, you will use the artwork to stimulate
ideas for writing.

The Cases of Personal Pronouns

At one time nouns in the English language had special endings to show how they were used within a sentence. Several hundred years ago, however, English nouns began to drop those endings. Now the word *boy,* for example, is the same whether it is a subject or an object. The only time the form changes is when a noun is used to show possession. Then *boy* becomes *boy's.*

Pronouns did not follow suit. Therefore, you must use *he* for a subject, *him* for an object, or *his* to show possession. These changes occur because all nouns and pronouns have case.

Case is the form of a noun or pronoun that indicates its use in a sentence.

Nouns and pronouns in English have three cases: the nominative case, the objective case, and the possessive case. Pronouns usually change form for each of the cases.

NOMINATIVE CASE
(Used for subjects and predicate nominatives)
SINGULAR   I, you, he, she, it
PLURAL   we, you, they
OBJECTIVE CASE
(Used for direct objects, indirect objects, and objects of prepositions)
SINGULAR   me, you, him, her, it
PLURAL   us, you, them
POSSESSIVE CASE
(Used to show ownership or possession)
SINGULAR   my, mine, your, yours, his, her, hers, its
PLURAL   our, ours, your, yours, their, theirs

You *and* it *are the same in both the nominative and objective cases.*

PRACTICE YOUR SKILLS

● Check Your Understanding
Determining Case

Contemporary Life

Write the personal pronouns in each sentence. Then identify the case of each pronoun, using *N* for nominative, *O* for objective, and *P* for possessive.

1. My sister and I will take the skates with us.
2. Did your brother see him at the skating rink on Friday?
3. They haven't repaired their skates yet.
4. He told me that her skates had been broken for some time.
5. Did she tell them that the in-line skates are his?
6. Take ours or theirs.
7. We want to go skating at this new rink.
8. I gave the knee pads to her yesterday.
9. Our team won the skating competition.
10. We spoke to him briefly after his winning performance.

▶ The Nominative Case

The **nominative case** is used for subjects and predicate nominatives.

The nominative case pronouns are *I, you, he, she, it, we,* and *they.*

Pronouns Used As Subjects

A **pronoun** can be the subject of either an independent clause or a subordinate clause.

INDEPENDENT CLAUSE
He is going with us.
We arrived at seven, but **they** came later.

SUBORDINATE CLAUSE	Jane said that **she** called about the trip.
	(*That she called about the trip* is the subordinate clause.)
	After **we** eat, let's go to the theater.
	(*After we eat* is the subordinate clause.)

Because selecting the correct pronoun in a compound subject can present a problem, you should follow two steps. First, check to make sure that you have selected a nominative case pronoun. Second, test your selection by saying each pronoun separately.

Matt and (he, him) are planning a trip.
He is planning a trip.
Him is planning a trip.

The nominative case *he* is the correct form to use.

Matt and **he** are planning a trip.

This test also works if both subjects are pronouns.

She and **I** are saving our money for this trip.
He and **they** are hoping to come too.

You can learn more about subordinate clauses on pages L155–L172.

PRACTICE YOUR SKILLS

● Check Your Understanding
Using Pronouns as Subjects

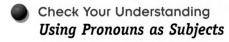 Contemporary Life **Write the correct form of the pronoun in parentheses.**

1. Allison and (me, I) are going to visit the Alamo over spring break.

2. (We, Us) hope to spend the whole week in San Antonio.

3. Brent and (him, he) hope to see the Riverwalk.

4. (Them, They) want to rent a boat.

5. My friend and (I, me) have been planning this trip for a long time.

6. Brenda and (she, her) are going to the San Antonio Zoo on Thursday.

7. (Me, I) want to see some of the other missions that are in the area.

8. (He, Him) will send lots of postcards to our history teacher.

9. (Her, She) will be pleased that we visited the Alamo.

10. Christopher and (he, him) will do all the driving.

11. (Us, We) washed cars and held bake sales to raise money for this trip.

12. Sabrina and (I, me) are going to do some research for a history report while (we, us) are there.

13. (Her, She) is writing a paper about the architecture of San Antonio.

14. (I, Me) will write about the Alamo.

15. (They, Them) hope it won't rain when (we, us) go to the amusement park.

Pronouns Used as Predicate Nominatives

A **predicate nominative** follows a linking verb and identifies or renames the subject.

That was **she** at the finish line.

The winner was **he**.

Each pronoun in a compound predicate nominative should be carefully checked to make sure it is in the nominative case.

The marathon winners were Tracy and **they.**
The runners not finishing were Paulo and **she.**

You can often avoid awkward-sounding expressions when writing if you reword a sentence, making the predicate nominative the subject.

| AWKWARD | The triathlon winner last year was **she.** |
| NATURAL | **She** was the triathlon winner last year. |

You can see page L26 for lists of common linking verbs. See pages L90–L91 for more information about predicate nominatives.

CONNECT TO SPEAKING AND WRITING

Nominative-case pronouns are not always used for predicate nominatives in casual conversation. You often hear people say, "It's me" instead of "It is I," or "That's him" instead of "That is he." Although this usage is common in conversation, it is not correct and should be avoided in written work.

PRACTICE YOUR SKILLS

● Check Your Understanding
Using Pronouns as Subjects and Predicate Nominatives

> Oral Expression **Read each sentence aloud, saying each pronoun separately. Then choose the correct pronoun and repeat the entire sentence.**

1. She and (I, me) entered the marathon.

2. (Him, He) and (I, me) hope to train every day.

3. (We, Us) and (they, them) are planning to enter the race as a group.

4. That was (he, him) and Sally running along the river last night.

5. It was Bob and (I, me) who decided to enter the triathlon instead of taking physical education.

6. (She, her) and Jim are running this afternoon.

7. The runners with the fastest practice time were (he, him) and Sue.

8. Stewart and (I, me) have noticed that (we, us) are in| better shape now.

9. The strongest competitors will be Cathy and (they, them).

10. The winners were (he, him) and Jonas.

● Check Your Understanding
Using Pronouns as Predicate Nominatives

Contemporary Life **Write the correct form of the pronoun in parentheses.**

11. The ushers at the talent show will be Nat Gardener and (I, me).

12. The best singer at rehearsal was (she, her).

13. The dancers in the duet were Marie and (he, him).

14. Standing outside the dressing room were Marsha and (she, her).

15. The people who practiced the most were (he, him) and (I, me).

16. The favorites for the show were the Bensons and (they, them).

17. The students who won were (he, him) and (she, her).

18. The performers in today's rehearsal are (they, them).

19. The most talented mimes are Lea and (he, him).

20. The boys seated in front were John and (they, them).

● Check Your Understanding
Supplying Pronouns in the Nominative Case

Contemporary Life **Complete each sentence by writing an appropriate pronoun in the nominative case. (Do not use *you* or *it.*) Then indicate how each pronoun is used by writing *S* for subject or *P* for predicate nominative.**

21. ■ are organizing the class elections this year.

22. Will you and ■ be running for treasurer again?

23. The new secretary is ■.

24. Mr. Handley promised that ■ would speak with you after school.

25. ■ will meet before school tomorrow.

26. I just found out that the announcers for the election will be ■.

27. The last student to vote is usually ■.

28. If ■ doesn't want to run for historian, ■ should try to convince him.

29. Without question, the best candidates this year are Reyna and ■.

30. The only candidate who I think is qualified for the job is ■.

● Connect to the Writing Process: Editing
Using Pronouns Correctly

Rewrite the sentences, correcting errors in pronoun case. If a sentence is correct, write C.

31. The O'Rileys and them made campaign posters over the weekend.

32. I think that our class president will be her.

33. We'll hang the posters in the hall after Rosie and she finish them.

34. Do you really think them are the right people to vote for?

35. Neither Conrad nor him made a speech today.

● Connect to the Writing Process: Drafting
Writing Sentences with Pronouns

Write two sentences for each of the following groups of words. In the first sentence, use the words as subjects. In the second sentence, use them as predicate nominatives.

36. you and I

37. he and she

38. we and they

APPLY TO WRITING

Campaign Speech: *Nominative Case Pronouns*

Your best friend is running for a class office. He or she has asked you to make a campaign speech that you will deliver to the entire student body at a pre-election pep rally. Write a speech that explains why you feel your friend would make a good officer. Be sure to use pronouns as subjects and predicate nominatives properly.

 The Objective Case

The **objective case** is used for direct objects, indirect objects, and objects of a preposition.

The objective case pronouns are *me, you, him, her, it, us,* and *them.*

Pronouns Used as Direct and Indirect Objects

If a pronoun answers the question *Whom?* after an action verb, it will be a direct object. A sentence that has a direct object can also have an indirect object. A pronoun used as an indirect object will come before the direct object and will answer the question *To whom?* or *For whom?* A pronoun used as a direct object or as an indirect object is in the objective case.

DIRECT OBJECTS	Carlos wants **them** to visit Mexico.
	Show **her** to the travel agent.
	You will drive **us** to the shop.
	Then drive **us** to the airport.

INDIRECT OBJECTS	Claire told **us** the details.
	(*Details* is the direct object.)
	Please write **me** an outline.
	(*Outline* is the direct object.)

You can learn more about direct and indirect objects on pages L86–L89.

Always check to see if the pronouns in a compound direct object are in the objective case. You can use the test you used to check compound subjects. Say each pronoun separately.

Did you interview Bill and (he, him) last night?
Did you interview **he** last night?
Did you interview **him** last night?

The objective case *him* is the correct form to use.

Did you interview Bill and **him** last night?

You can also use the same test to check the pronouns used in a compound indirect object.

Show Jessica and (I, me) the new research.
Show **I** the new research.
Show **me** the new research.

The objective case *me* is the correct form to use.

Show Jessica and **me** the new research.

PRACTICE YOUR SKILLS

● Check Your Understanding
Using Pronouns as Direct and Indirect Objects

Contemporary Life **Write the correct form of the pronoun in parentheses.**

1. Call (she, her) before you finish your science report tonight.

2. Show (him, he) your research on butterflies.

3. Andy wants (I, me) to explain the migration route to him.

4. Sheila told (we, us) and (they, them) about the monarch butterflies.

5. Did you see (them, they) when they flew through town last year?

6. My dad drove (us, we) to see the butterflies in Mexico last winter.

7. We thanked (he, him) for helping us with our project.

8. Susan helped the local scientists count (they, them) last spring.

9. The scientists offered (her, she) special information on butterflies.

10. Mrs. Johansen gave (she, her) the best grade for her research.

Pronouns Used as Objects of Prepositions

A prepositional phrase begins with a preposition and ends with a noun or pronoun called the **object of a preposition.** A pronoun used as the object of a preposition is in the objective case.

I hope Al takes Spanish class with **us.**

(With us is the prepositional phrase.)

The counselor spoke to **them.**

(To them is the prepositional phrase.)

A pronoun used as part of a compound object of a preposition can also be checked by saying each pronoun separately.

Mrs. Rivas always calls on Inez and (I, me).

Mrs. Rivas always calls on **I.**

Mrs. Rivas always calls on **me.**

The objective case *me* is the correct form to use.

> Mrs. Rivas always calls on Inez and **me.**

You can find a list of common prepositions on page L43. You can learn more about objects of prepositions on pages L44 and L111.

CONNECT TO SPEAKING AND WRITING

 In an effort to sound formal or correct, people will often use the nominative case pronouns after the preposition *between.* However, all pronouns used as objects of a preposition should be in the objective case.

INCORRECT	The contest was *between* **he** *and* **I.**
CORRECT	The contest was *between* **him** *and* **me.**

PRACTICE YOUR SKILLS

● Check Your Understanding
Using Objective Case Pronouns

> Oral Expression **Read each sentence aloud, saying each pronoun separately. Then choose the correct pronoun and repeat the entire sentence.**

1. The counselors gave Cara and (I, me) our new schedules for Spanish.

2. The secretary showed David and (he, him) to Spanish class.

3. I gave my report to (them, they) after I had finished writing it.

4. There was a debate between (us, we) and (they, them) in Spanish.

5. The teacher sent (him, he) to the office for the message.

6. I wanted (her, she) and (he, him) to take Spanish with me.

7. Mrs. Rivas assigned (me, I) and (she, her) a difficult dialogue project.

8. We must present it to (her, she) and (he, him) by the end of next week.

9. I will do most of the research for (she, her) because she is very sick.

10. Hector gave (her, she) some valuable information for our project.

● Check Your Understanding
Using Pronouns as Objects of Prepositions

Contemporary Life **Write the correct form of the pronoun in parentheses.**

11. My uncle and I are going to the state fair with my cousin and (she, her).

12. We are planning to give some of our tickets to Todd and (she, her).

13. Who is sitting between Pilar and (she, her) on the Ferris wheel?

14. Dad spoke with my sister and (I, me) about dangerous rides.

15. The beautiful carousel belongs to the Levinsons and (they, them).

16. The ticket money should be sent to (they, them) or (we, us).

17. Juana stood beside Justin and (he, him) at the new roller coaster.

18. Will you take a picture of (he, him) and (I, me) at the fair?

19. Did you give specific directions for getting to the fair to Lola and (she, her)?

20. Do you and your brother want to go to the fair with Claudia and (we, us)?

21. I will go on that ride with (her, she).

22. Get in line behind (them, they).

Supplying Pronouns in the Objective Case

Contemporary Life **Complete each sentence by writing an appropriate pronoun in the objective case. (Do not use *you* or *it*). Then indicate how each pronoun is used by writing *D* for direct object, *I* for indirect object, or *O* for object of the preposition.**

23. Will you call Matthew and ▨ when the race course is ready?

24. Please teach Angela and ▨ the official rules of sailboat racing.

25. Before the race, the coach praised ▨.

26. Those award ribbons and trophies belong to Charlotte and ▨.

27. Steve drove Brewster and ▨ to the lake for the afternoon race.

28. Landlubbers like ▨ shouldn't go in the water.

29. Give ▨ your ideas about the article that should be written about the race.

30. Mr. Lee called Chad and ▨ to the starting line.

31. Mr. Tobias has coached Kena and ▨ for the race.

32. This competition can be discussed among ▨.

Connect to the Writing Process: Editing
Using Objective Case Pronouns Correctly

Rewrite the sentences, correcting any pronoun errors.

33. Just between you and I, his race strategy will never work.

34. Please notify we crew members of the next race.

35. Mr. Dobson showed Rosa and I a beautiful sailboat sitting at the dock.

36. There were no other available crew members except Carlos and she.

37. Joyce found Warren and he at the dock.

Writing Sentences with Pronouns

Write five sentences, following the directions below.

38. Use *Kate and me* as a compound direct object.

39. Use *Roger and him* as a compound indirect object.

40. Use *Greg and her* as a compound object of a preposition.

41. Use *her and him* as a direct object.

42. Use *them and us* as a compound object of a preposition.

Communicate Your Ideas

APPLY TO WRITING

Friendly Letter: *Nominative and Objective Case Pronouns*

You have been accepted to a summer camp and have the opportunity to "meet" your roommate through the mail. Write a letter to your future roommate, describing yourself and your family members. Use pronouns in the nominative and objective cases properly.

QuickCheck   Mixed Practice

General Interest **Write each pronoun that is in the wrong case. Then write each pronoun correctly. If a sentence is correct, write C.**

1. Them and we are learning about the ancient city of Petra in geography class.

2. The people of Petra know that some interesting choices await they.

3. The city will be shared by the archaeologists and them.

4. The archaeologists are Don and her.

5. The city's history fascinated we.

6. Ask them or us anything you want to know about Petra.

7. Hamoudi and them gave up their nomadic lifestyle to help the archaeologists.

8. In recent years the government has squeezed tourists, archaeologists, and they into the ancient city.

9. The archaeologist asked him for permission to drink from the cistern.

10. The ancient people enjoyed spices and silks from the Chinese and they.

11. That's him entering the ancient tomb.

12. Ruth and me are doing a special photo essay about Petra.

13. The photographers and us shot pictures of the ancient city.

14. The archaeologists and her found a new artifact.

15. Every day they find something new.

Possessive Case

The **possessive case** is used to show ownership or possession.

The possessive case pronouns are *my, mine, your, yours, his, her, hers, its, our, ours, their,* and *theirs.* Some possessive case pronouns can be used to show possession before a noun or before a gerund. Others can be used by themselves.

BEFORE A NOUN	I enjoyed **her** project very much.
BEFORE A GERUND	**His** practicing the speech has helped.
BY THEMSELVES	Is this notebook **yours** or **mine?**

Notice on the following page that, unlike the possessive noun, the possessive pronoun does not have an apostrophe.

| Possessive Pronoun | **Her** project is late. |
| Possessive Noun | **Martha's** project is late. |

 CONNECT TO SPEAKING AND WRITING

Be very careful about confusing certain possessive pronouns with contractions. *Its, your, their* and *theirs* are possessive pronouns. *It's, you're, they're,* and *there's* are contractions. A good way to avoid using the wrong word is to substitute the full word for the contraction and say it aloud. If the sentence makes sense, use the contraction. If the sentence does not make sense, use the possessive pronoun.

(Your, You're) going on a trip tomorrow.
You are going on a trip tomorrow.

(The contraction *you're* is the correct form to use.)

When is (your, you're) trip?
When is **you are** trip?

(The possessive pronoun *your* is the correct form to use.)

PRACTICE YOUR SKILLS

● Check Your Understanding
Using Pronouns in the Possessive Case

Science Topic **Write the correct word in parentheses.**

1. The paleontologists say (their, they're) locating a mastodon is a great find.

2. The museum says the credit is (hers, her's).

3. Is this new find going to affect (your, you're) researching the topic?

4. San Bernardino County Museum personnel say (their, they're) very excited about this most recent discovery.

5. They say (its, it's) size is incredible.

6. The paleontologists welcomed (their, they're) contribution to the project.

7. I think (his, his's) information about the weather in ancient California is important.

8. The discovery was (ours, our's).

9. "The Valley of the Mastodons" is located near (your, you're) house.

10. My mom thinks (me, my) visiting the old tar pits to look for fossils is dangerous.

11. She fears the possibility of (us, our) getting stuck in the tar.

12. The next fossil found might be (my, mine).

13. There is little likelihood of (me, my) returning to the Valley.

14. I think (her, hers) worries are needless.

15. The final word, however, is (her, hers).

● Connect to the Writing Process: Editing
Using Possessive Pronouns Correctly

Rewrite the sentences, correcting any incorrect pronouns. If the sentence is correct, write C.

16. Did you enjoy they're presentation on the mammoths?

17. I found your research very thorough.

18. Its difficult to believe that giant elephants once lived in California.

19. They're careful analysis of the fossils helped the scientists.

20. That tool is our's.

21. Mammoths and mastodons have always been my favorite prehistoric mammals.

22. Theres is the saber-toothed tiger.

23. It's teeth were quite impressive.

24. Her favorite prehistoric mammal is the eohippus.

25. Its an ancestor of the horse.

APPLY TO WRITING
Proposal: *Possessive Pronouns*

You have just returned from a field trip to see a prehistoric dig site. You decide that you would like to have the paleontologist visit your school to talk about his work. You wish him to display some of the artifacts he has found, bringing both small, touchable objects and slides of some of his larger finds. Write a proposal to the PTA and your principal so that they will make the proper arrangements for this educational visitor. Be sure to use possessive pronouns correctly.

Contemporary Life

Write each pronoun that is in the wrong case. Then write each pronoun correctly. If a sentence is correct, write C.

1. Us and he froze like statues when the snake crossed our path.

2. There are some dry clothes in the tent for both Carrie and her.

3. The extra supplies will be split between them and we.

4. People like Arlene and he should be forest rangers.

5. We were proud of them climbing the mountain.

6. The leaders of the hike are Hans and him.

7. How do you stop them running through your tent?

8. The fireside meal pleased we and them.

9. Ask them or us anything you want to know about the terrain.

10. Ernie and him gave up their tent so they could sleep under the stars.

11. My parents squeezed my brother, my sister, the dog, and I into the car, and we headed to the campground.

12. He gave Lupe and I an extra stake for our tent.

13. Everybody ate toasted marshmallows except Otis and me.

14. Finally they found their seats around the campfire beside Maureen and he.

15. That's him at the cabin door.

16. He was pleased with me rappelling down the mountain.

17. Ruth and me are going canoeing tomorrow.

18. They and us climbed to the rim of the canyon.

19. Fortunately, Philip and her didn't lose their glasses on the trip.

20. It's them at the campsite on the east side.

People answering the phone in an office may say, "Whom shall I say is calling?" They really should say, "Who shall I say is calling?" Choosing between *who* and *whom* can be a problem. Another pronoun problem arises with an incomplete comparison that begins with the word *than*. Should you say "Carl is more alert than I" or "Carl is more alert than me"? Appositives present still another problem. Do you say "An explanation was given to we sophomores" or "An explanation was given to us sophomores"? All these problems will be explained in the following section.

 ## *Who* or *Whom*?

Who is a pronoun that changes its form depending on how it is used in a sentence. The singular and plural forms of *who* and its related pronouns, however, are the same.

NOMINATIVE CASE	who, whoever
OBJECTIVE CASE	whom, whomever
POSSESSIVE CASE	whose

The correct use of *who* is determined by how the pronoun is used in a question or a clause.

In questions *who* or one of its related pronouns is often used. The form of *who* you choose will depend on how the pronoun is used in the question. It is often easier to find the correct form if you put the sentence into its natural order.

NOMINATIVE CASE **Who** will take me to the dance?

(subject of a sentence)

OBJECTIVE CASE	**Whom** will you invite?
	(direct object)
	To whom were you speaking?
	(object of the preposition *to*)
POSSESSIVE CASE	**Whose** ticket is this?
	(shows possession)

PRACTICE YOUR SKILLS

● Check Your Understanding
Using Forms of **Who** *in Questions*

Write the correct form of the pronoun in parentheses. Then indicate how each pronoun is used by writing *S* for subject, *D* for direct object, or *O* for object of the preposition.

1. (Who, Whom) won the award for best athlete at the homecoming game?

2. For (who, whom) should I ask when I interview the team?

3. (Who, Whom) did you nominate for best float in the parade?

4. With (who, whom) are you going to the homecoming dance?

5. (Who, Whom) did the class choose for homecoming queen?

6. (Who, Whom) should be introduced first, the homecoming queen or her court?

7. To (who, whom) was the corsage sent?

8. (Who, Whom) will crown the new queen?

9. About (who, whom) were you speaking?

10. (Who, Whom) did she take to the dance?

In clauses forms of *who* are also used. The way *who* or one of its related pronouns is used in an adjective or a noun clause determines its case. The following examples show how forms of *who* are used in adjective clauses.

NOMINATIVE CASE	Mr. Johnson is the man **who organized the trip.**
	(*Who* is the subject of *organized*.)
OBJECTIVE CASE	A woman **whom we met in Washington** is visiting us.
	(*Whom* is the direct object of *met*. We met whom in Maine.)
	This is Mrs. Strohmeyer, **with whom I work.**
	(*Whom* is the object of the preposition *with*.)

The following examples show how *who* is used in noun clauses.

NOMINATIVE CASE	Make sure you show your ticket to **whoever stops you.**
	(*Whoever* is the subject of *stops*.)
	I don't know **who the leader of my group is.**
	(*Who* is a predicate nominative.)
OBJECTIVE CASE	Take **whomever you want to the senior prom.**
	(*Whomever* is the direct object of *want*.)
	Gary usually agrees with **whomever he is speaking to.**
	(*Whomever* is the object of the preposition *to*.)

You can learn more about adjective and noun clauses on pages L163–L172.

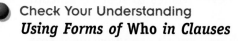

A parenthetical expression such as *I believe* may interrupt a clause. To decide on a nominative-case pronoun or an objective-case pronoun, say the sentence without the parenthetical expression.

> John Foster, (who, whom) I believe gave the best speech, didn't win the debate.

> John Foster, **who gave the best speech,** didn't win the debate.

> (With the parenthetical expression *I believe* removed, it is easy to see that *who* is the subject of *gave*.)

PRACTICE YOUR SKILLS

● Check Your Understanding
Using Forms of Who in Clauses

Contemporary Life **Write the correct form of the pronoun in parentheses. Then indicate how each pronoun is used by writing *S* for subject, *P* for predicate nominative, *O* for object of the preposition, or *D* for direct object.**

1. Mr. Fletcher has not said (who, whom) the committee will choose for the trip to Washington, D.C.

2. Ms. Davis has not said (who, whom) the chaperones will be.

3. Isaac is the student (who, whom) Miss Compton thinks should meet the president.

4. On the bus, snacks were given to (whoever, whomever) asked for them.

5. Alicia's mom is the person (who, whom) we chose to lead our group at the White House.

6. Those are the students (who, whom) will represent our school at the next session of Congress.

7. Speak to the Jacksons, with (who, whom) we will be sharing a room on the trip.

8. Is there any question about (who, whom) should go on the trip?

9. Anyone (who, whom) plans to go on the trip must sign up today.

10. Mr. Randall, (who, whom) I believe is organizing the trip, hired Ned as a counselor.

● Connect to the Writing Process: Editing
Using Who and Whom Correctly

Rewrite the following sentences, correcting errors with *who* or *whom*. If the sentence is correct, write C.

11. Give the brochure to whoever you like.

12. Whom is responsible for the hotel bill?

13. She is the one who needs to know about the trip.

14. We will take whomever wishes to see the Lincoln Memorial.

15. Mr. Thompson, whom won the congressional seat, met us.

Communicate Your Ideas

APPLY TO WRITING

Writer's Craft: *Analyzing an Author's Use of Pronouns*

Read the following passage from *The House on Mango Street* and answer the questions that follow.

> Then Uncle Nacho is pulling and pulling my arm and it doesn't matter how new the dress Mama bought is because my feet are ugly until my uncle who is a liar says, You are the prettiest girl here, will you dance, but I believe him, and yes, we are dancing, my Uncle Nacho and me, only I don't want to at first. My feet swell big and heavy like plungers, but I drag them across the linoleum floor straight center where Uncle wants to show off the new dance we learned. And Uncle spins

me, and my skinny arms bend the way he taught me, and my mother watches, and my little cousins watch, and the boy who is my cousin by first communion watches, and everyone says, wow, who are those two who dance like in the movies, until I forget that I am wearing only ordinary shoes, brown and white, the kind my mother buys each year for school.

—*Sandra Cisneros,* The House on Mango Street

- List all the pronouns and identify how they are being used.
- Rewrite a sentence or two using nouns instead of pronouns. What happens to the sentences?
- The author often substitutes pronouns for the characters' names. How does that affect the tone of the passage?

 ## Pronouns in Comparisons

Pronouns are often used when comparisons are made between two people. Problems arise, however, when a comparison is made but not said or written out completely, resulting in an elliptical clause. An **elliptical clause** is a subordinate clause that begins with *than* or *as.* Although words are omitted from an elliptical clause, they are still understood to be there.

Sue spends more time running with Jeff **than I.**
Sue spends more time running with Jeff **than me.**

Your choice of *I* or *me* in the preceding examples depends upon the meaning you wish to convey.

Sue spends more time running with Jeff **than *I* spend running with Jeff.**

Sue spends more time running with Jeff **than she spends running with** *me.*

I is correct in the first example on the preceding page because it is the subject of the clause. *Me* is correct in the second example because it is the object of the preposition *with*.

In an elliptical clause, use the form of the pronoun you would use if the clause were completed.

The best way to decide the case of a pronoun in an elliptical clause is to complete the clauses mentally. Then you can choose the form of the pronoun that expresses the meaning you want. Some elliptical clauses, of course, will express only one meaning.

PRACTICE YOUR SKILLS

● Check Your Understanding
Using Pronouns in Elliptical Clauses

Contemporary Life **Write each sentence, completing the elliptical clause. Then underline the pronoun you chose.**

1. Peg is almost as fast as (she, her).
2. Chuck throws the discus better than (I, me).
3. Willis is better than (he, him) in the high jump.
4. My brothers are stronger than (they, them).
5. No one works out harder than (he, him).
6. I know that I am a better relay runner than (he, him).
7. Jason prepared for the hurdles longer than (she, her).
8. Mary hands off the baton better than (he, him).
9. I think we were more nervous about the race than (they, them).
10. The coach spoke longer with Tina than (I, me).

● Connect to the Editing Process: Drafting
Writing Sentences with Elliptical Clauses

Write sentences that follow the instructions. Use elliptical clauses to express the comparisons.

11. Compare two school teams.

12. Compare a ballet dancer with an acrobat.

13. Compare ninth grade with tenth grade.

14. Compare roller skating with ice skating.

15. Compare in-line skating with roller skating.

Communicate Your Ideas

APPLY TO WRITING

Paragraph of Comparison: *Elliptical Clauses*

Your coach has just finished holding tryouts for the new season. As the captain of the team, your job is to rate the new players and recommend them for various positions. Write a paragraph of comparison for the coach that will help him place the new players in the positions they are most qualified for. Use elliptical clauses to make comparisons, and be sure to use pronouns correctly.

Pronouns and Appositives

In Chapter 3, you learned that an appositive is a noun or pronoun that identifies or explains another noun or pronoun in the sentence. When a pronoun is used with an appositive or as an appositive, make sure that it is in the correct case.

Pronouns Used with Appositives

Sometimes a noun appositive follows the pronouns *we* or *us.*

(We, Us) **sophomores** raised two thousand dollars.
The principal thanked (we, us) **volunteers.**

To decide whether to use the nominative-case *we* or the objective-case *us,* read the sentence without the noun appositives.

> (We, Us) raised two thousand dollars.
> The principal thanked (we, us).

Without the appositives, it is easy to see that the pronoun in the first sentence is used as the subject. As a result, the correct answer is *we* because subjects are in the nominative case. Because the pronoun in the second sentence is used as a direct object, the correct answer is *us* because direct objects are in the objective case.

> **We sophomores** raised two thousand dollars.
> The principal thanked **us volunteers.**

Pronouns as Appositives

Occasionally pronouns themselves can be used as appositives. To determine whether a pronoun used as an appositive should be in the nominative or objective case, first decide how the noun in front of it is used. If the noun is used as a subject or a predicate nominative, the pronoun appositive should be in the nominative case.

> The nominees, **Roberto and (she, her),** will give a speech at the next assembly.

Since *nominees* is the subject, the correct pronoun to use is *she.*

> The nominees, **Roberto and she,** will give a speech at the next assembly.

If a pronoun is used as an appositive to a direct object, an indirect object, or an object of a preposition, it should be in the objective case.

> Mr. Cain sent two students, **Mary and (I, me),** to the rally.

Since *students* is a direct object, the correct pronoun to use is *me.*

> Mr. Cain sent two students, **Mary and me,** to the rally.

You can learn more about appositives on pages L119–L120.

PRACTICE YOUR SKILLS

● Check Your Understanding
Using Appositives

Oral Expression **Trying each pronoun separately, read each sentence aloud without the noun appositives. Then read the sentence aloud again, using the correct pronoun.**

1. (We, Us) band students wanted to build extra practice rooms at our school.

2. The band director helped (we, us) band officers with our fund-raiser.

3. Mrs. Donovan sent two officers, Kendra and (he, him), to the principal.

4. Their job was to convince the accounting officers, Mr. Baker and (she, her), of the school board.

5. The principal thanked the two students, Bill and (she, her), for their input.

6. He decided that (we, us) band students could conduct a fund-raiser.

7. The officers, John and (she, her), thought a talent show would be successful.

8. Mrs. Donovan thanked (we, us) students for our efforts.

9. The best performers, John and (he, him), helped us raise the money we needed.

10. (We, us) band students raised more than three hundred dollars.

● Check Your Understanding
Using Pronouns with and as Appositives

Contemporary Life **Write the correct form of the pronoun in parentheses.**

11. Do your friends, Marla and (she, her), know where the school picnic is being held this year?

12. (We, Us) sophomores got to pick the location.

13. The newspaper representatives, David and (he, him), wanted to hold it at the city amusement park.

14. Jason asked the class officers, Joe and (she, her), if they would consider having it at the lake.

15. Finally Mrs. Fishburne told (we, us) students that we could hold it at the city park at no cost to the class.

16. Two volunteers, Jonathan and (she, her), went to the city council to reserve a date.

17. The city council thanked (we, us) students for promising to clean up the park when the picnic is over.

18. Mr. Boyd gave (we, us) students soft drinks at the picnic.

19. The newspaper representatives, Sheila and (she, her), sponsored a three-legged race.

20. The fastest students, Ben and (he, him), easily won the race.

Connect to the Writing Process: Drafting
Writing Sentences Using Appositives

Write sentences that use the following group of words with appositives or as appositives.

21. Julia and she

22. Ms. Masters and us

23. Davis and he

24. Monty and me

25. Shawna and her

Communicate Your Ideas

APPLY TO WRITING

Committee Report: *Appositives*

The chairman of the dance committee wants you to determine a theme that all the students will enjoy for the next school dance. Your job is to conduct a poll among your fellow classmates for possible suggestions. Write a brief report to the chairman that explains your findings. Use pronouns with and as appositives correctly.

Contemporary Life

Write each pronoun that is in the wrong case. Then write each pronoun correctly. If a sentence is correct, write C.

1. Between Bruce and I, we ate two dozen tacos at the school carnival.

2. Wasn't it him who held last year's record?

3. At the time I thought that them meeting you outside the school grounds was a good idea.

4. Sheila plays air hockey much better than I.

5. The two students who took part in organizing the carnival received an award.

6. Do you think you can eat more hot dogs than me?

7. We students expect to have a good carnival this year.

8. Whom do you suppose will be elected carnival queen?

9. I saw them at the dunk tank with Ashley and he.

10. Aren't you and I on the ring-toss booth committee?

11. Is Lee going to the carnival with Susanne and they?

12. A man who I knew from Knoxville helped us with our booth.

13. Is Carrie a better artist than her?

14. Many of we sophomores are inviting middle-school students to come to the carnival.

15. Erica and me helped him fix up the ticket booth.

16. That's them riding on the camel.

17. Did you hear whom the new carnival chairman will be?

18. The principal thanked we volunteers for our help.

19. She thinks that we should be cleaning up now.

20. For whom is she planning this carnival?

Pronouns and Their Antecedents

A pronoun and its **antecedent,** the word that the pronoun replaces or refers to, must agree in number and gender. **Number** is the term used to indicate whether a noun or a pronoun is singular or plural. The term **singular** indicates one; the term **plural** indicates more than one. **Gender** is the term used to indicate whether a noun or a pronoun is masculine, feminine, or neuter.

	GENDER		
MASCULINE	he	him	his
FEMININE	she	her	hers
NEUTER	it	its	

> A pronoun must agree in number and gender with its antecedent.

Agreement between a single-word antecedent and a pronoun usually does not present a problem.

> If **Dan** sets out the supplies, **he** doesn't have to clean up.
>
> The **artists** hung **their** work in the gallery.

If an antecedent is more than one word, however, you need to remember two rules.

> If two or more singular antecedents are joined by *or, nor, either/or,* or *neither/nor,* use a singular pronoun to refer to them.

All the conjunctions listed in the preceding rule indicate one *or* the other. Since *one* or *the other* is singular, the pronoun must be singular.

> Either **Bart** or **Claude** will sell us **his** paintings.

In this example Bart *or* Claude will sell his paintings—not both Bart and Claude. The pronoun, therefore, is singular.

> **If two or more singular antecedents are joined by *and* or *both/and,* use a plural pronoun to refer to them.**

The conjunctions listed in the preceding rule indicate more than one. Since *more than one* is plural, the pronoun must be plural.

> Both **Faye** and **Donna** signed **their** names to the mural.

In this example both Faye and Donna—two people—signed their names. The pronoun, therefore, is plural.

The gender of most antecedents is clear. Sometimes the gender of an antecedent is unknown. Standard English solves this agreement problem by using *his or her* to refer to such antecedents.

> Every **student** must turn in **his or her** painting on Friday.

Overusing **his or her** can make writing sound awkward. You can often avoid this problem by using all plural forms.

> All **students** must turn in **their** paintings on Friday.

PRACTICE YOUR SKILLS

  Check Your Understanding
Making Pronouns and Antecedents Agree

Contemporary Life **Write the pronoun that correctly completes each sentence.**

1. Neither Stanley nor Juan had signed ▦ painting.
2. Has your pot finished ▦ drying process yet?
3. Mix the paints and add ▦ to the others.
4. Either Maureen or Yvonne will lend you ▦ brush.
5. Since both Karen and Jane won the art competition, ▦ will be going on to the regional contest.
6. Will Fidel or Ralph display ▦ pottery at the show?

7. Students show ▩ artwork once a year.

8. Franklin said that ▩ would not finish.

9. The candidates must submit ▩ applications by Monday.

10. Mary and Beth displayed the paintings ▩ had finished in art class.

11. The two girls have not found ▩ paintings.

12. Many artists show ▩ work in a gallery.

13. After the students completed the paintings, ▩ put them away.

14. Either Roger or David will loan you ▩ canvas.

15. When Nancy learned about the art show, ▩ told our teacher.

16. After painting all afternoon, Paul and Leslie washed ▩ hands in the big sink.

17. It's easy to look at a painting and notice ▩ good qualities.

18. A child who enjoys drawing might see ▩ work in the art fair.

19. Neither Thomas nor Martin brought ▩ painting to the show Saturday.

20. Either the Coxes or the Cases will loan us ▩ easel.

● Connect to the Writing Process: Editing
Using Pronouns and Antecedents Correctly

Rewrite the following sentences, changing any pronouns that are used incorrectly. If a sentence is correct, write C.

21. Mart and Val wanted their paintings to win.

22. Neither Sal nor Aaron had prepared their canvases properly.

23. Every judge must complete their critique by the end of the evening.

24. Either Jimmy or Robert placed his easel by the door.

25. Sara and Tammy painted her favorite landscapes.

Indefinite Pronouns as Antecedents

The antecedent of a personal pronoun can be an indefinite pronoun. Agreement can be confusing because some singular indefinite pronouns suggest a plural meaning. Other indefinite pronouns can be either singular or plural.

The following list divides the common indefinite pronouns into three groups. A personal pronoun must be singular if its antecedent is a singular indefinite pronoun or plural if its antecedent is a plural indefinite pronoun. If the antecedent of a personal pronoun is one of the indefinite pronouns in the last group, the personal pronoun should agree in number and gender with the object of the preposition that follows the indefinite pronoun.

COMMON INDEFINITE PRONOUNS	
SINGULAR	anybody, anyone, each, either, everybody, everyone, neither, nobody, no one, one, somebody, someone
PLURAL	both, few, many, several
SINGULAR/PLURAL	all, any, most, none, some

Each of the girls was given **her** own uniform.

(singular)

Both of the players were praised for **their** talent.

(plural)

Some of the ice had melted at **its** edges.

(singular)

Some of the gloves have spots on **them**.

(plural)

Sometimes the gender of a singular indefinite pronoun is not indicated in a sentence. Standard English solves this agreement problem by using *his or her* to refer to such antecedents.

Everyone must have **his or her** physical by Thursday.

PRACTICE YOUR SKILLS

● Check Your Understanding
Making Pronouns Agree

Contemporary Life **Write the pronoun that correctly completes each sentence.**

1. One of your sisters found ▨ glove.
2. All of the players have stretched ▨ muscles.
3. One of the umpires found a rock in ▨ shoe.
4. Someone on the girls' softball team forgot ▨ glove.
5. Most of the pitcher's mound has lost ▨ contour over the winter.
6. Several of the fans complained about ▨ seats.
7. Few of my friends have ▨ own equipment.
8. Neither of the girls has finished ▨ warm-up.
9. Some of the coaches brought ▨ rosters.
10. Everyone on the baseball team will receive ▨ new uniform on Friday.
11. Many of the fields lost ▨ bases in the storm.
12. Both of the umpires had ▨ calls questioned.
13. Everyone in the men's softball division will be assigned ▨ starting time this afternoon.
14. Neither of the boys will tell ▨ view of the play.
15. Most of the players will receive ▨ trophies at the end of the season.
16. Each of my sisters has worn ▨ new sneakers.

17. Jackson told the coach that both of the shoes were missing ▓ labels.

18. All of the players can pick up ▓ uniforms next Wednesday after school.

19. We are all amazed that none of the fields have lost ▓ bases yet.

20. Either of the girls might pitch ▓ curve ball to the batter.

● Connect to the Writing Process: Editing
Using Pronouns and Antecedents Correctly

Rewrite the following sentences, correcting errors with pronouns and antecedents. If a sentence is correct, write C.

21. All of the coaches will finalize their rosters by this evening.

22. One of the girls sprained their ankle during last week's game.

23. Both of my friends rode her bikes to the game.

24. Any of the former players could submit his or her names to be an umpire.

25. Several of the fans brought their coolers filled with snacks to the game.

Communicate Your Ideas

APPLY TO WRITING

Instructions: *Pronouns and Antecedents*

Your cousin is coming to visit for the weekend and has never played your favorite game. Since you want to include your cousin in your planned activities, you decide to E-mail your cousin instructions for your favorite game. Use indefinite pronouns where appropriate and be sure to use correct antecedents with them.

Write the personal pronoun that correctly completes each sentence.

1. Neither Alan nor Ed has played ■ first game yet.

2. All of the coaches have promised ■ support.

3. Both the girls' team and the boys' team play most of ■ games at the field near my house.

4. If Leslie gets home early, tell ■ to hurry to the ball field.

5. Some people say that professional baseball has lost ■ appeal.

6. Either Dad or Uncle Frank will give ■ glove to you.

7. While the team was taking pictures, ■ ice packs melted.

8. One of the girls left ■ bag in the dugout.

9. Several of the coaches stopped ■ games during the thunderstorm.

10. David or Richard will loan you ■ camcorder to tape the game.

11. Both of the girls played ■ share of defense.

12. Every player on the team has had ■ fill of bubblegum.

13. One of the girls was late for ■ tryout with the team.

14. Sandy and Debbie enjoyed ■ first softball game of the season.

15. Neither Tony nor Jim ever loans out ■ glove.

16. I sat in the bleachers with ■ friend.

17. Sal and Jane quickly took ■ seats.

18. Each of the players stood when ■ name was called.

19. Bethany took ■ bat from the rack.

20. One of the other bats had fallen from ■ spot.

Unclear, Missing, or Confusing Antecedents

When you edit a story or report you have written, you should always check to see if the pronouns you used are in the correct case and if there is agreement between the pronouns and their antecedents. You should also check for any unclear or missing antecedents.

Every personal pronoun should clearly refer to a specific antecedent.

UNCLEAR	Although I had never skied in Colorado before, I liked **it.**
	(Although the antecedent of *it* is unclear, the context of the sentence suggests that the pronoun *it* refers to skiing.)
CLEAR	Although I had never skied in Colorado before, I liked **the skiing.**
UNCLEAR	In Colorado we visited Pike's Peak and saw where **they** mined for gold.
	(The antecedent of *they* is not clear, but the context of the sentence suggests that the antecedent of the pronoun *they* is the miners at Pike's Peak.)
CLEAR	In Colorado we visited Pike's Peak and saw where the **miners** dug for gold.
UNCLEAR	I like winter because **you** can go skiing then.
	(*You* is used incorrectly because it is not meant to refer to the person being spoken to. Instead the speaker intends to refer to himself or herself.)
CLEAR	I like winter because **I** can go skiing then.

MISSING	In Denver **they** can ski all year.
	(The antecedent of *they* is missing.)
CLEAR	**People in Denver** can ski all year.

CONFUSING	Sue visited Samantha before **she** left for Boulder.
	(Who left for Boulder, Sue or Samantha?)
CLEAR	Sue visited Samantha before **Sue** left for Boulder.

CONFUSING	Before you give the students their skis, check **them.**
	(What should you check, the students or the skis?)
CLEAR	Before you give the students their skis, check the **skis.**

PRACTICE YOUR SKILLS

● Check Your Understanding
Identifying Unclear, Missing, or Confusing Antecedents

Contemporary Life   **After each sentence, write *C* if the pronouns and antecedents are used correctly. Write *I* if they are used incorrectly.**

1. John's father was a ski instructor when he was only six years old.

2. Walter looked outside and knew you couldn't drive to the resort without snow tires.

3. I enjoy playing hockey because you're always getting plenty of exercise.

4. After the doctor had set Sherry's leg, she went home.

5. When Josh and Scott were on the slopes on Saturday, they were covered with snow.

6. My sister is studying to be a ski instructor, and she expects to like it very much.

7. I enjoy ice skating because it gives me a chance to be outside in the winter.

8. About an hour before we left for the slopes, Paul asked his father where his car keys were.

9. The ski lodge has a wood-burning stove in the lobby so that you can reduce your fuel bills.

10. Anne casually skated into the rink and knocked it right into the net for a goal.

11. Harriet visited Martha before she left for Denver for winter vacation.

12. I prefer to do my skiing in the morning because you have the whole day to ski then.

13. Jose took his brother to the beginner's slope, but he didn't ski.

14. Before you give those boots for skiing to Sara, check the straps.

15. I like skiing and skating because you can be outside.

● Connect to the Writing Process: Revising
Using Pronouns and Antecedents Correctly

16.–20. Choose any five of the incorrect sentences from above and rewrite them so that the antecedents are clear.

Communicate Your Ideas

APPLY TO WRITING

Summary: *Pronouns and Antecedents*

The student council is trying to decide on a destination for a class trip. You have just been to a wonderful vacation spot and would like to persuade the student council to book a class trip there. Write a summary of your vacation that will convince the student council that there are enough activities to keep the class occupied for a weekend trip. Use pronouns and antecedents correctly.

Using Pronouns

Write the correct form of the pronoun in parentheses.

1. The poetry slam contest is now only between you and (she, her).

2. Carl, Van, and (I, me) went bobsledding last winter in Colorado.

3. That was (he, him) on the high diving board.

4. Don't forget (we, us) hard workers.

5. Is that new car the Milligans' or (theirs, them)?

6. (Who, Whom) do you believe will be the team's most improved player?

7. My younger brother Chad is almost as tall as (I, me).

8. I will take Roger and (they, them) in the car with me.

9. The cheerleaders think that (them, their) shouting sometimes causes laryngitis.

10. The candidate (who, whom) the experts thought did not have a chance won by a landslide.

11. Will you take a picture of Amanda and (I, me) as we finish the race?

12. Maggie admitted that it was (she, her) behind the mask.

13. Steve prefers to play tennis with players who are better than (he, him).

14. The statue memorialized six original settlers, each of (who, whom) gave a great deal to the city.

15. (Him, His) singing that country song brought back old memories.

Making Pronouns and Antecedents Agree

Write the personal pronoun that correctly completes each sentence.

1. Neither Alex nor Edgar has had ▦ physical yet.
2. All of the candidates promised ▦ support.
3. Both the blue jay and the cardinal get most of ▦ food from our bird feeder.
4. If Lisa answers the phone, tell ▦ to take a message.
5. Some of the cheese has lost ▦ sharpness.
6. Either Mom or Aunt Betty will give ▦ alarm clock to you.
7. While our neighbors were on vacation, ▦ newspapers stacked up on the doorstep.
8. One of the women left ▦ briefcase in the conference room.
9. Several of the drivers stopped ▦ cars during the heavy downpour.
10. Dennis or Rico will loan you ▦ tape recorder.
11. Each of the students passed in ▦ research report on time.
12. All of the students were happy with ▦ grades.
13. Did you do ▦ math assignment last night?
14. The team members could not agree on ▦ practice time.
15. Most of the teachers are in ▦ classrooms.

Writing Sentences

Write five sentences that follow the directions below.

1. Write a sentence with a pronoun as a part of a compound subject.
2. Write a sentence with a pronoun as a part of a compound direct object.
3. Write a sentence with a pronoun as a part of an appositive.
4. Write a sentence that includes *who* or *whom* in a question.
5. Write a sentence that includes a pronoun in an elliptical clause.

Language and *Self-Expression*

Philip Evergood was born in New York City, but he moved with his family to England in 1909. His father was a painter who hoped his son would become a lawyer. Nevertheless, Evergood became a painter as well. When he returned to the United States in 1931, he was shocked to see the effects of the Great Depression on the people. Much of his work depicted the hunger, unemployment, and despair of the Depression and the results of racial discrimination.

The face of the girl in *Her World* is very thought-provoking. Imagine that you are able to see into her mind. What might she be thinking and feeling? Write a journal entry that the girl might write, describing her thoughts as she stands by the fence in the painting. Use various kinds of pronouns in your writing, and be sure your pronouns agree with your antecedents.

Prewriting You may want to make a character-traits chart for the girl in the painting. Write down details about her character, including her likes and dislikes, her feelings, and her desires for the future.

Drafting Use the character-traits chart as the basis for your journal entry. Try to write as the girl would write, explaining what events have led to her pensive look.

Revising Reread your journal entry carefully. Determine if you have captured the personality of the girl as she is depicted in the painting.

Editing Check your journal entry for errors in spelling and punctuation. Also make any changes necessary to correct your use of pronouns and their antecedents.

Publishing After you prepare a final copy of your journal entry, exchange entries with classmates. Discuss the different ways you and your classmates interpreted the character of the girl in the painting.

Another Look

Case is the form of a noun or pronoun that indicates its use in a sentence.

Cases of Personal Pronouns
The **nominative case** is used for subjects and predicate nominatives. The nominative case pronouns are *I, you, he, she, it, we,* and *they.* *(page L244)*

The **objective case** is used for direct objects, indirect objects, and objects of prepositions. The objective case pronouns are *me, you, him, her, it, us,* and *them.* *(page L250)*

The **possessive case** is used to show ownership or possession. The possessive case pronouns are *my, mine, your, yours, his, her, hers, its, our, ours, their,* and *theirs.* *(pages L257–L258)*

Pronoun Problems
The correct use of *who* is determined by how the pronoun is used in a question or clause. *(pages L262–L263)*

In an elliptical clause, use the form of the pronoun you would use if the clause were completed. *(pages L267–L268)*

Pronouns and Their Antecedents
A pronoun must agree in number and gender with its **antecedent,** the word that the pronoun refers to or replaces. *(page L274)*

If two or more singular antecedents are joined by *or, nor, either/or,* or *neither/nor* use a singular pronoun to refer to them. *(pages L274–L275)*

If two or more singular antecedents are joined by *and* or *both/and,* use a plural pronoun to refer to them. *(page L275)*

Every personal pronoun should clearly refer to a specific antecedent. *(pages L281–L282)*

Other Information About Pronoouns
Using pronouns with appositives *(pages L269–L270)*
Using pronouns as appositives *(page L270)*
Using indefinite pronouns as antecedents *(pages L277–L278)*

Directions

Read the passage and choose the pronoun that belongs in each underlined space. Write the letter of the correct answer.

EXAMPLE   **1.** __(1)__ has ever taken a ride on a ferry?

    1 A Who
       B Whoever
       C Whomever
       D Whom

ANSWER   **1 A**

The ferry between Grand Manan Island and New Brunswick is both functional and entertaining to __(1)__ riders. Many of the year-round inhabitants consider the ferry __(2)__ lifeline. To summer riders, however, the ferry ride is a nature voyage. Pods of dolphins swim alongside, flashing silver as __(3)__ leap into the air. Sometimes a whale will surface, blowing spray as __(4)__ surfaces. Both animals enjoy __(5)__ effect on the ferry riders.

One woman, __(6)__ didn't know much about wildlife, thought a dolphin was a shark! Her husband, even less informed than __(7)__, insisted the dolphin was some kind of sea serpent. Jon Uhrick, the ferry captain, couldn't help laughing at __(8)__. The first mate and __(9)__ explained that the dolphins like to play in the ferry's wake. The two passengers were embarrassed about __(10)__ mistake.

1	**A**	his		**6**	**A**	she
	B	their			**B**	who
	C	it's			**C**	whom
	D	its			**D**	her
2	**A**	his		**7**	**A**	her
	B	their			**B**	she
	C	its			**C**	him
	D	they			**D**	them
3	**A**	them		**8**	**A**	they
	B	he			**B**	their
	C	they			**C**	them
	D	it			**D**	theirs
4	**A**	it		**9**	**A**	him
	B	they			**B**	he
	C	them			**C**	them
	D	its			**D**	they
5	**A**	they		**10**	**A**	their
	B	his			**B**	they
	C	them			**C**	his
	D	their			**D**	them

CHAPTER 7

Subject and Verb Agreement

 **Pretest**

Directions
Read the passage and choose the word or group of words that belongs in each underlined space. Write the letter of the correct answer.

EXAMPLE

The largest earthquake of the twentieth century __(1)__ the South American coast of Chile in 1960.

1 **A** struck
  B have struck
  C are striking
  D were striking

ANSWER   1 **A**

When a large earthquake __(1)__ a coastal area, there __(2)__ often permanent changes in the coastline. After a strong earthquake, underwater slopes and mountains __(3)__ away in what is called "slumping." This is what geologists __(4)__ was the case, for example, in the 1999 earthquake in Turkey. Since then a team of geologists __(5)__ the quake. Twenty meters __(6)__ the highest wave height that they measured after that quake. Each of the waves __(7)__ changes in the coastline. __(8)__ these changes permanent? Nobody __(9)__ the answer yet. A number of scientists __(10)__ further study of these phenomena before a final decision is made.

1 **A** hits
   B are hitting
   C have hit
   D hit

2 **A** are
   B is
   C am
   D was

3 **A** slid
   B has slid
   C have slid
   D slide

4 **A** believes
   B believe
   C does believe
   D is believing

5 **A** has been studying
   B have been studying
   C are studying
   D were studying

6 **A** was
   B were
   C are
   D have been

7 **A** is causing
   B have caused
   C has caused
   D were causing

8 **A** Is
   B Am
   C Are
   D Was

9 **A** knows
   B know
   C is knowing
   D have known

10 **A** has planned
   B have planned
   C plan
   D was planning

Chuck Jones. *Love Is in the Hare,* 1998.
Limited edition giclée, 20 by 15 inches.
© Warner Bros.

Describe What does the cartoon show? How do you think color contributes to the ideas the cartoonist is expressing?

Analyze In what ways do you think the cartoonist uses exaggeration to add humor to the cartoon?

Interpret How does the title of the work use wordplay? In what way does the wordplay contribute to the humor of the work?

Judge What details in the cartoon do you find most amusing? Why?

At the end of this chapter, you will use the artwork to stimulate ideas for writing.

Agreement of Subjects and Verbs

When certain keys on a piano are played together, they create a pleasant, harmonious sound. Other keys played together cause people to wrinkle their foreheads and hold their ears. In this way language is similar to music. Some subjects and verbs go together. Others do not. When a subject and a verb fit together, they are in **agreement.** This chapter will show you how to make subjects and verbs agree. Keep in mind this one basic rule as you go through the chapter.

A verb must agree with its subject in number.

Number indicates whether a noun or pronoun is singular or plural. This term is also applied to verbs. **Singular** indicates one; **plural** indicates more than one.

Most nouns form their plurals by adding *–s* or *–es* to the singular form, but a few nouns form their plurals irregularly. Pronouns form their plurals by changing forms, except for *you,* which has the same form for both singular and plural.

NOUNS	
SINGULAR	boy, lunch, goose
PLURAL	boys, lunches, geese
PRONOUNS	
SINGULAR	I, you, he, she, it
PLURAL	we, you, they

Present tense verbs also have singular and plural forms. The third person singular form ends in *–s* or *–es*. Most verb forms that do not end in *–s* or *–es* are plural.

THIRD PERSON SINGULAR	(He, She, It) **eats.**
OTHERS	(I, You, We, They) **eat.**

The verbs *be, have,* and *do* have irregular singular and plural forms for the present tense. *Be* also has irregular forms for the past tense.

PRESENT TENSE	
SINGULAR	**PLURAL**
I **am, have, do**	we **are, have, do**
you **are, have, do**	you **are, have, do**
he, she, it **is, has, does**	they **are, have, do**
PAST TENSE	
SINGULAR	**PLURAL**
I **was**	we **were**
you **were**	you **were**
he, she, it **was**	they **were**

Because a subject and verb both have number, they must agree.

A singular subject takes a singular verb.

A plural subject takes a plural verb.

The **boy sings.**	The **boys sing.**
The **dance was** good.	The **dances were** good.
The **goose flies.**	The **geese fly.**
He is here.	**They are** here.
I was at the store.	**We were** at the store.

Be, have, and *do* are often used as helping verbs. When they are, they must agree in number with the subject.

The first helping verb must agree in number with the subject.

Kim **is** acting.	Kim and Andrew **are** acting.
She **does** act.	They **do** like to rehearse.

PRACTICE YOUR SKILLS

● Check Your Understanding
Making Subjects and Verbs Agree

General Interest **Write the form of the verb in parentheses that agrees with the subject.**

1. The lights (dims, dim).
2. The curtain (rises, rise).
3. It (begins, begin).
4. Musicians (plays, play).
5. Grace (does, do) sing.
6. They (is, are) dancing.
7. The lights (does, do) shine.
8. The actors (is, are) nervous.
9. The soloist (sings, sing).
10. It (has, have) begun.
11. I (performs, perform).
12. The audience (claps, clap).
13. The musicians (bows, bow).
14. The show (ends, end).
15. We (exits, exit).

● Connect to the Writing Process: Editing
Correcting Subject and Verb Agreement

Write the verbs that do not agree with their subjects. Then, write the verbs correctly. If the sentence is correct, write C.

16. Mr. Smith gives excellent acting advice.
17. He enjoy our acting class.
18. He is planning our next play.
19. Mr. Smith have the best ideas for plays.
20. I likes his class.

APPLY TO WRITING

Tongue Twisters: *Subject and Verb Agreement*

As part of your acting class, your teacher has asked you to devise your own vocal warm-up. Write ten original tongue twisters that will help you warm up your voice and concentrate. Write all ten in the present tense and make sure the subject and verb agree in each.

● Interrupting Words

The agreement of a verb with its subject is not changed by any interrupting words.

A verb always agrees with its subject—whether the verb comes right next to the subject or is separated from it by other words. If a phrase or a clause separates a subject and verb, a mistake in agreement sometimes occurs. The verb may be mistakenly made to agree with the object of a prepositional phrase or some other word that is closer to the verb.

The subjects and the verbs in the following examples are underscored and double underscored, respectively. Notice that they agree in number—despite the words that separate them.

PREPOSITIONAL PHRASE	The winds at the peak **were** howling.
	(The plural verb *were* agrees with the plural subject *winds,* even though *peak* is closer to the verb.)
PARTICIPIAL PHRASE	The backpack filled with ropes **was** put on the table.
	(*Was* agrees with the subject *backpack*—not with *ropes.*)

NEGATIVE STATEMENTS	David, not one of his brothers, **is** <u>going</u> to climb.
	(*Is* agrees with the subject *David*—not with *brothers.*)
ADJECTIVE CLAUSES	The <u>hikers</u> who are climbing the mountain <u>train</u> like athletes.
	(*Train* agrees with the subject *hikers*—not with *mountain.*)

Compound prepositions, such as *in addition to, as well as, along with,* and *together with,* often begin interrupting phrases. Make sure the verb always agrees with the subject, not with the object of the compound preposition.

<u>Eric</u>, together with his two cousins, **is** <u>coming</u> with us.

(*Is* agrees with the subject *Eric*—not with *cousins,* the object of the compound preposition *together with.*)

PRACTICE YOUR SKILLS

 Check Your Understanding
Making Interrupted Subjects and Verbs Agree

 General Interest **Write the subject in each sentence. Next to each, write the form of the verb in parentheses that agrees with the subject.**

1. Explorers' quests for adventure (leads, lead) to new discoveries.
2. Greg Child, together with his climbing team, (has, have) climbed in many unusual locations.
3. Mountaineering, not rock climbing, (is, are) the team's specialty.
4. The summit, partly hidden by clouds, (towers, tower) above everything else for miles.

Agreement of Subjects and Verbs **L297**

5. The mountains of Baffin Island (is, are) seldom climbed by anyone.

6. The hikers, not the leader, (decides, decide) which mountains they will climb.

7. The sheer height of the cliff (intimidates, intimidate) even the most seasoned climbers.

8. Many writers who work for the *National Geographic Magazine* (has, have) accompanied climbing expeditions.

9. The granite of Great Sail Peak, as well as its height, (makes, make) for difficult climbing.

10. The climbers on the team (was, were) finished climbing in twenty-three days.

11. The altitude, as well as the cold weather, (tests, test) the climbers' abilities.

12. The rugged terrain, in addition to the altitude, (is, are) another obstacle to success.

13. Supplies for the team (has, have) been flown in well before the climb begins.

14. The climber's backpack, which is filled with many unusual items, (has, have) been packed carefully for the challenging expedition.

15. The lead climber, together with his teammates, (was, were) in training for this climb months in advance.

16. Approximately six people in the world (has, have) climbed the Great Sail Peak in Baffin Island, Canada.

17. Greg Child, who accompanied the climbers, (is, are) also a writer.

18. Almost every person who climbs mountains (enjoys, enjoy) the experience.

19. Equipment once used by professional climbers (is, are) now available to anyone.

20. Many snowdrifts in the Baffin Island area (contain, contains) broken snowmobiles.

Correcting Subject and Verb Agreement

Write the verbs that do not agree with their subjects. Then write them correctly. If a sentence is correct, write C.

21. The pictures that Greg took on his last climb is in that album.

22. The winds blowing on the peak were incredibly strong.

23. Most accidents on a climb is the result of carelessness.

24. Two ropes from the climb is torn.

25. Greg Child, along with his team, have arrived at the summit of Great Sail Peak.

Communicate Your Ideas

APPLY TO WRITING

News Story: *Subject and Verb Agreement*

A group of students at your high school participated in a sporting event for charity. The editor of the school paper has asked you to write a feature article that highlights the members of the group as well as their achievements. As you write your feature story, be sure that the subjects and verbs agree.

 QuickCheck Mixed Practice

General Interest **Write the correct form of the verb in parentheses.**

1. Televisions (is, are) steadily increasing in size.

2. Television (has, have) been a major source of news and entertainment for many years.

3. The main feature of the auto channel (is, are) a tip for auto care.

4. The TV in our room (was, were) borrowed for us.

5. The list of tonight's programs (is, are) here in the newspaper.

6. A TV dinner (is, are) my favorite food.

7. The programs on Friday (was, were) not even remotely interesting.

8. One newscaster on that station (is, are) my cousin.

9. In the 1970s, cable (was, were) just beginning to reach many households.

10. Comedies (has, have) been popular programs for many years.

11. The sportscasters that work on the local station (works, work) just as hard as national broadcasters.

12. The Super Bowl (is, are) seen by millions of people each year.

13. People in the United States (views, view) many hours of television each year.

14. My cousins (likes, like) to watch music videos.

15. Television, like other forms of entertainment, (helps, help) people relax.

16. The first pictures from the moon (was, were) seen by millions of people, thanks to television.

17. Most people (owns, own) at least one TV set in their home.

18. An award of excellence (was, were) presented to our school by the local TV station.

19. One early performer who had a successful TV variety show (were, was) Milton Berle.

20. The two television sets that belong to my brother (is, are) broken.

Common Agreement Problems

In addition to interrupted subjects and verbs, there are other problems you should watch for when you edit your written work for agreement problems.

Compound Subjects

There are two rules to remember when a verb must agree with a compound subject.

When subjects are joined by *or, nor, either/or,* or *neither/nor,* the verb agrees with the closer subject.

This rule applies to any combination of compound subjects: two or more singular subjects, two or more plural subjects, or one singular and one plural subject. The verb always agrees with the subject closer to it.

Beth or Craig **is** going to buy a computer.

(*Is* agrees with *Craig,* the subject closer to the verb.)

Either the roads or the sidewalks **have** been slated for repaving.

(*Have* agrees with *sidewalks,* the subject closer to the verb.)

Neither Art nor his brothers **have** ever owned a car.

(*Have* agrees with *brothers,* the subject closer to the verb— even though *Art* is singular.)

Neither the Lings nor their son **is** planning to buy a car soon.

(In this case, *is* agrees with the singular subject *son* because that subject is closer to the verb.)

Different conjunctions are the basis of the second rule.

When subjects are joined by *and* or *both/and*, the verb is plural.

These conjunctions always suggest more than one. As a result, the verb is always plural—regardless of whether the individual subjects are singular, plural, or a combination of singular and plural.

Ted's shovel and rake **were** missing from the shed.

(Two things—the *shovel* and the *rake*—were missing. The verb must be plural to agree with them.)

A rose and two irises **were** chosen best in the garden show.

(Even though *rose* is singular, the verb is still plural because the *rose* and the two *irises*—together—were chosen best in the garden show.)

There are two exceptions to the second rule. On a few rare occasions, subjects joined by *and* refer to only one person or one thing. When this is the case, the verb must be singular.

The artist and gardener **was** given a standing ovation.

(The artist and gardener is the same person.)

Cheese and crackers **is** my favorite snack when I garden.

(*Cheese and crackers* is considered one item.)

The other exception to the second rule involves the words *every* and *each* when they come before a compound subject that is joined by *and*. In this situation, each subject is considered separately. As a result, a singular verb is needed.

Every man and woman **is** asked to vote for garden club president.

Each tree and bush **was** infested with bugs.

PRACTICE YOUR SKILLS

● Check Your Understanding
Making Verbs Agree with Compound Subjects

General Interest **Write the correct form of the verb in parentheses.**

1. Flowers or herbs (make, makes) nice arrangements for centerpieces.

2. Herbs and spices (is, are) often confused by novice gardeners.

3. The winner and president of the garden club (is, are) Ryan Anderson.

4. Neither the lilac bush nor apple trees (does, do) well in a subtropical climate.

5. Both professional and amateur gardeners (heeds, heed) the first signs of winter frost.

6. Both color and texture (was, were) considerations in the rose committee's selection of the winning rose.

7. Topsoil or mulch (needs, need) to be added to a garden every year.

8. Watering and weeding (is, are) my least favorite gardening chores.

9. Either Rebecca or her sister (is, are) going to weed the garden this weekend.

10. Each rose and iris (was, were) inspected for flaws at the garden show.

● Connect to the Writing Process: Editing
Correcting Errors in Agreement

Write the verbs that do not agree with their subjects. Then write the verbs correctly. If a sentence is correct, write C.

11. Each cup and saucer were used at the garden club reception.

12. Sandwiches and a fruit salad were served at the reception.

13. The guest speaker and president of the club were Mrs. Jan O'Reilly.

14. Either sugar or sweetener are needed to improve the iced tea.

15. Neither the violinists nor the harpists have arrived on time for the reception.

Indefinite Pronouns as Subjects

In the previous chapter, you learned that some indefinite pronouns are singular, some are plural, and some can be either singular or plural.

A verb must agree in number with an indefinite pronoun used as a subject.

COMMON INDEFINITE PRONOUNS	
SINGULAR	anybody, anyone, each, either, everybody, everyone, neither, no one, one, somebody, someone
PLURAL	both, few, many, several
SINGULAR/PLURAL	all, any, most, none, some

SINGULAR   One of the students **was** asked to be a member of the archaeology club.

PLURAL   Few of my friends **are** going to the lecture tomorrow night.

SINGULAR OR PLURAL   Some of the water **was** spilled.

     Some of the pyramids **were** looted.

PRACTICE YOUR SKILLS

● Check Your Understanding
Making Verbs Agree with Indefinite Pronoun Subjects

History Topic **Write the subject in each sentence. Then write the form of the verb in parentheses that agrees with the subject.**

1. Neither of the pyramids (was, were) filled with treasure.

2. Each of the tombs (contains, contain) evidence of looting.

3. Most of the artifacts (come, comes) from the Valley of the Kings.

4. All of the tombs (has, have) some sort of writing inside them.

5. Many of the old records (was, were) carefully preserved.

6. One of the Egyptologists (was, were) too exhausted to continue.

7. Any of these artifacts (is, are) considered very valuable.

8. Several of the tombs in the Valley of the Queens (was, were) filled with valuable hieroglyphics.

9. No one at the museum (was, were) surprised at the new discovery.

10. Everybody in my school (is, are) interested in ancient Egypt.

● Connect to the Writing Process: Revising
Correcting Subject and Verb Agreement

Rewrite the sentences that have verbs that do not agree with their subjects. If a sentence is correct, write C.

11. Both of my brothers is working in Egypt.

12. None of the recent finds was properly cleaned.

13. Few of the new reports has been read yet.

14. Some of the artifacts has been stolen.

15. Somebody on the expedition is responsible for taking care of a rare sarcophagus.

Subjects in Inverted Order

Most sentences are in natural order, with the subject coming before the verb. Some sentences, though, are in inverted order, with the subject following the verb or part of the verb phrase. Regardless of where a subject is located in a sentence, the verb must agree with it.

The subject and the verb of an inverted sentence must agree in number.

There are several types of inverted sentences. To find the subject in an inverted sentence, turn the sentence around to its natural order. In the following examples, each subject is underlined once, and each verb is underlined twice.

INVERTED ORDER	Hidden in the back of the closet **was** Kevin's painting.
	(Kevin's painting was hidden in the back of the closet.)
QUESTIONS	**Was** the art room cleaned today?
	(The art room was cleaned today.)
	Are the paints stored safely in the cabinet?
	(The paints are stored safely in the cabinet.)
SENTENCES BEGINNING WITH *HERE* OR *THERE*	Here **is** your clean paintbrush.
	(Your clean paintbrush is here.)
	There **were** too many people crowded into the gallery.
	(Occasionally you must drop *here* or *there* before putting the sentence into its natural order. Too many people were crowded into the gallery.)

Professional writers use sentences in both natural and inverted order. Changing the normal subject-verb order creates sentence variety and adds interest to writing. Notice Alan Paton's use of inverted order, primarily through the use of questions, to convey meaning in the following passage.

Have no doubt it is fear in the land. For what can men do when so many have grown lawless? Who can enjoy the lovely land, who can enjoy the seventy years, and the sun that pours down on the earth, when there is fear in the heart? Who can walk quietly in the shadow of the jacarandas, when their beauty is grown to danger? Who can lie peacefully abed, while darkness holds some secret?

–Alan Paton, Cry, the Beloved Country

PRACTICE YOUR SKILLS

● Check Your Understanding
Making Subjects and Verbs in Inverted Order Agree

Art Topic **Write the subject in each sentence. Then write the form of the verb in parentheses that agrees with the subject.**

1. There (is, are) about one hundred paintings included in this book.

2. Why (was, were) Picasso such a good artist?

3. In his artwork (is, are) many fascinating themes.

4. There (is, are) many paintings in his repertoire.

5. (Was, Were) he considered one of the most interesting artists of the twentieth century?

6. Why (have, has) you decided to study Picasso's work?

7. In his Blue Period (is, are) many paintings that feature the color blue.

8. (Does, Do) you know when his Rose Period began?

9. There (is, are) very few who can paint like Picasso.

10. Above the mantel (is, are) two Picasso paintings.

● Connect to the Writing Process: Drafting
Writing Sentences in Inverted Order

Use the instructions to write original sentences in inverted order. Be sure that the subjects and verbs agree.

11. Begin a sentence with *there*.

12. Write a question, using *does*.

13. Begin a sentence with the phrase *in the window*.

14. Begin a sentence with the phrase *hanging from the ceiling*.

15. Write a question, using *why*.

Communicate Your Ideas

APPLY TO WRITING

Art Critique: *Subject and Verb Agreement*

Pablo Picasso. *Portrait of a Young Girl, After Cranach the Younger, II,* 1958. Linoleum cut, printed in color, composition: 25¹¹/₁₆ by 21⁵/₁₆ inches. The Museum of Modern Art, New York.

Your art teacher has asked you to help out the local art gallery by writing a critique of a painting that it will have on display. You have been assigned to write about this piece by Picasso. Write a short description of the painting for the museum and its patrons, and discuss the good and bad qualities of the painting. Refer to an encyclopedia or to the Internet for background information about Picasso. Use subjects in inverted order in at least three sentences, and be sure your verbs and subjects agree.

QuickCheck Mixed Practice

Contemporary Life
Write the subject of each sentence and the verb in parentheses that agrees with the subject.

1. Why (is, are) you working so hard on that sculpture?

2. No one in the class (has, have) finished yet.

3. Both painting and sculpture classes (is, are) popular this year.

4. Several of the students (has, have) been selected to participate in the art festival this year.

5. Jenny and Meagan (win, wins) on a regular basis.

6. (Was, Were) you able to complete your painting on time this year?

7. Few of the artists (refuse, refuses) to show their work in the festival.

8. There (is, are) an extra place for your sculpture.

9. Painting or sculpture (is, are) featured in this year's contest.

10. Each of the sculptures (requires, require) its own special pedestal.

11. Hanging in the entrance to the hall (was, were) Marcia's painting.

12. (Does, Do) you know when the judging of the paintings will begin?
13. Most of the paintings (have, has) been signed.
14. Either my grandparents or my cousin (are, is) coming to the exhibit tonight.
15. The judge and art teacher (is, are) Sandra Pearson.

 ## Other Agreement Problems

Although less common, a few other special situations also may cause agreement problems. Look for these when you edit your written work.

Collective Nouns

A collective noun, as you know, names a group of people or things. How a collective noun is used will determine its agreement with the verb.

COMMON COLLECTIVE NOUNS			
audience	congregation	flock	league
band	crew	gang	orchestra
class	crowd	group	swarm
committee	faculty	herd	team
colony	family	jury	tribe

Use a singular verb with a collective noun subject that is thought of as a unit.

Use a plural verb with a collective noun subject that is thought of as a group of separate individuals.

The class **has** been out for ten hours.

(The class is acting together as a whole unit. Therefore, the verb is singular.)

The class **have** not been able to come to an agreement.

(Members of the class are acting as individuals—each with a separate opinion. Therefore, the verb is plural.)

Words Expressing Amounts or Times

Subjects that express quantities or times are usually considered singular, but they often have plural forms.

A subject that expresses an amount, measurement, weight, or time is usually singular and takes a singular verb.

QUANTITY   **Ten miles** is the distance from my house to my high school.

(one unit of distance)

Fifty dollars is the prize for first place in the essay contest.

Five pennies equals a nickel.

(one sum of money)

Three fourths of the class **is** going on the trip.

(one part of a group)

Fifty pounds is a heavy weight for many people.

(one unit of weight)

TIME   **Five minutes** was too long to wait for him.

Two weeks is a standard vacation.

(one period of time)

Use a singular verb when an amount tells *how much*. Use a plural verb when an amount tells *how many*.

Half of the meeting was devoted to questions.

Fifty percent of the meeting was devoted to speeches.

(How much of the meeting?)

Half of the students were not present.

Twenty percent of the students were ill that day.

(How many students?)

The Number of, A Number of

These two expressions present different problems in agreement.

Use a singular verb with *the number of* and a plural verb with *a number of*.

The number of girls taking drafting class **has** doubled this year.

A number of girls **are** taking drafting class this year.

Singular Nouns That Have Plural Forms

Words like *molasses, measles, economics,* and *physics* look plural because they end in *–s*. However, they name single things, such as one type of food, one disease, or one area of knowledge.

Use a singular verb with subjects that are plural in form but singular in meaning.

Mumps is a dangerous disease for adults to contract.

Physics is his major in college.

Molasses moves very slowly when it is poured.

PRACTICE YOUR SKILLS

● Check Your Understanding
Making Problem Subjects and Verbs Agree

Contemporary Life **Write the correct form of the verb in parentheses.**

1. Mathematics (has, have) been made easier by the use of pocket calculators.

2. A number of parents (has, have) requested more homework for their teenagers.

3. One third of the school year (is, are) over already.

4. The faculty (meets, meet) every Tuesday afternoon.

5. Four gallons of water (was, were) spilled in the science laboratory.

6. The number of eight-hour school days (is, are) increasing.

7. Only three fourths of the seats in the new auditorium (was, were) occupied during the assembly.

8. Twenty-five pounds (is, are) too much to carry in your backpack.

9. Television news (is, are) too condensed for history discussions.

10. The final two days before the school play (was, were) devoted to dress rehearsals.

11. Fifty dollars (was, were) all he could afford for a football jacket.

12. The male quartet from our school (is, are) singing at the assembly today.

13. Gymnastics (is, are) the featured sport at our school spirit day.

14. Four miles (is, are) the distance from my house to the high school.

15. In the main hall of our school, there (is, are) a large statue dedicated to the founder of the school.

Correcting Subject-Verb Agreement with Problem Subjects

Rewrite the following sentences, using the correct verbs. If a sentence is correct, write C.

16. Half of Chico's spare time is spent working on his chemistry homework.

17. Our football team are known as the Fighting Bears.

18. A number of tardy warnings has been posted.

19. Have anyone finished the assignment?

20. There is more students in the band than in the choir.

Doesn't or *Don't?*

When you write a contraction, always say the two words that make up the contraction. Then check for agreement with the subject.

The verb part of the contraction must agree in number with the subject.

Doesn't, isn't, wasn't, and *hasn't* are singular and agree with singular subjects. *Don't, aren't, weren't,* and *haven't* are plural and agree with plural subjects.

The <u>story</u> **does**<u>n't start</u> until four o'clock.

Do<u>n't</u> <u>you</u> <u>like</u> this novel?

<u>They</u> **have**<u>n't seen</u> the movie yet.

<u>Isn't</u> <u>he</u> a good actor?

Subjects with Linking Verbs

A verb always agrees with its subject—regardless of any other word in the sentence.

A verb agrees with the subject of a sentence, not with the predicate nominative.

> Historical <u>novels</u> **are** a good way to learn history.
>
> (The plural verb *are* agrees with the plural subject *novels*—even though the predicate nominative *way* is singular.)
>
> The major reading <u>problem</u> **is** motivation and time.
>
> (*Is* agrees with the subject *problem*—not with the compound predicate nominative, *motivation* and *time*.)

Titles

Although a title may have many words in it, it is considered singular because it is the name of one book or one work of art. Most multiword names of businesses and organizations are also considered singular.

A title is singular and takes a singular verb.

> *<u>Seven Gothic Tales</u>* **was** written by Isak Dinesen.
>
> <u>The Home Owners Association</u> **is** holding a book signing.

PRACTICE YOUR SKILLS

 Check Your Understanding
Making Subjects and Verbs Agree

General Interest **Write the correct form of the verb in parentheses.**

1. (Doesn't, Don't) you have to learn about the French Revolution in history?

2. *A Tale of Two Cities* (tells, tell) about some of the things that happened during the French Revolution.

3. Charles Dickens (wasn't, weren't) able to have a normal childhood.

4. Many people in my class (is, are) reading about Dickens's life.

5. The Readers' Club (is, are) sponsoring a panel discussion about his works.

6. (Doesn't, Don't) Mrs. Simer plan a big lesson about Charles Dickens?

7. Politics (was, were) a main issue in Dickens's life.

8. (Isn't, Aren't) you going to lead the discussion about *Oliver Twist?*

9. *Dombey and Son* (is, are) about a man's relationship with his daughter.

10. Dickens (wasn't, weren't) happy with the treatment of the poor.

● Connect to the Writing Process: Editing
Making Subjects and Verbs Agree

Write each sentence, correcting the underlined verb. If the verb in the sentence is correct, write C.

11. *Hard Times* are my favorite book by Charles Dickens.

12. A major problem during Dickens's lifetime was pollution.

13. Why wasn't you finished with your book project?

14. Journalism was Dickens's occupation before he became a novelist.

15. Dickens are considered one of the best writers of the 1800s.

Communicate Your Ideas

APPLY TO WRITING

Book Review: *Subject and Verb Agreement*

Your school librarian is starting a literacy program with the local elementary school. She has asked you to write a review of a book for students in the fifth grade. Write a review of a book that was a favorite of yours when you were younger. Include a summary of the plot and what you liked and did not like about it. Be sure to make your review interesting enough for fifth graders. Check to make sure that subjects and verbs agree.

 **QuickCheck** Mixed Practice

Write the verbs that do not agree with their subjects. Then write the verbs correctly. If a sentence is correct, write C.

1. Has everyone throughout the world heard of the Olympic Games?

2. The people in Greece was the originators of these games in 776 B.C.

3. In those days every boy were trained in running, jumping, and wrestling.

4. The ideal for all Greeks was a sound mind in a healthy body.

5. The modern Olympic Games are patterned after those held in ancient Greece.

6. There is, however, many important differences.

7. The games in the original competition was always held in Olympia, Greece.

8. Each of the modern competitions are held in a different city of the world.

9. In the early days, only young men of Greek descent was able to participate in the games.

10. A modern change in the games are events for women.

11. Now female winners in an event receive the same honors as men.

12. In the ancient games, there was honors for cultural achievements.

CheckPoint

Making Subjects and Verbs Agree

Write the correct form of the verb in parentheses.

1. The number of solar houses (is, are) steadily increasing.
2. (Doesn't, Don't) the red cedar have blue berries?
3. The main feature of the auto show (is, are) new compact cars.
4. The tent and the sleeping bag (was, were) borrowed from the Robinsons.
5. Here (is, are) the wood for the bookcase.
6. Macaroni and cheese (is, are) my favorite dish.
7. None of the tires (was, were) in good shape.
8. One of those lifeguards (is, are) my cousin.
9. In the 1950s, twenty-five cents (was, were) the price of a gallon of gasoline.
10. Neither Carrie nor Pedro (is, are) willing to run for class office.
11. *Little Women* (was, were) written by Louisa May Alcott.
12. Five dollars (seems, seem) like a fair price for the lamp.
13. In the stream (was, were) two beautiful rainbow trout.
14. Many of our early television programs (was, were) produced live.
15. Each quarter of a football game (is, are) fifteen minutes of play.
16. The choir (has, have) been measured for their new robes.
17. Neither milk nor juice (was, were) needed from the store.
18. Most of the houses on our street (has, have) no garage.
19. Either daisies or roses (is, are) needed for the bouquet.
20. There (is, are) millions of licensed drivers in the United States.

Correcting Subject–Verb Agreement

Find and write the verbs that do not agree with their subject(s). Then write them correctly. If a sentence is correct, write C.

1. Don't Barry play shortstop anymore?
2. The tomato plants in the field was thriving.
3. There is approximately 100,000 species of butterflies.
4. Five hundred dollars was raised by the students for the victims of the flood.
5. Leroy, with the rest of the team, are departing at noon in front of the gym.
6. Hot dogs and beans are my first choice for dinner.
7. A number of two-family houses has been recently built in this city.
8. Neither Marty nor his friends have ever performed in public before.
9. Every roll and piece of bread were eaten.
10. None of the water in the battery was left.

Writing Sentences

Write five sentences that follow the directions below. Then underline each subject once and each verb twice.

1. Write a sentence in which the subject is a sum of money.
2. Write a sentence in which *social studies* is the subject.
3. Write a sentence with a compound subject linked with the conjunction *neither/nor.*
4. Write a sentence in which the subject is an indefinite pronoun.
5. Write a sentence in which the subject is a collective noun.

Language and *Self-Expression*

Chuck Jones is a cartoonist who has done animation for many well-known cartoon characters—including Bugs Bunny, Daffy Duck, Road Runner, and Wile E. Coyote. He has won three Academy Awards for his work, which has been exhibited around the world.

Think of a favorite cartoon character. What makes the character funny? What aspects of his or her (or its) personality appeal to you and why? Write a description of the character without writing the character's name. Describe the traits and actions that define the character. Make sure your subjects and verbs agree. Then read your description aloud to the class and have class members guess who your cartoon character is.

Prewriting Make a character-traits web for your character. Include circles that describe physical traits, quirks, words or phrases the character is known for, and other identifying details.

Drafting Use the details from your web to write your first draft. Try to create a mental image of your character without revealing directly who it is.

Revising Read the first two sentences of your draft to a classmate. If your partner can guess your character, rewrite the description to make it a little less obvious. Then have your partner read your description and give you feedback.

Editing Check your description for errors in spelling and punctuation. Also make sure your subjects and verbs agree.

Publishing Make a clean copy of your description. Then read it aloud to the class. Have your classmates try to guess the subject of your description.

Another Look

Agreement of Subjects and Verbs

A verb must agree in number with its subject. *(page L293)*
A singular subject takes a singular verb. *(page L294)*
A plural subject takes a plural verb. *(page L294)*
The first helping verb must agree in number with the subject. *(page L294)*
The agreement of a verb with its subject is not changed by any
   interrupting words. *(pages L296–L297)*

Common Agreement Problems

When compound subjects are joined by *or, nor, either/or,* or *neither/nor,*
   the verb agrees with the closer subject. *(page L301)*
When compound subjects are joined by *and* or *both/and,* the verb is plural.
   (page L302)
When compound subjects joined by *and* refer to only one person or
   thing, the verb is singular. *(page L302)*
When the words *every* or *each* come before a compound subject that is
   joined by *and*, the verb is singular. *(page L302)*

Indefinite Pronouns as Subjects

A verb must agree in number with an indefinite pronoun used as a
   subject. *(page L304)*

Subjects in Inverted Order

The subject and the verb of an inverted sentence must agree in number.
   (page L306)

Collective Nouns

Use a singular verb with a collective noun subject that is thought of as a
   unit. *(pages L310–L311)*
Use a plural verb with a collective noun subject that is thought of as a
   group of separate individuals. *(pages L310–L311)*

Words Expressing Amounts or Times

A subject that expresses an amount, measurement, weight, or time is
   usually singular and takes a singular verb. *(page L311)*
Use a singular verb when an amount tells *how much*. Use a plural verb
   when an amount tells *how many*. *(page L312)*
Use a singular verb with *the number of* and a plural verb with *a number of*.
   (page L312)

 **Posttest**

Directions

Read the passage and choose the word or group of words that belongs in each underlined space. Write the letter of the correct answer.

EXAMPLE

My brother __(1)__ all of his time on the computer.

1 A am spending
  B are spending
  C spends
  D have spent

ANSWER **1 C**

My brother Luke __(1)__ a computer genius. His whole third-grade class __(2)__ more about computers than I do. One day __(3)__ all the time they needed to set up a class Web page. A number of third-graders __(4)__ teaching the upper-grade students how to create Web pages! My brother, not I, __(5)__ the contest to create a Website for our town. My sister Kathy, who is in college, __(6)__ Luke's skill both admirable and annoying. Both she and her college roommate __(7)__ Luke all the time to ask for help. Neither Kathy nor I __(8)__ any idea how to do many of the things he can do. None of Luke's classmates __(9)__ to worry about finding a job later. As long as computers are around, they __(10)__ incredibly marketable skills!

1. **A** are
   B am
   C is
   D were

2. **A** knows
   B know
   C have known
   D were knowing

3. **A** be
   B was
   C were
   D have been

4. **A** am
   B is
   C are
   D has been

5. **A** is entering
   B am entering
   C are entering
   D were entering

6. **A** find
   B finds
   C have found
   D have been finding

7. **A** call
   B is calling
   C calls
   D has called

8. **A** have
   B has
   C have had
   D is having

9. **A** need
   B needs
   C have needed
   D was needing

10. **A** has
    B have
    C has had
    D is having

Using Adjectives and Adverbs

• •

Directions

Read the passage and choose the word or group of words that belongs in each underlined space. Write the letter of the correct answer.

EXAMPLE   Our baseball team will win the championship because it is the __(1)__ in the league.

           1 A good
              B better
              C more good
              D best

ANSWER   **1 D**

    My team, the Mighty Warriors, practices __(1)__ than the other teams. Our coach is a woman, and she is __(2)__ than most men coaches. You should hear her yell. It is the __(3)__ yell I have ever heard come out of a coach's mouth. We learn __(4)__ from her. Ray, our pitcher, throws __(5)__ person on our team. We don't need __(6)__ relief pitchers when he plays in a game. He also throws the __(7)__ curve ball I've ever seen. No one can __(8)__ hit Ray's curve. I play outfielder. Without bragging too much, I must say that I am a __(9)__ outfielder than my friend Jason. During the championships, we'll all play the __(10)__ teams in the country.

1. **A** harder
   B hard
   C hardest
   D more hard

2. **A** tough
   B more tough
   C most tough
   D tougher

3. **A** loud
   B louder
   C loudest
   D most loudest

4. **A** good
   B better
   C best
   D well

5. **A** better than any
   B better than any other
   C more better than other
   D more better than any other

6. **A** any
   B none
   C no
   D some

7. **A** good
   B better
   C best
   D gooder

8. **A** never
   B ever
   C always
   D not

9. **A** good
   B better
   C more better
   D best

10. **A** good
    B better
    C best
    D bestest

Wang Yani. *Little Monkeys and Mummy,* 1980.
Ink and pigment on paper, 15 by 21 inches.
©Wang Shiquiang.
Courtesy of Byron Preiss
Visual Publications, Inc.
New China Pictures

Describe   How many monkeys are there in the painting? Describe them in terms of their size and position.

Analyze   What are the monkeys doing? What do you think is the overall tone of the painting? How do the colors affect the tone?

Interpret   What do you think the artist wanted viewers to think about the monkeys?

Judge   Do you find the painting appealing? Why or why not?

At the end of this chapter, you will use the artwork to stimulate ideas for writing.

Comparison of Adjectives and Adverbs

When you go to a restaurant, the first thing you probably do is look at the menu. You then might say to yourself, "Beef would taste *good,* but some fish would taste *better."* Then, after looking further, you might make your selection by saying, "Chicken, however, would taste *best* tonight." While making your selection, you would have used the modifier *good* and both of its forms of comparison. The different forms of comparison will be reviewed in this chapter, as well as some of the problems with comparisons.

To show degrees of comparison, most modifiers have three forms: the positive, the comparative, and the superlative. These forms are used to show differences in degree or extent.

Most modifiers show degrees of comparison by changing form.

The **positive degree** is the basic form of an adjective or an adverb. It is used when no comparison is being made.

> George is a **strong** singer.
> We live in an **old** house.

The **comparative degree** is used when two people, things, or actions are being compared.

> George is a **stronger** singer than Kent.
> Our house is **older** than the one across the street.

The **superlative form** is used when more than two people, things, or actions are being compared.

> George is the **strongest** singer in the choir.
> The house next door is the **oldest** on the block.

At the top of the following page are some additional examples of the three degrees of comparison.

POSITIVE	That was a **nice** concert. (adjective)
	Teddy practices **hard.** (adverb)
COMPARATIVE	That concert was **nicer** than yesterday's.
	Teddy practices **harder** than Brian.
SUPERLATIVES	That was the **nicest** concert so far this spring.
	Teddy practices **hardest** of all.

You can learn more about how adjectives and adverbs are used in a sentence on pages L30–L40.

PRACTICE YOUR SKILLS

 Check Your Understanding
Determining Degrees of Comparison

 **Write the underlined modifier in each sentence. Then label its degree of comparison *P* for positive, *C* for comparative, or *S* for superlative.**

General Interest

1. This music is very <u>loud</u>.

2. Mozart's compositions are the <u>most difficult</u> pieces I have ever played.

3. Some people think Beethoven composed music <u>more slowly</u> than Mozart.

4. Which of the two pieces is <u>quieter</u>?

5. When the music started, everyone <u>quickly</u> stopped talking.

6. The musicians played the Mozart concerto <u>more quietly</u> than they did the Beethoven sonata.

7. That was the <u>highest</u> note I have ever heard.

8. Some musicians believe that Mozart's music is <u>more complex</u> than Beethoven's.

9. I like Mozart <u>better</u> than Beethoven.

10. This is the <u>most interesting</u> concert I have ever attended.

 Regular and Irregular Comparison

Most modifiers form the comparative and the superlative degrees regularly, but a few modifiers form their comparisons irregularly.

Regular Comparisons

Most modifiers follow one of three rules to form their comparisons. The rules are based on the number of syllables in a modifier.

Add *–er* to form the comparative degree and *–est* to form the superlative degree of one-syllable modifiers.

ONE-SYLLABLE MODIFIERS		
Positive	**Comparative**	**Superlative**
old	older	oldest
clean	cleaner	cleanest
soon	sooner	soonest

Most two-syllable words form their comparative and superlative degrees in the same way. Some two-syllable words, however, sound awkward when *–er* or *–est* is added. For these modifiers, *more* or *most* should be added instead.

Use *–er* or *more* to form the comparative degree and *–est* or *most* to form the superlative degree of two-syllable modifiers.

More and *most* are always used with adverbs that end in *–ly*.

TWO-SYLLABLE MODIFIERS		
Positive	**Comparative**	**Superlative**
easy	easier	easiest
fragrant	more fragrant	most fragrant
sweetly	more sweetly	most sweetly

Let your ear be your guide when deciding between *er/est* and *more/most* with two-syllable modifiers. If adding *–er* or *–est* makes a word difficult to pronounce, use *more* or *most* instead. It is obvious, for example, that you would never say "gracefuller" or "aimlesser."

Use *more* to form the comparative and *most* to form the superlative degree of modifiers with three or more syllables.

MODIFIERS WITH THREE OR MORE SYLLABLES		
Positive	Comparative	Superlative
considerate	more considerate	most considerate
quietly	more quietly	most quietly

Use *less* and *least* to form the negative comparisons of adjectives and adverbs.

NEGATIVE COMPARISONS		
considerate	less considerate	least considerate
quietly	less quietly	least quietly

Irregular Comparisons

The comparative and superlative degrees of a few modifiers are formed irregularly.

IRREGULAR MODIFIERS		
Positive	Comparative	Superlative
bad/badly/ill	worse	worst
good/well	better	best
little	less	least
many/much	more	most

Be sure that you do not add the regular comparison endings to the comparative and the superlative degrees of these irregular modifiers. For example, *worse* is the comparative form of *bad*. You should never use "worser."

PRACTICE YOUR SKILLS

Check Your Understanding
Forming the Comparison of Modifiers

Write each modifier. Then write its comparative and superlative forms.

1. low		**11.** eager	
2. good		**12.** beautiful	
3. rapidly		**13.** lean	
4. bad		**14.** little	
5. rough		**15.** different	
6. fast		**16.** thin	
7. calmly		**17.** tasty	
8. many		**18.** slowly	
9. clever		**19.** tough	
10. well		**20.** dramatic	

Check Your Understanding
Using the Correct Form of Comparison

Contemporary Life **Write the correct form of the modifier in parentheses.**

1. Is Janelle the (faster, fastest) student on the basketball team?

2. Of the two sports, Janelle and I enjoy basketball (more, most).

3. Who runs the basketball court (faster, fastest), Mavis or Janet?

4. Of the two coaches, Ms. Thompson is the (friendlier, friendliest).

5. A lay-up is my (less, least) favorite shot.

6. Between basketball and football, I think basketball is the (better, best) sport.

7. Which team is the (more, most) prepared, the home team or the visitors?

8. Of the three players, who gets the (more, most) time on the court?

9. Anne made the (higher, highest) number of shots of all the players.

10. Was the (tougher, toughest) team the Bulls or the Rockets?

11. Which is (taller, tallest)—the boys' team or the girls' team?

12. Which of the two players on that team did you like (better, best)?

13. Practicing on another team's court is (worse, worst) than practicing on the home court.

14. That is absolutely the (more, most) aggressive team I have seen all year.

15. Which do you think is (more, most) interesting—girls' basketball or boys' basketball?

Connect to the Writing Process: Drafting
Writing Sentences with Forms of Comparison

Write each sentence according to the directions given.

16. Use the positive form of *calmly*.

17. Use the comparative form of *bad*.

18. Use the superlative form of *little*.

19. Use the comparative form of *different*.

20. Use the superlative form of *clever*.

21. Use the comparative form of *rapidly*.

22. Use the superlative form of *many*.

Using the Correct Form of Comparison

Write each incorrectly formed modifier and then write it correctly. If all modifiers within a sentence are correct, write C.

23. Jennifer is the taller person on the entire team this year.

24. The team is having a best year.

25. The girls have made rebounds quicklier than their opponents.

26. Last week they played the worse team in the district and won.

27. The girls will have to shoot most accurately in tonight's game than they did last week.

28. Don't you think they play gooder when they compete on their home court?

29. The boys' team is playing more games than the girls' team this semester.

30. That was the beautifulest shot I've ever seen in a basketball game.

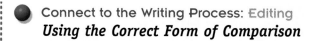

Communicate Your Ideas

APPLY TO WRITING

E-mail: *Forms of Comparison*

Your cousin is driving in to watch your basketball team play the championship game. She has never met the other players on the team. Since you would like her to know a little bit about your friends on the team, you decide to E-mail her.

Write her an E-mail message that describes your three best friends on the team, using comparative and superlative forms of adjectives and adverbs to describe the three players' height, speed, and style of play.

General
Interest **Write the correct form of the modifier in parentheses.**

1. I enjoy ancient history (more, most) than modern history.

2. In my opinion, the ancient Greeks were (smarter, smartest) than the Romans.

3. However, the Romans conquered (more, most) territory.

4. At the time, the Romans had the (better, best) organized army.

5. They built towns (more, most) rapidly than other civilizations at the time.

6. They also had some of the (higher, highest) taxes in the ancient world.

7. Some people feel that the ancient Greeks were (more, most) civilized than the Romans.

8. I like Greek architecture (better, best) than I like Roman architecture.

9. Which is (older, oldest), the Parthenon or the Coliseum?

10. Some scholars think that the Roman circus was the (worse, worst) form of entertainment the world has ever known.

11. The ancient Greeks gave us some of the (more, most) dramatic literature of all times.

12. I like *The Odyssey* (better, best) than *The Iliad*.

13. What is your (less, least) favorite aspect of ancient history?

14. Ancient Greek ruins are usually (older, oldest) than Roman ruins.

15. Some people think that the Romans were (tougher, toughest) than the Greeks.

Problems with Comparisons

When you compare people or things in your writing, watch out for the following special comparison problems.

Double Comparisons

Use only one method of forming the comparative or superlative form of a modifier. Never use both at the same time.

Do not use both *–er* and *more* to form the comparative degree, or both *–est* and *most* to form the superlative degree.

DOUBLE COMPARISON	I've never seen a **more funnier** postcard.
CORRECT	I've never seen a **funnier** postcard.
DOUBLE COMPARISON	Which is the **most highest** mountain?
CORRECT	Which is the **highest** mountain?

Illogical Comparisons

When you compare unrelated things, the comparison is illogical.

Compare only items of a similar kind.

ILLOGICAL COMPARISON	This **camper** is better than the **Hamiltons.** (A camper is being compared with people.)
LOGICAL COMPARISON	This **camper** is better than the **Hamiltons' camper.** (Now the camper is being compared with another camper.)

ILLOGICAL COMPARISON	The boys' **room** in the hotel is larger than the **girls.**
	(A room is being compared to girls.)
LOGICAL COMPARISON	The boys' **room** in the hotel is bigger than the girls' **room.**
	(Now two rooms are being compared.)

You can learn more about the use of an apostrophe with possessive nouns on pages L485–L486.

Other and *Else* in Comparisons

When a comparison is made, the similarities or differences between people or things are pointed out. Sometimes, however, a comparison is incorrectly made. This happens when people or things are compared with themselves as well as with other people or things. Using *other* or *else* will help you avoid this problem.

Add *other* or *else* when comparing a member of a group to the rest of the group.

INCORRECT	That jet is faster than any plane.
	(Since the jet is an airplane, it is incorrectly being compared with itself.)
CORRECT	That jet is faster than any **other** plane.
	(When the word *other* is added, the jet is being compared only with other planes.)
INCORRECT	Ed wins more points than anyone on the team.
	(Since Ed is on the team, he is being incorrectly compared with himself.)
CORRECT	Ed wins more points than anyone **else** on the team.
	(When the word *else* is added, Ed is being compared only with other members of the team.)

Problems with Modifiers

A few problems that cause confusion in writing or speaking may arise when you use modifiers.

Adjective or Adverb?

Adjectives and adverbs are both modifiers because they describe other words. As you probably remember, an adjective describes a noun or pronoun. Also, an adjective usually comes before the noun or pronoun it describes, or it follows a linking verb. Adjectives are easy to recognize because they answer the following questions:

WHICH ONE?	**This** bus will leave tomorrow.
WHAT KIND?	The suitcases are **new.**
HOW MANY?	**Ten** cameras sat on the window.
HOW MUCH?	The trip sounds **great.**

Remember that some verbs—such as *feel, smell,* and *taste*—can be either linking verbs or action verbs. When these verbs are used as linking verbs, they are often followed by an adjective.

LINKING VERB	The fries at the restaurant **smell** delicious.
	(*Smell* links *delicious* and *fries*—delicious fries.)
ACTION VERB	We **smell** the food from the bus.
	(*Food* is the direct object of *smell*. We smell what? food)

You can find lists of linking verbs on page L26.

Adverbs describe verbs, adjectives, and other adverbs. Although adverbs can be placed almost anywhere in a sentence, you can find them by asking the questions at the top of the next page.

WHERE?	Jenny looked **everywhere** for her new dance shoes.
WHEN?	David **always** sings when he is driving his car.
HOW?	Please move to the hall **quietly.**
TO WHAT EXTENT?	Everyone agrees that this summer has been **very** hot.
	Sue reads magazines **quite often.**

Because so many adverbs end in *–ly,* they are usually easy to recognize. Remember, however, that a few adjectives also end in *–ly.*

ADVERB	Even during summer vacations Dad rises **early.**
	(*Early* tells when he rises.)
ADJECTIVE	On Monday, Dad had an **early** meeting about our trip.
	(*Early* tells what kind of meeting it is.)

A few words—such as *first, hard, high, late,* and *long*—are the same whether they are used as adjectives or adverbs.

ADVERB	Tim works **hard** every day for the money for his trip.
	(*Hard* tells how he works.)
ADJECTIVE	He finished the **hard** assignment in time to mow Mr. Taylor's lawn.
	(*Hard* tells what kind of assignment it was.)

Special Problems

Some adjectives and adverbs present special problems.

Good or *Well?*

Good is always used as an adjective. *Well* is usually used as an adverb. However, when *well* means "in good health" or "attractive," it is an adjective.

ADJECTIVE	Your trip was very **good.**
ADVERB	The car ran **well.**
ADJECTIVE	I didn't feel **well,** so I had to miss the trip to Washington.
	(in good health)
ADJECTIVE	The exam was a **good** test of our reading and writing skills.
ADVERB	Kari did **well** on it.
ADJECTIVE	Jonathan didn't look **well** yesterday afternoon.
	(in good health)

Bad or *Badly?*

Bad is an adjective and often follows a linking verb. *Badly* is used as an adverb.

ADJECTIVE	The hamburger tasted **bad.**
ADVERB	He washed the car **badly.**

CONNECT TO SPEAKING AND WRITING

In casual conversation it is acceptable to use *bad* or *badly* after the verb *feel.* In writing, however, use *bad* as an adjective and *badly* as an adverb.

IN CONVERSATION	I feel **bad** about the argument.
	or
	I feel **badly** about the argument.
IN WRITING	I feel **bad** about the argument.

Double Negatives

The following words are all considered to be negatives.

COMMON NEGATIVES	
but (meaning "only")	none
hardly	not (and its contraction *n't*)
never	nothing
no	only
nobody	scarcely

Avoid using a double negative.

A double negative often cancels itself out, leaving you with a positive statement. For example, if you say, "We didn't meet nobody on the trail," you are actually saying, "We did meet somebody on the trail."

DOUBLE NEGATIVE	Dad says he does**n't** need **no** more mats for his car.
CORRECT	Dad says he does**n't** need any more mats for his car.
DOUBLE NEGATIVE	Did you know there is**n't hardly** any air in the tire?
CORRECT	Did you know there is **hardly** any air in the tire?
DOUBLE NEGATIVE	We did**n't** find **nothing** in the glove box.
CORRECT	We did**n't** find anything in the glove box.
CORRECT	We found **nothing** in the glove box.

CONNECT TO WRITER'S CRAFT

Occasionally, a writer may use double negatives to depict a character. This occurs frequently in dialogue. Notice in the excerpt at the top of the next page how Mark Twain uses double negatives in the conversation of a character.

He got up and looked distressed, and fumbled his hat, and says: "I'm sorry, and I warn't expecting it. They told me to. They all told me to. They all said kiss her; and said she'll like it. They all said it—every one of them. But I'm sorry ma'm, and I won't do it no more— I won't, honest."

—*Mark Twain*, The Adventures of Huckleberry Finn

PRACTICE YOUR SKILLS

● Check Your Understanding
Identifying the Correct Form of Modifiers

Contemporary Life **Write the correct form of the adjective or adverb in parentheses.**

1. Susan has been on more vacations than (anyone, anyone else) in our class.

2. These suitcases are bigger than the (Smiths, Smiths' suitcases).

3. Nancy said that she hoped that this trip would be more (enjoyable, enjoyabler) than last year's trip.

4. When I read in the car, I don't feel very (good, well).

5. I get so sleepy after lunch I (can, can't) hardly keep my eyes open.

6. My dog behaves (bad, badly) when I go away on long trips.

7. We (could, couldn't) hardly stand the heat in Death Valley.

8. From where we sat on the bus, we could see everything quite (good, well).

9. Our bus was more comfortable than (any, any other) bus.

10. A warm shower feels (wonderful, wonderfully) after a long day of travel.

Using Modifiers Correctly

Rewrite the sentences, correcting the forms of modifiers. If a sentence is correct, write C.

11. Mr. Harris remained calmer than anyone when we missed our bus.

12. Do you think the trip went good?

13. We never got no sleep during the trip.

14. The drive to Death Valley was the longest trip I have ever taken.

15. The boys' bus was noisier than the girls'.

Communicate Your Ideas

APPLY TO WRITING

Postcard: *Adjectives and Adverbs*

During your class trip, you decide to send a postcard like this one to your parents so that they can see the place you have been visiting. Write them a note, describing what you have been doing and what the place looks like. Be sure to use modifiers properly.

Geography
Topic

Rewrite the following sentences, correcting each mistake in the use of modifiers. If a sentence is correct, write C.

1. The desert is certainly more drier than the rain forest.

2. Which is farther north—the Sahara Desert or the Amazon Rain Forest?

3. The Amazon River is the longest river in the continent of South America.

4. The caravan hadn't scarcely begun when the windstorm started.

5. During desert windstorms, the sand blows rapid and with great force.

6. Covering an area the size of the United States, the Sahara is the world's largest desert.

7. The camel is meaner than any animal in the desert.

8. Whatever the rain forest hides, it hides good because it is so thick.

9. Of all the places on earth, the Amazon Rain Forest is the most interesting.

10. Some scientists think the rain forest is the most richest place on earth.

11. The fire in the Amazon was worse than the one in Mexico.

12. Towering high in the sky, the ancient trees were some of the tallest in the world.

13. More traders have crossed the Sahara Desert than any desert.

14. The dates from the oasis tasted good, but I didn't feel good after I ate them.

15. Of those three desert stories, I think *Lawrence of Arabia* is the better.

Using Adjectives and Adverbs Correctly

Write the following sentences, correcting each mistake. If a sentence is correct, write C.

1. Niagara Falls has a steadier flow of water than any waterfall in the world.
2. Who is the best diver, Jessie or Mark?
3. Tara learned the new signals easy.
4. Of all the cross-country runners, Phyllis wins races most consistently.
5. We hadn't but one hour to tour the assembly plant.
6. Our house isn't as large as the McDonalds.
7. I like Isaac Asimov's science fiction novels better than any books.
8. The fans groaned as Andrew, who usually plays good, fumbled the ball.
9. The youngest of the two Fletcher girls is going to college in the fall.
10. By the time Tim and I got to Kate's house, there wasn't no food left.
11. The grass is always greener on the other side of the fence.
12. I received an answer to my letter more quickly than I had expected.
13. One of the most busiest spots in the world is the intersection of State and Madison in downtown Chicago.
14. Manuel couldn't decide which of the six horses was the tamest.
15. The United States has more telephones than any country in the world.

Choosing Adjectives and Adverbs

Choose the word or words in parentheses that correctly completes each sentence.

1. That house is the (older, oldest) one on the block.
2. Nobody (has, hasn't) lived there for at least ten years.
3. Lanie thinks it looks (scary, scarier) than (any, any other) haunted house in a movie.
4. She got a (good, well) scare there last week.
5. She was walking past the house in the (most fast, fastest) pace she could manage.
6. Suddenly, a voice rang out, scaring her (bad, badly).
7. She looked to see to whom the voice was calling, but there was (nobody, nobody else) around.
8. She was so scared she (could, couldn't) scarcely breathe.
9. She ran away (quicklier, more quickly) than she could ever remember running before.
10. She took it pretty (good, well) when she learned that a new family had just moved into the house.

Writing Sentences

Write ten sentences that follow the directions below.

1. Include the comparative form of *little*.
2. Include the superlative form of *much*.
3. Compare one animal to another.
4. Compare one chore to another.
5. Compare one age to all others.
6. Include the comparative form of *rapidly*.
7. Include the superlative form of *bad*.
8. Include the negative comparative of *important*.
9. Include the negative superlative of *precisely*.
10. Include the comparative form of *well*.

Language and *Self-Expression*

Wang Yani began painting at the age of three and painted this work when she was just five. Her early paintings focused on animal groups, while her later work is more likely to show people and landscapes.

Little Monkeys and Mummy shows a family group of monkeys. There are many ways to compare and contrast the members of a family—you can do it with your own family. Think of ways you and your family members are both similar and different. Then write a brief essay comparing and contrasting two members of your family. Correctly use modifiers in your comparisons.

Prewriting You may want to make a Venn diagram. Each circle of the diagram can describe one family member. Where the two circles intersect, write traits that both family members share. Where they do not intersect, write traits that individual members have.

Drafting Use your Venn diagram to write the first draft of your essay. Focus on the traits and habits both family members share. Then describe how each member is also an individual.

Revising Reread your essay carefully. Check to see that you have focused on family members' shared and individual traits.

Editing Check your draft for errors in spelling and punctuation. Be sure you have added *–er* or *more* to form comparatives and *–est* or *most* to form superlatives.

Publishing Write a final draft of your essay. Show your writing to family members and see if they agree with your comparisons and contrasts.

Another Look

Most modifiers show **degrees of comparison** by changing form.

Comparison of Adjectives and Adverbs

The **positive degree** is used when no comparison is being made. *(page L327)*

The **comparative degree** is used when two people, things, or actions are being compared. *(page L327)*

The **superlative form** is used when more than two people, things, or actions are being compared. *(page L327)*

Regular and Irregular Comparisons

Add *–er* to form the comparative degree and *–est* to form the superlative degree of one-syllable modifiers. *(page L329)*

Use *–er* or *more* to form the comparative degree and *–est* or *most* to form the superlative degree of two-syllable modifiers. *(page L329)*

Use *more* to form the comparative degree and *most* to form the superlative degree of modifiers with three or more syllables. *(page L330)*

Use *less* and *least* to form the negative comparisons of adjectives and adverbs. *(page L330)*

The comparative and superlative forms of some modifiers are irregular. *(pages L330–L331)*

Problems with Comparisons

Do not use both *–er* and *more* to form the comparative degree, or both *-est* and *most* to form the superlative degree. *(page L335)*

Compare only items of a similar kind. *(pages L335–L336)*

Add *other* or *else* when comparing a member of a group to the rest of the group. *(page L336)*

Problems with Modifiers

Good is always used as an adjective. *Well* is usually used as an adverb; but when *well* means "in good health" or "attractive," it is an adjective. *(page L339)*

Bad is an adjective and often follows a linking verb. *Badly* is used as an adverb. *(page L339)*

Avoid using a **double negative.** *(page L340)*

 **Posttest**

Directions

Read the passage and choose the word or group of words that belongs in each underlined space. Write the letter of the correct answer.

EXAMPLE   A chinchilla is __(1)__ than a mouse.

     1 A large
        B more large
        C larger
        D largest

ANSWER   **1 C**

Chinchillas have more hair coming from each hair follicle than __(1)__ animal in the world. Chinchillas are __(2)__ than most other rodents. They are some of the __(3)__ rock climbers in the world. However, they also run on flat ground very __(4)__. The Andes, the chinchillas' home, is one of the __(5)__ mountain chains in the world. Chinchillas live __(6)__ in the Andes Mountains than almost any other animal. A mountain viscacha looks like the chinchilla but is __(7)__. Both of these animals climb __(8)__ on rocks. The Andean mountain cat is very __(9)__ at catching both chinchillas and viscachas. Some people believe that chinchilla fur is the __(10)__ fur in the world.

1	**A**	any	**6**	**A**	high
	B	any other		**B**	higher
	C	no		**C**	more high
	D	none		**D**	highest
2	**A**	quick	**7**	**A**	big
	B	more quick		**B**	more big
	C	quicker		**C**	bigger
	D	quickest		**D**	biggest
3	**A**	good	**8**	**A**	good
	B	better		**B**	better
	C	best		**C**	best
	D	well		**D**	well
4	**A**	good	**9**	**A**	good
	B	better		**B**	better
	C	best		**C**	best
	D	well		**D**	well
5	**A**	high	**10**	**A**	beautiful
	B	higher		**B**	more beautiful
	C	highest		**C**	most beautiful
	D	most high		**D**	beautifulest

A Writer's Glossary of Usage

The four preceding chapters in this book covered a number of usage elements. You learned how to use verbs and pronouns correctly, how to make the subject and verb agree, and how to form comparisons with adjectives and adverbs. A Writer's Glossary of Usage presents some other areas you might have difficulty with.

Within this glossary you will notice references to standard English and nonstandard English. **Standard English,** of course, refers to the rules and conventions of usage that are accepted and most widely used by English-speaking people throughout the world. On the other hand, **nonstandard English** has many variations because it is influenced by regional differences and dialects and by current slang. The term *nonstandard* does not mean that the language is wrong, but rather that it is inappropriate in certain situations. An example of such a situation would be a job interview. At a job interview or for a writing assignment, you should use standard English because nonstandard English lacks uniformity.

Two other references in this glossary are to formal and informal English. **Formal English** is used for written work because it follows the conventional rules of grammar, usage, mechanics, and spelling. Formal English is generally used in the workplace and in school. **Informal English** also follows the conventions of standard English, but informal English often includes words and phrases that might seem out of place in formal writing. Examples of informal English can generally be found in fiction, news articles, and magazines.

Notice that the items in this glossary have been arranged alphabetically so that you can use this reference easily.

a, an Use *a* before words beginning with consonant sounds and *an* before words beginning with vowel sounds. Always keep in mind that this rule applies to sounds, not letters. For example, *an hourglass* is correct because the *h* is silent.

> Today is **a** humid day.
> Within **an** hour, it will probably rain.

accept, except *Accept* is a verb that means "to receive with consent." *Except* is usually a preposition that means "but" or "other than."

> Everyone **accepted** the award **except** Tony.

advice, advise *Advice* is a noun that means "a recommendation." *Advise* is a verb that means "to recommend."

> Your **advice** saved me time and money.
> I hope you will **advise** me more often.

CONNECT TO SPEAKING AND WRITING

Note that *advice* and *advise* are not pronounced alike. *Advice* rhymes with *price; advise* rhymes with *prize.*

affect, effect *Affect* is a verb that means "to influence." *Effect* is usually a noun that means "a result" or "an influence." As a verb, *effect* means "to accomplish" or "to produce."

> The devastating **effects** of the hurricane **affected** the lives of everyone in the small coastal town.
> (*effects,* noun)
>
> As a result, the county council **effected** a change in the area's hurricane warning system.
> (*effected,* verb)

ain't This contraction is nonstandard English. Avoid using it in your writing.

> NONSTANDARD   That **ain't** my notebook.
> STANDARD   That **isn't** my notebook.

all ready, already *All ready* means "completely ready." *Already* means "previously."

> The actors behind the curtain were **all ready** for the second curtain call.

> They had **already** made the first one.

all together, altogether *All together* means "in a group." *Altogether* means "wholly" or "thoroughly."

> Is the camping equipment **all together** in the garage?

> I believe the camping trip to Yosemite National Park will be **altogether** successful.

a lot These two words are often written incorrectly as one. There is no such word as *alot*. *A lot,* even when written as two words, should be avoided in formal writing.

> INFORMAL   I like washing dishes **a lot.**
> FORMAL   I like washing dishes **very much.**

CONNECT TO SPEAKING AND WRITING

Do not confuse *a lot* with *allot,* which is a verb that means "to distribute by shares."

Were the chores **allotted** evenly?

among, between *Among* is used when referring to three or more people or things. *Between* is usually used when referring to two people or things. Both these words are prepositions.

> I divided my lunch **among** three of my friends.
> Please keep this information just **between** you and me.

amount, number *Amount* refers to a singular word. *Number* refers to a plural word.

> A large **number** of town merchants contributed a substantial **amount** of money to the scholarship fund.

anymore Do not use *anymore* for *now* or *nowadays. Anymore* is usually used in a negative statement.

NONSTANDARD	Most automobile manufacturers are interested in fuel efficiency **anymore.**
STANDARD	Most automobile manufacturers are interested in fuel efficiency **nowadays.**
STANDARD	Some manufacturers don't offer luxury cars **anymore.**

anywhere, everywhere, nowhere, somewhere Do not add *–s* to any of these words.

NONSTANDARD	Melissa said she can't go **anywheres** tonight.
STANDARD	Melissa said she can't go **anywhere** tonight.

as far as This expression is sometimes confused with "all the farther," which is nonstandard English.

NONSTANDARD	This is **all the farther** the new garden hose will go.
STANDARD	This is **as far as** the new garden hose will go.

at Do not use *at* after *where.*

NONSTANDARD	Do you know **where** he's **at?**
STANDARD	Do you know **where** he is?

awhile, a while *Awhile* is an adverb that stands alone and means "for a short period of time." *A while* is an expression made up of an article and a noun. It is used mainly after the preposition *for.*

After watching TV **awhile,** I fell asleep.

Later I complained for **a while** because I missed the show's ending.

PRACTICE YOUR SKILLS

● Check Your Understanding
Finding the Correct Word

Contemporary Life | **Write the word in parentheses that correctly completes each sentence.**

1. Plans for homecoming had (all ready, already) started.

2. (Anymore, Nowadays) homecoming dances offer students an opportunity to socialize in a formal setting.

3. The members of the homecoming committee had to decide (among, between) two possible themes.

4. (Accept, Except) for two members, the committee agreed on a "Tropical Nights" theme.

5. The school sponsor suggested that the students try to reach (a, an) unanimous decision.

6. The committee members debated the pros and cons for (a while, awhile).

7. A large (amount, number) of students bought tickets.

8. The students realized that the sponsor's (advice, advise) had been helpful.

9. (All together, Altogether) they eagerly joined in to decorate the ballroom on Saturday morning.

10. Within (a, an) hour the plain ballroom was transformed into a tropical paradise.

● Connect to the Writing Process: Revising
Recognizing Correct Usage

Rewrite the following paragraph, changing the words that are used incorrectly.

The final affect of the decorating was enchanting. That evening a lot of the students were visibly affected by the beautiful setting. Everywheres they looked, the stars twinkled from the ceiling all the farther the eye could see.

A large number of palm trees seemed to sway between the dancers, creating an tropical island illusion. A rustic straw hut was the stage where the musicians entertained at. When the evening ended, the committee members exchanged all together satisfied looks among themselves.

bad, badly *Bad* is an adjective and often follows a linking verb. *Badly* is used as an adverb.

NONSTANDARD	Henry feels **badly** today. (linking verb)
STANDARD	Henry feels **bad** today. (linking verb)
STANDARD	He hung the wallpaper **badly.** (action verb)

You can learn more about using adjectives and adverbs on pages L337–L339.

because Do not use *because* after the *reason*. Use one or the other in a sentence.

NONSTANDARD	The **reason** he left is **because** he had an important appointment this afternoon.
STANDARD	He left **because** he had an important appointment this afternoon.
STANDARD	The **reason** he left is **that** he had an important appointment this afternoon.

being as, being that These expressions should be replaced with *because* or *since*.

NONSTANDARD	**Being that** the air was cold, we went into the house.
STANDARD	**Because** the air was cold, we went into the house.

beside, besides *Beside* is always a preposition that means "by the side of." As a preposition, *besides* means "in addition to." As an adverb, *besides* means "also" or "moreover."

> Come sit **beside** me at the meeting. (by the side of)
>
> **Besides** the students, the faculty will also participate in the paper drive. (in addition to)
>
> They gave instructions and organized teams **besides.** (also)

both Never use *the* before *both*.

> NONSTANDARD   **The both** of them went to the concert.
> STANDARD   **Both** of them went to the concert.

bring, take *Bring* indicates motion toward the speaker. *Take* indicates motion away from the speaker.

> Please **bring** me a trash can liner.
> **Take** the trash out also.

can, may *Can* expresses ability. *May* expresses possibility or permission.

> Tammy **can** drive you to the airport. (ability)
>
> **May** I ride with you? (permission)

can't help but Use a gerund instead of *but*.

> NONSTANDARD   I **can't help but** miss them.
> STANDARD   I **can't help missing** them.

different from Use this form instead of *different than*.

> NONSTANDARD   Her pea soup tastes **different than** yours.
> STANDARD   Her pea soup tastes **different from** yours.

doesn't, don't *Doesn't* is singular and should be used only with singular nouns and the pronouns *he, she,* and *it. Don't* is plural and should be used with plural nouns and all other personal pronouns.

| NONSTANDARD | Dylan **don't** come here anymore. |
| STANDARD | Dylan **doesn't** come here anymore. |

| NONSTANDARD | Geometry **don't** come easily to me. |
| STANDARD | Geometry **doesn't** come easily to me. |

double negative Words such as *hardly, never, no,* and *nobody* are considered negatives. Do not use two negatives to express one negative meaning.

NONSTANDARD	I did**n't hardly** know what to say.
STANDARD	I did**n't** know what to say.
STANDARD	I **hardly** knew what to say.

You can learn more about double negatives on page L340.

emigrate, immigrate These words are both verbs. *Emigrate* means "to leave a country to settle elsewhere." *Immigrate* means "to enter a foreign country to live there." One emigrates *from* a country and immigrates *to* another country. *Emigrant* and *immigrant* are the noun forms.

> From 1892 to 1954, millions of people **emigrated** from a variety of countries and **immigrated** to the United States by way of Ellis Island.

etc. *Etc.* is an abbreviation for the Latin phrase *et cetera,* which means "and other things." Never use the word *and* with *etc.* If you do, what you are really saying is "and and other things." It is best, however, not to use this abbreviation at all in formal writing.

| INFORMAL | Remember to pack tents, sleeping bags, **etc.** |
| FORMAL | Remember to pack tents, sleeping bags, **and other necessities.** |

farther, further *Farther* refers to distance. *Further* means "additional" or "to a greater degree or extent."

> How much **farther** do we have to go before we get there?
> **Further** details will not be known until later.

fewer, less *Fewer* is plural and refers to things that can be counted. *Less* is singular and refers to quantities and qualities that cannot be counted.

> **Fewer** dollars were spent on education this year.
> There will be **less** equipment for the schools.

PRACTICE YOUR SKILLS

● Check Your Understanding
Finding the Correct Word

Speech Topic **Write the word in parentheses that correctly completes each sentence.**

1. A person who (doesn't, don't) know how to write and deliver a speech is lacking important skills.

2. Delivering a speech is (different from, different than) carrying on a conversation.

3. Although (both, the both) involve using words, delivering a speech is usually more formal.

4. (Don't ever, Don't never) give a speech before you consider your audience.

5. (Beside, Besides) giving a person confidence, the art of speaking serves useful purposes.

6. Types of speeches include reports, lectures, sermons, (and many others, etc.).

7. Maintaining eye contact with the audience (can, may) have a positive effect.

8. (Fewer, less) references to notes make a speech more effective.

9. A speech delivered (bad, badly) in practice needs more rehearsal time.

10. (Farther, Further) practice in front of a mirror should produce better results.

Writing Negatives Correctly

Rewrite each sentence in two different ways to eliminate the double negative construction.

11. Before entering a speech class, Chris hardly never spoke in front of an audience.

12. He didn't know nothing about speech preparation.

13. He hadn't no idea about the importance of visual aids.

14. Nobody hadn't taken the time to train him.

15. He wouldn't take no part in verbal presentations.

Communicate Your Ideas

APPLY TO WRITING

Persuasive Paragraph: *Repetition*

When a writer wishes to persuade an audience, one device often used is repetition of key words or phrases to create a certain tempo and to emphasize a point or theme. In this excerpt from "I Have a Dream," Martin Luther King, Jr., speaks about his hope for brotherhood among all races. Read the excerpt and then follow the instructions below.

> This is our hope. This is the faith that I go back to the South with. With this faith we will be able to hew out of the mountain of despair a stone of hope. With this faith we will be able to transform the jangling discords of our nation into a beautiful symphony of brotherhood. With this faith we will be able to work together, to pray together, to struggle together, to go to jail together, to stand up for freedom together, knowing that we will be free one day.
>
> *—Martin Luther King, Jr.,* "I Have a Dream"

- Identify the use of repetitive words and phrases. How do they help the author make his point?

- Now imagine you have been chosen to persuade lawmakers to lower or raise the driving age from the present one. Decide which viewpoint to endorse.
- Write a paragraph to convince the lawmakers to change the law. Include at least four of the correct forms of the following words, making sure you use the words more than once to emphasize your point or theme: *accept/except; advice/advise; affect/effect; can/may; fewer/less.*

good, well *Good* is an adjective and often follows a linking verb. *Well* is an adverb and often follows an action verb. However, when *well* means "in good health" or "attractive," it is used as an adjective.

> The recital was very **good.** (adjective)
>
> Heidi dances quite **well.** (adverb)
>
> She didn't feel **well** after the performance. (adjective)

CONNECT TO WRITER'S CRAFT

W riters often use mnemonic devices, such as a rhyme, to help determine proper word usage.

The mirror is **good** to tell
When I look and feel **well.**

You can learn more about using adjectives and adverbs on pages L337–L339.

have, of Never substitute *of* for the verb *have.* When speaking, many people make a contraction of *have.* For example, someone might say, "We should've gone." Because *'ve* sounds like *of, of* is often mistakenly substituted for *have* in writing.

> NONSTANDARD   We **couldn't of** known that at the time.
> STANDARD   We **couldn't have** known that at the time.

hear, here *Hear* is a verb that means "to perceive by listening." *Here* is an adverb that means "in this place."

> We can **hear** the music if we stand **here** on the lawn.

hole, whole A *hole* is an opening. *Whole* means "complete."

> Has this **hole** in the wall been here the **whole** time?

imply, infer Both these words are verbs. *Imply* means "to suggest" or "to hint." *Infer* means "to draw a conclusion by reasoning or evidence." A speaker *implies;* a listener *infers. Implication* and *inference* are the noun forms.

> Kent **implied** that he agreed with us.
> We **inferred** from Kent's remarks that he agreed with us.

in, into Use *into* when you want to express motion from one place to another.

> After going **into** the stadium, we sat **in** our seats.

its, it's *Its* is a possessive pronoun and means "belonging to it." *It's* is a contraction for *it is.*

> The committee will share **its** research when **it's** appropriate.

kind of, sort of Never substitute these expressions for *rather* or *somewhat.*

> NONSTANDARD   Your sister is **kind of** smart.
> STANDARD   Your sister is **rather** smart.
>
> NONSTANDARD   I feel **sort of** proud of my sister.
> STANDARD   I feel **somewhat** proud of my sister.

knew, new *Knew,* the past tense of the verb *know,* means "was acquainted with." *New* is an adjective that means "recently made" or "just found."

> From the beginning he **knew** which of the **new** bicycles he wanted for his birthday.

learn, teach Both these words are verbs. *Learn* means "to gain knowledge." *Teach* means "to instruct."

> NONSTANDARD   Leonard **learned** me how to speak German.
> STANDARD   Leonard **taught** me how to speak German.
> STANDARD   I have **learned** to speak German.

leave, let Both these words are verbs. *Leave* means "to depart" or "to go away from." *Let* means "to allow" or "to permit."

NONSTANDARD	**Leave** me help you with the dishes.
STANDARD	**Let** me help you with the dishes.
STANDARD	I can help until we **leave** for the airport.

lie, lay *Lie* means "to rest or recline." *Lie* is never followed by a direct object. Its principal parts are *lie, lying, lay,* and *lain. Lay* means "to put or set (something) down." *Lay* is usually followed by a direct object. Its principal parts are *lay, laying, laid,* and *laid.*

LIE	Please let me **lie** down for about an hour.
	The children are **lying** on the floor, watching television.
	I **lay** in bed for an extra hour yesterday morning.
	How long have I **lain** here on the couch?
LAY	Please **lay** the magazine on the coffee table.
	I'm **laying** the rest of the mail on the counter.
	Who **laid** the box on the wet floor?
	Have you **laid** the bills on my desk?

You can learn more about using the verbs lie *and* lay *on pages L209–L210.*

like, as *Like* is a preposition that introduces a prepositional phrase. *As* is usually a subordinating conjunction that introduces an adverb clause. In informal usage *like* is sometimes used as a conjunction. In formal usage avoid using *like* as a conjunction.

FORMAL	I came to help just **as** you asked. (clause)
FORMAL	Do you want the curtains hung **like** this? (prepositional phrase)

loose, lose *Loose* is usually an adjective that means "not tight." *Lose* is a verb that means "to misplace" or "not to have any longer."

Sew on that **loose** button, or you will **lose** it.

PRACTICE YOUR SKILLS

● Check Your Understanding
Finding the Correct Word

> General Interest **Write the word in parentheses that correctly completes each sentence.**

1. Have you ever thought about going (in, into) the field of court reporting?

2. (Its, It's) a challenging and interesting profession.

3. One of the things court reporters must (learn, teach) is the protocol for the courtroom.

4. They also must know how to listen (good, well).

5. Court reporters have a chance to (hear, here) a variety of testimony during trials.

6. Focusing on the testimony is essential to avoid (loosing, losing) concentration.

7. Remaining quiet and impartial during the (hole, whole) proceeding is also essential.

8. Disapproving expressions during testimony could (imply, infer) that the court reporter is biased.

9. From that careless expression, a jury might (imply, infer) a person's guilt or innocence!

10. Learning about a profession often provides you with a (knew, new) perspective.

● Connect to the Writing Process: Revising
Recognizing Correct Usage

Rewrite the following paragraph, changing the words that are used incorrectly.

Manual dexterity is kind of important when you take a court-reporting course. Once you get into the class, you must learn a form of shorthand. Acquiring a good command of language is also essential. Often the course requires students to familiarize themselves good with language in specialized fields. The instructor must explain good the phonetic spelling of words and phrases. The court reporter's machine has only twelve keys on its keyboard. Learning to use those twelve keys to record testimony is not easy, like you might think. To qualify for certification, you must build your speed up to 225 words per minute. Those who have difficulty developing the required speed often loose interest. Those who succeed find the hole process an interesting one.

of Prepositions such as *inside, outside,* and *off* should not be followed by *of*.

NONSTANDARD	Did you look **inside of** the box?
STANDARD	Did you look **inside** the box?

ought Never use *have* or *had* with *ought*.

NONSTANDARD	Jennifer **had**n't **ought** to sit long in the sun.
STANDARD	Jennifer **ought** not to sit long in the sun.

passed, past *Passed* is the past tense of the verb *pass*. As a noun *past* means "a time gone by." As an adjective *past* means "just gone" or "elapsed." As a preposition *past* means "beyond."

In the **past** I always drove **past** the park on the way to work. (*past* as a noun and then as a preposition)

I **passed** the exam for a new job this **past** month. (*past* as an adjective)

rise, raise *Rise* means "to move upward" or "to get up." *Rise* is never followed by a direct object. Its principal parts are *rise, rising, rose,* and *risen*. *Raise* means "to lift (something) up," "to increase," or "to grow something." *Raise* is usually followed by a direct object. Its principal parts are *raise, raising, raised,* and *raised*.

When the guest speaker arrived, the students **rose.**
She **raised** her hand to ask a question.
(*Hand* is a direct object)

You can learn more about using the verbs rise *and* raise *on page L210.*

-self, -selves A reflexive pronoun should not be used as a subject.
In addition, you should never use *hisself* or *theirselves.*

NONSTANDARD	Jean and **myself** met at the museum.
STANDARD	Jean and **I** met at the museum.

CONNECT TO WRITER'S CRAFT

W alt Whitman, a renowned nineteenth-century
American poet, uses the reflexive pronoun *myself* to
emphasize his topic. Notice the powerful opening three lines that
announce the theme of his poem.

> I celebrate myself, and sing myself,
> And what I assume you shall assume,
> For every atom belonging to me as good belongs to you.
> —*Walt Whitman, "Song of Myself"*

shall, will Formal English requires the use of *shall* with first
person pronouns and *will* with second- and third-person pronouns.
Today these words are used interchangeably with *I* and *we,* except
that *shall* is usually used for questions.

Shall we eat at seven?
He **will** join us soon.

sit, set *Sit* means "to rest in an upright position." *Sit* is rarely
followed by a direct object. Its principal parts are *sit, sitting, sat,*
and *sat.* *Set* means "to put or place (something)." *Set* is usually
followed by a direct object. Its principal parts are *set, setting, set,*
and *set.*

Sit down on the couch while I **set** your packages on
the table.

To avoid confusion between these two verbs and their principal parts, it might be helpful to notice that all principal parts of *set* retain the same letter, *e:* set, setting, set and set. For the word *sit,* neither the base word nor any of its principal parts contain the letter *e.*

You can learn more about using the verbs sit *and* set *on page L211.*

so *So* should not be used to begin a sentence.

NONSTANDARD	**So** why are you still here?
STANDARD	The plane was late, **so** we missed our connection. (coordinating conjunction)
STANDARD	I'm **so** tired of waiting that I might fall asleep. (adverb)

than, then *Than* is a subordinating conjunction and is used for comparisons. *Then* is an adverb and means "at that time" or "next."

Would you rather go to the skating rink **than** to the movies?
Then do you want to join the rest of the group?

that, which, who These words are often used as relative pronouns to introduce adjective clauses. *That* refers to people, animals, or things and always begins an essential clause. *Which* refers to animals and things. *Who* refers to people.

The man **that** just drove by is my math teacher.
Geometry, **which** is my first period class, is challenging.
Mr. Jenkins, **who** is my math teacher, designed this course.

their, there, they're *Their* is a possessive pronoun. *There* is usually an adverb, but it sometimes begins an inverted sentence. *They're* is a contraction for *they are.*

Don't worry about **their** late arrival.
There is a good reason why **they're** late.

theirs, there's *Theirs* is a possessive pronoun. *There's* is a contraction for *there is.*

> Our invitation came a week ago; **theirs** came later.
> **There's** a delicious turkey dinner waiting for us.

them, those Never use *them* as a subject or as an adjective.

NONSTANDARD	**Them** are the ones to get. (subject)
STANDARD	**Those** are the ones to get.
NONSTANDARD	Do you like **them** shoes? (adjective)
STANDARD	Do you like **those** shoes?

PRACTICE YOUR SKILLS

 Check Your Understanding
Finding the Correct Word

Literature Topic   **Write the word in parentheses that correctly completes each sentence.**

1. Stephen Crane, (that, which, who) is a widely acclaimed author today, struggled in his early career.

2. He (raised, rose) to literary fame through his novel *The Red Badge of Courage.*

3. Before (than, then), his first novel, *Maggie: Girl of the Streets,* was not well received by readers.

4. (Their, there, they're) disapproval was partially based on the subject matter.

5. In *The Red Badge of Courage,* Crane tells of the inward struggle (that, which, who) a young man suffers in war.

6. Crane never actually served in a war (himself, hisself).

7. For realistic details Crane studied (passed, past) war photographs and interviewed veterans of the Civil War.

8. Rather (than, then) romanticizing war, he presented a frank account of the horrors of war.

9. No one (shall, will) ever know what other literary works of art Stephen Crane might have given to the world.

10. His death at the age of twenty-eight left (them, those) types of questions unanswered.

● Connect to the Writing Process: Revising
Recognizing Correct Usage

Rewrite the following paragraph, changing the words that are used incorrectly.

Stephen Crane's life hadn't ought to be examined solely for his novel writing. Raised in a family of fourteen children, he and his family moved often. In college he appeared to work harder at baseball then at studying. Theirs evidence of his interest in writing from his first job. Them accounts that he wrote while a newspaper reporter showed his talent for details. The years he past living in the Bowery area of New York also inspired him. He sat them experiences down in his poems, short stories, and novels. Years later, as a correspondent on his way to Cuba, he was shipwrecked off of the Florida coast. So he hisself wrote a story, "The Open Boat," based on his experiences. There are also two volumes of poetry that he wrote in his short lifetime.

this, that, these, those *This* and *that* are singular and modify singular nouns. *These* and *those* are plural and modify plural nouns.

| NONSTANDARD | I don't like **these** brand of sneakers. |
| STANDARD | I don't like **this** brand of sneakers. |

this here, that there Avoid using *here* or *there* in addition to *this* or *that*.

NONSTANDARD	**This here** band is really good.
STANDARD	**This** band is really good.

threw, through *Threw* is the past tense of the verb *throw*. *Through* is a preposition that means "in one side and out the other."

Roseanne **threw** the basketball right **through** the hoop.

to, too, two *To* is a preposition. *To* also begins an infinitive. *Too* is an adverb. *Two* is a number.

Adam went **to** the library **to** study.
Studying for **two** hours straight is **too** difficult for me.

use to, used to Be sure to add the *–d* to *use*.

NONSTANDARD	I **use to** dislike math, but now I enjoy it.
STANDARD	I **used to** dislike math, but now I enjoy it.

CONNECT TO SPEAKING AND WRITING

When saying *used to,* clearly enunciate the *d* at the end of *used* so that your speech sounds correct.

way, ways Do not substitute *ways* for *way* when referring to a distance.

NONSTANDARD	You live a long **ways** from school.
STANDARD	You live a long **way** from school.

weak, week *Weak* is an adjective that means "not strong" or "likely to break." *Week* is a noun that means "a period of seven days."

Since you've been sick for a **week,** you must feel **weak.**

what Do not substitute *what* for *that*.

NONSTANDARD	The car **what** we want is too expensive.
STANDARD	The car **that** we want is too expensive.

when, where Do not use *when* or *where* directly after a linking verb in a definition.

NONSTANDARD	A talus is **when** rock fragments accumulate at the base of a cliff.
STANDARD	A talus is an accumulation of rock fragments at the base of a cliff.
NONSTANDARD	Boulder is **where** there is low humidity.
STANDARD	Boulder is a city **where** the humidity is low.

where Do not substitute *where* for *that*.

NONSTANDARD	I read **where** winters in the Midwest are going to be warmer.
STANDARD	I read **that** winters in the Midwest are going to be warmer.

who, whom *Who,* a pronoun in the nominative case, is used either as a subject or as a predicate nominative. *Whom,* a pronoun in the objective case, is mainly used as a direct object, an indirect object, or an object of a preposition.

Who went to the museum with you? (subject)

Whom did you see at the museum? (direct object)

You can learn more about using who *and* whom *on pages L262–L263.*

whose, who's *Whose* is a possessive pronoun. *Who's* is a contraction for *who is.*

Whose computer did you use?
Who's working in the lab with you?

your, you're *Your* is a possessive pronoun. *You're* is a contraction for *you are.*

You're sure this is the correct assignment?
Is **your** American history book at home?

PRACTICE YOUR SKILLS

● Check Your Understanding
Finding the Correct Word

Social
Studies
Write the word in parentheses that correctly completes each sentence.

1. The slaves (whose, who's) way to freedom was the Underground Railroad faced many dangers.

2. Some people today think the Underground Railroad (use to, used to) involve an actual train and tracks.

3. In truth, the Underground Railroad was simply the route that slaves took (to, too, two) the North in search of freedom.

4. Often slaves had to travel a long (way, ways).

5. The secret journey was partially made possible by those (who, whom) provided assistance to them.

6. Some of the people to (who, whom) they often owed their lives were white abolitionists.

7. Abolitionists who were former slaves played a major role (to, too, two).

8. (To, Too, Two) of the most famous black women abolitionists were Harriet Tubman and Sojourner Truth.

9. Harriet Tubman, (whose, who's) also referred to as the "Moses" of her people, led a total of almost three hundred slaves to freedom.

10. (Your, You're) likely to find her inspiring story in (your, you're) history book.

● Connecting to the Writing Process: Revising
Recognizing Correct Usage

Rewrite the following paragraph, changing the words that are used incorrectly.

Slaves and abolitionists use to speak in code about a planned escape. This type of secrecy was essential for success. The code name what escaping slaves were given was "passenger." People to who the passengers often turned to lead them were called "conductors," whom led them to a "safe" home. They usually traveled a long ways to reach a safe home, or a "station," where the slaves found food and shelter. To prevent capture, most slaves traveled threw the night after they left a station. Those recaptured used to be beaten or killed. On the other hand, only a jail sentence or fine faced white abolitionists who's involvement in an escape was determined. Because of her nineteen trips too the South helping slaves too escape, Harriet Tubman is known as the most successful conductor of the Underground Railroad.

Communicate Your Ideas

APPLY TO WRITING

Explanatory Paragraph: *Correct Usage*

When you read the information in the two preceding exercises, what kind of picture or pictures did you form in your mind? Quickly sketch what you "saw." Then write a paragraph that explains what you have sketched. Use any ten of the glossary words from *good/well* through *your/you're*. Before writing, consider the following questions about your images.

- Are your images clear or hazy?
- What words clearly illustrate the mood?
- Which adjectives might enhance sounds or silence?

When you have finished, underline the glossary words and check that you have used them correctly.

QuickCheck Mixed Practice

Write the word in parentheses that correctly completes each sentence.

1. The variety of extracurricular activities offered (anymore, nowadays) in high school is remarkable.

2. (Among, Between) those offered are drama clubs, honor clubs, service clubs, social clubs, surfing clubs, (and many others, etc.).

3. (Because, Being that) such a variety is available, (your, you're) offered almost unlimited opportunities to participate.

4. (Its, It's) often a matter of (your, you're) personal preference.

5. Some clubs offer tutoring to students (who, whom) are (weak, week) in a certain subject.

6. A large (amount, number) of clubs take part in community projects (as, like) building playgrounds and cleaning up the environment.

7. (Their, There, They're) are other types of support clubs, (which, who) some students prefer.

8. The members of these clubs go (in, into) the community to offer (their, there, they're) assistance to the elderly.

9. (Them, Those) organizations are often called service clubs.

10. Usually the bylaws (lay, lie) down the requirements for membership (in, into) a club.

11. For example, many clubs require attendance at meetings once a (weak, week).

12. Some even (set, sit) their meeting time during lunch.

13. (The reason they do is because, The reason they do is that) many students work after school.

14. No matter where or when they (meet, meet at), students (can, may) enjoy the fellowship.

15. Experiences such as these add a (knew, new) dimension to school life.

CHAPTER 9

Capital Letters

 **Pretest**

Directions

Read the passage. Choose the correct way to write each underlined part and write the letter of the correct answer. If the underlined part contains no error, write _D._

> EXAMPLE
> Here's a letter from <u>our Niece Tina</u>
>
> **1**   **A**   our Niece Tina   **(1)**
>   **B**   our niece Tina
>   **C**   Our Niece Tina
>   **D**   No error
>
> ANSWER
> **1**   **B**

<u>214 calkinstown rd.</u>
(1)
Sharon, CT 06406
May 24, 20—

<u>dear uncle will</u>,
    (2)
I enjoyed seeing you and <u>aunt di in california</u>. The <u>san</u>
                     (3)   **(4)**
<u>diego zoo</u> was terrific. When we <u>drove north, i</u> was amazed
                            (5)
at both the <u>pacific ocean</u> and the mountains. The <u>golden</u>
          (6)   **(7)**
<u>gate bridge</u> was also breathtaking. I enjoyed _<u>a man for all</u>_
                                    (8)
<u>seasons</u> at the theater despite the bad review in the _<u>san</u>_
                                         (9)
<u>francisco chronicle</u>. Thanks for having me!

<u>All my love</u>,
    (10)
Tina

1	**A**	214 Calkinstown rd.	6	**A**	Pacific ocean
	B	214 calkinstown Rd.		**B**	pacific Ocean
	C	214 Calkinstown Rd.		**C**	Pacific Ocean
	D	No error		**D**	No error

2	**A**	Dear Uncle Will,	7	**A**	Golden Gate Bridge
	B	Dear uncle Will,		**B**	Golden Gate bridge
	C	dear Uncle Will,		**C**	Golden gate bridge
	D	No error		**D**	No error

3	**A**	Aunt Di in california	8	**A**	*A Man For All Seasons*
	B	aunt di in California		**B**	*A Man for all Seasons*
	C	Aunt Di in California		**C**	*A Man for All Seasons*
	D	No error		**D**	No error

4	**A**	San diego zoo	9	**A**	*San francisco Chronicle*
	B	San Diego Zoo		**B**	*San Francisco Chronicle*
	C	San Diego zoo		**C**	*San Francisco chronicle*
	D	No error		**D**	No error

5	**A**	drove North, I	10	**A**	all my love,
	B	drove north, I		**B**	All My Love,
	C	Drove North, I		**C**	All my Love,
	D	No error		**D**	No error

Georges Seurat. *A Sunday on La Grande Jatte–1884*, 1884–1886.
Oil on canvas, 83 by 123¼ inches. The Art Institute of Chicago.

Describe   What does this painting show? Describe the
            scene's colors and characters.

Analyze   What details tell you that the scene in this
            painting takes place on a Sunday in the
            1800s?

Interpret   What do you think the artist is trying to say
            about the people in the painting? Explain.
            How might a writer express the same ideas?

Judge   Do you think you would enjoy sharing the
            kind of Sunday the painting's subjects are
            having? Why or why not?

At the end of this chapter, you will use the artwork to stimulate
ideas for writing.

Capitalization

A clear, detailed set of directions is extremely important if you are trying to find a friend's house for the first time. Capitalization and punctuation marks are like a good set of directions. As you read, they tell you when to go, when to slow down, and when to stop. These marks give you signals and clues that help you understand the meanings of sentences—just as directions give you signals and clues that help you find your way. Without directions you might not find your friend's house. Without capitalization and punctuation, you might not be able to find your way through even a short paragraph.

For many years you have been studying the rules for capitalization. Reviewing them in this chapter should help you use them correctly in your written work.

First Words and the Pronoun *I*

A capital letter is like a green light. It indicates that you can begin to move forward.

Sentences and Poetry

Capitalize the first word of a sentence and the first word of a line of poetry.

SENTENCE   The mountain view was spectacular.

LINES OF POETRY   Time, you old gypsy man,
                        Will you not stay,
                    Put up your caravan
                        Just for one day?
                            —Ralph Hodgson

A few modern poets deliberately misuse or eliminate capital letters. If you are quoting any poem, copy it exactly as the poet has written it.

"How Can I Lie to You"

now thread my voice
with lies
of lightness
force within
my mirror eyes
the cold disguise
of sad and wise
decisions.

—*Maya Angelou*

Parts of Letters

Capitalize the first word in the greeting of a letter and the first word in the closing of a letter.

SALUTATIONS AND CLOSINGS	
SALUTATIONS	**D**ear Diane, **D**ear Bob,
CLOSINGS	**Y**ours truly, **S**incerely yours,

Outlines

Capitalize the first word of each item in an outline and the letters that begin major subsections of an outline.

Wolves
I. **A**ppearance
   A. **S**imilar to sled dogs, huskies
      1. **N**arrower and leaner than domestic dogs
      2. **H**eavy for coats

The Pronoun *I*

Capitalize the pronoun *I*, both alone and in contractions.

CONTRACTION	**I**'m going to be ready on time.
ALONE	**I** had better hurry.

You can learn about capitalization of quotations on page L462.

PRACTICE YOUR SKILLS

● Check Your Understanding
Using Capital Letters

Write *a* or *b* to indicate the item that is correctly capitalized in each of the following pairs. Assume poetry is in traditional style.

1. a. the test is tomorrow.

   b. The test is tomorrow.

2. a. When you notice a cat in profound meditation,
     The reason, I tell you, is always the same:

                     —T. S. Eliot

   b. when you notice a cat in profound meditation,
     the reason, I tell you, is always the same:

                     —T. S. Eliot

3. a. Dear Phillip,

   b. dear Phillip,

4. a. sincerely yours,

   b. Sincerely yours,

5. a. II. Causes of the Civil War

       A. States' rights

       B. Slavery

   b. II. causes of the Civil War

       A. states' rights

       B. slavery

6. a. Yours Always,

   b. Yours always,

7. a. Stop Talking.

   b. Stop talking.

8. a. dear Grandma,

   b. Dear Grandma,

9. a. Whose woods these are I think I know.
   His house is in the village, though;

   —Robert Frost

   b. whose woods these are I think I know.
   his house is in the village, though;

   —Robert Frost

10. a. III. Types of birds

       A. songbirds

       B. raptors

   b. III. Types of birds

       A. Songbirds

       B. Raptors

11. a. Susan and Jim went to the dance.

   b. susan and Jim went to the dance.

12. a. Most Respectfully Yours,

   b. Most respectfully yours,

13. a. Dear Sir:

   b. dear Sir:

14. a. IV. Famous ancient ruins
       A. Stonehenge
       B. the Parthenon

   b. IV. Famous ancient ruins
       A. Stonehenge
       B. The Parthenon

15. a. Tyger! Tyger! Burning bright
      In the forests of the night,

                      —William Blake

   b. Tyger! Tyger! Burning bright
      in the forests of the night,

                      —William Blake

● Connect to the Writing Process: Editing
Using Capital Letters Correctly

Rewrite the following letter, correcting the errors in capitalization.

dear Jennifer,

    today in class we had to read a poem by William Shakespeare. it was a sonnet. my favorite part of it went something like this:

      "make thee another self, for love of me,
      that beauty still may live in thine or thee."

                    sincerely,

                    Mark

APPLY TO WRITING

Friendly Letter: *Capital Letters*

Your older sister, who is away at college, was always good at poetry. You are struggling with a poem in your English class, and you decide to ask for her help. Write her a letter and include a couple of lines from your poem. Be sure to use capitalization properly.

Proper Nouns

You may recall that a proper noun is the name of a particular person, place, or thing.

Capitalize proper nouns and their abbreviations.

The following proper nouns have been divided into groups to help you remember them easily.

Names of particular persons and animals should be capitalized. Also capitalize the initials that stand for people's names.

NAMES OF PERSONS AND ANIMALS	
PERSONS	Tad, Mary Lou Taylor, Carlos **T.** Rivera, Jr.
ANIMALS	Dusty, Duke, Mittens, Fang

Some surnames consist of two parts. You should usually capitalize the letter that follows *De, Mc, Mac, O', St.,* or *Von.* Since names do vary, however, it is always best to ask people how their names are capitalized.

NAMES WITH TWO CAPITALS
MacDonald, O'Reilly, St. James, Von Hussen

Geographical names, including particular places, bodies of water, and celestial bodies, should be capitalized.

GEOGRAPHICAL NAMES	
TOWNS, CITIES	Lincoln, **New York City (NYC)**, Terre Haute, Austin
STREETS, HIGHWAYS	Sterns Hill Road (Rd.), New York Freeway, Thirty-third Street (The second part of a hyphenated numbered street is not capitalized.)
COUNTIES, PARISHES, TOWNSHIPS	Gotland Township, St. Mary's Parish, Canby County
STATES	Pennsylvania (PA), North Dakota (ND), Arizona (AZ)
COUNTRIES	Brazil, Zaire, Egypt, United States (US)
SECTIONS OF A COUNTRY	the East, the Midwest, the Great Plains (Compass directions are not capitalized.)
CONTINENTS	South America, Asia, Australia
WORLD REGIONS	the Southern Hemisphere, the Far East, the South Pole
ISLANDS	Block Island, Canary Islands
MOUNTAINS	Mount (Mt.) Palomar, Rocky Mountains
PARKS	Glacier National Park, Bentley Park
BODIES OF WATER	Gulf of Mexico, Rio Grande, Atlantic Ocean, Chesapeake Bay, Lake Arthur
STARS	Vega, Polaris
CONSTELLATIONS	the Little Dipper, Orion, Ursa Major
PLANETS	Jupiter, Saturn, Mars, Neptune, Earth (Do not capitalize *sun* or *moon*. Also, do not capitalize *earth* if it is preceded by the word *the*.)

You should capitalize words such as *street, island, city, lake,* and *mountain* only when they are part of a proper noun.

> Which street runs parallel to Ames Street?

You can learn more about proper nouns on page L7 and about capitalizing the titles of persons on pages L396–L397.

PRACTICE YOUR SKILLS

● Check Your Understanding
Capitalizing Geographical Names

Write the following items, using capital letters where needed.

1. chicago, il
2. mt. etna
3. st. catherine parish
4. the north star
5. a city in louisiana
6. grand rapids, michigan
7. dade county, fl
8. the sun belt
9. the grand canyon
10. a nation in africa
11. the arctic ocean
12. sherwood island
13. forty-second street
14. south on rte. 66
15. the red bluff reservoir
16. the middle east
17. a pier in tampa bay
18. the sun and mars
19. a highway in seattle
20. north of lake huron

● Check Your Understanding
Using Capital Letters

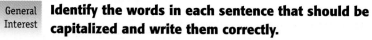

General Interest **Identify the words in each sentence that should be capitalized and write them correctly.**

21. recently in a letter from my aunt, I learned that the o'tooles have been traveling across the country.

22. they crossed the mississippi river last week.

23. The o'tooles have learned about the many countries that have influenced texas: spain, france, and mexico.

24. next week they are planning to visit sacramento, california.

25. last night they watched venus rise as they drove east on rte. 44.

26. we got a postcard from the painted desert.

27. the o'tooles plan to travel to china, japan, and parts of the middle east next year.

28. on their last trip, they saw the home of ulysses s. grant and discovered that his horse was named egypt.

29. over the holidays they visited the capital of the u.s., which is washington, d.c.

30. mrs. o'toole lives in st. mark's parish when she is not traveling.

31. she informed us that wheat is primarily a product of the midwest.

32. mr. o'toole's favorite part of new york city is the point at which seventh ave., forty-fourth st., and broadway cross each other at times square.

33. los angeles is one of the most populous cities in north america that they have not visited.

34. mr. o'toole would like to drive to visit some cities in central america.

35. last summer they got to see mercury and saturn from the top of the space needle in seattle.

36. what is the name of the river that separates manhattan from the bronx?

37. the smallest country that mrs. o'toole has visited is denmark.

38. how many people do you know who have visited switzerland?

39. mr. jones said he wants to visit the suez canal next summer.

40. soon I will be visiting carson city, nevada, for the first time.

Rewrite the following sentences, correcting the errors in capitalization. If a sentence is correct, write C.

41. When I travel, I board my dogs, Muffy and Tuffy.

42. Have you ever visited monaco?

43. The macfarlands left the northeast and headed for the smoky mountains.

44. At the mcdonald observatory in texas, we saw jupiter and its four moons.

45. Mrs. Smith likes to visit florida in the winter.

Communicate Your Ideas

APPLY TO WRITING

Informative Paragraph: *Capital Letters*

The mayor of your town would like to increase tourism to the area. In an effort to attract young people to visit your town, the mayor has asked the students at your school to create a travel brochure for students your age. Write an informative paragraph for the brochure that highlights major geographical points of interest. Be sure to capitalize all geographical names.

Names of groups, such as organizations, businesses, institutions, government bodies, political parties, and teams, should be capitalized.

NAMES OF GROUPS	
ORGANIZATIONS	Brentwood Civic Association (Assn.), the United Nations (UN)
BUSINESSES	Highland Motors, Serendipity Life Insurance Company (Co.)

INSTITUTIONS	West Virginia Institute of Technology, Canton High School, Westwood Hospital (Words such as *college, school,* and *hospital* are not capitalized unless they are part of a proper noun.)
GOVERNMENT BODIES AND AGENCIES	House of Representatives, Department of Commerce, the Supreme Court, the Environmental Protection Agency, the House of Commons, Parliament
POLITICAL PARTIES	the Democratic Party, a Republican
TEAMS	the Boston Celtics, the Smithville Colts, the Houston Astros

Specific time periods and events, including the days of the week, the months of the year, holidays, and special events, should be capitalized. Also capitalize the names of historical events, periods, and documents.

TIME PERIODS AND EVENTS	
DAYS MONTHS	Monday (Mon.), Friday (Fri.) January (Jan.), December (Dec.) (Do not capitalize the seasons of the year—such as winter and spring—unless they are part of a proper noun; e.g., Winter Festival.)
HOLIDAYS	Fourth of July, Labor Day, New Year's Day, Arbor Day
TIME ABBREVIATIONS	400 B.C., A.D. 1999, 1:30 A.M.
SPECIAL EVENTS	the Rose Bowl Parade, the Flower Show, the Olympics, the Kentucky Derby
HISTORICAL EVENTS	the War of 1812, the Battle of Bunker Hill
PERIODS	the Renaissance, the Space Age, the Middle Ages

DOCUMENTS	the **D**eclaration of **I**ndependence, the **B**ill of **R**ights, the **T**reaty of **V**ersailles, the **M**agna **C**arta

Notice that short prepositions are not capitalized. Also notice that A.D.—which stands for the Latin phrase *anno Domini* (meaning "in the year of the Lord")—is placed before the year, and B.C., meaning "before Christ," is placed after the year.

PRACTICE YOUR SKILLS

● Check Your Understanding

Using Capital Letters

Write *a* or *b* to indicate the item that is correctly capitalized.

1. **a.** Iowa state University
   b. Iowa State University

2. **a.** Thursday, May 6
   b. Thursday, may 6

3. **a.** Bapp Computer corp.
   b. Bapp Computer Corp.

4. **a.** The United Nations
   b. the United Nations

5. **a.** the Brady Bill
   b. the Brady bill

6. **a.** Sol airlines
   b. Sol Airlines

7. **a.** the Civil War
   b. the civil War

8. **a.** the Freeport vikings
   b. the Freeport Vikings

9. **a.** the parent-teacher association
   b. the Parent-Teacher Association

10. **a.** Tools Of The Stone Age
    b. tools of the Stone Age

11. **a.** members of the senate
    b. members of the Senate

12. **a.** Winter and Summer
    b. winter and summer

13. **a.** the Restoration
    b. the restoration

14. **a.** the Republican Party
    b. the republican party

15. **a.** a college in Utah
    b. a College in Utah

16. **a.** the Pittsburgh Steelers
    b. the pittsburgh steelers

17. a. a.d. 1066
   b. A.D. 1066

18. a. the Pecan st. festival
   b. the Pecan St. Festival

19. a. Valley High School
   b. Valley high school

20. a. 3:45 P.M.
   b. 3:45 p.m.

● Connect to the Writing Process: Editing
Using Capital Letters Correctly

Rewrite the following sentences, correcting the errors in capitalization. If a sentence is correct, write C.

21. In 1981, sandra day o'connor became the first female justice of the supreme court.

22. The Speedy Office Supply Co. is located on Ashburton Dr.

23. Sargent shriver was the first director of the peace corps.

24. in 1999, the denver broncos won the super bowl.

25. Legends tell that king Arthur lived during the dark ages, around a.d. 500.

Names of nationalities, races, languages, religions, religious holidays, and religious references should be capitalized. Some writers also capitalize pronouns that refer to the Deity.

NATIONALITIES, RACES, RELIGIONS, ETC.	
NATIONALITIES	an American, Russians, a Pole
RACES	Hispanic, Caucasian, Asian
LANGUAGES	English, French, German, Spanish
COMPUTER LANGUAGES	Java, C++, Visual Basic
RELIGIONS	Roman Catholicism, Judaism, Buddhism, Islam
RELIGIOUS HOLIDAYS	Christmas, Passover, Kwanza, Easter
RELIGIOUS REFERENCES	God, the Bible, Hanukkah, Allah, the Koran, Genesis, the Lord, Buddha (Do not capitalize *god* when it refers to a polytheistic god.)

Other proper nouns also begin with capital letters.

OTHER PROPER NOUNS	
Awards	Academy Award, Pulitzer Prize
Brand Names	Novac computer, New Foam soap (The product itself is not capitalized.)
Bridges and Buildings	Golden Gate Bridge, Cardan Building, Reunion Tower
Memorials and Monuments	Jefferson Memorial, Washington Monument
Vehicles	*Viking I*, the *Orient Express*
Names of Courses	Mathematics II, Art I, English
Technological Terms	E-mail, Internet, Web, World Wide Web, Website, Web Art, Web Page

Unnumbered courses, such as *history, woodworking,* and *science,* are not capitalized unless they are languages. Also, do not capitalize class names such as *sophomore* and *senior* unless they are part of a proper noun, such as the *Sophomore Class.*

Practice Your Skills

● Check Your Understanding
Capitalizing Proper Nouns

Write *a* or *b* to indicate the item that is correctly capitalized in each of the following pairs.

1. a. an italian
b. an Italian

2. a. Buddhism
b. buddhism

3. a. easter
b. Easter

4. a. the Grammy Awards
b. the grammy awards

5. a. the Lincoln Memorial
b. the lincoln memorial

6. a. the ship *titanic*
b. the ship *Titanic*

7. **a.** a Spaniard
   b. a spaniard

8. **a.** yom kippur
   b. Yom Kippur

9. **a.** the brooklyn bridge
   b. the Brooklyn Bridge

10. **a.** the holocaust museum
    b. the Holocaust Museum

11. **a.** a canadian
    b. a Canadian

12. **a.** chinese
    b. Chinese

13. **a.** a Greek goddess
    b. a Greek Goddess

14. **a.** green foam soap
    b. Green Foam soap

15. **a.** the forty-ninth st. bridge
    b. the Forty-ninth St. Bridge

16. **a.** algebra II
    b. Algebra II

17. **a.** Smartt Software Co.
    b. Smartt software co.

18. **a.** the Bible
    b. the bible

19. **a.** the sears tower
    b. the Sears Tower

20. **a.** the *maine*
    b. the *Maine*

● Check Your Understanding
Using Capital Letters

General Interest **Write *a* or *b* to indicate the sentence that is correctly capitalized in each of the following pairs.**

21. **a.** Last year we drove to Rhode island and spent the summer in the east.
    b. Last year we drove to Rhode Island and spent the summer in the East.

22. **a.** In 1960, the Submarine *Triton* circumnavigated the globe.
    b. In 1960, the submarine *Triton* circumnavigated the globe.

23. **a.** The national council of jewish women held its annual meeting in hartford, ct.
    b. The National Council of Jewish Women held its annual meeting in Hartford, CT.

24. **a.** The Monroe Doctrine warned European countries not to interfere in the Americas.
    b. The monroe doctrine warned european countries not to interfere in the americas.

25. a. Last spring I studied french, but now I wish I had taken Spanish instead.
  b. Last spring I studied French, but now I wish I had taken Spanish instead.

26. a. Everyone voted for Laurie as treasurer because she is a genius in Mathematics.
  b. Everyone voted for Laurie as treasurer because she is a genius in mathematics.

27. a. In 1913, the sixteenth amendment to the united states constitution introduced the income tax to the American people.
  b. In 1913, the Sixteenth Amendment to the United States Constitution introduced the income tax to the American people.

28. a. John F. Kennedy was the first Roman Catholic to be president.
  b. John F. Kennedy was the first Roman catholic to be president.

29. a. If you are taking History, Algebra, Chemistry, English Composition, and Art II, you're going to be busy!
  b. If you are taking history, algebra, chemistry, English composition, and Art II, you're going to be busy!

30. a. The space age began with the launching of *sputnik I,* the first artificial satellite.
  b. The Space Age began with the launching of *Sputnik I,* the first artificial satellite.

● Connect to the Writing Process: Editing
Using Capital Letters Correctly

Rewrite the following paragraphs, correcting the errors in capitalization.

The alamo, the old spanish mission founded in 1718 at

san antonio, texas, was the site of one of the most famous

sieges in all of united states history. The army of santa anna was made up of poorly trained and poorly equipped mexicans, plus some mayan indians who could not understand spanish. Such factors, however, had little effect on the outcome of the battle. The texans were too greatly outnumbered—fewer than 200 defenders to 6,000 troops from mexico.

The historic old church that stands at the alamo today looked quite different in 1836 when the battle took place. It is only one-ninth the size of the building that such famous men as davy crockett and jim bowie defended so many years ago. The old mission originally included not only the church but also the alamo city plaza park and several surrounding streets.

Communicate Your Ideas

APPLY TO WRITING

E-mail Message: *Capital Letters*

Your friend is having difficulty in history class. He has to write a research paper on a period of history that you are very familiar with. Write him an E-mail message that describes a historical event from that period in history. Mention the people and places associated with the event. Be sure to capitalize all proper nouns.

General Interest **Identify each word that should begin with a capital letter and rewrite the words correctly.**

1. abraham lincoln signed the emancipation proclamation on january 1, 1863.

2. the american revolution began in lexington, massachusetts, on april 19, 1775.

3. stone was rarely used in the construction of the earliest buildings of the egyptians, babylonians, and assyrians.

4. the washington redskins played the los angeles raiders in the 1984 super bowl; the raiders won.

5. has the chordalle company ever presented a piano to the white house?

6. the largest collection of baseball cards belongs to the metropolitan museum of art in new york city.

7. many of the cheese-making advances in the middle ages were made by monks.

8. the sides of *old ironsides* are actually made of wood.

9. this nupict camera has many innovative features that make photography easier.

10. the chicken was a common fowl in europe by the time of the roman empire.

11. rockefeller center in new york city extends from forty-eighth street to fifty-second street.

12. loy and sampson board games are popular with children and adults in many nations, including canada.

13. the gulf of bothnia separates sweden and finland.

14. three major airports serve washington, d.c.: Ronald Reagan national, dulles, and baltimore-washington.

15. unlike earth, jupiter radiates more heat back into space than it gets from the sun.

 Proper Adjectives

Proper adjectives are formed from proper nouns. Most proper adjectives are also capitalized.

PROPER ADJECTIVES	
Hawaiian pineapples	Danish accent
Roman citizen	American cities

Capitalize only the part of a compound adjective that is a proper noun or proper adjective.

COMPOUND ADJECTIVES		
pro-American	Mexican American	Japanese-made

PRACTICE YOUR SKILLS

 Check Your Understanding
Capitalizing Proper Adjectives

Write *a* or *b* to indicate the item that is correctly capitalized in each of the following pairs.

1. **a.** french pastries
   b. French pastries

2. **a.** a French Canadian
   b. a French canadian

3. **a.** hungarian waltz
   b. Hungarian waltz

4. **a.** German shepherd
   b. german shepherd

5. **a.** Irish Dancing
   b. Irish dancing

6. **a.** polish sausage
   b. Polish sausage

7. **a.** Canadian bacon
   b. Canadian Bacon

8. **a.** African American
   b. African american

9. **a.** Dutch cocoa
   b. dutch cocoa

10. **a.** Swedish Meatballs
    b. Swedish meatballs

11. a. Italian pasta **b.** italian pasta	**16. a.** Scottish Tartan **b.** Scottish tartan
12. a. mandarin collar **b.** Mandarin collar	**17. a.** spanish bullfighting **b.** Spanish bullfighting
13. a. Arabian horse **b.** Arabian Horse	**18. a.** swiss chocolates **b.** Swiss chocolates
14. a. Japanese-made car **b.** Japanese-Made car	**19. a.** English literature **b.** english literature
15. a. Russian accent **b.** russian accent	**20. a.** Alaskan Folklore **b.** Alaskan folklore

● Connect to the Writing Process: Drafting
Capitalizing Proper Adjectives

Write original sentences, using the following proper adjectives. Be sure to use capital letters correctly.

21. brazilian

22. hawaiian

23. greek

24. korean-made

25. american

▶ Titles

Capital letters indicate the importance of titles of persons, written works, and other works of art.

Capitalize titles of persons and of works of art.

Titles Used with Names of Persons

Capitalize a title showing office, rank, or profession when the title comes directly before a person's name. The same title is usually not capitalized when it follows a name.

BEFORE A NAME	Have you met **S**enator Ames?
AFTER A NAME	Harold Ames is our new **s**enator.
	I know Harold Ames, our new **s**enator.

Titles Used Alone

Capitalize a title that is used alone when it is substituted for a person's name in direct address. The titles *President, Vice President, Chief Justice,* and *Queen of England* are capitalized when they stand alone.

USED AS A NAME	I disagree with you, **G**overnor.
NOT USED AS A NAME	Who will our next **g**overnor be?
HIGH GOVERNMENT OFFICIAL	Has the **P**resident arrived yet?

President and *vice president* are capitalized when they stand alone only if they refer to the current president and vice president.

Titles Showing Family Relationships

Capitalize a title showing a family relationship when it comes directly before a person's name, when it is used as a name, or when it is substituted for a person's name.

BEFORE A NAME	Did you call **U**ncle David?
USED AS A NAME	Is **D**ad going too?
DIRECT ADDRESS	May I go with you, **M**om?

Do not capitalize titles showing family relationships when they are preceded by a possessive noun or pronoun—unless they are considered part of a person's name.

Jerry's **a**unt is visiting from Oklahoma.

Jerry's **A**unt Mildred is visiting from Oklahoma.
(*Aunt* is part of the name.)

Titles of Written Works and Other Works of Art

Capitalize the first, the last, and all other important words in the titles of books, stories, poems, newspapers, magazines, movies, plays, television productions, musical compositions, and other works of art. Do not capitalize a preposition, a conjunction, or an article—unless it is the first word in a title.

BOOKS AND CHAPTER TITLES	The first chapter in Charles Dickens's *A Tale of Two Cities* is called "The Period."
SHORT STORIES	I enjoyed reading "A Rose for Emily" in class.
POEMS	Have you read Coleridge's "The Rime of the Ancient Mariner"?
NEWSPAPERS AND NEWSPAPER ARTICLES	Today's *Washington Post* ran a story entitled "Volunteerism in Our High Schools."
MAGAZINES AND MAGAZINE ARTICLES	Did you read "A Harvest for the Hungry" in *Time?*
PLAYS	We saw *Death of a Salesman* on Broadway.
TELEVISION SERIES	My dad likes to watch *60 Minutes* after dinner.
WORKS OF ART	My favorite movement from Grofé's *Grand Canyon Suite is* "Painted Desert."

Usually you should not capitalize *the* as the first word of the name of a newspaper or a periodical.

The election was covered by the *Boston Globe* and the *Los Angeles Times.*

You can learn more about punctuating titles on page L457.

PRACTICE YOUR SKILLS

● Check Your Understanding
Capitalizing Titles

Write *a* or *b* to indicate the sentence that is correctly capitalized in each of the following pairs.

1. **a.** Have you ever read *The Last Of The Mohicans?*
   b. Have you ever read *The Last of the Mohicans?*

2. **a.** George gershwin wrote the music for the broadway musical *porgy and bess.*
   b. George Gershwin wrote the music for the Broadway musical *Porgy and Bess.*

3. **a.** I am sure I wasn't speeding, Officer.
   b. I am sure I wasn't speeding, officer.

4. **a.** The president spent last week at Camp David.
   b. The President spent last week at Camp David.

5. **a.** Franklin R. Marsh has run for Mayor three times.
   b. Franklin R. Marsh has run for mayor three times.

6. **a.** When General Lee surrendered, President Lincoln asked the band to play "Dixie."
   b. When general Lee surrendered, president Lincoln asked the band to play "dixie."

7. **a.** Call mom and tell her grandma Kay will be late.
   b. Call Mom and tell her Grandma Kay will be late.

8. **a.** *The Mouse Trap* by Agatha Christie is a great play.
   b. *The mouse trap* by Agatha Christie is a great play.

9. **a.** We will have to call my aunt jean "Senator Mason."
   b. We will have to call my Aunt Jean "Senator Mason."

10. **a.** I enjoy O. Henry's story "The Ransom of Red Chief."
    b. I enjoy O. Henry's story "the Ransom Of Red Chief."

11. **a.** Are you driving or flying to Cincinnati, Dad?
    b. Are you driving or flying to Cincinnati, dad?

12. **a.** In English class we read "Ode on a Grecian urn."
    b. In English class we read "Ode on a Grecian Urn."

13. a. Tim's cousin Michelle is a reporter for the *Miami Herald*.

  b. Tim's Cousin Michelle is a reporter for the *Miami herald*.

14. a. I enjoyed reading the article "At Home with Brad Pitt" in *People*.

  b. I enjoyed reading the article "At home with Brad Pitt" in *People*.

15. a. Verdi wrote the opera *Aïda* to commemorate the opening of the Suez Canal.

  b. Verdi wrote the opera *Aïda* to commemorate the opening of the suez canal.

● Connect to the Writing Process: Editing
Using Capital Letters Correctly

Rewrite the following sentences, correcting the errors in capitalization. If a sentence is correct, write C.

16. the review in the *springfield gazette* unfavorably criticized the movie at showtime cinema.

17. The theme song from *Butch Cassidy and the Sundance Kid* is "Raindrops Keep Falling On My Head."

18. today the president vetoed a bill passed by congress.

19. Both movies, *the wizard of oz* and *the secret garden*, have black-and-white and color sequences.

20. How often do you read *Newsweek*?

Communicate Your Ideas

APPLY TO WRITING

Summary: *Capital Letters*

Over the summer, you attended several cultural events that included music, dance, and art. You also read a great deal of literature. To your surprise, your principal will

allow you to receive some course credit if you write a
detailed summary of your experiences. Write a summary
of all the things you saw and read over the summer. After
you have finished, check that you have used capital
letters correctly.

✅ QuickCheck Mixed Practice

General Interest **Write each word that should begin with a capital letter. Then see if you can answer the questions!**

1. is the grand coulee dam in washington or oregon?

2. what time is it in london, england, when it is noon in sioux city, iowa?

3. who was the famous general from the south who led the confederate forces?

4. arizona, new mexico, utah, and which other state meet at the same point?

5. was dr. mccoy or dr. zorba the doctor aboard the *starship enterprise?*

6. who was the author of *the old man and the sea,* which won the pulitzer prize in 1954?

7. what are the first five words of lincoln's gettysburg address?

8. are the headquarters for the defense department in the pentagon or the united states capitol?

9. does the winner of the finals of the national hockey league win the stanley cup or the davis cup?

10. where can you see charles lindbergh's plane, *spirit of st. louis?*

Using Capital Letters

Write each word that should begin with a capital letter.

1. the surface of mercury is similar to that of the moon.

2. The movie *law and order* is about wyatt earp.

3. The area drained by the amazon river in south america would cover three fourths of the united states.

4. hattie wyatt caraway was the first woman to be elected to the united states senate.

5. the largest french-speaking population in the united states lives in louisiana.

6. The republican party is represented by an elephant.

7. the two most common languages spoken in the united states besides english are spanish and french.

8. during most of the pre-civil war period in the united states, james buchanan was president.

9. the last chapter in the book *tom sawyer* is called "respectable huck joins the gang."

10. In the early 1500s, peter henlein, a german locksmith, invented the first watch.

11. on the morning of may 20, 1927, charles lindbergh took off for paris from roosevelt field in new york.

12. the first battle of world war I was the battle of the marne.

13. polaris, also called the north star, is the end star in the handle of the little dipper.

14. the name of the first dog to orbit earth was laika.

15. the clock in the cathedral of notre dame in dijon, france, has struck the hour every hour since 1383.

Using Capital Letters

Write the following items, using capital letters only where needed.

1. lake michigan
2. queen elizabeth
3. a tour of the south
4. the lincoln park zoo
5. my uncle from iowa
6. typing and english
7. a lieutenant
8. the fourth of july
9. the moons of jupiter
10. south of portland
11. city of austin, tx
12. rio grande river
13. the earth and moon
14. a senator from montana
15. spring and fall
16. the pure food and drug act
17. president lincoln
18. the french and indian war
19. a high school in elwood
20. the sophomore class
21. the bank on main street
22. my brother clifford
23. *columbia's* orbit
24. the midwest
25. *romeo and juliet*

Writing Sentences with Capital Letters

At the library, find a fact that pertains to each of the following topics. Each fact should include a proper noun, a proper adjective, or a title.

1. science
2. the southern states
3. space travel
4. the Civil War
5. magazines
6. baseball
7. television
8. rodeos
9. the solar system
10. poetry

Language and *Self-Expression*

Georges Seurat was a French painter who worked during the late 1800s. He was a member of the Impressionist school of painting, a group of painters who tried to capture impressions of a time and a scene rather than depict it exactly as it appeared. Seurat pioneered the style known as *pointillism*, using thousands of tiny dots to build a painting.

Seurat has captured the feel of a formal Sunday afternoon in a French park. Write a description of a typical Sunday that you spend. Try to create an impression with your description, rather than telling exactly what happens or describing every detail. Use capital letters wherever needed.

Prewriting Create a sense star for your description. Label each of the five points in the star with a sense. Then, in each point, you can write details that appeal to that sense.

Drafting Use your sense star to help you write a first draft of your description. Do not try to be too specific as you describe your Sunday; just create an impression of the day for your reader.

Revising Ask a classmate to read your description. Have your partner tell you if your description creates an impression of a Sunday as you might experience it. Add details if necessary.

Editing Check your draft for errors in spelling and punctuation. Be sure you have used all capital letters correctly.

Publishing Place your Sunday description in a booklet with your classmates' descriptions. Title the booklet *Sundays*.

Another Look

Capitalizing First Words and the Pronoun *I*

Capitalize the first word of a sentence and of a line of poetry. *(page L377)*

Capitalize the first word in the greeting of a letter and the first word in the closing of a letter. *(page L378)*

Capitalize the first word of each item in an outline and the letters that begin major subsections of the outline. *(pages L378–L379)*

Capitalize the pronoun *I*, both alone and in contractions. *(page L379)*

Capitalizing Proper Nouns and Proper Adjectives

Capitalize the following kinds of proper nouns:

Names of particular persons and animals *(page L382)*

Geographical names *(pages L383–L384)*

Names of groups *(pages L386–L387)*

Specific time periods and events *(pages L387–L388)*

Nationalities, races, languages, religions, religious holidays, and religious references *(page L389)*

Awards, brand names, bridges and buildings, memorials and monuments, vehicles, names of courses, and technological terms *(page L390)*

Capitalize most proper adjectives. *(page L395)*

Capitalizing Titles

Capitalize titles of persons and of works of art. *(page L396)*

Capitalize a title showing office, rank, or profession when directly before a person's name. *(pages L396–L397)*

Capitalize titles used alone when substituted for a person's name in direct address. *(page L397)*

Capitalize titles showing family relationships when they come directly before a person's name, part of a name, or in place of a name, but not when they are preceded by a possessive noun or pronoun. *(page L397)*

Capitalize the first word, the last word, and all important words in titles of books, newspapers, periodicals, stories, poems, movies, plays, television productions, musical compositions, and other works of art. *(page L398)*

 **Posttest**

Directions

Read each sentence. Choose the correct way to write each underlined part and write the letter of the correct answer. If the underlined part contains no error, write _D_.

EXAMPLE

1. My <u>friend allie and I</u> read for a play.

  1 A Friend allie and I
  B friend Allie and I
  C Friend Allie and I
  D No error

ANSWER **1 B**

1. The tryouts for the play were held in the <u>matthewson center</u>.

2. It is located at the corner of <u>fifty-second street and main street</u>.

3. Allie and I both wanted the part of Anne Boleyn in the production <u>*anne of a thousand days*</u>.

4. As Allie tried out, she looked for the <u>director, Tim Cardoza</u>.

5. Finally she gave up and recited a passage from <u>shakespeare's macbeth</u>.

6. I read a scene from a <u>french play by molière</u>.

7. I admit I was never meant to play <u>Henry viii's wife</u>.

8. Allie had already been in a <u>winston civic association</u> production.

9. She starred in <u>*the King and I*</u>.

10. I told Allie that I'd be happier painting scenery for the <u>city's festival of spring</u>.

1 A Matthewson center
   B matthewson Center
   C Matthewson Center
   D No error

2 A Fifty-second street and Main street
   B Fifty-second Street and Main Street
   C Fifty-Second Street and Main Street
   D No error

3 A *Anne of a Thousand Days*
   B *Anne of a thousand days*
   C *Anne of a Thousand days*
   D No error

4 A Director, Tim Cardoza
   B director, tim Cardoza
   C Director, tim cardoza
   D No error

5 A Shakespeare's *Macbeth*
   B Shakespeare's *macbeth*
   C shakespeare's *Macbeth*
   D No error

6 A French play by molière
   B French Play by Molière
   C French play by Molière
   D No error

7 A Henry VIII's wife
   B henry VIII's wife
   C henry VIII's Wife
   D No error

8 A Winston Civic Association
   B Winston civic association
   C Winston Civic association
   D No error

9 A *the King and I*
   B *The King and I*
   C *The King And I*
   D No error

10 A City's Festival of Spring
   B city's Festival of Spring
   C city's Festival of spring
   D No error

CHAPTER 10

End Marks and Commas

 **Pretest**

Directions

Each sentence is missing an end mark or comma(s). Choose the mark that is needed. Then write the letter of the mark.

EXAMPLE	**1.** Have you ever worked as a lifeguard
	1 A period
	B comma(s)
	C exclamation point
	D question mark
ANSWER	**1 D**

1. I was a lifeguard at our town pool last summer

2. What an exciting job it turned out to be

3. Beginning with the first day I had work to do.

4. Children ran on the slippery tile and adults dove in the shallow water.

5. My instructions made very loudly never stopped.

6. Did anyone listen to me

7. It wasn't until a near tragedy that I was treated as an authority

8. The Thompson kids a pair of twins were horsing around near the diving board.

9. Did you see a diver land on top of one of them

10. I dove in swam as fast as I could and reached the twins in seconds.

1. **A** period
   B comma(s)
   C exclamation point
   D question mark

2. **A** period
   B comma(s)
   C exclamation point
   D question mark

3. **A** period
   B comma(s)
   C exclamation point
   D question mark

4. **A** period
   B comma(s)
   C exclamation point
   D question mark

5. **A** period
   B comma(s)
   C exclamation point
   D question mark

6. **A** period
   B comma(s)
   C exclamation point
   D question mark

7. **A** period
   B comma(s)
   C exclamation point
   D question mark

8. **A** period
   B comma(s)
   C exclamation point
   D question mark

9. **A** period
   B comma(s)
   C exclamation point
   D question mark

10. **A** period
    B commas(s)
    C exclamation point
    D question mark

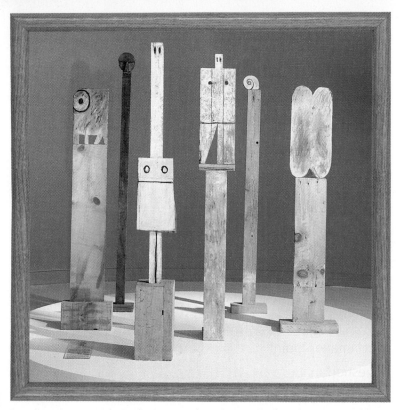

Francisco Matto. *Lamb, Mask, Venus, Universal Man, Snail, and Covenant Tablets,* from 1979.
Carved wood totems, painted with oil, height 71 to 83 inches. Courtesy of Cecilia de Torres, Ltd., New York City.

Describe What do you think each totem in the group represents? Can you recognize each totem?

Analyze What effect does the variety in size and shape of the totems have on the viewer?

Interpret What traditions do you think the totems symbolize? Why do you think the sculptor chose to include symbols from various cultures?

Judge Would you like to view this grouping of totems up close? Explain.

At the end of this chapter, you will use the artwork to stimulate ideas for writing.

Kinds of Sentences and End Marks

There are four basic kinds of sentences: declarative, imperative, interrogative, and exclamatory. Each of these kinds of sentences has a different purpose or function. The end mark you use at the end of a particular sentence is determined by that sentence's purpose or function.

One purpose of a sentence is to make a statement or to express an opinion.

A **declarative sentence** makes a statement or expresses an opinion and ends with a period (**.**).

The following examples are both declarative statements. Although the second example includes an indirect question, it is still a statement.

> The ancient Egyptians revered the cat**.**
>
> Mom asked me if I wanted to get a cat**.**
> (The direct question would be *Do you want to get a cat?*)

The second purpose of a sentence is to give directions, make requests, or give commands. *You* is usually the understood subject of these sentences.

An **imperative sentence** gives a direction, makes a request, or gives a command. It ends with either a period or an exclamation point (**.** or **!**).

If a command is spoken in a normal voice, it is followed by a period when written. However, if emotion is expressed, an exclamation point follows the command.

> Brush the cat**.**
>
> (normal voice)
>
> Look out for the cat**!**
>
> (emotional voice)

Sometimes an imperative sentence is expressed as a question but no reply is expected. Since the purpose of the sentence still remains a request or a command, the sentence is followed by a period or an exclamation point—not by a question mark.

> Will you please let the cat out.
>
> May I make my position clear.

The third purpose of a sentence is to ask a question.

> An **interrogative sentence** asks a question and ends with a question mark (**?**).

The following examples are all interrogative sentences. Although the second example is phrased as a statement, it is intended as a question. Even questions that are incompletely expressed, like the third example, should be followed by a question mark.

> Which is the largest breed of cat**?**
>
> You want me to believe that**?**
>
> The cat left after dinner. Why**?**

The fourth purpose of a sentence is to express a feeling such as joy, anger, or fear.

> An **exclamatory sentence** expresses strong feeling or emotion and ends with an exclamation point (**!**).

The first sentence in the following examples is an exclamatory sentence. The second sentence includes an interjection that is followed by an exclamation point.

> That cat bites**!**
>
> Oh**!** I forgot to call the vet**.**

You can learn about interjections on pages L49–L50.

PRACTICE YOUR SKILLS

● Check Your Understanding
Classifying Sentences

Contemporary Life **Read the following sentences, each of which lacks an end mark. Label each sentence *declarative*, *imperative*, *interrogative*, or *exclamatory*.**

1. Feed the cat after you brush her

2. The kitten likes to play with the paper bag

3. I thought your kitten was very cute

4. Will you please stop teasing the cat

5. Look at that cat run

6. Which kitten will shed the least fur

7. Clip her nails carefully

8. You asked if I found the cat's toys

9. The Siamese cat originated in Asia

10. Did you take the cat to the vet

● Connect to the Writing Process: Editing
Punctuating Sentences

11.–20. Rewrite the sentences above, adding the correct punctuation mark at the end of each sentence.

Communicate Your Ideas

APPLY TO WRITING

Instructions: *Kinds of Sentences*

Your younger brother, who is in kindergarten, wants to bring home the class pet for the weekend. His teacher will not allow him to do so until she is sure that he understands exactly how to care for a hamster. Write your brother a set of instructions that will help him take care of the hamster for the entire weekend. Be sure to use all four types of sentences in your instructions.

Other Uses of Periods

Periods are used in other places besides the ends of sentences.

With Abbreviations

Abbreviations can be a personal form of shorthand. Using them can help you take notes in class more quickly. Most abbreviations, however, should be avoided in formal writing.

Use a period after most abbreviations.

The following list contains some abbreviations that are acceptable in formal writing. For other acceptable abbreviations, look in a dictionary.

ABBREVIATIONS					
TITLES WITH NAMES	Mr.	Ms.	Rev.	Sgt.	Jr.
	Mrs.	Dr.	Gen.	Lt.	Sr.
INITIALS FOR NAMES	D.C. Rosen, Janet L. Lake, F. Scott Fitzgerald				
TIMES WITH NUMBERS	A.M.	P.M.	B.C.	A.D.	
ADDRESSES	Ave.	St.	Blvd.	Rt.	Dept.
ORGANIZATIONS AND COMPANIES	Co.	Inc.	Corp.	Assoc.	

You may have noticed that some organizations and companies are known by abbreviations that stand for their full names. The majority of these abbreviations do not use periods. A few other common abbreviations also do not include periods.

APO = Army Post Office
FBI = Federal Bureau of Investigation
NASA = National Aeronautics and Space Administration
rpm = revolutions per minute
cm = centimeter

A statement that ends with an abbreviation needs only one period. An interrogative or an exclamatory sentence that ends with an abbreviation needs both marks of punctuation.

The play begins at 8:30 P.M.

Does the play begin at 8:30 P.M.?

No, the play begins at 8:00 P.M.!

Today almost everyone uses the United States Postal Service's two-letter state abbreviations. They do not include periods. You can find a list of these abbreviations at the front of most telephone books. The following are a few examples.

STATE ABBREVIATIONS		
AR = Arkansas	FL = Florida	ME = Maine
AZ = Arizona	IA = Iowa	NY = New York
CA = California	ID = Idaho	OR = Oregon
DE = Delaware	MA = Massachusetts	VA = Virginia

With Outlines

Use a period after each number or letter that shows a division in an outline.

I. Greek Myths
   A. Used to teach in ancient times
      1. Explained a natural event
      2. Taught a moral lesson

   B. Taught as literature today
      1. Characteristics
      2. Structure

II. Roman Myths

You can learn about capitalization of outlines on pages L378–L379.

PRACTICE YOUR SKILLS

● Check Your Understanding
Identifying Correct Abbreviations

**Write *a* or *b* to indicate the abbreviation that is correctly
punctuated in each of the following pairs.**

1. a. BC   **8. a.** m.p.h.
   b. B.C.   **b.** mph

2. a. Jr.   **9. a.** AVE.
   b. JR   **b.** Ave.

3. a. U.S.   **10. a.** doz.
   b. US   **b.** DOZ

4. a. MA   **11. a.** Dr.
   b. Ma.   **b.** DR

5. a. Oct.   **12. a.** Inc.
   b. OCT   **b.** INC.

6. a. ml   **13. a.** F.L.
   b. ml.   **b.** FL

7. a. Assoc.   **14. a.** AM
   b. ASSOC   **b.** A.M.

● Connect to the Writing Process: Editing
Using Periods

**Rewrite the following sentences and correctly punctuate them.
If a sentence is correct, write *C*.**

15. Did you know that the President lives at 1600
Pennsylvania Ave?

16. The White House is located in Washington, D.C..

17. Dr and Mrs Rivera have been guests at the White House
on a regular basis

18. The White House was designed in AD 1792.

19. Has the head of NASA been invited to the White House
recently?

20. Where is the main office of the f.b.i.?

Communicate Your Ideas

APPLY TO WRITING

Invitation: *Abbreviations*

You are planning a surprise party to celebrate your parents' anniversary. Design an invitation and address it to one of their friends. Include information about where and when the party will be held. Be sure to use abbreviations correctly.

QuickCheck Mixed Practice

History Topic **Rewrite the following outline, adding periods where needed.**

   I   The Battle of Gettysburg
      A   Fought at Gettysburg, PA
      B   Occurred July 1–3, AD 1863
  II. Commanders
      A Confederate
          1   Gen. Robert E Lee
          2. Gen George Pickett
          3   Gen James Longstreet
      B. Union
          1. Gen George G Meade
  III The First Day

Commas That Separate

Basically a comma has two purposes. Commas are used to separate items, and commas are used to enclose items. Without commas, some items in a sentence would run into one another, causing confusion. The following are some situations in which commas should be used to separate items.

Items in a Series

Three or more similar items together form a series. Words, phrases, or clauses can be written as a series.

Use commas to separate items in a series.

WORDS	I need to buy sunscreen, sunglasses, a towel, and a hat. (nouns)
	Today I washed the boat, waxed the car, and repaired the trailer. (verbs)
PHRASES	Did you look on the deck, behind the mast, and under the boom? (prepositional phrases)
CLAUSES	I don't know what time the regatta is, where it is, or who will be there. (noun clauses)

Through common usage it has become acceptable to omit the comma before the conjunction that connects the last two items in a series. However, if that comma is omitted, some sentences could be misread. That is why it is better to include the comma before the conjunction.

CONFUSING	The restaurant had banana, bran, blueberry and raisin muffins.
CLEAR	The restaurant had banana, bran, blueberry, and raisin muffins.

If conjunctions connect all the items in a series, no commas are needed.

> We can go sailing on Friday **or** Saturday **or** Sunday.

Some words, such as *macaroni and cheese,* are thought of as a single item. If one of these pairs of words appears in a series, consider it one item.

> For breakfast I ordered juice, ham and eggs, and a muffin.

Adjectives Before a Noun

Sometimes a comma should separate two adjectives that are not connected by a conjunction.

> We followed the steep, narrow road to their beach house.

It is sometimes necessary to use a comma to separate two adjectives that precede a noun and are not joined by a conjunction.

There is a test that can help you decide if a comma is needed between two adjectives. If a sentence reads sensibly with *and* between the adjectives, a comma is needed.

COMMA	Don't lean on that old, rickety boat.
	(*Old **and** rickety boat* reads well.)
NO COMMA	Don't lean on that old green boat.
	(*Old **and** green boat* does not read well.)

Usually no comma is needed after a number or after an adjective that refers to size, shape, or age. For example, no commas are needed in the following expressions.

ADJECTIVE EXPRESSIONS	
two short messages	a tall elderly man
round green eyes	large red apples

PRACTICE YOUR SKILLS

● Check Your Understanding
Using Commas to Separate

Contemporary Life **Write *a* or *b* to indicate which sentence in each pair shows the correct use of commas.**

1. a. Dad's new sailboat turns well, sails fast, and attracts much attention on the lake.

 b. Dad's new sailboat turns well sails fast, and attracts much attention on the lake.

2. a. Jet skis, sailboards and motor boats are popular.

 b. Jet skis, sailboards, and motor boats are popular.

3. a. Catamarans are fast versatile boats.

 b. Catamarans are fast, versatile boats.

4. a. The cabin cruiser rolled pitched, and tossed in the stormy waters.

 b. The cabin cruiser rolled, pitched, and tossed in the stormy waters.

5. a. I don't know whether I should sail, whether I should water-ski, or whether I should swim.

 b. I don't know whether I should sail whether I should water-ski, or whether I should swim.

6. a. From the cliff we viewed the dark blue sea.

 b. From the cliff we viewed the dark, blue sea.

7. a. The skipper said to straighten the tiller, pull in the jib sheet, and coil the extra lines.

b. The skipper said to straighten the tiller, pull in the jib sheet and coil the extra lines.

8. a. Over the centuries ships have been made from such substances as wood, steel, and fiberglass.

b. Over the centuries ships have been made from such substances as wood steel and fiberglass.

9. a. Eager young sailors can learn to sail in a few days.

b. Eager, young sailors can learn to sail in a few days.

10. a. The harsh wind blew throughout the night, into the morning, and until three o'clock the following afternoon.

b. The harsh wind blew throughout the night into the morning, and until three o'clock the following afternoon.

11. a. Our sailing crew should include Jennifer Tim and David.

b. Our sailing crew should include Jennifer, Tim, and David.

12. a. Hot humid weather isn't good for sailing.

b. Hot, humid weather isn't good for sailing.

13. a. The captain should be experienced and reliable and intelligent.

b. The captain should be experienced, and reliable, and intelligent.

14. a. Tell me what you have planned for the regatta, what I can bring, and when you need it.

b. Tell me what you have planned for the regatta what I can bring, and when you need it.

15. a. Should we snack on nuts, cheese, and crackers or fresh fruit on the boat?

b. Should we snack on nuts, cheese and crackers, or fresh fruit on the boat?

Writing Sentences

Write sentences that follow each set of directions. Add commas where needed.

16. Include a series of verbs that describe the actions of someone diving off a high board.

17. Include a series of nouns that name what you ate for lunch yesterday.

18. Include a series of prepositional phrases that tell where you might look for a missing tennis ball.

19. Include a noun that is described by two adjectives separated with a comma.

20. Include a noun that is described by two adjectives that are *not* separated by a comma.

21. Include a series of verbs that tell what you did yesterday.

22. Include a series of prepositional phrases that tell why you like your favorite food.

● Connect to the Writing Process: Editing
Using Commas Correctly

Write each sentence, adding a comma or commas where needed. If a sentence does not need any commas, write C for correct.

23. We spent the hot July weekend at the beach.

24. Florida has some of America's best tourist attractions warmest weather and prettiest beaches.

25. Tourists enjoy that warm sunny weather.

26. Bob described scouting for fish, catching the fish, and cleaning the fish.

27. Do you want baked fish, fish and chips or poached fish for dinner?

28. Actually, I would prefer a bowl of cantaloupe, watermelon pineapple, and strawberries.

APPLY TO WRITING
Advertisement: *Commas*

Claude Monet. *Beach at Trouville*, 1870.
Oil on canvas, 21^{15}/$_{16}$ by 22^{5}/$_{8}$ inches. Wadsworth Atheneum, Hartford.

The year is 1870, and you work for an advertising agency in France. You have an assignment to design a tourism ad that will bring people to the beaches in Trouville. As you stroll along the beach depicted in the Monet painting, describe the scene in two paragraphs suitable for a travel brochure. Be sure to use commas properly.

Compound Sentences

A compound sentence becomes a run-on sentence when independent clauses are not separated. Using a conjunction and a comma is one way to correct run-on sentences.

Use a comma to separate independent clauses of a compound sentence if the clauses are joined by a coordinating conjunction.

A comma is usually placed before the conjunctions *and, but, or, nor, for, so,* and *yet* in a compound sentence.

> Come to my house, and we'll look at the turtle shell.
> The turtle swims quickly, but it walks slowly.

A comma is not needed in a very short compound sentence—unless the conjunction separating the independent clauses is *yet* or *for*.

> No Comma   The turtle moved but I stayed.
> Comma   I waited, for I was curious.

Be careful that you do not confuse a compound sentence with a simple sentence that has a compound verb. No comma comes before the parts of a compound verb unless there are three or more verbs.

> Compound Sentence   The scientist pitched the tent, and I built a fire.
> (A comma is needed.)
>
> Compound Verb   The scientist pitched the tent and built a fire.
> (No comma is needed.)

A compound sentence can also be joined by a semicolon. You can learn more about semicolons on pages L501–L505.

CONNECT TO WRITER'S CRAFT

Writers will sometimes deliberately use a run-on sentence to create a scene or mood. In the passage at the top of the next page, notice how Charles Dickens uses commas to separate pairs of independent clauses that show the opposites that exist in the two cities of London and Paris.

It was the best of times, it was the worst of times, it was the age of wisdom, it was the age of foolishness, it was the epoch of belief, it was the epoch of incredulity, it was the season of Light, it was the season of Darkness, it was the spring of hope, it was the winter of despair, we had everything before us, we had nothing before us, we were all going direct to Heaven, we were all going direct the other way.

—Charles Dickens, A Tale of Two Cities

You can learn more about run-on sentences on pages L183–L184.

PRACTICE YOUR SKILLS

● Check Your Understanding
Using Commas with Compound Sentences

Science Topic **Write *a* or *b* to indicate which sentence in each pair shows the correct use of commas.**

1. **a.** Look carefully, for turtles are hard to find.

   b. Look carefully for turtles, are hard to find.

2. **a.** Turtles are hard to find and, they like to hide in their shells.

   b. Turtles are hard to find, and they like to hide in their shells.

3. **a.** Snapping turtles look fearsome, yet they seldom bite people.

   b. Snapping turtles look fearsome yet, they seldom bite people.

4. **a.** Turtles like to sun themselves and eat plants, and fish.

   b. Turtles like to sun themselves and eat plants and fish.

5. **a.** Snapping turtles are to be feared, for they can sever fingers.

   b. Snapping turtles are to be feared for, they can sever fingers.

6. a. The turtle's shell was scaly and its feet had claws.

   b. The turtle's shell was scaly, and its feet had claws.

7. a. Many baby turtles are eaten by raccoons, so some kinds of turtles are scarce.

   b. Many, baby turtles are eaten by raccoons so some kinds of turtles are scarce.

8. a. Snapping turtles are loners, and often live quiet lives.

   b. Snapping turtles are loners and often live quiet lives.

9. a. Turtles and tortoises belong to the same family, but turtles live near the water.

   b. Turtles and tortoises belong to the same family but, turtles live near the water.

10. a. Be careful, for turtles can be trouble.

   b. Be careful for turtles, can be trouble.

● Connect to the Writing Process: Drafting
Writing Compound Sentences

Write one compound sentence for each of the following subjects. Make sure the clauses in each compound sentence are related. Add commas where needed.

11. turtles

12. fishing

13. water

14. scientists

15. boats

● Connect to the Writing Process: Editing
Using Commas in Compound Sentences

Write each sentence, adding a comma or commas where needed. If a sentence does not need any commas, write C for correct.

16. The scientists were close to the turtle's nest but they turned back because of bad weather.

17. They plowed through the underbrush and made their way to a clearing.

18. You need to move more quickly or you will miss the turtles hatching.

19. All the eggs have hatched and the baby turtles have left the nest.

20. Photograph these baby turtles now, for tomorrow they will be gone.

Introductory Elements

Certain words, phrases, and clauses that come at the beginning of a sentence need to be separated from the rest of the sentence by a comma.

Use a comma after certain introductory elements.

The following are examples of introductory elements that should be followed by a comma.

WORDS	**Why,** surely you've studied the material. *(No, now, oh, well,* and *yes* are other introductory words—unless they are a part of the sentence; for example, *Why didn't you go?)*
PREPOSITIONAL PHRASES	**After five hours of studying,** I never wanted to sit down again. (A comma comes after more than one prepositional phrase or a prepositional phrase of four or more words.)
PARTICIPIAL PHRASES	**Opening my grammar book,** I found my missing class notes.
ADVERB CLAUSE	**Since the day was overcast,** I took an umbrella to school with me.

Notice on the next page that the punctuation of shorter phrases varies. Also, never place a comma after phrases followed by a verb.

In Room 151, one hundred persons were gathered.

(A comma follows a phrase that ends with a number.)

Behind Ben, Stanley paced back and forth.

(A comma is used to prevent confusion.)

In the center of the room were the tests.

(No comma is used because the verb follows the introductory phrases.)

PRACTICE YOUR SKILLS

● Check Your Understanding
Using Commas with Introductory Elements

Contemporary Life **Write *a* or *b* to indicate which sentence in each pair shows the correct use of commas.**

1. a. Now, this is your last chance.

　 b. Now this, is your last chance.

2. a. Without studying, for the test you cannot hope to pass.

　 b. Without studying for the test, you cannot hope to pass.

3. a. Since the beginning of the year, Sheila has been using Gary's notes.

　 b. Since the beginning, of the year Sheila has been using Gary's notes.

4. a. Reading far into the night we often had to stop, and rest.

　 b. Reading far into the night, we often had to stop and rest

5. a. Along with Jan Jo decided to stop studying.

　 b. Along with Jan, Jo decided to stop studying.

6. a. After studying for eight hours straight, we were exhausted.

   b. After studying for eight hours straight we were exhausted.

7. a. Now is the time to take the test.

   b. Now, is the time to take the test.

8. a. In the back of the room were some extra pencils.

   b. In the back of the room, were some extra pencils.

9. a. During a test I feel more confident if I have studied.

   b. During a test, I feel more confident if I have studied.

10. a. No, I do not know the correct answer to the essay question.

   b. No I do not know the correct answer, to the essay question.

● Connect to the Writing Process: Drafting
Writing Sentences

Write sentences that follow each set of directions. Add commas where needed.

11. Begin a sentence with the introductory word *well*.

12. Begin a sentence with a three-word prepositional phrase.

13. Begin a sentence with a prepositional phrase of four or more words.

14. Begin a sentence with a participial phrase.

15. Begin a sentence with an adverb clause.

● Connect to the Writing Process: Editing
Using Commas with Introductory Elements

Write each sentence, adding a comma or commas where needed. If a sentence does not need any commas, write C for correct.

16. Among the thirty-five students in our class twenty-five got an A on the test.

17. After English math is my favorite subject.

18. According to Mrs. Wood Shakespeare was the greatest playwright ever.

19. Dating back to the sixteenth century Shakespeare's work contains themes that still apply today.

20. While I was studying for my English test I discovered that my notes were incomplete.

⏵ Commonly Used Commas

There are a few other rules for commas that you use almost daily.

With Dates and Addresses

Commas are most commonly used to separate the elements of dates and addresses.

Use commas to separate the elements in dates and addresses.

Notice in the following examples that a comma is used to separate a date or an address from the rest of the sentence. No comma, however, separates the state and the ZIP code.

DATE   On Saturday, March 9, 1975, my parents were married in a small ceremony.

ADDRESS   We are ordering invitations for an anniversary party from Paper Products, 1330 West 11th Street, Cleveland, Ohio 44113, today.

When only the month and year are stated, the commas may be omitted.

My parents were married in March 1975.

By July 1976, my aunt and uncle were married as well.

In Letters

Commas are also used to separate the salutation and the closing from the body of a letter.

Use a comma after the salutation of a friendly letter and after the closing of all letters.

SALUTATIONS AND CLOSINGS		
SALUTATIONS	Dear Mom,	Dear Kathy,
CLOSINGS	Love,	Sincerely yours,

Often the use of too many commas is as confusing as not using enough commas. Use commas only where a rule indicates they are needed. In other words, use commas only where they make your writing clearer.

PRACTICE YOUR SKILLS

 Check Your Understanding
Using Commas

General Interest **Write *a* or *b* to indicate which sentence in each pair shows the correct use of commas.**

1. a. On March 12 1888, a terrible blizzard struck New York City.

   b. On March 12, 1888, a terrible blizzard struck New York City.

2. a. Belfast, Ireland, is the largest linen manufacturer in the world.

   b. Belfast Ireland, is the largest linen manufacturer in the world.

3. a. Send all travel inquiries to Martha Witt, 3297 Princeton Drive, Mobile, Alabama 36618, before May 1.

   b. Send all travel inquiries to Martha Witt 3297 Princeton Drive, Mobile Alabama 36618, before May 1.

4. a. I was amazed to learn that the temperature near Death Valley reached a record high of 134 degrees in July 1913.

b. I was amazed to learn that the temperature near Death Valley reached a record high of 134 degrees in July, 1913.

5. a. On October 1 1908, Henry Ford introduced his famous Model T Ford.

b. On October 1, 1908, Henry Ford introduced his famous Model T Ford.

6. a. All final sales reports for the past season are due on Mrs. Johannsen's desk by Friday, February 6.

b. All final sales reports for the past season are due on Mrs. Johannsen's desk by Friday February, 6.

7. a. On May 14, 1948, the new state of Israel was proclaimed in Tel Aviv.

b. On May 14, 1948 the new state of Israel, was proclaimed in Tel Aviv.

8. a. The first professional football game was played on September, 3 1895 in Latrobe Pennsylvania.

b. The first professional football game was played on September 3, 1895, in Latrobe, Pennsylvania.

9. a. On Sunday, May 18, 1980, Washington's Mount St. Helens erupted.

b. On Sunday May 18, 1980, Washington's Mount St. Helens erupted.

10. a. General Lee met General Grant in Appomattox, Virginia, to discuss terms of the Confederate Army's surrender.

b. General Lee met General Grant in Appomattox Virginia to discuss terms of the Confederate Army's surrender.

Rewrite the following letter, adding commas where needed.

> 1251 Smith Street
>
> Dimebox TX 78934
>
> March 15 1999

Dear Beth

    We have been looking forward to your visit. It is hard to believe that a year has passed since you were here.

    Mom says to tell you that you can take a cab from the airport to Aunt Velma's house. Just tell the driver to stop at 642 Main Street Selma Texas.

    I can hardly wait to see you.

> Your cousin
>
> Sara

Communicate Your Ideas

APPLY TO WRITING

E-Mail: *Commas*

You and your best friend have decided to go ice skating at a local skating rink. Write an E-mail to your friend, providing information about the day, date, time, and place where he or she should meet you. Be sure to use commas correctly to separate addresses and dates.

General Interest **Write the paragraphs that follow, adding commas where needed.**

On May 6 1929 a group of athletes lined up at City Hall in New York City. They were waiting for the start of a footrace across the country to San Francisco California. Among the eager group of participants was sixty-year-old Abraham Lincoln Monteverde. Although he was older than the other contestants he was a competitor to be reckoned with. Monteverde had been running for years and he had completed more than one hundred marathons.

During the 3,145 miles of the course Monteverde's younger competitors dropped out, one by one. When Monteverde neared San Francisco he found that he had no company at all. Everyone else had quit the race. By reaching San Francisco's City Hall at 7:10 P.M., on July 24 Monteverde had crossed the country in seventy-nine days ten hours and ten minutes. Monteverde's experience and determination had paid off!

Commas That Enclose

One or two commas are used to set off, or enclose, some expressions that interrupt the flow of a sentence. These expressions generally add information that is not needed to understand the main idea of a sentence. If one of these interrupters comes in the middle of a sentence, two commas are needed to set it off from the rest of the sentence. If an interrupter comes at the beginning or at the end of a sentence, only one comma is needed to set it off.

 ## Direct Address

Names, titles, or other words used to address someone directly are set off by commas. These expressions are called nouns of **direct address.**

> Use commas to set off nouns of direct address.

Randy, do you know who got the part?
The players, **Mr. Director,** are ready.
Thanks for the theater tickets, **my friends.**

 ## Parenthetical Expressions

A parenthetical expression provides additional information that can easily be removed without changing the meaning of a sentence.

> Use commas to set off parenthetical expressions.

Consequently, the show started two hours late.
Mona, **like Samantha,** is a soprano.
Reserved seats are extra, **according to the brochure.**

The following list contains common parenthetical expressions.

COMMON PARENTHETICAL EXPRESSIONS		
after all	for instance	of course
at any rate	generally speaking	on the contrary
by the way	I believe (guess,	on the other hand
consequently	hope, know, think)	moreover
however	in fact	nevertheless
for example	in my opinion	to tell the truth

Occasionally, one of the parenthetical expressions listed in the preceding box does not interrupt a sentence. In that case, the expression should not be enclosed in commas.

COMMAS   The actors, **I believe,** are not ready.

(*I believe* interrupts the sentence.)

NO COMMAS   **I believe** everything you said.

(*I believe* is necessary for the meaning of the sentence.)

Contrasting expressions, which usually begin with *not,* are also considered parenthetical expressions.

Dramas, **not comedies,** are her favorite plays.

● Appositives

An appositive with its modifiers identifies or explains a noun or pronoun in a sentence.

Use commas to set off most appositives and their modifiers.

Mr. Roberts, **our drama coach,** just got married.
We listened to "Memory," **a song from *Cats.***

Commas are not used with an appositive if it identifies a person or thing by answering the question *Which one?* or *Which ones?* Usually these appositives are names and have no modifiers.

I enjoyed the play **Hamlet.**

(Which play?)

The color **blue** has many shades.

(Which color?)

Titles and degrees that follow a name are also set off by commas.

Lawrence T. Mahoney, **Jr.,** was elected drama club treasurer.

Jennifer Morgan, **Ph.D.,** will introduce the show.

You can learn more about appositives on pages L119–L120.

PRACTICE YOUR SKILLS

 Check Your Understanding
Using Commas with Interrupters

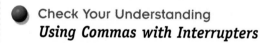 Contemporary Life **Write *a* or *b* to indicate which sentence in each pair shows the correct use of commas.**

1. a. Mr. Donaldson, the most ambitious drama coach at our school, wants to direct a musical.

   b. Mr. Donaldson, the most ambitious drama coach at our school wants to direct a musical.

2. a. A musical is after all, one of the most challenging forms of theater.

   b. A musical is, after all, one of the most challenging forms of theater.

3. a. Randy, not Stewart, is being considered for the lead.

   b. Randy not Stewart, is being considered for the lead.

4. a. Have you ever heard him sing Mara?

   b. Have you ever heard him sing, Mara?

5. a. Mr. Donaldson wants to put on the musical *Camelot*.

   b. Mr. Donaldson wants to put on the musical, *Camelot*.

6. a. Maria, is Dr. Angelo S. DeVito Jr. your voice coach or your acting coach?

   b. Maria, is Dr. Angelo S. DeVito, Jr., your voice coach or your acting coach?

7. a. I hope everyone will work hard on the musical.

   b. I hope, everyone will work hard on the musical.

8. a. Julia, has had many more years of performing experience moreover.

   b. Julia has had many more years of performing experience, moreover.

9. a. My oldest brother Joey hopes to work on the stage crew.

   b. My oldest brother, Joey, hopes to work on the stage crew.

10. a. Our production of *Camelot*, unlike our last production, will open on a Friday.

   b. Our production of *Camelot* unlike our last production, will open on a Friday.

● Connect to the Writing Process: Drafting
Writing Sentences with Interrupters

Write sentences that follow each set of directions. Add commas where needed.

11. Write a sentence that uses a direct address at the beginning of the sentence

12. Write a sentence that uses a parenthetical expression at the end of a sentence.

13. Write a sentence using an appositive in the middle of the sentence.

14. Write a sentence using a title or degree as an appositive.

15. Write a sentence using a contrasting expression as a parenthetical expression.

Write each sentence, adding a comma or commas where needed. If a sentence does not need any commas, write C for correct.

16. Despite popular belief many theater superstitions are completely unfounded.

17. The play *Macbeth* is thought to be cursed.

18. Jennifer please post the cast list for the musical.

19. Stewart one of the best actors did not get a role in the new musical.

20. Tracy Bedford Ph.D. will attend our evening performance.

● Nonessential Elements

Sometimes a participial phrase or a clause is not essential to the meaning of a sentence.

Use commas to set off nonessential participial phrases and nonessential clauses.

A participial phrase or a clause is **nonessential** if it provides extra, unnecessary information. As a test, read the sentence without the phrase or clause. If the phrase or the clause could be removed without changing the basic meaning of the sentence, it is nonessential. A phrase or clause that modifies a proper noun is almost always nonessential.

NONESSENTIAL PARTICIPIAL PHRASE

Roy Pierce, **standing by the door,** is a Revolutionary War expert.

(*Roy Pierce is a Revolutionary War expert* is the only essential information in this sentence.)

NONESSENTIAL ADJECTIVE CLAUSE	In school we studied the Declaration of Independence, **which was written in 1776.**
	(In school we studied the Declaration of Independence is the only essential information in this sentence.*)*

No commas are used if a participial phrase or a clause is essential to the meaning of a sentence. An **essential** phrase or clause usually identifies a person or thing and answers the question *Which one?* Adjective clauses that begin with *that* are usually essential.

ESSENTIAL PARTICIPIAL PHRASE	The student **standing by the door** is Roy Pierce.
	(Standing by the door is essential because it is needed to identify which student.*)*
ESSENTIAL ADJECTIVE CLAUSE	The Betsy Ross story **that you told** was fascinating.
	(That you told is essential because it tells which Betsy Ross story was fascinating.*)*

Nonessential and essential elements are also called nonrestrictive *and* restrictive.

PRACTICE YOUR SKILLS

● Check Your Understanding
Using Commas with Nonessential Elements

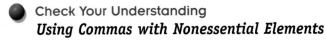 History Topic **Write *a* or *b* to indicate which sentence in each pair shows the correct use of commas.**

1. **a.** The words written in the Declaration of Independence should be known by every American.

   b. The words, written in the Declaration of Independence, should be known by every American.

2. **a.** George Washington, who led the American troops to victory, later became this country's first president.

b. George Washington who led the American troops to victory later became this country's first president.

3. a. The Liberty Bell cracked on one side is a popular tourist attraction.

b. The Liberty Bell, cracked on one side, is a popular tourist attraction.

4. a. Philadelphia, which is called the City of Brotherly Love, is where the Declaration of Independence was signed.

b. Philadelphia which is called the City of Brotherly Love is where the Declaration of Independence was signed.

5. a. The document that was written by Thomas Jefferson remains one of the most important pieces of writing in American history.

b. The document, that was written by Thomas Jefferson, remains one of the most important pieces of writing in American history.

6. a. The first Independence Day celebrated in 1776 was truly a historic occasion.

b. The first Independence Day, celebrated in 1776, was truly a historic occasion.

7. a. The Declaration of Independence, signed by many influential colonists, got King George's attention.

b. The Declaration of Independence signed by many influential colonists got King George's attention.

8. a. The signature, that was written by John Hancock, was the boldest.

b. The signature that was written by John Hancock was the boldest.

9. a. The possibility of a war with England, which had been escalating for years, became a certainty.

b. The possibility of a war with England which had been escalating for years became a certainty.

10. a. The Declaration of Independence, displayed in Philadelphia, is an important part of our history.

b. The Declaration of Independence displayed in Philadelphia, is an important part of our history.

Writing Sentences

Write sentences that follow each set of directions. Add commas where needed.

11. Write a sentence using a nonessential participial phrase.

12. Write a sentence using a nonessential adjective clause.

13. Write a sentence using an essential participial phrase.

14. Write a sentence using an essential adjective clause.

15. Write a sentence using a nonessential participial phrase.

● Connect to the Writing Process: Editing
Using Commas with Nonessential Elements

Write the paragraphs below, adding commas where needed.

Just before the Declaration of Independence was signed, three men visited a woman named Betsy Ross. She was a seamstress in Philadelphia. These men were members of the flag committee of the Continental Congress commissioned in 1776. The men asked her to sew the first flag which was sketched on a piece of paper.

In fact, there was no official flag committee in 1776, and this event never happened. Almost one hundred years later, William J. Canby who was Betsy Ross's grandson first told the story about his grandmother's making the flag. However, there is no written proof, and none of Betsy's other relatives ever remembered seeing her make the first Stars and Stripes!

Communicate Your Ideas

APPLY TO WRITING
News Article: *Commas with Nonessential Elements*

You have traveled back in time to your favorite period in history. Since you know your friends will never believe that you witnessed a historical event, you decide to write a newspaper article. Be sure that your news article covers the event thoroughly and uses commas with participial phrases and adjective clauses correctly.

QuickCheck Mixed Practice

Sports Topic **Write the paragraph below, adding commas where needed.**

At the closing ceremony of the 1912 Olympic Games in Stockholm Sweden the King of Sweden spoke with Jim Thorpe a young American Indian. The king praised Thorpe for being the greatest athlete in the world and the American certainly was. Thorpe who had studied at Carlisle Institute excelled in boxing wrestling lacrosse gymnastics swimming hockey handball football track and baseball. Indeed many authorities rate Thorpe as the finest football player who ever lived. Playing on his college team Thorpe scored twenty-five touchdowns and made 198 points in a single season. When Thorpe was thirty-two he got into professional football and pro football's Hall of Fame eventually made him a member.

Using Commas Correctly

Write each sentence, adding commas where needed.

1. Everyone has heard of Samuel F. B. Morse the inventor of the telegraph.

2. He was born on April 27 1791 in Charlestown MA.

3. For many years during his life Morse was a respectable gifted painter.

4. Eventually he became tired of painting portraits of men women and children.

5. While he was on a trip from France to New York Morse got the idea for a magnetic telegraph.

6. Morse created a prototype which used magnetic transmitters and receivers to send signals across a wire.

7. With further work on his invention he then developed a language of dots and dashes known as Morse Code.

8. His first efforts to sell his invention however were met with disbelief.

9. Years passed but he finally secured money from Congress.

10. A public test of his telegraph was held on May 24 1844.

11. A long-distance wire was strung between posts in Baltimore Maryland and Washington D.C.

12. The test was a great success and Morse became quite famous after that.

13. Yes Morse also became a rich man.

14. By the time Morse died in 1872 the telegraph was being used around the globe.

15. Forgetting about his early career as a painter the history books talk only about Mr. Morse the inventor.

Understanding Kinds of Sentences and End Marks

Write an appropriate end mark for each sentence. Then label each sentence *declarative, imperative, interrogative,* or *exclamatory.*

1. Be prepared for some surprises

2. For example, is a peanut a nut

3. No, it's a seed like a pea or a bean, but it looks and tastes like a nut

4. Have you ever wondered why root beer has the word *root* in it

5. Take a good guess

6. Yes, root beer is made from a root, the root of the sassafras tree

7. When you eat mushrooms, you're not eating a plant; you're eating a fungus

8. Does the cinnamon you sprinkle on applesauce come from a cinnamon plant

9. No, cinnamon actually comes from the bark of the cinnamon tree

10. Be careful what you eat in the future

Writing Sentences with Commas

Write sentences that follow the directions below.

1. Write a sentence that includes a series of nouns.

2. Write a sentence that includes two or more adjectives before a noun.

3. Write a sentence that has two independent clauses joined by a coordinating conjunction.

4. Write a sentence that includes an introductory participial phrase.

5. Write a sentence that includes an introductory adverbial clause.

Language and *Self-Expression*

Francisco Matto is a sculptor from Uruguay. After he taught himself to paint, he became a member of the *Taller Torres-García,* a group of artists who expressed themselves through painting, sculpture, wood and iron reliefs, architecture, furniture, and murals.

Matto's sculptures are totems, symbols used to represent certain subgroups in a culture. Think of a totem that has an impact on your life, such as an advertising logo or a school or team mascot. Write an essay describing the totem and explaining its symbolic meaning and its meaning to the group it represents. Use end marks and commas correctly in your essay.

Prewriting Create a word web around the symbol you have chosen to describe. Your web can include descriptive information about the symbol, analysis of its symbolic meaning, explanations of when and where it is used, and a description of its meaning to the group it represents.

Drafting Use your word web as the basis for a draft of your essay. Be sure you explain in the essay why the symbol you have chosen is a totem; that is, explain why it represents a cultural group.

Revising Reread your essay carefully. Have you given a complete description and analysis of the totem you have chosen? Be certain that readers will understand why you have chosen the symbol you did. Add any additional information that will clarify your choice.

Editing Go over your essay for errors in spelling and punctuation. Be sure your sentences end with the appropriate punctuation and check your use of commas.

Publishing Make a final copy of your essay. Read it aloud to the class, and encourage discussion of your choice of totem. Does the class agree that it represents a cultural group?

Another Look

Kinds of Sentences and End Marks

A **declarative sentence** makes a statement or expresses an opinion and ends with a period.

An **imperative sentence** gives a direction, makes a request, or gives a command. It ends with either a period or an exclamation point.

An **interrogative sentence** asks a question and ends with a question mark.

An **exclamatory sentence** expresses strong feeling or emotion and ends with an exclamation point.

Other Uses of Periods

Use a period after most abbreviations. *(pages L414–L415)*

Use a period after each number or letter that shows a division in an outline. *(page L415)*

Commas That Separate

Use commas to separate items in a series. *(pages L418–L419)*

Use a comma sometimes to separate two adjectives that precede a noun and are not joined by a conjunction. *(pages L419–L420)*

Use a comma to separate the independent clauses of a compound sentence if the clauses are joined by a coordinating conjunction. *(pages L423–L425)*

Use a comma after certain introductory elements. *(pages L427–L428)*

Use commas to separate the elements in dates and addresses. *(page L430)*

Use a comma after the salutation of a friendly letter and after the closing of all letters. *(page L431)*

Commas That Enclose

Use commas to set off nouns of direct address. *(page L435)*

Use commas to set off parenthetical expressions. *(pages L435–L436)*

Use commas to set off most appositives and their modifiers. *(pages L436–L437)*

Use commas to set off nonessential participial phrases and nonessential clauses. *(pages L439–L440)*

Posttest

Directions

Read the passage. Each underlined part is missing punctuation. Write the letter of the correct way to write each part. If the underlined part contains no error, write *D*.

EXAMPLE   Have you learned about <u>the beginnings of World</u>
                                                      (1)
           <u>War I!</u>

1 **A** the beginnings, of World War I?

   B the beginnings of World War I.

   C the beginnings of World War I?

   D No error

ANSWER   **1 C**

On <u>June 28 1914</u> an event occurred in <u>Sarajevo the capital</u> of
      (1)   (2)
Bosnia and Herzegovina, that changed the world. The heir to the

throne of <u>Austria Archduke Francis Ferdinand</u> was assassinated. The
                          (3)
assassin was a Serbian nationalist, one of <u>many who were opposed</u>
                                                              (4)
to Austrian rule. As a result, the Austrian government wanted to

discipline the <u>Serbian nationalists and the government</u> issued an
                               (5)
ultimatum demanding an end to all anti-Austrian activities by

Serbs.

1 **A** June 28 1914,

   B June 28, 1914,

   C June, 28, 1914,

   D No error

2 **A** Sarajevo, the capital

   B Sarajevo, the capital,

   C Sarajevo the capital,

   D No error

3 **A** Austria, Archduke Francis Ferdinand

   B Austria, Archduke Francis Ferdinand,

   C Austria Archduke Francis Ferdinand,

   D No error

4 **A** many, who were opposed

   B many who, were opposed

   C many who were, opposed

   D No error

5 **A** Serbian nationalists, and the government

   B Serbian nationalists and, the government

   C Serbian nationalists and, the government,

   D No error

CHAPTER 11

Italics and Quotation Marks

Pretest

Directions

Read the passage. Each underlined part may contain errors in the use of italics and/or quotation marks. Choose the best way to write each part and write the letter of the correct answer. If the underlined part contains no error, write *D*.

EXAMPLE

My favorite science fiction story is <u>The Veldt.</u>
(1)

1 A "The Veldt."

B *The Veldt.*

C the "Veldt."

D No error

ANSWER **1 A**

<u>"Did you see the new science fiction movie"? Jamal</u>
(1)
<u>asked Nia.</u>

<u>"No, Nia said "but I read about in the New York Times."</u>
(2)
<u>Jamal exclaimed, "Those movie critics never like anything!</u>
(3)
Nia replied, "The newspaper critic and the <u>Newsweek</u>

<u>writer of the article Too Many Special Effects</u> both agreed.
(4)
<u>"There's too much action she added and too little story."</u>
(5)

1 **A** "Did you see the new science fiction movie"?
          Jamal asked, Nia.

   B "Did you see the new science fiction movie?"
          Jamal asked Nia.

   C "Did you see the new science fiction movie,"
          Jamal asked Nia?

   D No error

2 **A** "No." Nia said, "but I read about it in *the New York Times*."

   B "No," Nia said, "but I read about it in the 'New York Times'."

   C "No," Nia said, "but I read about it in the *New York Times*."

   D No error

3 **A** Jamal exclaimed! "Those movie critics never like anything."

   B Jamal exclaimed, "Those movie critics never like anything!"

   C Jamal exclaimed. "Those movie critics never like anything"!

   D No error

4 **A** *Newsweek* writer of the article 'Too Many Special Effects'

   B *Newsweek* writer of the article *Too Many Special Effects*

   C "Newsweek" writer of the article *Too Many Special Effects*

   D No error

5 **A** "There's too much action," she added. "And too little story."

   B "There's too much action," she added, "and too little story."

   C There's too much action, she added, and too little story."

   D No error

Leo and Diane Dillon. Illustration from *Why Mosquitoes Buzz in People's Ears*, by Verna Aardema.
Watercolor, pastel, and ink.

Describe What do you see in this illustration? What animals are portrayed?

Analyze Describe the style the artist uses in her illustration. What effect does the style have?

Interpret What do you think the lion might be saying to the monkey? What might the monkey be answering?

Judge What details appeal to you? Do you like the illustration? Why or why not?

At the end of this chapter, you will use the artwork to stimulate ideas for writing.

Italics (Underlining)

A novel without any conversation would probably be rather dull. Conversation, or dialogue, adds realism to characters in stories and books. A report without references to factual evidence could be questioned or not taken seriously. Stating what authorities say can add support and verification to a report. Since both of these situations involve quotations, learning to punctuate quotations properly is an important skill to master.

This chapter will cover the uses of quotation marks with direct quotations, as well as with titles. First, however, the uses of italics will be reviewed.

You probably already know that italics are printed letters that slant to the right. If you are using a computer, you need to highlight what should be italicized and then use the command for italics. If you are writing by hand, you need to underline whatever should be italicized.

| ITALICS | I have read *The Odyssey* by Homer. |
| UNDERLINING | I have read The Odyssey by Homer. |

Certain letters, numbers, words, titles, and names should be italicized (underlined).

Italicize (underline) letters, numbers, and words when they are used to represent themselves. Also italicize (underline) foreign words that are not generally used in English.

LETTERS, NUMBERS	You never cross your *t*'s or write your *2*s correctly.
WORDS, PHRASES	You never cross your t's or write your 2s correctly.
	I often get chose and choose mixed up.
FOREIGN WORDS	What does *merci beaucoup* mean?

Notice that only the *t* and the *2* in the first example above are underlined or italicized—not the 's or s.

You can learn when to add 's or just s with letters and numbers on pages L497 and L542.

Italicize (underline) the titles of long written or musical works that are published as a single unit. Also italicize the titles of paintings and sculptures and the names of vehicles.

Long written works include books, magazines, newspapers, full-length plays, and long poems. Long musical compositions include operas, symphonies, ballets, and albums. Vehicles include airplanes, ships, trains, and spacecraft. Titles of movies and of radio and TV series should also be italicized (underlined).

ITALICIZED TITLES	
BOOKS	*The Pearl* All Quiet on the Western Front
MAGAZINES	*Sports Illustrated* National Geographic
NEWSPAPERS	*Butler Eagle* Oak Hill Gazette
PLAYS AND MOVIES	*The Crucible* Braveheart
TELEVISION SERIES	*Friends* The Brady Bunch
LONG MUSICAL COMPOSITIONS	*Don Giovanni* Swan Lake
WORKS OF ART	*The Thinker* The Boardwalk at Sainte-Addresse
NAMES OF VEHICLES	the *Mayflower* the Challenger

You can learn more about capitalizing titles on page L398.

PRACTICE YOUR SKILLS

● Check Your Understanding
Using Italics (Underlining)

Write *a* or *b* to indicate which item in each pair is correctly underlined.

1. **a.** Drums Along the Mohawk
   b. Drums Along the Mohawk

2. **a.** the Mona Lisa
   b. the Mona Lisa

3. **a.** the New York Daily News
   b. the New York Daily News

4. **a.** the film Quo Vadis
   b. the film Quo Vadis

5. **a.** an Italian luxury liner, the Andrea Doria
   b. an Italian luxury liner, the Andrea Doria

6. **a.** Strength is an eight-letter word.
   b. Strength is an eight-letter word.

7. **a.** Charles Dickens's A Tale of Two Cities
   b. Charles Dickens's A Tale of Two Cities

8. **a.** the expression sic transit gloria mundi
   b. the expression sic transit gloria mundi

9. **a.** The Reader's Digest
   b. The Reader's Digest

10. **a.** the French dish ratatouille
    b. the French dish ratatouille

● Connect to the Writing Process: Editing
Using Underlining

Rewrite the following sentences, underlining the words that should be italicized.

11. Susan likes to watch the reruns of Fame on TV.

12. My sister always dances the role of Clara in The Nutcracker.

13. The 2s in the program look like s's.

14. Did you know that the ship Titanic is the basis of a Hollywood movie and a Broadway play?

15. Did you pay for your subscription to Dancer?

Communicate Your Ideas

APPLY TO WRITING
Summary: *Italics (Underlining)*

The Morton H. Meyerson Symphony Center in Dallas, Texas.

Your humanities teacher is planning field trips to a local museum, library, and concert hall. Your principal will allow the trips only if you can write a report that shows the educational benefits of the trips. Write a summary of the works you will see or experience on one of the trips. Be sure to italicize or underline properly.

Quotation Marks

Quotation marks come in pairs. They are placed at the beginning and at the end of uninterrupted quotations and certain titles.

Quotation Marks with Titles

Titles of long works of art and of publications such as newspapers or magazines are italicized (underlined). Most of these long works, however, are made up of smaller parts. The titles of these smaller parts should be enclosed in quotation marks.

Use quotation marks to enclose titles of songs, chapters, articles, stories, one-act plays, short poems, and songs.

Smaller parts of long works include episodes from a TV series and movements from long musical compositions. Titles of essays should also be enclosed in quotation marks.

CHAPTER IN A BOOK	In your textbook *Earth Science,* read the chapter "Atoms to Minerals" for homework.
POEM IN A BOOK	Mr. Sullivan's favorite poem from The Essential Blake is "The Tyger."
ARTICLE IN A MAGAZINE OR NEWSPAPER	Did you read the article "The Art of Winning" in *U.S. News and World Report?*
A TELEVISION EPISODE	My Dad watched "A Bluegrass Tribute to Bill Monroe" on Austin City Limits.
A SONG	Not many people can sing "The Star Spangled Banner" well.

PRACTICE YOUR SKILLS

● Check Your Understanding
Using Quotation Marks with Titles

General Interest **Write *a* or *b* to indicate which sentence in each pair uses quotation marks correctly.**

1. **a.** The Allure of Fiber Optics was an interesting article in a recent issue of "Time."
   b. "The Allure of Fiber Optics" was an interesting article in a recent issue of Time.

2. **a.** "Home, Sweet Home" is the only song that John Howard Payne ever wrote.
   b. Home, Sweet Home is the only song that John Howard Payne ever wrote.

3. **a.** Autumn Reflection is a poem published in "Prominent Voices in American Poetry."
   b. "Autumn Reflection" is a poem published in Prominent Voices in American Poetry.

4. **a.** "The Nature of Dreams" is the best chapter in the book The Forgotten Language.
   b. The Nature of Dreams is the best chapter in the book "The Forgotten Language."

5. **a.** "The Bear" is probably William Faulkner's most famous story.
   b. The Bear is probably William Faulkner's most famous story.

● Connect to the Writing Process: Editing
Using Quotation Marks with Titles

Write the following sentences, correcting the use of quotation marks. If a sentence is correct, write *C*.

6. The one-act play To the Chicago Abyss is by Ray Bradbury.

7. One of my favorite episodes of The X-Files is called "Traveler."

8. <u>On the Trail</u> is the best-known movement from the <u>Grand Canyon Suite</u>.

9. "The Yellow Rose of Texas" and <u>My Wild Irish Rose</u> are among the many song titles that refer to roses.

10. The poem <u>Richard Cory</u> by Edwin Arlington Robinson can be found in the book titled <u>Modern American Poetry</u>.

11. The chapter "The Changing City" in our social studies textbook <u>World Geography</u> took me less than an hour to read.

12. Mary was busy watching the "War Stories" episode of <u>Cosby</u> last night.

13. Did you read the article "<u>Cuba Capitalizes</u>" in today's paper?

14. God Save the Queen and My Country 'Tis of Thee share the same tune.

15. The Open Boat by Stephen Crane is a thought-provoking story.

Communicate Your Ideas

APPLY TO WRITING

Bibliography: *Quotation Marks*

One of your friends is putting together a presentation and report that focuses on the culture of a particular period in American history. Help your friend with the research part of the project. Write a bibliography for your friend that lists at least six possible sources of information for the report and presentation. Include the titles of magazine or newspaper articles, song titles, poetry titles, short story titles, essay titles, or titles of book chapters that might be helpful. Be sure to punctuate the titles correctly.

● Quotation Marks with Direct Quotations

Only a **direct quotation**—the exact words of a person—is enclosed in quotation marks.

> Use quotation marks to enclose a person's exact words.

> Amber said, "I will be late for the meeting."

Quotation marks are not used, however, with an **indirect quotation,** a paraphrase of someone's words.

> Amber said that she will be late for the meeting.

Notice that the word *that* often signals an indirect quotation.

> Bill said **that** he might have to miss the meeting.

A one-sentence direct quotation can be written in several ways. It can be placed before or after a speaker tag, such as *she said* or *Bob asked*. When the quotation comes before the speaker tag, quotation marks enclose the person's exact words from beginning to end.

> "The meeting is important," April commented.
>
> April commented, "The meeting is important."

A speaker tag can interrupt a one-sentence quotation. Two pairs of quotation marks are needed in such a situation because quotation marks enclose only a person's exact words—not the speaker tag.

> "The meeting," April commented, "is important."

If you are quoting more than one sentence, place quotation marks at the beginning and at the end of the entire quotation. It is not necessary to put quotation marks around each sentence within a quotation—unless a speaker tag interrupts.

> "The meeting is important," April commented. "I hope that everyone will make a special effort to attend."

PRACTICE YOUR SKILLS

● Check Your Understanding
Using Quotation Marks with Direct Quotations

History Topic **Read each of the following sentences. Write *I* if the quotation marks are used incorrectly and *C* if they are used correctly.**

1. Martin Luther King, Jr., once said, "Injustice anywhere is a threat to justice everywhere."

2. "Why is Dr. King considered such a great leader? Wendy asked."

3. I believe, Edmund stated, "it was because he was such a powerful speaker."

4. Toby said, "I think it was because he demonstrated that nonviolence is effective."

5. He was a great inspiration to us all, "Susan said." He helped change history.

6. "He gave the Civil Rights movement a voice." "People took notice of his presence at a demonstration," Bart explained.

7. "There have been few men as charismatic as Dr. Martin Luther King," said Tanya.

8. "My uncle says he met Dr. King once, mused Benjamin. It was in Memphis."

9. Toby said "that Dr. King was an unusually courageous man."

10. "I don't think we can ever forget Dr. Martin Luther King. He was a tremendous person," Benjamin explained.

● Connect to the Writing Process: Editing
Using Quotation Marks

11.–16. Rewrite the incorrect sentences from the preceding exercise, using quotation marks correctly.

Capital Letters with Direct Quotations

Begin each sentence of a direct quotation with a capital letter.

"**J**ogging regularly has changed my life," she said.

If a quotation follows a speaker tag, two capital letters are needed—one for the first word of the sentence and one for the first word of the quotation.

She said, "**J**ogging regularly has changed my life."

If a single-sentence quotation is interrupted by a speaker tag, only one capital letter is needed—at the beginning of the sentence. In the following example, it would not make sense to capitalize *has,* because it comes in the middle of the sentence.

"**J**ogging regularly," she said, "has changed my life."

PRACTICE YOUR SKILLS

● Check Your Understanding
Using Capital Letters with Direct Quotations

Geography Topic **Write *a* or *b* to indicate which sentence in each pair is correctly capitalized.**

1. **a.** "is the Sears Tower the highest building in the world?" Edward asked.
   b. "Is the Sears Tower the highest building in the world?" Edward asked.

2. **a.** Sal said, "I think so."
   b. Sal said, "i think so."

3. **a.** "which is the windiest city in the United States?" Melba asked.
   b. "Which is the windiest city in the United States?" Melba asked.

4. **a.** "Most people think it's Chicago," Lucy said, "But it's really Great Falls, Montana."
   b. "Most people think it's Chicago," Lucy said, "but it's really Great Falls, Montana."

5. **a.** "I was really surprised!" Devin exclaimed. "The city of Chicago is called the Windy City."
   b. "I was really surprised!" Devin exclaimed. "the city of Chicago is called the Windy City."

● Connect to the Writing Process: Editing
Using Capital Letters with Direct Quotations

Rewrite the following sentences, correcting errors in the use of capital letters with quotation marks. If a sentence is correct, write C.

6. Marty said, "some of the best blues music can be found in Chicago."

7. "Did you know that Chicago sits on Lake Michigan?" Asked Brenda.

8. "My favorite place to visit," commented Shari, "Is the Museum of Contemporary Art."

9. "The Great Chicago Fire occurred in October of 1871," explained our tour guide.

10. "As a result," He continued, "Chicago created one of the first modern fire departments in America."

11. "The smallest of the Great Lakes is Lake Ontario," Terry reported.

12. Then she asked, "which is the largest of the Great Lakes?"

13. "Lake Michigan," Rob stated, "Is the answer to your question."

14. "can you name all the lakes of the Great Lakes?" asked Martin.

15. "Huron, Ontario, Michigan, Erie, and Superior," Terry explained, "Are the names of the Great Lakes."

Commas with Direct Quotations

Your voice naturally pauses between a direct quotation and a speaker tag when you speak. In written material these pauses are indicated by commas.

Use a comma to separate a direct quotation from a speaker tag.

Mom said, "The groceries are still in the car."

"The groceries are still in the car," Mom said.

(The comma goes *inside* the closing quotation marks.)

"The groceries," Mom said, "are still in the car."

(The first comma goes *inside* the closing quotation marks.)

Notice in the last example that two commas are needed because the one-sentence quotation is interrupted.

PRACTICE YOUR SKILLS

● Check Your Understanding
Using Commas with Direct Quotations

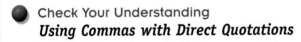 **If the use of commas in a sentence is incorrect, write *I.* If the use of commas is correct, write *C.***

 1. Casey Stengel joked, "Ability is the art of getting credit for all the home runs somebody else hits."

 2. "Words are the most powerful drug used by mankind" said Rudyard Kipling.

 3. "Do what you can," Theodore Roosevelt stated "with what you have, where you are."

 4. "The price of greatness is responsibility," said Winston Churchill.

5. "People who say they sleep like a baby" Leo Burke joked, "don't have one."

6. "Ours is the only country deliberately founded on a good idea," John Gunther stated.

7. An old Vermont proverb says "Don't talk unless you can improve the silence."

8. Sir Richard Steele announced, "Reading is to the mind what exercise is to the body."

9. Paul Signac said about Monet "He paints as a bird sings."

10. "Double—no, triple—our troubles," Ronald Reagan stated "and we'd still be better off than any other people on Earth."

● Connect to the Writing Process: Editing
Using Commas with Direct Quotations

11.–16. Rewrite the incorrect sentences from the preceding exercise, using commas with quotation marks correctly.

End Marks with Direct Quotations

When a direct quotation comes at the end of a sentence, it must have an end mark. A period follows a quotation that is a statement or an opinion.

Place a period inside the closing quotation marks when the end of the quotation comes at the end of a sentence.

Susan said, "The reports are due tomorrow**.**"

(The period goes *inside* the closing quotation marks.)

A one-sentence quotation that is interrupted by a speaker tag is still one sentence. Therefore, the period comes at the end of the sentence—inside the closing quotation marks.

"The reports," Susan said, "are due tomorrow."

If a quotation comes at the beginning of a sentence, the period follows the speaker tag.

"The reports are due tomorrow," Susan said.

If a quotation has more than one sentence, a period comes at the end of each sentence.

"The reports are due tomorrow," Susan said. "Mr. David wants them typed. I am typing mine now."

(The last period goes *inside* the closing quotation marks.)

Place a question mark or an exclamation point inside the closing quotation marks when it is part of the quotation.

Mary asked, "Did you find the materials you needed for your report?"

"Did you find the materials you needed for your report?" Mary asked.

"Did you find the materials you needed for your report," Mary asked, "or should we plan a return trip to the library?"

Leon shouted, "Don't touch that computer on Ms. Scott's desk!"

"Don't touch that computer on Ms. Scott's desk!" Leon shouted.

A question mark and an exclamation point are placed *inside* the closing quotation marks when they are part of the quotation. Occasionally, a question or an exclamation may include a direct quotation. When such a situation occurs, the question mark or the exclamation point goes *outside* the closing quotation marks. Placing the end mark outside the quotation marks shows that the whole sentence, rather than the quotation, is a question or an exclamatory statement.

Who said, "Give me liberty or give me death"**?**

(The whole sentence, not the quotation, is the question.)

I'll never forget the day that the president looked at me and said, "Hello"**!**

(The whole sentence, not the quotation, is exclamatory.)

In the two examples above, notice that the end marks for the quotations are omitted. Two end marks would be confusing to a reader.

PRACTICE YOUR SKILLS

● Check Your Understanding
Using End Marks with Direct Quotations

Contemporary Life **Write *a* or *b* to indicate which sentence in each pair is correctly punctuated.**

1. a. Pamela said, "I just learned that Sydney is the largest city in Australia."
 b. Pamela said, "I just learned that Sydney is the largest city in Australia".

2. a. "Your geography reports are due on Friday." Mr. David stated.
 b. "Your geography reports are due on Friday," Mr. David stated.

3. a. Rachel asked, "Mr. David, is the Missouri River the second-longest river in the United States?"
 b. Rachel asked, "Mr. David, is the Missouri River the second-longest river in the United States"?

4. a. "Are there really palm trees in Dublin?" Sean asked.
 b. "Are there really palm trees in Dublin," Sean asked?

5. a. "I think you have your topics for your reports now." revealed Mr. David.
 b. "I think you have your topics for your reports now," revealed Mr. David.

6. a. "How long do our reports have to be." asked Pamela.
   b. "How long do our reports have to be?" asked Pamela.

7. a. Mr. David replied, "You need five hundred words".
   b. Mr. David replied, "You need five hundred words."

8. a. "Five hundred words!" Sean exclaimed.
   b. "Five hundred words," Sean exclaimed!

9. a. "I can't wait," Rachel said, "to start my research!"
   b. "I can't wait," Rachel said, "to start my research"!

10. a. "As you're preparing your reports," Mr. David told the class, "be sure to keep track of your sources".
   b. "As you're preparing your reports," Mr. David told the class, "be sure to keep track of your sources."

● Connect to the Writing Process: Editing
Using End Marks with Quotations

Rewrite the following sentences, using end marks correctly. If a sentence is correct, write C.

11. Donald shouted, "Mine is finally finished"!

12. Did Mr. David say, "Read the next chapter in your textbook?"

13. "The busiest time of the year," Anton stated, "is the month when we are writing reports".

14. "Where are my note cards?" Maxine asked. "I haven't seen them all day."

15. I was shocked when Mr. David remarked, "Class will be dismissed early today!"

16. I was glad to hear Mr. David say, "Your reports will not be due until Monday."

17. "Can you believe that he actually extended a deadline" Paula asked.

18. Did the librarian say, "The reference section is closed today."

19. Danny exclaimed, "There was more information than I needed on the Internet"!

20. "I hope this is our last report for a while," said Rita, "I am tired of writing so much".

APPLY TO WRITING

E-mail: *End marks and Quotations*

Your best friend was unable to go to school today. Unfortunately, your teacher was conducting an oral review for a big test. Write an E-mail message for your friend that includes some of the dialogue that formed the review. Be sure to use end marks with quotations properly.

 QuickCheck Mixed Practice

General Interest **Rewrite the following sentences, adding capital letters, quotation marks, and other punctuation marks where needed.**

1. Shakespeare wrote shall I compare thee to a summer's day

2. genius is 10 percent inspiration and 90 percent perspiration said Thomas Edison

3. I have nothing to offer Winston Churchill declared but blood, toil, tears, and sweat
4. don't give up the ship Captain Lawrence shouted
5. Ben Franklin said nothing is certain but death and taxes
6. love doesn't make the world go 'round Franklin Jones said love is what makes the world worthwhile
7. these are the times Thomas Paine warned that try men's souls
8. when did Commodore Perry say we have met the enemy and they are ours
9. Elizabeth Barrett Browning wrote how do I love thee let me count the ways
10. did Gertrude Stein write a rose is a rose is a rose

Other Uses of Quotation Marks

Before you write a story with dialogue or a report in which you quote long passages from a book or periodical, you should be aware of some special applications of quotation marks.

Unusual Uses of Words

Quotation marks can draw attention to a word that is used in an unusual way.

Use quotation marks to enclose slang words, technical terms, and other uses of unusual words.

SLANG	"In hog heaven" and "in the bag" are two slang expressions in the *Thesaurus of American Slang*.
TECHNICAL TERMS	"Online," "Website," and "logging on" are Internet terms I just learned.

OTHERS   "Brillig" is a word that Lewis Carroll made up.

Dictionary Definitions

You will use both italics and quotation marks when writing a dictionary definition within a piece of writing.

When writing a word and its definition in a sentence, italicize (underline) the word but use quotation marks to enclose the definition.

DEFINITIONS
OF WORDS   The word *languid* means "lacking energy or vitality; weak."

Dialogue

Stories often include **dialogue**—a conversation between two or more people. Dialogue is written in a special way so that readers know who is speaking.

When writing dialogue, begin a new paragraph each time the speaker changes.

The following conversation takes place between a husband and wife. Each quotation follows the rules you have just studied, but each time the speaker changes, a new paragraph begins.

> She turned to him wildly. "I have—I have—I've lost Mme. Forestier's necklace."
> He stood up, appalled. "What! . . . How? . . . Impossible! You're sure you had it on when you left the ball?"
> "Yes, I felt it in the vestibule of the Ministry."
>
> —*Guy De Maupassant,* "The Necklace"

Long Passages

Reports sometimes include quotations of more than one paragraph to support a particular point.

When quoting a passage of more than one paragraph, place quotation marks at the beginning of each paragraph—but at the end of only the last paragraph.

Closing quotation marks are omitted at the end of each paragraph, except the last one, to indicate to the reader that the quotation is continuing.

"In the 1950s and 1960s, rock 'n' roll music blasted its way across the United States. Teenagers loved it; adults hated it. Today people are collecting these early records.

"The big names in those days were Chuck Berry, Little Richard, Fats Domino, and Buddy Holly. The early records of these singers are worth the most money. They might sell for two to twenty-five dollars each.

"Prices for old forty-five-rpm records and albums change a great deal. A book called *Collectible Rock Records* by Randal C. Hill gives today's prices, as well as a big list of people and stores that buy and sell records. This book can be found in most libraries."

Another easy way to quote a long passage is to set it off from the rest of the text by indenting both left and right margins. If you are using a computer, you could also set the passage in a smaller type size. When you use this method of quoting a long passage, no quotation marks are needed.

Quotations Within Quotations

To distinguish a quotation within a quotation, use single quotation marks to enclose the inside quotation.

Tim stated, "I heard Ms. Brown say, 'This set of literature tests is the best work I've ever seen.'"

Notice that the closing single quotation mark and the double quotation marks come together.

A direct quotation sometimes contains another title with quotation marks.

Mr. Ray said, "Ed, read the poem 'The Raven' to us."
"My favorite song is 'The Little Man' by Alan Jackson," said Marie.

PRACTICE YOUR SKILLS

● Check Your Understanding
Using Quotation Marks Correctly

Contemporary Life **Write *a* or *b* to indicate which sentence in each pair uses quotation marks correctly.**

1. **a.** Mrs. Brocklehurst said, "I want all of you to read 'The Rime of the Ancient Mariner' for homework this weekend."
   b. Mrs. Brocklehurst said, I want all of you to read 'The Rime of the Ancient Mariner' for homework this weekend.

2. **a.** The word *misoneism* means "a hatred, fear, or intolerance of innovation or change."
   b. The word "misoneism" means "a hatred, fear, or intolerance, of innovation or change."

3. **a.** Robert Heinlein invented the word *grok* for his book *Stranger in a Strange Land.*
   b. Robert Heinlein invented the word "grok" for his book *Stranger in a Strange Land.*

4. **a.** "He's all that" is a slang expression.
   b. 'He's all that' is a "slang expression."

5. a. Jane said, "I was very happy when Edward said, "I love you."

b. Jane said, "I was very happy when Edward said 'I love you.'"

6. a. The word "jabberwocky" is a nonsense word.

b. The word 'jabberwocky' is a nonsense word.

● Connect to the Writing Process: Editing
Punctuating Dialogue

Rewrite the following dialogue between Sherlock Holmes and John Clay, a criminal whom Holmes has just captured. Add punctuation and indentation where needed.

It's no use, John Clay said Holmes blandly. You have no chance at all. So I see Clay answered with the utmost coolness. I fancy that my pal is all right. There are three men waiting for him at the door said Holmes.

—*Sir Arthur Conan Doyle,* "The Red-Headed League"

Communicate Your Ideas

APPLY TO WRITING

Documentation: *Long Quotations*

While writing a biography for your English class, you discover that a passage in your history textbook would support your topic very well. Write a passage of two or more paragraphs from your history book as they would appear as part of your research paper. Be sure to follow the rules for quoting long passages.

Contemporary Life | **Write the following sentences, using underlining or adding quotation marks, commas, capital letters, and end marks where necessary.** (Only a sentence with a speaker tag should be considered a direct quotation.)

1. Justin, are you going to the dance, Ashley asked.

2. Justin replied is that an invitation

3. Homecoming activities Debbie announced will be handled by Fred this year.

4. For English class I read the short story The Cask of Amontillado by Edgar Allan Poe.

5. Have you read Poe's short story The Pit and the Pendulum inquired Tina.

6. Stephen Sondheim wrote the music for the musical A Little Night Music as well as the lyrics for the song Send in the Clowns.

7. I would like to visit Paris so that I could see the painting the Mona Lisa.

8. Did you say bonjour to the new French teacher?

9. Mrs. Johnsen wants you to write your 7s more neatly in her math class.

10. Our reading teacher, Mrs. Smythe, told us that the word munition means rampart.

Punctuating Titles Correctly

Write each sentence, adding quotation marks and underlining or italics where needed. (None of the following sentences should be considered direct quotations.)

1. In the Shakespearean play <u>Julius Caesar</u>, I played the part of Cassius.

2. Clickety-clack, Toy Trains are Back was an interesting article in this issue of the magazine called Smithsonian.

3. For homework I have to read the chapter Human Heredity in my science book <u>Biology for Today</u>.

4. When You Wish upon a Star is the Oscar-winning song from the 1940 movie Pinocchio.

5. I wrote an essay about the poem The Centaur by May Swenson.

6. Have you seen The Starry Night, a painting by Vincent van Gogh?

7. Ski Season Has Rocky Start was the lead story in the <u>Manchester Daily News</u> today.

8. I recently heard a recording of Invasion from Mars, the one-act radio play that made people believe Martians had landed.

9. Read the definition of the word <u>differential</u> from the <u>American Heritage Dictionary</u>.

10. Columbus's ships were the Santa Maria, the Pinta, and the Niña.

11. Tomorrow is a song that was made famous in the musical <u>Annie</u>.

12. Ebenezer Scrooge is the miserly old man in Dickens's story A Christmas Carol.

13. Samuel Taylor Coleridge wrote the poem Kubla Khan.

14. The word tam-o'-shanter is the name for a Scottish woolen cap with a wide crown and a pom-pom.

15. My favorite short story by Edgar Allan Poe is The Pit and the Pendulum.

Punctuating Direct Quotations

Write each quotation, adding capital letters, quotation marks, and other punctuation marks where needed.

1. the blue whale is the largest animal ever known to have lived on Earth Mrs. Jennings said

2. blue whales sometimes measure over one hundred feet long she continued and weigh one hundred tons on average

3. the blue whale is larger than the largest dinosaurs she exclaimed

4. she explained in comparison, the extinct Apatosaurus was only seventy-five feet long and weighed about thirty-five tons

5. a newborn blue whale is twenty-three feet long she added

6. a newborn blue whale is much bigger than a full-grown elephant Mrs. Jennings elaborated

7. she added these giant whales eat tiny animals called krill krill consist mostly of shrimp-like crustaceans about two inches long

8. krill abound in polar waters she continued

9. the whales graze in floating krill pastures she explained much like cattle browse in a grassy meadow

10. a blue whale may eat two or three tons of krill at a single meal Mrs. Jennings concluded dramatically

Writing Sentences with Quotation Marks

Write a short dialogue using the following topic or one of your choice: a conversation between you and a fictional person, such as a character from a movie; a television series; or a book. Punctuate the dialogue correctly.

Language and *Self-Expression*

The book from which this illustration was taken, *Why Mosquitoes Buzz in People's Ears,* was written by Verna Aardema and illustrated by the husband-and-wife team of Leo and Diane Dillon. In 1976, the book won the Caldecott Medal, an award for the best illustrations in a children's book.

Why Mosquitoes Buzz in People's Ears is a retelling of an African folktale. Think of a folktale or fairy tale you have enjoyed hearing or reading. Then write your own retelling of the tale. As you write, use italics (underlining) and quotation marks correctly.

Prewriting Create a Sequence-of-Events chart for your folktale or fairy tale. Describe the setting, characters, main problem, major events, and solution in your chart.

Drafting Write a first draft of your folktale or fairy tale. Use your Sequence-of-Events chart to help you organize the events in the tale. Be sure to include dialogue in your tale.

Revising Reread your tale. Have you retold it so that readers can understand it? Are the events of the tale in sequence? Make any changes necessary to make your tale clear and entertaining.

Editing Check your spelling and punctuation. Have you underlined titles or placed them in quotation marks? Have you punctuated any dialogue correctly?

Publishing Make a final copy of your tale. Place it with classmates' tales in a class book of folktales and fairy tales.

Another Look

Italics (Underlining)

Italicize (underline) letters, numbers, and words when they are used to represent themselves. Also italicize (underline) foreign words that are not generally used in English. *(page L453)*

Italicize (underline) the titles of long written or musical works that are published as a single unit. Also italicize (underline) titles of paintings and sculptures and the names of vehicles. *(page L454)*

Quotation Marks

Use quotation marks to enclose the titles of chapters, articles, stories, short poems, and songs. *(page L457)*

Use quotation marks to enclose a person's exact words. *(page L460)*

Begin each sentence of a direct quotation with a capital letter. *(page L462)*

Use a comma to separate a direct quotation from a speaker tag. Place the comma inside the closing quotation marks. *(page L464)*

Place a period inside the closing quotation marks when the end of the quotation comes at the end of the sentence. *(pages L465–L466)*

Place a question mark or exclamation point inside the closing quotation marks when it is part of the quotation. *(pages L466–L467)*

Other Uses of Quotation Marks

Use quotation marks to enclose slang words, technical terms, and other uses of unusual words. *(pages L470–L471)*

When writing a word and its definition in a sentence, italicize (underline) the word but use quotation marks to enclose the definition. *(page L471)*

When writing dialogue, begin a new paragraph each time the speaker changes. *(page L471)*

When quoting a passage of more than one paragraph, place quotation marks at the beginning of each paragraph—but at the end of only the last paragraph. *(page L472)*

To distinguish a quotation within a quotation, use single quotation marks to enclose the inside quotation. *(pages L472–L473)*

 **Posttest**

Directions

Read the passage. Each underlined part may contain errors in the use of italics and/or quotation marks. Choose the best way to write each part and write the letter of the correct answer. If the underlined part contains no error, write _D_.

EXAMPLE   "I met a <u>television star!" Joe exclaimed.</u>
                            (1)

    1   **A**   television star," Jo exclaimed.
        B   television star," Jo exclaimed!
        C   television star." Jo exclaimed!
        D   No error

ANSWER   **1   D**

Lewis Murdoch, the star of <u>the television series Long Ago and</u>
                                            (1)
<u>Far Away,</u> gave a performance at our school.

<u>"I'm here" he said, "To show you the sort of thing an actor</u>
                    (2)
<u>does to succeed on the stage.</u> He sang <u>The Street Where You Live</u>
                                                            (3)
<u>from My Fair Lady</u> and then recited a soliloquy from _Hamlet_.

At the end of his performance, Murdoch took questions. "What
was your most memorable <u>stage performance, one student asked?</u>
                                            (4)
Murdoch laughed. <u>"Once when I was performing in Molière's</u>
                                            (5)
<u>play The Imaginary Invalid, my powdered wig slid off my head"!</u>

1 **A** the television series "Long Ago and Far Away,"

   B the television series *Long Ago and Far Away,*

   C the television series "Long Ago and Far Away",

   D No error

2 **A** "I'm here," he said, "to show you the sort of thing an actor does to succeed on the stage."

   B "I'm here," he said. "To show you the sort of thing an actor does to succeed on the stage."

   C "I'm here," he said, to show you the sort of thing an actor does to succeed on the stage."

   D No error

3 **A** "The Street Where You Live" from *My Fair Lady*

   B *The Street Where You Live* from "My Fair Lady"

   C "The Street Where You Live" from "My Fair Lady"

   D No error

4 **A** stage performance," one student asked?

   B stage performance, one student asked?"

   C stage performance?" one student asked.

   D No error

5 **A** "Once when I was performing in Molière's play "The Imaginary Invalid," my powdered wig slid off my head"!

   B "Once when I was performing in Molière's play *The Imaginary Invalid,* my powdered wig slid off my head!"

   C "Once when I was performing in Molière's play 'The Imaginary Invalid,' my powdered wig slid off my head"!

   D No error

CHAPTER 12

Other Punctuation

Pretest

Directions

Read the passage. Each underlined part contains mistakes in punctuation. Write the letter of the correct way to write each underlined part.

EXAMPLE   My <u>father a lover of antique autos—</u>
(1)
often takes me to car shows.

1 **A** father a lover of antique autos

   B father—a lover of antique autos

   C father, a lover of antique autos

   D father: a lover of antique autos

ANSWER   1 **B**

This week we saw <u>Watkins Glens yearly classic car show.</u>
(1)
There were many exotic kinds of <u>cars Dusenbergs Model A</u>
(2)
<u>Fords a beautiful, ancient Stutz Bearcat and a 1919 Auburn</u>
<u>Speedster.</u> However, the car that raised <u>everyones eyebrows</u>
(3)
<u>was a pre war Rolls-Royce Phantom.</u> We could easily picture

the past while looking at these cars. <u>A gangster from the</u>
(4)
<u>thirties could have driven one another</u> could easily have

carried a president to the White House. Next year <u>well go</u>
(5)
<u>back again Ive heard theres</u> a better show to come.
(5)

1 **A** Watkins Glens yearly classic car show.
   B Watkins Glen's yearly classic-car show.
   C Watkins' Glens yearly classic car show.
   D Watkins Glens yearly classic (car) show.

2 **A** cars Dusenbergs Model A Fords a beautiful, ancient Stutz Bearcat and a 1919 Auburn Speedster.
   B cars—Dusenbergs, Model A Fords—a beautiful, ancient Stutz Bearcat; and a 1919 Auburn Speedster.
   C cars: Dusenbergs; Model A Fords; a beautiful, ancient Stutz Bearcat; and a 1919 Auburn Speedster.
   D cars (Dusenbergs, Model A Fords, a beautiful, ancient Stutz Bearcat, and a 1919 Auburn Speedster).

3 **A** everyones eyebrows was a pre war Rolls-Royce Phantom.
   B everyones eyebrows—was a pre war Rolls-Royce Phantom.
   C everyones eyebrow's was a pre war Rolls-Royce Phantom.
   D everyone's eyebrows was a pre-war Rolls-Royce Phantom.

4 **A** A gangster from the thirties could have driven one another
   B A gangster from the thirties could have driven one—another
   C A gangster from the thirties could have driven one; another
   D A gangster from the thirties could have driven one: another

5 **A** well go back again Ive heard theres
   B we'll go back again: I've heard theres
   C w'ell go back again I've heard there's
   D we'll go back again; I've heard there's

Grant Wood. *Parson Weems' Fable,* 1939
Oil on canvas, 38⅜ by 50⅛ inches. Amon Carter Museum, Fort Worth, Texas. 1970.43

Describe What well-known story does the painting show?

Analyze Who is the figure in the foreground? What is he doing?

Interpret What moral lesson do you think the painting shows? How does it portray the lesson? What kind of stories do writers use to teach lessons?

Judge Do you think this painting is effective in both telling a story and portraying a message? Explain.

At the end of this chapter, you will use the artwork to stimulate ideas for writing.

Apostrophes

Punctuation marks are a fairly modern invention. The colon is said to have first been introduced about 1485, but the semicolon did not appear until almost a century later. Without these and other marks of punctuation, imagine how difficult it must have been to decipher written material. Likewise, imagine how difficult it would be for people to decipher your written work if needed punctuation were missing! This chapter will cover apostrophes, semicolons, colons, hyphens, and two less commonly used marks of punctuation, dashes and parentheses.

The first section of this chapter will show the uses of apostrophes. Apostrophes are used most frequently with contractions, but they are also commonly used with nouns and some pronouns to show ownership or relationship.

Apostrophes to Show Possession

Nouns and pronouns have a special form to show possession or relationship. An apostrophe is used to form the possessive of nouns and some pronouns.

Possessive Forms of Nouns

The first step in forming the possessive of any noun is to decide whether the noun is singular or plural.

Add 's to form the possessive of a singular noun.

Remember to write a singular noun—without adding or omitting any letter. Then just add 's at the end.

> man + 's = man's   Is this a man**'s** shirt?
>
> Carla + 's = Carla's   I think you have Carla**'s** glove.

Singular compound nouns and the names of most businesses and organizations form the possessive the way other singular nouns do.

> A two-year-old's soccer skills are limited.
>
> I enjoy looking at A Sport Place's catalog for sports equipment.
>
> Christopher Reilly's business sold a variety of sporting goods.

The possessive form of a plural noun is formed differently.

Add only an apostrophe to form the possessive of a plural noun that ends in s.

> balls + ' = balls'   All of the balls' stitches are becoming loose.
>
> players + ' = players'   The players' rights were spelled out in the contract.

A few plural nouns do not end in s. The possessive of these nouns should be formed the way singular nouns are—by adding 's.

> women + 's = women's   The women's uniforms arrived today.
>
> mice + 's = mice's   The infield crew disturbed the mice's home.

Be careful that you do not confuse a plural possessive with the simple plural form of a noun.

> POSSESSIVE   The outfielders' practice session was much too long.
>
> PLURAL   The outfielders practiced for an extremely long time.

You can learn more about plural nouns on pages L537–L544.

PRACTICE YOUR SKILLS

● Check Your Understanding
Using Possessive Nouns

Contemporary
Life

Write the possessive form of each underlined word or words.

1. After a <u>year</u> practice, Susan joined the high school tennis team.

2. The <u>players</u> equipment is being kept in the coach's office.

3. Jogging is <u>Eric</u> main interest right now.

4. Have you ever gone swimming in the <u>St. John</u> River?

5. The <u>athletes</u> records were astounding.

6. <u>Ralph</u> bowling average is 150.

7. The <u>coach</u> office is located next to the gym.

8. Where can I play <u>women</u> softball?

9. Roberta will play on her <u>sister-in-law</u> team next summer.

10. At halftime the <u>game</u> score was 3–2.

● Check Your Understanding
Forming Possessive Nouns

Write the possessive form of each noun.

11. committee	**21.** monkey
12. Graves	**22.** whale
13. women	**23.** Sarah
14. Cohen	**24.** dogs
15. governors	**25.** Boise
16. tomato	**26.** city
17. teachers	**27.** brother
18. children	**28.** computer
19. sister	**29.** pen
20. boys	**30.** boxes

31.–35. Choose five possessive forms from the preceding exercise and use them in sentences of your own.

Rewrite the following sentences, correcting any errors in the use of possessive nouns. If a sentence is correct, write C.

36. Have you signed up for our towns' softball team?

37. The attorney-at-law's office will sponsor the team.

38. You can get your uniform at Rudolphs Sporting Goods.

39. The newspapers front page featured the new coach.

40. Mr. Griffin will be the team's coach this year.

Possessive Forms of Pronouns

Unlike a noun, a personal pronoun does not use an apostrophe to show possession. Instead, it changes form. Notice that none of the following possessive pronouns include apostrophes.

POSSESSIVE PRONOUNS			
my, mine	his	its	their, theirs
your, yours	her, hers	our, ours	

Also notice that the possessive *its* is different from *it's,* which is a contraction of *it is.*

Do not add an apostrophe to form the possessive of personal pronouns.

Her book is on the desk, and **yours** is on the floor.

Instead of changing form the way a personal pronoun does, an indefinite pronoun forms the possessive the same way a singular noun does—by adding 's.

Add 's to form the possessive of indefinite pronouns.

> Anyone's guess is as good as mine.
>
> Has everyone's test been graded?

You can find a list of common indefinite pronouns on page L15.

PRACTICE YOUR SKILLS

● Check Your Understanding
Using Possessive Pronouns

Contemporary Life

Write *a* or *b* to indicate which sentence in each pair uses possessive pronouns correctly.

1. a. Someone's art sketchbook is in my car.
   b. Someones art sketchbook is in my car.

2. a. These are my notes, but which are your's?
   b. These are my notes, but which are yours?

3. a. If this enormous project is going to succeed, we need everyone's cooperation.
   b. If this enormous project is going to succeed, we need everyones' cooperation.

4. a. Have you finished your history assignment yet?
   b. Have you finished yours history assignment yet?

5. a. My art easel cost fifty dollars, but her's cost less.
   b. My art easel cost fifty dollars, but hers cost less.

6. a. Nobodys supplies were forgotten on the first day of school.
   b. Nobody's supplies were forgotten on the first day of school.

7. a. That trophy is theirs.
   b. That trophy is their's.

8. a. Our's were the only poems that were read aloud.
   b. Ours were the only poems that were read aloud.

9. a. A mouse has built its nest in the corner of the cafeteria.
   b. A mouse has built it's nest in the corner of the cafeteria.

10. a. No one's project was damaged when the pipes burst in the art room.
   b. No ones' project was damaged when the pipes burst in the art room.

● Connect to the Writing Process: Editing
Using Possessive Pronouns

Rewrite the following sentences, adding or deleting apostrophes where needed. If a sentence is correct, write C.

11. Everybodys short story was chosen for the school literary magazine.

12. Hers was the only letter to the editor about the chaperones at the school dance.

13. The team had it's best season yet.

14. Did he leave his's notes on the bus again?

15. The jacket left at the game last week could have been anybodys.

Apostrophes to Show Joint or Separate Ownership

Apostrophes distinguish between joint and separate ownership.

Add 's only to the last name to show joint ownership.

These are Lenny and Harold**'s** props.

(The props belong to both Lenny and Harold.)

If one of the words in a phrase showing joint ownership is a possessive pronoun, the noun must also show possession.

These are Lenny**'s** and **his** props.

Separate ownership is indicated in a different way.

Add **'s** to show separate ownership.

These are Lenny**'s** and Harold**'s** props.

(Both Lenny and Harold have their own props.)

PRACTICE YOUR SKILLS

● Check Your Understanding
Using Apostrophes to Show Joint Ownership

Contemporary Life **Write *a* or *b* to indicate which sentence in each pair uses apostrophes correctly. Be prepared to explain your answer.**

1. a. Rhonda and Kenneth's great performances saved the show.
  b. Rhonda's and Kenneth's great performances saved the show.

2. a. Kent and Martha's old sofa was donated for the school play.
  b. Kent's and Martha's old sofa was donated for the school play.

3. a. Troy's and Jon's acting skills contributed greatly to the show's success.
  b. Troy and Jon's acting skills contributed greatly to the show's success.

4. a. These are Sophie's and hers costumes.
  b. These are Sophie's and her costumes.

5. a. Are these black gloves Ray or Gerald's?
  b. Are these black gloves Ray's or Gerald's?

Apostrophes with Nouns Expressing Time or Amount

When you use a noun that expresses time or amount as an adjective, write the noun in the possessive form.

> Use an apostrophe with the possessive form of a noun that expresses time or amount.

> Have you made this month's vacation plans?
>
> Please buy ten dollars' worth of stamps.

Other words that express time include *minute, hour, day, week,* and *year.*

PRACTICE YOUR SKILLS

● **Check Your Understanding**
Using Apostrophes Correctly

 Write the possessive form of each underlined word or words.

1. Sandra purchased <u>travelers</u> checks for her trip.
2. In a <u>weeks</u> time, she will be sailing to the Bahamas.
3. The two <u>days</u> planning should enable her to be prepared.
4. Sandra needed three <u>years</u> savings to pay for the trip.
5. Her mother bought her seventy <u>dollars</u> worth of clothes.
6. A <u>months</u> vacation should help Sandra relax.
7. Sandra has packed her suitcases so well that there is not a <u>centimeters</u> worth of room to spare.
8. A typical <u>evenings</u> activities include shows, dinner, and dancing.
9. The first <u>days</u> itineraries seem to be filled with tourist activities on the islands.
10. The last <u>weeks</u> schedule is the most relaxing of all.

Using Apostrophes with Time or Amounts

Rewrite the following sentences, correcting the use of apostrophes. If a sentence is correct, write C.

11. Did you remember to get sixty cents worth of stamps for postcards?

12. I brought along ten dollar's worth of quarters for the washing machines.

13. An hours worth of work was all that I could stand on the night before vacation.

14. Did you check this morning's weather report?

15. Ten miles distance separates us from the new airport.

Communicate Your Ideas

APPLY TO WRITING
Postcard: *Apostrophes*

You are on vacation and wish to send the above postcard to your friends. Write a short message for the back of this postcard, describing some of the activities you are taking part in. Be sure to use apostrophes correctly.

General Interest **Correctly write each underlined word as a possessive form.**

1. My dog picture was in this morning *Herald*.
2. A years worth of hard work has finally paid off.
3. The judges opinion was that my dog should win.
4. No ones surprise was greater than mine.
5. Gregs Dalmatian was awarded second place.
6. Mandys and her poodles were disqualified after they bit the judge.
7. Training dogs for shows used to be considered men work, but now there are many women trainers.
8. During March, everyone attention will be on the Westminster Kennel Club and it annual dog show.
9. Due to budget cuts, the dog show entry fee will have to be increased this year.
10. Is that golden retriever your brother or your father?
11. Are you interested in earning a week salary by working as an usher at the show this evening?
12. The MacGregor spaniel and the Gordon collie have impressive pedigrees.
13. Mom and Dad passes need to be updated so they can go to the show tomorrow.
14. Mrs. Masters knack for picking the winner is well known.
15. Please remember to buy fifty cents worth of doggie treats for my dog before the show starts.

▶ Other Uses of Apostrophes

In addition to showing possession, an apostrophe has several other uses.

Apostrophes with Contractions

A contraction combines two words into one. An apostrophe is added to take the place of the missing letter or letters.

Use an apostrophe in a contraction to show where one or more letters have been omitted.

CONTRACTIONS	
We ~~a~~re = we're	there ~~i~~s = there's
let ~~u~~s = let's	it ~~i~~s = it's
can~~not~~ = can't	~~of the~~ clock = o'clock

Usually no letters are added and no letters are moved around in a contraction. There is, however, one exception: *will not = won't*.

CONNECT TO SPEAKING AND WRITING

When you are speaking, contractions and possessive pronouns sound the same. However, when you are writing, do not confuse a contraction with a possessive pronoun.

CONTRACTIONS	it's, you're, they're, there's, who's
POSSESSIVE PRONOUNS	its, your, their, theirs, whose

PRACTICE YOUR SKILLS

● Check Your Understanding
Writing Contractions

Write the contraction for each pair of words.

1. you are	**6.** is not	**11.** I would	**16.** it is
2. will not	**7.** I have	**12.** I am	**17.** there is
3. has not	**8.** they are	**13.** who is	**18.** we will
4. that is	**9.** do not	**14.** let us	**19.** did not
5. we have	**10.** have not	**15.** does not	**20.** were not

Distinguishing Between Contractions and Possessive Pronouns

Contemporary Life **Write the word in parentheses that correctly fills each blank.**

1. (who's, whose) ▓ driving? ▓ is that car?
2. (it's, its) Don't let ▓ looks deceive you; ▓ a gem under the hood.
3. (you're, your) ▓ judging the car only with ▓ eyes.
4. (they're, their) Because ▓ experienced mechanics, I asked for ▓ advice.
5. (their, there's) ▓ a trophy for ▓ race team too.
6. (it's, its) ▓ one of the most popular sports today because of ▓ excitement.
7. (who's, whose) ▓ is the car we are looking for, and ▓ going to be driving?
8. (there's, theirs) ▓ a finishing time. Is it ▓ ?
9. (you're, your) If ▓ wise, you'll have ▓ engine checked before the race.
10. (they're, their) ▓ going to introduce ▓ new driver for the race in Daytona.

● Connect to the Writing Process: Editing

Using Contractions and Possessive Pronouns

Rewrite the following sentences for correct use of contractions and possessives. If a sentence is correct, write C.

11. If your going to race today, you'd better tell the track steward.
12. Its going to be a great race today. Don't you think it will be?
13. I've been a fan of NASCAR for the past five years.
14. Whose your favorite driver?
15. I dont want to miss any of today's race.

Apostrophes with Certain Plurals

To prevent confusion, certain items form their plurals by adding 's.

> **Add 's to form the plural of lowercase letters, some capital letters, and some words used as words.**

> Your *k*'**s** and *h*'**s** look exactly the same.
>
> Form your *I*'**s** carefully.

The plurals of most other letters, symbols, numbers, and words used as words can be formed by adding *s*.

> There are too many *and***s** and *or***s** in that paragraph.
>
> Young learners often have difficulty with *6***s** and *9***s.**

Notice that in the previous examples, the letters, words, and numbers are all italicized. However, the 's or s with each of those letters and words is *not* italicized.

You can learn more about the use of italics or underlining in such situations on pages L453–L454.

PRACTICE YOUR SKILLS

● Check Your Understanding
Using Apostrophes

Correctly write each underlined letter, symbol, or word that needs either an apostrophe, an *s*, or an apostrophe and an *s*.

1. You shouldn't use so many *and* and *well* in your paper.

2. Bart never crosses his *t* or dots his *i*.

3. The ¶ indicate where new paragraphs should begin.

4. A hyphen is only one -, but a dash is two -.

5. How many *A* are on that report card?

6. Be sure to use " " properly when you write dialogue.

7. Well-placed , help readers understand your writing.

8. Why do you make your *l* so big in your name?

9. I can never write *Q* very well in cursive.

10. You shouldn't use so many *but* in your paper.

Apostrophes with Certain Dates

An apostrophe is also used when numbers are dropped from a date.

Use an apostrophe to show that numbers were omitted in a date.

She hopes to run for president in '04. (2004)

My brother was born in '63. (1963)

PRACTICE YOUR SKILLS

● Check Your Understanding
Using Apostrophes

Contemporary Life **Write *a* or *b* to indicate which sentence in each pair uses apostrophes correctly.**

1. a. Do you remember what happened in '76?
   b. Do you remember what happened in 76?

2. a. I think it was in 19'72 that Jennifer was born.
   b. I think it was in '72 that Jennifer was born.

3. a. It was in '64 that the Beatles came to America.
   b. It was in '1964 that the Beatles came to America.

4. a. Did your brother graduate in '96?
   b. Did your brother graduate in 96'?

5. a. The class of 2'000 was highly regarded.
   b. The class of '00 was highly regarded.

6. a. The flood of October 98' was pretty bad.
   b. The flood of October '98 was pretty bad.

7. **a.** The '98–'99 school year was an interesting one.
   b. The 98–'99 school year was an interesting one.

8. **a.** Julia wants to be class president in 99'.
   b. Julia wants to be class president in '99.

9. **a.** Mrs. Richter was Teacher of the Year in '82.
   b. Mrs. Richter was Teacher of the Year in 19'82.

10. **a.** The class of '80 will hold its reunion in the gym.
    b. The class of 80 will hold its reunion in the gym.

● Connect to the Writing Process: Editing
Using Apostrophes

Rewrite and edit the sentences below for proper use of apostrophes. If a sentence is correct, write C.

11. Did you forget what happened in 77?

12. *The Empire Strikes Back* was released in '80, I think.

13. The '89–90 school year was Mr. Thompson's first year of teaching.

14. The class of 87' will host a benefit for the incoming freshmen.

15. My sister got married in '90, and my niece was born the following year.

Communicate Your Ideas

APPLY TO WRITING

Autobiography: *Apostrophes*

Your English teacher has recommended you for an internship on the local newspaper. Before you can apply for the post, you must submit a brief autobiography that details your school activities and grades for the past five years. Write a short autobiographical paragraph for the personnel director of the local newspaper. Be sure to include dates and use apostrophes correctly.

General
Interest **Correctly write each word that needs an apostrophe, an *s,* or an apostrophe and an *s.***

1. In your report change some of those *and* and *but* to *although, when, because,* or *since.*

2. I think Ive read somewhere that the mud in beavers dams is held together by roots, leaves, and grasses.

3. Sybilla Masters device for reducing corn into meal and Margaret E. Knight machine for cutting shoes are two important American inventions.

4. The class of 98 had its picture taken for publication in the local paper.

5. Mom and Dad station wagon needs new tires before the vacation trip starts.

6. No one claim to the man enormous fortune held up in court.

7. The McDuff sons and the Smith daughters always manage to make the honor roll.

8. Gary house is just around the corner from Lee grocery store.

9. Arent there three *r* in the word *preferred?*

10. Martina and his stories were read aloud in class.

11. Is that striped blouse your mother or your sister?

12. In most tennis tournaments, the women play-offs are held before the men.

13. Due to the tax increase, the firefighters salaries were raised this year.

14. I told my parents that Im going to try to make straight *A* during this school year.

15. During September, everyone picture will be taken for the yearbook.

Semicolons and Colons

The most common use for a semicolon (**;**) is to separate the independent clauses of a compound sentence. A colon (**:**), on the other hand, is used mainly to introduce a list of items.

Semicolons

The independent clauses of a compound sentence can be joined in several ways. You have already learned that a comma and a conjunction can join the clauses.

> Tara's skating routine had six triples, **and** she made all of them.

Clauses in a compound sentence can also be joined by a semicolon.

> Tara's skating routine had six triples; she made all of them.

Use a semicolon between the clauses of a compound sentence that are not joined by a conjunction.

> Kristi is an artistic skater; Michelle is an artistic skater, too.

You can learn about using semicolons to correct run-on sentences on page L183.

PRACTICE YOUR SKILLS

 Check Your Understanding
Using Semicolons

General Interest **Write *I* if the compound sentence is incorrectly punctuated. Write *C* if it is correct.**

1. Ice skates did not originate in Holland, roller skates did.

2. Ice balls will not form if the ground temperature is below freezing; hail rarely falls during the winter months.

3. My new skates were paid for by my grandmother, I paid only for the laces.

4. Skating rinks can be used for ice hockey, figure skating, and curling they have other uses as well.

5. Lydia works hard at her figure skating lessons, and she has earned many skating trophies.

6. A well-rehearsed skating routine can look very easy; not everyone can skate well enough to perform, though.

7. The rink is available for our skating party on Saturday, December 19, I hope everyone can come.

8. The members of the skating team are planning a special surprise for all of us we are all waiting to see what the surprise will be.

9. I need new skates, new gloves, and a new hat; I will be ready for the party then.

10. Gina's skating routine lasts for six minutes, but Marty's lasts only three.

● Connect to the Writing Process: Editing
Punctuating Compound Sentences

11.–15. Rewrite the incorrect sentences in the preceding exercise, correcting the use of punctuation in a compound sentence.

Semicolons with Conjunctive Adverbs and Transitional Words

The following lists contain conjunctive adverbs and transitional words that, with a semicolon, can be used to combine the independent clauses of a compound sentence.

COMMON CONJUNCTIVE ADVERBS		
accordingly	furthermore	otherwise
also	hence	similarly
besides	however	still
consequently	instead	therefore
finally	nevertheless	thus

COMMON TRANSITIONAL WORDS		
as a result	in addition	in other words
for example	in fact	on the other hand

Use a semicolon between clauses in a compound sentence that are joined by certain conjunctive adverbs or transitional words.

Notice in the following examples that the conjunctive adverb *nevertheless* and the transitional words *as a result* are preceded by a semicolon and followed by a comma.

I have not had much time to devote to my studies; **nevertheless,** I will take the test on Tuesday.

I have been spending all my free time working; **as a result,** I have not read the assigned chapters.

You can learn more about independent clauses on page L155 and pages L176–L177.

Some of the conjunctive adverbs and transitional words listed in the box can also be used as parenthetical expressions within a single clause.

JOINING CLAUSES	I needed more time to study; **in fact,** I was willing to sacrifice sleep.
WITHIN A CLAUSE	It was David, **in fact**, who suggested the extra study time.

You can learn more about parenthetical expressions on pages L435–L437.

PRACTICE YOUR SKILLS

● Check Your Understanding
Using Semicolons

General
Interest **Write *I* if the compound sentence is incorrectly punctuated. Write *C* if it is correct.**

1. Snow will not lie on the ground if the temperature has not been below freezing on a regular basis, consequently, there is seldom measurable snowfall in Austin, Texas.

2. Peanuts can be used to make oil, cheese, ink, and soap; in addition, they have more than 300 other uses.

3. Men have walked on the moon; nevertheless parts of Greenland have never been explored.

4. Many people; however, do not see the need to fund such expeditions.

5. Human life expectancy in Hawaii is high, moreover, its life expectancy is higher than that of any other state.

6. The iguana has one of the most rugged bodies of any living creature nevertheless it is very timid.

7. A housefly beats its wings up to 190 times a second, however, a honeybee beats its wings 250 times a second.

8. Sunglasses are nothing new, for example; tinted lenses were common during the sixteenth century.

9. Many of the most popular commercials use classical music, in fact many people recognize Mozart's music from TV ads.

10. The French people; nevertheless, are the world's greatest cheese eaters.

● Connect to the Writing Process: Editing
Using Punctuation with Compound Sentences

11.–19. Rewrite the incorrect sentences from the preceding exercise, correcting the use of punctuation.

Semicolons to Avoid Confusion

A semicolon is substituted for a comma in two situations.

Use a semicolon instead of a comma between the clauses of a compound sentence if there are commas within a clause.

Don't make tacos, pizza, or chili; for Robert hates tomatoes.

We cooked rice, vegetables, and chicken; but we could not eat all of it.

Use semicolons instead of commas between items in a series if the items themselves contain commas.

Next week the President will visit Norfolk, Virginia; Cincinnati, Ohio; and San Antonio, Texas.

The polls indicate that the President has received great support from the voters in Miami, Florida; Los Angeles, California; and New York, New York.

You can learn more about using commas on pages L418–L440.

CONNECT TO WRITER'S CRAFT

Author Alexandre Dumas uses semicolons to connect phrases in a series in a long sentence that has additional commas. Notice how the semicolons draw attention to how the character is feeling. The semicolons are in **bold** type for emphasis.

> . . . Alone, in the presence of all the luxury which surrounded him; alone, in the presence of his power; alone, with the part he was about to be forced to act, Philippe for the first time felt his heart, and mind, and soul expand beneath the influence of a thousand varied emotions, which are the vital throbs of a king's heart.
>
> —*Alexandre Dumas,* The Man in the Iron Mask

PRACTICE YOUR SKILLS

● Check Your Understanding
Using Semicolons

General | **Write *a* or *b* to indicate the sentence in each pair that**
Interest | **is correctly punctuated.**

1. a. Michelangelo was a painter; sculptor, and architect, and he was also a poet.
  b. Michelangelo was a painter, sculptor, and architect; and he was also a poet.

2. a. The four state capitals that have been named after presidents are Jackson; Mississippi, Lincoln; Nebraska, Jefferson City, Missouri; and Madison; Wisconsin.
  b. The four state capitals that have been named after presidents are Jackson, Mississippi; Lincoln, Nebraska; Jefferson City, Missouri; and Madison, Wisconsin.

3. a. George Lucas is a director, producer, and writer; and he owns his own production company.
  b. George Lucas is a director, producer, and writer and he owns his own production company.

4. a. The states that make up the Four Corners are Utah; Colorado; New Mexico; and Arizona.
  b. The states that make up the Four Corners are Utah, Colorado, New Mexico, and Arizona.

5. a. Before the summer is over, a large number of tourists will have visited Paris, France; London, England; and Dublin, Ireland.
  b. Before the summer is over, a large number of tourists will have visited Paris, France, London, England; and Dublin, Ireland.

● Connect to the Writing Process: Editing
Using Semicolons

Rewrite the following sentences, using semicolons correctly. If a sentence is correct, write C.

6. You bring the silverware, cups, and napkins; and I will bring the food.

7. The barbecue cook-off will be held in Kansas City; Missouri, Dallas, Texas and Yuma; Arizona.

8. Donald ate five hot dogs three chicken wings three hamburgers two ears of corn and an apple for he was hungry.

9. The cook-off sponsors will supply the grill; the charcoal; and the utensils; but you will have to bring your own meat.

10. Next year we plan to go to the chili cook-offs that will be held in El Paso, Texas; Santa Fe, New Mexico; and Phoenix, Arizona.

 ## Colons

A colon points ahead—usually to a list of items that is about to follow.

Use a colon before most lists of items, especially when a list comes after the expression *the following*.

> You can respond by using one of the following**:** telephone, letter, or personal interview.
>
> There are four principal forms of clouds**:** cumulus, stratus, cirrus, and nimbus.

Notice that commas separate the items in the series.

When you write a list, do not place a colon after a verb or a preposition.

> No Colon Our high school colors are red, white, and blue.
>
> Colon Our high school has three colors: red, white, and blue.

You can learn more about using commas with items in a series on pages L418–L419.

Colons are also used in a few other situations.

Use a colon to introduce a very long formal quotation.

Oscar Wilde, in *The Picture of Dorian Gray,* said this of books: "There is no such thing as a moral or an immoral book. Books are well written, or badly written. That is all."

Use a colon in certain special situations.

COLON USAGE	
Between Hours and Minutes	3:30 P.M.
Between Biblical Chapters and Verses	Psalms 62:5 Genesis 1:10
Between Title and Subtitle	*Star Wars: The Phantom Menace*
After Salutations in Business Letters	Dear Sir or Madam: Dear Mr. Johnson:

Practice Your Skills

● Check Your Understanding
Using Colons

General Interest

Write *I* if a sentence is punctuated incorrectly. Write *C* if a sentence is punctuated correctly.

1. Common breeds of cats include the following: Siamese, Persian, Angora, and Manx.

2. The term *precious stones* actually only applies to: diamonds, rubies, sapphires, and emeralds.

3. If you want to be there on time, you will need to set your alarm for 5:30 A.M.

4. Almost everyone knows that water may appear in three forms; solid, liquid, and gas.

5. My favorite Bible verse is: 1 Corinthians 13, 4.

6. The nine English words most often used are: *and, be, it, of, the, will, I, have,* and *you.*

7. For English class we are using *From Beowulf to the Beatles: Approaches to Poetry.*

8. Horace Mann had this to say "Do not think of knocking out another person's brains because he differs in opinion from you. It would be as rational to knock yourself on the head because you differ from yourself ten years ago."

9. Dear Ms. Dell,
   I would be very interested in learning more about the summer internship program.

10. The costume committee still needs to find the following items, a top hat, a pair of gloves, a red cape and a feather scarf.

Connect to the Writing Process: Editing
Using Colons

11.–17. **Rewrite the incorrect sentences in the preceding exercise, punctuating them correctly.**

Communicate Your Ideas

APPLY TO WRITING

Business Letter: *Colons and Semicolons*

The director of the summer camp has chosen you as a potential camp counselor. In order to secure your position, you decide to send a letter to the camp director and describe some of the ideas and schedules you have for working with this year's six-year-olds. After you finish, be sure to check that you used colons and semicolons correctly throughout your letter.

Contemporary Life **Write the following sentences, adding semicolons, commas, and colons where needed. If a sentence is correct, write C.**

1. We heard Katherine sing last night furthermore, we thought she was fantastic!

2. Arlene is not a junior cellist she's a sophomore.

3. I must find my music, my stand, and my flute and then I will be ready to go.

4. All musicians need the following a good teacher, regular practice time, and a sense of timing.

5. The are no violins in our jazz band they play only in the orchestra.

6. Tonight's soloists are Tran Lo, a senior Carla Totara, a junior, and Jeff Higgins, a sophomore.

7. Dear Mr. John Williams,

8. Our band has enjoyed playing your music.

9. Television can be very informative for instance, last night I watched a program about Handel.

10. Our orchestra teacher composed a piece of music entitled "Summer Respite A Solitary Journey."

11. I did not know how to play the viola I had to be taught by a private tutor.

12. By the end of our first performance, we had lost half of the audience nevertheless we were not discouraged.

13. Mary's cello lesson was scheduled for 415 P.M.

14. Did you know that Kyle wrote some violin music for Psalms 2 1?

15. On our band trip, we wanted to go to Maine, instead, we decided to go to Wisconsin.

16. Among the many words associated with music are the following *crescendo, pianissimo, treble,* and *largo.*

Although you may use hyphens, dashes, and parentheses less often than other marks of punctuation, you should know the rules for using them.

 Hyphens

A hyphen **(-)** is most often used to divide words at the end of a line.

Hyphens with Divided Words   Although you should avoid dividing words when possible, sometimes it is necessary to divide words in your writing.

Use a hyphen to divide a word at the end of a line.

The following guidelines will help you to divide words correctly.

DIVIDING WORDS

1. Divide words only between syllables.
production: pro-duction or produc-tion

---

2. Never divide a one-syllable word.

strap	pour	match	wrist

---

3. Never separate a one-letter syllable from the rest of the word.
For example, the following words should never be divided:

a-mong	e-ven	u-nite

---

4. Two-letter divisions are permissible at the end of a line, but two-letter word endings should not be carried over to the next line.

Break	in-fant	de-fense	en-dear
Do Not Break	loss-es	ful-ly	mon-ey

---

5. Divide words containing double consonants between the double consonants.

tomor-row   shim-mer   run-ning   oc-cur

6. Divide hyphenated words only after the hyphens.

mother-in-law   double-decker   flip-flop

7. Do not divide a proper noun or a proper adjective.

Henderson   Pacific   Detroit   American

Remember that you can always look in a dictionary to find out where words can be divided into syllables.

PRACTICE YOUR SKILLS

● Check Your Understanding
Using Hyphens to Divide Words

Write *a* or *b* to indicate the word in each pair that shows where a word may be correctly hyphenated for division at the end of a line.

1. **a.** ent-hrone
   b. en-throne

2. **a.** en-velop
   b. enve-lop

3. **a.** even
   b. ev-en

4. **a.** he-ather
   b. heather

5. **a.** mid-way
   b. midwa-y

6. **a.** might
   b. mig-ht

7. **a.** nec-es-sar-y
   b. nec-es-sary

8. **a.** neg-a-tive
   b. ne-gative

9. **a.** prin-ce
   b. prince

10. **a.** prin-ter
    b. printer

11. **a.** pro-xy
    b. proxy

12. **a.** rapp-ort
    b. rap-port

13. **a.** re-com-mend
    b. rec-om-mend

14. **a.** Rogers
    b. Rog-ers

15. **a.** sec-ret
    b. se-cret

16. **a.** ser-i-ous
    b. se-ri-ous

17. **a.** stretch
    b. str-etch

18. **a.** thr-ee-ring
    b. three-ring

19. **a.** tro-pical
    b. trop-i-cal

20. **a.** well-wisher
    b. well-wis-her

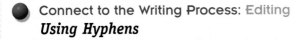

Connect to the Writing Process: Editing
Using Hyphens

Rewrite the following words, hyphenating them correctly as if they were to appear at the end of a line. If a word cannot be hyphenated at the end of a line, write C.

21. tonight

22. president

23. son-in-law

24. dazzle

25. Hawaii

26. enter

Hyphens with Certain Numbers   Hyphens are needed when you write out numbers.

Use a hyphen when writing out the numbers twenty-one through ninety-nine.

Sixty-two people attended the skating trials.

Only twenty-eight skaters attended last year.

Hyphens with Some Compound Nouns and Adjectives
Some compound nouns and adjectives need one or more hyphens.

Use one or more hyphens to separate the parts of some compound nouns and adjectives. Also use one or more hyphens between words that make up a compound adjective in front of a noun.

COMPOUNDS	
Compound Nouns	father-in-law, stand-in, pom-pom
Compound Adjectives	far-off, fast-food, do-it-yourself

A hyphen is used only when a compound adjective comes before a noun—not when it follows a linking verb and comes after the noun it describes.

ADJECTIVE BEFORE A NOUN	I believe that my report about the Olympics is a **well-written** paper.
ADJECTIVE AFTER A NOUN	I believe that my paper is **well written.**

A hyphen is used only when a fraction is used as an adjective—not when it is used as a noun.

FRACTION USED AS AN ADJECTIVE	Jane owned a **two-thirds** share of the family farm.
FRACTION USED AS A NOUN	The farmhand mowed **two thirds** of the pasture quickly.

Hyphens with Certain Prefixes
Certain prefixes and the suffix -*elect* are separated from their base words by a hyphen.

> Use a hyphen after the prefixes *ex-, self-,* and *all-* and before the suffix -*elect.*

Also use a hyphen with all prefixes before a proper noun or a proper adjective.

HYPHENS WITH PREFIXES AND SUFFIXES		
ex-pilot	self-addressed	president-elect
ex-mayor	self-satisfied	senator-elect
all-out	mid-October	
all-American	mid-Pacific	
pre-Civil War		
pro-American		

PRACTICE YOUR SKILLS

● Check Your Understanding
Using Hyphens

Contemporary Life
Write *a* or *b* to indicate which sentence in each pair uses hyphens correctly.

1. a. Allie saw the pre Olympic trials for figure-skating.
   b. Allie saw the pre-Olympic trials for figure skating.

2. a. Three fourths of the proceeds went toward expenses for the Olympic team members.
   b. Three-fourths of the proceeds went toward expenses for the Olympic team members.

3. a. Twenty-five years from now, these skaters will be forty-one years old.
   b. Twenty five years from now, these skaters will be forty-one years old.

4. a. Greg, the ex-captain of the River City High School hockey team, is an all-around athlete.
   b. Greg, the ex captain of the River City High School hockey-team, is an all-around athlete.

5. a. The president elect of the Olympic-committee will take office in January.
   b. The president-elect of the Olympic committee will take office in January.

● Connect to the Writing Process: Editing
Using Hyphens

Rewrite the following sentences, using hyphens correctly. If a sentence is correct, write C.

6. By the time I am forty-nine years old, I will have seen at least four different Olympics.

7. Two-thirds of my allowance is spent on sporting events.

8. Sabrina gave an all out performance for the judges.

9. By mid February, the winter Olympics are under way.

10. My brother-in law, who is an athlete, does not eat fast food often.

Dashes and Parentheses

In some situations a dash (—) and parentheses ( ) are used like commas, because they separate certain words or groups of words from the rest of the sentence. There are, however, some distinctions among the uses of these marks of punctuation.

Dashes

Dashes indicate a greater separation between words than commas do. They can be used in the following situations.

Use dashes to set off an abrupt change in thought.

> The Caspian Sea—the name *sea* is misleading—is by far the largest lake in the world.

Use dashes to set off an appositive that is introduced by words such as *that is, for example,* or *for instance.*

> Some family names—for example, Baker, Butler, and Gardner—come from occupations.

> Some plants—for instance, the pitcher, the sidesaddle, and the sundew—devour insects.

Use dashes to set off a parenthetical expression or an appositive that includes commas.

> Thomas Jefferson—scientist, architect, philosopher—was truly a great person.

> Three scientists—Finlay, Reed, and Theiler—are responsible for conquering yellow fever.

If you do not know how to make a dash on the computer, you can place two hyphens together. Do not leave space before or after the hyphens.

Professional writers sometimes use dashes in a character's dialogue. A dash in dialogue can indicate an abrupt change in thought, or it can reveal something about the way a character speaks. Notice the effect that dashes have on the speech of Finny in *A Separate Peace*.

> "Well of course," Finny said with an exasperated chuckle, "of course *I* was in the tree—oh you mean Gene?—he wasn't in—is that what you mean, or—" Finny floundered with muddled honesty between me and my questioner.
>
> *John Knowles*, A Separate Peace

Parentheses

When using parentheses, remember that they come in pairs.

Use parentheses to enclose information that is not closely related to the meaning of the sentence.

To decide whether or not you should use parentheses, read the sentence without the parenthetical material. If the meaning and structure in the sentence are not changed, then add parentheses. Just keep in mind that parenthetical additions to sentences tend to slow readers down and interrupt their train of thought. As a result, you should always limit the amount of parenthetical material that you add to any one piece of writing.

> The ostrich **(**often pictured with its head in the sand**)** can run faster than any other bird.

Sometimes the closing parenthesis comes at the end of a sentence. When this happens, the end mark usually goes outside of the parenthesis. However, occasionally, the end mark goes inside the parenthesis if the end mark actually belongs with the parenthetical material—for example, if the parenthetical material forms a complete sentence.

> Admission to the zoo is $6.95 for adults and $1.95 for children (under 12**)**.
>
> Your ticket entitles you to free parking. (Present the stub to the attendant on your way out.**)**

Commas, dashes, and parentheses are all used to enclose parenthetical material. When you are trying to determine which mark of punctuation to use, remember that dashes are stronger than commas while parentheses are weaker than commas.

PRACTICE YOUR SKILLS

Check Your Understanding
Using Dashes and Parentheses

Science Topic **Write *I* if a sentence is incorrectly punctuated. Write *C* if a sentence is correct.**

1. We saw twenty-four—yes, we counted them, bluebirds.

2. Is it true that some African animals, (for instance camels and tigers), once roamed the American continent?

3. Some reptiles—for example—the turtle and the alligator may live twenty-five years or more.

4. Several birds—(for example, the cassowary and the kiwi), have lost the ability to fly.

5. The gestation period (the time from conception to birth) is almost two years for an elephant.

6. Many animals—the cow, the goat, the reindeer, the yak, the llama, and the buffalo—give milk for human consumption.

7. A shark, as any scientist can tell you—has a seemingly endless supply of teeth.

8. The lobster (which is a favorite food of many) has five pairs of legs.

9. Some large birds, for example, the eagle, the hawk, and the falcon—have some of the keenest eyesight.

10. The whale shark—the name *whale* refers to its size) is one of the largest fish in the world.

● Connect to the Writing Process: Editing
Using Dashes and Parentheses

11.–17. Rewrite the incorrect sentences in the preceding exercise, using dashes and parentheses correctly.

Communicate Your Ideas

APPLY TO WRITING

Explanatory Paragraph: *Dashes and Parentheses*

Your local zoo has a special summer program that will allow you to work with the animal of your choice. In order to work with your favorite animal, you must show the head zookeeper that you know enough about that animal to care for it. Write a paragraph that names your favorite animal. Explain what you know about that animal and give specific reasons you have for choosing it. Be sure to use dashes and parentheses correctly.

Contemporary Life **Write each sentence, adding or changing punctuation marks where needed. If a sentence is correct, write C.**

1. Three people in my class Sharon, Christopher, and Guy have to work on the Fourth of July.

2. There were twenty-five people left in the store when it closed.

3. The average American sixteen year old finds it difficult to balance a job and schoolwork.

4. Wade McGee, however, owns a one-sixth share in his father's company.

5. When I get my first paycheck which should be soon I plan to put half the money in the bank.

6. I am planning on starting a new job at a restaurant in mid August.

7. Wendy was the store's all around best salesperson last week.

8. My brother in law wants me to work for him.

9. Two thirds of the people in my class have been hired for summer jobs.

10. Jonathan is three-fourths of the way through his training.

11. A job can teach a person to be self sufficient.

12. My cousin is going to work as a clerk for an attorney at law.

13. The newspaper *Pravda* which means "truth" in Russian is sold at the newsstand where Sam works.

14. The mayor-elect came into our store last night to hand out campaign literature.

15. Twenty five dollars was all I was able to save after I paid my mom back.

Science Topic **Write the following paragraphs, adding punctuation marks where needed.**

If the crust of the earth werent mostly solid, it would be shaking constantly. There are places they are technically called faults in the rocks of the earths crust where it isnt held together. Sometimes, along one of these breaks in the crust, one rock mass will rub against another with tremendous force. The energy of this rubbing is then changed to vibration in the rocks consequently an earthquake is formed.

There are two ways in which an earthquake is described in terms of size one is by noting the force of the earthquake itself, and the other is by reporting the amount of damage it does. The greatest earthquake in North American history occurred in San Francisco, California, in 1906. Seven hundred people died property damage amounted to about $425 million. More recently earthquakes in the Los Angeles and San Francisco areas caused more than a billion dollars worth of damage. Other great earthquakes have occurred in Lisbon Portugal Sicily Italy and Tokyo Japan.

Using Correct Punctuation

Write each sentence, adding punctuation where needed.

1. We will be taking our vacation in mid August.

2. Isnt your appointment at 930 A.M.?

3. A number of chickens I estimated at least sixteen have escaped through a hole in the fence.

4. Egg drop soup is made from the following ingredients eggs, chicken broth, and noodles.

5. That rabbits foot is Mikes good luck charm.

6. A lobster has five pairs of legs four pairs are used for walking.

7. Horse shows will be held in Pittsburgh Pennsylvania Dayton Ohio and Richmond Virginia.

8. Its an hours drive from Concord New Hampshire to my grandparents house.

9. The four fastest growing products in the United States are computers air conditioners video recorders and boats.

10. Garlic probably first grew in southern Siberia however it is now found in Asia and the Mediterranean area.

11. For our new apartment, we had to buy new curtains bedspreads and towels but we bought them all on sale.

12. Sharks teeth replace themselves as they wear out.

13. A two thirds majority voted for passage of the amendment.

14. Have you seen Dan and his fathers new boat?

15. Many languages for example, English German Swedish French and Italian come from a common source.

Editing for Correct Punctuation

Write the following paragraphs, adding punctuation where needed.

Charles Hatfield, modern historys greatest rainmaker, built his reputation by doing the following filling lakes, saving crops, and ending droughts. His greatest feat occurred in 1916 in San Diego, California. He promised to fill the citys reservoir for ten thousand dollars however, he wouldnt accept payment if no rain fell. Hatfields offer was instantly accepted. After all, the reservoir had never been more than one third filled since it was built.

Five days after Hatfield had prepared his special mixture it worked through a process of chemical evaporation rain began to fall. Twenty one days later the rain stopped all but five inches of the reservoir had been filled. His all out effort had been enormously successful! The members of the City Council, however, were not pleased in fact, they refused to pay Hatfield. The rain had caused enormous damage such as two hundred destroyed bridges, thousands of demolished houses, and miles of ruined railroad tracks.

Writing Sentences with Punctuation Marks

Write sentences that follow the directions below.

1. Write a sentence that includes a series of dates.
2. Write a sentence that includes joint ownership of a thing.
3. Write a sentence that includes *two thirds* as an adjective.
4. Write a sentence that includes a dash or two dashes.
5. Write a sentence that includes parentheses.

Language and *Self-Expression*

Grant Wood studied art in France and Germany, but he eventually returned to his roots in Iowa. From there he drew many of the subjects of his paintings. His work focuses on simple, ordinary subjects and often reveals his own sense of humor. In the painting *Parson Weems' Fable,* Wood shows Parson Mason Locke Weems, the author of the story about George Washington chopping down the cherry tree.

Tales about famous historical figures often become important, whether they are true or not. The story about the cherry tree is one such story. Think of another historical figure about whom a story is told. The story can be a true account or a form of fable, like George Washington's. Write your own version of the story, using various kinds of punctuation in your sentences.

Prewriting Create a story map to outline the details of the story you will tell. Describe the setting, characters, complication, turning point, falling action, and ending on your map.

Drafting Use your story map to write a first draft of your story. Tell what happened to the historical figure. Include your interpretation of what the events reveal about your subject and why the story is popular.

Revising Have a classmate read your story. Encourage that person to assess whether you have told the story in a way that will hold readers' interest and whether you have adequately explained the impact of the story events on your subject's role in history.

Editing Check your story for errors in spelling and capitalization. Be sure you have used apostrophes, semicolons, colons, and other punctuation correctly.

Publishing Read your story aloud to the class without identifying your subject. Encourage classmates to guess the identity of your subject.

Another Look

Using Apostrophes

Add *'s* to form the possessive of a singular noun. *(page L485)*

Add only an apostrophe to form the possessive of a plural noun that ends in *s*. Add *'s* to form the possessive of a plural noun that does not end in *s*. *(page L486)*

Add *'s* to form the possessive of indefinite pronouns. *(page L489)*

Use an apostrophe with the possessive form of a noun that expresses time or amount. *(page L492)*

Use an apostrophe in a contraction to show where one or more letters have been omitted. *(page L495)*

Using Semicolons and Colons

Use a semicolon between the clauses of a compound sentence that are not joined by a conjunction. *(page L501)*

Use a semicolon between clauses in a compound sentence that are joined by certain conjunctive adverbs or transitional words. *(pages L502–L503)*

Use a semicolon instead of a comma between the clauses of a compound sentence if there are commas within a clause. *(page L505)*

Use semicolons instead of commas between the items in a series if the items themselves contain commas. *(page L505)*

Use a colon before most lists of items, especially when the list comes after the expression *the following*. *(page L507)*

Use a colon to introduce a very long, formal quotation. *(page L508)*

Using Hyphens

Use a hyphen to divide a word at the end of a line. *(pages L511–L512)*

Use a hyphen when writing out certain numbers. *(page L513)*

Use a hyphen after the prefixes *ex-, self-,* and *all-* and before the suffix *-elect*. Also use a hyphen with all prefixes before a proper noun or a proper adjective. *(page L514)*

Using Dashes and Parentheses

Use dashes to set off an abrupt change in thought. *(page L516)*

Use dashes to set off an appositive that is introduced by words such as *that is, for example,* or *for instance*. *(page L516)*

Use dashes to set off a parenthetical expression or an appositive that includes commas. *(page L516)*

Use parentheses to enclose information that is not related closely to the meaning of the sentence. *(page L517)*

Posttest

Directions

Read the passage. Each underlined part contains mistakes in punctuation. Write the letter of the correct way to write each underlined part.

EXAMPLE

<u>Carrie Watson's friends</u> encouraged her to join
(1)
the talent contest.

1   **A**   Carrie Watson's friends
       B   Carrie Watsons' friends
       C   Carrie Watsons friends'
       D   Carrie Watsons friends

ANSWER   1   **A**

Carrie Watson signed up to be a <u>part of Glendales All City</u>
(1)
<u>Talent Show.</u> The winner would get the following <u>prizes a years</u>
(2)
<u>worth of free pizzas a hundred dollar gift certificate at a clothing</u>
<u>store</u> and an appearance on the local cable television show. Carrie
planned to perform a song from *Miss Saigon*. There were many
kinds of talent at the <u>show tap dancers a magician ballet dancers</u>
(3)
and one very odd, interesting tuba solo. <u>Carrie nervous but self</u>
(4)
<u>assured sang beautifully</u>. Afterward the crowd's applause <u>rang out</u>
(5)
<u>in fact</u> it was thunderous. Carrie was thrilled when she won the
contest!

1   **A**   part of Glendales All City Talent Show.

   B   part of Glendales' All City Talent Show.

   C   part of Glendale's All-City Talent Show.

   D   part of Glendales' All-City Talent-Show.

2   **A**   prizes a years worth of free pizzas a hundred dollar gift certificate at a clothing-store

   B   prizes—a years worth of free pizzas, a hundred dollar gift-certificate at a clothing store,

   C   prizes: a year's worth of free pizzas, a hundred-dollar gift certificate at a clothing store,

   D   prizes - a years worth of free pizzas: a hundred dollar gift certificate at a clothing store;

3   **A**   show tap dancers a magician ballet dancers

   B   show: tap dancers a magician ballet dancers

   C   show: tap dancers; a magician; ballet dancers;

   D   show; tap dancers; a magician; ballet dancers;

4   **A**   Carrie nervous but self assured sang beautifully.

   B   Carrie—nervous but self-assured—sang beautifully.

   C   Carrie nervous but self-assured—sang beautifully.

   D   Carrie; nervous but self assured; sang beautifully.

5   **A**   rang out in fact,

   B   rang out—in fact

   C   rang out; in fact,

   D   rang out: in fact,

A Writer's Guide to Citing Sources

When you use someone else's words or ideas in your own report, you must give that person proper credit. One way to cite sources is to use the guidelines of the Modern Language Association (MLA), which incorporate parenthetical citations.

Parenthetical citations give the reader just enough information to identify the source of the material. They should appear as close as possible to the words or ideas being cited. The reader then refers to the works-cited page at the end of the research paper for complete source information. The following examples will help you format parenthetical citations.

BOOK BY ONE AUTHOR	Give author's last name and page number(s): (Werbach 99–101).
BOOK BY MORE THAN ONE AUTHOR	Give both authors' names and page number(s): (Dunn and Kinney 147).
ARTICLE WITH AUTHOR NAMED	Give author's last name and page number(s): (Cox 51).
ARTICLE WITH AUTHOR UNNAMED	Give a shortened form of the title (unless full title is already short) and page number(s): ("Citizen Activism" 1).
ARTICLE IN A REFERENCE WORK; AUTHOR UNNAMED	Give title (full or shortened) and page number(s); if the article is a single page from an encyclopedia, no page number is needed: ("Rain Forest").

If a parenthetical citation falls at the end of a sentence, place it before the period. If you have used quotation marks, place the citation after the closing quotation mark and before the period.

Some teachers may prefer that you use **footnotes** or **endnotes**. Footnotes and endnotes mark borrowed material with a small number, or superscript, set halfway above the line, immediately after the borrowed material. It corresponds with a number at the bottom of the page—a footnote—or at the end of the paper—an endnote.

[1]Adam Werbach, <u>Act Now, Apologize Later</u> (NY: Harperperennial, 1998) 73.

A **works-cited page** is an alphabetical list of all sources in a research paper. The sources are alphabetized by the author's last name (or by title if no author is given). In the following examples, note the order of information, the indentation, and the punctuation.

GENERAL REFERENCE WORK	"Rain Forest." <u>Encyclopedia Americana</u>. 1999 ed.
BOOK BY ONE AUTHOR	Werbach, Adam. <u>Act Now, Apologize Later</u>. New York: HarperPerennial, 1998.
BOOK BY TWO OR MORE AUTHORS	Dunn, James R., and John E. Kinney. <u>Conservative Environmentalism</u>. Westport, CT: Quorum, 1996.
ARTICLE IN A MAGAZINE; AUTHOR NAMED	Cox, J. Robert. "Making Democracy Work." <u>Sierra</u> July–Aug. 1996: 51–2.
ARTICLE IN A NEWSPAPER	Malcolm, Andrew H. "Persuade the Children to Recycle, and They'll Teach the Adults." <u>New York Times</u> 7 Apr. 1992, late ed.: B5+.
INTERVIEW	Setchell, Linda. Telephone interview. 14 July 1999.
ARTICLE FROM A CD-ROM	"Deforestation." <u>Encyclopedia of Science</u>. CD-ROM. Version 2.0. New York: Dorling Kindersley, 1996.
ARTICLE FROM AN ON-LINE DATABASE WITH A PRINT VERSION	Knight, Robin. "Call of the Wild." <u>Time Magazine</u>. 21 June 1999: 7 pars. 7 Sept. 1999 <http://www.pathfinder. com/time/magazine/articles/ 0,3266,27563,00.html>.
ARTICLE FROM AN ON-LINE DATABASE WITHOUT A PRINT VERSION	Roach, John. "Natural Repellant Could Save Endangered Tree." <u>Environmental News Network</u>. 7 Sept. 1999: 10 pars. 7 Sept. 1999 <http://enn.com/news/enn-stories /1999/09/090799/cedar_5466.asp>.

Spelling Correctly

· ·

Directions

Read the passage. Write the letter of the answer that correctly spells each underlined word. If the word contains no error, write *D*.

EXAMPLE   Gymnastics is an <u>enjoyable</u> way to stay fit.
                                            (1)

          1 A enjoiable

             B enjoyble

             C enjoyabel

             D No error

ANSWER   **1 D**

To stay fit, many people are turning to an <u>excercise</u> we
                                                        (1)
<u>ordinaryly</u> associate with the Olympics. Gymnastics is an
(2)
<u>efficeint</u> way to increase your heart rate and improve your
(3)
grace and balance. Although at one time gymnastics classes

were the realm of <u>childrun</u>, now many of their parents are
                          (4)
<u>comitted</u> to this form of physical activity.
(5)
          In a typical class, people warm up to the <u>accompanyment</u>
                                                              (6)
of music. Movements are <u>controled</u>, and <u>instructors</u> help pose
                                (7)   **(8)**
students who are having trouble. Each <u>manuever</u> on an
                                              (9)
apparatus is <u>similarally</u> observed and assisted.
                    (10)

1	A	exersize	6	A	accompaniment
	B	exercise		B	acompanyment
	C	excersize		C	acompaniment
	D	No error		D	No error

2	A	ordinarily	7	A	controlied
	B	ordinarally		B	controlled
	C	ordinaryally		C	conntroled
	D	No error		D	No error

3	A	efficiant	8	A	instructers
	B	effisient		B	innstructors
	C	efficient		C	instructres
	D	No error		D	No error

4	A	children	9	A	maneuver
	B	childs		B	maneuvre
	C	childeren		C	manuver
	D	No error		D	No error

5	A	comited	10	A	similarily
	B	commited		B	similarly
	C	committed		C	similarrly
	D	No error		D	No error

Strategies for Learning to Spell

Learning to spell involves a variety of senses. You use your senses of hearing, sight, and touch to spell a word correctly. Here is a five-step strategy that many people have used successfully as they learned to spell unfamiliar words.

1 Auditory
Say the word aloud. Answer these questions.
- Where have I heard or read this word before?
- What was the context in which I heard or read the word?

2 Visual
Look at the word. Answer these questions.
- Does this word divide into parts? Is it a compound word? Does it have a prefix or a suffix?
- Does this word look like any other word I know? Could it be part of a word family I would recognize?

3 Auditory
Spell the word to yourself. Answer these questions.
- How is each sound spelled?
- Are there any surprises? Does the word follow spelling rules I know, or does it break the rules?

4 Visual/Kinesthetic
Write the word as you look at it. Answer these questions.
- Have I written the word clearly?
- Are my letters formed correctly?

5 Visual/Kinesthetic
Cover up the word. Visualize it. Write it. Answer this question.
- Did I write the word correctly?
- If the answer is no, return to step 1.

Spelling Strategies

Good spelling is important if you want to communicate effectively in writing. Your readers will find it easier to understand your message if you spell words correctly. Misspellings distract readers. The strategies and instruction in this chapter will help you improve your spelling and communicate more clearly.

STRATEGY **Use a dictionary.** If you are not sure how to spell a word, or if a word you have written does not "look right," check the word in a dictionary or use a spell checker on a computer.

STRATEGY **Proofread your writing carefully.** Be on the lookout for misspellings and for words you are not sure you spelled correctly. You can place a check mark over a word that you are not sure of and look it up when you finish writing.

PRACTICE YOUR SKILLS

● Check Your Understanding
Recognizing Misspelled Words

Write the letter of the misspelled word in each set. Then write the word correctly.

1. (a) leather   (b) Wensday   (c) surgeon
2. (a) changable   (b) schedule   (c) practical
3. (a) awkward   (b) develope   (c) annual
4. (a) transferred   (b) category   (c) obsticle
5. (a) labratory   (b) accommodate   (c) jealous
6. (a) basicly   (b) marriage   (c) separate
7. (a) preferred   (b) movement   (c) disatisfied
8. (a) fiery   (b) twelth   (c) equipment
9. (a) dominent   (b) martyr   (c) meant
10. (a) fulfill   (b) advertisment   (c) business

Be sure you are pronouncing words correctly.
"Swallowing" syllables or adding extra syllables can cause
you to misspell a word.

PRACTICE YOUR SKILLS

● **Check Your Understanding**
Pronouncing Words

| Oral Expression | **Practice saying each syllable in the following words to help you spell the words correctly.** |

1. nine•ty
2. ath•let•ics
3. vo•cab•u•lar•y
4. Feb•ru•ar•y
5. lat•er•al

6. ex•cel•lent
7. in•te•grate
8. fa•mil•iar
9. re•mem•ber
10. prob•a•ble

Make up mnemonic devices. A sentence like "Do not
bi**cy**cle when it's **icy**" can help you remember an important
sequence of letters in *bicycle*. "Will you (**u**) vol**u**nteer?" can
help you remember that the unstressed vowel sound in
volunteer is spelled with *u*.

Keep a spelling journal. Use it to record the words that
you have had trouble spelling. Here are some suggestions for
organizing your spelling journal.

- Write the word correctly.
- Write the word again, underlining or circling the part of
  the word that gave you trouble.
- Write a tip to help you remember how to spell the word.

| laboratory | laboratory | We labor in the laboratory. |
| fulfill | fulfill | One, two—first one l, then two |

Becoming familiar with spelling generalizations can help you improve your spelling ability. Some spelling generalizations are based on spelling patterns, such as the choice between *ie* and *ei*. Other generalizations are concerned with forming plurals and adding prefixes and suffixes.

▶ Spelling Patterns

The following spelling patterns are useful to know because they apply to many words.

Words with *ie* and *ei*

When you spell words with *ie* or *ei*, *i* comes before *e* except when the letters follow *c* or when they stand for the long *a* sound.

	IE AND *EI*			
EXAMPLES	ie		ach**ie**ve	hyg**ie**ne
	ei after **c**		dec**ei**t	conc**ei**ted
	sounds like long **a**		f**ei**gn	sl**ei**gh
EXCEPTIONS	anc**ie**nt	effic**ie**nt	conterf**ei**t	s**ei**zure
	consc**ie**nce	spec**ie**s	prot**ei**n	w**ei**rd
	suffic**ie**nt		sover**ei**gn	

The generalization about *ie* and *ei* applies only when the letters occur in the same syllable and spell just one vowel sound. It does not apply when *i* and *e* appear in different syllables.

IE AND *EI* IN DIFFERENT SYLLABLES			
de ity	re inforce	juici er	soci ety

Words ending in *–sede, –ceed,* and *–cede*

Words that end with a syllable that sounds like "seed" are usually spelled with *–cede*. Only one word in English is spelled with *–sede,* and only three words are spelled with *–ceed.*

	–SEDE, –CEED, AND –CEDE			
EXAMPLES	ac**cede**	pre**cede**	inter**cede**	se**cede**
EXCEPTIONS	super**sede**	ex**ceed**	pro**ceed**	suc**ceed**

PRACTICE YOUR SKILLS

● Check Your Understanding
Using Spelling Patterns

Write each word correctly, adding *ie* or *ei*.

1. hyg ■ ne
2. dec ■ t
3. sl ■ gh
4. for ■ gn
5. s ■ ge
6. conc ■ t
7. bel ■ ve
8. th ■ r
9. med ■ val
10. perc ■ ve

11. f ■ gn
12. ch ■ f
13. p ■ rce
14. n ■ ghbor
15. w ■ ght
16. l ■ utenant
17. conc ■ vable
18. s ■ zure
19. counterf ■ t
20. rec ■ pt

Write each word correctly, adding *–sede, –ceed,* or *–cede*.

21. pro ■
22. re ■
23. con ■
24. super ■
25. se ■

26. ac ■
27. pre ■
28. ex ■
29. suc ■
30. inter ■

Social Studies **Find and rewrite the ten words that have been spelled incorrectly.**

The medieval period is excedingly appealing to many people. They percieve it as a time when everyone's cheif interest was doing noble deeds. I conceed that the Middle Ages have thier charm, but I find the idea of living in that period inconceivable. The appalling sanitary conditions in medieval towns were superceded only by a happy disregard for personal hygeine. Those heroic knights wore armor that couldn't be pierced with a sword, but it also wieghed a great deal and was exceedingly hot. Imagine attending a medieval banquet with knights. Then remember that a day of jousting in the sun would have preceeded the banquet!

Word Alert
! The words *proceed* and *precede* are sometimes confused.

proceed—[verb] to advance or go on; to move along

She **proceeded** to tell me the whole story.

precede—[verb] to be, come, or go before

Darkness **preceded** the rainstorm.

● **Plurals**

As you know, the word *plural* means "more than one." Although many nouns form their plurals by adding *s* or *es* to the word, not all do. There are several spelling generalizations that can help you form the plural of most nouns.

Regular Nouns

To form the plural of most nouns, simply add *s*.

MOST NOUNS				
Singular	dentist	character	column	niece
Plural	dentists	characters	columns	nieces

If a noun ends in *s*, *ch*, *sh*, *x*, or *z*, add *es* to form the plural.

S, CH, SH, X, AND Z				
Singular	genius	clutch	sash	waltz
Plural	geniuses	clutches	sashes	waltzes

Nouns Ending in *y*

Add *s* to form the plural of a noun ending in a vowel and *y*.

VOWELS AND Y				
Singular	tray	holiday	attorney	decoy
Plural	trays	holidays	attorneys	decoys

Change the *y* to *i* and add *es* to a noun ending in a consonant and *y*.

CONSONANTS AND Y				
Singular	tendency	family	accessory	delivery
Plural	tendencies	families	accessories	deliveries

PRACTICE YOUR SKILLS

 Check Your Understanding

Forming Plurals

Write the plural form of each noun.

1. salary	**8.** marsh	**15.** speech
2. turkey	**9.** breeze	**16.** juror
3. watch	**10.** fossil	**17.** alloy
4. college	**11.** glass	**18.** valley
5. jockey	**12.** ranch	**19.** lunch
6. society	**13.** hoax	**20.** opportunity
7. constable	**14.** delay	

 Connect to the Writing Process: Editing

Spelling Plural Nouns

General
Interest
Rewrite this paragraph, changing the underlined nouns from singular to plural.

On Halloween 1940, many Americans were the victim of one of the greatest unintentional hoax of all times. On that night, the Mercury Theater of the Air presented a radio play based on *War of the Worlds,* one of H. G. Wells's popular science fiction story. Few play have ever had such an impact on people. *War of the Worlds* used what sounded like actual news broadcast and eyewitness report to tell the story of a Martian invasion of Earth. Listener who tuned in late and missed the introductory speech believed they were hearing report about actual event. People panicked, thinking that the United States was being overrun by army of aliens.

Nouns Ending with *o*

Add *s* to form the plural of a noun ending with a vowel and *o*.

VOWELS AND *O*			
SINGULAR	radio	portfolio	cameo	shampoo
PLURAL	radios	portfolios	cameos	shampoos

Add *s* to form the plural of musical terms ending in *o*.

MUSICAL TERMS			
SINGULAR	piano	trio	soprano	piccolo
PLURAL	pianos	trios	sopranos	piccolos

The plurals of nouns ending in a consonant and *o* do not follow a regular pattern.

CONSONANTS AND *O*			
SINGULAR	hero	potato	photo	memo
PLURAL	heroes	potatoes	photos	memos

Nouns Ending in *f* or *fe*

To form the plural of some nouns ending in *f* or *fe*, just add *s*.

F OR FE			
SINGULAR	roof	waif	clef	belief
PLURAL	roofs	waifs	clefs	beliefs

For some nouns ending in *f* or *fe,* change the *f* to *v* and add *es* or *s.*

	F OR FE TO V			
SINGULAR	cal**f**	thie**f**	sel**f**	wol**f**
PLURAL	cal**ves**	thie**ves**	sel**ves**	wol**ves**

PRACTICE YOUR SKILLS

● Check Your Understanding
Forming Plurals

Write the plural form of each noun. Check a dictionary to be sure you have formed the plural correctly.

1. folio   **4.** alto   **7.** chef   **10.** elf

2. ego   **5.** rodeo   **8.** shelf   **11.** brief

3. igloo   **6.** studio   **9.** gulf   **12.** wolf

● Connect to the Writing Process: Editing
Spelling Plural Nouns

Contemporary Life   **Rewrite this paragraph, correcting ten spelling errors.**

We went to an outdoor concert on a summer evening. We positioned ourselfs on a blanket and got ready to take some photoes and to listen. I said to my friend, "If it doesn't rain, we don't need rooves over our heads."

The orchestra began with two concertoes—one for two pianos, the other for violin. Next was a new composition for a trio of celloes. I love the cello, and all cello players are my heros. When the cellos started playing, we were having the time of our lifes, but that soon changed. Halfway through, the celloes were drowned out by the annoying buzzing of mosquitos! My friend wailed, "I knew we should have stayed home and listened to the concert on our radioes!"

Compound Nouns

Most compound nouns are made plural in the same way as other nouns.

MOST COMPOUND NOUNS				
SINGULAR	baby-sitter	go-between	stand-in	rooftop
PLURAL	baby-sitter**s**	go-between**s**	stand-in**s**	rooftop**s**

When the main word in a compound noun appears first, that word becomes plural.

OTHER COMPOUNDS			
SINGULAR	bird of prey	lily of the valley	son-in-law
PLURAL	bird**s** of prey	lil**ies** of the valley	son**s**-in-law

Numerals, Letters, Symbols, and Words as Words

To form the plurals of numerals, letters, symbols, and words used as words, add an *s*. To prevent confusion, it's best to use an apostrophe and *s* with lowercase letters, some capital letters, and some words used as words.

EXAMPLES Sometimes 7**s** are mistaken for cursive *T*s.
She used &**s** instead of *and*s in her note.

EXCEPTIONS How do you write your *a*'**s** and *g*'**s**?
She signed the note with lots of *X*'**s** and *O*'**s**.

PRACTICE YOUR SKILLS

● Check Your Understanding
Forming Plurals

Write the plural form for each item.

1. sergeant-at-arms
2. passerby
3. *I*
4. editor in chief
5. grandparent
6. *A* and *B*
7. 1900
8. 1890
9. *pro* and *con*
10. signpost
11. teaspoonful
12. newcomer
13. snowman
14. byline
15. *
16. *s*
17. sister-in-law
18. drive-in
19. 52
20. table of contents

● Connect to the Writing Process: Editing
Spelling Plural Nouns

Language Arts — **Write each sentence, changing the underlined items to plural from singular.**

1. Here are some *do* for choosing books.
2. Titles can be signpost, so look for titles that sound interesting.
3. Then you should learn what you can about story line or contents.
4. Dust jacket usually have information that can help you.
5. Use the table of contents of nonfiction books to tell you what topics are covered.
6. If you like history, many books have been written about the 1950 and the 1960.
7. The biographies are arranged alphabetically on the bookshelf.
8. Check various Website for recently published titles.
9. Newspaper are a good source for reviews and recommendations.
10. Ask the clerks who work at the bookstore which titles have been well received.

Other Plural Forms

Irregular plurals are not formed by adding *s* or *es*.

IRREGULAR PLURALS					
SINGULAR	tooth	man	ox	foot	woman
	child	goose	mouse	louse	
PLURAL	tee**th**	m**en**	ox**en**	f**ee**t	wom**en**
	child**ren**	g**ee**se	m**ice**	l**ice**	

Some nouns have the same form for singular and plural.

SAME SINGULAR AND PLURAL		
Chinese	sheep	scissors
Japanese	moose	headquarters
Swiss	salmon	series
Sioux	species	politics

Words from Latin and Greek

Some nouns borrowed from Latin and Greek have plurals that are formed as they are in the original language. For a few Latin and Greek loan words there are two ways to form the plural.

LATIN AND GREEK NOUNS				
EXAMPLES	vertebra	stimulus	synops**is**	parenthes**is**
	vertebr**ae**	stimul**i**	synops**es**	parenthes**es**
EXCEPTIONS	index		focus	
	index**es** or ind**ices**		focus**es** or fo**ci**	

Check a dictionary when forming the plural of words from Latin and Greek. When two forms are given, the first one is preferred.

PRACTICE YOUR SKILLS

● Check Your Understanding
Forming Plurals

Write the plural form of each item. Use a dictionary to check the spelling.

1. pliers
2. Danish
3. corps
4. foot
5. ox
6. synthesis
7. woman
8. fulcrum
9. alumna
10. Chinese

11. goose
12. matrix
13. stylus
14. pants
15. sheep
16. shad
17. series
18. shears
19. moose
20. headquarters

● Connect to the Writing Process: Editing
Forming Plurals

General Interest **Decide if the underlined plurals are formed correctly. If any are incorrect, write the correct form.**

The 1960s are remembered as a time of change. Not
only did the curriculum change in many schools but also
the clotheses young peoples were allowed to wear to school
changed. Students could wear sneakers to class, and young
mens could wear jeanses. Young woman still had to wear
skirts, which used to be long enough to touch the tops of
their bobby socks. In the 1960's, skirts were getting shorter
and shorter, and the medium reported that skirts had
become a dress-code problem. Some school officials came

up with an ingenious test. They would ask the young womens to kneel on the floor. If the hems of their skirts touched the floor, the length was okay. If they didn't, with no ifes, and's, or buts, they were sent home to change into something more suitable.

Communicate Your Ideas

APPLY TO WRITING
Persuasive Letter: *Plurals*

Although dress codes may not be as strict today as they were in the past, most schools still have some restrictions about what students may and may not wear to class. Many schools are even returning to school uniforms. What is your opinion? Do you think students should have the freedom to wear what they wish, or do you think there is some benefit to having students wear uniforms? Express your opinion in a letter to the editor of your school newspaper. Use at least ten plural nouns in your paragraph.

Write the plural form of each word. Use a dictionary whenever necessary.

1. alumnus
2. thesis
3. trousers
4. child
5. alto
6. potato
7. roof
8. *how*
9. 1860
10. avocado

11. clef
12. 50
13. octopus
14. *I*
15. sheep
16. formula
17. index
18. aquarium
19. species
20. son-in-law

Spelling Numbers

When you want to use numbers in sentences, you may not be sure whether you should write the number in numerals or in words. The following generalizations can help guide you.

Numerals or Number Words

Spell out numbers that can be written in one or two words. Use numerals for other numbers. Always spell out a number that begins a sentence.

> We stood in line for **three** hours to get the concert tickets.
>
> There were **268** people ahead of us in line.
>
> **Three hundred thirty-four** people bought concert tickets for the first show.

When you have a series of numbers, and some are just one or two words while others are more, use numerals for them all.

> The month of February has **29** days in a leap year, and so the entire year has **366** days instead of **365.**

Ordinal Numbers

Always spell out numbers that are used to tell the order.

> This is the **third** time someone has asked that question.
> The meeting is held the **second** Tuesday of each month.

Numbers in Dates

Use a numeral for a date when you include the name of the month. Always use numerals for the year.

EXAMPLES	Armistice Day marked the end of World War I on **November 11, 1918.**
	The name of the holiday was changed to Veterans' Day in **1954.**
EXCEPTION	In Canada, the **eleventh** of November is called Remembrance Day.
	(Always spell out ordinal numbers.)

PRACTICE YOUR SKILLS

● Check Your Understanding
Spelling Numbers

Use the correct form of the number given in parentheses to complete each sentence.

1. (1) New Year's Day is always the ▓ of January.

2. (2) Groundhog Day is February ▓.

3. (3) Presidents' Day is the ▓ Monday in February.

4. (300) Columbus Day was first celebrated in 1792, ▇ years after Columbus landed in the Bahamas.

5. (117) ▇ years later, in 1909, Columbus Day was officially recognized as a holiday.

6. (12) October ▇, 1909, was the first time Columbus Day was celebrated as holiday.

7. (15) Martin Luther King, Jr., was born on January ▇.

8. (3) The ▇ Monday in January is the day we celebrate Martin Luther King's life and achievements.

9. (14) June ▇ is Flag Day.

10. (1877) Flag Day was first celebrated in ▇.

11. (100) It had then been ▇ years since the design of the flag had been adopted.

12. (1949) Flag Day became an official holiday in ▇.

13. (22) George Washington was born on the ▇ of February in 1732.

14. (1796) His birthday became a holiday in ▇.

15. (3) Washington's birthday became a holiday ▇ years before his death.

● Connect to the Writing Process: Editing
Writing Numbers Correctly

General Interest **Rewrite this paragraph, correcting any mistakes in writing numbers.**

There are 365 days in a year, and on every day something important happened. Take September, for example. On the 1st of September, World War II began in 1939; and in 1985, Dr. Robert Ballard located the *Titanic* on the bottom of the Atlantic Ocean. Queen Liliuokalani, the last monarch of the Hawaiian Islands, was born on the 2nd of September. The Treaty of Paris was signed on September 3rd, 1783, ending the American colonies' 8-year struggle for independence. On September 4, 1888, George Eastman patented his camera. The 5th of September is the birthday of the outlaw Jesse James. The Pilgrims set sail for the New World on September 6, 1620, and 368 years later, on the 6th of September, an 11-year-old boy named Thomas Gregory swam the English Channel.

Prefixes and Suffixes

A **prefix** is one or more syllables placed in front of a base word to form a new word. When you add a prefix, the spelling of the base word does not change.

PREFIXES	
in + definite = **in**definite	**un** + opened = **un**opened
pre + view = **pre**view	**over** + look = **over**look
dis + appoint = **dis**appoint	**mis** + guided = **mis**guided
re + assess = **re**assess	**il** + logical = **il**logical

A **suffix** is one or more syllables placed after a base word to change its part of speech and possibly also its meaning.

Suffixes –*ness* and –*ly*

The suffixes –*ness* and –*ly* are added to most base words without any spelling changes.

–*NESS* AND –*LY*	
kind + **ness** = kind**ness**	kind + **ly** = kind**ly**
sad + **ness** = sad**ness**	sad + **ly** = sad**ly**

Words Ending in *e*

Drop the final *e* in the base word when adding a suffix that begins with a vowel.

SUFFIXES WITH VOWELS	
note + **able** = not**able**	relate + **ion** = relat**ion**
antique + **ity** = antiqu**ity**	tone + **al** = ton**al**

However, keep the final *e* in a word that ends in *ce* or *ge* if the suffix begins with *a* or *o*. Notice in the following words that the *e* keeps the sound of the *c* or *g* soft.

CE OR *GE*	
manage + **able** = manage**able**	trace + **able** = trace**able**
notice + **able** = notice**able**	courage + **ous** = courage**ous**

Keep the final *e* when adding a suffix that begins with a consonant.

SUFFIXES WITH CONSONANTS		
EXAMPLES	home + **like** = home**like**	use + **ful** = use**ful**
	place + **ment** = place**ment**	care + **less** = care**less**
EXCEPTIONS	argue + **ment** = argu**ment**	awe + **ful** = aw**ful**
	judge + **ment** = judg**ment**	true + **ly** = tru**ly**

When you add *–ly* to form an adverb, make sure you are adding the suffix to the correct word. The adverbs *formerly* and *formally* are often confused.

formally— [formal + ly] in a formal manner; with regard for form
Everyone at the ball was dressed *formally*.

formerly— [former + ly] in the past
The restaurant had *formerly* been called Max's Place.

PRACTICE YOUR SKILLS

● Check Your Understanding
Adding Suffixes

Combine the base words and suffixes. Remember to make any necessary spelling changes.

1. real + ity
2. improve + ment
3. open + ness
4. account + able
5. pronounce + able
6. insure + ance
7. inflate + ion
8. rude + ly
9. together + ness
10. courage + ous
11. true + ly
12. sure + est
13. grace + ful
14. sane + ity
15. mourn + ful

● Connect to the Writing Process: Drafting
Using Words with Prefixes and Suffixes

Add a prefix or suffix to each word as indicated in parentheses. Then write a sentence using each word.

16. regard (suffix)
17. lingual (prefix)
18. argue (suffix)
19. appear (prefix)
20. mobile (prefix)
21. instrument (suffix)
22. nerve (suffix)
23. merry (suffix)
24. regular (prefix)
25. elect (prefix)

● Connect to the Writing Process: Editing
Spelling Words with Prefixes and Suffixes

History Topic **Find the words in this paragraph that have prefixes or suffixes, and correct those that are spelled incorrectly.**

In 1936, Berlin was the locateion for the international Olympic Games. Two years before, Adolf Hitler had taken control of the goverment in Germany. It was Hitler's outragous belief that the so-called Aryan race, which he called the "master race," should have dominateon over people of every other ethnicity. He thought that the Olympic Games would prove the correctness of his ideas. He was hopful that German athletes would be succesful in winning all the events. But that year something happened that Hitler found unbelieveable. To his amazment, Jesse Owens, an African American, won four gold medals and set records that stood for twenty years. Jesse Owens's achievment was a great disappointment for Hitler but a victory for those who believed in equallity.

Words Ending with *y*

To add a suffix to most words ending with a vowel and *y*, keep the *y*.

SUFFIXES WITH VOWELS AND Y		
EXAMPLES	employ + **able** = employ**able** delay + **ing** = delay**ing** convey + **ance** = convey**ance**	play + **ful** = play**ful** joy + **ous** = joy**ous** buy + **er** = buy**er**
EXCEPTIONS	day + **ly** = da**ily**	gay + **ly** = ga**ily**

To add a suffix to most words ending in a consonant and y, change the *y* to *i* before adding the suffix.

SUFFIXES WITH CONSONANTS AND Y	
read**y** + **ly** = read**ily** den**y** + **al** = den**ial** friendl**y** + **er** = friendl**ier**	slopp**y** + **ness** = slopp**iness** hurr**y** + **ed** = hurr**ied** twent**y** + **eth** = twent**ieth**

If the suffix begins with an *i*, do not change the *y* to an *i*.

SUFFIXES WITH *I*	
study + **ing** = study**ing**	baby + **ish** = baby**ish**

Doubling the Final Consonant

Sometimes the final consonant in a word is doubled before a suffix is added. This happens when the suffix begins with a vowel, and the base word satisfies both of these conditions: (1) it has only one syllable or is stressed on the final syllable; and (2) it ends in one consonant preceded by one vowel.

DOUBLE CONSONANTS	
ONE-SYLLABLE WORDS	win + ing = wi**nn**ing shop + ed = sho**pp**ed big + est = bi**gg**est
FINAL SYLLABLE STRESSED	occur + ence = occu**rr**ence corral + ed = corra**ll**ed regret + able = regre**tt**able infer + ing = infe**rr**ing

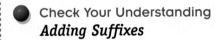

PRACTICE YOUR SKILLS

● Check Your Understanding
Adding Suffixes

Combine the base words and suffixes. Remember to make any necessary spelling changes.

1. silly + ness
2. forget + able
3. refer + al
4. shy + ness

5. joy + ful
6. compel + ing
7. deny + able
8. fancy + ful

9. red + ish
10. clumsy + ly
11. comply + ance
12. mercy + less

Adding Suffixes

General
Interest
Rewrite this story beginning, correcting the words with suffixes that are spelled incorrectly.

The young man stood outside the door, clumsyly fumbling with an armload of packages as he tryed ineptly to ring the doorbell. His actions betrayed his uneasyness. He was paying a call on Miss Emily Ames. The enormity of his admiration for her had compeled him to come bearing gifts. He fancyed that gifts would make her more complyant and receptive to his courtship.

Hidden by the leafyness of the potted plants, Mrs. Ames slily spied on him. Studying his face, she admitted that he lacked the homelyness ordinaryly found in people of humbler origins. Some might even say he possessed boyish good looks. In her snobish way, Mrs. Ames thought wrily that he would be a wonderful "catch"—for someone else's daughter.

Communicate Your Ideas

APPLY TO WRITING
Narrative: *Suffixes*

You have been asked to continue the story about Miss Emily Ames's young suitor and Mrs. Ames, her mother, for publication in a literary magazine for high school students. What happens when the young man finally manages to ring the bell? How will he be received in the house? Use five of the following words with suffixes in your writing.

- icy + ly
- regret + able
- dizzy + ly
- nerve + ous
- lovely + ness

- steady + ly
- deny + al
- shabby + ness
- courage + ous
- commit + ed

✓ QuickCheck Mixed Practice

Add the prefix or suffix to each base word and write the new word.

1. pre + arrange
2. notice + able
3. transmit + al
4. day + ly
5. plain + ness
6. occur + ence
7. permit + ed
8. il + legal
9. innovate + ive
10. simple + ly
11. coy + ly
12. merry + ment
13. re + apply
14. joy + ful
15. happy + ness

16. final + ly
17. begin + er
18. odd + ly
19. worry + some
20. argue + ment
21. re + arrange
22. lively + ness
23. strange + ness
24. ir + replace + able
25. acquit + al
26. commit + ment
27. true + ly
28. anti + bacterial
29. un + easy
30. like + able

WORDS TO MASTER

Make it your goal to learn to spell these fifty words this year. Use them in your writing and practice writing them until spelling them correctly comes automatically.

ac**cc**ompan**i**ment	empl**oy**a**b**le	man**eu**ver
ac**cu**mulate	**exer**cise	mischi**evo**us
appl**ica**tion	fals**ify**	omit**t**ed
basic**ally**	fi**e**ry	ordinar**ily**
benefi**t**ed	forf**eit**	peac**e**able
carr**y**ing	fund**a**men**tally**	practic**ally**
chang**e**able	grammatic**ally**	prefer**e**nce
civi**lly**	guid**ance**	publi**c**ly
cla**nn**ish	hind**ra**nce	refer**e**nce
commi**tt**ed	hyg**ie**ne	refer**r**ing
compa**rat**ive	inartistic**ally**	relig**ious**
compa**ris**on	infer**r**ed	remem**br**ance
cons**cious**ness	infer**e**nce	satisfactor**ily**
controlled	light**ni**ng	signifi**c**ance
counterf**eit**	likel**i**hood	sk**ii**ng
disas**trou**s	livel**i**est	veng**e**ance
empha**ses** (*pl.*)	maint**en**ance	

Recognizing Misspelled Words

Write the letter of the misspelled word in each group. Then write the word, spelling it correctly.

1. (a) cemetery (b) brilliant (c) foreign
   (d) arguement (e) obstacle

2. (a) disarray (b) perceive (c) dissimilar
   (d) exceed (e) seperate

3. (a) excitable (b) potatoes (c) temperture
   (d) siege (e) attorneys

4. (a) seizure (b) families (c) occuring
   (d) bicycle (e) courageous

5. (a) conscience (b) vinegar (c) tommorrow
   (d) weird (e) foxes

6. (a) friendlier (b) illiterate (c) athletics
   (d) subtle (e) maintainance

7. (a) baby-sitter (b) Wednesday (c) concede
   (d) pianoes (e) awkward

8. (a) achieve (b) noticable (c) nuisance
   (d) thieves (e) bookkeeper

9. (a) tradgedy (b) sophomore (c) reenact
   (d) fulfill (e) sleigh

10. (a) transmittal (b) either (c) neighbor
    (d) twelfth (e) passerbys

Another Look

Spelling Patterns

When you spell words with *ie* or *ei*, *i* comes before *e* except when the letters follow *c* or when they stand for the long *a* sound. *(page L535)*

Words that end in a syllable that sounds like "seed" are usually spelled with *–cede*. Only one word in English is spelled with *–sede*, and only three words are spelled with *–ceed*. *(page L536)*

Plurals

If a noun ends with *s, ch, sh, x,* or *z,* add *es* to form the plural. *(page L538)*

Add *s* to form the plural of a noun ending with a vowel and *y*. *(page L538)*

Change *y* to *i* and add *es* to nouns ending in a consonant and *y*. *(page L538)*

Add *s* to form the plural of a noun ending with a vowel and *o*. *(page L540)*

Add *s* to form the plural of musical terms ending in *o*. *(page L540)*

The plurals of nouns ending in a consonant and *o* do not follow a regular pattern. *(page L540)*

For some nouns ending in *f* or *fe*, change the *f* to *v* and add *es* or *s*. *(pages L540–L541)*

When the main word in a compound word appears first, that word becomes plural. *(page L542)*

Spelling Numbers

Spell out numbers that can be written in one or two words. Always spell out a number that begins a sentence. *(page L547)*

Always spell out numbers that are used to tell the order, or ordinal numbers. *(page L548)*

Use a numeral for a date when you include the name of the month. Always use numerals for the year. *(page L548)*

Prefixes and Suffixes

The suffixes *–ness* and *–ly* are added to most base words without any spelling changes. *(page L550)*

Drop final *e* in a base word when adding a suffix that begins with a vowel. *(page L551)*

Keep final *e* in a word that ends in *ce* or *ge* if the suffix begins with *a* or *o*. *(page L551)*

Keep final *e* when adding a suffix beginning with a consonant. *(page L553)*

To add a suffix to most words ending in a consonant and *y*, change the *y* to *i* before adding the suffix. *(pages L553–L554)*

Directions

Read the passage. Write the letter of the answer that correctly spells each underlined word. If the word contains no error, write D.

EXAMPLE   A <u>guidence</u> counselor's job is to point
                    (1)
               students in the right direction.

        1 **A** guidance
               B guideance
               C giudance
               D No error

ANSWER   **1 A**

Many students have <u>beneffitted</u> from a good relationship with
                          (1)
their school counselor. Counselors can ensure that students are

<u>emploiable</u> and have <u>markettable</u> skills. They can guide students
   (2)   (3)
through the battery of <u>acheivement</u> tests and <u>applycations</u> that are
                           (4)   (5)
required by colleges. They can show students <u>comparesons</u> of
                                                  (6)
colleges that can help the students and their <u>familys</u> decide on the
                                                   (7)
right place for them.

    Counselors stay informed about job <u>opportunities</u> in a variety
                                            (8)
of fields. They advise, offer opinions, provide <u>referrences</u>, or just
                                                    (9)
listen. Counselors may be the unsung <u>heros</u> of high school.
                                         (10)

1	A	benefited	6	A	comparasons
	B	bennefitted		B	comparisons
	C	benafited		C	comparrisons
	D	No error		D	No error

2	A	employabel	7	A	famalies
	B	employable		B	familyes
	C	employble		C	families
	D	No error		D	No error

3	A	marketable	8	A	oppertunities
	B	marketble		B	opportunitys
	C	marketible		C	opportunaties
	D	No error		D	No error

4	A	achevement	9	A	references
	B	acheifment		B	referances
	C	achievement		C	refferrances
	D	No error		D	No error

5	A	applications	10	A	heri
	B	aplications		B	heroes
	C	appleications		C	herroes
	D	No error		D	No error

A Study Guide for Academic Success

Academic success depends a great deal on preparation. You must be familiar with the material presented in textbooks and in the classroom; you must also be aware of various test-taking strategies. In some ways, preparing for a test is like learning to play football. You can't simply grab the ball and run with it. You must first learn the rules of the game and strategies for offense and defense. If you learn the strategies and apply helpful pointers, for example, you can become both a better football player and a better test taker. Also, the more practice you have, the better prepared you are to play a difficult game or take an important test.

In the following chapter you will become familiar with the different kinds of questions asked on standardized tests. Pay close attention to the "rules" for each type of question and the strategies used to master them. These lessons and practice exercises will help you develop your test-taking muscles.

Keep in mind that the abilities you acquire in this chapter will carry over into homework and daily classroom assignments—and even into areas outside of school. Learning how to read for various types of information and how to approach different kinds of questions and problems will sharpen the critical thinking skills you use when you participate in classroom discussions, play sports, and make important life decisions.

Learning Study Skills

Applying good study habits helps you in taking tests as well as in completing daily classroom assignments. Begin to improve your study habits by using the following strategies.

> **Strategies for Effective Studying**
> - Choose an area that is well lighted and quiet.
> - Equip your study area with everything you need for reading and writing, including a dictionary and a thesaurus.
> - Keep an assignment book for recording assignments and due dates.
> - Allow plenty of time for studying. Begin your reading and writing assignments early.
> - Adjust your reading rate to suit your purpose.

 ## Adjusting Reading Rate to Purpose

Your reading rate is the speed at which you read. Depending on your purpose in reading, you may choose to read certain materials quickly or slowly.

If your purpose is to get a quick impression of the contents of a newspaper, you should scan the headlines. If you want to learn the main ideas of a certain article, you should skim it. On the other hand, if your purpose is to learn new facts or understand details, then you might choose to read the article closely.

Whether you are reading a newspaper, an article in a periodical, or a textbook, you can read with greater effectiveness if you adjust your reading rate to suit your purpose in reading.

Scanning

Scanning is reading to get a general impression and to prepare for learning about a subject. To scan, you should read the title, headings, subheadings, picture captions, words and phrases in boldface or italics, and any focus questions. Using this method, you can quickly determine what the reading is about and what questions to keep in mind. Scanning is also a way to familiarize yourself with everything a book has to offer. Scan the table of contents, appendix, glossary, and index of a book before reading.

Skimming

After scanning a chapter, section, or article, you should quickly read or skim the introduction, the topic sentence of each paragraph, and the conclusion. **Skimming** is reading quickly to identify the purpose, thesis, main ideas, and supporting ideas of a selection.

Close Reading

Close reading means reading to locate specific information, follow the logic of an argument, or comprehend the meaning or significance of information. After scanning the selection or chapter, read it more slowly, word for word.

Reading a Textbook

In studying a textbook, the techniques of scanning, skimming, and close reading are combined in the *SQ3R* study strategy. This method helps you understand and remember what you read. The *S* in *SQ3R* stands for "Survey," *Q* for "Question," and *3R* for "Read, Recite, and Review."

THE SQ3R STUDY STRATEGY	
SURVEY	First get a general idea of what the selection is about by scanning titles, subtitles, and words that are set off in a different type or color. Also look at maps, tables, charts, and other illustrations. Then read the introduction and conclusion or summary.
QUESTION	Decide what questions you should be able to answer after reading the selection. You can do this by turning the headings and subheadings into questions or by looking at any study questions in the book.
READ	Now read the selection. As you read, try to answer your questions. In addition, find the main idea in each section and look for important information that is not included in your questions. After reading, review the important points in the selection and take notes. *(pages 565–568)*
RECITE	Answer each question in your own words by reciting or writing the answers.
REVIEW	Answer the questions again without looking at your notes or at the selection. Continue reviewing until you answer each question correctly.

 **Taking Notes**

Taking notes when reading a textbook or listening to a lecture will help you identify and remember important points. Three methods for taking notes are the modified outline, the graphic organizer, and the summary.

In an **informal outline,** you use words and phrases to record main ideas and important details. Notes in this form are helpful in studying for an objective test because they emphasize specific facts.

In a **graphic organizer,** words and phrases are arranged in a visual pattern to indicate the relationships between main ideas and supporting details. This is an excellent tool for studying information for an objective test, for an open-ended assessment, or for writing an essay. The visual organizer allows you, instantly, to see important information and its relationship to other ideas.

In a **summary** you use sentences to express important ideas in your own words. A summary should not simply restate the ideas presented in the textbook or lecture. Instead, a good summary should express relationships between ideas and draw conclusions. For this reason, summaries are useful in preparing for an essay test.

In the following passage from a history textbook, the essential information for understanding the Great Compromise is underlined. Following the passage are examples of notes in modified outline, graphic organizer, and summary form.

Model: Essential Information

The Great Compromise, proposed by Roger Sherman of Connecticut at the Constitutional Convention in 1787, offered a way to ensure fair representation for all the states. The compromise provided that Congress have two houses, as the Virginia Plan had proposed. Voters in each state would choose representatives for two-year terms. The number of representatives from a state would be based on population, a provision that satisfied the larger states. Each state would also have two senators, regardless of the state's population. Like the New Jersey Plan, this provision gave all states an equal voice, at least in one branch of Congress. The provision satisfied the smaller states. Legislators in each state would choose senators for six-year terms.

The Great Compromise

INFORMAL
OUTLINE:

1. Satisfied large and small states by guaranteeing fair representation

2. Provided two houses of Congress

3. Number of representatives in Congress based on state's population

4. Two senators in Congress regardless of state's population

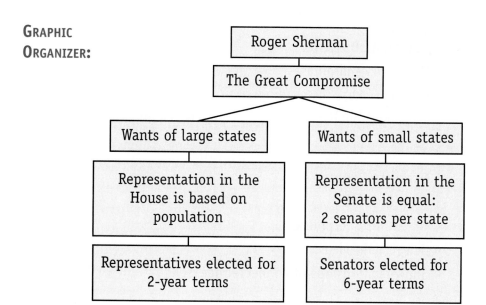

The Great Compromise

SUMMARY: The Great Compromise satisfied both the large and
the small states by guaranteeing fair representation.
The compromise provided for two houses of Congress.
The number of representatives in Congress from each
state would vary according to each state's population,
but the number of senators from each state would be
the same regardless of population.

Whichever note-taking method you use, the following strategies
will help you make those notes clear and well-organized.

 Strategies for Taking Notes

- Label your notes with the title and page numbers of the
  chapter or the topic and date of the lecture.
- Record only the main ideas and important details.
- Use the titles, subtitles, and words in special type to help
  you select the most important information.
- Use your own words; do not copy word for word.
- Use as few words as possible.

Informal Outline

- Use words and phrases.
- Use main ideas for headings.
- List any supporting details under each heading.

Graphic Organizer

- Draw a visual.
- Use words and phrases.
- Select main ideas.
- Show relationships of connected ideas.

Summary

- Write complete sentences, using your own words.
- Show the relationship between ideas, being careful to use only the facts stated in the textbook or lecture.
- Include only essential information.
- Organize ideas logically.

Preparing Subject-Area Assignments

The strategies you have learned in this chapter for reading textbooks and taking notes can be applied to assignments in any subject area.

Mathematics and science textbooks often list rules, formulas, equations, or models. In these subjects, you should focus on applying the rules or models to solve a problem or to show the truth of a scientific principle.

History, government, and economics classes, on the other hand, emphasize reading and interpreting maps, charts, graphs, time lines, documents, and statistical data. In preparing for these assignments or tests, you should pay special attention to information provided in those formats.

 Tips for Preparing Subject-Area Assignments

- Carefully read and follow directions.
- Adjust your reading rate to suit your purpose.
- In reading your textbook, use the SQ3R method. *(page 565)*
- Take notes from readings. Organize your notebook by keeping notes on the same topic together.
- For review keep a separate list of vocabulary, key terms and concepts, or rules and equations.
- Keep a list of questions you think of as you read, listen, or review. Seek answers promptly.
- Participate in study groups, following the principles of cooperative learning.
- Leave ample time to study for tests. Anticipate and answer the questions you think will be asked.

Taking Standardized Tests

A standardized test measures your academic progress, skills, and achievement in such a way that results can be compared with those of other students who have taken the same test. Standardized tests that assess your ability to use language—or verbal—skills, include vocabulary tests, analogy tests, reading tests, sentence-completion tests, and tests of standard written English.

The best way to do well on standardized tests is to work consistently on your school subjects throughout the year, to read widely, and to learn the strategies of test taking.

Strategies for Taking Standardized Tests

- Read the test directions carefully. Answer the sample questions to be sure you understand what the test requires.
- Relax. Although you can expect to be a little nervous, concentrate on doing the best you can.
- Preview the whole test by skimming to get an overview of the kinds of questions on the test.
- Plan your time carefully, allotting a certain amount of time to each part of the test.
- Answer first the questions you find easiest. Skip hard questions, coming back to them later if you have time.
- Read and reread all choices before you choose an answer. If you are not sure of the answer, try to eliminate choices that are obviously wrong. Educated guessing often helps.
- If you have time, check your answers. Be sure you have not made a mistake in marking your answer sheet.

⏵ Vocabulary Tests

One kind of vocabulary test asks you to find antonyms—words most nearly opposite in meaning. For instance, in the following test item, you must find the antonym for *temporary* among the five choices.

> TEMPORARY:
> (A) portable (B) permanent (C) reliable
> (D) patriotic (E) momentary
>
> (The answer is *(B)* because *permanent* is an antonym for *temporary*. The other choices are wrong for various reasons. The word *momentary* is a synonym for *temporary*, not an antonym. None of the other three choices means the opposite of *temporary*.)

Synonym items have the same format as antonym items, but instead of choosing the answer that means the opposite of the word in capital letters, you choose the word that means the same. For example, in the following item, the answer is *(D) clear,* which means the same as *lucid.*

> LUCID:
> (A) polite (B) vague (C) simple
> (D) clear (E) strange
>
> Always consider every choice carefully. You can often figure out the meaning of a word by using a prefix, a root, or a suffix as a clue.

PRACTICE YOUR SKILLS

● Check Your Understanding
Recognizing Antonyms

Write the letter of the word that is most nearly opposite in meaning to the word in capital letters.

1. TRANQUIL:
   (A) old-fashioned (B) troubled (C) pleasant
   (D) steady (E) famous

2. DEVIOUS:
    (A) tricky   (B) reckless   (C) handsome
    (D) straightforward   (E) skillful

3. ORNATE:
    (A) plain   (B) amusing   (C) fancy
    (D) strong   (E) variable

4. RELINQUISH:
    (A) upset   (B) surrender   (C) disagree
    (D) keep   (E) praise

5. NOVICE:
    (A) beginner   (B) coward   (C) veteran
    (D) bravery   (E) praise

6. ROTUND:
    (A) square   (B) long   (C) short
    (D) heavy   (E) slender

7. INEXHAUSTIBLE:
    (A) twisted   (B) endless   (C) limited
    (D) easy   (E) energetic

8. REMOTE:
    (A) close   (B) exact   (C) full
    (D) noisy   (E) dim

9. TANGIBLE:
    (A) parallel   (B) unreal   (C) flavorless
    (D) touching   (E) loose

10. CONSTRAINT:
    (A) pressure   (B) thought   (C) pleasure
    (D) freedom   (E) irritation

Recognizing Synonyms

Write the letter of the word that is most nearly the same in meaning as the word in capital letters.

11. AGILE:
   (A) free   (B) active   (C) speedy
   (D) fearful   (E) dishonest

12. HUMANE:
   (A) unwilling   (B) moody   (C) absurd
   (D) caring   (E) mean

13. OVERT:
   (A) strong   (B) brave   (C) innocent
   (D) terrible   (E) open

14. CONVENE:
   (A) dismiss   (B) oppose   (C) assemble
   (D) refuse   (E) select

15. PRECARIOUS:
   (A) brilliant   (B) postponed   (C) safe
   (D) forewarn   (E) dangerous

16. INCONCEIVABLE:
   (A) illogical   (B) unbelievable   (C) realistic
   (D) meaningless   (E) unplanned

17. EXPOUND:
   (A) illustrate   (B) uncover   (C) explain
   (D) search   (E) select

18. DESIST:
   (A) stop   (B) want   (C) continue
   (D) search   (E) select

19. PALATABLE:
   (A) smooth   (B) painted   (C) portable
   (D) filling   (E) tasty

20. FLIMSY:
   (A) silly   (B) fluffy   (C) humorous
   (D) frail   (E) flat

Analogies

Analogy questions test your skill at figuring out relationships between words. The first step is to decide how the given words—the first, capitalized pair of words—are related to each other. The next step is to decide which other pair has the same kind of relationship as the given pair.

The punctuation in an analogy question stands for the words *is to* and *as*.

FURNACE : FIRE :: reservoir : water

The above example reads, "A furnace is to fire as a reservoir is to water." That is, a furnace has the same relationship to fire as a reservoir has to water. A furnace and a reservoir are both containers for natural elements—fire and water. Explaining an analogy to yourself in one sentence can help you to figure out the answer. In the following example, you might say, "One kind of flower is a tulip."

FLOWER : TULIP ::
(A) deer : buffalo   (B) fever : virus
(C) automobile : station wagon   (D) plumber : wrench
(E) oak : tree

(The answer, *(C) automobile : station wagon*, expresses the same category-to-item relationship.)

Keep in mind that the word order in analogy is very important. If the given pair of words in the analogy expresses a part-to-whole order, for example, the words in the correct answer should also be taken in order of part to whole.

Some analogies are written in sentence form.

> *Urbane* is to *polite* as *verbose* is to ■.
> (A) outstanding   (B) bitter   (C) wordy
> (D) brief   (E) calm
>
> (The first two italicized words are synonyms. Therefore, the correct answer is *(C) wordy,* a synonym for *verbose.*)

Knowing some of the common types of analogies, like those in the following chart, will help you figure out word relationships.

COMMON TYPES OF ANALOGIES

Analogy	Example
word : synonym	slim : slender
word : antonym	exciting : dull
part : whole	wing : airplane
cause : effect	drought : famine
worker : tool	carpenter : hammer
worker : product	baker : bread
item : purpose	ruler : measure
item : category	robin : bird

PRACTICE YOUR SKILLS

● Check Your Understanding
Recognizing Analogies

Write the letter of the word pair that has the same relationship as the word pair in capital letters.

   1. TARNISH : SILVER ::
   (A) tape : music   (B) ending : story
   (C) salesperson : bonus   (D) decay : organism
   (E) peace : treaty

2. PUBLISHER : NEWSPAPER : :
(A) ink : paper   (B) book : writer
(C) farmer : crops   (D) hockey : puck
(E) needle : thread

3. CRIME : PUNISHMENT : :
(A) chinchilla : fur   (B) rat : rodent
(C) client : attorney   (D) game : tennis
(E) tornado : destruction

4. TAXI : TRANSPORT : :
(A) president : democracy   (B) scene : play
(C) fence : enclose   (D) evade : avoid
(E) architecture : profession

5. ENGINE : AUTOMOBILE : :
(A) teacher : student   (B) dog : cat
(C) sail : boat   (D) lamp : light
(E) telephone : message

6. COBRA : SNAKE : :
(A) tree : leaves   (B) run : baseball
(C) collie : dog   (D) water : dissolve
(E) greasy : oily

7. JUBILANT : MOROSE : :
(A) car : tire   (B) passive : active
(C) pencil : lead   (D) meddle : interfere
(E) pilot : plane

8. DECK : SHIP : :
(A) portion : segment   (B) roof : house
(C) picture : frame   (D) computer : printer
(E) iron : ore

9. LEASH : DOG : :
(A) rein : horse   (B) bicycle : tire
(C) gold : money   (D) key : chain
(E) hand : finger

10. MODERATE : REASONABLE : :
(A) jeweler : gem   (B) flag : nation
(C) conquer : vanquish   (D) spoon : chef
(E) silver : chain

Completing Analogies

Complete the analogy with the choice that correctly completes the second pair.

11. *Bandage* is to *protect* as *knife* is to ■.
(A) pain   (B) cut   (C) cook   (D) grate   (E) sell

12. *Condemn* is to *approve* as *reject* is to ■.
(A) hurt   (B) blame   (C) pity
(D) sympathize   (E) accept

13. *Flour* is to *bread* as *cloth* is to ■.
(A) trade   (B) heel   (C) flag   (D) sell   (E) color

14. *Fan* is to *breeze* as *radio* is to ■.
(A) dial   (B) satellite   (C) television
(D) sound   (E) DJ

15. *Beetle* is to *insect* as *snow* is to ■.
(A) flake   (B) snowman   (C) precipitation
(D) rain   (E) winter

16. *Pliers* is to *electrician* as *ink* is to ■.
(A) pen   (B) stamp   (C) printer
(D) plumber   (E) writing

17. *Result* is to *outcome* as *real* is to ■.
(A) film   (B) genuine   (C) article
(D) victory   (E) fiction

18. *Tree* is to *pine* as *clothes* is to ■.
(A) red   (B) closet   (C) wardrobe
(D) trousers   (E) silk

19. *Metal* is to *copper* as *shellfish* is to ■.
(A) ocean   (B) oyster   (C) catfish
(D) pearl   (E) amphibian

20. *Horse* is to *equine* as *cow* is to ■.
(A) bovine   (B) milk   (C) farm
(D) sheep   (E) veterinarian

⏵ Sentence-Completion Tests

Sentence-completion tests measure your ability to comprehend what you read and to use context correctly. Each item consists of a sentence with one or more words missing. First read the entire sentence. Then read the answer choices and select the one that completes the sentence in a way that makes sense. For example, in the following item, read the sentence and then find the word that most appropriately completes the sentence.

> Our tour of the two-hundred-foot Pyramid of the Sun in Mexico, which included climbing and ▨ the steep stairs, took more than an hour.
> (A) completing   (B) scaling   (C) descending
> (D) constructing   (E) ascending
>
> (The answer is *(C) descending,* the opposite of *climbing.* Because the sentence refers to climbing steep stairs, a choice of either *scaling* or *ascending* to complete the sentence is repetitive. *Scaling* and *ascending* both mean the same as *climbing.* A choice of either *completing* or *constructing* is incorrect because neither word makes sense in the context of the sentence.)

Some sentence-completion questions have two blanks in the same sentence, with each answer choice including two words. Find the correct answer in this example.

> The invention of barbed wire, a ▨ in the history of the American West, ▨ the cattle industry, ending the era of the open range and bringing about great change.
> (A) plan . . . surprised   (B) mistake . . . hurt
> (C) landmark . . . transformed   (D) note . . . pleased
> (E) milestone . . . ended
>
> (The answer is *(C) landmark . . . transformed.* The other choices do not make sense. The invention of barbed wire was not a plan, mistake, or a note in American history. It revolutionized the cattle industry, but it did not end it.)

PRACTICE YOUR SKILLS

● Check Your Understanding
Completing Sentences

Write the letter of the word that best completes each of the following sentences.

1. Grackles are blackbirds with plumage so glossy it ▧.
   (A) glides (B) sheds (C) disappears
   (D) shimmers (E) wrinkles

2. While to an observer the pitch of a train whistle seems to change as the train passes, to a passenger on the train the pitch remains ▧.
   (A) louder (B) constant (C) harsh
   (D) variable (E) faint

3. James Thurber's humorous writings are among the most ▧ and popular literary works of the twentieth century.
   (A) awkward (B) delightful (C) incomprehensible
   (D) serious (E) threatening

4. Far north of Fairbanks, Alaska, on the icy shores of the Arctic Ocean, lies the ▧ village of Prudhoe Bay.
   (A) barren (B) tropical (C) inland
   (D) popular (E) brutal

5. Ida Tarbell led the muckraking movement, which attacked dishonesty and other ▧ in business and politics.
   (A) debt (B) corruption (C) freedom
   (D) fairness (E) progress

6. With the development of the tiny silicon chip, the ▧ of electronic equipment proceeded rapidly.
   (A) disappearance (B) banning (C) destruction
   (D) shelving (E) miniaturization

7. In the early 1900s, a Texas League baseball player set a ▧ record; he hit eight home runs in eight times at bat.
   (A) remarkable (B) humdrum (C) daily
   (D) broken (E) common

8. Today the ■ city of Williamsburg, Virginia, looks much as it did in the eighteenth century.
(A) active   (B) local   (C) restored
(D) major   (E) crowded

9. The ■ appears at front of a book and contains information about the author and the work.
(A) table of contents   (B) introduction   (C) index
(D) biography   (E) dedication

10. Although the *Titanic* was heralded as the unsinkable ship, the luxury liner soon ■ this claim by sinking on its first voyage.
(A) disobeyed   (B) proved   (C) invalidated
(D) upheld   (E) mistook

● Check Your Understanding
Completing Sentences with Two Blanks

Write the letter of the words that best complete each of the following sentences.

11. Chocolate has been a ■ product throughout history; the Aztecs even used the ■ cacao beans as currency.
(A) known . . . worthless   (B) dangerous . . . valuable
(C) cherished . . . precious (D) aromatic . . . significant
(E) legendary . . . treasured

12. To picture the ■ size of the sequoia tree, consider that a single branch can be longer than the ■ American elm.
(A) minute . . . greatest
(B) unknown . . . unaccountable
(C) historical . . . protected
(D) immense . . . tallest
(E) statuesque . . . tiniest

13. Pearl Buck, the first American woman to win the ■ Nobel Prize, was honored for her novels promoting peace and ■ relations with China.
(A) coveted . . . ending   (B) infamous . . . beneficial
(C) valuable . . . difficult   (D) renowned . . . friendly
(E) distinguished . . . destroying

14. The crowded gym was full of ■ students and ■ players, all waiting anxiously to see if the last shot would drop into the basket.
(A) noisy . . . active
(B) watchful . . . attentive
(C) cheering . . . relaxed
(D) bored . . . silent
(E) sleepy . . . angry

15. Beginning in 1885, the czars of Russia gave ■ eggs, created by the ■ jeweler Carl Fabergé, as gifts at Easter.
(A) cracked . . . eccentric
(B) wonderful . . . talented
(C) amazing . . . disobedient
(D) dyed . . . court
(E) chicken . . . famous

16. As the dying embers of the fire ■, the bitter cold began to ■ the cabin.
(A) raged . . . surround
(B) faded . . . invade
(C) glowed . . . soak
(D) roared . . . leave
(E) smoldered . . . light

17. The ■ secret of silk making was ■ guarded by the Chinese for hundreds of years.
(A) important . . . loosely
(B) trivial . . . jealously
(C) great . . . casually
(D) dark . . . carefully
(E) valuable . . . vigilantly

18. The antique table, with its surface ■ and its leg ■, will require careful restoration.
(A) new . . . sound
(B) polished . . . injured
(C) dull . . . flawless
(D) scarred . . . broken
(E) dusty . . . dirty

19. My mother ■ vegetable peels, egg shells, and coffee grounds and buries them in the garden to ■ the soil.
(A) conserves . . . contaminate
(B) keeps . . . taint
(C) saves . . . enrich
(D) trashes . . . improve
(E) stores . . . grow

20. The team became ■ when their right forward fell and their goalie ■ the ball.
(A) ecstatic . . . dropped
(B) upset . . . injured
(C) joyous . . . passed
(D) anxious . . . blocked
(E) distressed . . . missed

Reading Comprehension Tests

Reading comprehension tests assess your ability to understand and analyze written passages. The information you need to answer the test questions may be either directly stated or implied in the passage. You must study, analyze, and interpret a passage in order to answer the questions that follow it. The following strategies will help you answer questions on reading tests.

> ### Strategies for Reading Comprehension Questions
> - Begin by skimming the questions that follow the passage.
> - Read the passage carefully and closely. Notice the main ideas, organization, style, and key words.
> - Study all possible answers. Avoid choosing one answer the moment you think it is a reasonable choice.
> - Use only the information in the passage when you answer the questions. Do not rely on your own knowledge or ideas on this kind of test.

Most reading questions focus on one or more of the following characteristics of a written passage.

- **Main idea** At least one question will usually focus on the central idea of the passage. Remember that the main idea of a passage covers all sections of the passage—not just one section or paragraph.

- **Supporting details** Questions about supporting details test your ability to identify the statements in the passage that back up the main idea.

- **Implied meanings** In some passages not all information is directly stated. Some questions ask you to interpret information that the author has merely implied.

- **Purpose and tone** Questions on purpose and tone require that you interpret or analyze the author's purpose for writing and the author's attitude toward his or her subject.

● Check Your Understanding
Reading for Comprehension

Read the following passage and write the letter of each correct answer to the questions that follow.

The emperor Nero didn't fiddle while Rome burned in A.D. 64—fiddles hadn't been invented—but some historians believe he played the bagpipes. It would not be very surprising. Everything about the bagpipes is a bit odd, including its history.

No one is certain just where and when the bagpipes came into being. Early classical writings and the Bible mention an instrument that loosely resembles the bagpipes, and ancient stoneware and pottery depict musicians playing pipes that look like the instrument. Still, it is not until the late Middle Ages that bagpipes suddenly become positively recognizable in artworks and illustrations throughout Europe. During the reign of the Spanish king Alfonso the Wise (1221–1284), the *Cantigas de Santa María,* one of the largest collections of solo songs of the Middle Ages, was written. Among the illustrations are some of musicians playing bagpipes. In the fifteenth century, the bagpipes, which are today associated almost exclusively with Scotland, achieved popularity in that country. The earliest definitive description of bagpipes is in 1619, in the *Syntagma Musicum* of Michael Praetorius, a German composer and theorist.

Such a sketchy history is explainable when one considers that bagpipes began as instruments of the "common" people. They were used roughly and out of doors; they were not collected and preserved. Any that might have been passed down in families would not have lasted long— the organic materials of which they were made would soon have deteriorated. Because bagpipes were in no way involved in life as it was lived at court—or in politics, warfare, or religion—they were of as little interest to early writers as peasants' shoes. Thus there is scanty evidence for historians to examine. However, the bagpipes, or *Tibia Utricularis*, as the Romans called them, are known to be among the oldest continuously played instruments in the world.

1. The best title for this passage is
   (A) A History of Musical Instruments.
   (B) Nero Played the Bagpipes.
   (C) Instruments of the Middle Ages.
   (D) How to Play the Bagpipes.
   (E) The Short History of the Bagpipes.

2. The idea that Nero played the bagpipes as Rome burned is
   (A) supported by eyewitness accounts.
   (B) supported by some historians.
   (C) ridiculed by music historians.
   (D) opposed by written records.
   (E) opposed by most people.

3. The main purpose of paragraph 2 is to
   (A) describe the bagpipes.
   (B) provide contrasting details.
   (C) assert the idea that bagpipes are difficult to play.
   (D) support the main idea of the passage.
   (E) provide fictional examples.

4. The passage indicates that bagpipes were
   (A) of little interest to peasants.
   (B) written about infrequently.
   (C) usually played by kings and emperors.
   (D) invented in the Middle Ages.
   (E) taken from Spain to Scotland and then to Germany.

5. This passage would most likely appear in
   (A) a Scottish travel brochure.
   (B) a biography of Nero.
   (C) a book on the history of instruments.
   (D) a textbook on the history of Europe.
   (E) the introduction to *Cantigas de Santa Maria*.

The Double Passage

You may also be asked to read two paired passages, called the **double passage,** and answer questions about each passage individually and about how the two passages relate to each other. The two passages may present similar or opposing views or may complement each other in other ways. A brief introduction preceding the passages may help you anticipate the relationship between them.

All of the questions follow the second passage. The first few questions relate to Passage 1, the next few questions relate to Passage 2, and the final questions relate to both passages. You may find it helpful to read Passage 1 first and then immediately find and answer those questions related only to Passage 1. Then read Passage 2 and answer the remaining questions

PRACTICE YOUR SKILLS

 Check Your Understanding
Reading for Double-Passage Comprehension

The following passages are about *suffrage*—the right to vote—in the United States. The first passage is from Frederick Douglass's 1866 "An Appeal to Congress for Impartial Suffrage." The second is from an address to the first Women's Rights Convention in 1848, delivered by Elizabeth Cady Stanton. Read each passage and answer the questions that follow.

Passage 1

A very limited statement of the argument for impartial suffrage, and for including the negro in the body politic, would require more space than can be reasonably asked here. It is supported by reasons as broad as the nature of man, and as numerous as the wants of society. Man is the only government-making animal in the world. His right to a participation in the production and operation of government is an inference from his nature, as direct and self-evident as is his right to acquire property or education. It is no less a crime against the manhood of a man, to declare that he shall not share in the making and the directing of the government under which he lives, than to say he shall not acquire property and education. The fundamental and unanswerable argument in favor of the enfranchisement of the negro is found in the undisputed fact of his manhood. He is a man, and by every fact and argument by which any man can sustain his right to vote, the negro can sustain his right equally. It is plain that, if the right belongs to any, it belongs to all.

Passage 2

. . . [W]e are assembled to protest against a form of government existing without the consent of the governed— to declare our right to be free as man is free, to be represented in the government which we are taxed to support. . . . And, strange as it may seem to many, we now demand our right to vote according to the declaration of the government under which we live. This right no one pretends to deny. . . . We have no objection to discuss the question of equality, for we feel that the weight of the argument lies wholly with us, but we wish the question of equality kept distinct from the question of rights, for the proof of one does not determine the truth of the other. All white men in this country have the same rights, however they may differ in mind, body, or estate. The right is ours. The question now is: how shall we get possession of what rightfully belongs to us? . . . The right is ours. Have it, we must. Use it, we will.

1. According to the author of Passage 1, which of the following best explains the reason African American (referred to as "negro" in the passage) men must be allowed to vote?
   (A) If one man is allowed to vote, all men must be allowed to vote.
   (B) Society needs more voters.
   (C) African American men are property holders.
   (D) African American men are as educated as white men.
   (E) African American men should be held responsible for the government and its laws.

2. The purpose of Passage 1 is to
  (A) display Frederick Douglass's talents as a writer.
  (B) persuade Congress that all people deserve the right to vote.
  (C) complain to readers about the sad state of the American government.
  (D) show why African American men must be allowed to vote.
  (E) inform readers about their rights.

3. According to the author of Passage 2, which of the following best describes the purpose of the meeting?
  (A) to argue for equality.
  (B) to demonstrate the talent of white women for public speaking.
  (C) to persuade men that white women should be allowed to vote.
  (D) to decide whether all women should be allowed to vote.
  (E) to protest against the government and determine a course of action.

4. The tone of Passage 2 is
  (A) lighthearted.
  (B) emphatic.
  (C) ironic.
  (D) sarcastic.
  (E) melodramatic.

5. Which of the following arguments for extending the vote is not used by either author?
  (A) People who pay taxes to support a government must be allowed a voice in that government.
  (B) The vote is a right as fundamental as the right to education.
  (C) If one man may vote, then all men may vote.
  (D) Allowing white women to vote will ensure that Democrats are supported.
  (E) African American citizens have the same rights and responsibilities as white citizens.

Tests of Standard Written English

Objective tests of standard written English assess your knowledge of the language skills used for writing. They contain sentences with underlined words, phrases, and punctuation. The underlined parts will usually contain errors in grammar, usage, mechanics, vocabulary, or spelling. You are asked to find the error in each sentence, or, in some tests, to identify the best way to revise a sentence or passage.

Error Recognition

The most familiar way to test a student's grasp of grammar, usage, capitalization, punctuation, word choice, and spelling is through an error-recognition sentence. A typical test item of this kind is a sentence with five underlined choices. Four of the choices suggest possible errors in the sentence. The fifth states that there is no error. Read the following sentence and identify the error, if there is one.

> The <u>bay</u> of Fundy, between Nova Scotia and New <u>Brunswick,</u>
>   **A**   **B**
> has <u>the</u> highest tides in the <u>world.</u> <u>No error</u>
>   **C**   **D**   **E**
> (The answer is A. The word *bay* should be capitalized as part of the proper name, the Bay of Fundy.)

The following list identifies some of the errors you should look for on a test of standard written English.

- lack of agreement between subject and verb
- lack of agreement between pronoun and antecedent
- incorrect spelling or use of a word
- missing, misplaced, or unnecessary punctuation
- missing or unnecessary capitalization
- misused or misplaced italics or quotation marks

Sometimes you will find a sentence that contains no error. Be careful, however, before you choose *E* as the answer. It is easy to overlook a mistake, since common errors are the kind generally included on this type of test.

Remember that the parts of a sentence that are not underlined are presumed to be correct. You can use clues in the correct parts of the sentence to help you search for errors in the underlined parts.

PRACTICE YOUR SKILLS

● Check Your Understanding
Recognizing Errors in Writing

Write the letter of the underlined word or punctuation mark that is incorrect. If the sentence contains no error, write *E*.

(1) A large amount of modern transportation routes
  A
follow old Indian trails. (2) The New York State Thruway,
  B   C   D   A   B
for example, parrallels the path once used by the Iroquois.
             C   D
(3) Like the Iroquois who preceded them, early explorers
                       A   B
traveling west often journeyed by canoe up the
         C
Mohawk river. (4) When the river became unnavigable,
         D   A   B
these explorers decided that the Indian foot trails were
      C
preferrable. (5) The Erie Canal opened in 1825; following
      D   A   B
the route that the Iroquois had been using for centuries.
                          C   D
(6) Eventually railroads were built close to the canal, and
    A   B   C
began to take business away from it. (7) Roads for horses,
      D
wagons, and stagecoaches followed this route; one road
  A   B   C
became route 5. (8) Those who planned the state thruway
  D   A
found that their was no better path than the old familiar
        B   C   D
one. (9) Parallel waterways, roads, and railroad tracks now
                A
follows the original Iroquois route. (10) Only the airways,
  B   C   D
heedless of the lay of the land, have broke the pattern set
                                A   B   C
so long ago.
  D

Sentence-Correction Questions

Sentence-correction questions assess your ability to recognize appropriate phrasing. Instead of locating an error in a sentence, you must select the most appropriate and effective way to write the sentence.

In this kind of question, a part of the sentence is underlined. The sentence is then followed by five different ways of writing the underlined part. The first way shown, (A), simply repeats the original underlined portion. The other four give alternative ways of writing the underlined part. The choices may involve grammar, usage, capitalization, punctuation, or word choice. Be sure that the answer you choose does not change the meaning of the original sentence.

Look at the following example.

> The task of exploring the depths of <u>the Ocean has seen great advances</u> over the past fifty years.
> (A) the Ocean has seen great advances
> (B) the Ocean, has seen great advances
> (C) the Ocean had seen great advances
> (D) the ocean has seen great advances
> (E) the ocean, has seen great advances
>
> (The answer is *(D)*. *Ocean* is a common noun, so it should not be capitalized. Choice *(E)* corrects the capitalization problem but introduces a comma problem.)

PRACTICE YOUR SKILLS

● Check Your Understanding
Correcting Sentences

Write the letter of the correct way, or the best way, of phrasing the underlined part of each sentence.

1. Although an old wives' tale states that the dots on a <u>ladybird's back reveals its age,</u> these dots actually denote a ladybird's species.
   (A) ladybird's back reveals its age,
   (B) ladybirds' back reveals its age,
   (C) ladybirds' back reveals their age,
   (D) ladybird's back reveal its age,
   (E) ladybird's back reveal it's age,

2. The fruit of the prickly pear cactus is edible and tastes like a cross between a watermelon and a strawberry.
(A) the prickly pear cactus is edible and tastes
(B) the Prickly Pear cactus is edible and tastes
(C) the prickly-pear-cactus is edible and tastes
(D) the prickly pear cactus are edible and tastes
(E) the prickly pear cactus is edible and taste

3. Ballroom dancing has become a popular sport where many couples compete for titles and prizes.
(A) where many couples compete for titles and prizes.
(B) where many couples competes for titles and prizes.
(C) in which many couples compete for titles and prizes.
(D) during which many couples compete for titles and prizes.
(E) when many couples competes for titles and prizes.

4. The older of the three fossils we found along the cliffs dates back hundreds of years.
(A) The older of the three fossils we found
(B) The older of the three fossils we found,
(C) The oldest of the three fossils we found
(D) The oldest of the three fossils we found,
(E) The most old of the three fossils we found

5. As I was buying some groceries, a shoplifter and a security guard flew passed me to the door.
(A) flew passed me to the door.
(B) flew passed me, to the door.
(C) flew, passed me, to the door.
(D) flew past me, to the door.
(E) flew past me to the door.

6. I saw the statues of Queen Mary Queen Margot and Queen Catherine as I strolled through the museum.
(A) statues of Queen Mary Queen Margot and Queen Catherine
(B) Statue of Queen Mary Queen Margot and Queen Catherine
(C) statue of Queen Mary, queen Margot and queen Catherine
(D) statues of Queen Mary, Queen Margot, and Queen Catherine

(E) statues of Queen Mary, Queen Margot, and Queen Catherine,

7. Some of his favorite activities include reading science fiction novels, playing soccer, and to go to the movies.
  (A) reading science fiction novels, playing soccer, and to go to the movies.
  (B) reading Science fiction novels, playing soccer, and to go to the movies.
  (C) reading, science fiction novels, playing soccer and go to the movies.
  (D) reading science fiction novels, playing soccer, and going to the movies.
  (E) reading Science Fiction novels, playing soccer, and going to the movies.

8. Of Mark and Loi, Loi is the more experienced rock climber.
  (A) Loi is the more experienced rock climber.
  (B) Loi are the more experienced rock climber.
  (C) Loi is the most experienced rock climber.
  (D) Loi is the best rock climber.
  (E) Loi has the most experience at rock climbing.

9. Here are the collection of coins I mentioned.
  (A) Here are the collection
  (B) Here is the collection
  (C) There are the collection
  (D) There is the collections
  (E) Here, are the collection,

10. Wang Yani a Chinese artist, began painting when she was only three years old.
  (A) Wang Yani a Chinese artist,
  (B) Wang Yani, a Chinese artist,
  (C) Wang yani, a chinese artist,
  (D) Wang yani, a Chinese artist,
  (E) Wang Yani a Chinese artist

11. In the 1800s, the german archaeologist Heinrich Schliemann became a scholar and discovered an ancient land.
  (A) german archaeologist Heinrich Schliemann became a scholar and discovered an ancient land.
  (B) german archaeologist Heinrich Schliemann became

a Scholar, and discovered an ancient land.
- (C) German archaeologist Heinrich Schliemann became a scholar, and discovered an ancient land.
- (D) german archaeologist Heinrich Schliemann became a scholar and discovered an Ancient Land.
- (E) German archaeologist Heinrich Schliemann became a scholar and discovered an ancient land.

12. As a child he read the storys told by the Greek poet Homer in the *Odyssey*.
- (A) storys told by the Greek poet Homer in the *Odyssey*.
- (B) stories told by the Greek poet Homer in the *Odyssey*.
- (C) storys told by the greek poet Homer in the Odyssey.
- (D) stories told by the greek poet Homer in the *Odyssey*.
- (E) storys told by the Greek poet Homer in the Odyssey.

13. His plan to discover the lost city of Troy seemed impossible; his family was poor, and had no money for education.
- (A) lost city of Troy seemed impossible; his family was poor, and had no money
- (B) lost City of Troy seemed impossible; his family was poor, and had no money
- (C) lost city of Troy seemed impossible: his family was poor and had no money
- (D) lost city of Troy seemed impossible; his family was poor and had no money
- (E) lost City of Troy seemed impossible: his family was poor and had no money

14. Schliemann educated himself, and set out to find Troy on the coast of Asia Minor.
- (A) himself, and set out to find Troy on the coast of Asia Minor.
- (B) himself and set out to find Troy on the coast of Asia Minor.
- (C) himself, and set out to find Troy, on the Coast of Asia Minor.
- (D) himself and set out to find Troy on the Coast of Asia Minor.
- (E) himself, and set out to find Troy on the Coast of Asia Minor.

15. His reading of Homer <u>had been correct; there were a group of cities buried on that spot, filled with things</u> Homer had described.

(A) had been correct; there were a group of cities buried on that spot, filled with things

(B) had been correct; there was a group of cities buried on that spot, filled with things

(C) had been correct, there were a group of cities buried on that spot, filled with things

(D) had been correct; there was a group of Cities buried on that spot filled with things

(E) had been correct, there was a group of Cities buried on that spot, filled with things

Revision-in-Context

Another type of multiple-choice question that appears on some standardized tests is called revision-in-context. These questions are based on a short reading that is meant to represent an early draft of student writing. The questions following the reading ask you to choose the best revision of a sentence, a group of sentences, or the essay as a whole or to clearly identify the writer's intention. This type of test assesses your reading comprehension, your composing skills, and your understanding of the conventions of standard written English.

MODEL: Correcting Sentences

(1) In Alice Walker's short story "Everyday Use," a conflict arises between two sisters who are very different. **(2)** The sisters are Dee and Maggie. **(3)** Dee is the "successful" child who has used her intelligence, looks, and determination to leave the small farm. **(4)** Maggie is shy, scarred, and slow. **(5)** Remaining on the farm is Maggie. **(6)** When Dee returns home for a visit, she has changed her name to Wangero and has changed her mind about the house and life she used to hate.

1. In relation to the rest of the passage, which of the following best describes the writer's intention in sentence 6?

(A) to restate the opening sentence
(B) to interest the reader in the story
(C) to provide examples
(D) to summarize the paragraph
(E) to offer contradictory evidence

(The correct answer is *(B)*, which can be determined by the process of elimination. Sentence 5 does not restate the opening, provide examples, summarize, nor offer contradictory evidence.)

2. Which of the following is the best revision of sentence 5?

(A) Remaining on the farm is she.
(B) Staying on the farm, Maggie remains.
(C) Maggie is remaining on the farm.
(D) Maggie remains on the farm.
(E) Staying on the farm is Maggie.

(The correct answer is *(D)*. The sentence and choices *(A)* and *(E)* are inverted and awkward. Choice *(B)* contains unnecessary repetition, and choice *(C)* uses the wrong verb tense.)

3. Which of the following is the best way to combine sentences 1 and 2?

(A) In Alice Walker's short story "Everyday Use," there are differences between two sisters.
(B) In "Everyday Use" a mother observes a conflict between her two different daughters, Dee and Maggie.
(C) In "Everyday Use" Dee and Maggie, Mama's two very different daughters, fight.
(D) In Alice Walker's short story "Everyday Use," the reader observes the differences and the conflict between two girls.

(E) In Alice Walker's short story "Everyday Use," a
conflict arises between two sisters, Dee and Maggie.
(The answer is *(E)*. The other choices all leave out
information.)

PRACTICE YOUR SKILLS

● Check Your Understanding
Correcting Sentences

**Carefully read the following passage. Write the letter of the
correct answer to the questions that follow.**

(1) In Zora Neale Hurston's book *Their Eyes Were
Watching God,* the main character, Janie Crawford, goes on a
journey to find her true self. (2) One beautiful spring day
the young girl dreams under a pear tree of real love and real
marriage. (3) This passage of Hurston's book is the first
moment of change for Janie. (4) The image of Janie under
the pear tree gives us the impression of youth through the
tree's green leaves and of blossoming womanhood through
the flowers on the tree.

(5) It is not long after this that Janie leaves her
grandmother's home. (6) She leaves her home in order to
marry a man she does not love. (7) The arrangement to
marry this man makes her extremely angry, but because she
loves her grandmother, she marries Logan Killicks.

(8) Janie is miserable with this new husband. (9) Her
new life is full of doing chores all day long on the farm that
Logan owns. (10) Logan treats her fairly enough. (11)

However, Janie does not love him or the life he provides her.

(12) It is not long after this that Janie walks out of the farm gate forever, tossing her apron onto a bush on the side of the road. **(13)** Janie is a new woman, and she has gone to meet the man of her dreams, Joe Starks. **(14)** She believed that her "true self" was surely in this new way of life with Joe. **(15)** He had fancy ways. **(16)** Joe wanted to get rich. **(17)** He promised Janie that she would be the queen of a town soon.

1. What is the purpose of sentence 1?
   (A) to provide support for the essay
   (B) to provide analysis for the essay
   (C) to set up a thesis for the essay
   (D) to describe Janie Crawford
   (E) to mark how important the opening paragraph is

2. The purpose of sentence 3 is—
   (A) to provide examples of the previous point
   (B) to summarize the events under the pear tree
   (C) to begin the analysis of the event
   (D) to show how Janie is unhappy
   (E) to provide a topic sentence for the paragraph

3. What is one of the purposes of sentence 4?
   (A) It summarizes the events under the tree.
   (B) It is the first sentence of the analysis of the pear-tree passage.
   (C) It draws the reader's interest into the essay.
   (D) It restates the opening sentence.
   (E) It provides examples from the novel to support the point.

4. What is the best phrasing of sentences 5 and 6?
- (A) It is not long after this that Janie leaves her grandmother's home. Because she wants to marry a man she does not love.
- (B) It is not long after this that Janie leaves her grandmother's home, hoping to marry a man she does not love.
- (C) It is not long after this that Janie leaves her grandmother's home to marry a man she does not love.
- (D) It is not long after this that Janie leaves her grandmother's home; in order to marry a man she does not love.
- (E) acceptable as is

5. Sentences 5, 6 and 7 serve what purpose in the essay?
- (A) They provide literary analysis of Janie.
- (B) They give the reader a summary of the events in the book.
- (C) They give the reader insight into the style of the author.
- (D) They provide examples of the main idea of the sentence.
- (E) They tell the reader what is going to happen in the next section.

6. What is the best way to combine sentences 10 and 11?
- (A) Logan treats her fairly enough. However, Janie does not love him or the life he provides her.
- (B) Although Logan treats her fairly enough, Janie does not love him or the life he provides her.
- (C) Logan treats her fairly enough because Janie does not love him or the life he provides her.
- (D) Logan treats her fairly enough, even though Janie does not love him or the life he provides her.
- (E) Since Logan treats her fairly enough, Janie does not love him or the life he provides her.

7. Sentence 14 is important to the essay because—
- (A) it refers back to the main point in the opening sentence.
- (B) it makes the writer appear intelligent.
- (C) it offers a key piece of evidence to the main point.
- (D) it makes the reader aware of the events of the book.
- (E) it summarizes the preceding paragraph.

8. The best revision of sentences 15, 16 and 17 is—
- (A) He had fancy ways, he wanted to get rich. Therefore, he promised Janie that she would be the queen of a town soon.
- (B) He had fancy ways, he wanted to get rich, and he promised Janie that she would be the queen of a town soon.
- (C) He promised Janie that she would be the queen of a town soon in spite of his fancy ways and his wanting to get rich.
- (D) He had fancy ways, he wanted to get rich; he promised Janie that she would be the queen of a town soon.
- (E) acceptable as is

Taking Essay Tests

Essay tests are designed to assess both your understanding of important ideas and your ability to see connections, or relationships, between these ideas. To do well, you must be able to organize your thoughts quickly and to express them logically and clearly.

Kinds of Essay Questions

Always begin an essay test by carefully reading the instructions for all the questions on the test. Then, as you reread the instructions for your first question, look for key words, such as those listed in the following box. Such key words will tell you precisely what kind of question you are being asked to answer.

KINDS OF ESSAY QUESTIONS	
ANALYZE	Separate into parts and examine each part.
COMPARE	Point out similarities.
CONTRAST	Point out differences.
DEFINE	Clarify meaning.
DISCUSS	Examine in detail.
EVALUATE	Give your opinion.
EXPLAIN	Tell how, what, or why.
ILLUSTRATE	Give examples.
SUMMARIZE	Briefly review main points.
TRACE	Show development or progress.

As you read the instructions, jot down everything that is required in your answer or circle key words and underline key phrases in the instructions, as in the following example.

(Explain) the theory of geographic determinism, the process by which the climate and the geography of the earth determines the distribution of the world's population centers. Write three paragraphs, giving (specific examples) or illustrations.

PRACTICE YOUR SKILLS

● Check Your Understanding
Interpreting Essay Test Items

Write the key direction word in each item. Then write one sentence explaining what the question asks you to do.

EXAMPLE   Trace the life cycle of a frog.

POSSIBLE ANSWER   Trace—Show the development, in order, of the stages in the life of a frog.

1. In your own words, define *plate tectonics.*

2. How does the appearance of a timber rattlesnake compare with that of a diamondback rattlesnake?

3. Briefly summarize one of the acts in Shakespeare's play *Julius Caesar.*

4. James Thurber wrote, "Humor is emotional chaos remembered in tranquility." Discuss his meaning.

5. Evaluate one of Edgar Allan Poe's short stories.

6. Trace the history of the Mexican flag.

7. Explain how a tornado forms and moves.

8. Briefly analyze the scientific contributions of Marie Curie.

9. In a three-paragraph essay, contrast a desert and a tundra.

10. From your study of literature, explain and illustrate one of the following: simile, metaphor, or personification.

◉ Writing an Effective Essay Answer

The steps in writing a well-constructed essay are the same for an essay test as they are for a written assignment. The only difference is that in a test situation you have a strict time limit for writing. As a result you need to plan how much time you will spend writing each answer and how much time you will devote to each step in the writing process. As a rule of thumb, for every five minutes of writing, allow two minutes for planning and organizing and one minute for revising and editing.

Prewriting Writing Process

Begin planning your answer by brainstorming for main ideas and supporting details. Then organize your main ideas into a simple informal outline. Your outline will help you to present your ideas in a logical order, to cover all your main points, and to avoid omitting important details.

OUTLINE: **Geographic Determinism**

(thesis)

1. explanation of theory

2. climate as a determining factor

3. geography as a determining factor

(conclusion)

GRAPHIC
ORGANIZER:

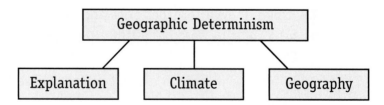

Your next step is to write a thesis statement that states your main idea and covers all your supporting ideas. Often you can write a suitable thesis statement by rewording the test question.

ESSAY QUESTION:	Explain the theory of geographic determinism, the process by which climate and the geography of the earth determined the distribution of the world's population centers.
THESIS STATEMENT:	The theory of geographic determinism states that population distribution was determined by climate and by geography.

Drafting ◁ **Writing Process**

As you write your essay answer, keep the following strategies in mind.

> **Strategies for Writing an Essay Answer**
> - Write an introduction that includes the thesis statement.
> - Follow the order of your outline. Write one paragraph for each main point, beginning with a topic sentence.
> - Be specific. Support each main idea by using supporting details such as facts and examples.
> - Use transitions to connect your ideas and examples.
> - End with a strong concluding statement that summarizes your thesis.
> - Write clearly and legibly because you will not have time to copy your work.

THESIS STATEMENT:

The theory of geographic determinism states that population distribution was determined by climate and by geography. One proof of this theory is the fact that the world's present population centers are not evenly distributed. Almost half of the world's population live on less than 10 percent of the total land area. The two main causes of high population density in some areas and low population density in others are climate and geography.

Climate affects where people live. For example, few people live in the far north of North America, because it is cold there for several months of the year. As a result, the growing season is too short to supply adequate food for a large population. Similarly, in parts of the Middle East and northern Africa, the climate is too hot and dry to produce enough food to feed large populations.

Geography also has a significant effect on where people live. For example, mountainous areas in North and South America have sparse populations. Because most farming is difficult in mountainous terrain, people who live in such areas support themselves mainly by animal husbandry. In contrast, broad, fertile river valleys and less mountainous land with abundant natural resources have always attracted large populations. Europe, for example, with its water supply, rich soil, and mineral wealth, is one of the most densely populated areas of the world.

CONCLUSION:

In conclusion, the evidence that shows that climate and geography have affected the distribution of the world's population centers supports the theory of geographic determinism.

Revising Writing Process

Leave time to revise and edit your essay answer. To keep your paper as neat as possible, use proofreading symbols to mark any corrections or revisions. As you revise, think of the following questions.

- Did you follow the instructions completely?
- Did you interpret the question accurately?
- Did you begin with a thesis statement?
- Did you include facts, examples, or other supporting details?
- Did you sequence your ideas and examples logically in paragraphs according to your modified outline?
- Did you use transitions to connect ideas and examples?
- Did you end with a strong concluding statement that summarizes your thesis?

Editing Writing Process

After you have made any necessary revisions, quickly read your essay to check for mistakes in spelling, usage, or punctuation. As you edit, check your work for accuracy in the following areas:

- agreement between subjects and verbs *(pages L293–L315)*
- comparative and superlative forms of adjectives and adverbs *(pages L327–L336)*
- capitalization of proper nouns and proper adjectives *(pages L382–L390)*
- use of commas *(pages L418–L440)*
- use of apostrophes *(pages L485–L498)*
- division of words at the end of a line *(pages L511–L512)*

APPLY TO WRITING
Prewriting: *Essay Test Question*

Some parents complained that the same athletes are filling up all of the positions on the basketball, football, baseball, and volleyball teams. In response to this, your school district wants to change the way team members are selected for all of the sports teams. They are proposing that each person in the school can play only one sport. They believe that this change will give more students the opportunity to play varsity sports. Several of your classmates disagree with this, stating that all it will do is make your school's teams weaker. What do you think? Use the organizer below to think about both sides of the argument.

```
        ┌─────────────────────────────┐
        │   ONE SPORT PER ATHLETE      │
        └─────────────────────────────┘
          ┌────────┐        ┌────────┐
          │  PROS  │        │  CONS  │
          └────────┘        └────────┘


    ┌──────────────────────────────────────────────┐
    │  FREE CHOICE IN NUMBER OF SPORTS PER ATHLETE   │
    └──────────────────────────────────────────────┘
          ┌────────┐        ┌────────┐
          │  PROS  │        │  CONS  │
          └────────┘        └────────┘
```

Timed Writing

Throughout your school years, you will be tested on your ability to organize your thoughts quickly and to express them in a limited time. Your teacher may ask you to write a twenty-minute, two-hundred-word essay that will then be judged on how thoroughly you covered the topic and organized your essay. To complete such an assignment, you should consider organizing your time in the following way.

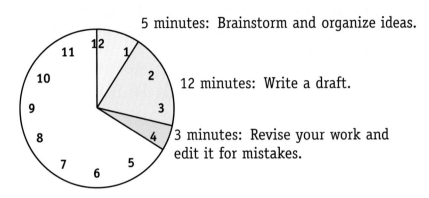

5 minutes: Brainstorm and organize ideas.

12 minutes: Write a draft.

3 minutes: Revise your work and edit it for mistakes.

The more you practice writing under time constraints, the better you will be able to apply these effective writing strategies during timed tests.

> ## Strategies for Timed Test
> - Listen carefully to instructions. Find out if you may write notes or an outline on your paper or in the examination book.
> - Find out if you should erase mistakes or cross them out by neatly drawing a line through them.
> - Plan your time, keeping in mind your time limit.

APPLY TO WRITING

Prewriting, Drafting, Revising, Editing: *Timed Writing*

Choose one side of the one sport per one athlete argument.
Then give yourself twenty minutes to write a response.
Begin by writing an informal outline and a thesis
statement. As you draft your essay, follow the Strategies
for Writing an Essay Answer on page L603. Be sure to
revise and edit your essay answer.

Abbreviation shortened form of a word.

Abstract summary of points of writing, presented in skeletal form.

Action verb word that tells what action a subject is performing.

Active voice the voice a verb is in when it expresses that the subject is performing action.

Adequate development quality of good writing in which sufficient supporting details develop the main idea.

Adjective word that modifies a noun or a pronoun.

Adjective clause subordinate clause that is used like an adjective to modify a noun or a pronoun.

Adjective phrase prepositional phrase that is used to modify a noun or a pronoun.

Adverb word that modifies a verb, an adjective, or another adverb.

Adverb clause subordinate clause that is used like an adverb to modify a verb, an adjective, or an adverb.

Adverb phrase prepositional phrase that is used like an adverb to modify a verb, an adjective, or an adverb.

Alliteration repetition of a consonant sound at the beginning of a series of words.

Analogies logical relationships between pairs of words.

Antecedent word or group of words that a pronoun replaces or refers to.

Antonym word that means nearly the opposite of another word.

Appositive noun or a pronoun that identifies or explains another noun or pronoun in a sentence.

Audience person or persons who will read your work or hear your speech.

Autobiography written account of a person's life.

B **Body** one or more paragraphs made up of details, facts, and examples that support the main idea.

Brainstorming prewriting technique of writing down everything that comes to mind about a subject.

Business letter writing form that uses formal language and contains six parts: the heading, inside address, salutation, body, closing, and signature.

C **Case** form of a noun or a pronoun that indicates its use in a sentence. In English there are three cases: the nominative case, the objective case, and the possessive case.

Cause and effect method of development in which details are grouped according to what happens and why it happens.

Characterization variety of techniques used by writers to show the personality of a character.

Chronological order order in which events occur.

Clarity the quality of being clear.

Classification method of development in which details are grouped together into categories.

Clause group of words that has a subject and a verb and is used as part of a sentence.

Clause fragment subordinate clause standing alone.

Cliché overused expression that is no longer fresh or interesting to the reader.

Clustering a visual form of brainstorming that is a technique used for developing supporting details.

Coherence logical and smooth flow of ideas connected with clear transitions.

Colloquialism informal phrase or colorful expression appropriate for conversation but not for formal writing.

Comparative degree modification of an adjective or adverb used when two people, things, or actions are compared.

Comparison and contrast method of development in which details are grouped according to similarities and differences.

Complement word that completes the meaning of an action verb.

Complete predicate all the words that tell what the subject is doing or that tell something about the subject.

Complete subject all the words used to identify the person, place, thing, or idea that the sentence is about.

Complex sentence one independent clause and one or more subordinate clauses.

Composition writing form that presents and develops one main idea in three or more paragraphs

Compound-complex sentence two or more independent clauses and one or more subordinate clauses.

Compound noun word made up of two smaller words that can be separated, hyphenated, or combined.

Compound sentence two or more independent clauses.

Compound subject two or more subjects in one sentence that have the same verb and are joined by a conjunction.

Compound verb two or more verbs that have the same subject and are joined by a conjunction.

Concluding sentence a strong ending added to a paragraph that summarizes the major points, refers to the main idea, or adds an insight.

Conclusion paragraph that completes an essay and reinforces its main idea.

Conjunction word that joins together sentences, clauses, phrases, or other words.

Connotation the meaning that comes from attitudes attached to a word.

Context clue clues to a word's meaning provided by the sentence, the surrounding words, or the situation in which the word occurs.

Contraction word that combines two words into one using an apostrophe to replace one or more missing letters.

Cooperative learning strategy in which a group works together to achieve a common goal or accomplish a single task.

Coordinating conjunction a single connecting word used to join words or groups of words.

Correlative conjunction pairs of conjunctions used to connect compound subjects, compound verbs, and compound sentences.

Creative writing writing style in which the writer creates characters, events, and images within stories, plays, or poems to express feelings, perceptions, and points of view.

D **Dangling modifier** phrase that has nothing to describe in a sentence.

Dash punctuation mark that indicates a greater separation of words than a comma.

Declarative sentence statement or expression of opinion. It ends with a period.

Demonstrative pronoun word that substitutes for a noun and points out a person or a thing.

Denotation the literal meaning of a word.

Descriptive writing writing that creates a vivid picture of a person, an object, or a scene.

Developmental order information that is organized so that one idea grows out of the preceding idea.

Dewey decimal system system by which nonfiction books are arranged on shelves in numerical order according to ten general subject categories.

Dialect regional variation of a language distinguished by distinctive pronunciation and some differences in word meanings.

Dialogue a conversation between two or more persons.

Direct object a noun or a pronoun that receives the action of a verb.

Direct quotation passage, sentence, or words written or spoken exactly as a person wrote or said them.

Double negative use of two negative words to express an idea when only one is needed.

Drafting stage of a writer's process in which he or she draws together ideas on paper.

E | **Editing** the stage of a writer's process in which the writer polishes his or her work by correcting errors in grammar, usage, mechanics, and spelling.

Elaboration addition of explanatory or descriptive information to an essay, such as supporting details, facts, and examples.

Elliptical clause subordinate clause in which words are omitted but understood to be there.

E-mail electronic mail that can be sent all over the world from one computer to another.

Emoticons symbols used by E-mail users to transmit emotion.

Encyclopedia print or online reference that contains general information about a variety of subjects.

Essay composition that presents and develops one main idea in three or more paragraphs.

Essential phrase or clause group of words essential to the meaning of a sentence and therefore not set off with commas.

Etymology history of a word, from its earliest recorded use to its present use.

Exclamatory sentence expresses strong feeling. It ends with an exclamation point.

Expository paragraph paragraph that explains or informs with facts and examples or gives directions.

F | **Fact** statement that can be proved.

Fiction prose works of literature, such as short stories and novels, that are partly or totally imaginary.

Figurative language imaginative, nonliteral use of language.

Footnote complete citation of the source of borrowed material at the bottom of a page in a research report.

Free verse poetry without meter or a regular, patterned beat.

Freewriting prewriting technique of writing freely about ideas as they come to mind.

G | **Gerund** a verb form ending in *-ing* that is used as a noun.

Glittering generality word or phrase that most people associate with virtue and goodness.

H **Helping verb** auxiliary verb that helps make up a verb phrase.

Hyphen used to divide words at the end of a line.

I **Idiom** phrase or expression that has a meaning different from what the words suggest in their usual meanings.

Imperative sentence a direction, a request, or a command. It ends with either a period or an exclamation point.

Indefinite pronoun word that substitutes for a noun and refers to an unnamed person or thing.

Independent clause group of words that stands alone as a sentence because it expresses a complete thought.

Indirect object a noun or a pronoun that answers the question *to or for whom?* Or *to or for what?* after an action verb.

Infinitive a verb form that usually begins with *to* and is used as a noun, an adjective, or an adverb.

Inquiring a prewriting technique in which the writer asks questions such as *Who? What? Where? Why?* and *When?*

Interjection a word that expresses strong feeling.

Internet a worldwide network of computers (see also "Basic Internet Terminology" in *A Writer's Guide to Using the Internet,* pp. C722–C768).

Interrogative pronoun word used to ask a question.

Interrogative sentence a question. It ends with a question mark.

Intransitive verb action verb that does not have an object.

Introduction paragraph in an essay that introduces a subject, states or implies a purpose, and presents a main idea.

Irregular verb does not form its past and past participle by adding *–ed* or *–d* to the present.

J **Jargon** specialized vocabulary used in particular professions.

Journal daily notebook in which a writer records thoughts and feelings.

L **Linking verb** verb that links the subject with another word in the sentence. This other word either renames or describes the subject.

Literary analysis interpretation of a work of literature supported by appropriate responses, detail, and quotations.

Loaded words subjective words that are interjected into a seemingly objective context to sway the audience emotionally without the audience knowing it.

M **Metaphor** figure of speech that compares by implying that one thing *is* another.

Meter rhythm of stressed and unstressed syllables in each line of a poem.

Misplaced modifier phrase or a clause that is placed too far away from the word it modifies, thus creating an unclear sentence.

Mood overall atmosphere or feeling created by a work of literature.

N **Narrator** the person whose voice is telling the story.

Narrative writing writing that tells a real or an imaginary story.

Nonessential phrase or clause group of words that is not essential to the meaning of a sentence and is therefore set off with commas.

Nonfiction prose writing that contains facts about real people and real events.

Noun a word that names a person, a place, a thing, or an idea. A *common noun* gives a general name. A *proper noun* names a specific person, place, or thing and always begins with a capital letter. A *collective noun* names a group of people or things.

Noun clause subordinate clause that is used like a noun.

Novel a long work of narrative fiction.

O **Objective** not based on an individual's opinions or judgments.

Observing prewriting technique that helps a writer use the powers of observation to gather details.

Occasion motivation for composing; the factor that prompts communication.

Onomatopoeia the use of words whose sounds suggest their meaning.

Opinion a judgment that varies from person to person.

Oral interpretation performance or expressive reading of a literary work.

Order of importance order in which supporting evidence is arranged from least to most (or most to least) important.

Outline information about a subject organized into main topics and subtopics.

P **Paragraph** group of related sentences that present and develop one main idea.

Parenthetical citation source title and page number given in parentheses within a sentence to credit the source of the information.

Participial phrase participle with its modifiers and complements—all working together as an adjective.

Participle verb form that is used as an adjective.

Passive voice the voice a verb is in when it expresses that the action is being performed upon its subject.

Peer conference meeting with one's peers, such as other students, to share ideas and offer suggestions for revision.

Personal writing writing that expresses the writer's personal point of view on a subject drawn from the writer's own experiences

Personal pronoun a pronoun that refers to a particular person, place, thing, or idea.

Persuasive writing writing that expresses an opinion on a subject and uses facts, examples, and reasons to convince readers.

Phrase group of related words that functions as a single part of speech and does not have a subject and a verb.

Plagiarism act of using another person's words, pictures, or ideas without giving proper credit.

Play composition written for dramatic performance on the stage.

Plot sequence of events leading to the outcome or point of the story.

Poem highly structured composition with condensed, vivid language, figures of speech, and often the use of meter and rhyme.

Point of view vantage point from which a writer tells a story or describes a subject

Portfolio collection of work representing various types of writing and progress made on them.

Possessive pronoun pronoun used to show ownership or possession.

Predicate part of a sentence that gives information about the subject.

Predicate adjective adjective that follows a linking verb and modifies the subject.

Predicate nominative noun or a pronoun that follows a linking verb and identifies, renames, or explains the subject.

Prefix one or more syllables placed in front of a root or base word to modify the meaning of the root or base word or to form a new word.

Preposition word that shows the relationship between a noun or a pronoun and another word in the sentence.

Prepositional phrase group of words that has no subject or verb and that modifies, or describes, other words in a sentence.

Prewriting invention stage in the writing process in which the writer plans for drafting based on the subject, occasion, audience, and purpose for writing.

Principal parts of a verb the *present*, the *past*, and the *past participle*. The principal parts help form the tenses of verbs.

Pronoun word that takes the place of one or more nouns.

Proofreading final stage of editing: carefully rereading and making corrections in grammar, usage, spelling, and mechanics.

Propaganda effort to persuade by distorting and misrepresenting information or by disguising opinions as facts.

Proper adjective adjective formed from a proper noun.

Protagonist the principal character in a story.

Publishing stage of a writer's process in which the writer may choose to share the work with an audience or make the work "public."

Purpose reason for writing and speaking.

R | **Readers' Guide to Periodical Literature** an index of magazine and journal articles.

Reflecting act of thinking quietly and calmly about an experience.

Reflexive pronoun pronoun formed by adding *–selves* or *–self* to a personal pronoun and used to reflect back to another noun or pronoun.

Relative pronoun pronoun that relates an adjective clause to the modified noun or pronoun.

Research paper a composition of three or more paragraphs that uses information from books, magazines, and other sources.

Revising stage of a writer's process in which the writer rethinks what is written and reworks it to increase its clarity, smoothness, and power.

Rhyme scheme regular pattern of rhyming in a poem.

Root the part of a word that carries the basic meaning.

Run-on sentence two or more sentences that are written as one, separated by a comma or with no mark of punctuation at all.

S | **Sensory details** details that appeal to one of the five senses: seeing, hearing, touching, tasting, and smelling.

Sentence group of words that expresses a complete thought.

Sentence base a subject, a verb, and a complement.

Sentence combining method of combining short sentences into longer, more fluent sentences by using phrases and clauses.

Sentence fragment group of words that does not express a complete thought.

Sequential order order in which details are arranged according to when they take place or where they are done.

Setting environment (location and time) in which the action takes place.

Short story short work of narrative fiction.

Simile figure of speech comparing two unlike objects using the words *like* or *as*.

Simple predicate main word or phrase in the complete predicate.

Simple sentence one independent clause.

Simple subject main word in a complete subject.

Slang nonstandard expressions developed and used by particular groups.

Sound devices ways to use sounds in poetry to achieve certain effects.

Spatial order order in which details are arranged according to their location.

Speech oral composition presented by a speaker to an audience.

Style visual or verbal expression that is distinctive to an artist or writer.

Subject word or group of words that names the person, place, thing, or idea that the sentence is about; topic of a composition.

Subordinate clause group of words that cannot stand alone as a sentence because they do not express a complete thought.

Subordinating conjunction single connecting word used in a complex sentence to introduce an adverb clause.

Suffix one or more syllables placed after a root or base word to change the word's part of speech and possibly also its meaning.

Summary information written in a condensed, concise form, touching only on the main ideas.

Superlative degree modification of an adjective or adverb used when more than two people, things, or actions are compared.

Supporting sentences specific details, facts, examples, or reasons that explain or prove a topic sentence.

Synonym word that has nearly the same meaning as another word.

T **Tense** the form a verb takes to show time. The six tenses are the *present, past, future, present perfect, past perfect,* and *future perfect.*

Theme underlying idea, message, or meaning of a work of literature.

Thesaurus specialized print or online dictionary of synonyms.

Thesis statement statement of the main idea that makes the writing purpose clear.

Tone writer's attitude toward the subject and audience of a composition.

Topic sentence statement of the main idea of the paragraph.

Transitions words and phrases that show how ideas are related.

Transitive verb an action verb that has an object.

U **Understood subject** unstated subject that is understood.

Unity combination or ordering of parts in a composition so that all the sentences or paragraphs work together to support one main idea.

V **Verb** word that expresses action or a state of being.

Verbal verb form used as some other part of speech.

Verb phrase main verb plus any helping, or auxiliary, verbs.

Voice particular sound and rhythm of language that the writer uses.

W **World Wide Web** network of computers within the Internet, capable of delivering multimedia content and text over communication lines into personal computers all over the globe.

Working thesis statement that expresses the possible main idea of a composition or research paper.

Works-cited page an alphabetical listing of sources cited in a research paper.

Writing process the recursive series of stages a writer proceeds through when developing ideas and discovering the best way to express them.

Note: Italic locators (page numbers) indicate skill sets

Note: Italic locators (page numbers) indicate skill sets

Note: Italic locators (page numbers) indicate skill sets

INDEX

Note: Italic locators (page numbers) indicate skill sets

INDEX

Note: Italic locators (page numbers) indicate skill sets

Note: Italic locators (page numbers) indicate skill sets

Note: Italic locators (page numbers) indicate skill sets

Note: Italic locators (page numbers) indicate skill sets

INDEX

vertical file, C686
World Wide Web and online
    services, C525, C661,
    C744–C768
Informative messages
    organizing, C391, C592–C596
    preparing, C110–C127, C144,
    C382–C399, C414
    presenting, C598–C599
Informative presentations
    evaluating presentations of
    peers, public figures, and
    media, C591,C609, *C615*
Informative writing, C96–161,
    C376–C419. *See also* Literary
    analysis; Research report.
    audience, C386
    body, C403–C407
    cause-and-effect writing,
        C157–C158, C161
    checklist, C161
    coherence, C138, C404
    compare-and-contrast writing,
        C156, C161
    conclusion, C407–C409
    defined, C110, C382
    definition writing, C159–C160,
        C161
    details, C404
    drafting, C129–C134, C144,
        C400–C410, C414
    editing, C143, C144, C412,
        C414
    evaluating, *C101*
    exercises, *C145, C148, C415,*
        C419
    gathering information, C386
    model, C387
    how-it-works writing,
        C153–C154, C161
    how-to writing, C151–C152,
        C161
    introduction, C402
    model, C120
    organizing, C391
    outlining, C397
    prewriting, C110–C127, C144,
        C382–C399, C414
    publishing, C144, C413, C414
    revising, C134–C143, C144,
        C410–C412, C414
    supporting points, C404
    thesis statement, C388, C400,
        C407
    transitions, C404
    uses, C381
    A Writer's Guide, C147–C161
Inquiring, C30
Insert editing, of video, C718
Inside address, business letter,
    C570, C572
Interfaces, on Website, C720

Interjection, L49
    identifying, *L50, L51, L53*
Internet
    browser, C726
    chat rooms, C727, C741,
        C742, C743
    E-commerce, C734
    E-mail, C730, C738–C744
    free programs and services,
        C734
    games, C734
    guidelines, C735–C736
    history, C724
    HyperText Markup Language
        (HTML), C721
    HyperText Transfer Protocol
        (http), C726
    Internet Relay Chat (IRC),
        C741
    Internet Service Provider
        (ISP), C723, C725, C740
    mailing lists, C731, C738,
        C742
    newsgroups, C731, C738,
        C743, C744
    research, C525, C665–C674,
        C676, C677, C679, C680,
        C681, C682, C683, C730,
        C731, C744–C768
    search engine, C115, C746
    search page, C745
    as study tool, C733
    terminology, C727–C729
    URL, C723, C726
    usage, C729, C737
    A Writer's Guide, C724–C768
Interrogative pronoun, L16
Interrogative sentence, L71,
    L412, L414
Interrupting words, subject-verb
    agreement, C44, L296, L321
Into, in, L361
Intransitive verb, L22
Introduction
    in book, as research tool,
        C675
    composition, C196, C211
    and conclusion, C408
    descriptive writing, C283
    functions, C214, C402
    model, C222, C403
    paragraph, C196
    persuasive writing, C426
    progress report,
    readers' attention, C402, C410
    research report, C537
    setting a scene, C321
    short story, C321, C339
    speech, C596
    techniques for writing, C339,
        C402
    thesis statement, C402

tone, C402
Introductory elements, commas
    and, L427
Inverted order of sentence, C80,
    L70–L71, L98, L306, *L307,*
    L308, L321
IRC, defined, C741
Irregular comparison of
    modifiers, L330, L347
Irregular verbs, L142, L199,
    L200, L202–L203,
    L205–L207, L216, L237
ISP, C723, C725, C728, C740
Italics (underlining),
    L453–L456, L479
    exercises, *L455, L456, L475,*
        L480
Items in a series, C86, L418,
    L505, L507

J Jargon, defined, C636
       Journal. *See* Writer's
       Journal.

K *Keep,* principal parts of,
       L200
       Keyword, in online
    search, C665, C673, C728,
    C745
Kind of, sort of, L361
Knew, new, L361
Know, principal parts, L203

L *Lay, lie,* L209, *L211,*
       L237, L362
       Layout
    book, C20
    captions and titles, C708
    charts and graphs, C707
    clip art, C706
    color, C704
    drawings, C706
    font selection, C701–C703
    font size, C703
    icons, C707, C709
    planning, C20
    photographs, C707
    preset page layouts, C704
Lead, principal parts of, L200
Learn, teach, L361
Learning log, as prewriting
    strategy, C16
Leave, let, L362
Leave, principal parts, L200
Less, fewer, L358
Let, principal parts of, L199
Letter of request, C573, C579,
    C585
Letters. *See* Business letters.
Library/media center
    arrangement of fiction, C661

Note: Italic locators (page numbers) indicate skill sets

Note: Italic locators (page numbers) indicate skill sets

Note: Italic locators (page numbers) indicate skill sets

Note: *Italic locators (page numbers) indicate skill sets*

Note: Italic locators (page numbers) indicate skill sets

INDEX

Note: Italic locators (page numbers) indicate skill sets

INDEX

Note: Italic locators (page numbers) indicate skill sets

INDEX

Note: Italic locators (page numbers) indicate skill sets

Note: Italic locators (page numbers) indicate skill sets

INDEX

Note: Italic locators (page numbers) indicate skill sets

INDEX

Note: Italic locators (page numbers) indicate skill sets

INDEX

Note: Italic locators (page numbers) indicate skill sets

Note: Italic locators (page numbers) indicate skill sets

INDEX

Note: Italic locators (page numbers) indicate skill sets

Barrett Kendall Publishing has made every effort to trace the ownership of all copyrighted selections in this book and to make full acknowledgment of their use. Grateful acknowledgment is made to the following authors, publishers, agents, and individuals for their permission to reprint copyrighted material.

Composition

C3: From *On Being a Writer,* Writer's Digest Books, a division of F&W Publications, Inc. © Lois Rosenthal. **C55:** "The Fifth Chinese Daughter", from *The Immigrant Experience* by Thomas C. Wheeler. Copyright © 1971 by Doubleday, a division of Bantam Doubleday Dell Publishing Group, Inc. Used by permission of Doubleday, a division of Random House, Inc. **C97:** From *Annals of the Former World,* by John McPhee. Farrar, Straus and Giroux. **C163:** Excerpt from "West With the Night" from *West With the Night* by Beryl Markham. Copyright © 1942, 1983 by Beryl Markham. Reprinted by permission of North Point Press, a division of Farrar, Straus and Giroux, LLC. **C207:** Copyright © 1976 by the New York Times Co. Reprinted by permission. **C213:** "A Worn Path", by Eudora Welty from *The Collected Stories of Eudora Welty*. Harcourt Brace. **C241, C261:** "The Jacket" by Gary Soto. Text copyright © 1986 by Gary Soto. Used with permission of the author and BookStop Literary Agency. All rights reserved. **C277:** N. Scott Momaday/LIFE Magazine. © Time Inc. Reprinted by permission. **C309:** *Made with Words* by May Swenson. University of Michigan Press. **C351:** From *The Piano Lesson* by August Wilson, copyright © 1988, 1990 by August Wilson. Used by permission of Dutton Signet, a division of Penguin Putnam Inc. **C366:** From *Collected Poems* by Wallace Stevens. Copyright 1954 by Wallace Stevens. Reprinted by permission of Alfred A. Knopf, a Division of Random House, Inc. **C367:** "Strawberrying" from *In Other Words* by May Swenson. Alfred A. Knopf Publishing. **C368:** "This is Just to Say" by William Carlos Williams, from *Collected Poems: 1909–1939,* Volume I, copyright © 1938 by New Directions Publishing Corp. Reprinted by permission of New Directions Publishing Corp. **C377:** From "The Mind of the Chimpanzee" in *Through a Window* by Jane Goodall. Copyright © 1990 by Soko Publications, Ltd. Reprinted by permission of Houghton Mifflin Company. All rights reserved. **C421:** © Tribune Media Services, Inc. All rights reserved. Reprinted with permission. **C467:** "Courage," from *The Awful Rowing Toward God* by Anne Sexton. Copyright © 1975 by Loring Conant, Jr., Executor of the Estate of Anne Sexton. Reprinted by permission of Houghton Mifflin Co. All rights reserved. **C469:** "The Courage That My Mother Had" by Edna St. Vincent Millay. From *Collected Poems*, HarperCollins. Copyright © 1954, 1982 by Norma Millay Ellis. All rights reserved. Reprinted by permission of Elizabeth Barnett, literary executor. **C476:** From *The Poetry of Robert Frost,* edited by Edward Connery Lathem. Henry Holt and Company, LLC. **C476:** "The Explorer" by Gwendolyn Brooks. © Gwendolyn Brooks. **C508:** From *The Poems, Prose and Plays of Alexander Pushkin,* translated by Babette Deutsch. Copyright © 1936 and renewed 1964 by Random House, Inc. Reprinted by permission of Random House, Inc. **C515:** Copyright © 1999 by the New York Times Co. Reprinted by permission. **C539:** From *Genealogy Online,* Elizabeth Powell Crowe, McGraw-Hill, © 1996. Reprinted by permission of The McGraw-Hill Companies. **C589:** Reprinted by arrangement with The Heirs to the Estate of Martin Luther King, Jr., c/o Writers House, Inc. as agent for the proprietor. Copyright 1963 by Martin Luther King, Jr., copyright renewed 1991 by Coretta Scott King. **C621:** "Freedom from English" from *The World in So Many Words: A Country-by-Country Tour of Words That Have Shaped Our Language* by Allan Metcalf. Copyright © 1999 by Allan A. Metcalf. Reprinted by permission of Houghton Mifflin Company. All rights reserved. **C631:** From *The House on Mango Street*. Copyright © 1984 by Sandra Cisneros. Published by Vintage Books, a division of Random House, Inc., and in hardcover by Alfred A. Knopf in 1994. Reprinted by permission of Susan Bergholz Literary Services, New York. All rights reserved. **C683:** From Marquis *Who's Who in America,* 51st edition. Reprinted by permission.

Language

L143: From: "Stopping by Woods on a Snowy Evening" from *The Poetry of Robert Frost,* edited by Edward Connery Lathem, Copyright 1951 by Robert Frost. Copyright 1923, © 1969 by Henry Holt and Company, LLC. Reprinted by permission of Henry Holt and Company, LLC. **L359:** Reprinted by arrangement with The Heirs to the Estate of Martin Luther King, Jr., c/o Writers House, Inc. as agent for the proprietor. Copyright 1963 by Martin Luther King, Jr., copyright renewed 1991 by Coretta Scott King. **L365:** From *Walt Whitman: Leaves of Grass,* Reader's Comprehensive Edition, New York University Press. **L378:** From *Just Give Me a Cool Drink of Water 'Fore I Diiie* by Maya Angelou. Copyright © 1971 by Maya Angelou. Reprinted by permission of Random House, Inc. **L380:** From: "Stopping by Woods on a Snowy Evening" from *The Poetry of Robert Frost,* edited by Edward Connery Lathem, Copyright 1951 by Robert Frost. Copyright 1923, © 1969 by Henry Holt and Company, LLC. Reprinted by permission of Henry Holt and Company, LLC.

PHOTO CREDITS

Key: (t) top, (c) center, (b) bottom, (l) left, (r) right.

Composition

C6: © Todd Gibstein/Corbis. **C27:** © Dereck M. Allan/Corbis. **C55:** © Aaron Haupt/Stock Boston Inc./PictureQuest. **C60:** The Metropolitan Museum of Art, gift of Mrs. John H. Ballantine, 1947. (47.75.1). Photograph © 1990 The Metropolitan Museum of Art. **C163, C165:** Corbis/Bettmann–UPI. **C185:** © Mike Kelly. **C199:** Photo by George Holmes, © 1998 Blanton Museum of Art, University of Texas. **C209:** © Tony Freeman/PhotoEdit/PNI. **C273:** © Jonathan Blair/Corbis. **C277:** © Jan Butchofsky-Houser/Corbis. **C279:** © William Hart/Fine Art Photog[...] **C273:** Private collection/SuperStoc[...] **C423:** © American R[...] Photography. **C470:** Christie's Images/Su[...] Brussels/Artists Rig[...] © Kevin McDonnell/[...] Kennan Ward/Corbi[...] **C589:** © Bettmann[...] **C621:** © Michael N[...]

ments